Handbook of Juvenile Justice

Theory and Practice

PUBLIC ADMINISTRATION AND PUBLIC POLICY

A Comprehensive Publication Program

Executive Editor

JACK RABIN
Professor of Public Administration and Public Policy
School of Public Affairs
The Capital College
The Pennsylvania State University—Harrisburg
Middletown, Pennsylvania

Assistant to the Executive Editor
T. Aaron Wachhaus, Jr.

1. *Public Administration as a Developing Discipline,* Robert T. Golembiewski
2. *Comparative National Policies on Health Care,* Milton I. Roemer, M.D.
3. *Exclusionary Injustice: The Problem of Illegally Obtained Evidence,* Steven R. Schlesinger
5. *Organization Development in Public Administration,* edited by Robert T. Golembiewski and William B. Eddy
7. *Approaches to Planned Change,* Robert T. Golembiewski
8. *Program Evaluation at HEW,* edited by James G. Abert
9. *The States and the Metropolis,* Patricia S. Florestano and Vincent L. Marando
11. *Changing Bureaucracies: Understanding the Organization before Selecting the Approach,* William A. Medina
12. *Handbook on Public Budgeting and Financial Management,* edited by Jack Rabin and Thomas D. Lynch
15. *Handbook on Public Personnel Administration and Labor Relations,* edited by Jack Rabin, Thomas Vocino, W. Bartley Hildreth, and Gerald J. Miller
19. *Handbook of Organization Management,* edited by William B. Eddy
22. *Politics and Administration: Woodrow Wilson and American Public Administration,* edited by Jack Rabin and James S. Bowman
23. *Making and Managing Policy: Formulation, Analysis, Evaluation,* edited by G. Ronald Gilbert
25. *Decision Making in the Public Sector,* edited by Lloyd G. Nigro
26. *Managing Administration,* edited by Jack Rabin, Samuel Humes, and Brian S. Morgan
27. *Public Personnel Update,* edited by Michael Cohen and Robert T. Golembiewski
28. *State and Local Government Administration,* edited by Jack Rabin and Don Dodd
29. *Public Administration: A Bibliographic Guide to the Literature,* Howard E. McCurdy
31. *Handbook of Information Resource Management,* edited by Jack Rabin and Edward M. Jackowski
32. *Public Administration in Developed Democracies: A Comparative Study,* edited by Donald C. Rowat
33. *The Politics of Terrorism: Third Edition,* edited by Michael Stohl

34. *Handbook on Human Services Administration,* edited by Jack Rabin and Marcia B. Steinhauer

36. *Ethics for Bureaucrats: An Essay on Law and Values, Second Edition,* John A. Rohr

37. *The Guide to the Foundations of Public Administration,* Daniel W. Martin

39. *Terrorism and Emergency Management: Policy and Administration,* William L. Waugh, Jr.

40. *Organizational Behavior and Public Management: Second Edition,* Michael L. Vasu, Debra W. Stewart, and G. David Garson

43. *Government Financial Management Theory,* Gerald J. Miller

46. *Handbook of Public Budgeting,* edited by Jack Rabin

49. *Handbook of Court Administration and Management,* edited by Steven W. Hays and Cole Blease Graham, Jr.

50. *Handbook of Comparative Public Budgeting and Financial Management,* edited by Thomas D. Lynch and Lawrence L. Martin

53. *Encyclopedia of Policy Studies: Second Edition,* edited by Stuart S. Nagel

54. *Handbook of Regulation and Administrative Law,* edited by David H. Rosenbloom and Richard D. Schwartz

55. *Handbook of Bureaucracy,* edited by Ali Farazmand

56. *Handbook of Public Sector Labor Relations,* edited by Jack Rabin, Thomas Vocino, W. Bartley Hildreth, and Gerald J. Miller

57. *Practical Public Management,* Robert T. Golembiewski

58. *Handbook of Public Personnel Administration,* edited by Jack Rabin, Thomas Vocino, W. Bartley Hildreth, and Gerald J. Miller

60. *Handbook of Debt Management,* edited by Gerald J. Miller

61. *Public Administration and Law: Second Edition,* David H. Rosenbloom and Rosemary O'Leary

62. *Handbook of Local Government Administration,* edited by John J. Gargan

63. *Handbook of Administrative Communication,* edited by James L. Garnett and Alexander Kouzmin

64. *Public Budgeting and Finance: Fourth Edition,* edited by Robert T. Golembiewski and Jack Rabin

65. *Handbook of Public Administration: Second Edition,* edited by Jack Rabin, W. Bartley Hildreth, and Gerald J. Miller

67. *Handbook of Public Finance,* edited by Fred Thompson and Mark T. Green

68. *Organizational Behavior and Public Management: Third Edition,* Michael L. Vasu, Debra W. Stewart, and G. David Garson

69. *Handbook of Economic Development,* edited by Kuotsai Tom Liou

70. *Handbook of Health Administration and Policy,* edited by Anne Osborne Kilpatrick and James A. Johnson

71. *Handbook of Research Methods in Public Administration,* edited by Gerald J. Miller and Marcia L. Whicker

72. *Handbook on Taxation,* edited by W. Bartley Hildreth and James A. Richardson

73. *Handbook of Comparative Public Administration in the Asia-Pacific Basin,* edited by Hoi-kwok Wong and Hon S. Chan

74. *Handbook of Global Environmental Policy and Administration,* edited by Dennis L. Soden and Brent S. Steel

75. *Handbook of State Government Administration,* edited by John J. Gargan

76. *Handbook of Global Legal Policy,* edited by Stuart S. Nagel

78. *Handbook of Global Economic Policy,* edited by Stuart S. Nagel

79. *Handbook of Strategic Management: Second Edition,* edited by Jack Rabin, Gerald J. Miller, and W. Bartley Hildreth

80. *Handbook of Global International Policy,* edited by Stuart S. Nagel
81. *Handbook of Organizational Consultation: Second Edition,* edited by Robert T. Golembiewski
82. *Handbook of Global Political Policy,* edited by Stuart S. Nagel
83. *Handbook of Global Technology Policy,* edited by Stuart S. Nagel
84. *Handbook of Criminal Justice Administration,* edited by M. A. DuPont-Morales, Michael K. Hooper, and Judy H. Schmidt
85. *Labor Relations in the Public Sector: Third Edition,* edited by Richard C. Kearney
86. *Handbook of Administrative Ethics: Second Edition,* edited by Terry L. Cooper
87. *Handbook of Organizational Behavior: Second Edition,* edited by Robert T. Golembiewski
88. *Handbook of Global Social Policy,* edited by Stuart S. Nagel and Amy Robb
89. *Public Administration: A Comparative Perspective, Sixth Edition,* Ferrel Heady
90. *Handbook of Public Quality Management,* edited by Ronald J. Stupak and Peter M. Leitner
91. *Handbook of Public Management Practice and Reform,* edited by Kuotsai Tom Liou
92. *Personnel Management in Government: Politics and Process, Fifth Edition,* Jay M. Shafritz, Norma M. Riccucci, David H. Rosenbloom, Katherine C. Naff, and Albert C. Hyde
93. *Handbook of Crisis and Emergency Management,* edited by Ali Farazmand
94. *Handbook of Comparative and Development Public Administration: Second Edition,* edited by Ali Farazmand
95. *Financial Planning and Management in Public Organizations,* Alan Walter Steiss and Emeka O. Cyprian Nwagwu
96. *Handbook of International Health Care Systems,* edited by Khi V. Thai, Edward T. Wimberley, and Sharon M. McManus
97. *Handbook of Monetary Policy,* edited by Jack Rabin and Glenn L. Stevens
98. *Handbook of Fiscal Policy,* edited by Jack Rabin and Glenn L. Stevens
99. *Public Administration: An Interdisciplinary Critical Analysis,* edited by Eran Vigoda
100. *Ironies in Organizational Development: Second Edition, Revised and Expanded,* edited by Robert T. Golembiewski
101. *Science and Technology of Terrorism and Counterterrorism,* edited by Tushar K. Ghosh, Mark A. Prelas, Dabir S. Viswanath, and Sudarshan K. Loyalka
102. *Strategic Management for Public and Nonprofit Organizations,* Alan Walter Steiss
103. *Case Studies in Public Budgeting and Financial Management: Second Edition,* edited by Aman Khan and W. Bartley Hildreth
104. *Handbook of Conflict Management,* edited by William J. Pammer, Jr. and Jerri Killian
105. *Chaos Organization and Disaster Management,* Alan Kirschenbaum
106. *Handbook of Gay, Lesbian, Bisexual, and Transgender Administration and Policy,* edited by Wallace Swan
107. *Public Productivity Handbook: Second Edition,* edited by Marc Holzer
108. *Handbook of Developmental Policy Studies,* edited by Gedeon M. Mudacumura, Desta Mebratu and M. Shamsul Haque
109. *Bioterrorism in Medical and Healthcare Administration,* Laure Paquette
110. *International Public Policy and Management: Policy Learning Beyond Regional, Cultural, and Political Boundaries,* edited by David Levi-Faur and Eran Vigoda-Gadot
111. *Handbook of Public Information Systems, Second Edition,* edited by G. David Garson

112. *Handbook of Public Sector Economics,* edited by Donijo Robbins
113. *Handbook of Public Administration and Policy in the European Union,* edited by M. Peter van der Hoek
114. *Nonproliferation Issues for Weapons of Mass Destruction,* Mark A. Prelas and Michael S. Peck
115. *Common Ground, Common Future: Moral Agency in Public Administration, Professions, and Citizenship,* Charles Garofalo and Dean Geuras
116. *Handbook of Organization Theory and Management: The Philosophical Approach, Second Edition,* edited by Thomas D. Lynch and Peter L. Cruise
117. *International Development Governance,* edited by Ahmed Shafiqul Huque and Habib Zafarullah
118. *Sustainable Development Policy and Administration,* edited by Gedeon M. Mudacumura, Desta Mebratu, and M. Shamsul Haque
119. *Public Financial Management,* edited by Howard A. Frank
120. *Handbook of Juvenile Justice: Theory and Practice,* edited by Barbara Sims and Pamela Preston

Available Electronically

Principles and Practices of Public Administration, edited by Jack Rabin, Robert F. Munzenrider, and Sherrie M. Bartell

Handbook of Juvenile Justice

Theory and Practice

edited by

Barbara Sims
Penn State Harrisburg
Middletown, Pennsylvania

Pamela Preston
Penn State Schuylkill
Schuylkill Haven, Pennsylvania

Taylor & Francis
Taylor & Francis Group
Boca Raton   London   New York

CRC is an imprint of the Taylor & Francis Group,
an informa business

Published in 2006 by
CRC Press
Taylor & Francis Group
6000 Broken Sound Parkway NW, Suite 300
Boca Raton, FL 33487-2742

International Standard Book Number-10: 1-57444-557-X (Hardcover)
International Standard Book Number-13: 978-1-57444-557-2 (Hardcover)
Library of Congress Card Number 2006040776

Library of Congress Cataloging-in-Publication Data

Sims, Barbara.
    Handbook of juvenile justice : theory and practice / Barbara Sims and Pamela Preston.
       p. cm. -- (Public administration and public policy)
    Includes bibliographical references.
    ISBN 1-57444-557-X (alk. paper)
    1. Juvenile justice, Administration of--United States. 2. Juvenile delinquency--United States. I. Preston, Pamela. II. Title. III. Series.

HV9104.S56 2006
364.360973--dc22   2006040776

Taylor & Francis Group
is the Academic Division of Informa plc.

Visit the Taylor & Francis Web site at
http://www.taylorandfrancis.com

and the CRC Press Web site at
http://www.crcpress.com

Preface

This project of collected works in the area of juvenile law and justice came about as a result of the lead editor's dissatisfaction with current books of a similar nature now in print. All too often instructors are left to find additional reading in a juvenile law and justice course or a juvenile delinquency course because a textbook does not give adequate coverage to the literature on many subjects of importance. The work presented here represents our best effort at providing comprehensive coverage of a vibrant field of study.

Once we started down the path to identifying issues that need coverage in a text of this sort, however, we quickly realized just how broad the subject matter is. The inclusion of those issues covered within these pages is a direct result of hours of discussions between the two of us related to what can be considered the most pressing or critical issues associated with the modern-day juvenile justice system. Once those issues had been identified, the next task was assembling a list of possible contributors, those individuals who were recognized as experts on the subject matter. For some chapters, we went to colleagues with whom one of us is acquainted, and for others we examined the annual meeting programs of both the American Society of Criminology and the Academy of Criminal Justice Sciences as a means of identifying papers that dealt with the topics we needed covered. Sometimes our first contact with an individual yielded information about other possibilities and our follow-up conversations with those new contacts more often than not produced yet another willing contributor.

Producing a project of this magnitude was quite a daunting task. We were fortunate, however, to have chosen excellent writers and a group of contributors who were willing to cooperate with us through the review and editing process. In the end, we regard this handbook as a group effort, with all contributors playing an equal role in its completion. Although one would view this book as rather substantial when it comes to issues covered and page length, it has the benefit of providing the reader with a truly comprehensive review of the best literature available on the subject.

Acknowledgments

The editors would like to express their sincere gratitude and appreciation to all the authors who contributed to this project. Without their willingness to produce a quality chapter and to cooperate with us in a timely manner through the review and revision process we would not have been able to complete our work. We also would like to thank our family, friends, and colleagues who encouraged us and who recognized our need to be pulled away from other commitments in order to work on the handbook. And we would be remiss to neglect to extend a thank you to our school director, Dr. Steve Peterson (School of Public Affairs, Penn State University, Harrisburg, Pennsylvania) for his continual support of all of our efforts. Thanks also to Erin Arthur, graduate assistant in the MACJ Program at Penn State–Harrisburg, for her assistance early in the project. The lead editor extends a hearty thank you to Dr. Pam Preston for her willingness to be involved in the project and for being an excellent colleague and friend throughout the doing of the hard work associated with it.

Contributors

Janice Ahmad is an assistant professor in the Department of Criminology and Criminal Justice at the University of Texas at Arlington.

Earl Angel, B.S., is a research associate in the Center for Criminal Justice Education and Research in the Department of Correctional and Juvenile Justice Studies at Eastern Kentucky University.

Katherine Bennett, Ph.D., is a professor of criminal justice at Armstrong Atlantic State University in Savannah, Georgia where she is currently serving as director of institutional research.

Lisa Bond-Maupin, M.S.W, Ph.D., is an associate professor in the Department of Criminal Justice at New Mexico State University where she also serves as the indergraduate internship coordinator.

Amanda Burgess-Proctor is a doctoral candidate in the School of Criminal Justice at Michigan State University. Her primary research interests include the areas of criminological theory, feminist criminology, domestic violence, and intersections of race, class, and gender.

Catherine E. Burton, Ph.D., is an assistant professor of criminal justice in the Department of Political Science and Criminal Justice at The Citadel in Charleston, South Carolina.

Carrie M. Butler, Ph.D., is an assistant professor in the College of Criminal Justice at Sam Houston State University. She also serves as the principal investigator for a federal initiative called Project Safe Neighborhoods through the U.S. Attorney's Office in Houston for the Southern District of Texas.

Timothy S. Bynum is a professor in the School of Criminal Justice at Michigan State University and the director of the Michigan Justice Statistics Center. His research centers on the evaluation of criminal justice policies and interventions.

Tory J. Caeti is an associate professor in the Department of Criminal Justice at the University of North Texas. He currently serves as a senior executive advisor for the Office of Antiterrorism Assistance, Bureau of Diplomatic Security, Cyber Training Program, for the United States Department of State, teaching in the Cyber-Terrorism Executive Seminar.

Ernest L. Cowles, Ph.D., is the director of the Institute for Social Research and professor of sociology at California State University, Sacramento. His current research interests include: substance abuse policy, correctional treatment, and organizational change.

Gordon A. Crews, Ph.D., is an associate professor in the Department of Criminal Justice at Washburn University in Topeka, Kansas. Dr. Crews' current research interests focus on an international comparison of police and societal responses to individuals involved in alternative belief systems and practices (e.g., Satanism, Wicca, Goth, etc.).

R. Gregg Dwyer, M.D., Ed.D., a former special agent with the United States Naval Criminal Investigative Service, is currently the chief resident of the Child and Adolescent Psychiatry Residency at the University of South Carolina's School of Medicine/Palmetto Health Alliance, and an associate medical staff member of the Columbia Behavioral Health System in Columbia, South Carolina.

Thomas Ellsworth, Ph.D., is professor and chairperson at the Department of Criminal Justice Sciences at Illinois State University. He specializes in juvenile justice.

Marilyn Chandler Ford, Ph.D., is assistant director of the Volusia County Division of Corrections located in Daytona Beach, Florida. She is also a certified jail manager and adjunct professor at the University of Central Florida.

Eric J. Fritsch, Ph.D., is an associate professor of criminal justice in the Department of Criminal Justice at the University of North Texas where he also serves as graduate advisor.

Edward J. Girard, MPA, is an adjunct instructor of social sciences at Lackawanna College, Hazleton, Pennsylvania. He served in law enforcement for 31 years in both the U.S. Coast Guard and the Pennsylvania Bureau of State Parks.

James L. Hague, J.D., LLM, was the director of the Graduate Program in Criminal Justice at Virginia Commonwealth University for over 20 years. He is currently professor emeritus and teaches part-time. Also, he is a former special agent with the FBI. His teaching and research interests are in law and legal systems.

Craig Hemmens, J.D., Ph.D., is chairperson and professor in the Department of Criminal Justice Administration at Boise State University, Boise, Idaho.

Mary Hjelm, Ph.D., is an associate professor of English at the University of South Carolina–Salkehatchie in Allendale, South Carolina.

Kristi Holsinger, Ph.D., is an associate professor of criminal justice and criminology at the University of Missouri–Kansas City.

Beth M. Huebner, Ph.D., is an assistant professor of criminology and criminal justice at the University of Missouri–St. Louis. She received her doctorate from the School of Criminal Justice at Michigan State University.

Suman Kakar, Ph.D., is an associate professor of criminal justice in the College of Health and Urban Affairs and School of Policy and Management at Florida International University.

Victor E. Kappeler, Ph.D., is the graduate program director and professor of criminal justice and police studies at Eastern Kentucky University.

Kate King, Ph.D., is an associate professor and director of criminal justice at Murray State University, Murray, Kentucky.

Rebekah J. Lanphierd, M.A., is a visiting research data analyst at the Institute for Legal and Policy Studies, a unit of the Center for State Policy and Leadership at the University of Illinois at Springfield.

Scott LeGrand, LCSW, is a program manager for the Devereux Foundation in Florida with the Specialized Therapeutic Group Homes in Chuluota and Cocoa, Florida. His current interests relate to treatment approaches with juvenile sexual offenders, model programming for milieu and community reintegration.

Deborah L. Laufersweiler-Dwyer, Ph.D., is an associate professor of criminal justice in the College of Professional Studies at the University of Arkansas at Little Rock.

Robert L. Marsh is an associate professor of criminal justice administration in the Department of Criminal Justice at Boise State University, Boise, Idaho. He is actively involved in research in child sex abuse, disparity in the juvenile justice system, and drug courts. He is also a private consultant.

John D. McCluskey, Ph.D., is an Assistant Professor in the Department of Criminal Justice at the University of Texas at San Antonio. He received his doctorate in Criminal Justice from the University at Albany.

E. K. McIntyre, M.A., is the clinical director at Devereux-Texas, Victoria, and serves as a research associate at the Devereux Institute of Clinical Training and Research.

J. Mitchell Miller is associate professor of criminology and social work and director of drugs and addictions studies at the University of South Carolina. Dr. Miller is the current editor of the *Journal of Criminal Justice Education*.

Karen S. Miller, Ph.D., is an assistant professor of sociology at Eastern Kentucky University.

Kevin Minor, Ph.D., is professor and chairperson of the Department of Correctional and Juvenile Justice Studies at Eastern Kentucky University.

David Mueller is associate professor of criminal justice administration at Boise State University, Boise, Idaho.

David Olveda, M. A., M.S., is a disability claims representative for the Social Security Administration in San Antonio, Texas, and is completing his M.B.A.

Leanne Owen is an assistant professor of criminal justice in the School of Arts and Sciences at Holy Family University in Philadelphia, Pennsylvania, where she also serves as the faculty moderator for Alpha Phi Sigma.

Justin W. Patchin, Ph.D., is an assistant professor of criminal justice in the Department of Political Science at the University of Wisconsin–Eau Claire. He received his doctorate from the School of Criminal Justice at Michigan State University.

Allan L. Patenaude, Ph.D., is an associate professor and director of the Justice Studies Department at Westminster College in Salt Lake City, Utah. A graduate of the School of Criminology at Simon Fraser University, Dr. Patenaude taught at the University of Arkansas at Little Rock for seven years prior to moving to Westminster College. His primary areas of research are corrections, Aboriginal peoples and criminal justice, and qualitative research.

Steven B. Patrick, Ph.D., is an associate professor of sociology in the School of Social Sciences and Public Affairs at Boise State University, Boise, Idaho. He is also an independent program consultant.

Everette B. Penn is assistant professor of criminology at the University of Houston, Clear Lake, Texas. He is the author of several publications including an edited volume with Taylor Greene and Gabbidon titled *Race and Juvenile Justice* from Carolina Academic Press.

Rebecca D. Petersen, Ph.D., is an assistant professor of criminal justice at Kennesaw State University in Kennesaw (metro Atlanta), Georgia.

Gary W. Potter, Ph.D., is a professor of criminal justice and police studies at Eastern Kentucky University.

Pamela Preston is an assistant professor of criminal justice at Pennsylvania State University, Schuylkill, Pennsylvania.

Johnny R. Purvis, Ed.D., is a professor in the Graduate School of Leadership and Management at the University of Central Arkansas in Conway, Arkansas.

Megan Reynolds recently graduated from Pennsylvania State University, Harrisburg, Pennsylvania, with her Master of Arts degree in criminal justice. She is currently at Temple University working towards her Ph.D.

James Ruiz, Ph.D., is an assistant professor of criminal justice in the School of Public Affairs at Pennsylvania State University, Harrisburg, Pennsylvania. He is also retired from the New Orleans Police Department.

Christopher J. Schreck is an assistant professor in the Department of Criminal Justice at the Rochester Institute of Technology. He is also the editor of the *Journal of Crime and Justice*.

Sarah Settles is a master's student in criminal justice at Southern Illinois University at Carbondale. She intends to seek her doctorate in criminal justice and work with juveniles.

John E. Shutt, J.D., M.C.J., is an adjunct professor at the University of South Carolina's Department of Criminology and Criminal Justice and a Ph.D. candidate at the University of South Carolina's Department of Sociology.

Barbara Sims, Ph.D., is an associate professor of criminal justice in the School of Public Affairs at Pennsylvania State University, Harrisburg, Pennsylvania, where she also serves as criminal justice program coordinator.

Benjamin Steiner is a research associate and doctoral candidate in the Division of Criminal Justice at the University of Cincinnati. He holds an M.A. from Boise State University. He worked as a juvenile probation officer in Idaho prior to entering graduate school. His publications have appeared in *Justice Quarterly* and *Juvenile and Family Court Journal*.

Sharon K. Tracy, D.P.A., is a professor of justice studies in the Department of Political Science at Georgia Southern University.

Sean P. Varano, Ph.D., is an assistant professor of criminal justice in the College of Criminal Justice at Northeastern University. He received his doctorate in Criminal Justice from Michigan State University.

Carol Veneziano, Ph.D., is a professor and graduate coordinator in the Department of Criminal Justice & Sociology at Southeast Missouri State University.

Louis Veneziano, Ph.D., is a clinical psychologist at Woodward State Hospital School.

Lisa Hutchinson Wallace, Ph.D., is an assistant professor of correctional and juvenile justice studies, where she serves as online coordinator.

Ted R. Watkins, D.S.W., has had a career as a therapist and administrator in social work practice in mental health, residential treatment of adolescents, and family counseling agencies. His academic career has included teaching, research, and administration in social work and criminal justice programs with emphasis on addictions, mental health, and youth services.

Michael Weinberg, Ph.D., BCBA, is the vice president of Professional Education Resource and Conference Services (PERCS), in Milford, MA, and owner and CEO of Orlando Behavior Health in Florida. He received his Ph.D. in 1985 in the experimental analysis of behavior program at Temple University in Philadelphia, and is a Board Certified Behavior Analyst.

James B. Wells, Ph.D., is professor and director of the Center for Criminal Justice Education and Research in the Department of Correctional and Juvenile Justice Studies at Eastern Kentucky University.

Karan Kell White has a B.A. in sociology from Louisiana Technical University and an M.A. in criminal justice from the University of Louisiana at Monroe. She is employed by the State of Louisiana at Swanson Center for Youth, Office of Youth Development as a social services counselor.

Table of Contents

Part I   The Development of a Separate Justice System for Juveniles

1   History of the Treatment of and Attitudes toward Children...3
Allan L. Patenaude

1.1   Introduction 3
1.2   Children in Biblical Times 5
1.3   Children during the Middle Ages and the Renaissance 8
1.4   Children during the Age of Enlightenment and
      Industrial Revolution 10
1.5   Children in America's Century of Juvenile Justice 16
      1.5.1   Balancing Protection and Punishment (1899–1966) 16
      1.5.2   Arguing for Formality in an Informal Process
              (1966–1975) 20
      1.5.3   The Balance Tips toward Punishment (1975–2003) 21
1.6   Children at the Dawn of the 21st Century —
      Are We Giving Up on Them? 24
1.7   Conclusion 26
References 26
Cases Cited 29
Notes 29

**2   Nineteenth Century Antecedents to the
Twentieth Century Juvenile Court 31**
James L. Hague

2.1   Introduction 31
2.2   Nineteenth-Century Reformers 35
2.3   The Progressive Era 42
2.4   Creation of a Separate Justice System for Juveniles 44
References 46
Cases Cited 47

3   The Extension of Constitutional Rights to Juveniles 49
Katherine Bennett

    3.1   Introduction 49
    3.2   *Haley v. Ohio*, 332 U.S. 596 (1948):
         Fourteenth Amendment Guarantees 51
    3.3   *Gallegos v. Colorado*, 370 U.S. 49 (1962) 53
    3.4   *Kent v. United States*, 383 U.S. 541 (1966):
         Juvenile Court Waivers 53
    3.5   *In re Gault*, 387 U.S. 1 (1967):
         Paving the Road for Constitutional Protections 55
    3.6   *In re Winship*, 397 U.S. 358 (1970):
         Standard of Proof in Juvenile Court Proceedings 57
    3.7   Sixth Amendment Rights for Juveniles 59
         3.7.1 *McKeiver v. Pennsylvania*, 403 U.S. 528 (1971):
                   Trial by Jury 59
         3.7.2 *Davis v. Alaska*, 415 U.S. 308 (1974) 60
    3.8   Fifth Amendment Protections:
         Double Jeopardy and Self-Incrimination 61
         3.8.1 *Breed v. Jones*, 421 U.S. 519 (1975): Double Jeopardy ... 61
         3.8.2 *Fare v. Michael C.*, 442 U.S. 707 (1979):
                   Self-Incrimination 63
    3.9   *Smith v. Daily Mail Publishing Company*, 443 U.S. 97 (1979) 64
    3.10 *Schall v. Martin*, 467 U.S. 253 (1984) 65
    3.11 Constitutional Rights of Juveniles in Educational Institutions 66
         3.11.1 First Amendment Rights and Juveniles 66
                 3.11.1.1 *West Virginia State Board of Education*
                           v. Barnette, 319 U.S. 624 (1943) 66
                 3.11.1.2 *Tinker v. Des Moines School District*,
                           393 U. S. 503 (1969) 67
             3.11.2 *Goss v. Lopez*, 419 U.S. 565 (1975): Fourteenth
                 Amendment Due Process Rights in School Suspensions 68
             3.11.3 *New Jersey v. T.L.O.*, 469 U.S. 325 (1985):
                 Fourth Amendment Rights and Juveniles 68
    3.12 Conclusion 70
    References 70
    List of Cases 70

Part I   Conclusion

Part II   Explaining Delinquency: Theory and Practice

4   Theoretical Explanations for Juvenile Delinquency 77
Barbara Sims

    4.1   Introduction 77
    4.2   Classical Deterrence Theory 78

4.3   Biological Theory 79
       4.3.1   Modern-Day Biological Theory 79
4.4   Psychological Explanations for Delinquency 80
4.5   Sociological Theories of Delinquency: Macro Perspectives 81
       4.5.1   Strain, Subcultural, and Differential Opportunity Theories.... 82
       4.5.2   Social Disorganization Theory 83
4.6   Sociological Theories of Delinquency: Micro Perspectives 84
       4.6.1   Differential Association and Social Learning Theory......... 84
       4.6.2   Social Control Theories of Delinquency.......... 85
               4.6.2.1   Self-Control Theory 86
4.7   Symbolic Interaction and Labeling Theory 86
4.8   Conflict and Critical Theories of Delinquency 87
4.9   Other Theories of Juvenile Delinquency..................... 88
       4.9.1   General Strain Theory 88
       4.9.2   A Systemic/Social Disorganization Model of Delinquency.... 88
       4.9.3   Crime, Shame, and Reintegration 89
4.10   Conclusions 89
References 90

5   **Delinquent Girls** **93**
    Suman Kakar

    5.1   Introduction 93
    5.2   What Do We Know about Female Delinquents? 94
           5.2.1   What Type of Crimes Do Girls Commit?........ 95
           5.2.2   What Age Group Are These Girls? 97
           5.2.3   Minorities Are Overrepresented 97
           5.2.4   Upward Trend in Female Delinquency Underrated.......... 98
           5.2.5   Juvenile Justice System Biased against Female Delinquents ... 98
    5.3   Childhood Maltreatment and Female Delinquency..................... 100
           5.3.1   Female Delinquents Internalize Their Victimization,
                   Threaten Their Own Well-Being...................... 100
           5.3.2   School Discipline Problems and
                   Poor Academic Performance 100
    References... 104

6   **Gender-Specific Intervention for Female Delinquents**.........**109**
    Kristi Holsinger

    6.1   Introduction 109
    6.2   A Brief History of Correctional Interventions for Girls 110
    6.3   Components of Gender-Specific Services 113
           6.3.1   Abuse.. 113
           6.3.2   Problematic Family Relationships................. 114
           6.3.3   Drug and Alcohol Use.................................... 115
           6.3.4   Health and Mental Health Issues 115
           6.3.5   Parenting and Childcare................................ 116
           6.3.6   Academic and Economic Challenges............. 117
           6.3.7   Self-Esteem and Gender Socialization 118

6.4 Other Issues in the Development and Implementation of
Gender-Specific Services.. 119
6.5 Conclusion 121
References.. 122

7 **The Relationship between Childhood Maltreatment
and Delinquency** **127**
Marilyn Chandler Ford

7.1 Introduction 127
7.2 Legally Defining Child Maltreatment... 128
7.3 Issues Associated with Identifying Abuse and Neglect.............. 130
    7.3.1 Reporters of Abuse 130
    7.3.2 Data Sources... 131
7.4 A Profile of Child Maltreatment 132
    7.4.1 Type of Maltreatment... 132
    7.4.2 Child Fatalities.. 132
    7.4.3 Victim–Offender Relationship.. 133
    7.4.4 Other Correlates of Maltreatment.................................... 133
7.5 Responses to Child Maltreatment... 134
7.6 Explanations of Abuse and Neglect.. 137
7.7 The Link between Abuse or Neglect and Delinquency.............. 138
7.8 Future Needs.. 139
References.. 141
Notes 143

8 **Effective Social Control Measures in School and
Community Programs: Implications for Policy
and Practice** **145**
Carrie M. Butler and Ted R. Watkins

8.1 Introduction 145
8.2 Theoretical Perspectives.. 146
    8.2.1 Control Theory.. 147
8.3 The Present Study 147
    8.3.1 Methodology.. 148
    8.3.2 Measures.. 149
    8.3.3 Dependent Variables... 150
        8.3.3.1 Gang Participation... 150
        8.3.3.2 Delinquency 150
        8.3.3.3 Peer Association 150
    8.3.4 Independent Variables 151
        8.3.4.1 Involvement in School and Community Programs. 151
        8.3.4.2 Social Control.. 152
        8.3.4.3 School Social Control.. 152
        8.3.4.4 Community Social Control................................ 152
        8.3.4.5 Social Accountability... 153
        8.3.4.6 Adult Supervision 153

8.4   Data Analysis 153
      8.4.1   Results 154
      8.4.2   Hypothesis 1 154
           8.4.2.1   Gang Participation 156
           8.4.2.2   Drug-Related Crimes 156
           8.4.2.3   Property Crimes 157
           8.4.2.4   Violent Crimes 158
      8.4.3   Hypothesis 2 159
           8.4.3.1   School Social Control on Gang Participation ... 159
           8.4.3.2   School Social Control on Delinquency 160
           8.4.3.3   Community Social Control on Gang
                     Participation 160
           8.4.3.4   Community Social Control on Delinquency 161
      8.4.4   Hypothesis 3 162
           8.4.4.1   Adult Supervision on Gang Participation 162
           8.4.4.2   Adult Supervision on Delinquency 163
      8.4.5   Hypothesis 4 163
           8.4.5.1   Social Accountability on Gang Participation 163
           8.4.5.2   Social Accountability on Delinquency 163
      8.4.6   Hypothesis 5 163
8.5   Discussion: Policy and Practice Implications 164
8.6   Conclusion 166
References 166

Part II   Conclusion

Part III   The Extent and Nature of Juvenile Delinquency

9   The Myth of the Juvenile Superpredator **173**
Karen S. Miller, Gary W. Potter, and Victor E. Kappeler

9.1   Introduction 173
9.2   The Myth of a Juvenile Crime Wave 176
9.3   Getting Tough on Juvenile Crime:
       Reconstructing the Juvenile Justice System 179
9.4   Lock 'Em Up and Throw Away the Key: Juveniles in Custody 182
9.5   Treating Juveniles as Adults: Does It Work? 183
9.6   Blaming the Victims: Crime against Juveniles 185
9.7   Conclusion 187
References 189

10   The Emerging Problem of Preppie Gangs in America **193**
Gordon A. Crews, Johnny R. Purvis, and Mary Hjelm

10.1   Introduction 193
10.2   Characteristics of Preppie Gangs 194
10.3   Types of Preppie Gangs and Member Characteristics 195

10.3.1 Delinquent or Criminal Gangs 197
10.3.2 Ideological Gangs 198
10.3.3 Occult-Based/Goth Groups 199
10.4 Demonstrated Behaviors within a Psychosocial Perspective 200
10.5 Possible Causes of Involvement 201
10.6 Attitude of Parents/Guardians 204
10.7 Reactions of the Law Enforcement Community 205
10.8 Games Played with the Law Enforcement Community 206
10.9 Dangers of Preppie Gangs 207
10.9.1 Criminal Activity Associated with Preppie Gangs 207
10.9.2 Preppie Gang-Related Violence 208
10.10 Preppie Gang Migration 210
10.10.1 Member Migration vs. Concept Migration 212
10.11 Responsible and Accountable 215
10.12 Conclusion 216
References 217

11   Juvenile Cybercrime: An Exploration of Theoretical and Legal Implications

Edward J. Girard

11   Juvenile Cybercrime: An Exploration of Theoretical and Legal Implications 219

11.1 Introduction 219
11.2 A Theoretical Examination of Cybercrime 221
11.2.1 The Classical Perspective 221
11.2.2 The Biopsychosocial Approach 222
11.2.3 The Social Learning Viewpoint 223
11.2.4 Social Bonding Approach 224
11.2.5 Strain and Anomie Theories 225
11.2.6 Other Control Theories 227
11.2.7 Social Disorganization and the Chicago School 227
11.2.8 Developmental Theories 228
11.3 Putting It All Together 229
11.4 Legal Problems and Implications 230
11.5 Conclusion 231
References 231

12   Juvenile Stalkers: An Introduction 235
Deborah L. Laufersweiler-Dwyer and R. Gregg Dwyer

12.1 Introduction 235
12.2 Stalking Defined 235
12.2.1 Technical Definitions 235
12.2.2 Legal Definitions 236
12.2.3 Behavioral Definitions 237
12.3 Stalking in Adults 237
12.3.1 Prevalence 237
12.3.2 Adult Typologies 239

12.4 Stalking by Children and Adolescents... 240
    12.4.1 Prevalence 240
    12.4.2 Obsessional Behaviors 241
12.5 Theoretical Explanations and Typologies for Child and
    Adolescent Stalking 243
    12.5.1 Typologies 243
12.6 Theoretical Models 244
    12.6.1 Behavioral Models 244
    12.6.2 Psychodynamic Model... 244
    12.6.3 Functional Analysis.. 245
    12.6.4 Communications Theory 245
12.7 Conclusion... 246
References.. 246

Part III Conclusion

Part IV Policing and Prosecuting the Youthful Offender

13 Police Organizations and Problem-Solving Strategies for Juvenile Intervention: Identifying Crucial Elements............255
John D. McCluskey, Timothy S. Bynum, Sean P. Varano,
Beth M. Huebner, Justin W. Patchin, and Amanda Burgess-Proctor

13.1 Introduction.. 255
13.2 Early Onset.. 256
13.3 Essential Elements for Programmatic Innovation 257
    13.3.1 Integration of Key Policymakers (Stakeholders) 257
    13.3.2 Communication and Shared Vision.............................. 258
    13.3.3 Assessment and Evaluation... 260
13.4 Site Descriptions.. 262
13.5 Data and Methods.. 263
    13.5.1 Measures 264
    13.5.2 Analysis 265
13.6 Conclusion... 270
    13.6.1 Future Directions... 271
References.. 271
Notes 273

14 Juvenile Curfews: The Recent Increase of Their Use 275
Janice Ahmad and James Ruiz

14.1 Introduction.. 275
14.2 Purpose and Extent of Youth Curfews.................................... 276
    14.2.1 Examples of Curfew Programs..................................... 279
14.3 Legal Issues... 279
14.4 Research on Curfew Laws and Enforcement............................ 283
14.5 The Role of the Police... 287
14.6 Policy Issues and Conclusion 289

References 291
Cases Cited 293

15 Prosecuting Juvenile Offenders 295
Leanne Owen

15.1 Introduction 295
15.2 Distinguishing between What Prosecutors Do and
      Who They (Think They) Are 297
15.3 The Origins of the Prosecutorial Job 298
      15.3.1 An Advocate for the Public: The Prosecutor as
             Elected Official 298
      15.3.2 "Doing More": Ideals of Community Justice and
             Community Prosecution 299
15.4 "Should We or Shouldn't We?" — The Decision to Charge 301
      15.4.1 Prosecutorial Constructions of Juvenile Offenders
             and Their "Just Deserts" 301
      15.4.2 Prosecutorial Considerations and Formulation
             of Concepts 303
      15.4.3 Goodness and Badness: Considering
             the Juvenile's Behavior 305
      15.4.4 Adulticism and Infanticism: Considerations of Maturity ... 306
      15.4.5 Salvageability and Disposability: Rehabilitative Prospects .. 307
15.5 Conclusion 309
References 309
Notes 310

16 Issues Associated with Juvenile Waiver 311
Craig Hemmens and Benjamin Steiner

16.1 Introduction 311
16.2 The Juvenile Court 312
16.3 Challenges to the Juvenile Court 313
16.4 Public Support for Juvenile Waiver 315
16.5 Effects of Juvenile Waiver 316
16.6 Forms of Juvenile Waiver 317
      16.6.1 Prosecutorial Waiver 318
      16.6.2 Judicial Waiver 318
      16.6.3 Legislative Waiver 324
16.7 Conclusion 328
References 329
Cases Cited 330

**17 Status Offenders: Early History and
     Contemporary Policies and Programs 331**
Catherine E. Burton and Sharon K. Tracy

17.1 Introduction 331
17.2 Background 332

17.3 The Impact of the Juvenile Justice and
Delinquency Act of 1974 on Status Offenders 332
17.4 Contemporary Status Offenses and Status Offender Programs:
An Examination of Curfew Violations and Truancy 334
17.5 Conclusion 339
References 341
Cases Cited 342

Part IV   Conclusion

Part V   Special Juvenile Populations

18 The Disabled Juvenile Offender 347
Pamela Preston

18.1 Statement of the Problem 347
18.2 Types of Disability 348
18.3 The Prevalence of Disability in the Juvenile Offender Population .. 350
18.4 Programming 352
18.5 Conclusion 357
References 358

19 Juvenile Sex Offenders: An Overview 359
R. Gregg Dwyer and Deborah L. Laufersweiler-Dwyer

19.1 Introduction 359
19.2 Definitions 360
      19.2.1 Offenders 360
      19.2.2 Gender 360
      19.2.3 Age 361
      19.2.4 Socioeconomic Status 361
      19.2.5 Psychiatric Diagnosis 362
      19.2.6 Socialization 363
      19.2.7 Abuse History 364
      19.2.8 School Difficulties 365
      19.2.9 Family Functioning 365
      19.2.10 Substance Abuse 365
19.3 Victims 366
      19.3.1 Gender 366
      19.3.2 Age 366
      19.3.3 Relationship to Offender 367
19.4 Offenses 367
19.5 Causes for Offending 368
      19.5.1 Sexual Victimization 369
      19.5.2 Psychiatric Diagnosis 369
      19.5.3 Substance Abuse 370
      19.5.4 Developmental Factors 370
      19.5.5 Socialization 371

19.6 Summary 371
References 372

20 The Treatment of Adolescent Sex Offenders 375
Louis Veneziano and Carol Veneziano

20.1 The Epidemiology of Juvenile Sex Offending 375
20.2 Characteristics of Juvenile Sex Offenders 377
20.3 Typologies of Juvenile Sex Offenders 380
20.4 Assessment of Juvenile Sex Offenders for Treatment 381
20.5 Treatment of Adolescent Sexual Offenders 381
20.6 Conclusions: A Practical Orientation 384
References 385

**21 Utilizing Applied Behavior Analysis with Juvenile
Sexual Offenders 391**
Scott LeGrand, Michael Weinberg, and E. K. McIntyre

21.1 Introduction 392
21.2 PBS: A Service Delivery Model 395
21.3 Origin of PBS 396
21.4 Goals of PBS 396
21.5 Assumptions and Characteristic of PBS 397
21.6 PBS: A Service-Delivery Model 398
21.7 Victim to Victimizer: A Behavioral Analytic Formulation 399
21.8 Relational Frame Theory 400
21.9 Assessment Process and Treatment Issues:
     Functional Assessment 402
21.10 Clinical Behavior Analysis 403
21.11 Conclusion 405
References 406

**22 The Complexities of Juvenile Justice and Delinquency
Research in American Indian Communities 409**
Lisa Bond-Maupin

22.1 Introduction 409
22.2 Policy and Legal Context for Understanding Jurisdiction and
     Juvenile Justice in American Indian Communities 411
     22.2.1 Introduction 411
     22.2.2 The Transformation of Legal Forms and Structures
            in Indian Nations 412
22.3 Resisting Generalization 419
22.4 Research on American Indian Delinquency and Juvenile Justice .. 421
     22.4.1 Introduction 421
     22.4.2 Review of the Literature 421
     22.4.3 Limitations of Prior Research and Implications for
            Ongoing Research 425

22.5 The Future of Juvenile Justice for American Indian Youths 427
References 428

**23 Using Culture and Social Structure to Predict Gang
Affiliation among Mexican American Adolescent Females....431**
Rebecca D. Petersen and David Olveda

23.1 Introduction 431
23.2 Review of the Literature 433
23.3 Measurements 435
23.4 Methods and Setting 436
23.5 Analysis 438
23.6 Findings 439
23.7 Summary and Conclusion 443
Acknowledgments 444
References 444
Notes 447

**24 Understanding and Treating the Substance-
Addicted Juvenile 449**
Ernest L. Cowles and Rebekah J. Lanphierd

24.1 Introduction 449
    24.1.1 The Treatment Context 450
24.2 What Do We Need to Treat? 451
    24.2.1 Risk and Protective Factors 451
    24.2.2 Key Factors in the Developmental Approach 452
        24.2.2.1 Genetics and Personality 452
        24.2.2.2 Personality and Self-Medication 453
        24.2.2.3 The Gateway Hypothesis 454
        24.2.2.4 Environmental Factors 455
    24.2.3 The Relationship between Delinquency and
        Substance Use 457
24.3 Prevention and Treatment 458
References 463
Notes 468

Part V   Conclusion

Part VI   Juvenile Corrections

25 Juvenile Diversion Programs 473
Robert L. Marsh and Steven B. Patrick

25.1 Introduction 473
25.2 Juvenile Court Discretion 476
25.3 Theories of Diversion 476

25.3.1 The Social Learning Theory 476
25.3.2 The Labeling Theory 476
25.3.3 The Social Control Theory 477
25.3.4 The Differential Association Theory 477
25.4 The Rationale of Diversion Programs 478
25.5 Types of Diversion Programs 479
25.5.1 Group Homes 479
25.5.2 Behavioral Contracts 479
25.5.3 Scared Straight Programs 479
25.5.4 Public Service 479
25.5.5 Education 480
25.5.6 Restitution 480
25.6 Summary of Research on Diversion Programs 481
25.7 Conclusions of Past Research 482
25.7.1 One Example of a Longitudinal Study 482
25.8 Demographics: Who Are These First-Time Offenders? 483
25.8.1 Ethnicity 483
25.8.2 Age 484
25.8.3 Gender 484
25.8.4 Outcomes 484
25.8.4.1 Tobacco or Alcohol 485
25.8.4.2 Recidivated for Drugs 485
25.8.4.3 Recidivated for Non-Alcohol-Related
Traffic Offenses 485
25.8.4.4 Recidivated for Violent Crimes 485
25.8.4.5 Recidivated for Property Crimes 485
25.8.4.6 Recidivism for Running Away from Home .. 485
25.8.5 Bivariate Findings 486
25.9 Summary 486
25.10 The Future of Diversion 486
References 487

26 Juvenile Placement and Programming 491
Kate King and Sarah Settles

26.1 Introduction 491
26.2 Private Juvenile Facilities 492
26.3 Public Institutions 493
26.4 Types of Programs 495
26.4.1 Treatment 495
26.4.2 Educational or Vocational Programs 496
26.5 Juveniles with Special Needs 498
26.5.1 Substance Abuse 498
26.5.2 HIV/AIDS 499
26.5.3 Mental Illness 499
26.5.4 Violent Recidivists 500

26.6 What Works?.. 501
26.7 What Does Not Work?.. 503
26.8 What Is Promising? 503
    26.8.1 Aftercare 504
26.9 Conclusion 505
References.. 506

27 Restorative Justice Programming 509
Karan Kell White

27.1 Introduction... 509
27.2 Restorative Justice: A Balanced Approach.............................. 510
    27.2.1 History 510
    27.2.2 Traditional Justice.. 511
    27.2.3 Restorative Justice 511
    27.2.4 The Legislative Basis — Federal Law..................... 512
        27.2.4.1 Juvenile Justice and Delinquency Prevention
                 Act of 1974... 512
        27.2.4.2 Victim's Rights and Restitution Act.............. 512
        27.2.4.3 Balanced and Restorative Justice Project 512
    27.2.5 Accountability-Based Sanctions for Juveniles................ 513
        27.2.5.1 Criticisms of Victim Offender Mediation for
                 Juveniles 513
        27.2.5.2 Net Widening... 514
        27.2.5.3 Fairness and Adequacy of Punishment......... 514
27.3 Restorative Justice Project: Louisiana Department of
Public Safety and Corrections 515
    27.3.1 Initiative #7 for the Eight-Year Document 515
    27.3.2 California Youth Authority Program............................. 517
27.4 Conclusion 517
References.. 518

28 Capital Punishment and Juveniles.............................521
Allan L. Patenaude and Megan Reynolds

28.1 Introduction... 521
28.2 Juveniles and Capital Punishment...................................... 522
28.3 The Juvenile Death Penalty vs. Evolving Standards of Decency 523
28.4 Recent Legal History on the Death Penalty for
Juvenile Offenders 526
28.5 Does a Juvenile's Moral Development Correspond to
an Adult's Mental Retardation?... 529
    28.5.1 The U.S. Supreme Court Bans the Execution of Juveniles... 531
28.6 Conclusion 532
References.. 533
Cases Cited.. 534
Notes 534

29 Job Satisfaction and Organizational Commitment among Staff of Juvenile Correctional Facilities 537
Kevin I. Minor, James B. Wells, and Earl Angel

29.1 Introduction and Literature Overview.................................. 537
29.2 Method... 539
    29.2.1 Participants 539
    29.2.2 Data... 539
        29.2.2.1 Job Satisfaction Data 541
        29.2.2.2 Organizational Commitment Data 541
29.3 Results... 542
29.4 Discussion.. 546
References.. 551
Notes 552

Part VI Conclusion

Part VII Other Critical Issues in Juvenile Justice

30 Increases in School Violence: Myth or Reality?....................559
Lisa Hutchinson Wallace

30.1 History of the Socialization of Children.............................. 559
30.2 Changing Roles of Adolescents in the Family 560
30.3 Changing Roles of Adolescents in Society......................... 560
30.4 Changing World of Schools... 562
30.5 The Sensationalism of School Violence 565
30.6 Explaining School Violence... 566
    30.6.1 Individual Explanations 566
    30.6.2 Family Explanations.. 569
    30.6.3 Peer-Related Explanations 571
    30.6.4 School-Related Explanations................................. 573
    30.6.5 Community Explanations 575
30.7 Responses to School Violence 577
    30.7.1 Current Responses 577
30.8 What Works.. 579
30.9 What Does Not Work.. 581
30.10 Recommendations for Future Responses............................ 583
References.. 585
Notes 601

31 The Adolescent Victim of School Violence: Social and Situational Risk Factors 603
Christopher J. Schreck, Thomas Ellsworth, John E. Shutt, and
J. Mitchell Miller

31.1 Introduction... 603
31.2 Trends and Patterns in School Victimization...................... 604

31.3   Theoretical Framework 605
  31.3.1   Routine Activities 605
    31.3.1.1   Exposure Factors.............................. 606
    31.3.1.2   Target Attractiveness Factors...................... 606
    31.3.1.3   Guardianship Factors 606
  31.3.2   Social Bonds and Vulnerability................... 607
31.4   The Present Study.. 608
  31.4.1   Dependent and Independent Variables 608
    31.4.1.1   Victimization 608
    31.4.1.2   Demographic Controls............................ 609
    31.4.1.3   School Environment Characteristics............ 609
    31.4.1.4   Delinquency 609
    31.4.1.5   Social Bonds 609
    31.4.1.6   Peer Associations 610
    31.4.1.7   Absences from School........................... 610
31.5   Findings... 610
31.6   Conclusion and Policy Implications........................... 613
  31.6.1   Policy Implications 614
References.. 615

32   Juvenile Justice: Answering the Question of Black Disproportionality...619
Everette B. Penn

32.1   Introduction.. 619
32.2   African Americans and the Juvenile Justice System 620
32.3   Defining Black and White in the United States 621
  32.3.1   Arrests... 621
  32.3.2   Detained Prior to Court Disposition.................... 622
  32.3.3   Petitioned Cases 622
  32.3.4   Adjudicated Cases... 623
32.4   Origin of the American Juvenile Justice System..................... 624
32.5   Traditional Answers to Disproportionality in Juvenile Justice.. 624
32.6   Black Criminology 625
32.7   Social Disorganization in the Black Community..................... 626
32.8   The Development of Black Social Disorganization and Delinquency.. 627
32.9   Child Saving or Child Slaving?.................................... 628
32.10 Continuing a Social Disorganizational Cycle 629
32.11 Conclusion.. 631
References.. 632
Notes 635

33   Kids, Cops, and School-Based Drug Prevention: The Legacy of Drug Abuse Resistance Education (DARE)....637
David Mueller

33.1   Introduction.. 637
33.2   One Step Forward, Two Steps Back 638

33.3 Where Drug War Dollars Are (and Are Not) Going 641
33.4 Drug Abuse Resistance Education (DARE) 641
33.5 Sticks and Stones, Slander and Suits 645
33.6 Science vs. Symbolic Politics 646
33.7 Conclusion 647
References 648
Notes 651

34 Is It Time to Abolish the Juvenile Justice System? 653
Tory J. Caeti and Eric J. Fritsch

34.1 Introduction 653
34.2 Arguments for Abolishing the Juvenile Justice System 654
    34.2.1 The Changing Landscape of Juvenile Justice 654
        34.2.1.1 The "New" Juvenile Criminal and
              the Wave of Violent Juvenile Crime 655
    34.2.2 The Juvenile Justice System Does Not Reflect
        the Goals of the Founders 655
    34.2.3 Juveniles Are Denied Basic Due Process Rights 658
        34.2.3.1 Right to a Jury Trial 659
        34.2.3.2 Role of Counsel in Juvenile Courts:
              A Good Thing? 660
    34.2.4 The Punitive Juvenile Justice System:
        Harsher than the Adult System? 661
    34.2.5 A Unified System 661
34.3 Arguments against Abolishing the Separate Juvenile
    Justice System 662
    34.3.1 Lessened Responsibility 663
    34.3.2 Greater Rehabilitation Potential 664
        34.3.2.1 Lower Recidivism 664
        34.3.2.2 State of Adult System: Warehousing Inmates .. 665
    34.3.3 Protections of the Juvenile Justice System 665
        34.3.3.1 Bail 665
        34.3.3.2 Harsher Penalties 666
        34.3.3.3 Criminal Records 667
    34.3.4 Maintaining a Separate System 667
        34.3.4.1 The Juvenile Justice Process Is Still More
              Benign than the Criminal Justice Process 668
    34.3.5 Success of the Juvenile Justice System 669
34.4 Conclusions 669
References 671
Cases Cited 673

Part VII Conclusion

    Index **677**

Part I

THE DEVELOPMENT OF A SEPARATE JUSTICE SYSTEM FOR JUVENILES

Throughout history, how the public thinks about children has greatly influenced approaches to handling the problem child. To a certain extent, even modern-day attitudes toward children are based on the Biblical notion of "spare the rod, spoil the child." In colonial America, some people believed that children who "acted up" were possessed by the devil. Throughout the history of America, it was believed that children were basically young adults, and accountable for their actions if they were beyond the age of seven or so. In Part 1, the authors examine some of this early history (Chapter 1) and demonstrate how attitudes and policies toward children have changed over time, leading up to a separate justice system for juveniles in Cook County (IL) in 1899 (Chapter 2). Further, Chapter 3 demonstrates that, over time, juveniles have been given some of the same constitutional rights as have adults, although some of those rights have yet to be extended to juveniles. Collectively, these chapters demonstrate that the public and policy makers alike have evolved in their thinking about young people, including support for the notion that some miscreant children are salvageable.

Chapter 1

History of the Treatment of and Attitudes toward Children

Allan L. Patenaude

1.1 Introduction

During the movie *Robin Hood — Prince of Thieves* (starring Kevin Costner and Morgan Freeman), many Americans were shocked by the scene showing a young child among those individuals who were about to be hanged as outlaws. Looking at this scene through the eyes of a person living in the United States at the dawn of the 21st century, such a reaction is not totally unexpected. Looking at the same scene through the eyes of someone from 12th-century England, however, would result in a dramatically different perspective. The events portrayed in this movie were, indeed, quite typical of state intervention during that period and for several centuries afterward (Ariès, 1973; Junger-Tas, 2002; Krisberg and Austin, 1978).

Age was not a major consideration in determining punishment for crime. Neither was it considered in determining who should be protected from abuse. Today, we need to ask ourselves two interrelated questions:

1. At what point should we, the nation-state, intervene in the life of a child to improve his or her lot in life?
2. Which form of intervention offers the most promise of success?

From antiquity to the start of the 21st century, the ways in which we have treated the youngest and most vulnerable members of our society have been reflective of both the dominant mode of production and the prevailing view of the role of the state in what many people consider to be "family matters." The delineation between the private and public spheres in matters involving children has changed considerably over time. During the 19th century, for example, society had few problems with having a child work 12 or more hours in a factory; such would not be the case in today's society. So, too, are there differences of opinion divided along class, racial/ethnic, urban/rural, and other lines concerning how best to treat children who are delinquent or in need of protection. Having a child step outside the house to gather a switch (or small branch) from a tree and return to be beaten across the buttocks with it may be acceptable to some members of contemporary society, but such punishment is clearly regarded as abuse by others within the same society.

This chapter explores the treatment of children and juveniles in Western society and, in particular, the United States from a historical perspective. Interwoven throughout is a discussion of the attitudes prevalent during each period that either supported such treatment or gave rise to changes from it. In so doing, this chapter traces the legal position of children from biblical times through the Middle Ages to the Industrial Revolution and, finally, to postindustrial American society of the 21st century. The treatment of both delinquent and nondelinquent children has varied within individual countries over time and between countries at any given time, making it appropriate in the context of this discussion to employ both temporal and spatial analyses. Although societies have generally approached the treatment of the delinquent from a common sense perspective, it is important to note that "common sense may exist in all cultures, but it is not the same from culture to culture" (Pye, 1981, p. 20). Whether the treatment of children, especially those who came into conflict with the law, during each of these periods was effective will become evident throughout this chapter.

1.2 Children in Biblical Times

Although no single mode of production was dominant during the biblical period of Western society, there were similarities in the manners by which children were perceived in the Western and Near-Eastern worlds. Around the coastlines and rivers of the Fertile Crescent region (formed by the Nile River, eastern Mediterranean, and Tigris–Euphrates rivers), hunting and gathering had generally been replaced by transhumance (migrating herds) and horticulture (small gardens), which were, in turn, in the process of being replaced by small-scale agriculture and the light industry that was developing in towns and villages along the coastline and rivers (Chard, 1975; Flannery, 1969, 1973). Among these societies, regardless of the mode of production, children were often raised in a multigenerational, extended family setting in which extreme sex-role differentiation was being enculturated and subsequently maintained within patriarchal power structures that spanned both the private and public spheres of social life.

The monotheistic religions of Christians and Jews as well as the polytheistic religions of Babylonia, Greece, and Rome all provided religious foundations for the treatment of children during this period. Children were regarded not merely as the next generation, but as proof of prosperity and a method of ensuring that the needs of parents would be met when they could no longer provide for themselves because of old age and infirmity (Eisenstadt, 1956; Lowie, 1961). When discussing the treatment of children and juveniles in a society, there can be little doubt that most parents love their offspring and attempt to act in the best interests of the child, the family, and society as a whole.

Proper child rearing was deemed essential for survival. Rules for the proper rearing of children were contained within the androcentric dogma of each religion and reflected in the respective legal codes of the various nation-states. Although no definitive age was encoded in the laws of the period, children were generally regarded as infants until the age of 7 years and were exempt from legal action, whereas children over the age of 7 were generally treated as miniature adults (Griffin and Griffin, 1978; Krisberg and Austin, 1978). Even in societies that permitted physical means to control children, it was found that parents were often reported to love their children and the society itself expressed devotion for its children. Biblical fathers, such as the patriarch Abraham, are referred to as being torn between loving a child or a God when asked to sacrifice a child for the favor of their God (Genesis 22: p. 16–18).

Throughout the Western and Near-Eastern worlds of this same period, children were regarded as legal property belonging to a father if free or to a master if they were born to a slave parent (Oppenlander, 1981). This legal status of "nonperson" was present within the Code of Hammurabi, the Mosaic Code, the Qur'an, and both the Twelve Tables and Corpus Juris Civilis of Rome (Lévy-Bruhl, 1961; Meek, 1958; Oppenlander, 1981). Each of these legal codes contained rules for acceptable social behavior in an androcentric and patriarchal society and the punishments for those persons who transgressed them. The Qur'an, for example, explicitly states how marriage is to be solemnized, children to be raised, orphans to be provided with the necessities of life, and how transgressors are to be judged, convicted, and punished in Islamic society (Pickthall, 1957; Taqi-ud-Din Al-Hilali and Khan, n.d.).

Interesting delineations are present in the Jewish Talmud and the Qur'an concerning the punishment of "sons" (including daughters by extension) who transgress one of the laws. These delineations are the earliest attempts to separate children from adults in terms of legal responsibility. Minor and petty crimes were often resolved between the parties (often families), whereas major crimes were publicly resolved. In rabbinic law, for example, Griffin and Griffin (1978, p. 6) noted the existence and recognition of three categories, namely: "(1) infant (up to age 6), (2) prepubescent (age 7 to puberty), and (3) adolescent (puberty to age 20)." As the maturity level increased, so, too, did the measures of responsibility and punishment. Similarly, within Islamic society, sons under the age of 4 or 5 were judged incapable of commiting a crime, but older sons were regarded as smaller adults who were dealt with by their fathers or, when a serous sin (*barâm*) had been committed, by a religious scholar acting as a judge (*faqîh*) (Pickthall, 1957; Taqi-ud-Din Al-Hilali and Khan, n.d.). As with an adult, a son whose offense was a serious sin was liable to harsh corporal punishment or death.

The legal philosophies enacted during the middle and later periods of the Roman Empire, however, have had the greatest impact on the status of the child in most Western civilizations. Roman law was both sexist and paternalistic as seen in the Twelve Tables (circa 455 BC). As with the Code of Hammurabi, they codified earlier Roman customary law and continued many of the principles and practices prevailing in Roman society. These included (1) *patriae potestas*, (2) *jus vitae necisque*, and (3) *a fortiori*. The principle that the father's power was absolute within the family and over family matters, *patriae potestas*, was the philosophical foundation upon which all Roman law was built (Oppenlander, 1981). The Roman father was free to make unimpeded decisions over the household and its members. It was he, for example, who could decide to sell family members into bondage and slavery or to arrange the marriages of his children. Within the principle of *patriae potestas* were subsumed the practices of *a fortiori* and *jus vitae necisque*. *A fortiori* was the power of handing out unlimited corporal punishment to control or correct the behavior of family members, whereas the ultimate expression of *patriae postestas* was found in *jus vitae necisque*. This latter principle gave a father the power of life or death over his spouse, children, and slaves (Oppenlander, 1981).

These principles, as well as the practices they engendered, would continue throughout the next 1000 years until the proclamation of the Corpus Juris Civilis (code of civil law) by the Roman Emperor Justinian (483–565 AD), and although Roman society evolved considerably during the millennium that passed between the enactments of the Twelve Tables and the Corpus Juris Civilis, the legal status of Roman children did not change.

Justinian's Corpus Juris Civilis guided Roman society until its end and continued to form the basis for several legal systems that emerged after its fall. The Corpus Juris Civilis comprised three distinct parts: the Codex (compilation of all previous Roman law), the Digest (case law or jurisprudence), and the Institutes (legal procedures and principles) (Gibbon, 1993; Moyle, 1896). The four books (or sections) of Institutes offer examples of the continuing androcentric nature of law during this period. For example, Book I, Section ix-iii notes that children, grandchildren born of a son, and all other descendants (except those born of a married daughter) are within the power of a father.

More important, for the purposes of this chapter, is the legal delineation between infants, children, and adults. Infants up to the age of 7 years were believed to lack the mental capacity to understand the wrongful nature of their actions. Unlike rabbinic law, Roman law employed chronological age and physical development, the nature of the offense, and the mental development of the child, rather than chronological age alone, in determining an individual's legal responsibility (Griffin and Griffin, 1978). In keeping with previous Roman law, fathers could punish children for their misdeeds, whereas the Roman state could publicly punish mature children over that age as adults (Halsall, 1996).

1.3 Children during the Middle Ages and the Renaissance

Although the laws and legal principles contained within Justinian's Corpus Juris Civilis were specific to Rome in the 6th century AD, they were constructed in such a manner that they also provided a foundation that supported the dogma of the emerging Christian church. Indeed, the Roman Catholic church of the 11th century AD employed these laws (alongside the Bible) as a cornerstone of its church or canon law (Vago, 2003). The civil laws of most Catholic nation-states across Western Europe followed this tradition, which, when coupled with German common law, led to the development of a new legal system: the Romano–Germanic system.

This system of law may be seen as "private law" because it regulates private relations, e.g., contracts and civil relations between individuals rather than between the state and individuals (Vago, 2003). With such a private-relations focus entrenched in the civil law, it does not require a large leap of legal reasoning to understand how the punishment of delinquent children remained within the institution of the family, where they continued to be treated as property. This leap is especially easy to accomplish when one examines the sociopolitical systems in Europe during this period (Ariès, 1973; Junger-Tas, 2002; Krisberg and Austin, 1978; LaMonte, 1949).

Most European countries were feudal states during the Middle Ages (approximately 500–1500 AD). Feudalism involved the fidelity of the populace to their local liege (or lord) who, in turn, owed loyalty to a superior lord and, eventually, to the king. Both the secular and non-secular followed this model as seen in the organization of the Catholic Church of Rome as well as the kingdoms throughout Europe. Both expected the kings and princes of the church (as the cardinals were known) to act in the best interests of those who owed them loyalty, in much the same manner as a father would watch over his children. Thus, the notion of *parens patriae* (from the Latin root *parentis*, meaning parent, and *patria*, meaning homeland or country) emerged whereby the nation-state as represented by the king had the responsibility to intervene in the lives of lesser lords and peasants in the best interests of the kingdom.

Children were considered the property of their father, in keeping with the traditions of Romano-Germanic law and the doctrines of the Roman Catholic Church (Ariès, 1973; LaMonte, 1949; Ludgwig, 1955; Vago, 2003). During the latter part of the Middle Ages, for example, children under the age of 7 years had absolute immunity from criminal liability because of the belief that they lacked the ability to form the necessary intent. Similarly, children between the ages of 7 and 14 years were generally believed to be incapable of forming intent but would be held criminally liable if it could be shown that they were sufficiently developed to form such intent (LaMonte, 1949). Along with childhood, such absolute and conditional immunity ended at the age of 14 years.

The Renaissance (French for rebirth) began at the end of the 15th century and saw the emergence of new perspectives on the treatment of children and the institutions to provide it. In Renaissance England, for example, the criminal liability of children was a mirror of the manner in which children were regarded on the European continent. Absolute immunity existed for children under the age of 7 years accompanied by conditional liability between the ages of 7 and 14 years. Children aged 7–14 years, if shown to understand the offense, were tried as adults and were liable to receive the same punishments as adults, including a number of corporal punishments, transportation to Australia or Van Dieman's Land (Tasmania), and the death penalty (Sanders, 1970).

During the Renaissance, however, there were a number of innovations introduced by both the church and the state. One of the effects of the frequent wars, plagues, and famines that marked the 16th and 17th centuries in Europe was the large number of children who roamed the continent, begging and stealing. Almshouses, hospices, indentured servitude, and transportation were a few of the methods used to combat this growing phenomenon.

Religious orders and the nation-states established almshouses, orphanages, and hospices to deal with children who were either in need of protection or were delinquent, or both (Ariès, 1973; Cavan, 1962; Somerville, 1982). During 1552, for example, Christ's Hospital was established in London to care for 400 abandoned children and was extremely successful in providing them with good-quality care and education (Sommerville, 1982).

In addition to the establishment of almshouses, orphanages, and hospices, the other major social policy for dealing with wayward children was through forced apprenticeships and indenturing of children over 10 years of age, as well as by sending them to sea as boy-sailors in the nation's navy or as drummer boys and boy-soldiers in the nation's army (Ariès, 1973; Junger-Tas, 2002; Zietz, 1969). England passed a number of so-called "poor laws" including the Statute of Artificers (1563) and the Vagabonds Act (1597) during the 16th century.

The former act authorized the indenture of poor and neglected children to families of substance who would provide training in domestic service, agriculture, or manufacturing, whereas the latter act authorized both corporal punishment and detention in workhouses and debtor's prisons for such children and youths. Such indentured service continued until the youth reached the age of 21 years; this ensured that the number of roaming children was reduced and that the national labor pool increased (Zietz, 1969). Similar efforts were undertaken by governments in both France and the Netherlands (Junger-Tas, 2002).

Throughout the Renaissance, responsibility for a child's misbehavior was placed upon the parent rather than the child (if the child lived within a family unit). Parents were legally responsible for both the misdeed and its correction. Although fathers could impose extreme physical punishments on their children, in keeping with the earlier Roman practice of *a fortiori*, there does not appear to be evidence indicating that they held *jus vitae necisque* (the power of life and death) during either the Middle Ages or the Renaissance (Ludwig, 1955; Sanders, 1970).

1.4 Children during the Age of Enlightenment and Industrial Revolution

Throughout the period that would become known as the Age of Enlightenment (approximately 1500–1800 AD), the religious views on childhood and delinquency would be challenged far more than in any other period. While the emerging views of Rousseau, Montesquieu, Bentham, and other philosophers concerning the rights of man and free will challenged the religious and political status quo, they were also influencing the way children and youths in conflict with the law were perceived and treated by society (Sanders, 1970; Schlossman, 1995).[1]

The emergence of new philosophies concerning the causes of crime and the methods for the treatment of adult criminals would trickle downwards, so to speak, and have an eventual effect on the treatment of children and youths. The reorganization of national criminal codes in Europe, based on new ideas of rehabilitation and resocialization, would result in the limiting of corporal and capital punishment and the emergence of incarceration as a form of penal sanction (Ariès, 1973; Hawes, 1971).

Methods that appeared to be more humane for dealing with delinquent and wayward children were also emerging during the Age of Enlightenment. Based on the dual notions that the environment rather than innate sin caused delinquency and that the best way to deal with delinquency was through correct and proper socialization, the almshouses, orphanages, and hospices were revisited and the new "juvenile institution" emerged (Ariès, 1973; Junger-Tas, 2002; Postman, 1994; Sanders, 1970; Schlossman, 1995).

During 1704, the Catholic Church established a hospice at San Michele outside Rome. This hospice was the first juvenile correctional institution, according to Cavan (1962, p. 5), created "for the correction and instruction of profligate youth, that they who when idle were injurious may, when taught, become useful to the state." Although the population of the hospice comprised children and youths under the age of 20 years who had either committed a criminal offense or were beyond their parent's ability to control, the architecture and operation was a direct precursor to the adult penitentiary, with its small cells, rule of silence, and congregate work regime (Cavan, 1962; Barnes and Teeters, 1959). During 1788, a juvenile institution was established by the London Philanthropic Society to provide similar corrective services for both delinquent and abandoned children in the nation's capital. This same society expanded its juvenile services and operate a number of institutions (similar to the large-scale orphanages of the day) and youth farms in southern England over the next 50 years (Griffin and Griffin, 1978; Schlossman, 1995). England's first juvenile reformatory was established on the Isle of Wight in 1838, based on the success of these farms and institutions. Coupled with the existing practices of forced apprenticeships and indentured service, the use of large institutions set the tone for British and Dutch government intervention in the 1900s. Both governments shared a desire to provide a structured and orderly upbringing for delinquent and wayward children, as well as to reduce crime and unemployment by providing them with basic work skills (Ariès, 1973; Junger-Tas, 2002; Schlossman, 1995).

With regard to law and justice, the 13 English-speaking colonies in America were simply extensions of the mother country, Great Britain. The philosophical and legal statuses of delinquent children varied from colony to colony due, for the most part, to the differences in the dominant modes of production in the colonies (Griffin and Griffin, 1978). There were distinct differences and similarities, for example, between how the northern colonies (Connecticut, Maine, Massachusetts, New Hampshire, New Jersey, New York, Pennsylvania, and Vermont) and the southern colonies (Georgia, Maryland, North and South Carolina, and Virginia) treated children who had offended against the social order.

For the most part, there was very little serious crime in colonial America, and those children and youth who did commit crime were subject to both English common law and natural law punishments (Bernard, 1992; Griffin and Griffin, 1978). Corporal punishments and imprisonment were heavily relied upon to correct the behavior of delinquents during this time. Both philosophically and legally, responsibility for the misbehavior and correction of children under the age of 7–10 years (depending on the colony or state) continued to reside with the father. Generally, children under this age were regarded as sinners and lacking the powers of free will or self-determination, whereas children over the age of 10 were regarded as miniature adults who possessed powers of reasoning when they committed a crime. The prevailing view that children aged 10–17 years were miniature adults was not a surprising one, given the notions concerning free will and determinism and the modes of production that were emerging and would become dominant during the Industrial Revolution.

During the period of industrialization in America (approximately 1750–1900 AD), the generally accepted views of how best to correct delinquent children would undergo a gradual shift, with the locus of control moving from the parents and family to the state. In the north, misbehaving children under the age of 7 years were given total immunity from legal responsibility. Because children were seen as sinners, the responsibility for such bad conduct and its correction fell to the parents rather than the errant child. The Quakers, for example, often held public meetings to discuss the correction of children, a responsibility that they then delegated to the family, whereas states such as New York laid stress on teaching a trade as a corrective measure (Griffin and Griffin, 1978). Many northern colonies or states lacked distinct legislation to deal with crime committed by children or youths and favored the idea of the family correcting such behaviour. However, these same colonies or states expressed no remorse when removing children from homes where the family was considered as incapable, negligent, or indulgent in alcohol and placing them in "proper" homes; thus removed, such children became the property of the state (Hawes, 1971). Imprisonment and other formal methods of social control were reserved for youths found committing serious crime.

The slave-owning southern colonies took a different approach to child misbehavior and crime, in part due to their largely slave-based plantation economies and history of slave ownership. Similar to their northern neighbors, southern legislators granted total legal immunity to children under the age of 7 years while continuing to treat children and youths over that age as miniature adults. This attitude was not surprising in light of the slave economy of the period because freeborn children were punished in the same manner as young slaves — brutally and with the purpose of ensuring compliance with the rules of society (Griffin and Griffin, 1978; Krisberg and Austin, 1978).

The 19th century was a time of rapid social, economic, and political change throughout the fledgling United States. Industrialization and urbanization brought large numbers of people from the farms and outlying areas into the cities and a demand for new skills and abilities. The need for increased literacy was most keenly felt among the working classes and immigrants as mechanization demanded the ability to read gauges and follow written instructions. The demand for child labor had increased in the same manner as it had in Great Britain, because their small physical stature enabled children to move deftly around and within the great machines of the day. Interestingly enough, however, both the northern and southern colonies and states regarded youths over 7 years of age as serving two masters: their fathers and their employers. This was due to the patriarchal structure of both societies and the fact that many children worked to support themselves or to assist their family (Krisberg and Austin, 1978).

Throughout the 19th century, states on both sides of the Mason–Dixon line embraced the concept of the juvenile institution in much the same manner as had Great Britain and Europe (Krisberg and Austin, 1978; Platt, 1969). Many children who were too young or too frail to work were left alone for long periods of time while their parents and older siblings worked one or more jobs to support the family. The truism that "idle minds are the devil's workshop" was often evident as many unsupervised children formed criminal and noncriminal gangs and roamed their respective neighborhoods, seeking ways to entertain themselves. If they were apprehended by the police, charged, and convicted of criminal offenses, children under the age of 10 were often sent to state-run institutions; youths over 10 years of age were often imprisoned alongside adult offenders, including the insane, manipulative, exploitative, and violent inmates of both sexes (Krisberg and Austin, 1978; Platt, 1969).

No distinction was made by the states in their treatment of abused, neglected, and delinquent juveniles during the first half of the 19th century. The emerging *parens patriae* attitude emphasized "teaching of lower-class skills and middle-class values" (Platt, 1969, p. 69) to the children and youths committed to these "one-size-fits-all" juvenile institutions. Although the nomenclature for these juvenile institutions varied within and between states, they were generally referred to as reformatories, reform schools, or houses of refuge (Platt, 1969). Such institutions were typically located in or near large urban centers, operated along militaristic lines, and provided basic literacy and trades training to the hundreds of juveniles confined within them (Platt, 1969). The regimes in such institutions were often described as "minor penitentiaries" and "hundreds of youths were there congregated under lock and key" (Platt, 1969, p. 69).[2]

The prevailing attitude of the state was that the juveniles needed to be protected from their environment and any potential criminality that might ensue; an attitude that was supported in the courts. In *Ex parte Crouse* (1838), the court rejected arguments from the father of a young girl, who had been committed by her mother to the Philadelphia House of Refuge, that the Bill of Rights applied to juveniles and that her committal to the house of refuge was done without due process and that the institution was itself a prison rather than a school. Although *Ex parte Crouse* (1838) would continue to be the standard employed by many states to legitimize their approaches to *parens patriae* well into the reconstruction period following the U.S. Civil War even without proof that their treatment of juveniles was successful in reducing crime among that age group.

During the three decades following the Civil War, the sentencing practices of many states contributed to the appearance of many cracks that appeared in the judicial wall that separated juvenile and adult offenders. Shelden (2001) and Watkins (1998) both noted, for example, that children were jailed alongside adults for petty offenses and sentenced to lengthy prison terms and even death for more serious offenses (see Platt, 1969 for a discussion of 14 juvenile cases involving the death penalty between 1800–1882). For example, the belief that juveniles needed to be protected from their social environments and any potential criminality, which was given credence in *Ex parte Crouse* (1838), was challenged and refuted in *People v. Turner* (1879). In this case, which was nearly identical to *Ex parte Crouse* (1838), court ruled that the juvenile was being punished rather than treated in the Chicago House of Refuge. This decision was based on the realities of daily life in that institution and the lack of due process protections that were afforded to the juvenile in this case. As seen in the previous discussion, there was little proof offered by the states that their treatment of juveniles was successful in reducing crime among children and youths.

However, the walls of juvenile justice were just as often reinforced by lower-court decisions, practices in other states, and well-intentioned (albeit sometimes misguided) social reformers. The United States was subject to large waves of European immigration, internal migration, and unemployment during the Reconstruction. Sheldon (2001) noted that many trade unions began to exclude juvenile "helpers" from their ranks, claiming that they affected the wage-earning abilities of younger trades-men; this practice displaced the juvenile worker into either dead-end jobs in local factories or unemployment. As a result of these factors, most states continued to use urban-based juvenile institutions (now known as "industrial" or "training" schools, within which little more than service or trades training and military discipline were taught), whereas a few states initiated rural-based training schools that merely substituted agricultural training for the service and trades training offered by their urban cousins! Their inmates were just as likely to have been criminalized and committed for their juvenile status (loitering, vagrancy, incorrigibility, promiscuity, etc.) rather than for a criminal conviction. It was against this backdrop that the drama of the child-saving move-ment was played out and the juvenile court was born (Platt, 1969).

The child-saving movement was born out of the cruel conditions faced by the poor of the era and the Victorian belief that the middle and upper classes should help those persons who were less fortunate than themselves. In Chicago, for example, upper-class women took it as their maternal mission to save the children of the poor (whether they wanted to be saved or not). Platt (1969, p. 79) noted that the argument used by many child-savers of the day was, "if a woman's place was in the home, she was certainly entitled to give her opinion on garbage disposal, cleanliness of the streets, and the care and education of children." Their activities were supported by a soft deter-minism that was loosely based on a misinterpretation of Charles Darwin's theory of evolution applied to the social environment. Indeed, they perceived that the social environment was the cause of delin-quency. Sheldon (2001, p. 218) noted that:

> The existing social [class] structure was held as good and necessary, but that there was a need to lead those who went astray back so that they could "fit" into the existing social order and class system. Unfortunately, the only place where they were permitted to "fit" was at or near the bottom of that order.

The child-savers advocated a rejection of the urban industrial school in favor of individual rehabilitation and treatment to assist juveniles to "fit" into society (Krisberg and Austin, 1978; Platt, 1969;

Sheldon, 2001). This was attempted by the individualized placement of children from the lower classes into middle-class families through an increasing number of children's aid societies, combined with calls for changes in the regimes within the existing industrial and training schools. There is little evidence that supports the effectiveness of these actions on the reduction of juvenile crime during this period despite the growth in the number of children's aid societies, industrial and training schools, and the creation of the first juvenile court in Cook County (IL) on July 1, 1899.

1.5 Children in America's Century of Juvenile Justice

1.5.1 Balancing Protection and Punishment (1899–1966)

The juvenile court heralded into existence nearly a century of justice for juveniles that sought to provide for the needs of the juvenile in the first instance, followed by the needs of society. The first juvenile court was as much a product of the child-saving movement as it was the result of a number of conditions that were coalescing in American society during the 1880s. These factors included: increased immigration, increased urbanization, dissatisfaction with the violence found in many juvenile institutions, and an increasing number of state and federal court decisions in which the lack of due process and the appalling conditions in juvenile institutions were condemned (Griffin and Griffin, 1978; Krisberg and Austin, 1978; Platt, 1969).

The creation of the juvenile court was accompanied by a number of changes that continue in either the same or a similar form to the present day. First and foremost was the exclusive jurisdiction of juvenile courts over the lives of children and juveniles. These early courts acted in much the same manner as the earlier English chancery courts and intervened in the lives of abused, delinquent, and neglected children and juveniles, their best interests uppermost in the hearts and minds of those involved (Griffin and Griffin, 1978; Platt, 1969).

The age jurisdiction of these courts varied between states. Most states granted total legal immunity to children under the age of 12 years, although a large number of states had a lower limit of 10 years of age for such immunity. A new class of legal status, the juvenile, was created for those who had reached this age but had not yet reached the age of criminal responsibility at either 16, 17, or 18 years of age (depending upon the state in which he or she resided). Although both children and juveniles could be adjudicated, labeled as delinquents, and placed in the care of the state by these courts for a broad range of criminal and noncriminal activities, juvenile delinquents were granted a limited form of legal immunity by the juvenile courts in that they could not receive the same sanctions that adults might receive for the same offense (Griffin and Griffin, 1978; Wheeler, 1983). Indeed, most states permitted a juvenile court to hold jurisdiction over a juvenile until he or she had reached the age of 21 years.

The second major change was brought about by the informality of the juvenile court. Early juvenile courts dispensed with the use of the formal courtroom and the adversarial process found in the criminal courts and, instead, sought to act in the juvenile's best interests (Griffin and Griffin, 1978; Platt, 1969). This goal was accomplished through the use of a working group comprising the juvenile court judge, prosecuting attorney, and probation officer, who would meet with the juvenile and, in many cases, his or her parents to determine what course of action should be taken. A number of authors have indicated, however, that this trend toward informality was far from uniform across the country (cf. Colomy and Kretzmann, 1995; Platt, 1969; Rothman, 1977, 1980; Schlossman, 1995). According to sociologists Paul Colomy and Martin Kretzmann (1995), for example, the early juvenile courts ranged between an informal social work style of proceedings that were often held in the judge's chambers and a formal judicial style of proceeding that was nearly indistinguishable from the adult criminal courts. Although the notion and practice of informality was at philosophical odds with the adult criminal courts and their constitutional requirements and safeguards, it remained unchallenged until the two decades between 1955 and 1975.

The third major change was the shift in focus from punishment to treatment and rehabilitation based on the emerging social work beliefs and methods of the period. Diagnosis of individual pathologies and the social conditions that contributed or maintained them was one of the goals of juvenile justice throughout this period. Once the problem was identified, the juvenile court then turned to existing social and mental health services to deal with the juvenile delinquent. According to Bernard (1992), those services that the juvenile courts "offered" to the juvenile and his or her parents were both coercive in nature and tended to be attempts at finding the best fit for the largest number of juveniles (rather than tailoring services to meet individual needs). Although conditions improved slightly, it was ironic that training and reform schools, as well as other group-oriented services, continued to be relied on to help the individual delinquent.

The only individual-oriented service that the juvenile court provided (in the broadest sense of the word) was probation (Bernard, 1992).

Building on the positive experiences of the Boston Municipal Court with the conditional release of offenders to John Augustus, juvenile probation as a rehabilitative sanction for juveniles became extensive throughout this period as every state authorized juvenile probation programs and personnel to operate them. According to juvenile programs specialist Patricia Torbet (1996, pp. 1–2), juvenile probation:

> … is the oldest and most widely used vehicle through which a range of court-ordered services is rendered. Probation may be used at the "front end" of the juvenile justice system for first-time, low-risk offenders or at the "back end" as an alternative to institutional confinement for more serious offenders. In some cases probation may be voluntary, in which the youth agrees to comply with a period of informal probation in lieu of formal adjudication. More often, once adjudicated and formally ordered to a term of probation, the juvenile must submit to the probation conditions established by the court.

The goals of juvenile probation as seen here and according to Vito et al. (1998) are, thus, community protection, individual accountability, and rehabilitation of the juvenile by equipping him or her with skills for living productively in the community.

In theory, probation officers could provide individual needs assessments and tailor their counseling and supervision activities to best meet the needs of their juvenile clients. In practice, however, probation caseloads began to increase to the point where the ability of many juvenile probation officers to diagnose individual needs was severely restricted and the amount of contact with, and supervision of, juvenile probationers had become similar to that provided to adult probationers in the criminal justice system. To meet this challenge, the position of intake officer was created and adopted by most juvenile courts. Although this new position did not reduce the number of juveniles supervised by a probation officer, it did provide a few more moments for client contact, supervision, and paperwork because they no longer had to perform the initial needs assessment of their clients.

During the 1960s, the effectiveness of large juvenile institutions was called into question. Indeed, many of these institutions had not changed since they were first opened as reform schools during the late 19th century. Krisberg and Austin (1993) noted that the juveniles warehoused in many state-run institutions still received little care and were often brutalized during their time in the state's care even after 100 years of operation. These conditions led to a brief movement, beginning in Massachusetts and sweeping across the nation, which closed many reform and training schools. Accompanying the closure of many large institutions was the creation of smaller, group homes or halfway houses as well as forestry and wilderness camps in which the structure permitted closer relationships between the juvenile and staff members and promoted change.

Although the percentage of juveniles committed to institutions remained small in comparison to those who received community sanctions, Griffin and Griffin (1978, p. 346) noted that "many authorities have argued that the institutionalization of youths is an unworkable, ineffective treatment strategy. The general consensus is that juvenile correctional institutions probably do more harm that good." This is a difficult position to support. Using 1975 data (in the absence of earlier data), it is possible to note that less than 25 percent of juveniles returned to custody during that same year, for example, were returned to custody by either the juvenile courts (8 percent) or an aftercare or parole agency (16 percent) (Griffin and Griffin, 1978, p. 347). Another attempt to promote Martinson's (1974) argument that "nothing works" has been attempted by examining the number of individuals who had served time in a juvenile institution and had been subsequently incarcerated in an adult correctional facility. Although Griffin and Griffin (1978) offered anecdotal information to show that nearly half of such individuals served time in an adult facility, such data as this fails to recognize that the effectiveness of juvenile institutions cannot be measured by examining variables outside the control of that system.

Prior to the 1960s, the effectiveness of juvenile probation was accepted by most Americans. Similar to the doubts regarding the effectiveness of juvenile institutions, this sanction also came to be questioned during the first half of that decade. Many lay persons, practitioners, academics, and the media began to view juvenile probation through glasses with Martinsonian lenses and cry "nothing works" and "probation is too lenient" (Junger-Tas, 2002). The notion of leniency was especially galling to some critics for whom punishment, the harsher the better, was equated with justice. Thus, any form of leniency was regarded as inefficient despite the fact that most juvenile probationers successfully completed their term of probation and avoided further conflict with the law during this same period (Griffin and Griffin, 1978).

1.5.2 Arguing for Formality in an Informal Process (1966–1975)

Although the philosophical shift may have been toward treatment and rehabilitation, dissatisfaction with the juvenile court's lack of the constitutional due process remained. This was seen not only in the *In re Holmes* (1955), but in a number of landmark U.S. Supreme Court decisions that examined due process protections for juveniles between 1955 and 1975.

As mentioned previously, the Supreme Court refused to explore the need for due process protections for juveniles in the case of *In re Holmes* (1955). In that case, the Court clearly stated its belief that the guarantees of protection granted to adults in the Second, Fifth, Sixth, Seventh, and Eighth amendments did not need to be applied to juveniles, because the role of the juvenile court was to help juveniles rather than to determine guilt and punish offenders as was the case in the adult criminal courts. In so doing, the Supreme Court reinforced not only the existing state practices of *parens patriae* but also that of age discrimination when it declined to rule on the applicability of the Bill of Rights to juvenile proceedings in the case of *In re Holmes* (1955).

Although the Supreme Court refused to apply the Bill of Rights in a *carte blanche* fashion to the juvenile justice system during 1955, it nevertheless was quite amenable to dispensing with its previous hands-off policy when confronted with egregious abuses of a juvenile's rights such as in *Gallegos v. Colorado* (1962). In that case, the Supreme Court ruled that the isolation of a juvenile for a prolonged period of time with the hope of obtaining a confession was tantamount to coercion. Any subsequent confession, the Court stated, would be deemed as having been involuntarily obtained and in contravention of the Fifth Amendment. Yet, the Supreme Court provided limited due process protections in four landmark decisions over the next 13 years, namely: *Kent v. United States* (1966), *In re Gault* (1967), *In re Winship* (1970), and *Breed v. Jones* (1975) (see Chapter 3 for an in-depth discussion of these cases).

Although these cases were decided during the 20-year period between 1955 and 1975, they nonetheless provided the precedents that most juvenile cases have referred to since that time. The juvenile justice system remains caught between the desire to provide informal hearings and services in the best interests of the juvenile and the desire to provide formal, evidence-based hearings with full due process protections. Overlaying this dynamic is the desire to punish offenders regardless of their age and to protect society from juvenile offenders, especially those who commit violent offences. The following section discusses the past quarter century of juvenile justice in the United States. In so doing, it explores the notion that the juvenile justice system is becoming more formal and punitive in its approach to juvenile delinquency and how the effects of this philosophical shift are being reflected in our treatment of juvenile offenders.

1.5.3 *The Balance Tips toward Punishment (1975–2003)*

Although Supreme Court decisions between 1965 and 1975 brought some hope that the juvenile justice system would provide juveniles with full due process protections, that hope was not realized (Junger-Tas, 2002; Krisberg and Austin, 1993). The juvenile justice system reinvented itself in ways that began to mirror the adult criminal justice system, with an emphasis on punishment and incapacitation based on the notions that juveniles were capable of self-determination and that society needed to be protected from juvenile offenders. Indeed, developments within the juvenile justice system during the latter part of this period appeared to have blurred many of the lines that separate the juvenile and adult justice systems to such an extent that Junger-Tas (2002, p. 31) argued: "it also meant the disintegration of the essentially protective system based on the principle that that the delinquent was primarily a victim of circumstances and environment." A new consensus was emerging that placed punishment and accountability ahead of treatment and rehabilitation for juvenile offenders.

Throughout the last quarter of the 20th century, probation remained the workhorse of the juvenile justice system (see Torbet, 1996; Snyder and Strickland, 1999), but its worth as an effective sanction for juvenile offenders was questioned. The methodological problem of quantifying rehabilitation in terms of providing skills for productive living was ignored in favor of employing recidivism as the measure of success in juvenile probation.

During the first half of this period (1975–1992), juvenile justice practitioners sought out new and innovative ways to deal with the increasing number of juveniles who were being processed by the juvenile courts. For example, juvenile probation agencies collaborated with adult correctional departments and experimented with the notion of tough love. Notable among these was New Jersey's Scared Straight program, which brought juvenile probationers and inmates serving life sentences together at the Rahway State Prison wherein they were confronted with the realities of prison life. Similarly, many probation departments experimented with wilderness challenge programs (modeled on the highly effective Outward Bound programs), which sought to reduce juvenile crime by increasing self-confidence and proper decision making among the participants. The effectiveness and life span of these programs did not live up to expectations due, mainly, to the lack of follow-up support for teens who were returned to their criminogenic environments.

At the other end of the treatment spectrum were found a number of "boot camp" programs that also emerged during this same period. Modeled on the military recruit school, this intermediate sanction placed juvenile and young adult offenders into a paramilitary environment where the program included limited skills training and self-improvement. Generally, boot camp programs ranged from 90 to 120 days in length. Although boot camps decreased the number of juveniles detained and the length of their stay, these programs suffered from the same design problems as the earlier Scared Straight and wilderness challenge programs.

Treatment activities that were proactive rather than reactive in nature were also developed in line with current criminological theories. These theories and the programs built upon them included such things as differential association (introduction to and mentoring in the arts), differential reinforcement (intensive aftercare supervision), and social bonding (after-school programs that sought to help juveniles succeed in academics and to reduce the dropout rate).

The enactment of the federal Juvenile Justice and Delinquency Prevention Act (hereafter JJDP Act, 1974) removed one of the great millstones that had hung around the neck of the juvenile justice system since its inception: status offenses. Prior to the passage of this act, juvenile court judges routinely mixed abused, neglected, and delinquent juveniles together in state-run institutions and programs. Status offenders would now be referred to family courts rather than juvenile courts. This act required that all nondelinquent children be deinstitutionalized and that delinquent juveniles also be protected from the influences of adult offenders by ensuring that juvenile and adult offenders were housed separately.

During the second half of this period (1993–2003), legislators and juvenile justice practitioners ignored the notion that just as there is no single cause for juvenile delinquency, there is also no single cure for it. Probation continued to be the primary method of dealing with juvenile delinquents during the early 1990s. The juvenile probation officer was heavily relied on to facilitate change in the juvenile and to protect society. Innovative supervision techniques were attempted within juvenile probation at this time. Intensive supervision probation (ISP) was developed, whereby a team of juvenile probation officers would provide higher levels of supervision for a smaller number of juvenile probationers and enhance the accountability of probation as a sanction. Unfortunately, the underlying goal was to put the "get-tough" rhetoric into action by providing increased protection to society rather than to increase opportunities for the rehabilitation of the juvenile offender. Similar practices have been adapted for the intensive supervision of high-risk juveniles in gangs and at schools (see Altschuler and Armstrong, 1994; Krisberg et al., 1994).

As had happened during the first half of this period, new programs and activities were explored to reduce both the juvenile court's reliance on probation and the number of juvenile offenders. Diversion and restorative justice programs were explored, for example, as possible methods to accomplish these goals while reducing the workload of the juvenile courts and avoiding the stigma of a conviction for the juvenile. Building on the early successes of restorative justice programs in Maine, Minnesota, and Florida, Balanced and Restorative Justice (BARJ) programs emerged in many parts of the United States. These programs sought to hold the juvenile accountable for his or her actions, ensure safety for the community, and help the juvenile develop new coping and decision-making skills (see Bazemore and Umbreit, 1997).

Specialty courts for first-time and nonviolent juvenile offenders also came into being during this time. Although teen courts were developed during the 1970s as an alternative to the increasingly formal juvenile courts, they proliferated throughout the late 1980s and 1990s. Similar to BARJ programs, teen courts stress accountability, personal growth, and empowerment while providing appropriate sanctions to many minor, first-time offenders (see Harrison et al., 2001). Similar in approach to teen courts, drug courts emerged during the 1990s to deal with first-time offenders, both juvenile and adult, whose offense was drug related. Originating in Florida during 1989, there are now over 600 drug courts operating across the United States, which have as their mandate:

> ... to use the authority of the court to reduce crime by changing defendants' drug-using behavior. Under this concept, in exchange for the possibility of dismissed charges or reduced sentences, defendants are diverted to drug court programs in various ways and at various stages of the judicial process, depending on the circumstances. (US GAO, 1997, p. 5)

The central tenet within both teen and drug courts is the notion of offender accountability, as demonstrated by the frequent court appearances, the use of graduated sanctions and rewards, and the provision of individualized services or treatment.

In its 1993 iteration, for example, the JJDP Act sought to deal effectively with serious, violent, and chronic juvenile offenders. Indeed, the JJDP Act (1993) has incorporated language that effectively treats juvenile offenders as miniature adults. In the face of increasing rates of violent juvenile crime, it was not surprising that federal and state governments enacted legislation that created harsher penalties and onerous processes for juveniles accused and convicted of violent crimes. Indeed, legislators feel vindicated in their efforts to reduce juvenile crime through the so-called "get-tough" efforts because the juvenile rates of violent crime dropped during the last 5 years of the 1990s.

1.6 Children at the Dawn of the 21st Century — Are We Giving Up on Them?

The extremely small, albeit tragic, number of school shootings during the last few years and the media coverage of those events have contributed to what criminologist Stanley Cohen (1972) described as a moral panic, whereby:

> A condition, episode, person or group of persons emerges to become defined as a threat to societal values and interests; its nature is presented in a stylized and stereotypical fashion by the mass media; the moral barricades are manned by editors, bishops, politicians, and other right-thinking people. (Cohen, 1972, p. 9)

The maintenance of such themes often leads to a sense of moral indignation and (for some) a sense of fear that is created, made public, and reproduced for a short period of time. Violent crime committed by juveniles is one such moral panic that has lasted most of the past decade.

As the legislation and the attitudes of many juvenile courts have illustrated, the American juvenile justice system appears to have returned to the situation mentioned in the opening paragraph of this chapter. Punishment and retribution are gradually replacing rehabilitation and treatment as the underlying philosophies of the juvenile justice system. Juvenile delinquents are being regarded less as dependents (owing to their age and relative states of mental development), and more as "young adults" whose status lacks the due process rights guaranteed by the Constitution to adults charged with the same offenses. The increasing numbers of juveniles certified as adults and transferred to the adult criminal courts and the growing number of states that have created blended sentencing legislation are indicative of this "get-tough" trend in juvenile justice.

As noted by Bishop (2000), the number of juveniles who were certified as adults and transferred to the adult criminal courts has increased by nearly 50 percent across the nation during the last decade (Bishop, 2000; FBI, 1989–1998). We cannot determine the actual number of juveniles who have arrived in front of an adult court judge owing to the number of states that exercise prosecutorial discretion in determining if a case falls within the jurisdiction of a juvenile court or whether it is statutorily excluded (Bishop, 2000).

Two recent developments in the sentencing of juvenile offenders have even greater potential to impact negatively on juveniles and society as a whole, namely, statutory reverse onus in waiver process and blended sentencing. In the past, the juvenile waiver hearing explored the maturity of the juvenile, his or her amenability to treatment, and the seriousness of the offense to determine if the best interests of the juvenile would be served by keeping him or her within the jurisdiction of the juvenile court. As a result of an increase in violent and serious crimes committed by juveniles (and an attendant moral panic), a number of states have enacted legislation that focuses on the seriousness of the offense and social defense. Such legislation requires the juvenile's attorney to argue how the best interests of society, rather than the best interests of the juvenile, are better served if the juvenile remains within the juvenile justice system.

The notion of social defense is clearly visible in the development and application of blended sentences in over 20 states. Designed to control serious and violent juvenile offenders, blended sentences permit the imposition of sentences similar in length to those imposed by the adult criminal courts for a similar offense. The juvenile is confined within a juvenile institution until the age of 18 or 21 years, at which time he or she is transferred to an adult correctional institution to serve the remainder of his or her sentence. Although it is cloaked in the rhetoric of accountability, the use of blended sentencing is clearly based on the notions of punishment and incapacitation. In his analysis of the shifting attitudes in juvenile legislation and juvenile court practices, Sheldon (2001, p. 227) noted that it is as if they have said: "We give up! We have done everything we can think of to help you."

1.7 Conclusion

Society's attitudes and its treatment of its youngest members have not always been in their best interests. We have seen how children and juveniles have been treated differently from adults in different societies over time. Indeed, the legal definition of when childhood ends and adulthood begins has been debated in numerous courts and in many countries. Children, in spite of their ages, have been considered to be the property of their father and/or the state under the *parens patriae* doctrine. They have also been granted absolute immunity from criminal responsibility as children and limited immunity as juveniles. When it comes to punishment, however, we have treated them as miniature adults who are whipped, incarcerated, and executed in the same manner as their larger comrades. We have also treated them as persons who, because of their level of moral development, are dependent and need strict guidance.

Just as there is no single cause of juvenile delinquency, there has also not been a single method used to treat and rehabilitate juvenile offenders. Americans have relied, however, on state-run juvenile institutions that have changed little since their inception a century ago. One can only hope that the next century of juvenile justice will witness the juvenile justice pendulum swinging to reach a balance between rehabilitation and incapacitation, whereby the needs of the juveniles and those of society are truly met.

References

Ariès, Philippe. 1973. *L'enfant et la Vie Familiale sous l'Ancien Régime.* (Nouvelle édition). Paris, France: Éditions du Seuil.

Altschuler, David M., and Troy L. Armstrong. 1994. *Intensive Aftercare for High-Risk Juveniles: A Community Care Model.* Washington, D.C.: Office of Juvenile Justice and Delinquency Programs.

Barnes, Harry E. and Negley K. Teeters. 1959. *New Horizons in Criminology,* 3rd ed. Englewood Cliffs, NJ: Prentice-Hall.

Bazemore, Gordon and Mark S. Umbreit. 1997. *Balanced and Restorative Justice for Juveniles.* Washington, D.C.: Office of Juvenile Justice and Delinquency Programs.

Bernard, Thomas J. 1992. *The Cycle of Juvenile Justice.* New York: Oxford University Press.

Bishop, Donna M. 2000. Juvenile Offenders in the Adult Criminal Justice System. In Michael Tonry (Ed.), *Crime and Justice: A Review of Research,* Vol. 27. Chicago, IL: University of Chicago Press. pp. 81–167.

Cavan, Ruth S. 1962. *Juvenile Delinquency.* Philadelphia, PA: Lippincott.

Chard, Chester S. 1975. *Man in Prehistory,* 2nd ed. New York: McGraw-Hill.

Cohen, Stanley. 1972. *Folk Devils and Moral Panics: The Creation of the Mods and Rockers.* Oxford: Basil Blackwell.

Colomy, Paul and Martin Kretzmann. 1995. Projects and institution building: Judge Ben B. Lindsey and the juvenile court movement. In *Social Problems,* Vol. 42(2), 191–215.

Eisenstadt, Shmuel N. 1956. *From Generation to Generation: Age Groups and Social Structure.* New York: The Free Press.

Federal Bureau of Investigation. 1989–1998. *Uniform Crime Reports for the United States.* Washington, D.C.: Department of Justice.

Flannery, Kent V. 1969. Origins and ecological effects of early domestication in Iran and the near east. In Peter J. Ucko and Geoffrey W. Dimbleby (Eds.), *The Domestication and Exploitation of Plants and Animals.* London: Gerald Duckworth and Company. pp. 73–100.

Flannery, Kent V. 1973. The origins of agriculture. In *Annual Review of Anthropology,* Vol. 2, 271–310.

Gibbon, Edward. 1993. *The Decline and Fall of the Roman Empire.* New York: Alfred A. Knopf.

Griffin, Brenda S. and Charles T. Griffin. 1978. *Juvenile Delinquency in Perspective.* New York: Harper and Row.

Halsall, Paul. 1996. *Medieval Sourcebook: The Institutes, 535 CE.* Online Document. Available at: http://www.fordham.edu/halsall/basis/535institutes.html #III.%20The%20Lex%20Aquili. Accessed December 29, 2002.

Harrison, Paige, James R. Maupin, and F. Larry Mays. 2001. Teen courts: an examination of processes and outcomes. In *Crime and Delinquency,* Vol. 47(2), 243–264.

Hawes, Joseph M. 1971. *Children in Urban Society: Juvenile Delinquency in Nineteenth-Century America.* New York: Oxford University Press.

Jenkins, Richard L., Preben H. Heidemann, and James A. Caputo. 1985. *No Single Cause: Juvenile Delinquency and the Search for Effective Treatment.* College Park, MD: American Correctional Association.

Juvenile Justice and Delinquency Prevention (JJDP) Act of 1993, as amended, Public Law 93-415, 42 U.S.C. 5601 et seq.

Junger-Tas, Josine. 2002. The juvenile justice system: past and present trends in Western society. In Ido Weijers and Antony Duff (Eds.), *Punishing Juveniles: Principle and Critique.* Oxford: Hart Publishing. pp. 23–44.

Krisberg, Barry and James F. Austin. 1993. *Reinventing Juvenile Justice.* Newbury Park, CA: Sage Publications.

Krisberg, Barry and James F. Austin. 1978. *The Children of Ishmael: Critical Perspectives on Juvenile Justice*. Palo Alto, CA: Mayfield Publishing.

Krisberg, Barry, Deborah Neuenfeldt, Richard Wiebush, and Orlando Rodriguez. 1994. *Juvenile Intensive Supervision: Planning Guide*. Washington, D.C.: Office of Juvenile Justice and Delinquency Programs.

LaMonte, John L. 1949. *The World of the Middle Ages: A Reorientation of Medieval History*. New York: Appleton-Century-Crofts.

Lévy-Bruhl, Henri. 1981. *Sociologie du droit*. Sixiéme ed. Paris, France: Presses universitaires de France.

Lowie, Ralph H. 1961 *Primitive Society*. New York: Harper and Brothers.

Ludwig, Frederick J. 1955. *Youth and the Law: Handbook on Laws Affecting Youth*. Mineola, NY: Foundation Press.

Meek, Theophile J. 1958. The code of Hammurabi. In James B. Pritchard (Ed.), *The Ancient Near East: An Anthology of Texts and Pictures*. Princeton, NJ: Princeton University Press. pp. 138–167.

Moyle, B. 1896. *The Institutes of Justinian*. 3rd ed. Oxford: Oxford University Press.

Oppenlander, Nan. 1981. The evolution of law and wife abuse. In *Law and Policy Quarterly*, Vol. 3(4), 382–405.

Pickthall, Marmaduke W. 1957. *The Glorious Koran*. London: George Allen and Unwin.

Platt; Anthony. 1969. *The Child Savers: The Invention of Delinquency*. Chicago, Illinois: University of Chicago Press.

Postman, Neil. 1994. *The Disappearance of Childhood*. New York: Vantage Books.

Pye, Lucian. 1981. *Asian Power and Politics: The Cultural Dimensions of Authority*. Cambridge, MA: Harvard University Press.

Rothman, David J. 1977. *Love and the American Delinquent: The Theory and Practice of "Progressive" Juvenile Justice, 1825–1920*. Chicago, IL: University of Chicago Press.

Rothman, David J. 1980. *Conscience and Convenience: The Asylum and Its Alternatives in Progressive America*. Glenview, IL: Scott, Foresman and Company.

Sanders, Wiley B. 1970. *Juvenile Offenders for a Thousand Years*. Chapel Hill, NC: University of North Carolina Press.

Schlossman, Steven. 1995. Delinquent children: The reform school. In Norval Morris and David J. Rothman (Eds.), *The Oxford History of the Prison: The Practice of Punishment in Western Society*. Oxford: Oxford University Press. pp. 325–350.

Shelden, Randall G. 2001. *Controlling the Dangerous Classes: A Critical Introduction to the History of Criminal Justice*. Boston, MA: Allyn and Bacon.

Snyder, Howard N. and Melissa Strickland. 1999. Juvenile Offenders and Victims: 1999 National Report. Washington, D.C.: Office of Juvenile Justice and Delinquency.

Sommerville, J. 1982. *The Rise and Fall of Childhood*. Beverley Hills, CA: Sage.

Taqi-ud-Din Al-Hilali, Muhammad, and Muhammad Muhsin Khan.(n.d.) *Rough Translation of the Meaning of the Noble Quran*. Online document. Available at http://www.unn.ac.uk/societies/islamic/index.htm. Accessed October 12, 2002.

Torbet, Patricia McFall. 1996. *Juvenile Probation: The Workhorse of the Juvenile Justice System*. Washington, D.C.: Office of Juvenile Justice and Delinquency Programs.

United States General Accounting Office. 1997. *Drug Courts: Overview of Growth, Characteristics, and Results*. Washington, D.C.: United States General Accounting Office.

Vago, Steven. 2003. *Law and Society*. 7th ed. Upper Saddle River, NJ: Prentice-Hall.

Vito, Gennaro F., Richard Tewksbury, and Deborah G. Wilson. 1998. *The Juvenile Justice System: Concepts and Issues*. Prospect Heights, IL: Waveland Press.

Watkins, John C., Jr., 1998. *The Juvenile Justice Century: A Sociolegal Commentary on American Juvenile Courts*. Durham, NC: Carolina Academic Press.

Wheeler, Leslie. 1983. The orphan trains. In *American History Illustrated*, Vol. 18(8), 10–23.

Zietz, Dorothy. 1969. *Child Welfare: Services and Perspective*. New York: John Wiley & Sons.

Cases Cited

Breed v. Jones, 421 U.S. 517 (1975).
Ex parte Crouse, 4 Whart. 9 (Pa. 1838).
Gallegos v. Colorado, 370 U.S. 49 (1962).
In re Gault, 387 U.S. 1 (1967).
In re Winship, 397 U.S. 358 (1970).
Kent v. United States, 383 U.S. 541 (1966).
People v. Turner, 55 Ill. 280 (1879).
In re Holmes, 348 U.S. 973, 75 S.Ct. 535 (1955).

Notes

1. It was interesting to note that pioneering criminologists within both the classical and positivist schools were silent on the treatment of children. This may have been due to the absolute immunity of children under 10 years of age and the limited immunity of youths aged 10–17 years during the period. Neoclassical and neopositivist criminologists, however, have not been silent on the issues of delinquent children and those in need of protection as can be seen in the direction taken by juvenile justice policy in the United States during the last 20 years.

2. One interesting distinction was made, however, between orphans and delinquent children and youths during the mid-19th century. The New York City Children's Aid Society began a practice in the late 1850s that was similar to Britain's press-ganging of idle sailors into Royal Navy service; they organized a service of adoption that placed orphans into good homes (they were not as selective as one might have expected and often entered neighborhoods picking up unattended children). Due to the success of this local program, orphaned children were transported to Indiana, Illinois, Wisconsin, and the western territories aboard what became known as "orphan trains" (Wheeler, 1983). The Civil War ended the use of orphan trains and the adoption of juveniles, especially those in their teens; teenaged youths fought in both armies, as mature-looking juvenile offenders found themselves pressed into service by judges and magistrates.

Chapter 2

Nineteenth Century Antecedents to the Twentieth Century Juvenile Court

James L. Hague

2.1 Introduction

The purpose of this chapter is to describe and evaluate the nineteenth century antecedents of the juvenile court that developed at the beginning of the twentieth century. Was the juvenile court which began in 1899 in Cook County, Illinois, and which spread rapidly through the rest of the United States in the early part of the twentieth century, a radically new and innovative departure from the past? Or, was the new juvenile court similar in many ways to past practices and institutions but with the *parens patriae* power of the state in a new location?

It is difficult to gain a full historical picture of the new institution of the juvenile court and its antecedents with regard to its actual administration and impact on the people over which it exercised jurisdiction. A full historical study of the powerless in our society is usually unavailable. The available literature upon which this chapter is based is derived from studies of what is available such as statutes, cases, legislative histories, and historical accounts of individuals and institutions and so on, which do not give a full picture. This same literature does not cover everything that was going on throughout the United States but tends to focus on those states and major cities which led the way, such as New York, Boston, Chicago, and Philadelphia. Consequently, the picture is not a full one but is mostly an account of what was happening in some of America's major cities. Perhaps this is because these were the places where major social problems, such as crime and poverty, were most noticeable.

Not everyone who writes about the antecedents agrees on their meaning or relationships. Principal writers in this area often interpret the meaning, significance, and cause and effect relationships of these forerunners in different ways; however, they do identify as historical antecedents (and in the same way) most of the same things. (Fox, 1970; Platt, 1969; Rendleman, 1971).

This chapter deals mainly with the historical antecedents of the juvenile court of 1899 that developed during the nineteenth century beginning with the house of refuge in the 1820s. However, to understand these institutions of the nineteenth century, to put them in context and give them meaning, it is necessary to view the legal, institutional, and social underpinnings of even earlier times.

One of those underpinnings was the common law, which traces its beginnings at least to the 14th century, and in some ways, even earlier. Because there was very little government structure to administer agrarian England, one way in which English monarchs exercised their governing influence was through a rudimentary judicial system. Justices of the Peace or judges representing the monarch traveled about from community to community administering justice, criminal and civil. Rather than enforcing a set of codified laws, which generally did not exist, they administered the rules known to the common people, the common law. People knew the basic rules of right and wrong behavior based on their customs, mores, and biblical and church teaching. Over time, English judges wrote these "laws" down in reported decisions which could be accessed by others later. Their written decisions became case law precedent defining what the law would be in future similar situations. This is not to say that English monarchs issued no laws or that, later on, parliament, as it grew in importance, did not codify acts of parliament. But for a long time in England there was no central source of codified law as under the earlier Roman code or as there is in modern-day England and the United States. This English, common law system is the antecedent of the American legal system. Following the American Revolution, the newly formed states adopted the common law from England, but with the provision that they could abrogate all or parts of it.

In our common law system, there are two primary sources of law: case law, which is generally from published appellate court opinions, and statutory or codified law, which includes such things as statutes (passed by legislatures) and constitutions. Therefore, to obtain an answer as to what the law is on a particular subject a lawyer or judge would have to search both case and codified law. The legal answer may be found in either cases or codes or in both, e.g., when a court interprets a statute.

Both court-made law (cases) and legislation (statutes) from England influenced laws and institutions that developed in the nineteenth century in the United States. First, there was the development in the English court of chancery of the doctrine of *parens patrie*, the doctrine in law that the government can exercise parental powers over children. This occurred in medieval England which operated under a feudal system. The power base for an English monarch was the support he or she got from the local nobility. The feudal system required that local nobility swear allegiance to the monarch who, in turn, guaranteed them protection. The power of the nobility was in their land holdings. The common people, serfs, farmed the land as tenants of the noble families and swore allegiance to them in return for their own protection by the nobility. Class distinctions between the haves (nobles) and the have-nots (serfs) were significant. Sometimes a nobleman would die, leaving a young child as heir to his title. To protect the allegiance of that family to the monarch, the child needed legal and other protection. The legal protection came in the form of the *parens patriae* doctrine developed by the English court of chancery, which established a guardianship over the children of the nobility. There was no such doctrine applied to the poor classes of children; it was clearly a legal device to protect wealth and power (Rendleman, 1971; Task Force Report [President's Commission], 1967).

Protection of the poor classes, such as it was, came in the form of statutes passed by parliament as poor laws, which created poorhouses or almshouses during the sixteenth and seventeenth centuries. For example, in preindustrial England and the United States there was a considerable problem with poverty, most generally recognized in the cities as contributing to what was classified at that time as pauperism, vagrancy, and crime. The main institution relied on for social control was the family. Even if a child was caught by officials he might be referred to the family for discipline or he could be taken from his family and be placed out as an "apprentice" in another family. Failing that, families and children were placed in poor- or almshouses and work-houses and children could be separated from their pauper families and placed into apprenticeships. Poorhouses and apprenticeships became the institutional solutions applied to paupers (Rendleman, 1971). Pauperism and crime were seen as cause and effect.

If a child were to be caught committing a crime, he was subject to the criminal law and courts used for adults. Although there was no separate court for juveniles, there were provisions in the common law in England and the United States which treated children in ways different from adults, depending upon their age. In English and United States common law, and still treated as the law in most states today, children were not held responsible under the criminal law before certain ages. Below the age of seven, a child was conclusively presumed in the law to be incapable of forming criminal intent (*mens rea*). Under this rule, children up to 6 years of age could not be convicted of a criminal act. For ages 7 through 13, children were rebuttably presumed in law to be incapable of forming criminal intent. Unlike a conclusive presumption in the law, a rebuttable presumption against the capacity for criminal intent can be overcome by proof that the child knew his act was wrong. Children younger than 14 who could be proved to have had criminal intent and children 14 and older could be prosecuted under the same criminal laws and in the same courts as adults. If convicted, they were liable to the same punishment (such as public whipping, jail, and even death). While awaiting trial they were jailed with adults. There were many instances of these things being done, especially the use of jails for juveniles.

However, there is good evidence that in late-eighteenth- and early-nineteenth-century America, children were diverted from the adult system of criminal law and courts, at least in nonofficial ways (Fox, 1970). It was typical for children (especially in case of minor crimes) to be acquitted outright by juries, particularly for lack of knowledge. Apparently, citizens often did not report crimes by children, and officials often did not take action against children. Juries, officials, and nonreporting citizens all had knowledge of the potential consequences of conviction and punishment. Poor children could be placed in the county poorhouse from where they could then be placed out or the courts could place them out to families where they would work and be supported (a forerunner of foster homes). Children who committed serious crimes were likely to be dealt with under the criminal law. This was the situation prior to the first major reform movement in the nineteenth century, which culminated in the creation of a new institution, the house of refuge, in the 1820s in America.

2.2 Nineteenth-Century Reformers

Early-nineteenth-century reformers believed that there was a serious pauperism or poverty problem as well as a crime problem, particularly in the large cities. In their view, poverty or pauperism and crime were the cause and effect —pauperism caused, or was the precondition to, crime. They saw many homeless, vagrant, pauper children of impoverished and incapable families (who were most often immigrants) roaming the streets and committing crimes in large cities such as New York, Boston, and Philadelphia. Because impoverishment caused crime, they believed that children should be removed from these conditions while they were still predelinquent (Fox, 1970) so that they would not grow into adult criminals. Prisons were viewed as schools for criminals where children would come under the influence of adult criminals. Adult punishment and institutions were thought to be too harsh for all but the most serious juvenile criminals. They also recognized that other current methods of dealing with these problems, such as the use of poorhouses and acquitting juveniles or otherwise allowing crimes of guilty juveniles to go unpunished, was not working.

The reformers of the day were middle-class individuals holding middle-class values who usually were part of civic and philanthropic organizations and churches. Quakers such as Thomas Eddy played a prominent role in the reform movements, especially in New York and Pennsylvania (Fox, 1970). Quakers had for some time been involved in a number of societal reforms, including penological ones. They were highly influential in creating prisons as a new institution beginning in the 1790s. Prisons were developed as an alternative to the death penalty for many crimes and they replaced severe public, corporal punishment of others.

Reformers wanted to save or rescue children from pauperism, crime, and harsh treatment under the criminal law. Also, they believed that pauperism and the crime-prone children represented a threat to the safety of American society which needed protection from them. Goals such as these could be accomplished if they could rescue these pauper children while they were still predelinquent, i.e., while they were vagrants, idle, acting immorally, mendicant, and only engaged in minor crimes. These were salvageable, but juveniles engaged in serious crime were thought to be too far gone for reform (Fox, 1970).

Their solution was the house of refuge, an institution which spread throughout most of the country (except the South) during the first half of the 1800s but which began, most notably, in the 1820s in New York, Boston, and Philadelphia. Pauper children could be submitted through summary "legal" proceedings from almshouses, from court proceedings following trial and conviction, or from lower courts and judicial authorities through summary proceedings. Once the refuge received the juveniles it subjected them to its institutional reform program and/or outplaced them to families — the boys to work on farms and the girls to work in domestic situations, especially with rural families. The usual intent was to remove the juveniles from city life and to place them in a rural farming community, which was believed to have a better value system than that of the city. Often, children were placed out into other states and even the western states of the time.

The juveniles who remained in the institutions were subjected to a highly regimented and routinized regimen of work and schooling which also included meals and chapel services (Mennel, 1973). Because these were large institutions, children were marched from activity to activity in large groups and routine was strictly enforced. Discipline was often severe, including use of restraints and corporal punishments. Daily regimented routine started early in the morning and continued through the day and into the evening. Work and school were not so much about vocational training as they were about learning self-discipline, moral values, frugality, time management, and personal responsibility. The work or labor of the children was often contracted out to businesses such as shoemaking, clothes making, and chair caning. The girls were more likely to be engaged in domestic duties. Girls and boys were segregated from each other, as were the races. Most houses of refuge did not admit African Americans, and those that did treated them as inferiors. In the southern states, of course, there was slavery and no houses of refuge for anyone. The juveniles who were committed to the house of refuge were paupers who were either vagrant, neglected, dependent, incorrigible, or convicted of minor crimes. Rarely were those convicted of serious crimes accepted by houses of refuge because they were usually considered too far into a criminal career to be salvaged. After all, the purpose of the house of refuge was to reform and not to punish or imprison. When children were committed and or placed out, the assumption was that the pauper parents were incapable and that children should be separated from that bad influence; the parents lost any claim to custody or control over their children.

Although the statutes that created the house of refuge established their authority to commit children to their care and custody, often with only summary commitment proceedings, there was also judicial authority. In 1839 the Pennsylvania Supreme Court decided the case of *Ex parte Crouse*, 4 Whart.9 (PA 1839). Mary Ann Crouse was committed to the Philadelphia House of Refuge based on a summary proceeding before a justice of the peace who granted Mary Ann's mother's petition that claimed her daughter was incorrigible. Her father later challenged her commitment by *habeas corpus*, a legal remedy used to challenge the legality of someone's confinement. The basis of the challenge was constitutional. Under Pennsylvania's constitution, a jury trial right existed before someone could be sentenced to commitment for a crime. The Pennsylvania Supreme Court approved the summary commitment procedure by the justice of the peace based on the chancery doctrine of *parens patriae,* which it now used to justify the government's guardianship over the poor, even those with parents. This case was widely cited across the United States during the rest of the nineteenth century and was used as a justification for the new juvenile court that came into being at the turn of the twentieth century. In its justification the high court said:

> The object of charity is reformation, by training its inmates to industry; by imbuing their minds with principles of morality and religion; by furnishing them with means to earn a living; and, above all, by separating them from the corrupting influence of improper associates. To this end, may not the natural parents, when unequal to the task of education, or unworthy of it, be superseded by the *parens patriae,* or common guardian of the community? It is to be remembered that the public has a paramount interest in the virtue and knowledge of its members, and that of strict right, the business of education belongs to it. That parents are ordinarily entrusted with it is because it can seldom be put into better hands; but where they are incompetent or corrupt, what is there to prevent the public from withdrawing their faculties, held, as they obviously are, at its sufferance? The right of parental

control is a natural, but not an unalienable, one. It is not excepted by the declaration of rights out of the subjects of ordinary legislation; and it consequently remains subject to the ordinary legislative power which, if wantonly or inconveniently used, would soon be constitutionally restricted, but the competency of which, as the government is constituted, cannot be doubted. As to abridgement of indefeasible rights by confinement of the person, it is no more than what is borne, to a greater or less extent, in every school; and we know of no natural right to exemption from restraints which conduce to an infant's welfare. Nor is there a doubt of the propriety of their application in the particular instance. The infant has been snatched from a course which must have ended in confirmed depravity; and, not only is the restraint of her person lawful, but it would be an act of extreme cruelty to release her from it. (Lexus 171,2)

But houses of refuge had their problems, and these came to the surface from time to time throughout their history. By about the mid-nineteenth century there was growing and widespread disaffection with them. Conditions in some were chaotic, some were burned down due to the arson of their inmates, and there were escapes and violence. Discipline was often severe and even brutal. As institutions, they were generally seriously underfinanced owing to legislative parsimony. Efforts to train its inmates in job skills through contracts with manufacturers of goods like clothes and shoes turned into long hours and harsh working conditions. Rather than job-skill training, the contract-lease system of sending refuge children to manufacturers became a way for the houses of refuge to survive financially. Because refuges were large institutions with severe conditions and were severely underfinanced, many considered them nothing more than prisons for juveniles. Gradually, courts and other institutions which had put juveniles into houses of refuge began to use other alternatives. These included placing children out, especially with rural families, using almshouses or poorhouses (which continued to exist throughout the nineteenth century) and various other alternatives provided by churches and private philanthropic organizations.

Mid-nineteenth-century reformers or child savers (Platt, 1969) were usually associated with philanthropic societies that were in various ways connected to government. Sometimes they received some government funding or had state charters and were given actual or *de facto* legal authority. They went by various names, for example, children's aid societies, and were intent on reforming impoverished (pauper) destitute, vagrant, neglected, petty, offending, predelinquent children. They often were opposed to institutionalizing these children and assumed that the best reform would come through family life, especially the family life of a rural, farming family. Some of the children in their care, for example, in the care of the children's aid societies, were there "voluntarily," but most were committed to their care by other institutions such as almshouses and courts. These "commitments" were generally done by summary legal proceedings and the practices of separating poor children from their natural families continued. They placed out or indentured these big-city children to rural farming families in various states west of the east coast, believing that the children would be reformed in these families with a rural, farming, work-ethic value system. Of course, placing out was a continuation of a practice prevailing during the time of the houses of refuge and earlier, all the way back to the English poor laws, and it continues to this day in a similar fashion in the form of juvenile court placement in foster homes.

John Augustus is usually cited as the founder of the practice of probation (for adults as well as juveniles). He was a shoemaker in Boston during the middle of the nineteenth century who began to provide bail for adults accused of crime in Boston during the 1840s. He took on the supervision of some juveniles as well. His supervision took place during a sentence of probation by the Boston courts. This practice of probation for both adults and juveniles began to spread into other parts of the country during the remainder of the nineteenth century. Unlike many of the methods practiced on children such as placing out, probation seems to have been an innovation or an extension of earlier English bail practices. Historically, bail could be provided by someone other than the accused (still permitted today), but not only was the bail provider liable to monetary forfeiture if the accused absconded, but he or she had a personal responsibility for making certain that the accused appeared for trial. This was somewhat like personal, pretrial supervision. Under still-existing common law rules, bail bondsmen, who are private business people, have the right to arrest and bring before the court someone who absconds. The practice of probation did not end with John Augustus but continued in the second half of the nineteenth century, for example, through private philanthropic efforts.

The last half of the nineteenth century saw some institutional changes, as well as the continuation of past practices. Of primary significance was the expanded role of government involvement in the effort to reform children and adolescents. What were to be called reform schools were very likely to be government institutions of the state or of state and local governments, or local governments. They were still institutions for juveniles, and they mixed juvenile criminals (usually petty) with impoverished children, orphans, and truants, and neglected, abused, and incorrigible juveniles. However, governments were creating new institutions, such as orphanages and insane asylums, so that, where these were available, orphans and the insane could be institutionalized in these. Also many of the new reform schools emphasized schooling of their children, sometimes emphasizing vocational education. Moreover, many reform schools turned to a system of cottage units in order to emulate family settings as much as possible, believing that family was still the best social institution for reform. The cottage or "family" unit was administered locally and kept its own schedule even though it was usually one of a number of units within a larger institution. Also, as part of their emphasis on family, they continued the practice of placing out and had a preference for rural, farming family placement.

Reform schools generally continued the contract-lease system with manufacturers, and even though they were often intended to provide vocational training, the contract-lease system had the same problems as the houses of refuge (and the adult penitentiaries, where it was also used). Owing to governmental financial parsimony, institutions were underfunded and felt they needed the contract-lease system for financial support. Manufacturers were concerned about the bottom line so that both working conditions and discipline for falling short of production quotas were harsh. Poor overall conditions often prevailed and similar to other juvenile institutions in the first half of the nineteenth century, there were problems with escape, violence, and inmate arson.

To make matters worse, the second half of the nineteenth century included the Civil War and its aftermath, an event of no little significance. Because of enrollment in military service and the death toll of men during the war, a significant number of fathers were absent from their homes. Juvenile populations swelled in reform schools and other institutions (Mennel, 1973). Following the Civil War, there was great inflation, raising the cost of everything, but government support for reform schools did not keep pace with inflation. Because government was now more involved in the provision of social welfare by creating the new institutions mentioned earlier, there was more competition for limited funds.

In addition to the impact of the Civil War in the United States, the country was passing through a period of rapidly increasing industrialization and immigration, both of which contributed to the growth of cities, thus, contributing to crime, delinquency, and other social problems. These ultimately affected the governmental services involving reform schools, for example, reform school populations reflected the growth in new immigrant populations.

As with houses of refuge, reform schools continued to put the emphasis on receiving salvageable juveniles, and the cross section of those being admitted was similar to those entering the refuges: juveniles who were destitute, impoverished, neglected, abused, and incorrigible, and had committed petty crimes. The serious criminals would be more likely to be put in adult institutions. Owing to the intended emphasis in reform schools on schooling, they were perhaps more likely to receive truants, and since the advent of other new government institutions such as orphanages, they were less likely to receive orphans (Mennel, 1973). The same sources of commitment continued to commit juveniles — parents, almshouses, courts of general and limited jurisdiction, and police magistrates — and usually with the same summary legal procedures. Similar to the houses of refuge, the stated intention of reform schools was to reform predelinquent children and adolescents into useful and productive citizens by saving them from bad family, environmental, and parental influences. Instead, they would have training in self-discipline, responsibility, moral virtues, and middle-class rural values and vocations.

Similar to the refuges and other institutions of the first half of the nineteenth century, reform schools and other institutions of the second half of the nineteenth century also exercised broad jurisdiction and wide discretion over predelinquent children and adolescents as well as their families. As described earlier, the type of behavior for which reform schools and other institutions could separate children and adolescents from their families, institutionalize or place them out, was broadly and often vaguely described behavior or status. The "legal" procedures by which they received custody and control over children and adolescents were generally summary procedures that allowed a broad exercise of discretion by government and, sometimes, philanthropic organizations.

There was one significant legal event which ran contrary to the trend toward broad jurisdiction and exercise of discretion. It was the case of *People ex rel. O'Connell v. Turner* (SS Ill.280) decided by the Illinois Supreme Court in 1870. Daniel O'Connell had been committed to reform school by the Superior Court of Cook County (IL), not for a crime but for "misfortune," a vague term describing predelinquent behavior. His father sought *habeas corpus* from the Illinois court to release his son from illegal confinement on the theory that it was unconstitutional. The Illinois Supreme Court agreed. Under today's constitutional doctrine, the best way to understand the Illinois court's reasoning of 1870 is to say that the justices concluded that the grant of power under Illinois law to confine a juvenile for misfortune was too broad, as the term was void for its vagueness. The constitutional doctrine of *void for vagueness* holds that vague language describing the behavior (or status) of misfortune is so unclear that unwary citizens cannot know what behavior is prohibited, and government officials have unfettered discretion to decide that any type of behavior (or status) falls under their jurisdiction. However, *O'Connell v. Turner* seems to have been a legal anomaly. The Supreme Court of Illinois changed its mind about a decade later and other courts around the country did not hold similar opinions. In fact, the earlier broad grant of *parens patriae* power in *Crouse* continues to be the prevailing law in the United States. Consequently, the broad grants of jurisdiction and discretion continued by state statutes and case law for the remainder of the nineteenth century and most of the twentieth. It was not until much later that the U.S. Supreme Court, beginning with its decisions in *Kent v. U.S.* in 1966 and *in re Gault* in 1967, began to erode such broad grants of power as unconstitutional. The high court was criticizing this broad grant of power that was now located in the juvenile court rather than institutions such as reform schools.

Reform schools and other institutions of the latter half of the nineteenth century did not cease to exist with the advent of the twentieth century. Rather they continued, perhaps changing names from time to time to such things as training or industrial schools, well into the twentieth century. In fact, the industrial school was an institution developed for females in the latter part of the nineteenth century. It was, more or less, the female equivalent of the reform school for boys.

2.3 The Progressive Era

Reform schools in the nineteenth century often suffered from problems as noted earlier. When these problems came to be generally known, they led to disaffections on the part of the public, those who were charged with committing juveniles to them, and those who sought to reform these and other institutions dealing with children and adolescents. One effort was to place the authority to oversee these institutions in state boards of charity or charity and corrections. Although this was helpful, if the state government did not follow their recommendations regarding funding, nothing much changed except, perhaps, that names were changed to give the appearance of change. Sometimes change did occur and these boards may have contributed to changes in methods of organizing and managing these institutions and the professionalism of the staff. Perhaps this was one of the factors leading to the Progressive Era of the last decade of the nineteenth century and the first part of the twentieth century. The Progressive Era was basically a movement to professionalize and bureaucratize government institutions around the turn of the century (Fox, 1970).

There were efforts at reforming the ways in which society dealt with children and adolescents, especially those who were predelinquent, throughout the nineteenth century. Recall the efforts by the Quakers and other reformers in the early part of the century leading to the creation of houses of refuge and other kinds of changes. For the second half of the nineteenth century, reformers had generated the changes in reform schools, orphanages, girls' industrial schools, and other institutions. Now, in the last part of the nineteenth century, reformers sought to reform these institutions and this led to the creation of the juvenile court at the beginning of the twentieth century. Therefore, although the reformers or child savers of the late nineteenth century were mainly interested in institutional changes, they were ultimately instrumental in the creation of the juvenile court at the turn of the century (Fox, 1970).

Reformers of that era were remarkably similar to reformers of the past in terms of their claims and beliefs, but women now played a new and prominent role in the late nineteenth century. According to Platt (1969), there was a women's movement in child saving that was fueled by changes in the status of women together with the assertion of the traditional role of women. The view was that women, as child raisers and nurturers in the home and as school teachers, were naturally more skillful than men in the affairs of children. Feminists and antifeminists of the day seemed to agree on this. Also, the role of women was changing. They were better educated and had more leisure time than had been the case earlier. At least this seemed to be true for upper-middle-class women, and in this "natural role" for women in the affairs of children and adolescents, they would not be in competition with men. Platt (1969) describes the prominent role played by a number of women, particularly Louise Bowen and Jane Addams, who were socially and politically prominent through women's clubs and other philanthropic organizations and who were also influential with male bar associations and legislatures in passing reform legislation, including that of the juvenile courts.

Also, beginning in the late nineteenth century, a new view was developing of the causes and correlates of delinquency and predelinquency (Mennel, 1973). These were grounded in the newly emerging sciences of sociology, criminology, psychology, and psychiatry. These often diverged over whether behavior was caused by one's nature or the nurturing one received. Cesare Lombroso and others thought that there were criminal types who could be identified on the basis of atavistic physical characteristics that were a throwback to primitive man. Of course, later careful study showed this to be false. Other early attempts to explain criminal behavior attributed it to nurture in the family or poor physical and economic environments. Rather than behavior being determined by social and environmental forces as viewed by the sociologists, psychology and psychiatry looked for explanations within the person's psychological makeup. Some of the pioneers in studying delinquent behavior were physicians and professional penologists. What was changing, at least for those who were engaged in the new "scientific" efforts to explain behavior, was that there was a shift away from a free-will, moralistic explanation of predelinquency and delinquency to a deterministic one of social illness. Before and during the nineteenth century, efforts at reform were aimed at changing the moral point of view of children and adolescents. The new, deterministic theories of behavior considered that behavior was determined by causes like one's environment or by psychological determinants. This was analogous to catching a disease and needed the medical model approach of diagnosis, prescription, and treatment directed at those causes (*In re Gault*). This was to be influential in the development of the new juvenile courts.

2.4 Creation of a Separate Justice System for Juveniles

In 1899, in Cook County, Illinois, the first juvenile court was created with exclusive jurisdiction to deal with delinquent, neglected, and dependent children. All such matters belonged in the juvenile court rather than in other courts or in other agencies or institutions. The institution of the juvenile court spread rapidly in the United States and by 1925 all but two states had a juvenile court (Task Force Report [President's Commission], 1967). Of course, there was a great deal of dissimilarity between the states and even within the same state in what was termed a juvenile court. About half of the states placed the juvenile court at the level of a trial court of general jurisdiction, whereas the other half considered them trial courts of limited jurisdiction. Rural and urban juvenile courts within the same state were typically different. Often, the juvenile court in rural America was part of the local county court and one judge wore many hats with jurisdiction (on different days of the week) over civil, traffic, adult criminal, and juvenile cases. In larger cities, the juvenile court was more likely to have full-time, specialized judges and a separately identified juvenile court. It was not until the 1970s that many states actually developed a clearly separate and distinct juvenile court as part of a general trend in state courts to reform and reorganize themselves into unified state court systems. City juvenile courts usually had more resources available, for example, probation officers, than their rural counterparts who had little to no resources.

The new juvenile court was both a social welfare and a legal institution. Although it was to be different in purpose and procedure from an adult criminal court, it was a court nevertheless and had all the powers of a court. *Parens patriae* was now relocated from other institutions of the nineteenth century to be clearly located in the juvenile court (Mack, 1909). It was a very broad grant of power and discretion to the court, including the power of complete denial of natural parental rights of those the court found to be unfit. This broad grant of power and discretion was the same as that found in nineteenth-century institutions (Rendleman, 1971).

Its grant of subject matter jurisdiction was also broad and covered the same delinquent and predelinquent offenders who had been included in the institutions of the nineteenth century (Fox, 1970; Rendleman, 1971): petty criminal, dependent, neglected, truant, and incorrigible; however, now its jurisdiction also included the serious juvenile criminal (although serious felonies could be transferred to the adult criminal court).

Its "legal" procedures, even for criminal cases, were summary (Fox, 1970; Rendleman, 1971), just as they were in the institutions of the nineteenth century. Adult criminal procedure involved arrest, indict-ment, adversary criminal trials, juries, conviction, and sentence in a public forum. Juveniles might be taken into custody and adjudicated "not innocent" (rather than "convicted") in an informal, nonadversarial hearing without lawyers and without formal rules of evidence or procedure. Rather than convict or punish for purposes of retribution and deterrence as in the criminal court, the juvenile court was supposed to reform and save juveniles. Instead of focusing on the event of the crime and punishment of the guilty, the juvenile court sought to investigate the whole juvenile, his background, and what had led to his delinquent behavior, in order to diagnose his problems and develop a plan for his rehabilitation as a good, law-abiding citizen. Also, because of this noncriminal approach, it was thought that juveniles would not suffer from the stigma associated with the criminal courts. In fact, juvenile delinquency was treated as a civil matter.

The juvenile judge was to be at the heart of the juvenile court, exercising broad discretion in an informal setting. He or she was to act as a parent would with his or her own child, i.e., play a protective role in the best interests of the child (Ward and Flowers, 1973).

Unfortunately, the juvenile court frequently did not live up to its idealized role as described above (*Kent v. U.S.*), a subject dealt with in other chapters of this book. In its role as the latest of many efforts to divert children and adolescents from the adult criminal courts, it continued the practices of the past, of its nineteenth century anteced-ents. Although it used probation more often than did the institutions of the past, it still placed juveniles out (but now in foster homes) and it still committed juveniles to institutions such as reform schools. Although there was some reduction in some places in the placement of juveniles in jails, it still occurred with too much frequency. Through-out the nineteenth century, reformers had also been quite concerned with keeping juveniles out of jails and had some success at this before the advent of the juvenile court.

Even though the juvenile court was a new institution, it was in most ways similar to the institutions and practices of the past and was firmly rooted in its nineteenth-century antecedents.

References

Fox, S.J. (1970). Juvenile justice reform: an historical perspective. *Stanford LawReview 22,* 1187–1239.

Mack, J.W. (1909). The juvenile court. *Harvard Law Review 23,* 104.

Mennel, R.M. (1973). *Thorns and Thistles.* Hanover, NH: The University of New Hampshire.

Platt, A. (1969). *The Child Savers: The Invention of Delinquency.* Chicago, IL: University of Chicago Press.

Rendleman, D.R. (1971). Parens patriae: from chancery to the juvenile court. *South Carolina Law Review 23,* 205.

The Challenge of Crime in a Free Society. (1967). The President's Commission on Law Enforcement and Administration of Justice. Washington D.C.

Task Force Report: Juvenile Delinquency and Youth Crime. (1967). The President's Commission on Law Enforcement and Administration of Justice. Washington D.C.

Ward, R.H. and Flowers, A. (1973). *Children's Courts in the U.S.: Their Origin, Development, and Results Prepared for the International Prison Commission (1904)*. New York: AMS Press.

Cases Cited

Ex parte Crouse, 4 What. 9, Pa. LEXIS 171.

In Re Gault, 387 U.S. 1 (1967).

Kent v. U.S., 383 U.S. 541 (1966).

People ex. rel. O'Connell v. Turner, 55 Ill. 280 (1870).

Chapter 3

The Extension of Constitutional Rights to Juveniles

Katherine Bennett

3.1 Introduction

As noted in the previous chapters, until the early 19th century, juveniles over age seven were tried in criminal courts along with adults and imprisoned with them. Children over 14 were automatically deemed responsible for their criminal acts; prosecutors assessed on an individual basis whether juveniles between the ages of 7 and 14 were liable for their actions before they were prosecuted. However, during the 18th and 19th centuries, both actions of reformers and research from the emerging discipline of psychology influenced a shift in society's views concerning juveniles. An emphasis on the rehabilitation and protection of children began to overshadow traditional punitive thinking. There developed a belief that society had a responsibility to salvage the lives of juvenile offenders before they were lost to the criminal activity in which they were engaged.

In 1899, the Illinois Juvenile Court Act, followed by similar acts in other states, gave to juvenile courts jurisdiction over not only juveniles charged with crimes, but any child who is:

> homeless or abandoned; or dependent on the public for support; or has not proper parental care or guardianship; or who habitually begs or receives alms; or who is living in any house of ill fame or with any vicious or disreputable person; or whose home, by reason of neglect, cruelty, or depravity on the part of its parents, guardian, or other person in whose care it may be, is an unfit place for such a child; and any child under the age of eight who is found peddling or selling any article or singing or playing a musical instrument upon the street or giving any public entertainment. (Illinois Juvenile Court Act, 1899 Ill. Laws 132 *et seq.*, in Shepherd, 1999)

As discussed in Chapter 1, such acts reflect the *parens patriae* ("parent of the country") role of the juvenile justice system, in which the state assumes the duty of parenting the child. A feature of the *parens patriae* role of the juvenile court is that children are not entitled to liberty, but to custody (*In re Gault,* 387 U.S. 1 (1967), 17). Thus, court proceedings in cases involving juveniles are traditionally much more informal than adult criminal court proceedings, with juveniles essentially deprived of the "due process of law" rights clarified in the amendments to the U.S. Constitution. Juveniles are entitled to less constitutional protection than that given to adults suspected of criminal offenses because of the "special solicitude for juveniles" (*Kent v. United States,* 383 U.S. 541 (1967), 551–552) reflected in the concept of *parens patriae*. The theory behind this concept is that the juvenile court exists to determine both the child's needs and societal needs, "not to fix criminal responsibility, guilt, and punishment" (*Kent* at 554). Being adjudicated in juvenile court means that a child can be held only until he is 21, and the youth "is protected against consequences of adult conviction such as the loss of civil rights, the use of adjudication against him in subsequent proceedings, and disqualification for public employment" (*Kent* at 557). This also means that juveniles are "not entitled to bail; to indictment by grand jury; to a speedy and public trial; to trial by jury; to immunity against self-incrimination; to confrontation of his accusers; and, in some jurisdictions ... [juveniles are] not entitled to counsel" (*Kent* at 555).

By the mid-20th century, increased concerns that juveniles were being denied certain constitutional rights that were given to adults in court proceedings led to landmark Supreme Court decisions that began to make significant changes in the juvenile justice system. These cases specifically addressed the application of First, Fourth, Fifth, Sixth, Eighth, and Fourteenth Amendment rights and how juveniles were protected or, in some cases, not protected by these rights. This chapter discusses these landmark cases in chronological order, with the omission of Eighth Amendment cases. The Eighth Amendment guarantees against the implementation of cruel and unusual punishment have been addressed primarily at the Supreme Court level in the realm of capital punishment for juveniles and are discussed in depth in a later chapter. The first case discussed in this chapter was decided in 1948 and involved due process rights of juveniles during police custodial interrogations (*Haley v. Ohio* (1948)).

3.2 *Haley v. Ohio,* 332 U.S. 596 (1948): Fourteenth Amendment Guarantees

The Fourteenth Amendment establishes that: "No state shall make or enforce any law which shall abridge the privileges or immunities of citizens of the United States; nor shall any state deprive any person of life, liberty, or property, without due process of law; nor deny to any person within its jurisdiction the equal protection of the laws." Many of the constitutional rights extended to juveniles originate with challenges to the due process clause of the Fourteenth Amendment. The first occasion for the Supreme Court to address such constitutional protections for juveniles during police custodial interrogations came in 1948 in the case of *Haley v. Ohio.* A 15-year-old boy, John Haley, along with two other juveniles, was arrested for murder by the Ohio police in 1945. Apparently, John acted as a lookout during the robbery of a store in which the store owner was shot and killed. John was picked up by police around midnight. He was then questioned for 5 hours, without the presence of counsel or an advisor, by several police officers working in relays of two. He signed a confession after being shown the alleged confessions of his alleged accomplices. There was also some evidence suggesting that he was beaten. John was never informed of his right to counsel, and the only mention of any constitutional rights was a written statement presented to him right before he made his written confession. He was then jailed and not permitted to see either his lawyer or his mother for several days. The only outsider allowed to see him was a newspaper photographer who took his picture right after his confession. He was not formally charged with a crime for 3 days after his confession.

On appeal, John's attorney argued that the methods used by the police in obtaining his confession violated the due process clause of the Fourteenth Amendment. The Court of Appeals of Ohio sustained Haley's conviction and the state supreme court dismissed a subsequent appeal. However, the U.S. Supreme Court granted *certiorari* and reversed the lower court's decision, finding that, "the age of petitioner, the hours when he was grilled, the duration of his quizzing, the fact that he had no friend or counsel to advise him, the callous attitude of the police toward his rights combine to convince us that this was a confession wrung from a child by means which the law should not sanction" (*Haley* at 600–601).

Because the issue concerned custodial interrogations by police, the Supreme Court did not address specifically the concept of *parens patriae* and juvenile court procedures. The Court did make clear, however, that juveniles should be treated with special care when being interrogated by police:

> Age 15 is a tender and difficult age for a boy of any race. He cannot be judged by the more exacting standards of maturity. That which would leave a man cold and unimpressed can overawe and overwhelm a lad in his early teens. This is the period of great instability which the crisis of adolescence produces. A 15-year-old lad, questioned through the dead of night by relays of police, is a ready victim of the inquisition. Mature men possibly might stand the ordeal from midnight to 5 A.M. But we cannot believe that a lad of tender years is a match for the police in such a contest. He needs counsel and support if he is not to become the victim first of fear, then of panic. He needs someone on whom to lean lest the overpowering presence of the law, as he knows it, may not crush him. (*Haley* at 599–600)

Regardless of a suspect's age, however, the Court's final observation in this decision was that "[t]he Fourteenth Amendment prohibits the police from using the private, secret custody of either man or child as a device for wringing confessions from them" (*Haley* at 601). It would be 14 years before the Court would have occasion to address this issue again in the case of *Gallegos v. Colorado* (1962).

3.3 *Gallegos v. Colorado,* 370 U.S. 49 (1962)

In 1962, the Court followed its reasoning in *Haley* in *Gallegos v. Colorado.* A 14-year-old boy, Robert Gallegos, along with a younger brother and a juvenile cousin, robbed and assaulted an elderly man in 1958. Robert Gallegos was picked up by police about 12 days after the incident, and he admitted to assaulting and robbing the victim. The victim died about a month after the assault, at which time the youth was charged with first-degree murder. The boy was tried and found guilty, largely due to the fact that he had signed a formal confession. The confession had been signed, however, after Robert had been held for 5 days without seeing an attorney, parent, or other "friendly adult" (*Gallegos* at 50). Colorado's Supreme Court upheld the conviction, but the U.S. Supreme Court reversed, finding that "the totality of the circumstances" regarding the boy's interrogation and detention violated his Fourteenth Amendment right to due process.

The Court addressed the similarity between the *Haley* case and this one in that both involved a young boy "not equal to the police in knowledge and understanding of the consequences of the questions and answers being recorded and who is unable to know how to protect his own interests or how to get the benefits of his constitutional rights" (*Gallegos* at 54).

As mentioned previously, the Court relied primarily upon violations of the Fourteenth Amendment's due process protections in the preceding cases. Four years after *Gallegos,* the Supreme Court decided *Miranda v. Arizona* (1966). This decision established clearly that the Fifth Amendment constitutional protection against self-incrimination applied to custodial interrogations. In 1966, the Supreme Court also decided a landmark case dealing specifically with juveniles: *Kent v. United States* (1966) examined the constitutional rights accorded juveniles in jurisdictional hearings relating to waivers to adult criminal court.

3.4 *Kent v. United States,* 383 U.S. 541 (1966): Juvenile Court Waivers

In 1961, Morris Kent, Jr., a 16-year-old probationer in Washington, D.C., was arrested on charges of housebreaking, robbery, and rape. He was found guilty in the adult criminal court of six counts of housebreaking and robbery and sentenced to 30 to 90 years in prison. He was found not guilty by reason of insanity on the two rape charges and committed to a mental institution. Before Morris Kent's indictment in criminal court, his attorney had requested a jurisdictional hearing, assuming that the juvenile court was going to waive jurisdiction and refer Kent for trial in criminal court. The attorney also sought access to Morris' social services file in juvenile court. However, the juvenile court judge waived jurisdiction without a hearing, making no findings and giving no reasons for the waiver, noting only that the court made a "full investigation" (*Kent* at 541). No reference was made to Morris' attorney's motions. Further, the attorney was not provided with two reports containing information about Morris' deteriorating mental condition.

After Morris Kent was indicted in criminal court, his attorney sought to have the indictment dismissed on grounds that the juvenile court's waiver was invalid. This motion failed, and Morris was subsequently tried in criminal court and found guilty. His lawyer appealed on alleged grounds that Morris was denied due process in the juvenile court procedures waiving jurisdiction. The lower appellate court rejected this argument, and in 1966, the U.S. Supreme Court granted *certiorari*. The Supreme Court reversed the lower court's decision, ruling that juveniles facing waiver to criminal court were entitled to "the essentials of due process and fair treatment," including "representation by counsel, access to social services records, and a written statement of the reasons for waiver" (*Kent* at 542).

The Supreme Court emphasized that the autonomy given to juvenile courts does not go beyond procedural regularity and the basic requirements of due process and fairness. The decision to transfer juveniles to criminal court carries importance of such magnitude that there must be a hearing, effective assistance of counsel, access by counsel to records considered by the juvenile court judge, and a statement of reasons for the decision. Indeed, these requirements reflect "society's special concern for children" (*Kent* at 554). However, the liberty accorded juvenile courts is reflected in the Supreme Court's ruling that both the hearing and the statement of reasons may be "informal," and the statement need not include "conventional findings of fact" (*Kent* at 561).

The Court ruled only on the procedural errors of the juvenile court's waiver of jurisdiction. However, the Court did note that Morris' attorney was also challenging police procedures. Law enforcement officials interrogated Morris for 7 hours on the first day of being taken into custody and then again for several hours on the second day. The interrogations took place without the presence of either a parent or Morris' attorney. He was detained for a week with no arraignment and no judicial determination of probable cause as would be required for adults. He was not informed of his right to remain silent or his right to counsel, both of which are rights given to juveniles by the Juvenile Court Act of the District of Columbia. Morris was also certified at this time by a psychiatrist as suffering from a "severe psychopathology" (*Kent* at 545).

The Supreme Court acknowledged that juvenile courts are frequently unable to offer effective treatment and to act as a concerned parent and, in fact, juveniles get the "worst of both worlds" (*Kent* at 556). The Court still declined to rule that constitutional protections given to adults in criminal courts should be applied in juvenile court proceedings. The opportunity to remedy this "worst of both worlds" situation was expressly attempted in *In re Gault* the following year. By 1967, the Court made clear that juveniles are entitled to Miranda rights in its landmark decision in *In re Gault* (1967), delivered 1 year after the Miranda decision. "The Court's decision in *Gault* followed decisions in *Haley v. Ohio* and *Gallegos v. Colorado* in which the Court recognized that juveniles in custody need at least the same constitutional protections that adults enjoy and possibly more" (McGuire, 2000, p. 1357). *In re Gault* is perhaps the most significant case involving constitutional rights of juveniles.

3.5 *In re Gault*, 387 U.S. 1 (1967): Paving the Road for Constitutional Protections

In 1964, Gerald Francis Gault, 15 years old, was taken into custody by the sheriff of Gila County, AZ, because a neighbor had complained to authorities that Gerald had made an indecent telephone call to her. At the time, Gerald was on probation for theft. He was taken to the children's detention home, and a hearing was scheduled for the next day. His mother was at work and was not notified, learning of his detention only after sending an older brother to his friend's house to look for him when she came home from work and found Gerald missing. The mother and brother went to the detention home and were informed verbally of the hearing on the following day. The superintendent of the detention home filed a petition with the juvenile court that stated only that the "said minor is under the age of 18 and is in need of the protection of this Honorable Court; [and that] the said minor is a delinquent minor" (*Gault* at 5). The petition made no mention of the case that resulted in his detention.

At the first hearing before the juvenile judge on June 9, Gerald, his mother, his brother, and two probation officers were present. However, the neighbor who filed the complaint was not present, no one was sworn in at the hearing, and no transcript of the proceedings was taken. At the end of the hearing, the judge stated that he would "think about it" (*Gault* at 6). Gerald was sent back to the detention home and was not released until a few days later. There was no explanation as to why he was held after the hearing.

On June 15, another hearing was held regarding Gerald's case. As with the first hearing, no transcript was made, and at a later *habeas corpus* hearing witnesses would differ in their recollections of Gerald's testimony at the first two hearings. Specifically, Gerald's parents and the detention home superintendent agreed that Gerald did not admit to making the lewd remarks over the telephone, but the judge recalled that "there was some admission again of some of the lewd statements" (*Gault* at 7). Again, the neighbor who filed the complaint was not present and when Gerald's mother requested that the neighbor be required to appear, the judge stated that the complainant's presence was not necessary. At the conclusion of the June 15 hearing, the judge found Gerald to be delinquent and committed him to the State Industrial School for no more than 6 years (when he would turn 21.) An adult convicted of the same crime would have received a fine of $5 to $50 or no more than 2 months in jail.

Under Arizona law, no appeal was permitted in juvenile cases; so on August 3, a petition for a writ of *habeas corpus* was filed on Gerald's behalf. At the *habeas corpus* hearing in the Superior Court, the judge in Gerald's case testified that, based on the fact that Gerald was on probation at the time of his arrest, his own (the judge's) recollection of a previous incident involving Gerald, and Gerald's alleged admission of making other nuisance phone calls in the past, he determined Gerald to fall under the Arizona Code definition of a delinquent child who is "habitually involved in immoral matters" (*Gault* at 9). The writ was dismissed by both the Superior Court and, upon appeal, by the Arizona Supreme Court.

Gerald's attorneys argued that Arizona's Juvenile Code was unconstitutional because it did not require notification of specific charges or a formal notice of a hearing and because it did not allow for an appeal. They also contested the validity of the court's proceedings against Gerald, alleging several violations of due process, specifically a denial of adequate notice of the charge and the hearing, denial of right to counsel, rights of confrontation and cross-examination, and the privilege against self-incrimination; in addition, there was the admission of hearsay testimony and the failure to make a record of the proceedings. Arizona's Supreme Court found that the guarantee of due process is implied in the juvenile code but that Gerald's proceedings did not violate due process.

On appeal, however, the U.S. Supreme Court reversed the judgment of the state supreme court. Reviewing its decisions in a handful of previous cases involving juveniles, the High Court found that it is apparent that "neither the Fourteenth Amendment nor the Bill of Rights is for adults alone" (*Gault* at 13). The Court ruled that Gerald's rights had been violated in the proceedings against him and that he was entitled to:

- Adequate notice of the precise nature of the charges against him
- Notice of the right to counsel and to have counsel appointed if indigent
- The right to confront witnesses and have them cross-examined
- The privilege against self-incrimination

The Court also noted that "[u]nder our constitution, the condition of being a boy does not justify a kangaroo court" (*Gault* at 28). The Supreme Court's ruling in *In re Gault* began the transformation of a juvenile court system formed under the concept of *parens patriae* to a more adversarial, due process model (del Carmen, et al., 1998).

The decision in *In re Gault* made it clear that juveniles were entitled to "notice of charges, right to counsel, the rights of confrontation and examination, and the privilege against self-incrimination" (*In re Winship* (1970) at 368). Three years later, in *In re Winship* (1970), the Court would address whether the Fourteenth Amendment also entitles juveniles to the standard of proof beyond a reasonable doubt.

3.6 *In re Winship*, 397 U.S. 358 (1970): Standard of Proof in Juvenile Court Proceedings

In 1967, Samuel Winship, a 12-year-old boy in New York, was arrested and charged as a juvenile delinquent for stealing $112 from a woman's pocketbook. He was found guilty in a New York family court based on a preponderance of the evidence, but not guilty beyond a reasonable doubt. The higher burden of proof, guilt beyond reasonable doubt, is the required standard in adult criminal court proceedings. Samuel's attorney appealed this conviction, maintaining that proof beyond a reasonable doubt is one of the requirements of due process and fair treatment for a juvenile charged with an act that would be a crime if committed by an adult. Both of the lower appellate courts that heard this case rejected the appeal, and the U. S. Supreme Court granted *certiorari*. The Court reversed the lower courts' decisions, ruling that because of the loss of liberty involved, the higher standard of guilt beyond a reasonable doubt must be used for all criminal defendants, regardless of age.

The lower courts had argued in this case that due process does not apply to civil juvenile proceedings, but the high court noted that *Gault* made clear that the due process clause does apply because the loss of liberty at stake is similar to loss of liberty implicated in felony prosecutions. The lower courts also argued that requiring proof beyond a reasonable doubt destroys the "beneficial aspects of the juvenile process" (*Winship* at 366). The majority opinion noted, though, that juvenile hearings still remain confidential, informal, and more flexible that criminal proceedings. Further, "a wide-ranging review of the child's social history for his individualized treatment will remain unimpaired" (*Winship* at 366).

The dissenting opinion by Chief Justice Burger, joined by Justice Stewart, in *In re Winship* demonstrates the controversy regarding granting constitutional rights to juveniles. The dissent noted that when juvenile courts were first implemented, the concept of the juvenile court system centered on providing "a benevolent and less formal means than criminal courts could provide for dealing with the special, and often sensitive, problems of youthful offenders" (*Winship* at 376). The dissent objected to what they referred to as a "further straitjacketing of an already overly restricted system" (*Winship* at 376). Juvenile court judges would be better served by less legal procedures, according to the dissent, and this system could function as it was intended if judges "were not crushed by an avalanche of cases" (*Winship* at 376).

This dissenting opinion also expressed a concern that decisions granting juveniles more constitutional rights were transforming juvenile courts into criminal courts and would end "a generously-conceived program of compassionate treatment intended to mitigate the rigors and trauma of exposing youthful offenders to a traditional criminal court" (*Winship* at 377).

The next occasion for the U.S. Supreme Court to consider extending other constitutional rights to juvenile court proceedings came 1 year later in 1971 in *McKeiver v. Pennsylvania* and concerned the issue of whether a juvenile is entitled to a jury trial. *McKeiver* was followed 3 years later by *Davis v. Alaska* (1974). Both cases involved challenges to Sixth Amendment rights and are discussed in the following section.

3.7 Sixth Amendment Rights for Juveniles

3.7.1 McKeiver v. Pennsylvania, *403 U.S. 528 (1971): Trial by Jury*

The Sixth Amendment is a list of rights afforded the accused in criminal proceedings. These rights include a trial by jury, notification of the charges, the right to confrontation of witnesses against the accused, the right to call witnesses in his or her favor, and the assistance of counsel. Recall that *In re Gault* (1967) established that juveniles were entitled to three of these protections: notice of the charges, assistance of counsel, and the right to cross-examination of witnesses. However, *McKeiver v. Pennsylvania* (1971) addressed the right to a jury trial in juvenile court proceedings and, in this case, the Supreme Court declined to extend such a right. Joseph McKeiver, age 16, was charged in 1968 with robbery, larceny, and receiving stolen goods. However, specific details of the case indicated that Joseph, along with 20 or 30 other juveniles, chased 3 other juveniles and took 25 cents from them. This was Joseph's first arrest. He requested and was denied a jury trial at his hearing, where he was adjudicated delinquent and placed on probation. His appeal in the Superior Court was dismissed. His subsequent appeal to the state supreme court was combined with a case involving another Pennsylvania youth, Edward Terry, age 15, who was charged in 1969 with assault and battery on a police officer and conspiracy. Details indicated that Edward was an onlooker at a fight and hit the officer with his fists and a stick when the officer broke up this fight. Edward Terry also requested a jury trial, which was denied. On appeal to Pennsylvania's Supreme Court, the court ruled that a constitutional right to a jury trial does not exist in juvenile court.

A North Carolina case was attached to the Pennsylvania cases upon appeal to the U.S. Supreme Court. The North Carolina case concerned a group of black juveniles who, with a group of adults, were charged with "willfully impeding traffic" (*McKeiver* at 536) while they were protesting school assignments and a school consolidation plan in 1968. Request for a jury trial was made in each individual case and was denied. Each juvenile was adjudicated as delinquent and placed on probation. Both the appellate court and the Supreme Court of North Carolina affirmed the lower court's decision.

On appeal, the U.S. Supreme Court concluded that a jury trial in juvenile court adjudicatory proceedings was not required. The Court reasoned in part that requiring a jury trial might turn juvenile proceedings into an adversarial process, putting an end to the informal, idealistic tradition of the juvenile court (*McKeiver* at 545) and ignoring "every aspect of fairness, of concern, of sympathy, and of paternal attention that the juvenile court system contemplates" (*McKeiver* at 550). Requiring jury trials would result in states losing control over juvenile court procedures, thus losing the ability to experiment with finding answers to "the problems of the young" (*McKeiver* at 547). If aspects of the criminal court are incorporated in the juvenile system, then "there is little need for its separate existence," and the Court noted that it would only dissolve the juvenile court system at a time when complete disillusionment with the system existed (*McKeiver* at 551).

Another aspect of the Sixth Amendment as it applies to juveniles was addressed in 1974 in *Davis v. Alaska*, although this case involved adult criminal court proceedings. As in *McKeiver*, the Court's decision did not offer more protection for juveniles.

3.7.2 Davis v. Alaska, 415 U.S. 308 (1974)

Davis v. Alaska (1974) regards the confrontation clause of the Sixth Amendment as it applies to a juvenile witness. In 1970, a bar in Anchorage was broken into and the safe was removed. The same day, state troopers received word that an empty, pried-open, safe had been discovered near the home of Richard Green, a 16-year-old on probation for burglary. Green told troopers that he had seen and spoken with two men standing alongside a sedan near where the safe was later discovered. From photographs, Green identified Davis as one of the men and, the next day, picked Davis out of a lineup. Through this identification, Green became a crucial witness for the prosecution. Before testimony was taken at Davis' trial, the prosecutor moved for a protective order to prevent any reference to Green's juvenile record by the defense in the course of cross-examination.

The defense opposed the protective order, wishing to argue that Green acted out of fear or concern of possible jeopardy to his probation. Not only might Green have made a hasty and faulty identification of Davis in order to shift suspicion away from himself as the one who stole the safe from the bar, but he might have been pressured by police to identify Davis or be subject to a probation revocation. Davis' defense maintained that only as much of Green's juvenile record would be revealed as was necessary to probe for bias and prejudice and not generally to question his character.

However, the trial court granted the protective order and the Alaskan Supreme Court affirmed the order stating that trial transcripts indicated that the defense "was able adequately to question the youth in considerable detail concerning the possibility of bias or motive" (*Davis* at 315) without the need for revealing Green's prior adjudication as a delinquent. On appeal, the U.S. Supreme Court reversed this decision. In the Supreme Court's interpretation of the Sixth Amendment, "cross-examination is the principal means by which the believability of a witness and the truth of his testimony are tested" (*Davis* at 316). Introducing evidence of a witness' criminal past is one way of suggesting to the jury that the witness may be less trustworthy than a witness with no criminal record. The defense was denied its constitutional right of effective cross-examination in this case. On the issue of the importance of protecting the anonymity of juvenile offenders over allowing the defense to effectively cross-examine Green, the Supreme Court argued that the "right of confrontation is paramount to the State's policy of protecting a juvenile offender" (*Davis* at 319) and that the "temporary embarrassment" that might result from exposure of a juvenile record is outweighed by the defense's right to establish possible bias on the part of a crucial witness.

One year after *Davis*, in *Breed v. Jones* (1975), the Supreme Court decided a landmark case concerning a juvenile and regarding his Fifth Amendment protection against double jeopardy. Four years later the Court would address another Fifth Amendment protection, the right against self-incrimination, in *Fare v. Michael C.* Recall that protections against self-incrimination for juveniles had been addressed in the early cases of *Haley v. Ohio* (1948) and *Gallegos v. Colorado* (1962) and then again in *In re Gault* (1967). The decision in *Fare v. Michael C.* limits that Fifth Amendment protection. The following section discusses *Breed v. Jones* (1975) and *Fare v. Michael C.* (1979).

3.8 Fifth Amendment Protections: Double Jeopardy and Self-Incrimination

3.8.1 Breed v. Jones, *421 U.S. 519 (1975): Double Jeopardy*

The Fifth Amendment prohibition against double jeopardy protects a person from being subjected to trial and possible conviction more than once for an alleged offense. "The underlying idea ... is that the State with all its resources and power should not be allowed to make repeated attempts to convict an individual for an alleged offense, thereby subjecting him to embarrassment, expense, and ordeal and compelling him to live in a continuing state of anxiety and insecurity, as well as enhancing the possibility that even though innocent he may be found guilty" (*Green v. United States* 355 U.S. 184, 187–88 (1957)).

The case of *Breed v. Jones* (1975) concerns this prohibition as applied to a juvenile. In 1971, Jones, a 17 year old, was accused of robbery. At the adjudicatory hearing, in which testimony was given by two prosecution witnesses and Jones, the Court found the allegations to be true, and Jones was held over for sentencing as a juvenile. Three weeks later, at the sentencing hearing, the court found Jones to be "unfit for treatment as a juvenile," and ordered that he be prosecuted as an adult. Jones then filed a petition for a writ of *habeas corpus* in the juvenile court, raising the claim of double jeopardy. This petition was denied in the juvenile court, the California Court of Appeals, and the California Supreme Court. Jones was held for trial in adult court, in which he pleaded not guilty and also pleaded that he had already been placed once in jeopardy and convicted of the offense in the juvenile court. He was found guilty and was committed to the California Youth Authority. Jones, through his mother as guardian, filed another petition for a writ of *habeas corpus* in the U.S. District Court. In his petition, he alleged that his adjudicatory hearing and transfer to adult court and a subsequent trial constituted double jeopardy.

Because juvenile court proceedings are technically civil and not criminal, the California courts decided that Jones could not have suffered double jeopardy as he was tried only once in criminal proceedings. The U.S. Supreme Court saw the issue differently: "... in terms of potential consequences, there is little to distinguish an adjudicatory hearing such as was held in this case from a traditional criminal prosecution" (*Breed* at 530). Because the Court saw little ultimate difference between Jones' juvenile court trial, which included formal testimony of witnesses against him and adjudication as a delinquent, and his later criminal court trial for the same offense, the Court ruled that double jeopardy was violated in Jones' case. The significance of this case is that it further extends constitutional rights to juvenile proceedings and establishes juvenile court proceedings as equivalent to criminal court proceedings in terms of due process rights afforded.

3.8.2 **Fare v. Michael C., 442 U.S. 707 (1979):** *Self-Incrimination*

The privilege against self-incrimination comes from the maxim *nemo tenetur seipsum accusare* which means "no man is bound to accuse himself" (Amendment 5).

Cases previously discussed in this chapter have established that juveniles enjoy this privilege (*Haley v. Ohio* (1948), *Gallegos v. Colorado* (1962), *In re Gault* (1967)), but exactly how this right applies to juveniles was addressed again by the Supreme Court in 1979 in *Fare v. Michael C.* Michael C., 16 years old, was implicated in a murder. Before being questioned at the police station, he was fully advised of his Miranda rights. At the time of the questioning, Michael had a record of prior offenses and was on probation to the juvenile court. He immediately asked to see his probation officer. But when the police denied this request, he stated he would talk without consulting an attorney, and he then proceeded to make statements and draw sketches implicating himself in the murder. After being charged in the juvenile court with the murder, his counsel sought to suppress the incriminating statements and sketches on the grounds that they had been obtained in violation of Miranda, in that Michael's request to see his probation officer constituted an invocation of his Fifth Amendment right to remain silent, just as if he had requested the assistance of an attorney.

The court denied the motion, holding that the facts showed that Michael had waived his right to remain silent, notwithstanding his request to see his probation officer. The California Supreme Court reversed, holding that Michael's request for his probation officer was an invocation of Fifth Amendment rights in the same way that the request for an attorney was found to be in *Miranda*, regardless of what the interrogation otherwise might have revealed. This holding was based on the court's view that a probation officer occupies a position as a "trusted guardian figure" (*Fare* at 713) in a juvenile's life.

The U.S. Supreme Court found, however, that the Michael's request to see his probation officer was not equivalent to asking for a lawyer. "A probation officer is not … the same [as a lawyer] with regard to either the accused or the system of justice as a whole. … He does not assume the power to act on behalf of his client by virtue of his status as adviser nor are the communications of the accused to the probation officer shielded by the lawyer–client privilege." (*Fare* at 719) Also, because a probation officer is an employee of the State that is prosecuting the offender, he is seen as a peace officer and, therefore, allied with the prosecutorial side of the issue.

This case, as well as the previously discussed *McKeiver v. Pennsylvania*, can be viewed as an example whereby the Court has restricted the rights of juveniles. The Court decided another case this same year that involved a conflict between preserving the anonymity of juveniles charged with crimes and First Amendment freedom of the press (*Smith v. Daily Mail Publishing Company*, 443 U.S. 97 (1979)). The Court decided in favor of the press' First Amendment rights over protecting juveniles. This case is discussed in the next section.

3.9 *Smith v. Daily Mail Publishing Company,* 443 U.S. 97 (1979)

An important case regarding the conflict between preserving the anonymity of juveniles charged with crimes and the First Amendment rights of the press is *Smith v. Daily Mail Publishing Company* (1979). A West Virginia statute provided that "[N]or shall the name of any child, in connection with any proceedings under this chapter, be published in any newspaper without a written order of the court ..." (W. Va. Code 49-7-3 (1976)). When a student was shot and killed at a West Virginia high school, the alleged assailant, a classmate, was identified by seven different eyewitnesses and was arrested soon after the incident. Reporters for two local newspapers obtained the name of the accused simply by asking witnesses, the police, and an assistant prosecuting attorney. The boy's name was broadcast over the radio for 2 days following the homicide. The papers published the name in their morning and afternoon editions, reasoning that because the name was already public knowledge, there was no need to obtain court approval to publish it. The publishers were indicted for violating the aforementioned statute.

The publishers petitioned the West Virginia Supreme Court of Appeals, alleging that the statute violated the First and Fourteenth amendments. The Court of Appeals held that the "statute abridged the freedom of the press" and constituted a "prior restraint on speech" (*Smith* at 100) that could not be justified by the State's interest in protecting the anonymity of the juvenile. The Supreme Court agreed, stating that "if the information is lawfully obtained, as it was here, the State may not punish its publication except, when necessary, to further an interest more substantial than is present here" and "that the constitutional right must prevail over the State's interest in protecting juveniles" (*Smith* at 104). Another decision which further limits the rights available to juveniles was handed down by the Supreme Court 5 years later (*Schall v. Martin* (1984)).

3.10 *Schall v. Martin*, 467 U.S. 253 (1984)

In 1984, the U.S. Supreme Court decided a case pertaining to the constitutionality of a section of the New York Family Court Act that allows pretrial detention of alleged juvenile delinquents upon finding that there is a serious risk that the juvenile would commit a crime before the appearance in juvenile court. *Schall v. Martin* (1984) began as a class action *habeas corpus* petition filed in 1977 on behalf of juveniles held in juvenile detention facilities before their fact-finding hearings. The lower courts agreed with the appellants that preventive detention was unconstitutional because it constituted a punishment before the juvenile had been adjudicated as delinquent and guilt is established.

The Supreme Court, however, reversed the holding, engaging in a two-pronged analysis. First, did preventive detention serve a lawful and genuine State purpose? If so, were procedures authorizing detention adequate? The Court concluded that preventive detention served a "legitimate State objective" (*Schall* at 256–257) and that the procedures followed by the State before detaining juveniles fulfilled due process requirements of the Fourteenth Amendment.

The Court acknowledged its previous holdings establishing due process rights in juvenile proceedings, reviewing the holdings in several of the cases discussed in this chapter (*In re Gault*, (1967); *In re Winship* (1970); *Breed v. Jones* (1975); *McKeiver v. Pennsylvania* (1971)). One of the concerns noted by the Court has been how to maintain the *parens patriae* concept and "respect the 'informality' and 'flexibility' that characterize juvenile proceedings" (*Schall* at 263), while ensuring that the proceedings are fair and comply with the requirements of the due process clause. Because the preventive detention never exceeded 17 days and the conditions of confinement were not punitive and met the objectives of *parens patriae* (counseling, educational, recreational programs; dorm assignment according to age, size, and behavior, etc.), the majority opinion did not see the preventive detention as constituting punishment before adjudication.

The three dissenting justices in this case obviously had a different point of view. The dissenting opinion stated that, on the contrary, conditions in detention are often unpleasant and youths are exposed to assault, including sexual assault, by other juveniles (*Schall* at 290). Another concern voiced in the dissenting opinion was the fact that over half of the youths in this class action suit had never been adjudicated delinquent before. One family court judge admitted that he sometimes used preventive detention as punishment and other judges acknowledged that they usually released juveniles after they had been in preventive detention because they had been punished enough (*Schall* at 301). The dissent would have decided this case very differently and would have supported the lower courts' ruling that "punishment of juveniles before adjudication of their guilt violates the due process clause" (*Schall* at 302).

3.11 Constitutional Rights of Juveniles in Educational Institutions

Several leading Supreme Court cases have addressed constitutional rights of juveniles in the school setting. Because juveniles spend the majority of each day in school institutions, it bears review of how the Court has extended, or failed to extend, various rights to juveniles in these institutions. As the Supreme Court noted in one such case, *Tinker v. Des Moines School District* (1969), students "do not 'shed their constitutional rights' at the schoolhouse door" (*Tinker* at 506). The remainder of this chapter discusses important cases involving constitutional rights of juveniles in schools, beginning with First Amendment cases.

3.11.1 First Amendment Rights and Juveniles

The First Amendment includes several separate individual rights, including freedom of religion, freedom of speech, freedom of the press, and the right to assemble peaceably. Two important cases concern First Amendment rights of children in public schools.

3.11.1.1 West Virginia State Board of Education v. Barnette, 319 U.S. 624 (1943)

In *West Virginia State Board of Education v. Barnette* (1943), the state board of education instituted a program requiring that the Pledge of Allegiance and flag salute be part of the program of activities in all public schools. All teachers and pupils were required to participate and refusal was treated as "insubordination," punishable by expulsion and charges of delinquency. Jehovah's Witnesses challenged this program because, according to their literal interpretation of Exodus, Chapter 20, verses 4 and 5, the flag is a "graven image" and, therefore, they are forbidden by their religion to participate in the salute. The Court held that this compulsory pledge and salute was a violation of the First Amendment rights of the public schoolchildren. The Court argued "that no official, high or petty, can prescribe what shall be orthodox in politics, nationalism, religion, or other matters of opinion or force citizens to confess by word or act their faith therein" (*West Virginia State Board* at 642).

3.11.1.2 Tinker v. Des Moines School District, 393 U.S. 503 (1969)

The case of *Tinker v. Des Moines School District* (1969) concerns three students who, in the December of 1965, agreed to protest the Vietnam War by wearing black armbands during the Christmas season. The principals of the school district learned of the plan and adopted a policy that the armbands would be forbidden and that students who refused to remove the armband would be suspended until they returned without it. The reasoning behind the policy was to prevent possible disturbances at school. The students knew of the policy and chose to ignore it by wearing their armbands to school. They were suspended and did not return to school until after the Christmas season when the period for wearing armbands was over. A complaint was filed by the parents of the students. The district court dismissed the complaint saying that the actions of the principals were "reasonable in order to prevent disturbance of school discipline" (*Tinker* at 505). The court of appeals was divided on the issue, thus upholding the lower court's ruling. On appeal, the Supreme Court ultimately ruled that the wearing of armbands was "closely akin to 'pure speech'" (*Tinker* at 505), and is protected by the First Amendment. The Court noted that "[i]n wearing armbands, the petitioners were quiet and passive. They were not disruptive and did not impinge upon the rights of others. In these circumstances, their conduct was within the protection of the free speech clause of the First Amendment and the due process clause of the Fourteenth" (*Tinker* at 505–506). Although First Amendment rights of teachers and students may be circumscribed in special situations pertinent to the functioning of the school, in this case it was determined that the principals failed to show that the students' behavior was detrimental to school discipline.

In 1975, the Court had occasion to address the extent of due process rights of juveniles when receiving short-term suspensions in *Goss v. Lopez*.

3.11.2 Goss v. Lopez, 419 U.S. 565 (1975): *Fourteenth Amendment Due Process Rights in School Suspensions*

In 1971, various Columbus, OH, public schools were experiencing "widespread student unrest," resulting in several school suspensions (*Goss* at 569). Six students from one high school were suspended for 10 days for disruptive conduct, including demonstrating in a school auditorium. One student from another high school, Dwight Lopez, along with 75 other students, was suspended for disruptive conduct during a lunchroom disturbance, although Dwight testified later that he was an innocent bystander. The eighth student was suspended for 10 days from her junior high school after being arrested at a demonstration at another school. The ninth student was suspended from his school but no information was available in school files regarding his suspension. All of the students were suspended without hearings. The students filed a class action suit against school officials, alleging that suspensions without hearings, as permitted in an Ohio statute, violated their Fourteenth Amendment due process rights. The district court agreed, ruling that the Ohio statute was unconstitutional. The lower court further ordered all references to the suspensions be removed from the students' school records. School officials appealed this decision, but the U.S. Supreme Court affirmed the lower court's ruling.

This case holds only that in cases of short suspensions, students must be given notice and an opportunity to be heard at a hearing. The Court stopped short of holding that the due process clause requires giving students who are facing short suspensions the right to counsel, confront and cross-examine witnesses, and call their own witnesses.

3.11.3 New Jersey v. T.L.O., 469 U.S. 325 (1985): *Fourth Amendment Rights and Juveniles*

Whether the Fourth Amendment's prohibition against unreasonable search and seizure applies to the actions of a school official, such as a teacher or principal, was addressed by the Supreme Court in 1985. The landmark case addressing this issue is *New Jersey v. T.L.O.* (1985). T.L.O., a 14-year-old freshman, and a friend were caught smoking in a school bathroom by a teacher in 1980. As smoking was a violation of school rules, the teacher escorted the girls to the principal's office where they met with the assistant vice principal. When T.L.O. denied that she had been smoking and claimed that she did not smoke at all, the assistant vice principal demanded to see her purse. Upon opening the purse, he found a pack of cigarettes and also cigarette rolling papers that are commonly associated with the use of marijuana. He proceeded to search the purse thoroughly and found some marijuana, a pipe, plastic bags, a fairly substantial amount of money, an index card titled "People who owe me money" (*New Jersey* at 347), and two letters implicating T.L.O. in marijuana dealing.

The State brought delinquency charges against T.L.O. in the juvenile court, denying her motion to suppress the evidence on the grounds that the search violated her Fourth Amendment rights. The court held that "a school official may properly conduct a search ... if the official has reasonable suspicion that a crime has been committed or reasonable cause to believe that the search is necessary to maintain school discipline or enforce school policies" (*New Jersey* at 329) and that the search of T.L.O.'s purse constituted a reasonable one. She was adjudicated delinquent and sentenced to a year's probation.

On appeal, the New Jersey Supreme Court reversed and ordered the suppression of the evidence found in T.L.O.'s purse, holding that the search of the purse was unreasonable. Possession of cigarettes was not against school rules and "a mere desire for evidence that would impeach T.L.O.'s claim that she did not smoke cigarettes could not justify the search" (*New Jersey* at 331).

The U.S. Supreme Court granted *certiorari* and determined that the Fourth Amendment's prohibition on unreasonable searches and seizures does apply to searches conducted by public school officials and is not limited to searches carried out by law enforcement officers. However, the search in this case was not unreasonable under the definitions set forth in the Fourth Amendment. The initial search for cigarettes was reasonable in that the teacher reported to the assistant vice principal that T.L.O. had been smoking, and this warranted a reasonable suspicion that she had cigarettes in her purse, even though the presence of cigarettes would only represent "mere evidence" (*New Jersey* at 326) and not proof of a violation of the no-smoking rule. Discovery of rolling papers resulted in reasonable suspicion that T.L.O. also had marijuana in her purse, "and this suspicion justified the further exploration that turned up more evidence of drug-related activities" (*New Jersey* at 326).

The import of this decision lies in the fact that the Court clearly established that "reasonable suspicion" was enough to allow a warrantless search by public school officials. The higher standard of "probable cause" is usually the required standard for warrantless searches by law enforcement officials. The Court noted that this decision was in accord with most of the lower courts' decisions that weigh in favor of the "substantial need of teachers and administrators for freedom to maintain order in the schools" (*New Jersey* at 341) over privacy rights of juveniles.

3.12 Conclusion

This chapter has discussed the extension of constitutional rights to juveniles in 15 leading Supreme Court cases, spanning the years between 1943 and 1985. The discussion illustrates the often difficult attempts by the Supreme Court to balance the rights of juveniles with the concept of *parens patriae*, community and school safety, and legitimate government objectives. Despite criticisms of the juvenile court system, there is no indication that the system will be abolished or even modified in the near future, and most cases involving juvenile offenders are still heard in juvenile courts. Given the informality of juvenile court procedures, heavy caseloads, and scarce resources, it is logical to expect that less attention may be paid to protecting the rights of juveniles. Some legal scholars urge, however, that more constitutional protections should be granted juveniles, rather than fewer (see, e.g., McGuire, 2000). McGuire (2000) cautions against "sacrific[ing] constitutional rights for the sake of expediency" and states that "... we must pay special attention to the needs of juveniles in the justice system. America's children deserve nothing less" (McGuire, 2000, p. 1387).

References

Amendment 5 — Rights of Persons. (2002), p. 1392. Available online at http://www.gpoaccess.gov/constitution/pdf2002/023.pdf.

McGuire, R.E. (2000). A proposal to strengthen juvenile Miranda rights: requiring parental presence in custodial interrogations. *Vanderbilt Law Review*, 53, 1355–1387.

Shepherd, R.E., Jr. (December 1999). The juvenile court at 100 years: a look back. *Juvenile Justice*, VI(2), 13–21. Available online at http://www.ncjrs.org/pdffiles1/ojjdp/178255.pdf. Accessed July 23, 2004.

List of Cases

Breed v. Jones, 421 U.S. 519 (1975).
Davis v. Alaska, 415 U.S. 308 (1974).
Fare v. Michael C., 442 U.S. 707 (1979).

Gallegos v. Colorado, 370 U.S. 49 (1962).
Green v. United States, 355 U. S. 184, 187-88 (1957).
Goss v. Lopez, 419 U.S. 565 (1975).
Haley v. Ohio, 332 U.S. 596 (1948).
In re Gault, 387 U.S. 1 (1967).
In re Winship, 397 U.S. 358 (1970).
Kent v. United States, 383 U.S. 541 (1967).
McKeiver v. Pennsylvania, 403 U.S. 528 (1971).
Miranda v. Arizona, 384 U.S. 436 (1966).
New Jersey v. T.L.O., 469 U.S. 325 (1985).
Schall v. Martin, 467 U.S. 253 (1984).
Smith v. Daily Mail Publishing Company, 443 U.S. 97 (1979).
Tinker v. Des Moines School District, 393 U.S. 503 (1969).
West Virginia State Board of Education v. Barnette, 319 U.S. 624 (1943).

Part I Conclusion

DISCUSSION QUESTIONS FOR PART I

1. According to Patenaude, how have attitudes toward children and the treatment of the problem child changed over time in American society?
2. Hague discusses the context in which the new separate system for juveniles emerged in America. Discuss the implications of these antecedents for this new system of "justice."
3. Write a brief discussion paper that might be used to explain to the lay person just what rights juvenile offenders have when compared with the adult offender (see Chapter 3 by Bennett).

Part II

EXPLAINING DELINQUENCY: THEORY AND PRACTICE

Just as the public's thinking about children has changed over time, so too have explanations for why they commit delinquent acts. It is important to understand why young people commit delinquency, from a policy perspective, because much of how we deal with them once they come in contact with the justice system is based on what we believe about crime causation in general. For example, if an individual believes that crime or delinquency is the result of free will, with everyone being responsible for his or her behavior, then that person will more than likely agree that punishment as retribution ("just desserts") is the only option for dealing with delinquents. On the other hand, if individuals believe that crime or delinquency is the result of forces either internal or external to the delinquent (biological explanations, for example, or one's social environment), they may be more inclined to show some leniency toward the youthful offender and be more in favor of rehabilitation. This part focuses on explanations for delinquency, beginning with Chapter 4, and discusses a variety of criminological theories that have been developed over time. In Chapter 5 and Chapter 6, girl delinquency is examined, and Chapter 7 discusses the established relationship between childhood maltreatment and delinquency. Chapter 8 demonstrates the policy implications associated with social control as it relates to community programs aimed at reducing delinquency in a local community.

Chapter 4

Theoretical Explanations for Juvenile Delinquency

Barbara Sims

4.1 Introduction

Explanations for delinquency are an important area of inquiry in the field of juvenile justice. Under *parens patriae*, the juvenile justice system was created to identify the problems associated with troubled youths, under the assumption that each child's condition would be diagnosed and treated. From a policy perspective, the intent of this approach has been to drive the development of treatment programming, and it begins with an understanding of why young people get into trouble in the first place.

Juvenile delinquency is defined here as those acts that, if committed by an adult, would be considered crimes. Primarily, these acts include property, person, and drug offenses; status offenses such as truancy, running away from home, etc., are excluded from the discussion here. Explaining delinquency is a complex matter, and one would be hard pressed to find a source in the literature that would attribute such behavior to one single cause. Quite the contrary. Delinquency is influenced by multiple factors. Some of those factors could be internal to the individual, and others externally related to both the immediate environment of the individuals and the larger society in which they live.

The purpose of this chapter is to give a brief overview of the many theories of delinquency, concluding with a discussion on the importance of these theories to the field of juvenile justice.

4.2 Classical Deterrence Theory

Modern-day deterrence theory can be traced back to the work of Cesare Beccaria in the 18th century. In his treatise *On Crimes and Punishment*, Beccaria (1764) argued that crimes could be deterred if the punishment was just enough to cause rational individuals, through a process of weighing the possible negative consequences of such behavior against what was to be gained from it, to refrain from such activities. He believed that the punishment should fit the crime and that it should be swift and certain. All laws should be written down, along with a description of the punishment wrongdoers would receive, should they violate any one of them. Punishment should become strongly associated with crime and thus deter individuals from engaging in it.

Rational choice theory was developed by Cornish and Clark in 1986, drawing heavily from Beccaria's earlier work, as was routine activities theory developed by Cohen and Felson in 1979. These two theories form the basis of much of the current approach to delinquency in the United States today. Cornish and Clark (1986) argue that people break the law after deciding to ignore the fact that they could be punished for their actions if caught. Cohen and Felson (1979) suggest that delinquency occurs when there is a convergence in time and space of (1) motivated offenders, (2) suitable targets, and (3) the absence of capable guardians. Changing lifestyles in American society, with more people working outside the home, place people in the position of becoming a victim of crime.

This group of theories is centered around the notion of *free will*. Young people commit delinquent acts because they are freely choosing to do so, and they need to learn that "crime does not pay." This lesson can only be taught through swift action on the part of legal authorities, sending a message to both the individual (*specific deterrence*) and the wider community of young people (*general deterrence*) that they will not escape punishment. Further, people need to think twice about their surroundings, and engage in some target-hardening activities (extra locks on windows and doors, car alarms, etc.) to deter criminal activities.

4.3 Biological Theory

In the latter part of the 19th century, Cesare Lombroso suggested that criminals were nothing more than throwbacks in the evolutionary chain. He referred to this phenomenon as *atavism*, and argued that criminals could be identified through an examination of such physical characteristics as the shape of their ears, nose, mouth, cheekbones, or other *stigmata* such as extra toes or wide arm spans. Through an examination of Italian prisoners, as compared with military soldiers, he found that those who did possess some of these physical characteristics were statistically more likely to be of the criminal class than of the military class. Although much of this work has been discredited today due to problems with being unable to replicate his findings and because it has overtones of racism and sexism, the work of Lombroso did turn our attention to the study of the biological causes of crime. Lombroso himself did eventually see the role that one's environment can play in the production of crime, and most modern-day biological theorists approach the study of crime, delinquency, and deviance using a model that integrates biological causes with those found in the environment (see Lombroso, 1968).

4.3.1 Modern-Day Biological Theory

Throughout the first few decades of the 20th century, many theorists refrained from considering biological explanations for delinquency for fear they would be connected to Lombroso and his earlier work. Today, however, much has changed in that regard. Biocriminologists, according to Siegel and Senna (1988, p. 92), "believe that certain traits linked to criminal activity are inherently biological and therefore not related to socialization." They point out that antisocial behavior in young people has been attributed to certain body functions "controlled by diet, blood chemistry, hormonal imbalance, allergies, and so on" (Siegel and Senna, 1988, p. 92).

Chemical imbalances in the brain have also been linked to antisocial behavior in young people. Lower levels of such chemicals as serotonin, for example, have been linked to violent behavior, and the neurotransmitter dopamine to the abuse of illicit drugs and alcohol (Fishbein, 1990).

Fishbein (2001) has written extensively on the subject of biology, crime, and delinquency, providing some evidence that there may be a link between severe blows to the frontal lobe of the brain and antisocial behavior. Further, other brain damage caused by lack of oxygen *in utero* or during the birth process, or some other trama associated with the birth experience, could be linked to future delinquency (Fishbein, 2001). Adolescent problem behaviors have also been attributed to problems with individual *limbic systems,* "a structure surrounding the brain stem and the source of feelings of pleasure and pain" (Bohm, 1997, p. 41).

Delinquency has also been linked to low IQ scores, a controversial subject in the field of juvenile justice. It is difficult to make the argument that low IQ causes crime, but there are several empirical studies that demonstrate a correlation between the two (see Hirschi and Hindelang, 2003). The fact that intelligence is innate and, therefore, inherited from one's parents is highly contested, with many arguing that tests that measure innate intelligence are doing nothing more than measuring what persons have learned from their environment up to that point in their life. For example, might a fifth grader living in a middle- or upper-class household, the child of parents with a college education, and attending a well-resourced private school, be expected to perform better on a test of verbal or language skills than would a fifth grader living in an urban, socially disorganized neighborhood, parented by a single mother with a below-poverty income and a high school dropout, and attending an under-resourced public school?

Although there are some researchers who hold fast to the view that intelligence is indeed inherited and can be measured reliably with most modern-day IQ tests (Hirschi and Hindelang, 2003), there are others who argue otherwise. Even if IQ could be measured reliably, it could be that IQ indirectly affects delinquency by way of academic problems and eventually dropping out of school. In short, it could be that low IQ leads escalatingly to (1) problems in school, (2) the child dropping out, (3) being free to seek out others who have similar problems, and eventually (4) delinquency.

4.4 Psychological Explanations for Delinquency

Psychology has been applied widely to the study of juvenile delinquency and is used quite often when developing treatment programs for young offenders. Much of this approach is grounded in Sigmund Freud's psychoanalytic theory, the notion that personality traits are formed in early childhood as children go through several psychosexual stages of growth. Concepts from Freud's (1940) theory include the *id*, the *ego*, and the *superego*. An overactive id leads to unbridled pursuit of desires and pleasures, and can be held in check by the ego, which works as a go-between for the id and the superego, the seat of one's conscience. Freud believed that by the age of five or so, the seat of a child's personality was fully developed, and any emotional trauma during these formative years can have a long-lasting and negative influence on the child. Only through intense psychoanalysis can these deep-seated emotions be brought to the surface and sufficiently addressed.

In a similar vein, personality traits theory argues that certain characteristics are directly associated with problem youth. As early as 1950, the Gluecks, writing in *Unraveling Juvenile Delinquency*, discovered that problem youth were more "defiant, ambivalent about authority, extroverted, fearful of failure, resentful, hostile, suspicious, and defensive than the nondelinquents" (cited in Bartollas, 2001, p. 81). Since that time, others have reported similar findings, noting that delinquency can be attributed to emotional instability (Conger and Miller, 1966), a desire to engage in stimulating, sometimes risk-taking behavior (Cloninger, 1987), and hostility, self-centeredness, spitefulness, jealousy, and an indifference to others (Miller and Lynam, 2001).

4.5 Sociological Theories of Delinquency: Macro Perspectives

At the end of the 19th century, Emile Durkheim wrote about the changes that were taking place during the Industrial Revolution across parts of Europe. He noted that during times of rapid transition from one type of society to another, chaos and confusion can develop when individuals' appetites for certain material goods are not sufficiently controlled. With the move from an organic society and its emphasis on agriculture and a primarily rural lifestyle to a more mechanical society marked by the rise of factories and large cities, society loses control over its members. Durkheim (1893) coined the concept *anomie* to describe a society in which individuals lose sight of their moral compass under these conditions.

Studying such social facts as poverty, divorce rates, religiosity, etc., Durkheim was able to show a correlation between these phenomena and suicide rates. Through the scientific study of these social events, he was able to show that increases in poverty, higher divorce rates, and a seeming decrease in church-related activities led to higher rates of suicide. His work has been noted as providing the basic foundation for future works that turned away from thinking about crime causation from a biological or psychological perspective, and looked instead to factors external to the individual. This group of theories are known as structural theories, and they take a more macro approach to the study of crime and delinquency. Put another way, these theories consider the impact that social conditions might have on the production of crime and delinquency.

4.5.1 Strain, Subcultural, and Differential Opportunity Theories

Drawing heavily from Durkheim's earlier work, Merton (1938) used the concept of anomie in an article titled "Social Structure and Anomie." What has come to be known as *strain theory* suggests that crime or delinquency is the result of a disjunction between cultural goals and societal means. In other words, in an industrialized country, people are encouraged to succeed by going after certain success symbols (e.g., a good education, a high-paying career, certain material goods, etc.). Things are not, however, always equal, and there are some individuals who do not have the same means through which to achieve those goals as do their more affluent counterparts.

Thinking about delinquency, we could use strain theory to argue that young people who see their legitimate opportunities as limited might use illegitimate opportunities instead. Merton referred to this group of individuals as *innovators* or those people who accept the goals that society lays out for everyone but who are willing to break the law as a way of accumulating a certain amount of material success when they are unable to achieve a good education, a decent job, etc.

In 1955, Cohen used parts of Merton's strain theory to provide an explanation for the development of the delinquent subculture. In *Delinquent Boys: The Culture of the Gang* (1955), Cohen suggested that Merton was incorrect in his assumption that all delinquent acts were meant to assist young people in acquiring material success symbols. Instead, working-class youth run into problems when trying to live up to the middle-class measuring rod, primarily encountered in the local schools. They have difficulties when it comes to academic achievements or participation in extracurricular activities, many of which are costly and are not easily afforded by their families. When this occurs, status frustration results in the seeking out of other youth in a similar situation, and this is how the delinquent subculture arises. Status is achieved through other means such as being tough on the streets and able to take care of oneself, and through engagement in risk-taking behaviors, with less emphasis on achieving the materialistic success goals associated with the middle class.

Cloward and Ohlin (1960) further expanded Merton's strain theory in *Delinquency and Opportunity: A Theory of Delinquent Gangs*. Differential opportunity theory suggests that Merton was correct when it comes to the role that blocked opportunities can play in the production of delinquency but that we should not assume that illegal opportunities are available to all youth. In other words, young persons might wish to seek out illegitimate means as a way to accumulate certain success symbols but may find that delinquent youth may not accept them into their groups as easily as one might assume they would. Cloward and Ohlin argued that when this occurs, these young people may retreat from society altogether and instead of engaging in violence or other typical gang-like behaviors, become addicted to alcohol or illicit drugs.

4.5.2 Social Disorganization Theory

Building further on the earlier work of Durkheim, sociologists connected with the University of Chicago, now referred to as *The Chicago School*, studied the etiology of delinquency through carefully examining the negative social milieu of Chicago's urban areas. Shaw and McKay (1942) examined multiple years of data from the 1930s and early 1940s to explore the cause of high rates of delinquency within these communities. They pulled data from several sources and were able to show a relationship between high rates of delinquency and poverty, residential mobility, and lack of homogeneity within local neighborhoods. Shaw and McKay noted that in areas where more people lived below the poverty line, with higher rates of infant mortality, numbers of single-female households, and cases of tuberculosis and other diseases, delinquency rates were higher. Further, they were also able to demonstrate that within these high-delinquency census tracts, there were fewer homeowners, and the median rental value of properties was lower. Finally, Shaw and McKay were able to demonstrate higher rates of delinquency in census tracts where people were constantly moving in and out, and where several different cultures were coming in contact with each other (heterogeneity).

In short, Shaw and McKay's (1942) basic argument suggests that in communities where social institutions (e.g., schools, families, etc.) are in disarray and local residents are unable to realize a common value system, there are fewer individuals looking out after young people, and delinquency is likely to be the result. Social disorganization theory sought to dispel the myth that delinquency is a "those kinds of people" problem through demonstrating empirically that delinquency is a "that kind of place" problem.

4.6 Sociological Theories of Delinquency: Micro Perspectives

There are several explanations for delinquency that approach the issue from a more micro (individual) level. This group of theorists situate delinquency in something gone awry in the socialization process of young people. Social process theorists do not throw out structural or macro perspectives altogether, but they do argue, and have demonstrated empirically, that micro theories do a better job of explaining delinquency than do their more macro counterparts.

4.6.1 Differential Association and Social Learning Theory

One of the greatest predictors of delinquency is hanging out with delinquent friends. Sutherland's (1947) differential association theory poses that young people learn to engage in criminal activities the same as they learn any other type of behavior, primarily through observing other people's behavior. Sutherland (1947) believes that through imitating the behavior of intimate others (e.g., parents and other close family members or friends) over a period of time, a young person could come to see crime as acceptable behavior.

The major proposition of differential association theory is that people become delinquent when they receive more *definitions* (messages or symbolic interactions) that are favorable to law-breaking behavior than definitions favorable toward law-abiding behaviors. In other words, if a young person hangs around people who are engaging in law-breaking behavior or who express sentiments that it is okay to break the law, they probably will be swayed in that direction. This is especially true if the youths hold in high regard the individuals from whom they are getting these messages. On the other hand, if children are in the company of individuals who do not engage in crime and who reinforce the message that such behavior is inappropriate, then they are less likely to become delinquents.

In 1966, Burgess and Akers revised Sutherland's differential association theory by introducing concepts from sociopsychology, namely, those more readily associated with operant conditioning. Burgess and Akers argued that Sutherland had stopped short of explaining how learning, so important to his theory and to the production of delinquency, takes place. In their *differential association-reinforcement theory*, they outlined the role that positive and negative reinforcements play in the learning of inappropriate behaviors. For example, behavior is positively reinforced when a child benefits from engaging in minor theft of a friend's property, enjoying the procurement and use of the item. On the other hand, that behavior is negatively reinforced when a parent or close friend knows about the behavior but fails to take corrective action.

The theory developed by Burgess and Akers came to be known as social learning theory and was further revised by Akers (1985) in his work titled *Deviant Behavior: A Social Learning Approach*. As Bohm (1997, pp. 100–101) points out, learning theory posits that delinquency can be curbed through extinction or punishment:

> Extinction is a procedure in which behavior that previously was positively reinforced is no longer reinforced. Punishment is the presentation of aversive stimuli to reduce a response .... and to be effective must be applied consistently and immediately.

4.6.2 Social Control Theories of Delinquency

Social control theories suggest that young people are free to deviate in the absence of either external social controls or internal self-control. Early social control theorists (Albert Reiss, Jackson Toby, E. Ivan Nye, and Walter Reckless) began to question the major approach to the study of delinquency. Instead of asking "Why do people commit crime?" they asked, "Why don't more of us commit crime?" According to control theorists, the reason that most of us conform to societal norms is that we are bonded to society in such a way that does not allow us to deviate from the norm, or we have internalized those norms to the extent that our conscience will not allow us to be so engaged.

Perhaps the best known control theory is the social bonding theory, developed by Travis Hirschi in 1969. In *Causes of Delinquency*, Hirschi suggested that delinquency is the result of a child's bonds to society becoming weak or broken. The four elements of the bond — attachment, commitment, belief, and involvement — are equally important, and the weakening of any one of them could bring about the weakening of another, thus eventually leaving a child free to deviate. Basically, social bonding theory argues that the closer children are to their parents, extended family members, school teachers, etc., coupled with being actively involved in family- and school-related activities, the more likely they are to believe strongly in the value systems being posited by these social institutions and will become committed to conforming behaviors.

4.6.2.1 Self-Control Theory

In 1990, along with Gottfredson, Hirschi developed yet another control theory. This new theory came to be known as a *general theory of crime* and argues that delinquency is the result of inadequate socialization. Basically, parents have the primary responsibility to instill in their children a sense of delayed gratification, and this must take place in the first 10 years or so of a child's life. Gottfredson and Hirschi (1990) attribute delinquency to an absence of *self-control* that leaves a person unable to effectively differentiate between right and wrong. They suggest that low self-control can be seen in individuals who act impulsively, express a lack of sensitivity toward others, and engage frequently in risk-taking activities (Gottfredson and Hirschi, 1990).

4.7 Symbolic Interaction and Labeling Theory

George Herbert Mead (1934) used the concept of *symbolic interaction* to describe the importance of meaning that people attach to the messages they receive through communications with other people. These symbols of meaning can be either verbal expressions, or they can be expressed through nonverbal communication such as one's body language (smiles, frowns, rolling of the eyes, etc.). For Mead, our self-image is shaped by our interactions with others across a period of time, often referred to as the *looking-glass self* (Cooley, as cited in Bohm, 1997).

From the symbolic interaction perspective, labeling theory was developed. This group of theories calls attention to the role that society's reaction to delinquency might play in the production of subsequent delinquent behavior. Becker (1963) notes that behavior considered to be outside the norm of society's boundaries, referred to as *deviant behavior*, is whatever people say it is. Thus, it is the *moral entrepreneurs* in society who get to decide what is and is not deviant or inappropriate behavior. These individuals have a great deal of resources at their disposal and use those resources (money, power, etc.) to influence the law-making process.

Lemert (1951) has talked about primary and secondary deviance. Although labeling theory might not be able to explain the young persons' first acts of deviance, how their parents, teachers, or law enforcement agencies react to those first acts does in fact greatly influence subsequent deviant behavior. Once children feel singled out, and are labeled "bad kids," they could internalize such a label, and the *self-fulfilling prophecy* becomes realized. In other words, the children may begin to act according to the label that has been applied to them. For some labeling theorists, the less said about some childhood behavior the better. Or, at the very least, the more children that can be diverted from the juvenile justice system, the better chance they will have of escaping the labeling process.

4.8 Conflict and Critical Theories of Delinquency

The structural theories discussed above (namely, strain and social disorganization theory) are often referred to as *consensus* theories. Society is built around the notion that individuals have achieved a common agreement about what is inappropriate behavior. Drawing from Talcott Parsons' (1951) concept of *functionalism*, consensus theorists see society as a group of interrelated parts, with each system playing a vital role in the survival of the system. There may be some swaying of the pendulum to the right or to the left, but by and large it usually arrives back in the middle, striking a compromise among the various members of society and their corresponding views about how society should function on the whole.

Conflict theorists argue otherwise and suggest that society is not built at all around the notion of consensus. Rather, the organizing framework of most modern-day societies is conflict. There are many special interest groups, according to conflict theorists (Vold, 1958), and it is the dominant group that is able to decide which behaviors will be defined as *criminal*, and which will not. Those who do not have the power or the resources to fight the dominant group become part of the subordinate group, and are forced to abide by the rules of the former. Some conflict theorists argue that the juvenile justice system, and the adult system as well, are nothing more than tools of the controlling group, making sure that the position of the dominant group is protected.

Critical theory, an offshoot of conflict theory, finds roots in Marx's political theory, although Marx himself wrote very little about crime and justice. Marx believed that under capitalism, those who own the means to production, the *bourgeoisie*, run rough shod over the working class, often referred to as *proletariats*. In a system where a few people have a lot, and many more people have very little, delinquency is likely to be the result (Sims, 1997). In this type of system, rife with social alienation and isolation, young people are likely to suffer the psychological wound of *relative deprivation*, and do what people in the upper classes sometimes do to get ahead: prey on those individuals within their own class who are weaker than they are (Sims, 1997).

4.9 Other Theories of Juvenile Delinquency

Much has been written about the causes of juvenile delinquency, and the theories presented thus far lay the basic foundation for that literature. In the last decades of the 20th century and into the first few years of the 21st century there has been a great deal of theoretical reformulation. Just as Burgess and Akers revised Sutherland's differential association theory, theorists have taken other preexisting theories and reformulated them into new theories. Further, some theorists have merged two or more theories together through a process referred to as *theoretical integration* in an attempt to produce a theory that has more explanatory power than the individual theories alone.

4.9.1 General Strain Theory

Robert Agnew (1992) revised strain theory by introducing concepts from the sociopsychological literature. He suggests a more micro study of the role that individual stress (as opposed to societal strain) plays in the production of delinquency. For example, a child could suffer from the loss of a parent through death or divorce, or adolescents might have girl- or boyfriends break up with them, an experience that can be quite traumatic at any age. Further, the child who suffers either physical or sexual abuse is most certainly inundated with stressors that could very well influence delinquent behavior. With the removal of positive stimuli or the introduction of noxious stimuli, young people are likely to act out in anger (Agnew, 1992). How they will react to these stressors varies across individuals, so there is a need to better understand what causes some children to respond with anger, while others do not.

4.9.2 A Systemic/Social Disorganization Model of Delinquency

Social disorganization theory received a great deal of renewed attention beginning in the 1980s, much of this attention stemming from the work of Robert Sampson and Byron Groves (1989). Once again, a macro level (structural) theory of delinquency was revised to include micro (individual) level concepts. Sampson and Groves (1989) suggested that the major concepts of social disorganization theory (poverty, residential mobility, and lack of homogeneity) do influence delinquency, but perhaps indirectly. Rather, the extent to which these social phenomena will negatively impact a community could be mediated by the extent to which individuals who reside within these communities can (1) watch out over teenage peer groups, (2) muster a certain degree of neighborhood cohesion, and (3) participate in community programs and projects (Crime Watch programs, the local PTA, etc.). In their own research, Sampson and Groves (1989) found that the greatest predictor of a reduction in delinquency within these neighborhoods is more attention paid to teenage peer groups. This finding gets to the heart of Shaw and McKay's original theory of social disorganization.

4.9.3 Crime, Shame, and Reintegration

John Braithwaite (1989) disagrees somewhat with labeling theorists, suggesting that some form of *shaming* might actually work to reduce further delinquency. In this theory, quite often referred to as *reintegrative shaming*, Braithwaite combines major concepts from several theories, including social disorganization, differential opportunity, social bonding, strain, and subcultural theory. His basic premise is that when people are allowed to express remorse over the ills they have committed toward society, they should be successfully reintegrated back into a community that is willing to let bygones be bygones. Braithwaite argues that individuals are so enmeshed within interlocking segments of the local community that the only way they can ever become law-abiding, contributing citizens is when a sense of *communitarianism* exists. He uses the word *shaming* to describe a process whereby the local community lets the offenders know that it disapproves of their behavior, and this message to the offenders is meant to get the offenders to see the errors of their ways (Braithwaite, 1989).

If, however, the shaming process is stigmatizing, as opposed to reintegrative in nature, the young person could be driven even further down a path toward delinquency. In order for Braithwaite's reintegrative shaming theory to be useful in the juvenile justice policy arena, both the young person and the local community would have to come to some sort of agreement about the admission of guilt and the asking for and the simultaneous expression of forgiveness.

4.10 Conclusions

Many of the empirical tests of the theories outlined here have been used in the development of juvenile justice public policy. The major tenets of deterrence theory can be seen in the more recent "get tough" approach to juvenile offenders in the last decade or so. More and more juveniles are waived into the adult system under the perception that harsher treatment awaits them and that this harsh treatment will, in turn, deter their future behavior. (See Chapter 33, however, for a response to this argument.) Community-based corrections attempt to treat juvenile delinquents at the local level, hoping to divert them from secure, locked-down holding facilities. This group of programs can be said to be rooted in several theories of delinquency, including social disorganization, strain, labeling, and the individual or micro theories of psychology or general strain theory.

Any effort to divert a young person from the juvenile system finds root in labeling theory. As mentioned above, balance and restorative justice programs bring together the young offenders with their victims through mediation with an objective party attempt to shame the offender, without further stigmatization, thus trying to ward off the negative effects of labeling.

Efforts at separating delinquent peers, and restricting who young people can and cannot hang around with, fit squarely with differential association, learning, and subcultural theories. Further, recall that the revisions of social disorganization theory by Sampson and Groves (1989) include measures of supervision over teenage peer groups.

All of these programs are commonsense approaches to curbing juvenile delinquency. There is, however, a sufficient body of empirical works available for juvenile justice policy makers and practitioners alike through which to judge which of these approaches holds the most promise for preventing delinquency in the first place.

References

Agnew, R. 1992. Foundation for a general theory strain theory of crime and delinquency. *Criminology* 30: 47–87.

Akers, R.L. 1985. *Deviant Behavior: A Social Learning Approach*, 3rd ed. Belmont, CA: Wadsworth.

Bartollas, C. 2001. *Juvenile Delinquency*, 6th ed. New York: Allyn and Bacon.

Beccaria, C. (1764) 1975. see *On Crimes and Punishment*. Trans. with introduction by, Harry Paolucci. Indianapolis, IN: Bobbs-Merrill.

Becker, H.S. 1963. *The Outsiders: Studies in the Sociology of Deviance*. New York: Free Press.

Bohm, R.M. 1997. *A Primer on Crime and Delinquency*. Belmont, CA: Wadsworth.

Braithwaite, J. 1989. *Crime, Shame and Reintegration*. Cambridge, MA: Cambridge University Press.

Burgess, R.L. and Akers, R.L. 1966. A differential association-reinforcement theory of criminal behavior. *Social Problems*, 14: 128–147.

Cloninger, C.R. 1987. A systematic method for clinical description and classification of personality variants. *Archives of General Psychiatry*, 44: 573–588.

Cloward, R.A. and Ohlin, L.E. 1960. *Delinquency and Opportunity: A Theory of Delinquent Gangs*. New York: Free Press.

Cohen, A.K. 1955. *Delinquent Boys: The Culture of the Gang*. New York: Free Press.

Cohen, L.W. and Felson, M. 1979. Social change and crime rate trends: a routine activity approach. *American Sociological Review*, 44: 588–608.

Conger, J.J.and Miller, W.C. 1966. *Personality, Social Class, and Delinquency*. New York: John Wiley & Sons.

Cornish, D. and Clarke, R., Eds., 1986. *The Reasoning Criminal: Rational Choice Perspectives on Offending*. New York: Springer-Verlag.

Durkheim, E. 1893. *Suicide*. New York: Free Press.

Freud, S. 1940. (reprint) *An Outline of Psychoanalysis*, translated by James Strachey. New York: W.W. Norton, 1963.

Fishbein, D.H. 1990. Biological perspectives in criminology. *Criminology*, 28: 27–72.

———. 2001. *Biobehavioral Perspectives in Criminology*. Belmont, CA: Wadsworth Press.

Glueck, S.and Glueck, E. 1950. *Unraveling Juvenile Delinquency*. Cambridge, MA: Harvard University Press.

Gottfredson, M.R. and Hirschi, T. 1990. *A General of Crime*. Stanford, CA: Stanford University Press.

Hirschi, T. 1969. *Cause of Delinquency*. Berkley, CA: University of California Press.

Hirschi, T. and Hindelang, M.J. 2003. Intelligence and delinquency: a revisionist review. In Renzetti, C.M., Curran, D.J., and Carr, P.J., Eds., *Theories of Crime: A Reader*. Boston, MA: Allyn and Bacon. pp. 37–50.

Lemert, E.M. 1951. *Social Pathology: A Systematic Approach to the Theory of Sociopathic Behavior*. New York: McGraw-Hill.

Lombroso, C. 1968. *Crime: Its Causes and Remedies*. Trans. Henry P. Horton, Montclair, NJ: Patterson Smith.

Mead, G.H. 1934. *Mind, Self, and Society*. Chicago, IL: University of Chicago Press.

Merton, R.K. 1938. Social structure and anomie. *American Sociological Review*, 3: 672–682.

Miller, J. and Lynam, D. 2001. Structural models of personality and their relation to antisocial behavior: a meta-analytic review. *Criminology*, 39: 765–798.

Parsons, T. 1951. *The Social System*. New York: Free Press.

Sampson, R.J. and Groves, W.B. 1989. Community structure and crime: testing social disorganization theory. *American Journal of Sociology*, 94: 774–802.

Shaw, C.R. and McKay, H.D. 1942. *Juvenile Delinquency in Urban Areas*. Chicago, IL: University of Chicago Press.

Siegel, L.J. and Senna, J.J. 1988. *Juvenile Delinquency: Theory, Practice and Law*. St. Paul, MN: West Publishing.

Sims, B. 1997. Crime, punishment, and the American dream: toward a marxist integration. *Journal of Research in Crime and Delinquency*, 3(1): 5–24.

Sutherland, E.H. 1947. *Principles of Criminology*, 4th ed. Philadelphia, PA: J.B. Lippencott.

Vold, G.B. 1958. *Theoretical Criminology*. New York: Oxford University Press.

Chapter 5

Delinquent Girls

Suman Kakar

5.1 Introduction

Understanding antisocial and delinquent behavior among children and young adults has been the subject of social science research for quite some time. Generally, delinquency has been considered to be a male phenomenon. More recent statistics have demonstrated that females are not impervious to delinquency. However, much of the research in the area of juvenile delinquency has focused on understanding male delinquent behavior. Very little, if any, attention has been devoted to understanding the development of similar behavior among girls (Kakar et al., 2002). Until recently, it has been believed that the delinquent behavior of girls does not cause serious problems, because girls have historically constituted a very small proportion of the offender population, and have committed minor and far fewer crimes than boys.

Many of the studies conducted so far have documented that girls get into trouble more quietly than boys, and in most cases, are victims themselves before they become offenders (Prescott, 1997; Girls, Inc., 1996; Davis et al., 1997). Some research suggests that anger may make girls strike inward (Belknap, 1996). Angry girls may not seem dangerous to society because it is believed that they are more likely to threaten their own well-being than others'. Consequently, there has been a general perception that intervention in female delinquent or criminal behavior was unnecessary for two apparent reasons: (1) only small numbers of females were involved, and (2) the few who got involved in illegal activities engaged in nonserious and nonthreatening crimes. Because such offenses were primarily sexual in nature, female offenders were the exception, and their criminality was assumed to be a manifestation of an extreme form of psychological deviance (Widom, 2000). As a result, girls' needs have been overlooked (Chesney-Lind, 1988), and they have been the afterthought of a juvenile justice system designed to deal with boys (Bergsmann, 1989; Miller et al., 1995).

However, the demographics are beginning to change. Girls and women are the fastest growing segments of the juvenile and criminal justice system (Acoca, 1999). The national arrest rate for girls has steadily climbed over the last decade. The arrests for violent crimes such as aggravated and simple assault increased a total of 36 percent among girls between 1994 and 1998 compared to a negligible increase or decline in those violent crimes for boys, according to the figures released by the federal Office of Juvenile Justice and Delinquency Prevention (OJJDP).

5.2 What Do We Know about Female Delinquents?

Although research about delinquency among girls is still scarce and most of it is descriptive, focusing on documenting the extent and type of crimes committed by girls (Kakar et al., 2002), existing literature on female delinquents presents some incontrovertible facts and answers many frequently asked questions. A summary of these emergent facts and themes is presented here.

First and foremost, the literature presents undeniable facts about the extent of female involvement in delinquency. One of the most important and recurring themes is that female delinquency is a serious problem, and that girls are a substantial and growing proportion of the juvenile justice population. The most recent Federal Bureau of Investigation (FBI) report released on October 27, 2003, revealed that females make up 25 percent of all the crimes committed in the United States.

Girls' involvement in delinquency and crime, though still less than boys', appears to have increased significantly in the last two decades. Although more than three quarters of juvenile arrests and juvenile court delinquency cases involve males (Snyder, 1997), female involvement in crimes has evolved into a significantly growing trend (Budnick and

Shields-Fletcher, 1998). During the decade from 1983 to 1993, arrests of female juveniles increased by 31 percent (compared to 21 percent for boys). In 1999, the FBI noted that girls account for one out of four arrests of young people in America (Chesney-Lind, 2001). In California in 2000, a quarter of the state's misdemeanor and 17 percent of its felony arrests were young women.

However, the literature also reveals that some of the more dramatic increases involving female juvenile offenders earlier in the decade have begun slowing down. For example, in Florida there were 28,531 females involved in delinquent acts in the fiscal year 2000 to 2001, accounting for 28.6 percent of 99,770 total juveniles referred for delinquency that year. A 44 percent increase in the number of girls arrested annually for committing crimes has occurred during the past decade in Florida. The number of boys arrested annually rose 12.5 percent during the same period. However, during the past 3 years, the number of girls arrested in the state has evened out to around 28,000 (Department of Juvenile Justice, 2003).

5.2.1 What Type of Crimes Do Girls Commit?

A comprehensive literature review indicates that not only have the rates for female involvement in crime and delinquency changed but there has also been a difference in the type of offenses committed. There is a trend towards more serious crimes. During the past decade girls have been increasingly involved in the juvenile justice system and have been charged with crimes that are traditionally committed by boys.

Traditionally, a large proportion of females entered the system for nonviolent offenses. For example, according to OJJDP (2000), girls were involved in 41 percent of the status offenses and in only 23 percent of the delinquency cases that ended in trial during 1996. However, the pace at which girls are being convicted of serious offenses is picking up faster than the pace at which boys are convicted. During the decade from 1983 to 1993, female juvenile arrests increased by 31 percent (compared to 21 percent for boys). Between 1989 and 1993, the relative growth in juvenile arrests involving females was 23 percent, more than double the 11 percent growth for males (Poe-Yamagata and Butts, 1996) The FBI noted that girls account for one out of four arrests of young people in America (Chesney-Lind, 2001). Despite a reported general decline in juvenile crime, girls are the fastest-growing segment of the juvenile population (American Bar Association [ABA] and National Bar Association [NBA] Report, 2001). This report states that although juvenile crime rates, especially for violent crimes, have decreased in general since peaking in 1994, data show an increase in the number and percentage of girls in the juvenile justice system. According to Snyder (1997), between 1994 and 1995 alone, girls' arrests increased by 3 percent for aggravated assault (vs. a decline of 4.5 percent for boys), by 7.7 percent for other assaults (vs. a 1.8 percent increase for boys), and by 26.6 percent for drug abuse violations (vs. a 16.7 percent increase for boys). The results of several research studies indicate that over the past 25 years there has been an exponential increase in the number of girls in detention facilities, jails, and prisons. Similarly, arrest rates for girls in all offense categories have increased disproportionately. In 1999, law enforcement agencies reported 670,800 arrests of girls under the age of 18 (27 percent of the total juvenile arrests that year). Another study reported that between 1988 and 1997, female delinquency cases increased by 83 percent. This increase was across all racial categories — 74 percent for white, 106 percent for black, and 102 percent for other races.

Consequently, there has been a growing interest in the number of young females involved in delinquent behavior. Female involvement in crimes, once seen as an anomaly, has evolved into a significantly growing trend (Budnick and Shields-Fletcher, 1998).

The National Center for Juvenile Justice (NCSS) reported that between 1992 and 1996, the number of arrests of female juveniles for violent crime index offenses increased by 25 percent, compared with no increase in the arrests of male juveniles. Similarly, property crime index arrests of juvenile females went up by 21 percent, while arrests of males declined by 4 percent.

Girls are involved in more violent crimes than they were a decade ago. For example, their murder arrest rate increased by 64 percent (Chesney-Lind and Brown, 1999). According to the OJJDP, arrests for violent crimes such as aggravated and simple assault increased by a total of 36 percent among girls between 1994 and 1998 compared with a negligible increase or decline in those violent crimes for boys.

Just as some of the more dramatic increases involving female juvenile offenders in general criminal activities earlier in the decade have begun slowing down, a similar trend is seen in their involvement in violent crimes. The number of girls arrested for violent felony offenses almost doubled over the past decade in Florida. There were 3044 females involved in violent felony offenses in the fiscal year 2000 to 2001, compared to 1609 in the fiscal year 1991 to 1992. However, in the past 3 years the number of female juvenile offenders arrested for violent felonies has begun to level off, in this case, at slightly more than 3000. The national arrest rate for girls steadily climbed from 21 percent in 1983 to 27 percent in 1999 and evened out in 2002.

5.2.2 *What Age Group Are These Girls?*

A typical female juvenile offender is aged 14 to 16, from an ethnic minority, lives in a poor neighborhood with a high crime rate, and has experienced physical, sexual, and/or emotional abuse, according to Peters (1998). Nationwide, girls are becoming involved with the justice system at a younger age. From 1987 to 1991, the number of 13- and 14-year-old girls in juvenile court increased by 10 percent (Bergsmann, 1994). One in five girls in secure confinement is now aged 14 or younger.

5.2.3 *Minorities Are Overrepresented*

Another fact that emerges from the literature is that ethnic minorities are disproportionately represented in the female offender population (Bergsmann, 1989; Campbell, 1995; Community Research Associates, 1997). African American girls are overrepresented in the criminal and juvenile justice systems. Data from several sources indicate that minority females are more likely to be victimized by violence. According to the 1999 National Crime Victimization Survey data, the violence victimization rate for female African American youth was almost double that of white female youth and about 25 percent greater than that of African American males and white teens. The violent victimization rate for African American girls between ages of 12 and 15 exceeded that of African American girls between the ages of 16 and 19 by more than one third. African American youth comprise nearly half of those in secure detention and Hispanics 13 percent (Bergsmann, 1994).

Although 65 percent of the population is Caucasian, only 34 percent of girls in detention are Caucasian. Seven out of every ten cases involving white girls are dismissed, compared to three out of every ten cases dismissed for black girls. According to the 2000 Census, African American girls form 29.4 percent of the population of girls under age 18 but are overrepresented among those involved in or impacted by the criminal and juvenile justice systems. According to Krisberg and Temin (2001), Black children are nine times more likely to have an incarcerated parent than white children. Another study conducted by ABA and NBA (2001), revealed that the number of delinquency cases involving Black girls increased by 106 percent between 1988 and 1997. During those years, Black girls were detained at a rate three times greater than the rate for white girls (OJJDP, 2000). Black girls from all ethnic backgrounds have a collective history of unequal sentencing and treatment by justice system, as well as victimization because of their double status as a black person and a female in American society (National Council on Crime and Delinquency [NCCD], 2002). Several reports issued by the Building Blocks for Youth Initiative indicate that African American girls are more likely to be detained, formally charged, tried as adults, and locked up in state and federal facilities than white youth who commit similar crimes. These reports also reveal that although minority youth represent only 34 percent of the population, they represent 67 percent of the youth committed to its public facilities.

5.2.4 Upward Trend in Female Delinquency Underrated

The literature suggests that, historically, this increase has not been taken seriously, perhaps because girls who break the law have not been perceived as a danger to society. Traditionally, girls have come into contact with the courts for nonviolent status offenses such as curfew violations, running away, or unruly behavior (Chesney-Lind, 1988). Theft cases have accounted for nearly one fourth of girls' arrests (Bergsmann, 1994).

According to the FBI Uniform Crime Report, in 1995, 23.5 percent of the arrests of girls under 18 were for larceny thefts. During the same year, 32.5 percent of all juvenile theft arrests involved girls. Even today, in spite of the increased crime rate among girls, they are almost always invisible when the delinquency "problem" is discussed, and largely forgotten when the programs for delinquents are crafted (Chesney-Lind, 2001). It is only recently that researchers and policymakers have started paying attention to the problem.

5.2.5 Juvenile Justice System Biased against Female Delinquents

Another important aspect revealed in the literature is a system bias against female delinquents. Several studies report that females, as compared with males of similar age and to severity of their crimes, are disproportionately charged with status offenses. According to data collected by Juvenile Detention Alternative Initiative (JDAI), girls are detained at a higher rate than boys for minor offenses such as public disorder, probation violations, status offenses, and traffic violations (29 percent for girls vs. 19 percent for boys). Girls are overrated in the justice system, and their arrests are more likely to occur for status offenses such as running away, incorrigibility, etc. (Peters and Peters, 1998). Although their offenses are typically less violent, girls who break the law are sometimes treated more harshly than boys who commit the same type of crime (Davidson, 1982). In 1999, although they comprised only 27 percent of the juveniles arrested, girls accounted for 59.5 percent of juvenile arrests for running away, and 54 percent of juvenile arrests for prostitution. Girls are twice as likely to be detained, with detention lasting five times longer than boys. In addition, girls are detained for less serious offenses. In 1987, 9 percent of girls in training schools were committed for status offenses compared to 1.5 percent of boys (Girls Incorporated, 1996). Between 1988 and 1997, the use of detention for girls increased by 65 percent compared with a 30 percent increase for boys.

Because most of the crimes committed by girls are status offenses and are not considered to be of much significance to the safety of the society, female juvenile delinquents have been an invisible minority whose needs, histories, and issues have gone largely undocumented for decades (Belknap, Holsinger, and Dunn, 1997). Girls who have broken the law have entered a juvenile justice system that was designed to cater to boys. The literature and analysis of data indicate that boys commit an overwhelming number of juvenile crimes and that their offenses tend to be more violent and dangerous than the status offenses committed by girls. This is, perhaps, one of the most important reasons why female delinquents have been overlooked and neglected.

Recent changes, however, are apparent as society has taken note of the fact that girls' arrests, in spite of constituting only about one fourth of all juvenile arrests, have increased at an alarming rate. More girls are entering the juvenile justice system at younger ages, they are committing more violent crimes such as assault, and some are involved in gangs, previously thought to be male turf (Peters, 1998). Although female offenders have been called "the forgotten few" (Bergsmann, 1989), they are fast becoming too numerous, and their problems too serious, to ignore.

5.3 Childhood Maltreatment and Female Delinquency

Existing research confirms that in most cases, girls are victims themselves before they become offenders (Prescott, 1997; Girls Inc., 1996; Davis et al., 1997). Similarly, according to Dembo et al. (1993), a substantial proportion of girls in the juvenile justice system report a history of childhood victimization through physical and/or sexual abuse. Chesney-Lind and Brown (1999) also report that young females in the correctional system are mostly poor, undereducated girls of color who have complex histories of trauma and substance abuse. The literature suggests that family factors play a significant role in influencing the girls' criminal behaviors. There is some evidence that dysfunctional living environments and exposure to childhood abuse can be significant variables in the development of conduct disorders and increased propensity toward commission of violent crime (Kaplan et al., 1998). A more recent study by Kakar et al. (2002) revealed that chaotic family environments and academic failure were pervasive in most delinquent girls' lives. Most of the girls that were studied in their experiment were poor, of minority status, and had histories of childhood victimization and alcohol and substance abuse.

5.3.1 Female Delinquents Internalize Their Victimization, Threaten Their Own Well-Being

Many of the studies conducted so far reveal that girls in crisis are more likely to threaten their own well-being than others', they may not seem dangerous to society. As mentioned earlier, delinquency by females has been overlooked, and there is a lack of adequate programs for girls who get in trouble with the system. The existing juvenile justice system was designed to deal with boys (Bergsmann, 1989; Miller et al., 1995) is forced to accommodate a new segment of the population — girls.

5.3.2 School Discipline Problems and Poor Academic Performance

Girls in the juvenile justice system generally perform poorly in school and have a history of discipline problems and substance abuse. Researchers have found that these factors are interrelated. For example, up to 70 percent of female delinquents have a history of sexual abuse, which can result in academic failure, teenage pregnancy, low self-esteem, substance abuse, and mental health problems, which in turn are found to be associated with delinquency and crime.

In conclusion, the literature suggests that more girls are becoming involved in the justice system and at a younger age, and for more violent offenses. Minorities are disproportionately represented, and female delinquents have fewer placement options than their male peers. These girls are often poor, undereducated, have experienced childhood victimization, and come from families that are full of chaos. It is believed that a number of interconnected risk factors, rather than one single factor, contribute to adolescent girls' being at risk of delinquency. A complex interaction of environmental (social, familial, economic) and personal factors (aptitude, maturity, psychopathology) seems to be connected with the appearance and occurrence of juvenile delinquency (Rutter, 1995; Smith, 1995). The literature also indicates that the indicators of female delinquency are different from those of male delinquency and that existing programs need to be adjusted to girls' needs.

Despite the fact that there have been indications that girls can and do get involved in delinquent and criminal activities, the needs of girls have largely been ignored. The common challenges facing the juvenile justice system today include a growing number of young female offenders committing more serious crimes, resulting in a greater number of juveniles in custody; a limited understanding of what works for girls; and a demand for comprehensive needs assessments that identify gaps in the provision of services for girls, the need to develop and implement gender-specific services and programs designed to meet the unique needs of girls, and competition for scarce resources in implementing these programs and policies (Budnick and Shields-Fletcher, 1998).

Although most research about delinquency among girls focuses on the extent and type of offenses they commit (Kakar et al., 2002), more recently, researchers have begun investigating (Belknap et al., 1998) and identifying developmental pathways most likely to lead girls to delinquency (Peters, 1998). By focusing specifically on girls, researchers are gaining a better understanding of female adolescent development and the factors that put girls at risk of delinquency, as well as identifying protective measures. More recent empirical studies that included findings on adolescent girls and boys suggest that significantly different risk factors for delinquency exist for girls (Simone et al., 2000). Results

Table 5.1   Risk Factors for Female Delinquency

Family Factors	Individual Factors	Community Factors
Family conflict	Childhood maltreatment	Residence in a disadvantaged neighborhood
Family management problems	Low self-esteem	Low neighborhood attachment
Parent or sibling history of criminal or violent behavior	Poor mental health Developmental or learning disabilities	Community disorganization
Parental attitudes favorable to involvement in problem behavior	Sexual activity at an early age	Extreme economic deprivation
Family violence	Pregnancy	Unsafe or inadequate housing
Antisocial parents	Gang involvement	
Substance-abusing parents	Personality disorder	Availability of firearms and drugs
Large family size		
Parental incarceration		Immigration problems
Social Factors	*System Factors*	*Education Factors*
Social norms	Bias	Truancy
Neighborhood characteristics	Inadequate resources	Poor academic performance
Distressed neighborhoods	Lack of adequate understanding of girls' needs	School discipline problems
Lack of supportive role models		Dropout
	Unresponsiveness to girls' needs and problems	Learning disabilities
		Negative attitude toward school

of these studies also suggest that early predictors of male conduct disorder and delinquency are not as reliable when applied to females (Chamberlain and Reid, 1994; Stattin and Magnusson, 1996).

Based on the literature reviewed, it can be hypothesized that the most significant risk factors that affect female personality and behavior development can be grouped into six categories. These risk factors, listed in Table 5.1, are based on our understanding of the developmental, psychological, social, educational, systemic, and cultural characteristics of female juveniles, and the need to provide collaborative and comprehensive services to female youth and their families in a continuum of care.

Even though girls and young women represent a minority within the juvenile justice system, there is little justification for the overall lack of policy, programs, and research attention given to this neglected population, and there is a general consensus that federal, state, and local strategies should invest in programs and policies for girls. In order to be responsive to the realities of girls involved in the juvenile justice system, a comprehensive and systematic research and data collection are needed. Systematic research grounded in theory will provide a full and accurate understanding of girls' needs. This genuine understanding is imperative for promoting gender-responsive policies and practices. For example, earlier research largely ignored female delinquency under the pretext that female offenders were "on the whole, a sorry lot" (Glueck and Glueck, 1934). Other researchers, such as Smith (1962), focused on girls' "precocious sexual development" as the root cause of their delinquency. Thus, many existing policies written specifically for females focus only on pregnancy-related issues with no recognition of other gender-specific needs (Bloom et al., 2002), whereas (as discussed earlier) delinquent girls' needs go beyond sexual deviance and pregnancy.

Another important fact to be noted is that most of the existing programs for girls place a strong emphasis on family reunification, and efforts are made to place girls in a facility close to home. This ignores the fact that many females have been physically or sexually abused at home and, consequently, family reunification services may not be beneficial (Bloom et al., 2002).

The changing demographics of girls who get in trouble and come under the care of the juvenile justice system indicate not only a need for gender-specific treatment programs and other mental health services, but that these programs and services should also be culturally competent. Much of the research on ethnicity and culture states that these factors affect individual behavior significantly. Thus, for programs to be effective, it is imperative that culture and ethnicity are taken into consideration.

Gender-specific programming should focus on some of the societal problems that challenge girls. These, as discussed earlier, include childhood maltreatment, domestic violence, high-risk sexual behavior, the incarceration of close family members, gang involvement, the use of alcohol, tobacco, or drugs, and adolescent health issues.

Based on existing literature, it can be concluded that girls and their needs have been basically disregarded in the development of policy and programs. The contemporary juvenile justice system is not adequately equipped to deal with the risks and needs of girls, and there are no appropriate and effective community-based prevention and early intervention programs for them. Inadequate planning and funding, the absence of a continuum of care, and the general lack of gender-appropriate programs, placement, detention, and aftercare services is further evidence of this apathy (Bloom et al., 2002).

As mentioned earlier, professionals in the juvenile justice system need to focus far more intensely on the role of family and its influence on girls. Most treatment programs greatly neglect the family perspective. The development of prevention programs aimed at reducing crime in this age and gender group need to be based on a broad understanding of the complex relationship of emotional, social, and family factors. Better knowledge about family dynamics through future research, especially as they relate to ethnicity, will be imperative for the informed development of rehabilitation programs for this growing segment of delinquents (Kakar et al., 2002). For programs to be effective, they have to be multipronged and tailored to the unique situations and problems encountered by girls who are at risk.

References

Acoca, L. (1999). Investing in girls: a 21st century strategy. *Juvenile Justice 4(1),* 3–13.

American Bar Association and the National Bar Association (2001). Justice by Gender: The Lack of Appropriate Prevention and Treatment Alternatives for Girls in the Juvenile System. A Report Jointly Issued by the American Bar Association and the National Bar Association.

Belknap, J. (1996). *The Invisible Woman: Gender, Crime and Justice.* Belmont, CA: Wadsworth.

Belknap, J., Holsinger, K., and Dunn, M. (1997). Understanding incarcerated girls: the results of a focus group study. *The Prison Journal, 77(4),* 381–404.

Bergsmann, I.R. (March 1989). The forgotten few: juvenile female offenders. *Federal Probation, 53(1),* 73–78.

Bergsmann, I. (1994). Establishing a foundation: just the facts. 1994 Juvenile Female Offenders Conference: A Time for Change pp. 3–14. Lanham, MD: American Correctional Association.

Bloom, B., Owen, B., Deschenes, E., and Rosenbaum, J. (2002). Moving towards justice for female juvenile offenders in the new millennium: modeling gender-specific policies and programs. *Journal of Contemporary Criminal Justice, Vol. 18(1),* 40–57.

Budnick, K.J. and Shields-Fletcher, E. (1998). What about girls. OJJDP Fact Sheet. Washington, D.C.: U.S. Department of Justice, Office of Justice Programs, Office of Juvenile Justice and Delinquency Prevention.

Bureau of Justice Statistics (1998). National Corrections Reporting Program, 1992 and 1996 [United States], prison admissions data [machine readable data files]. Washington, D.C.: BJS.

Bureau of Justice Statistics (2000). 1999 National Crime Victimization Survey, Washington, D.C.: BJS.

Campbell, J.R. (February 1995). Conference focuses on issues facing female juvenile offenders. *Corrections Today, 57(1),* 72.

Chamberlain, P. and Reid, J.B. (1994). Difference in risk factors and adjustment for male and female delinquents in treatment foster care. *Journal of Child and Family Studies, 3,* 23–39.

Community Research Associates (1997). Juvenile Female Offenders: A Status of the States Report. Northglenn, CO.

Chesney-Lind, M. (February 2001). What about the girls? Delinquency programming as if gender mattered. *Corrections Today,* 38–45.

Chesney-Lind, M. and Brown, M (1999). Girls and violence: an overview. In Flannery, D.J. and Huff, C.R., Eds., *Youth Violence: Prevention, Intervention, and Social Policy.* Washington, D.C., American Psychiatric Press, 171–199.

Chesney-Lind, M. (1988). Girls and status offenses: is juvenile justice still sexist? *Criminal Justice Abstracts, 20(1),* 144–165.

Davidson, S. (1982). *Justice for Young Women.* Tucson, AZ: New Directions for Young Women.

Davis, K., Schoen, C., Greenberg, L., Desroches, C., and Abrams, M. (1997). The Commonwealth Fund Survey of the Health of Adolescent Girls. New York: Commonwealth Fund.

Dembo, R., Williams, L., and Schmeidler, J. (1993). Gender differences in the mental health service needs among youth entering a juvenile detention center. *Journal of Prison and Jail Health 12,* 73–101.

Federal Bureau of Investigation (1999). Uniform Crime Reports for the United States, 1998–1999. Washington, D.C.: FBI U.S. Department of Justice. U.S. Government Printing Office.

Florida Department of Juvenile Justice (2003). Juvenile Justice Statistics. Girls Incorporated. (1996). Prevention and Parity: Girls in Juvenile Justice. Washington, D.C.: U.S. Department of Justice, Office of Juvenile Justice and Delinquency Prevention.

Glueck, S. and Glueck, E. (1934). *Five Hundred Delinquent Women,* New York: A.A. Knopf.

Kakar, S., Louise Friedmann, and Linda Peck (2002). Girls in detention: the results of focus group discussion interviews and official records review. *Journal of Contemporary Criminal Justice, 18(1),* 57–73.

Kaplan, S., Pelcovitz, D., Salzinger, S., Weiner, M., Mandel, F., Lesser, M., and Labruna, V. (1998). Adolescent physical abuse: risk for adolescent psychiatric disorders. *American Journal of Psychiatry, 155(7)*, 954–959.

Krisberg, B. and Temin, C. (2001). The Plight of Children Whose Parents are in Prison. National Council on Crime and Delinquency.

Miller, D., Trapani, C., Fejes-Mendoza, K., Eggleston, C., and Dwiggins, D. (1995). Adolescent female offenders: unique considerations. *Adolescence, 30(118)*, 429–435.

Office of Juvenile Justice and Delinquency Prevention. (1998). Women in Criminal Justice: A Twentieth Year Update.Washington, D.C: U.S. Department of Justice.

Office of Juvenile Justice and Delinquency Prevention. (2000). *Fact Sheet No.16*. Washington D.C.: U.S. Department of Justice.

Peters, R.S. (1998). Guiding Principles for Promising Female Programming. Washington, D.C.: U.S. Department of Justice, Office of Justice Programs, Office of Juvenile Justice and Delinquency Prevention.

Peters, S. and Peters, S. (1998). Violent adolescent females. *Corrections Today, 60(3)*, 28–29.

Poe-Yamagata, E. and Butts, J.A. (1996). Female Offenders in the Juvenile Justice System: Statistics Summary. Washington, D.C.: U.S. Department of Justice, Office of Juvenile Justice and Delinquency Prevention.

Prescott, L. (1997). Adolescent Girls with Co-occurring Disorders in the Juvenile Justice System. New York: Policy Research.

Rutter, M. (1995). Causal concepts and their testing. In Rutter, M. and Smith, D.J., Eds., *Psychosocial Disorders in Young People: Time Trends and Their Causes,* John Wiley & Sons, Manchester, U.K., pp. 7–35.

Simone, A.M., Lenssen, E.V, Theo, A.H. Doreleijers, Mirjam E. Van Dijk, and Catharina A. Hartman (2000). Girls in detention: what are their characteristics? A project to explore and document the character of this target group and the significant ways in which it differs from one consisting of boys. *Journal of Adolescence, 23*, 287–303.

Smith, A.D. (1962). *Women in Prison*, London: Stevens and Sons.

Smith, D.J. (1995). Youth crime and conduct disorders: trends, patterns and causal explanations. In Rutter M. and Smith, D.J., Eds., *Psychosocial Disorders in Young People: Time Trends and Their Causes,* John Wiley & Sons, Manchester, U.K. pp. 389–490.

Snyder, H.N. (1997). Juvenile Arrests 1996 Bulletin. Washington, D.C.: U.S. Department of Justice, Office of Justice Programs, Office of Juvenile Justice and Delinquency Prevention.

Stattin, H. and Magnusson, D. (1996). Antisocial development: a holistic approach. *Developmental Psychology*, 8: 617–645.

U.S. Census Bureau. Population Division, Population Projections Branch (2000). U.S. Populations by Estimates by Age, Sex, Race, and Hispanic Origin. Available http://www.cnesus.gov/population.

Widom, C. (2000). Report of the Coordinating Council on Juvenile Justice and Delinquency Prevention Quarterly Meeting, March 31, 2000, p. 6.

Chapter 6

Gender-Specific Intervention for Female Delinquents

Kristi Holsinger

6.1 Introduction

An examination of the history of juvenile delinquency, from theory development and testing to the establishment of treatment programs and services, reveals a nearly exclusive focus on boys. An examination of the minimal attention given to girls shows limited, and often sexist, ideas regarding their pathways to delinquency. When females' deviant behavior was not being ignored for its less threatening nature, it was being conceptualized as an extreme and often sexual type of psychological problem. As for correctional interventions, females were either expected to fit into programming designed for males or were treated in ways consistent with prevailing ideas about the unique factors that propel them into delinquent behavior. For example, it was thought that by returning girls to their "proper" gender role, their deviant behavior would be eliminated.

Fortunately, since the 1990s, there has been a growing movement toward the provision of more accurate theoretical perspectives and equitable treatment for girls in the juvenile justice system. In part, the renewed interest is due to the accelerated rate with which girls are entering the juvenile justice system (Acoca, 1999). Another contributing factor is research that is increasingly being conducted to examine the realities of girls' lives, instead of relying on stereotypical assumptions about them (see Holsinger, 2000). These developments have led to the creation of gender-specific interventions, a term which up to this point has been used to refer to programs and services for girls and women. These approaches, although still in the early stages of development, are examined, as are the research and theoretical perspectives they have been based on. Barriers to implementation and recommendation for research are presented in order to further discussion regarding programs and services that can sufficiently respond to the needs of system-involved girls.

6.2 A Brief History of Correctional Interventions for Girls

Popularly held notions regarding the "appropriate" characteristics of females and males have influenced the development of correctional institutions over the last two centuries. These historical realities have affected, in turn, how girls' institutions presently function. In many ways, correctional facilities for girls have mirrored the problems of correctional facilities for women. Women prisoners receive less attention and resources than their male counterparts due to the small proportion they make up of the total jail and prison population as well as the lesser seriousness of their criminality (Belknap, 2000). Women have typically had fewer vocational, educational, and recreational programs compared to men (Morash et al., 1994). The quality of programs provided for women has been based on stereotyped gender roles that have failed to provide women with adequate skills to emerge from prison and support themselves. Throughout history, the treatment and rehabilitation of women in prison has been geared toward teaching them to conform to the desired role for women as wives, mothers, and homemakers, whereas men were more likely to receive valuable vocational training (Feinman, 1984; Morash et al., 1994).

Institutions for delinquent girls experienced many of these same problems. Facilities for girls, compared to facilities for boys, provide half as many treatment services, require longer waits for services, deliver shorter, less intensive programs, and have fewer certified teachers on staff (Wells, 1994). By reinforcing stereotypical gender roles and applying policies in sexist ways, correctional facilities for girls reinforced and rewarded appropriate gender role behavior. This gendered treatment occurred by offering programs to girls that focused on skills such as emotional development and cooking (Gelsethorpe, 1989). Feinman (1984) argued that attempts to improve the treatment of females will continue to fail as long as they are based on stereotypical gender roles rather than on the unique needs of this population.

Initially, institutions created for juveniles emphasized treatment, not punishment (Chesney-Lind and Shelden, 1998). The history of the first reform school for girls, detailed by Brenzel (1983), described the creation of this Massachusetts institution as a response to the need to control poor minority girls who did not conform to the white, middle-class cultural norms. The primary concern appeared to be with the girls' "morality." Parents were often convinced to cooperate with the State, given its promises to protect their vulnerable daughters from further corruption (Brenzel, 1983).

Special attention to what is considered by some to be normal teenage rebellion and what has been classified as "status offenses" by the juvenile justice system, has been given in the case of girls (e.g., running away, truancy, disobedience to authority). Historically, attempts to control girls' morality (particularly their sexuality) have resulted in more arrests, adjudications, and harsher punishments for these status offenses when compared to boys (see reviews of processing studies in Belknap, 2000 and Chesney-Lind and Shelden, 1998). Self-report studies have found similar rates for girls and boys for these types of offenses, revealing bias in the system (see for example, Canter, 1982). Status offenses have been and continue to be an important factor in understanding female delinquency due to their greater application to girls by juvenile justice professionals (Chesney-Lind and Shelden, 1998).

In an attempt to respond to the discriminatory practices in the treatment of girls, particularly around the issue of status offenses, the Juvenile Justice Delinquency Prevention Act (JJDP Act) of 1974 was passed. One goal of this legislative act was to divert and deinstitutionalize status offenders from the juvenile justice system. Even with provisions for minimal financial incentives to jurisdictions that complied, the JJDP Act was met with resistance (Chesney-Lind and Shelden, 1998). Setbacks have included get-tough policies that disproportionately affect females, sexism in diversion practices, reclassification of female status offenders as violent offenders, the medicalization of female delinquency, and the phenomenon of net-widening (Chesney-Lind and Okamoto, 2000). It has been suggested that since the JJDP Act, youth have been increasingly institutionalized in "hidden" institutions, such as mental health, child welfare, and chemical dependency systems (Federle and Chesney-Lind, 1992). Ultimately, the JJDP Act fell short of achieving its desired goals, particularly for girls.

An examination of the influence of race on the history of juvenile institutions finds that, from their inception, juvenile institutions have been based on not just sexist themes, but racist themes as well (Young, 1994). For example, the deinstitutionalization movement begun by the JJDP Act has not affected racial groups similarly. Minority youth are more likely to be disproportionately represented in public detention facilities, whereas white youths are more likely to be released or institutionalized in private mental health or treatment facilities (Federle and Chesney-Lind, 1992). However, white girls have been more likely to be referred to court for status offenses and receive harsher treatment compared to African American girls (Belknap, 2000). Harsher processing for status offenses has been linked to greater expectations for white girls to conform to gender stereotypical roles. However, for other types of offenses, research has consistently supported that females of color are given less chivalrous treatment by the justice system than white females (Belknap, 2000). Differences in socialization may make African American females more likely to violate stereotypic gender roles than white girls, resulting in harsher treatment by the juvenile justice system.

During the 1992 Reauthorization of the JJDP Act of 1974 (Section 223 [a] [8] of the JJDP Act, as modified in 1992), Congress listened to professionals who identified a need to address the gender-specific needs of girls. This amendment represents the first official acknowledgment of the need to examine the unique programmatic needs of girls involved in the juvenile justice system. Thus, grants were authorized to address many areas and one of the most popular areas, in terms of state interest (24 states applied), was gender bias and the improvement (or creation of) gender-specific services (Budnick and Shields-Fletcher, 1998). Individual state efforts included assessment of current programs, public education and community mobilization, staff training, program evaluation, and various other research projects (Community Research Associates, 1998). Several nationally-funded research efforts followed, including a gender-specific training and technical assistance grant allowing for the identification of best practices (Greene et al., 1998) and the development of technical assistance and training curricula to aid those agencies serving girls (Greene et al., 2000). Similar themes, discussed below, emerge from this body of work. Although the 1992 Reauthorization of the JJDP Act of 1974 provided initial momentum, there is much yet to be done to identify and respond to the gender-specific needs of delinquent girls.

6.3 Components of Gender-Specific Services

There is a growing literature base reflecting not only gender differences in girls' pathways to crime and delinquency, but also gender differences in development and experiences. The recent movement toward creating a gender-specific focus for female delinquents and their unique needs has resulted in recommendations by feminist scholars on ways to improve programs for girls. Gender-specific programming refers to program models and services that comprehensively address the special needs of a targeted gender group (Greene et al., 1998, p. 17). Another definition notes that gender-specific services should be designed to meet the unique needs of female offenders, value the female perspective, celebrate and honor the female experience, respect and take into account female development, and empower young women to reach their full potential (Girls Incorporated, 1996, p. 24). The evolution of gender-specific services for girls is well underway. The question that remains is how are these general objectives best achieved or what, specifically, should gender-specific services look like. Research involving practitioners who work with girls and the girls themselves reveals several important and often overlapping components.

6.3.1 Abuse

Although physical and sexual abuse and neglect are important issues in the delinquency of boys, studies have shown that these problems are more common, start at an earlier age, and last longer for girls (Chesney-Lind 1989; Miller et al., 1995). Estimates regarding the prevalence of girls' abuse in the general population are approximately 25 percent, whereas abuse estimates of girls in the juvenile justice system range between 40 and 73 percent (Chesney-Lind and Shelden, 1998). Abused and neglected girls were twice as likely to be arrested as juveniles, twice as likely to be arrested as adults, and almost two and a half times more likely to be arrested for violent crimes compared to nonabused girls (Widom, 2000). Much of the research suggests that girls and boys respond differently to abuse, with boys engaging in externalizing behaviors (e.g., violence) and girls tending to internalize behaviors (see for example, Chandy et al., 1996). More recent research suggests, however, that these generalizations may not apply across racial groups (Holsinger and Holsinger, 2005).

There is a unique pathway into delinquency for girls, in which abuse or a harmful home environment leads to running away and subsequent involvement in the juvenile justice system, either for status offenses or criminal ones such as prostitution or theft (Janus et al., 1987). Therefore, correctional programs need to address the unique needs of girls in their families, who have problems resulting from physical violence and sexual victimization (Artz, 1998). Issues of home-lessness, housing, and independent living skills may also need to be addressed for girls who will not be able to return to their homes. In the meantime, it is paramount for correctional facilities to provide emotional and physical safety for a population where the majority have experienced abuse of some kind (Acoca and Dedel, 1998).

6.3.2 Problematic Family Relationships

Girls tend to come from extremely troubled homes and report more negative family experiences than boys (Belknap et al., 1997; Holsinger et al., 1999). In fact, girls' offenses are often related to conflict in their family relationships (Acoca and Dedel, 1998). Additionally, girls in the system are often the daughters of a parent, or have a close family member, who has experienced incarceration (Holsinger et al., 1999). Staff who work with girls often hold blaming and punitive attitudes toward the girls' parents due to their advocacy role with the girls (Freitas and Chesney-Lind, 2001; Belknap et al., 1997). Although parents may be a part of the problem in girls' lives, their ultimate involvement is paramount.

Programs should be holistic in their approach and address all relevant domains of a girl's life, including her family (Greene et al., 1998; Marcus-Mendoza and Briody, 1996). Family reunification is typically a goal of social service and juvenile justice systems. Programming that addresses the needs of the family is critical. Family-focused services are needed to help girls counteract family patterns that are damaging to them. Research on the generational pattern of incarceration in families and how to best break the cycle is also needed.

6.3.3 Drug and Alcohol Use

Understanding gender differences in drug and alcohol use requires an examination of differences in development. For example, research on girls has revealed that they are more likely than boys to give up their sense of self to be in a relationship (Gilligan, 1982). Girls may use alcohol or other drugs to maintain valued relationships with boys (Covington, 1999). Childhood abuse and neglect is also related to drug and alcohol use or abuse and leads to subsequent involvement in the juvenile or criminal justice system (Bodinger-de Uriarte and Austin, 1991; McClellan et al., 1997).

Females and males often use drugs and/or alcohol for different reasons (Miller et al., 1995). Girls are more likely to misuse substances they can purchase legally and tend to use other substances moderately as a way to self-medicate (Girls Incorporated, 1996). Girls are more likely than boys to report being addicted, experiencing withdrawal symptoms, and initiating use because of a boyfriend or to cope with depression (Holsinger et al., 1999). Males are more likely to use drugs for pleasure and at the prompting of peers (Holsinger et al., 1999).

Most substance abuse programs have been developed for boys (Owen and Bloom, 1999). Programs for girls should be designed to address their unique risk factors for use. The American Correctional Association (1990) found that half of state training schools report more than 60 percent of girls are in need of substance abuse treatment. Other studies have also noted the need for substance abuse treatment that is designed around girls' unique motivations and patterns of use (Girls Incorporated, 1996; Marcus-Mendoza and Briody, 1996).

6.3.4 Health and Mental Health Issues

Medical needs for females have typically been ignored by the correctional systems in the United States (Acoca, 1998; Belknap, 1996; Belknap et al., 1997). The health problems experienced by incarcerated females may be exacerbated by their poverty and the resulting low access to health care over the life course. The stress of incarceration itself can worsen overall health (Ingram-Fogel, 1991). Several state-initiated research projects found that facilities serving girls were less likely than those serving boys to provide treatment for physical and mental health problems, and girls were less likely to report that medical services were available when needed (Holsinger et al., 1999; Kempf-Leonard et al., 1997). In interviews with incarcerated women, unaddressed medical concerns included infectious and communicable diseases, reproductive health issues, and mental health disorders (Acoca, 1998).

Given the statistics on the physical and sexual abuse of girls, it is not surprising that many girls in the juvenile justice systems have mental health needs (Federle and Chesney-Lind, 1992). Sexual abuse in children has been shown to influence a child's mental health negatively and increase rates of posttraumatic stress disorder (Miller et al., 1995; Wolfe et al., 1989). A national study of girls in juvenile correctional settings found that 54 percent had attempted suicide (American Correctional Association, 1990). In particular, girls are at an increased risk of internalizing problems, which is frequently manifested by withdrawal, depression, emotional problems, and self-destructive behaviors due to their gender socialization (Miller et al., 1995; Wells, 1994). Although revealing, this research has not paid close attention to racial differences between girls, which point to these issues being more prevalent for white girls compared to African American girls (Holsinger and Holsinger, 2005).

Mental-health-oriented programming is clearly needed to address abuse issues (Chesney-Lind and Shelden, 1998). Identifying and treating these youths may help to prevent suicide attempts and other damaging outcomes in youth with mental disorders. In addition, health care services are needed that have been developed with the needs and concerns of girls at the center. It has been recommended that programs for girls also promote general health through good nutrition and exercise — services that are often lacking for girls (Girls Incorporated, 1996). Girls, specifically, need more education about their bodies, especially that related to pregnancy and contraception, diseases and how they spread, and the mixed cultural messages they receive about their sexuality (Marcus-Mendoza and Briody, 1996; Girls Incorporated, 1996).

6.3.5 Parenting and Childcare

Approximately 19 percent of girls in correctional settings were mothers at the time of their incarceration (American Correctional Association, 1990). Pregnancy has presented a host of problems for incarcerated women and girls. One study of state prisons found that less than half of the institutions even had written policies regarding the care of pregnant inmates (Wooldredge and Masters, 1993). Often, pregnant women have not received adequate prenatal care and in some cases, have been prescribed drugs inappropriate or dangerous for pregnant women (McHugh, 1980).

Separation of mothers from their infants is another psychological health issue that has not been addressed (Austin et al., 1992; Wooldredge and Masters, 1993). Several studies have supported the idea that one of the most severe deprivations suffered by incarcerated women, if not the most severe, was the separation they experienced from their families (Jones, 1993). Women are also more likely to have been the primary source of financial and emotional support for their children before their imprisonment, making parenting issues more relevant for women offenders (Belknap, 1996).

One of the recommendations made in a final report by the Task Force on Federally Sentenced Women in Canada suggested that changes be made to alleviate the hardship of mothers' separation from their children (Miller-Ashton, 1993). Allowing mothers and young children to remain together, allowing more regular visitation, or expanding sentencing alternatives to include community-based sanctions would help preserve female offenders' families.

6.3.6 Academic and Economic Challenges

School failure has been related to the early violent offending of girls (Sommers and Baskin, 1994). Bjerregaard and Smith (1993) found that school expectations was the only variable that differentiated between females' and males' likelihood of joining a gang. Having low expectations of completing school increased the chances of gang membership by 20 percent for females but only by 1 percent for males. Gender differences exist for the reasons given for dropping out of or quitting school. Incarcerated girls are more likely than boys to report leaving school because they had trouble keeping up, had run away from home, experienced boredom, felt that no one cared if they learned, or were not liked by others at school (Belknap, Holsinger, and Dunn, 1997). When asked about programming they had received, girls reported receiving fewer programs to help them become better students when compared to boys. Programming that allows girls to receive needed academic and career skills are clearly lacking in the juvenile justice system. Of 18 possible programs, 72 percent of incarcerated girls named "learning job or career skills" as the program they most desired, making this the most frequently desired need (Belknap, Holsinger, and Dunn, 1997).

Because of the serious disadvantage academic failure creates for youth, there is reason to provide additional academic assistance to girls. In reinforcing traditional gender roles, females have rarely been given the opportunity to develop skills which may facilitate gainful employment and provide the means for economic survival (Chesney-Lind and Shelden, 1998). Incarcerated women learn fewer marketable skills compared to incarcerated men (Morash et al., 1994). One of the most important needs of girls is an economic means of survival, and many services undermine rather than encourage girls' independence. Too often it is assumed that girls in the justice system will not achieve more than a high-school education and a low-paying job. Yet, studies with girls have indicated their potential as the girls challenge many of the stereotypes commonly held regarding their intelligence and capabilities (Belknap et al., 1997). Building academic and job-related skills should be integrated with treatment and must appeal to various learning styles.

6.3.7 Self-Esteem and Gender Socialization

During adolescence, girls experience a decrease in self-concept, whereas boys experience improved self-concept and self-esteem (Miller et al., 1995). A national study by the American Association of University Women (1991) found that although girls report lower self-esteem than boys, there are important variations based on ethnicity. African American girls reported much higher levels of self-esteem in the areas of personal and family importance but felt worst about their academic experience compared to the other groups of girls. Latina girls had the overall worst self-esteem problem in familial, personal, and academic areas.

Gender-specific services should include the development of program components that promote a positive gender identity during girls' formative years (Greene et al., 1998). This involves a close look at the socialization of girls and the extent to which they have accepted stereotypical gender roles that may be destructive for them. Girls need help in seeing who they are sexually; they should not see themselves as objects and should be helped to realize that their sexuality can be a positive part of who they are. This can be done, in part, by addressing power and the abuse of power in male–female relationships (Greene et al., 1998). It has also been recommended that programs teaching empowerment strategies to girls must focus on improving their self-esteem (Greene et al., 1998; Miller-Ashton, 1993).

The correctional system needs to recognize the influence of socialization. Many of the problems experienced by girls are due to the unique cultural pressures on girls. Virtually all girls would be helped by prevention programs that enhance their skills and knowledge (Girls Incorporated, 1996). Reitsma-Street and Offord (1991) suggest that "the priorities for practice shift from changing the deviant, different females to changing the political, economic, and social arrangements that make females bear such high costs for the commonalities they experience, especially when they deviate from what is expected of a female" (p. 23).

6.4 Other Issues in the Development and Implementation of Gender-Specific Services

A gender-specific focus begins with the assumption that girls and boys have differences, so services provided should also be different. In the past, equality has been the goal in the treatment of delinquents. However, the goal of equality has not always been beneficial for girls. Equal treatment has often meant less than adequate care for females, as treatment for males was used as the standard for equality and important gender differences were ignored. Equality must be redefined as providing opportunities (which may be different) to girls and boys that mean the same to each gender (Belknap et al., 1997).

Programs for girls and boys should be needs-based, not offense-based. Needs-assessment should be used to develop individualized treatment plans (Hoge, 2001). Assessments at intake are needed for classification and treatment purposes. However, it has been assumed that criminogenic risk factors are a relatively uniform set of concepts. Much more research needs to be conducted in the area of offender assessment with regard to female offenders before this assumption can be accepted. Further, issues of potential racial or ethnic differences in criminogenic assessment need to be explored within the female offender population. Programming should also pay attention to the strengths present in the girls' lives and work to build on these strengths. Competency-based programming is also frequently advocated in order to focus on skill development.

Incarcerated women's perceptions of programming needs vary by race (Belknap, 1996). Very little is known about these types of racial differences that may exist in program needs for girls in the system. There is a also a need for programs and services that are culturally sensitive and diverse (Belknap et al., 1997; Greene et al., 1998; Miller-Ashton, 1993). Good gender-specific services require well-trained, competent staff who are willing to look at their own behavior for any signs of racism and sexism and who have an awareness of gender, class, and racial differences. Due to the lack of research on this issue, a clear implication is the expansion of research on girls to include those from different cultural and socioeconomic groups (Freitas and Chesney-Lind, 2001).

More work needs to be done in the area of offender responsivity, within the female offender population. By focusing on responsivity — how offenders respond to different programming strategies, curricula, and counselor style or characteristics — much light may be shed on the issue of correctional programming for girls. Interpersonal relationships are key to understanding female development (Acoca and Dedel, 1998). Girls need more one-on-one relationships and emotional support (according to staff who work with them) (Bloom et al., 2002). Girls need the opportunity to develop positive relationships, including cross-gender relationships. This may include the use of counseling and mentoring programs that would helps girls learn how to have healthy relationships of all types. Gender-specific programs should be responsive to girls by addressing their need for, and responsiveness to, relationships.

Little has been done to incorporate knowledge about gender-specific services in existing correctional-treatment literature. It is important to blend these two perspectives. For example, the principles of effective intervention and meta-analyses have determined what type of treatment works best for offenders (Palmer, 1992). These principles should also guide the development of gender-specific services for youth.

Many scholars in this area have come to the conclusion that delinquent girls should be involved in developing and evaluating treatment programs (Fejes and Miller, 2002; Greene et al., 1998). By listening to girls' voices, Artz (1998) noted that during the time of her study, the girls were not involved in fights, which indicated the benefits of being listened to and treated with respect as a way to counteract violence. This was consistent with the Ohio girls' repeated comments about needing to be listened to and respected (Belknap et al., 1997; Bloom et al., 2002). Another study on the subculture of incarcerated juveniles supports this recommendation: Zingraff (1980) found that youth, both girls and boys, were more likely to engage in an oppositional subculture that worked against the goals of the correctional facility when they were denied participation in determining some of the operations of the facility.

Secure facilities should be seen as the last resort. The development of alternative community-based programming for girls is needed to reduce incarceration (Beger and Hoffman, 1998; Chesney-Lind and Shelden, 1998). Inadequate community-based options for girls was found to be a factor in girls receiving longer sentences than boys (Beger and Hoffman, 1998). In general, a wider range of programs is needed, from prevention to intervention to aftercare (Girls Incorporated, 1996). Aftercare is an important correctional component that is virtually nonexistent in correctional programming for girls. It is a critical need, as many girls identify their greatest fear as what will happen to them upon release (Belknap et al., 1997; Owen and Bloom, 1997).

Finally, the professionals who work with girls should have an interest in them, enjoy working with them, and have a basic understanding of their needs. Girls will learn the most about healthy relationships from these professionals. Many studies reveal that professionals working with girls do not meet these criteria and perceive girls as more difficult than boys to work with (Belknap et al., 1997; Bloom et al., 2002). On the bright side, most staff desire training (Bloom et al. 2002). As such, training should be provided in the following areas: gender identity, female adolescent development, and cross-gender supervision (Freitas and Chesney-Lind, 2001). Girls are aware of institutional gender bias and staff must be wary of the gendered messages they may be sending to girls (Belkap et al., 1997).

6.5 Conclusion

Gender-specific services do not currently exist on a large scale. Existing services do not meet the needs of girls, making the juvenile justice system ill-equipped to adequately respond (Bloom et al., 2002). Young female offenders have been even more invisible than women offenders, and girl-specific research is needed to make delinquent girls' lives more visible to researchers, policy makers, professionals, and the public.

Although many authors have previously called for additional funding for more research in the area of gender-specific programming and services, as mentioned, many needs in this area remain unfulfilled. Questions are being raised about what additional assessment tools, case-planning techniques, or other resources will be needed in order to more fully round out the capabilities of the juvenile justice system to adequately address the unique experiences of girls.

There is a clear and present need for program evaluation pertaining to the correctional rehabilitative programs serving girls in the juvenile and criminal justice systems. Rehabilitative programs should be examined regarding the extent to which they incorporate all of the above recommendations. Program evaluations would ideally offer a measure of a program's effectiveness, while presenting recommendations for improvement. Although there have been some recent improvements in the type and form of curricula that are available for programs serving girls, there may be a need for additional changes based on the results of program evaluations.

Although much work needs to be done, much is known about how to more appropriately address the needs of girls in the system. The conclusions that have been reached regarding the development and implementation of gender-specific services are largely consistent. The question now is one of priorities. In choosing to move forward with these recommendations, the priorities of the juvenile justice system will shift, ultimately improving the treatment of girls in the juvenile justice system.

References

Acoca, L. (1999). Investing in girls: a 21st century strategy. *Juvenile Justice*, 6(1), 3–13.

Acoca, L. (1998). Defusing the time bomb: understanding and meeting the growing health care needs of incarcerated women in America. *Crime and Delinquency*, 44(1), 49–69.

Acoca, L. and Dedel, K. (1998). No Place to Hide: Understanding and Meeting the Needs of Girls in the California Juvenile Justice System. The National Council on Crime and Delinquency.

American Association of University Women (1991). Shortchanging Girls, Shortchanging America: Executive Summary. Washington D.C.: Author.

American Correctional Association (1990). The Female Offender: What Does the Future Hold? Laurel, MD: Author.

Artz, S. (1998). *Sex, Power, and the Violent School Girl.* Toronto: Trifolium Books.

Austin, J., Bloom B., and Donahue, T. (1992). Female Offenders in the Community: An Analysis of Innovative Strategies and Programs. San Francisco, CA: National Council on Crime and Delinquency.

Belknap, J. (2000). The Invisible Woman: Gender, Crime and Justice. Belmont, CA: Wadsworth.

Belknap, J. (1996) Access to programs and health care for incarcerated women. *Federal Probation*, 60(4), 34–39.

Belknap, J. and Holsinger, K. (1998). An overview of delinquent girls: how theory and practice have failed and the need for innovative changes. In R. Zaplin (Ed.), *Female Crime and Delinquency: Critical Perspectives and Effective Interventions,* pp. 31–64. Gaithersburg, MD: Aspen.

Belknap, J., Holsinger, K., and Dunn, M. (1997). Understanding incarcerated girls: the results of a focus group study. *Prison Journal*, 77(4), 381–404.

Beger, R.R. and Hoffman, H. (1998). Role of gender in detention dispositioning of juvenile probation violators. *Journal of Crime and Justice*, 21(1), 173–188.

Bjerregaard, B. and Smith, C. (1993). Gender differences in gang participation, delinquency, and substance use. *Journal of Quantitative Criminology,* 9(4), 329–355.

Bloom, B., Owen, B., Deschenes, E.P., and Rosenbaum, J. (2002). Moving toward justice for female juvenile offenders in the new millennium: Modeling gender-specific policies and programs. *Journal of Contemporary Criminal Justice,* 18(1), 37–56.

Bodinger-de Uriarte, C. and Austin, G. (1991). Substance Abuse Among Adolescent Females. Prevention Research Update. Portland, OR: Northwest Regional Educational Laboratory.

Brenzel, B.M. (1983). *Daughters of the State: A Social Portrait of the First Reform School for Girls in North America 1856–1905.* Cambridge, MA: MIT Press.

Budnick, K.J. and Shields-Fletcher, E. (1998). What about Girls? (OJJDP Fact Sheet No. 84). Washington, D.C.: U.S. Department of Justice, Office of Justice Programs, Office of Juvenile Justice and Delinquency Prevention.

Canter, R.J. (1982). Sex differences in self-report delinquency. *Criminology,* 20, 373–393.

Chandy, J.M., Blum, R.W., and Resnick, M.D. (1996). Gender-specific outcomes for sexually abused adolescents. *Child Abuse and Neglect,* 20(12), 1219–1231.

Chesney-Lind, M. (1989). Girls' crime and woman's place: Toward a feminist model of female delinquency. *Crime and Delinquency,* 35(1), 5–29.

Chesney-Lind, M. and Okamoto, S. (2000). Gender matters: Patterns in girl's delinquency and gender-responsive programming. *Journal of Forensic Psychology Practice,* 1(3), 1–28.

Chesney-Lind, M. and Shelden, R. (1998). *Girls, Delinquency, and Juvenile Justice.* Belmont, CA: West/Wadsworth.

Community Research Associates (1998). *Female Juvenile Offenders: A Status of the States Report.* Washington D.C.: U.S. Department of Justice, Office of Justice Programs, Office of Juvenile Justice and Delinquency Prevention.

Covington, S. (1999). *Helping Women Recover: A Program for Treating Substance Abuse.* San Francisco, CA: Jossey-Bass.

Federle, K.H. and Chesney-Lind, M. (1992). Special issues in juvenile justice: gender, race, and ethnicity. In Schwartz, I.M. Ed., *Juvenile Justice and Public Policy: Toward a National Agenda,* New York: Macmillian. pp. 165–195.

Feinman, C. (1984). An historical overview of the treatment of incarcerated women: myths and realities of rehabilitation

Fejes, K.E. and Miller, D. (2002). Assessing gender-specific programming for juvenile female offenders: Creating ownership, voice and growth. *Journal of Correctional Education,* 53(2), 58–64.

Freitas, K. and Chesney-Lind, M. (2001). Difference doesn't mean difficult: Practitioners talk about working with girls. *Women, Girls and Criminal Justice,* 2(5), 65–66: 77–80.

Gelsethorpe, L. (1989). *Sexism and the Female Offender.* Aldershot, U.K.: Gower.

Gilligan, C. (1982). *In a Different Voice: Psychological Theory and Women's Development.* Cambridge, MA: Harvard University Press.

Girls Incorporated (1996). *Prevention and Parity: Girls in Juvenile Justice.* Washington, D.C.: Office of Juvenile Justice and Delinquency Prevention.

Greene, Peters and Associates (2000). *Paving a Way for Female Development: Gender-Specific Programming.* Washington, D.C.: Office of Juvenile Justice and Delinquency Prevention.

Greene, Peters and Associates (1998). *Guiding Principles for Promising Female Programming: An Inventory of Best Practices.* Washington, D.C.: Office of Juvenile Justice and Delinquency Prevention.

Hoge, R.D. (2001). Case management instrument for use in juvenile justice systems. *Juvenile and Family Court Journal,* 52(2), 25–32.

Holsinger, K. (2000). Feminist perspectives on female offending: examining real girls' lives. *Women and Criminal Justice,* 12(1), 23–51.

Holsinger, K. and Holsinger, A. (2005). Differential pathways to violence and self-injurious behavior: African-American and white girls in the juvenile justice system. *Journal of Research in Crime and Delinquency,* 42(2), 211–242.

Holsinger, K., Belknap, J., and Sutherland, J. (1999). Assessing the Gender Specific Program and Service Needs for Adolescent Females in the Juvenile Justice System. Columbus, OH: Ohio Office of Criminal Justice Services.

Ingram-Fogel, C. (1991). Health problems and needs of incarcerated women. *Journal of Prison and Jail Health,* 10(1), 43–57.

Janus, M.D., McCormack, A., Burgess, A.W., and Hartman, C. (1987). *Adolescent Runaways: Causes and Consequences.* Lexington, MA: Lexington Books.

Jones, R.S. (1993). Coping with separation: adaptive responses of women prisoners. *Women and Criminal Justice,* 5(1), 71–97.

Kempf-Leonard, K., Peterson, E.S.L., and Sample, L.L. (1997). *Gender and Juvenile Justice in Missouri.* Jefferson City, MO: Missouri Department of Public Safety.

Marcus-Mendoza, S. and Briody, R. (1996). Female inmates in Oklahoma: an updated profile and programming assessment. *Journal of the Oklahoma Criminal Justice Research Consortium,* 3, 85–105.

McClellan, D.S., Farabee D., and Crouch, B.M. (1997). Early victimization, drug use and criminality: a comparison of male and female prisoners. *Criminal Justice and Behavior,* 24(4), 455–476.

McHugh, G.A. (1980). Protection of the rights of pregnant women in prisons and detention facilities. *New England Journal on Prison Law,* 6, 231–263.

Miller, D., Trapani, C., Fejes-Mendoza, K., Eggleston, C., and Dwiggins, D. (1995). Adolescent female offenders: unique considerations. *Adolescence,* 30(118), 429–435.

Miller-Ashton, J. (1993). Canada's new federal system for female offenders. In *Female Offenders: Meeting Needs of a Neglected Population,* Laurel, MD: American Correctional Association. pp. 105–111.

Morash, M., Harr, R.N., and Rucker, L. (1994). A comparison of programming for women and men in U.S. prisons in the 1980s. *Crime and Delinquency,* 40(2), 197–221.

Owen, B. and Bloom, B. (1999). Planning for gender-specific services in juvenile justice. *Corrections Management Quarterly,* 3(4), 63–72.

Palmer, T. (1992). *The Re-emergence of Correctional Intervention.* Newbury Park, CA: Sage.

Reitsma-Street, M. and Offord, D.R. (1991). Girl delinquents and their sisters: a challenge for practice. *Canadian Social Work Review,* 8(1), 11–27.

Sommers, I. and Baskin, D.R. (1994). Factors related to female adolescent initiation into violent street crime. *Youth and Society* 25(4), 468–489.

Wells, R.H. (1994). America's delinquent daughters have nowhere to turn for help. *Corrections Compendium,* 19(11), 4–6.

Widom, C.S. (2000). Childhood victimization and the derailment of girls and women to the criminal justice system. In Research on Women and Girls in the Justice System: Plenary Papers of the 1999 Conference on Criminal Justice Research and Evaluation–Enhancing Policy and Practice Through Research, Vol. 3, pp. 27–36. Washington, D.C.: National Institute of Justice.

Wooldredge, J. and Masters, K. (1993). Confronting problems faced by pregnant inmates in state prisons. *Crime and Delinquency,* 39(2), 195–203.

Wolfe, V.V., Gentile, C., and Wolfe, D.A. (1989). The impact of sexual abuse on children: a PTSD formulation. *Behavior Therapy,* 20, 215–228.

Young, V.D. (1994). Race and gender in the establishment of juvenile institutions: the case of the south. *The Prison Journal,* 73(2), 244–265.

Zingraff, M.T. (1980). Inmate assimilation: a comparison of male and female delinquents. *Criminal Justice and Behavior,* 7(3), 275–292.

Chapter 7

The Relationship between Childhood Maltreatment and Delinquency

Marilyn Chandler Ford

7.1 Introduction

The issue of child maltreatment first intruded into the public consciousness in the 1960s with the "discovery" of the battered child syndrome.
Child abuse was exposed when Kempe and his colleagues (1962) challenged the ubiquitous "unspecified trauma" terminology that was used
to refer to child injuries seen in emergency rooms and doctors' offices
across the country. The media's discovery of the issue soon led to public
policy and government initiatives in the 1970s and into the 1980s.

As with most social issues, the prominence of abuse and neglect
waxes and wanes. Awareness of child abuse and neglect may be
heightened by a daytime talk show or a serious news report, or it may
remain on the periphery of public interest. A childhood marred by

maltreatment, with the subject later linked to a sensational crime is sure to heighten media and public interest. The catastrophic failure of a state agency to protect a child also galvanizes public attention. In Florida, the disappearance of Rilya, a little girl placed in a foster home under the supervision of the state's child protective system (CPS), led to intense scrutiny and staff turnover at the highest levels in state government.

Although the media's voice has been crucial in focusing interest on child maltreatment, the media tends to rely on sound bites and hype to convey information. This chapter will provide a more detailed review of abuse and neglect behaviors — the story behind the headlines. In this review, the incidence of child abuse, the causes of child abuse, and the link between maltreatment and delinquency is considered. This chapter concludes with a discussion of critical issues that warrant further attention.

7.2 Legally Defining Child Maltreatment

Child maltreatment is an overarching descriptor for the more commonly used terms, child abuse and neglect. Legally, both abuse and neglect result in harm to the child, but abuse is characterized by action, whereas neglect is based on inaction. In both abuse and neglect the harm is by an adult, typically the parent or guardian. Newer statutory formulations recognize the caretaker role instead of relying solely upon birth or blood relationships to define the parental responsibility. Persons who stand in *loco parentis*, even temporarily, are subject to prohibitions on abuse and neglect. Thus, for example, day-care workers, recreation leaders, teachers, and anyone in a custodial relationship may be charged if a complaint of abuse or neglect surfaces. A distinguishing feature of child sexual abuse is that it is the only act in the abuse–neglect continuum where a complaint commonly involves a stranger.

Abuse implies a degree of willfulness in conduct. Physical abuse, including sexual abuse, is nonaccidental injury that occurs when a parent or caregiver willfully injures, causes injury, or allows a child to be injured. Many states permit the prosecution of a parent or caregiver who had knowledge of the possibility of injury, but failed to protect his or her child from such abuse (National Victim Assistance Academy, 2002, p. 6). Neglect may or may not include the component of willfulness. In some situations, a parent willfully fails to provide for the basic needs of the child; in other instances, the parent or caretaker may not have intended to directly harm the child.

Abuse can take two forms: physical or emotional abuse. Sexual abuse is a specific type of child physical abuse. Sexual exploitation is included in some statutory formulations due to the link between missing children and their sexual exploitation.

Legal neglect may involve physical, emotional, medical, and educational aspects. Many states also include abandonment in the definition of neglect (National Clearinghouse on Child Abuse and Neglect Information, 2002). Physical neglect occurs when a parent or custodian fails to provide basic necessities for the child, such as food, shelter, or clothing. Neglect can also be of a child's right to thrive or to be nurtured. Educational neglect may be one part of the failure to provide a nurturing environment.

An interesting medical neglect issue arises when a decision about medical care intersects with parental religious beliefs. Is it neglect for a parent to refuse to seek or to ignore medical assistance for a sick child due to his or her religious convictions? In a recent survey of state statutes, 31 states provided a religious exemption for parents who choose not to seek medical care for their children due to religious beliefs (National Clearinghouse on Chiild Abuse and Neglect Information, 2002).

Maternal drug or alcohol addiction triggers another medically relevant child abuse issue. When a female substance abuser is pregnant and continues to use illegal drugs, there is a likelihood that her child will be born addicted to alcohol or drugs. It is estimated that 40 percent of confirmed cases of child abuse are related to substance abuse (Children of Alcoholics Foundation, 1996). An estimated 11 percent of pregnant women are substance abusers, and 300,000 infants are born each year to mothers who abuse crack cocaine (Blau et al., 1994).

Concerns about child abuse and neglect are increasingly being reflected in the law. Child abuse and neglect, once legally treated as *mala prohibita,* are increasingly seen as *mala in se* offenses. This was not always the case. In the dawn of society, children were considered the property of their parents. Parental regulation of all aspects of a child's conduct was the norm; corporal punishment and a disregard for a child's individuality and needs were common. It has only been within the past 100 years, with the increase in industrialization and developments in psychology and sociology, that childhood and adolescence have come be to regarded as separate life stages. In addition, the impact of criminal-activity environments upon child abuse and neglect is attracting increased attention. For example, children located at clandestine methamphetamine labs are now being treated as potential victims of abuse, neglect, or endangerment (Swetlow, 2003).

As a final note on the definition of child abuse and neglect, it is important to remember Bethea's (1999) observation that child maltreatment is a legal finding and not a diagnosis. National organizations and the federal government have established a set of common working definitions of abuse and neglect. Yet, identification of children who have been abused and neglected is conditioned by two principles. First, specific acts constituting maltreatment are defined by states and, thus, vary from one jurisdiction to another. Second, real-world identification of child abuse and neglect requires working definitions that are often refined by culture and bureaucracy and by the sensitivity and priority accorded to child abuse and neglect by field personnel.

7.3 Issues Associated with Identifying Abuse and Neglect

A consistent theme in this review is that whereas child maltreatment awareness has increased, knowledge of child maltreatment remains superficial. Particularly for law enforcement personnel, child abuse and neglect are not considered "core" offenses. Street crime, property offenses, and the most violent of person offenses — murder and sexual assault — are considered the "meat and potatoes" of crime. This is paradoxical. Although the incidence of street crime and property crime may justify their place as core crimes, the long-term effects of those offenses at the micro (i.e., the individual) level are arguable when compared with child maltreatment. The perception of enforcement personnel that child abuse and neglect are unimportant can lead to limited detection and identification of such misconduct.

7.3.1 Reporters of Abuse

State laws set out who is required to report suspected maltreatment. Typically, such formulations require police, social workers, teachers, and physicians to report suspicions about abuse and neglect. Hardly surprising is the fact that schools generate more referrals to CPS than all other community agents combined. With compulsory education laws, children are more likely to be regularly observed and, hence, suspected maltreatment is more likely to be identified (Sedlak and Broadhurst, 1996).

A broad picture of abuse and neglect is easily drawn but, as with numerous social issues, "the devil is in the details." Counts of child abuse and neglect vary considerably according to the definitions and methodologies employed to gather and compile the data. National-level figures vary from one study to the next and from those compiled by advocacy groups (e.g., NCANDS, 2002; Child Welfare League of America, 2002). This also makes it difficult to make comparisons across years (see Hopper, 2005, for an in-depth discussion).

Gaps in data also may be due as much to a state or agency's inability to report in categories defined by external researchers as to their unwillingness to provide information that may reveal the system's failings. To illustrate, the Child Welfare League of America conducts an annual survey of state child welfare agencies, which reports, among other information, substantiated cases of maltreat-ment. Review of their annual data reveals that an average of 15 states regularly fail to provide figures to the collection effort (Child Welfare League of America, 2002).

7.3.2 Data Sources

A key data source for information on child maltreatment is the National Incidence Study of Child Abuse and Neglect, popularly known as NIS-3, the numeral indicating that it is the third national incidence study of its type. In addition to gathering data from state child protective agencies, reports are obtained from community professionals (called "sentinels") who are likely to come into contact with maltreated children (e.g., police, teachers, day-care personnel, hospitals, etc.).[1]

NIS-3 estimated that there were 3 million maltreated or endangered children in 1993 (Sedlak and Broadhurst, 1996). This was a sizeable increase over NIS-2, which had been conducted 7 years earlier. NIS-3's increase was two to four times greater than in the prior survey. Despite the fluidity in definitions and methodologies, the upward trend of maltreatment cases from the mid-1980s into the 1990s is supported by a variety of studies. So too is the downward trend experienced since NIS-3. Data from state child protective agencies for 1998 showed just over 903,000 substantiated cases of child abuse and neglect (National Victim Assistance Academy, 2002) and for 2002, the corresponding number was approximately 896,000 (NCANDS, 2004).

7.4 A Profile of Child Maltreatment

The rate of child victimizations per 1,000 children declined from 15.3 victims in 1993 to 11.8 victims in 1999. The victimization rate increased slightly to 12.3 per 1,000 children in 2002 (NCANDS, 2004).[2] It not clear whether the upward swing first evidenced in 2000 and continuing into 2002 signals a trend shift or not.

7.4.1 Type of Maltreatment

A majority of maltreated children are victims of neglect. The NIS-3 estimated neglect victims were nearly double the abuse victims (Sedlak and Broadhurst, 1996). Data for 2000 and 2002 align; 60 to 63 percent of the substantiated reports involved child victims of neglect (NCANDS, 2002 and 2004). National Victim Assistance Academy (2002, p. 8) estimates are widely divergent; they estimate there are five times more cases of neglect than abuse.

NIS-3 data indicate that more than half of all victims (55 percent) experienced serious or moderate harm as a result of maltreatment. Those with fatal or serious injuries were more likely to have suffered at the hands of birth parents than others (Snyder and Sickmund, 1999, p. 42).

7.4.2 Child Fatalities

Data from the Federal Bureau of Investigation (FBI) provide a companion view of child abuse. The FBI's Supplementary Homicide Reporting (SHR) Program provides detailed information about the most serious of child victimizations, homicide and sexual assault. In 1997, there were 2,100 juvenile murder victims, or 11 percent of all persons murdered were under the age of 18 (Snyder and Sickmund, 1999, p. 17). This equated to six juveniles murdered daily. In 2000 there were approximately 1,200 child fatalities (Child Welfare League, 2002; NCANDS, 2002), and by 2002 the estimate was at 1,400 child fatalities (NCANDS, 2004). This was a rate of 1.71 children per 100,000 children in the population for 2000, and for 2002 it was 1.98 (NCANDS, 2002; NCANDS, 2004). Not unexpectedly, the youngest children are the most vulnerable. Children younger than 1 year accounted for 41 percent of child fatalities; 76 percent of child fatalities were of children younger than 6 years old (NCANDS, 2004).

U.S. child homicide rates exceed the rates of other industrialized countries. For homicide victims 4 years old and younger, the U.S.

homicide rate is 4.10 per 100,000 children. The comparative rate for other countries is 0.95. For homicide victims between the ages of 5 to 14, the U.S. rate per 100,000 children is 1.75 compared to 0.30 for other foreign nations (Snyder and Sickmund, 1999, p. 25).

The FBI's National Incident-Based Reporting System (NIBRS) is another rich source of information about crime against juveniles.[2] NIBRS data for 1991 through 1996 show young juveniles (persons under the age of 12) were the victims in 5.5 percent of all violent crime incidents reported to police (Snyder and Sickmund, 1999, p. 29). Young victims were more common in some crime types than others: kidnapping (21 percent), sexual assault (32 percent), aggravated assault (4 percent), and simple assault (4 percent). More than one third of the child victims were younger than seven (Snyder and Sickmund, 1999).

7.4.3 Victim–Offender Relationship

Detailed data on relationships of victims to their offenders and the location of the crimes aligns with earlier research on sexual assault events. Perpetrators were about evenly divided between a family member and an acquaintance for victims under the age of 12, and most incidents occurred in a residence (Snyder and Sickmund, 1999). CPS data for 2002 show more than 80 percent of victims were abused by a parent or parents (NCANDS, 2004). Children victimized by birth parents are more likely to experience neglect than abuse, whereas those victimized by other categories of parents are more like to be abused (Snyder and Sickmund, 1999).

There is consistent evidence that perpetrators are more likely to be female, except in the case of child sexual assault. Data from 2000 are illustrative of the pattern: 60 percent of the perpetrators were female and 40 percent were male (NCANDS, 2002). Mothers acting alone were responsible for 47 percent of neglect cases and 32 percent of physical abuse cases. Nonrelatives, fathers acting alone, and other relatives were responsible for 29 percent, 22 percent, and 19 percent, respectively, of sexual abuse cases (NCANDS, 2002).

7.4.4 Other Correlates of Maltreatment

Race has not been consistently linked to child abuse and neglect (Sedlak and Broadhurst, 1996). Maltreatment has been linked to family size. Children from large families, defined as those with four or more children, were physically neglected more often than those from smaller families (Snyder and Sickmund, 1999; Sedlak and Broadhurst, 1996).

Children of single parents are at higher risk of maltreatment. They also are overrepresented among the seriously injured, moderately injured, and endangered children (Sedlak and Broadhurst, 1996). Among single-parent households, those living only with their fathers are more likely to be physically abused than those living only with their mothers (Sedlak and Broadhurst, 1996).

Abuse and neglect cuts across socioeconomic lines; those in medium- and upper-income groups are not immune to it. However, there is significant evidence that the income level of the family is correlated with child abuse and neglect. The NIS studies have consistently documented that maltreatment is more likely for children living in poverty (Sedlak and Broadhurst, 1996). Children from lower-income families had higher abuse rates, higher rates of neglect, and higher injury rates in every category (endangered, inferred, moderate, serious) except in fatalities (Snyder and Sickmund, 1999).

7.5 Responses to Child Maltreatment

The NIS provide a mechanism to accurately assess the "dark figure" of child maltreatment not apparent from official measures. Indeed, one of the continuing findings of the NIS is the gap between the number of maltreatment cases reported and the number of cases that had CPS investigations. Less than half of the instances of maltreatment identified by the sentinel respondents were investigated by CPS (Sedlak and Broadhurst, 1996, p. 18).

A related issue is whether those children who die from maltreatment are already known to CPS. One estimate is that almost 50 percent of the maltreated children who died were known to child protection (National Victim Assistance Academy, 2002). The 2001 State Child Welfare Agency survey suggests that this is a much lower figure (Child Welfare League of America, 2002). In only 18.3 percent of the fatalities was the child a subject of an open case at the time of death. Nearly 19 percent of the fatalities were of children previously known to the child welfare agency, but the case was inactive (closed) at the time of death. Nearly two thirds (63 percent) of the child abuse and neglect fatalities were of children never known to the state child welfare agency (Child Welfare League of America, 2002).

Reports of abuse and neglect come to the attention of CPS units via police, teachers, and other mandated reporters, as well as from private citizens. Centralized registries for abuse and neglect reports and 24-h hot lines for reporting abuse are of relatively recent vintage — within the last 25 years. The most typical chain of events following a report of maltreatment is for a CPS worker to meet with the child and parent to assess the situation. In situations where harm has already occurred or where it is imminent, removal of the child from the home may occur. Such removal is temporary and conditioned by court restrictions. Court-appointed special advocates (CASAs) or *guardian ad litems* may be used by the court to secure and represent the child's interests.

There are three typical outcomes for abuse and neglect complaints. A report or an allegation may be: (1) substantiated (founded), (2) not substantiated (unfounded), or (3) indicated. The last finding means that there was some evidence to support the allegation, but it did not rise to the level of substantiation. In 2000, three million referrals concerning the welfare of five million children were made to CPS (NCANDS, 2002). This number represents 4 to 7 percent of the child population of the United States. Approximately one third of all reports are substantiated (NCANDS, 2002).

Child maltreatment occasions simultaneous responses from law enforcement agencies, medical providers, social services, and other victim assistance workers. The child protection system and the criminal justice system are complex parallel systems. Yet CPS operated in a singular and linear fashion until only recently. It was not until the late 1970s and early 1980s that the interdisciplinary or multidisciplinary model was embraced by the child welfare community (Untalan and Mills, 1992). Given divergent and yet overlapping purposes in investigating and processing child maltreatment cases, professionals have come to recognize the benefits of an interdisciplinary approach.

A refinement to the multidisciplinary approach has been the creation of child advocacy centers in some jurisdictions. Children's advocacy center programs allow law enforcement, social services, medical and mental health personnel, and child protection workers to interview children and provide services in a single, child-friendly location (U.S. Department of Justice, 1999). The benefits of a coordinated approach are many. Joint efforts can ease the trauma of the child victim by reducing multiple interviews and exams as a case passes through the civil and criminal systems. Communication is enhanced as information, expertise, and experiences are shared by the responding professionals. Service duplication is reduced, thereby resulting in greater cost efficiencies (National Victim Assistance Academy, 2002).

Services for child victims and their families are varied and aimed not only at addressing the immediate problem but also at preventing further maltreatment (for a comprehensive review, see National Victims Assistance Academy, 2002). Clinical treatment is a traditional service for child abuse and neglect victims. Such programs may include therapeutic day-school programs, day-hospital programs, residential programs, and treatment in home and clinic settings (Donnelly, 1997).

Parents or caretakers may be required to attend parenting classes or anger management courses, be placed in substance abuse treatment, engage in mental health counseling, or receive employment training. In-home or day respite care for parents may be offered as a means to reduce the stress on individuals who are overwhelmed with child rearing responsibilities (Donnelly, 1997). The newest model for processing child abuse and neglect cases that involve substance abuse by the child's parents or caregivers is the family dependency treatment court, which is modeled after the relatively new drug court models (U.S. Department of Justice, 2004).

Foster care placement and termination of parental rights are at the extreme end of the CPS continuum. CPS traditionally has subscribed to a philosophy of keeping families together and reunifying families that have been temporarily disrupted due to abuse or neglect.

The financial impact of interventions in abuse and neglect cases is large. In an interesting exercise, Fromm (2001) attempted to estimate the costs of child abuse and neglect. The cost of the child welfare system was estimated to be $14.4 billion. Law enforcement costs were estimated to be $24.7 million and judicial costs were estimated at $340 million. Other direct costs, which included hospitalization, chronic health problems, and mental health care totaled $9.5 billion. Total direct costs were $24.38 billion. Indirect costs were another $69.7 billion (Fromm, 2001).

Given the media-induced outrage against CPS when an egregious instance of abuse occurs, and the ensuing attention to the inner workings of the CPS, caseload data for CPS is revealing. The State Child Welfare Agency survey relies on states to voluntarily report caseload and programmatic data. Noteworthy is the fact that the agencies are most likely to report the variety of programs offered rather than caseload counts (Child Welfare League of America, 2002).

The average caseload for CPS (investigations and assessments) was 16 per professional caseworker. However, only 9 states, or 19 percent of the existing agencies, reported caseload data in 1999 and 2000. More interesting is the comparison with data for caseworkers for other types of cases. Professional caseworkers handling placement and foster care cases had a median caseload of 25, and for adoptions, the caseload was 20. The number of states reporting the latter measures was nearly double that reporting CPS caseload data (Child Welfare League of America, 2002).

Over 50 percent of the child victims referred to CPS — nearly a half a million — received services (NCANDS, 2002). One fifth (20 percent) of these victims were removed from their homes and placed in foster care as a result of a CPS investigation. In addition, 19 percent of referred children received services, although they were not determined to be victims.

7.6 Explanations of Abuse and Neglect

A recent book reviews 46 theoretical perspectives on child maltreatment (Jackson et al., 1991). Jackson and his colleagues organize the perspectives into nine general theoretical paradigms, which fall along three bipolar continuums. These continuums include: (1) the individual–cultural continuum, (2) the individual–family continuum, and (3) the sociobiological–sociopsychological continuum. Each of the theoretical perspectives is supported by some data and yet, each is also inconsistent with other research findings. Just as a singular theory of delinquency has not been found, there is no singular theory to explain child abuse and neglect. Research on the causes of child maltreatment has, thus, recently undergone a paradigm shift. The movement has been away from simple cause-and-effect models, which tended to have a narrow focus on parents and be overly static (Bethea, 1999, p. 3); in their place an ecologic model has been substituted.

The ecologic model considers the origins of child abuse to be a complex interactive process. Child abuse and neglect may be seen within a system of risk and protective factors interacting across: (1) the individual, (2) the family, (3) the community, and (4) society (National Research Council, 1993). For example, individual explanations of child maltreatment may pertain to the victim (the child) or to the abuser (the parent or caregiver). For children, individual-level factors include premature birth and physical or mental handicap. For parents or families, individual-level factors include: teenage parents, emotional immaturity, lack of parenting skills, personal history of substance abuse (Bethea, 1999). Family-related risk factors also include a personal history of physical or sexual abuse as a child.

Social learning theory is sometimes used to describe the transmission of a culture of violence or what Straus (1983) termed the "cycle of violence." Community and societal risk factors encompass conditions outside the family unit that create sufficient strain that abuse or neglect may occur. The more frequent and persistent of these social factors is poverty. Allied societal factors are a high crime rate and a lack of, or inadequacy of, social services. Social isolation, which may be a by-product of poverty or a different, individual-level variable, may contribute to stress and factor into the abuse–neglect profile.

As is evident, the variety of disciplinary orientations yields varying concepts of causation. Most importantly, different models of causation translate into different prevention and treatment strategies.

7.7 The Link between Abuse or Neglect and Delinquency

As our understanding of the dynamics of child abuse has grown, so too has our awareness of the long-term impact this offense occasions. The link between early adversity and maltreatment in all of its forms and later psychopathology in its many forms is well accepted. Maltreatment during childhood has been shown to result in acting out and in varied self-destructive behaviors. Such behavior may include running away, adolescent pregnancy, suicide attempts and self-mutilation (Green, 1978; Post et al., 1981).

Kilpatrick, Saunders, and Smith (2003) found child victimization to be a risk factor for adolescents in developing major mental health problems and abuse of alcohol. Agnew's (2002) work suggests that the victimization does not need to be one-on-one, but that vicarious victimization—witnessing maltreatment of a family or friend—may suffice to influence later lawbreaking behavior.

Studies of sexual abuse victims indicate that these children may experience extreme emotional distress, low self-image, impulsive behavior, and post-traumatic stress disorder (Mullen et al., 1993). Physical and psychological damage are not limited to victims of child sexual abuse (Mullen et al., 1996). Research indicates that physically abused children tend to be aggressive toward peers and adults and to display a diminished capacity of empathy for others (English, 1998; National Council of Child Abuse and Family Violence, n.d.) Other studies of victims of emotional abuse in childhood suggest that victims encounter difficulty developing healthy intimate relationships with adults.

Widom's (1992) landmark work indicates that childhood abuse increased the odds of future delinquency and adult criminality overall by 40 percent.[3] Childhood abuse and neglect increased the likelihood of arrest as a juvenile by 53 percent, and as an adult by 38 percent.

Child sexual abuse victims similarly were at higher risk of adult criminality than individuals who were not physically or sexually abused as children (Widom, 1995). However, victims of sexual abuse, when compared with youths victimized by other forms of abuse or neglect, were no more likely to engage in subsequent deviant behavior. In sum, Widom found that it is the general rather than the specific that applies: it is maltreatment in its many forms that is the precursor, rather than the potency of one type of maltreatment over another, in shaping the law-breaking trajectory. Kilpatrick et al.'s (2003) findings from adolescents align.

Findings from studies of prisoner populations are also consistent. A study of 6,000 inmates confined in local correctional institutions found that a higher percentage of inmates reported being victims of physical or sexual abuse as children (Harlow, 1998).

Yet, although researchers agree that there is a link between abuse or neglect and delinquency, several studies challenge the strength of the cycle of violence. As Zingraff et al. (1993, p. 175,176) illustrate, major methodological shortcomings of abuse–neglect designs put their findings on less than firm terrain. Their own well-designed study illustrated how uncertain the relationship between abuse and delinquency can be (Zingraff et al., 1993).

7.8 Future Needs

Looking to the future, there are three areas ripe for further attention from researchers, CPS workers, and policy makers. These relate to the state of knowledge about the incidence of abuse and neglect, the maltreatment–criminality link, and system performance in responding to suspected abuse and neglect reports.

Child abuse and neglect are not easily defined. There is tremendous heterogeneity in child maltreatment. Complicating the issue is the fact that maltreatment is not a diagnosis but a legal status. In addition, the vast majority of maltreatment complaints do not result in a CPS-substantiated finding or court intervention. The implications of these elements are staggering. If child maltreatment cannot be uniformly measured and if official responses are not consistently forthcoming, a large dark figure of maltreatment will go uncounted and unchecked. As a consequence, our understanding of the problem remains compromised.

An important start would be a national data collection effort. In this regard, the NIS provide valuable information and, because they include sentinel reports in addition to CPS records, our knowledge of the incidence of child maltreatment is enhanced. Unfortunately, the NIS rely on congressional authorization. It has been a decade since the NIS-3 and it was 7 years between NIS-2 and NIS-3. It would be desirable to develop a data system, much like the FBI's Uniform Crime Reporting System, for child abuse and neglect information. Although information on abuse and neglect is now partially accessible through the NIBRS data set and the Supplementary Homicide Reporting Program of the FBI, the information is still quite restrictive. An annual data collection effort, with information fields tailored to abuse and neglect and child protection issues, would be a good start to improving our understanding of maltreatment over time.

Another pressing issue is the relationship between child maltreatment and criminality. Retrospective studies of individuals in the juvenile and criminal justice systems demonstrate the abuse–criminality connection. However, prospective studies indicate that a majority of maltreated children do not progress to minor or sustained criminality. These contraindications point to the importance of identifying the intermediating variables that lead from maltreatment to criminality. Studies employing more rigorous designs are needed. So too are studies that demonstrate the effectiveness of interventions.

Finally, and arguably, the most critical problem is how to get a CPS to perform at a generally agreed–upon level of effectiveness and efficiency. This is the age of privatization. A number of correctional and social services have privatized service delivery functions.[4] Although the turn toward privatization has been prompted by the failures of state CPS, in time the attraction may seem more illusory than real. Privatization may be akin to balkanization, that is, an invitation for each agency to "do its own thing." As a result, the service delivery system becomes fragmented.

In addition, private companies tend to focus on the bottom line. It is hard not to expect that bottom-line concerns may intrude and shape the handling of victims. Even with oversight via a state regulatory agency, disparities in handling abuse and neglect cases is likely to occur. Although there surely is considerable room for improvement in the current CPS system, it is not clear that the privatization trend will achieve greater effectiveness or efficiency. This is an area that calls for continued monitoring by consumers, the general public, and policy makers. Failure to remain vigilant about the impact of privatization may result in the next media sound bite about child maltreatment.

References

Agnew, R. (2002). Experienced, vicarious, and anticipated strain: an exploratory study on physical victimization and delinquency. *Justice Quarterly, 19,* 603–632.

Bethea, L. (March 15, 1999). Primary prevention of child abuse. *American Family Physician,* 1–12.

Blau, G.M., Whewell, M.C., Gullotta,T.P., and Bloom, M. (1994). The prevention and treatment of child abuse in households of substance abusers: a research demonstration progress report. *Child Welfare, 73,* 83–94.

Child Welfare League of America. (2002). 2001 State Child Welfare Agency Survey. National Data Analysis System. http://ndas.cwla.org.

Children of Alcoholics Foundation (1996). Helping Children Affected by Parental Addiction and Family Violence: Collaboration, Coordination, and Cooperation. New York: Children of Alcoholics Foundation.

Donnelly, C. (1997). An Approach to Preventing Child Abuse. Chicago, IL: Prevent Child Abuse America.

English, D.J. (1998). The extent and consequences of child maltreatment. In *The Future of Children: Protecting Children from Abuse and Neglect.* Los Altos, CA: The David and Lucille Packard Foundation.

Fagan, A.A. (2001). Gender cycle of violence: comparing the effects of child abuse and neglect on criminal offending for males and females. *Violence and Victims, 16,* 457–474.

Fromm, S. (2001). Total Estimated Cost of Child Abuse and Neglect in the United States: Statistical Evidence. Chicago, IL: Prevent Child Abuse America.

Green, A.M. (1978). Self-destructive behavior in battered children. *American Journal of Psychiatry, 135,* 5.

Harlow, C.W. (1998). Profile of Jail Inmates, 1996. U.S. Department of Justice. Washington, D.C.

Hopper, Jim. (2005). Child Abuse: Statistics, Research and Resources. Retrieved February 8, 2005 from http://www.jimhopper.com/abstats.

Jackson, J.W., Karlson, H.C., and Tzeng, O.C.S. (1991). *Theories of Child Abuse and Neglect: Differential Perspectives, Summaries, and Evaluations.* Westport, CT: Greenwood Publishing Group.

Kempe, C.H., Silverman, F.N., Steele, B.F., Droegemuller, W., and Silver, H.K. (1962). The battered-child syndrome. *Journal of the American Medical Association, 181,* 105–112.

Kilpatrick, D., Saunders, B., and Smith, D.W. (2003). *Prevalence and consequences of child victimization: Results from a national survey of adolescents.* National Institute of Justice Research Preview. Washington, D.C.

Mullen, P.E., Martin, J.L., Anderson, J.C., Romans, S.E., and Herbison, G.P. (1993). Childhood sexual absue and mental health in adult life. *British Journal of Psychiatry, 163,* 721–732.

Mullen, P.E., Martin, J.L., Anderson, J.C., Romans, S.E., and Herbison, G.P. (1996). The long-term impact of the physical, emotional and sexual abuse of children: a community study. *Child Abuse and Neglect, 20,* 7–22.

NCANDS (April, 2002). Summary of Key Findings from Calendar Year 2000. National Child Abuse and Neglect Data System. Retrieved February 8, 2005 from http://nccanch.adf.hhs.gov.

National Child Abuse and Neglect Data System (NCANDS) (2004). Child Maltreatment 2002. Washington D.C.: U.S. Government Printing Office. http://nccanch.adf.hhs.gov.

National Clearinghouse on Child Abuse and Neglect Information (February, 2002). Child Abuse and Neglect Statutes: At a Glance. Washington D.C. Retrieved February 8, 2005 from http://nccanch.adf.hhs.gov.

National Clearinghouse on Child Abuse and Neglect Information (2004). Child Abuse and Neglect Fatalities: Statistics and Interventions. Retrieved February 8, 2005 from http://www.calib.com/nccanch.

National Council of Child Abuse and Family Violence. Facts About Child Abuse and Neglect. Washington D.C. Retrieved January 21, 2003 from http://www.nccafv.org.

National Research Council (1993). *Understanding Child Abuse and Neglect.* Panel on Research on Child Abuse and Neglect, Commission on Behavioral and Social Sciences and Education. Washington, D.C.: National Academy Press.

National Victim Assistance Academy (2002). Retrieved December 27, 2002 from http://www.ojp.gov/ovc/assist/nvaa.

Post, R.D., Willett, A.B., Franks, R.D., House, R.M., and Black, S.M. (1981). Childhood exposure to violence among victims and perpetrators of spouse battering. *Victimology, 6,* 156–166.

Sedlak, A.J. and Broadhurst, D.D. (1996). The Third National Incidence Study of Child Abuse and Neglect (NIC-3). National Center on Child Abuse and Neglect. Washington, D.C.: U.S. Department of Health and Human Services.

Snyder, H. and Sickmund, M. (1999). Juvenile Offenders and Victims: 1999 National Report. Office of Juvenile Justice and Delinquency Prevention. Washington, D.C.

Straus, M.A. (1983). Ordinary violence, child abuse, and wife-beating: what do they have in common? In Finkelhor, D., Gelles, R.J., Hotaling, G.T., and Straus, M.A. (Eds.), *The Dark Side of Families: Current Family Violence Research.* Beverly Hills, CA: Sage.

Swetlow, K. (June, 2003). OVC Bulletin: Children at Clandestine Methamphetamine Labs: Helping Meth's Youngest Victims. Washington, D.C.: U.S. Department of Justice.

Untalan, F.F. and Mills, C.S. (Eds.) (1992) *Interdisciplinary Perspectives in Child Abuse and Neglect.* Westport, CT: Praeger.

U.S. Department of Justice (1999). Regional and Local Children's Advocacy Centers. Washington, D.C.

U.S. Department of Justice (December, 2004). Family Dependency Treatment Courts: Addressing Child Abuse and Neglect Cases Using the Drug Court Model, Monograph. Washington, D.C.: Bureau of Justice Assistance.

Wang, C.T. and Harding, K. (1999). Current Trends in Child Abuse Reporting and Fatalities: The Results of the 1998 Annual Fifty State Survey. Chicago, IL: Prevent Child Abuse America.

Widom, C.S. (1992). Cycle of Violence. National Institute of Justice. Washington, D.C.

Widom, C.S. (March 1995). *Victims of Childhood Sexual Abuse and Later Criminal Consequences.* National Institute of Justice Research in Brief. Washington, D.C.

Zingraff, M.T., Leiter, J., Myers, K.A., and Johnson, M.C. (1993). Child maltreatment and youthful problem behavior. *Criminology, 31,* 171–202.

Notes

1. NIS studies are conducted upon congressional mandate. The most recent NIS occurred in 1993. The data are unique in that they do not reflect just the official reports of child maltreatment. Sentinel reports provide a more comprehensive measure of the scope of child abuse and neglect because children who were not referred to CPS or who were screened out by CPS without investigation are included in developing the national estimates. Another important aspect of the NIS methodology is that although only unduplicated counts of child victims are included, each incident of abuse or neglect is also considered.

2. The FBI's NIBRS system collects detailed data on crimes reported to law enforcement. Participation in the NIBRS program, like the FBI's Uniform Crime Reporting Program, is voluntary, and participation by states has been limited. Data on 1.1 million incidents of violence have been collected for 1991 through 1996

3. An interesting outgrowth of the abuse–criminality model is the rise of child maltreatment as a defense to mitigate sentencing decisions. Child abuse or neglect has been cited as a reason to mitigate punishment in capital crimes (see, for example, *Roger Lee Cherry v. Michael Moore,* FL Sup Ct, NSC01-2862). Case law indicates that although the argument is made with some frequency, it generally does not prevail (see, for example, decisions out of Arizona and the Armed Forces).

4. This is not to ignore that the juvenile justice and social welfare systems have frequently used private institutions and treatment providers.

Chapter 8

Effective Social Control Measures in School and Community Programs: Implications for Policy and Practice

Carrie M. Butler and Ted R. Watkins

8.1 Introduction

Juvenile gang activity and delinquency present problems for public school personnel in that they are often associated with truancy, school crime, and victimization. Many students resort to delinquency or gang activity as protective mechanisms and feel the need to carry weapons on campus. Thereby, these behaviors transform into self-defeating patterns that ultimately perpetuate the cycle of violence in schools and communities (Baker et al., 2001).

According to the Bureau of Justice Statistics (1989), approximately 13 percent of all public middle and high school students reported being physically attacked or being involved in a fight in which a weapon was used. Stephens (as in Goldstein and Huff, 1993) claims that students carry weapons for protection, to fit in, and to intimidate others, and it seems that formal punishments for carrying weapons are not serving as deterrents for this behavior. In 1999, approximately 18 percent of students reported carrying weapons both to school and after school during a 1-month period (Bureau of Justice Statistics, 1989). Students' perceptions of discipline consistency and enforcement procedures contribute to components of school violence and students' feelings of insecurity (McDaniel, 1994; Nuttal and Kalesnik, 1987). School-related crimes not only instill the fear in students that they may become victims of violent crimes, but these crimes also make it difficult for them to concentrate on their academics (Bureau of Justice Statistics, 1989; Stern, 1992). Many of the students who fear for their safety believe that joining a gang will help them to feel protected at school. About 19 percent of middle school and high school students reported gang presence in their schools (Bureau of Justice Statistics, 1989). Schools serve as central meeting locations for students, especially because of the laws and policies for mandatory attendance.

8.2 Theoretical Perspectives

Social systems theory combines the body of juvenile delinquency literature into an understandable whole. It provides a meta-level explanation of the interaction among systems (van Gigch, 1991). Macro-level systems incorporate issues that affect masses of people, such as subcultural group membership, social class, and other demographic variables. Infiltration from macro-level systems to mediating-level systems may determine how effectively lower-level systems operate. Macro-level systems directly affect mediating levels but only indirectly affect micro levels. The mediating level consists of law enforcement, social agencies, and schools and is directly affected by the macro level but also directly affects the micro level. The micro level includes family and peer systems; the micro level is considered to include relationships closest to the individual. There is merit in each of these perspectives. Each level of a social system interacts with the others, thus compounding or reducing delinquency; however, the mediating level at this point in our society provides the best avenue to control volatile juvenile activity.

8.2.1 Control Theory

There are equally diverse suggestions regarding effective intervention and prevention measures. Control theory suggests that individuals engage in deviant behavior as a result of weakening social controls (Ward et al., 1994). Youths are more likely to engage in deviance when controls in the forms of parents, schools, or other social institutions fail to hold them accountable for their actions. Control theory provides a useful framework for studying the effects of mediating systems of after-school programs that attempt to deter young people from delinquency.

Longres (1990, p.44) defines social control as "the processes through which a person's participation in a system is limited or constrained. Social control may be implemented through positive or negative means. Often systems of reward are devised to assure compliance with group expectations." Social control variables that help individuals conform to societal expectations will facilitate positive peer socialization. Social controls that influence youth on a daily basis may either promote or deter them from engaging in gang and delinquent activity, depending on the consistency of the social control influence. Social control factors in after-school programs may help to serve as deterrents to delinquency within those programs. Specifically, these forms of social control in after-school programs can be identified as police visibility, presence of adults, accountability for behavior through adult supervision, and parental reinforcement of negative consequences.

8.3 The Present Study

There is minimal research regarding the effects of social control variables in after-school and community-based activities on gang involvement in youth. Esbensen et al. (1993) examined adolescents' involvement in conventional activities without identifying critical differences in program structure. They reported that there were no significant differences among gang members, street offenders, and nonoffenders in their participation in conventional activities. However, Ekland-Olson (1982) maintained that involvement of youth in conventional activities establishes prosocial interpersonal bonds with peers and adults. This chapter will examine the effect of youths' participation in conventional activities on outcomes of gang participation and delinquency, in conjunction with key social control components that can explain the differences between effective and ineffective programming. The analysis consists of the following hypotheses:

- H1 (a) Participation in extracurricular activities decreases the likelihood of gang participation.
- H1 (b) Participation in extracurricular activities decreases the likelihood of delinquency.
- H2 (a) Students who participate in after-school activities at school have lower levels of gang participation than students who participate in community programs.
- H2 (b) Students who participate in after-school activities at school have lower levels of delinquency than students who participate in community programs.
- H3 (a) Visibility of adult supervision decreases adolescents' gang participation.
- H3 (b) Visibility of adult supervision decreases adolescents' delinquent activity.
- H4 (a) Accountability of behavior through adult supervision during school and in after-school activities decreases the likelihood of adolescent gang participation.
- H4 (b) Accountability of behavior through adult supervision during school and in after-school activities decreases the likelihood of adolescent delinquent activities.
- H5 Participation in school and community activities contributes to a higher sense of commitment to positive peers.

8.3.1 Methodology

A large Texas suburban school district and the city police department formed a partnership for a project to study the factors associated with criminal activities at a local high school in which high levels of delinquency (gang activity, truancy, and criminal mischief) were reported. The goal of the current study was to determine, by using secondary data from the local project, what school and community programs were associated with lower levels of gang involvement during truant episodes.

A survey design was employed to examine students' outcomes of gang participation and delinquency in relation to their involvement in conventional activities. Survey items regarding students' involvement in after-school activities were included to target social control variables that deter youth from gang activity and delinquency as well as build a sense of belonging to school and community. Social control items were developed

Table 8.1 Percentages of Sample and Population Composition for the APD School-Based Partnership Project Student Survey by Gender and Ethnicity

	Sample			Population		
Ethnicity	*Male*	*Female*	*Ethnicity*	*Male*	*Female*
American Indian	1	1	American Indian	1	1
African American	12	14	African American	14	16
Hispanic	12	14	Hispanic	13	15
Caucasian	12	14	Caucasian	15	14
Asian	7	5	Asian	5	6
Other	3	5			

based on literature supporting mediating systems' influences on youths' behavior. The instrument was piloted on a group of ten student volunteers and then revised prior to distribution to the larger sample.

A convenience sample of 400 students (from the total student body of 2296) from grades 9 through 12 was selected from the target school. The sample consisted of students in selected history and government classes and was selected by a school administrator based on convenience of location. Resource, or special learning, classes were not represented in the sample. Classroom teachers explained the instructions to students, distributed the surveys, and were present in the classrooms while students completed the surveys. Teacher presence during survey administration might be a source of bias because these were questions about illegal conduct.

The survey was distributed to 400 students; however, only 353 surveys were used for this analysis. Surveys were not included if they were incomplete or illegible. The student survey sample was highly representative of the whole student body in terms of ethnic and gender variables (see Table 8.1).

8.3.2 Measures

The survey questionnaire used a Likert format and contained items addressing the constructs "involvement in school and community programs," social control variables of "school social control," and "community social control," "adult supervision," "social accountability," and "peer socialization." Construct validity was established by determining factor loadings or "item groupings" that reflect the independent variables, social control variables in school and community-based programs, and the dependent variable, gang participation.

8.3.3 Dependent Variables

8.3.3.1 Gang Participation

The Texas State Penal Code (70.01) defines a street gang as "three or more people, with common identifiable signs or symbols, with identifiable leaderships, who regularly associate in the commission of criminal activity." This definition was used in reference to gang participation. Students responded to one item based on self-interpretation of their gang participation. Common offenses committed by gangs include graffiti, illegal drug use and drug sales, carrying and selling weapons illegally, shoplifting, vandalism, and burglary. The dependent variable delinquency will be considered as acts that violate the school code (i.e., truancy, skipping class, carrying weapons to school) and other violations of the law (i.e., burglary, vandalism, theft, and graffiti).

8.3.3.2 Delinquency

Delinquency included the frequency of participation in school violations or law-related offenses during truant episodes at school. School violations are defined as those actions that violate the school code of conduct (skipping class, truancy from school, and fighting). Law-related offenses included those actions that violate the Texas State Penal Code or federal law (misdemeanors and felonies). Examples of misdemeanors may include, but are not limited to, loitering, damaging property with graffiti, and hassling customers at local businesses. Felonies may include, but are not limited to, assaulting someone, taking something from someone using physical force, and taking something from someone using a weapon.

8.3.3.3 Peer Association

This construct represented students' association with peers involved with gang activity or other forms of delinquent behavior. Students responded to items in Likert scale format on their association with gang peers and law violators.

Peers serve as strong influences on individual behavior (Brown, 1982; Chess and Norlin, 1991; Keenan et al., 1995). Students who associate with negative peers are more likely to engage in negative behaviors, and likewise, students who associate with peers who do not engage in negative behaviors are more likely to associate with positive peers. Thus, students indicating low levels of association with delinquent peers reflect a greater likelihood of positive peer socialization.

8.3.4 *Independent Variables*

8.3.4.1 *Involvement in School and Community Programs*

The construct "involvement in school and community programs" represents activities that youth are involved in at the school setting after school hours, community programs, and youth church programs. After-school activities at school include after-school sports such as basketball, volleyball, football, track, and others. As programs operated by the school system, after-school school programs offer high degrees of social control through disciplinary measures and behavioral standards. Community programs include local YMCA programs, Boys and Girls Clubs of America programs, recreation center programs, and the like. Involvement in community activities provides social control through supervised programs that reinforce participants' conforming to group rules and standards. Church youth activities include programs and events hosted by church organizations or other religious groups. They incorporate high degrees of social control on youths by providing structured activities that reinforce prosocial behaviors through religious standards.

Students were asked to identify their participation in these activities by frequency of involvement. They were coded (1) never, (2) once per month, (3) one to two times per week, (4) three or more times per week, and (5) every day. The three variables for school and community programs are (1) after-school sports (basketball, track, etc.), (2) community activities (Boys and Girls Club, YMCA, recreation centers, etc.), and (3) youth church activities.

Responses on school and community programs were summed into a composite score for the multiple regression analyses on gang participation. All activities combined revealed an alpha coefficient of 0.50, indicating weak to moderate levels of intercorrelation among items.

8.3.4.2 Social Control

The "social control" construct is represented by items on adult supervision and accountability for behavior. Social control was divided into two categories to analyze differences in "school social control" and "community social control." Theoretically, schools have higher degrees of social control owing to the representation of more adults (i.e., teachers, administrators, and police officers) and stricter policies about academic expectations and behavioral standards (i.e., student codes of conduct) than community programs, which may have fewer guidelines. School and community social control variables produced a composite reliability alpha coefficient of 0.82. The school and community social control variables were also run separately in the multiple regression analysis to determine the unique effects of school and community forms of social control in after-school programs on gang participation.

8.3.4.3 School Social Control

Social control in after-school programs at school was represented by five items on adult supervision and behavioral accountability. Students were asked to respond — (1) never, (2) hardly ever, (3) sometimes, (4) mostly, or (5) always — to items such as "If I get into trouble after school while participating in a school program my parents are likely to find out about it," and "The adults present during after-school activities at school pay attention to students and make sure there is no trouble and no fighting." Answers were summed into a composite score. An alpha coefficient of 0.66 was achieved for this variable, indicating moderate intercorrelations among items.

8.3.4.4 Community Social Control

Community social control included four items on adult supervision and behavioral accountability in after-school community programs. Sample questions were "While participating in a community program after school I have noticed more than one adult present" and "There is at least one police officer present on a regular basis where I participate in community programs after school." These four items attained a reliability coefficient of 0.67, indicating moderate to high levels of intercorrelation among items.

A factor analysis was also performed on the scale. An oblique rotation was conducted to simplify the pattern factor matrix, which produced three factors, but loaded highly on two. One factor contained items on parents' likelihood of finding out about troublesome behavior during school and community programs, being held responsible for troublesome behavior during after-school activities at school and in the community, and noticing adults present during the activities. This construct was named "social accountability." The other factor loaded highly on items about noticing adults present during after-school programs at school and in the community, presence of police officers at after-school programs at school and in the community, and adults properly monitoring the programs to keep the activities under control. This construct was named "adult supervision." Each construct was used in multiple regression analyses on the dependent variable gang participation.

8.3.4.5 Social Accountability

Social accountability represented social control in these programs in terms of parental intervention for problem behaviors, students' likelihood of accountability for behavioral problems during these programs, and presence of supervising adults.

8.3.4.6 Adult Supervision

The construct, adult supervision, is represented by social control factors in school, community, and youth church activities: visibility of adults, presence of police officers, and attentiveness of adults to disruptions during activities. Students were asked to indicate if they noticed police officers present on a regular basis during these programs and if the adults attended to students during community programs to ensure a safe environment.

8.4 Data Analysis

Multiple regression analyses were used to analyze scales of involvement in school- and community-based programs, adult supervision, social accountability, peer association, and demographic variables (age, sex, ethnicity, and grade point average) on gang participation during truant episodes. The two scales of adult supervision and social accountability on gang participation and delinquency were used for hypotheses 3(a), 3(b), 4(a), and 4(b). For all hypotheses, demographic variables (ethnicity, grade point average, sex, and age) were controlled for by inclusion.

Cross-tabulation analyses examined differences among school, community, and youth church activities. Cross tabulations were run separately for each category with gang participation and delinquency measures. Delinquency was classified into three distinct categories: drug offenses, property crimes, and violent crimes. Gang participation was represented by one item on level of gang participation, and the categories for delinquency were represented by level of involvement.

Effects on involvement in after-school programs at school, community programs, youth church activities, and during-school programs on delinquency were analyzed separately according to types of crime (drug, property, or violent) by first using cross tabulations. Then, school and community programs, school and community social control, adult supervision, and social accountability were analyzed on delinquency items as a composite score.

8.4.1 Results

In this section, the results of hypotheses 1 through 5 will be discussed. Hypotheses 1(a) and 1(b) are related to participation in after-school programs at school and in the community and the likelihood of gang participation and delinquency. Hypotheses 2(a) and 2(b) compare social control variables in after-school activities at school with social control variables in community programs and the likelihood of students engaging in gang activity and delinquency. Hypotheses 3(a) and 3(b) examine the effect of social control in the form of adult supervision on gang participation and delinquency. Hypotheses 4(a) and 4(b) include the accountability of behavior through adult supervision (i.e., social accountability) on gang participation and delinquency. The fifth and final hypothesis examines the effects of school and community activities on peer socialization.

8.4.2 Hypothesis 1

Hypotheses 1(a) and 1(b) were analyzed by using multiple regression and cross-tabulation analyses. Hypothesis 1(a) was unsupported in the multiple regression and in cross-tabulation analyses as no significant relationships were established for school and community activities on gang participation (see Table 8.2). Hypothesis 1(b) was supported using cross-tabulation analyses on specific categories of crime for school and community programs; however, no significant relationships were found using multiple regression analyses on them as a composite variable (see Table 8.3).

Table 8.2   Activity Level Associated with Gang Participation

Measure Variables	No Criminal Activity			Criminal Activity			
	Low	High	N	Low	High	N	p^a
After-school activities at school	55.2	44.8	288	54.3	45.7	35	NS[b]
Community programs	81.5	18.5	287	74.3	25.7	35	NS[b]
Youth church activities	71.2	28.8	285	74.3	25.7	35	NS[b]
During-school activities	65.0	35.0	286	80.0	20.0	35	NS[b]

[a]Chi-square test.

[b]NS = not significant at .05 level.

Table 8.3   Multiple Regression Analysis of the Effect of Involvement in School and Community Programs on Gang Participation

Measure Variables	Gang Participation ($R^2 = 0.060$)		
	Beta	(SEB)[b]	p Value
School and community activities[c]	0.022	0.240	.705
Age	0.104	0.666	.065
Gender	0.199	1.570	.000[a]
African American	0.092	2.120	.165
Hispanic	0.015	2.190	.820
Asian	0.045	2.790	.480
Other	0.077	2.940	.204

[a]Chi-square test.

[b]SEB = standard error beta.

[c]School and community activities = after school sports, Boys' and Girls' Clubs, and YMCA programs; combined variable.

Table 8.4   Activity Level Associated with Drug and Alcohol Use

After-School Activities at School

	No Drug Use			Drug Use			
Measure Variable	Low	High	N	Low	High	N	P[a]
Used alcohol	54.7	45.3	256	56.2	43.8	73	NS[b]
Smoked marijuana	50.4	49.6	246	70.4	29.6	71	.005[c]
Used illegal drugs	52.3	47.7	264	71.7	28.3	46	.05[c]

[a]Chi-square test.

[b]NS = not significant at .05 level.

[c]Significant at .05 level.

8.4.2.1 Gang Participation

Table 8.2 indicates that no significant differences were found between level of involvement in activities and the reports of gang activity. Extracurricular school activities revealed highest percentages of involvement for both non-gang- (44.8 percent) and gang-involved youth (45.7 percent), indicating that these students are equally likely to participate in school programs. Nongang youth reported lower levels of participation in community programs, whereas gang youth reported higher involvement in community programs and youth church activities. Additionally, gang-involved youth reported lower levels of involvement in during-school activities.

8.4.2.2 Drug-Related Crimes

For extracurricular school activities, Table 8.4 indicates that marijuana and illegal drug use revealed significant differences between users and nonusers. Drug-related crimes included use of alcohol, marijuana, and other illegal drugs. For nonusers, 49.6 percent reported being highly active in after-school activities at school, whereas 29.6 percent of marijuana users reported being highly active in these activities. For those who reported illegal drug use, 28.3 percent of them were highly involved in after-school activities at school, whereas 47.7 percent of nonusers were highly involved in these activities. An important finding from these results indicates that involvement in school activities is associated with lower student reports of marijuana and other illegal drug use, although no significant differences were reported between alcohol users and nonusers and their level of their involvement in extracurricular school programs.

For effects of alcohol and drug use on involvement in after-school community programs, no significant differences were reported between users and nonusers. Percentages of those highly involved in community programs were greater for those who reported marijuana and illegal drug use than for nonusers who were highly involved in community programs, such as Boys' and Girls' Clubs of America and YMCA programs. Consequently, students who participate in community programs show greater risk for using illicit drugs.

Involvement in youth church activities revealed no significant differences between users and nonusers. For marijuana and other illegal drug users, more students reported lower levels of activity in youth church programs than did nonusers.

Involvement in during-school activities and students' use of alcohol and drugs revealed no significant differences between users and nonusers. For nonusers, students were more likely to be highly involved in during-school activities than users of alcohol, marijuana, and other illegal drugs.

8.4.2.3 Property Crimes

Students' reports of participation in community programs revealed significant differences between offenders and nonoffenders in certain crime categories (see Table 8.5). For damaging property with graffiti, significant differences in percentages were reported between nonoffenders (17.2 percent) and offenders (37.1 percent) for high levels of involvement in community programs. Students who damage property with graffiti reported higher levels of participation in community programs than nonoffenders. Likewise, for setting something on fire, significant differences were reported between nonoffenders (17.9 percent) and offenders (35.1 percent) for high levels of involvement in community programs, indicating that students who set things on fire were more likely to participate more frequently in community programs than nonoffenders.

Students' reports of involvement in extracurricular school activities, youth church activities, and during-school activities revealed no significant differences between property crime offenders and nonoffenders

Table 8.5   Activity Level Associated with Property Crimes

After-School Community Programs

Measure Variable	No Criminal Activity			Criminal Activity			p^a
	Low	High	N	Low	High	N	
Damaged school property	82.8	17.2	285	71.7	28.3	46	NS
Damaged someone else's property	82.3	17.7	277	76.5	23.5	51	NS
Stolen any item	82.4	17.6	272	73.2	26.8	56	NS
Broken into a vehicle	81.4	18.6	301	77.3	22.7	22	NS
Stolen a vehicle	80.8	19.2	297	78.3	21.7	23	NS
Burglarized a house or apartment	82.0	18.0	294	74.1	25.9	27	NS
Been a passenger in a stolen vehicle	81.2	18.8	287	81.8	18.2	33	NS
Damaged property with graffiti	82.8	17.2	285	62.9	37.1	35	.005^a
Set something on fire	82.1	17.9	280	64.9	35.1	37	.05^a

^{a}Chi-square test.

(see Table 8.5). Students' reports of frequent participation in extra-curricular school activities revealed the highest percentages for both offenders and nonoffenders, thereby indicating that many of these students were more likely to participate in school activities.

8.4.2.4 Violent Crimes

For all categories of conventional activities, only community programs revealed significant differences between offenders and nonoffenders for fighting, robbery, and aggravated robbery. Table 8.6 shows that offenders were more likely than nonoffenders to be highly active in these programs. No significant differences were reported between violent crime offenders and nonoffenders for their involvement in extracurricular school activities, youth church activities, and during-school activities.

Table 8.6 Activity Level Associated with Violent Crimes

	After-School Community Programs						
	No Criminal Activity			*Criminal Activity*			
Measure Variable	*Low*	*High*	*N*	*Low*	*High*	*N*	*p*[a]
Carried a gun or weapon	81.6	18.4	288	76.5	23.5	34	NS
Been in a fight	83.3	16.7	257	70.0	30.0	60	.05[a]
Taken something using physical force	82.1	17.9	279	67.6	32.4	37	.05[a]
Taken something using a weapon	82.6	17.4	299	52.4	47.6	21	.001[a]
Assaulted someone	81.8	18.2	286	72.7	27.3	33	NS
Threatened to hurt someone	80.8	19.2	266	80.0	20.0	55	NS
Hassled customers	81.6	18.4	282	70.6	29.4	34	NS

[a]Chi-square test.

8.4.3 Hypothesis 2

Hypotheses 2(a) and 2(b) and hypotheses 3(a) and 3(b) were analyzed using multiple regression analyses. Variables for school social control and community social control were analyzed separately to determine their unique effects on gang participation and delinquency in order to avoid multicollinearity.

8.4.3.1 School Social Control on Gang Participation

School social control, gender, and ethnicity had significant effects on gang participation ($p < .001$) (see Table 8.7). These variables demonstrated moderate relationships with gang participation. School social control had a negative effect on gang participation, indicating that it successfully controls gang-related behavior. Consistent with previous literature on juvenile gang activity and delinquency, males and African Americans were more vulnerable to gang participation than females and other

Table 8.7 Multiple Regression Analysis of the Effect of School Social Control on Gang Participation and Delinquency

Measure Variable	Gang Participation ($R^2 = 0.105$)			Delinquency ($R^2 = 0.169$)		
	Beta	(SEB)	P Value	Beta	(SEB)	p Value
School social control	0.226	0.012	.000[a]	0.326	0.180	.000[a]
Age	0.079	0.044	.164	0.092	0.630	.083
Gender	0.127	0.106	.025[a]	0.166	1.500	.002[a]
African American	0.187	0.141	.005[a]	0.097	2.010	.122
Hispanic	0.101	0.141	.134	0.002	2.010	.979
Asian	0.045	0.184	.474	0.062	2.610	.288
Other	0.071	0.199	.245	0.060	2.840	.300

[a]Significant at .05 level.

ethnic groups. The R^2 revealed that 10.5 percent of the variance in gang participation was attributable to gender, ethnicity, and school social control.

8.4.3.2 School Social Control on Delinquency

Similar to the findings for gang activity, school social control and gender demonstrated significant effects on delinquency ($p < .01$); school social control appears to also successfully deter delinquency (see Table 8.7). Relationships between gender and delinquency were weak to moderate, but a moderately strong relationship was shown between school social control and delinquency. The R^2 revealed that 16.9 percent of the variance in delinquency was attributable to gender and school social control.

8.4.3.3 Community Social Control on Gang Participation

Community social control, gender, and ethnicity demonstrated significant effects on gang participation ($p < .05$) (see Table 8.8). The results indicated that as community social control in after-school community programs increased, gang participation decreased. Similar to school social control, males and African Americans were more vulnerable to

Table 8.8   Multiple Regression Analysis of the Effect of Community Social Control on Gang Participation and Delinquency

Measure Variable	Gang Participation (R² = 0.078)			Delinquency (R² = 0.105)		
	Beta	(SEB)	P Value	Beta	(SEB)	p Value
Community social control	0.136	0.013	.019ᵃ	0.207	0.184	.000ᵃ
Age	0.096	0.046	.097	0.097	0.659	.080
Gender	0.149	0.111	.010ᵃ	0.173	1.570	.002ᵃ
African American	0.177	0.149	.010ᵃ	0.087	2.110	.187
Hispanic	0.124	0.149	.074	0.000	2.110	.997
Asian	0.044	0.196	.491	0.069	2.760	.265
Other	0.066	0.207	.295	0.057	2.940	.349

[a]Significant at .05 level.

gang participation than females or other ethnic groups. The R^2 showed that 7.8 percent of the variance in gang participation was attributable to gender, ethnicity, and community social control.

8.4.3.4 Community Social Control on Delinquency

Community social control and gender demonstrated significant effects on delinquency ($p < .01$) (see Table 8.8). A moderate relationship was established between community social control and delinquency, and weak-to-moderate relationships were shown between males and delinquency. The results indicated that as social control in community programs increased, students' reports of delinquency decreased. The R^2 demonstrated that 10.5 percent of the variance in delinquency was attributable to gender and community social control.

Hypothesis 2 stated that participation in after-school programs at school has a greater likelihood of decreasing gang participation and delinquency than participation in community programs that have less visible signs of social control. Although both school social control and community social control appeared to control outcomes of gang participation delinquency, school social control appeared to have stronger effects and accounted for more variance in the dependent variables than community social control.

Table 8.9 Multiple Regression Analyses of the Effect of Adult Supervision on Gang Participation and Delinquency

Measure Variable	Gang Participation $(R^2 = 0.093)$			Delinquency $(R^2 = 0.141)$		
	Beta	(SEB)	p Value	Beta	(SEB)	p Value
Adult supervision	0.169	0.011	.005[a]	0.275	0.162	.000[a]
School programs	0.033	0.038	.608	0.024	0.535	.697
Community programs	0.110	0.056	.080	0.089	0.775	.130
Youth church activities	0.003	0.051	.958	0.045	0.728	.440
Age	0.088	0.046	.132	0.085	0.665	.126
Gender	0.150	0.114	.013[a]	0.199	1.620	.001[a]
African American	0.163	0.150	.020[a]	0.068	2.130	.300
Hispanic	0.120	0.150	.089	0.015	2.150	.819
Asian	0.051	0.194	.439	0.068	2.750	.274
Other	0.062	0.207	.335	0.048	2.960	.428

[a]Significant at .05 level.

8.4.4 Hypothesis 3

Hypotheses 3(a) and 3(b) on effects of adult supervision in youth programs on gang participation and delinquency were examined by multiple regression analyses. Results showed that as adult supervision in school and community programs increased, gang participation and delinquency decreased for truants.

8.4.4.1 Adult Supervision on Gang Participation

Similar to other social control measures, adult supervision, gender, and ethnicity demonstrated significant effects on gang participation ($p < .01$) (see Table 8.9), and adult supervision demonstrated an ability to effectively control gang participation in student activities. The R^2 demonstrated that 9.3 percent of the variance in gang participation was accounted for by gender, ethnicity, and adult supervision.

8.4.4.2 Adult Supervision on Delinquency

Adult supervision and gender demonstrated significant moderate effects on delinquency ($p < .01$) (see Table 8.9). Although female gang activity has increased in recent years, results of these findings are consistent with previous literature on males being disproportionately represented in gangs. The R^2 indicated that 14.1 percent of the variance in delinquent behavior is accounted for by adult supervision and gender.

Hypotheses 3(a) and 3(b) were supported as effects of adult supervision on delinquency were significant on gang participation and delinquency. These findings substantiate the important role of adult supervision as an effective deterrent for juvenile criminal behavior.

8.4.5 Hypothesis 4

Hypotheses 4(a) and 4(b) were supported by multiple regression analyses. Similar to other social control variables, results indicated that as social accountability increased in school and community programs, gang participation and delinquency for truants decreased.

8.4.5.1 Social Accountability on Gang Participation

Social accountability, gender, and ethnicity showed significant effects on gang participation ($p < .05$) (see Table 8.10). The independent variables indicated moderately strong relationships. Social accountability had a negative effect on gang participation, therefore serving as an effective deterrent to gang participation in student activities. The R^2 indicated that 11.2 percent of the variance in gang participation was attributable to gender, ethnicity, and social accountability.

8.4.5.2 Social Accountability on Delinquency

Similarly, social accountability and gender also revealed significant effects on delinquency ($p < .001$) (see Table 8.10). Social accountability therefore was demonstrated to be an effective deterrent for both gang participation and delinquency. The R^2 indicated that 13.1 percent of the variance in delinquency was attributable to social accountability and gender.

8.4.6 Hypothesis 5

Results from multiple regression analysis uncovered a unique finding for Hypothesis 5. Students' reports of involvement in community activities

Table 8.10   Multiple Regression Analyses of the Effect of Social Accountability during After-School Programs at School and in the Community on Gang Participation and Delinquency

Measure Variable	Gangs Participation ($R^2 = 0.112$)			Delinquency ($R^2 = 0.131$)		
	Beta	(SEB)	p Value	Beta	(SEB)	p Value
Social accountability	0.217	0.011	.000[a]	0.241	0.162	.000[a]
School programs	0.043	0.037	.498	0.063	0.526	.301
Community programs	0.113	0.056	.066	0.093	0.782	.115
Youth church activities	0.018	0.051	.768	0.089	0.730	.131
Age	0.092	0.047	.113	0.083	0.667	.138
Gender	0.132	0.115	.026[a]	0.188	1.630	.001[a]
African American	0.155	0.149	.025[a]	0.077	2.110	.238
Hispanic	0.141	0.150	.043[a]	0.016	2.150	.814
Asian	0.048	0.198	.456	0.061	2.800	.327
Other	0.067	0.208	.285	0.071	2.970	.240

[a]Significant at .05 level.

revealed a significant positive relationship to negative peer association ($p < .05$ level) (see Table 8.11). Consequently, youth who participated in community activities, especially male youth, were more vulnerable than youth who participated in other youth programs to develop delinquent peer networks. The R^2 indicated that 5.5 percent of the variance in association with negative peers was attributable to involvement in community programs and gender. This finding has important implications regarding the standards required to prevent antisocial values and behaviors in youth-geared programs. Based on results of this study, strengthening social control measures in community programs, such as increasing adult supervision and attending to social accountability, should be considered.

8.5 Discussion: Policy and Practice Implications

Results of this study indicate that mediating systems with high levels of social control in school and community programs show promise as

Table 8.11 Multiple Regression Analyses of the Effect of Involvement in School and Community Programs on Peer Association

Measure Variable	Negative Peer Association $(R^2 = 0.055)$		
	Beta	(SEB)	p Value
Social programs	0.080	0.065	.185
Community programs	0.116	0.099	.048[a]
Youth church activities	0.038	0.094	.531
During school activities	0.052	0.066	.376
Age	0.018	0.083	.750
Gender	0.114	0.208	.051
African American	0.115	0.272	.085
Hispanic	0.155	0.279	.023
Asian	0.009	0.357	.889
Other	0.083	0.370	.174

[a]Significant at .05 level.

effective deterrents to youth gang participation and delinquency. Important implications can be drawn for minority youth. In particular, African American and Hispanic males appear more likely than Caucasian males to engage in gang activity and delinquency. Perhaps more adult representation of these ethnic groups in after-school programs, in combination with tighter social controls, may serve to accommodate the needs of minority participants.

Mediating and micro-level systems play important roles in deterring young people from gang participation and delinquency through socialization processes. Schools and community programs offer opportunities for peer networking and prosocial activities. In addition, youth programs may be the best hope for success for some individuals; particularly if parental role models are inattentive, negative, or nonexistent. Families who incorporate and reinforce appropriate levels of adult supervision and guidance will help young people to establish healthy and productive lifestyles. Families and schools can work together to facilitate positive peer socialization.

Institutional policies that include standards for organizing and managing youth group activities should be implemented and continually revised. Given the changing nature of our society, regular evaluation of youth programs can help schools and communities successfully address rising challenges. Several years ago, the National School Safety Center (1988) recommended consistent enforcement of school code policies, in conjunction with prevention and intervention efforts. Law enforcement agencies can play important roles in this process by expanding prevention programs in the schools (i.e., the Gang Resistance Education and Training program), in addition to other suppression efforts.

8.6 Conclusion

Mediating systems such as schools and community organizations either intentionally or unintentionally promote or deter delinquency in youth subcultures. Presumably, micro-level systems have the most influence over individual choice and behavior; however, mediating-level systems provide the greatest source of social control. Social control variables in conventional activities can minimize youth gang participation and delinquency. Schools appear to more effectively control for negative group socialization than community programs. The evaluation of group interaction in community programs can reveal important implications for social control strategies to reduce negative peer networking. In order to consistently provide prosocial youth activities, schools and community organizations should assess and evaluate key social control strategies. It seems imperative for schools and community organizations to invest their time, money, and efforts in "going the extra mile," given the detrimental consequences of offering hit-or-miss approaches.

References

Baker, M.L., Sigmon, J.N., and Nugent, M.E. (2001). Truancy Reduction: Keeping Students in School. U.S. Department of Justice, Office of Juvenile Justice and Delinquency Prevention, NCJ 184176. Washington, D.C.

Bureau of Justice Statistics, U.S. Department of Justice. (1989). Weapons In School. NCJ-116498. Washington, D.C.

Ekland-Olson, S. (1982). Deviance, social control, and social networks. *Research in Law, Deviance, and Social Control*, 4, 271–299.

Esbensen, F.A., Huizinga, D., and Weiher, A.W. (1993). Gang and non-gang youth: differences in explanatory factors. *Journal of Contemporary Criminal Justice*, 9(2), 94–116.

Goldstein, A.P. and Huff, C.R. (1993). *The Gang Intervention Handbook.* Champaign, IL: Research Press.

Keenan, K., Loeber, R., Zhang, Q., Stouthemer-Loeber, M., and Van Kammen, W.B. (1995). The influence of deviant peers on the development of boys' disruptive and delinquent behavior: A temporal analysis. *Development and Psychopathy,* 7: 715–726.

Longres, J.F. (1990). *Human Behavior in the Social Environment.* Itasca, IL: F.E. Peacock.

McDaniel, T.R. (1994). A back-to-basics approach to classroom discipline. *The Clearing House,* 67(5): 254–256.

Nuttal, E.V. and Kalesnik, J. (1987). Personal violence in the schools: the role of the school counselor. *Journal of Counseling and Development,* 65: 372–375.

Stern, D. (1992). Structure and spontaneity: teaching with the student at risk. *English Journal,* 81(6): 49–55.

Texas State Penal Code (1996). *Texas Criminal Law and Motor Vehicle Handbook.* Longwood, FL: Gould.

van Gigch, J.P. (1991). *System Design Modeling and Metamodeling.* New York: Plenum.

Ward, D.A., Carter, D.J., and Perrin, R.D. (1994). *Social Deviance: Being, Behaving, and Branding.* Boston, MA: Allyn and Bacon.

Part II Conclusion

DISCUSSION QUESTIONS FOR PART II

1. In Chapter 4, Sims introduces a brief discussion of the various theories used to explain juvenile delinquency. With which theories do you most agree? Why?

2. Kakar (see Chapter 5) argues that until recently very little attention has been given to girls and delinquency. According to this author, what type of crimes do girls commit? What explanations are given by Kakar for these behaviors?

3. In Chapter 6, Holsinger discusses the need for gender-specific approaches to treating female delinquents. What recommendations does the author make about the type of programs needed for the female delinquent? Why is it important to recognize that the same type of programs that might work with male delinquents might not work with female delinquents?

4. What is the extent and nature of child abuse and neglect in the U.S. today (see Chapter 7 by Chandler Ford)? How does Chandler Ford link child abuse or maltreatment to delinquency?

5. What is the major purpose of the research conducted by Harter and Watkins in Chapter 8? Discuss their major findings.

Part III

THE EXTENT AND NATURE OF JUVENILE DELINQUENCY

The next four chapters address several key issues currently considered to be hot topic issues in juvenile delinquency. There continues to exist a percpeption that juvenile "superpredators" are wreaking havoc on American society. Miller-Potter et al. attempt to dispel this perception in Chapter 9. Crews points out in Chapter 10 that gang activity is not restricted to urban youth in his examination of the rise of surburban "Preppie Gangs." Girard, in Chapter 11, tackles the ever-increasing problem of cybercrime among juveniles, and Laufersweiler-Dwyer and Dwyer provide an overview of the literature on juvenile stalkers in Chapter 12.

Chapter 9

The Myth of the Juvenile Superpredator

Karen S. Miller, Gary W. Potter, and Victor E. Kappeler

"It is very, very hard for me, knowing I'm going to spend the rest of my life in prison. I'm still a kid, and kids make mistakes. We can learn from our mistakes. But nowadays, all people want to do is send a kid to prison and throw away the key."
— S.S., 16-year-old sentenced to life without parole.

— From *The Beat Within* (1998), a writing and conversation program (and weekly magazine) for detainees in juvenile halls

9.1 Introduction

In the 1990s, a media frenzy fueled by the predictions of a few social scientists led to great concern over an allegedly developing group of juvenile *superpredators* (Glassner, 1999; Steinberg, 1999). These super-predators were described before a U.S. Senate Subcommittee on Youth Violence by James Wootton, president of the Safe Streets Coalition, as committing brutal crimes against other people, operating with no remorse, and being the ultimate urban nightmare (Federal Document Clearing House, 1997). Wootton also warned the senate subcommittee that the number of these superpredators is growing. This testimony was based largely on a 1995 report for the Council on Crime in America, a conservative special-interest group, and the work of Professor John DiIulio. This report advised of a "ticking time bomb" that would explode as the juvenile population of the United States increased over the next few years (Butterfield, 1996, p. 6). DiIulio (1995, p. 15) predicted that the "large population of 7- to 10-year-old boys now growing up fatherless, godless, and jobless; and surrounded by deviant, delinquent, and criminal adults; will give rise to a new and more vicious group of predatory street criminals than the nation has ever known." DiIulio's predictions were widely disseminated by both print- and broadcast-media outlets (Schiraldi and Keppelhoff, 1997).

The media, always receptive to sensationalized crime news, reported these indicators of a juvenile crime wave with great enthusiasm. Both television and print media widely disseminated reports of violent kids committing horrifying acts of depredation. In his book *Culture of Fear* (1999), Professor Barry Glassner described the results of studies that monitored the presentation of children and images of juvenile crime by the media. This research demonstrated that 40 percent of the stories about children in major newspapers and 48 percent of stories about children on the three major networks' evening newscasts were reports of crime and violence. Glassner argued that these types of stories contained two common elements: They depict juveniles and their crimes using vivid language, and they report a dramatic increase in juvenile crime.

These media presentations depicted juveniles as violent, aimless predators who acted with total disregard for human life. With each new school shooting, the news media included a timeline of school shootings occurring across the country, implying both a pervasiveness of this conduct and a level of incidence out of all proportion to the relatively infrequent events they were reporting. The locations of these shootings became etched into our collective psyche. West Paducah, KY, Jonesboro, AK, and Littleton, CO, are often referred to as proof of increasing rates of senseless violence among America's youth. Unfortunately, the reports did not include the numbers of inner-city children who died at their schools in the 1980s. Nor did they reveal the number of children killed by their parents or guardians, and the number of children who die of gun injuries across the country every day. In short, these reports were indicative of a highly selective presentation of facts by journalists, designed to both frighten and titillate the general populace.

The fear generated because of these sensationalized reports soon led politicians to take up the cause of protecting our society from its children. Arizona's assistant attorney general reported:

> A tidal wave of juvenile crime and violence is gathering force. Criminologists have variously called it an epidemic, a ticking time bomb, the calm before the storm, and a long descent into night …

> Over the next 10 years, the population of 14 to 17 year olds will grow 23 percent, and the current generation of juveniles has already brought us the worst juvenile crime rates in recorded history …

> The increasing juvenile murder rate coincides with an increase in "stranger murders" … now four times as common as killings by family members (Thomas, 1995).

Similar politically inspired affirmations of impending doom were repeated at various hearings in support of new legislation across the country. The arguments in support of reformed juvenile delinquency statutes consistently utilized similar language, often referring to juveniles as superpredators (Schiraldi and Keppelhoff, 1997; Torbet et al., 1996).

In the throes of a media-created frenzy and public fear of violent youngsters, states revamped their systems of juvenile justice. Between 1992 and 1997, 44 states and the District of Columbia passed laws that make it easier for juveniles to be tried as adults (Sickmund, 1998). These included 28 states that expanded their lists of crimes eligible for waiver. The changes in laws were not grounded in reality; they were not based on reflective deliberation, but as Franklin Zimring reports, they "bordered on hysteria — not just public hysteria. It was official hysteria" (cited in Mills, 1999, p. 3). This hysteria and its products were largely based on the projections of a small number of crime control advocates in the social science community who had misread, misinterpreted, and misunderstood a hypothetical prediction that suggested an unprecedented, yet hypothetical, increase in the number of juveniles in the United States. Unfortunately for the children subsequently processed under these new provisions, this huge increase is not happening. According to the Office of Juvenile Justice and

Delinquency Prevention (1999), the juvenile population is increasing at a far slower rate than any other segment of the population. It is anticipated that the juvenile population will increase only 8 percent by 2015. Perhaps the real issue for the omniscient criminologists who made these claims is the fact that the number of minority juveniles is expected to have the highest increase, with the number of black juveniles increasing 19 percent, Native American juveniles 17 percent, and Hispanic juveniles 59 percent (OJJDP, 1999). If so, it would seem that the same type of racial stereotyping that so discredits the work of the criminal justice system has now spread to a handful of crime-control-oriented scholars.

As a result of sweeping legislative changes, juvenile court proceedings increasingly resembled those of adult criminal offenders. The reports of various criminologists and the media's highly sensationalized reports of juvenile violence greatly impacted the response by politicians. The changes in legislation essentially began a "war" on juveniles.

9.2 The Myth of a Juvenile Crime Wave

The media and "official" hysteria surrounding juvenile crime in the 1990s was based on the belief of an increase in the rates of violent crimes committed by juveniles. This raises an interesting question: Are juveniles committing more acts of violence? The key issue here may not be the amount of crime but the status of being a juvenile. One very simple fact is that juvenile crime is related to age. When there are more juveniles in a society there will be more juvenile crime. It is this "obvious" truth that is the foundation for the hysteria surrounding superpredators and the juvenile crime wave (Barkan, 1997, p.78; Lotke, 1997). Because crime peaks at ages 17 or 18 and declines from that point forward, more juveniles implies more crime (Barkan, 1997). What is important, however, is that higher numbers do not imply higher rates.

The violent-crime arrest rate for juveniles increased 62 percent between 1980 and 1994 (OJJDP, 2002a). During the same period, the rate for adults in their 30s increased 74 percent. These increases in arrests may be related more to police practices than actual increases in certain types of behavior (Kappeler et al., 2000). Since 1994, however, the arrest rate of juveniles for violent offenses has decreased 44 percent while decreasing 19 percent for adults in their 30s (OJJDP, 2002a). To broaden the perspective, between 1980 and 2000, the Violent Crime Index arrest rates for juveniles aged 15 to 17 decreased 10 percent. On the other hand, the rates for adults increased: 12 percent for those of ages 25 to 29, 31 percent for ages 30 to 34, 44 percent for ages 35 to 39, 38 percent for ages 40 to 44, and 8 percent for ages 60 to 64. Despite the increase in index-crime arrests among the elderly, we have not seen Congressional action, media exposes, or bad social science suggesting that special provisions should be enacted for handling geriatric predators. Perhaps the implementation of draconian practices in dealing with juveniles, despite their declining rates of crime, has more to do with their lack of political and economic power than their potential for criminality.

Arrest data are, of course, only indicative of police practices. The Uniform Crime Report, which provides arrest statistics, is the most common source of this information. While those data certainly have flaws, they indicate that the proportion of violent crimes cleared by an arrest of a juvenile has decreased in recent years (Snyder, 1998). In fact, other sources indicate that overall crime rates have decreased since 1975. Bernard (1999) reviewed the National Crime Victim Survey data to examine changes in juvenile crime rates. He found that in 1975 there were 128.9 personal crimes for every 1000 people. By 1992, this had decreased by 30 percent. Bernard (1999) concluded that the proportion of offenses being committed by young people has changed little since the late 1970s.

Another area necessary for review in determining if a juvenile crime wave occurred in the 1990s is self-report surveys. These surveys are designed to determine the true rates of delinquency through questionnaires and interviews administered to juveniles. Although these instruments have some methodological problems, they are widely accepted as reliable instruments for measuring crime incidence and trends (Hindelang, Hirschi and Weis, 1981; Huizinga and Elliot, 1981; Rouse, Kozel and Richards, 1985). One of the strengths of self-report studies relates to the information provided about the dark figure of crime, that which is not known to the police. Although these surveys indicate that a majority of delinquency is not reflected in official statistics, they do not show an increase in the overall rates of delinquency. The University of Michigan's Institute for Social Research conducts a Monitoring the Future study and has large samples for the years 1975 to 1996. The information provided by this survey has not indicated an increased tendency toward criminality among juveniles (Bachman and O'Malley, 1998). Other studies have also indicated that delinquency rates have stabilized since 1975 (Sarri, 1983; Osgood et al., 1989)

The exception to this stable rate of juvenile crime is homicide, which increased during the 1980s and early 1990s. In the 10-year period between 1984 and 1994, the juvenile homicide rate nearly tripled. It is important to note, however, that even with this increase, only 16 percent of all homicides involved juvenile offenders (Sickmund et al., 1997; Kappeler et al., 2000). This percentage decreased to 12 by 1998 (UCR, 1999) and to 9 by 2000 (OJJDP, 2002b). The initial increase in homicides by juveniles was associated with the use of firearms. During the same 10-year period, non-gun-related homicides by juveniles declined.

After peaking in 1994, juvenile homicide rates have continued to decline; in fact, the rate has dropped 40 percent (Snyder, 1998). Whereas the superpredator was presented as a national crisis, data indicate that juvenile homicide is not a national problem. It is heavily concentrated in urban areas. Sickmund et al. (1997) report that 84 percent of counties in the United States reported no juvenile homicide offenders in 1995, 10 percent reported only 1; however, five counties accounted for 25 percent of all known juvenile homicide offenders. These counties contain the cities of Chicago, Detroit, Houston, Los Angeles, and New York.

In addition to the predictions surrounding the increase in the juvenile population leading to a mass of superpredators and the increase in juvenile homicides in the early 1990s, reports of school violence also impacted the myth of a juvenile crime wave. The school shootings in Pearl, MS, in 1997, West Paducah, KY, in 1997, Springfield, OR, in 1998, Jonesboro, AK, in 1998, and Littleton, CO, in 1999 fueled the hysteria surrounding the dangerousness of juveniles. The media coverage of the events created the impression that public schools are dangerous places where children and employees are no longer safe. It is often reported that children are afraid to attend school and are even arming themselves out of fear of being victimized at school (Arnette and Walsleben,1998). Upon reviewing the data on school violence, it appears that this fear a media creation, not what is occurring in schools.

Homicide at school is a rare event. The probability of a child dying as a result of school-based violence is less than one in a million. In 1992 and 1993, less than 1 percent of the children murdered were killed on school property (federal departments of education and justice, 1998, pp. 8–9). The National School Safety Center reports that out of approximately 52 million students in the United States, about 24 are killed each year at school. That stands in stark contrast to the estimated 2000 to 3000 children murdered each year by their parents (Males, 1998). Surveys conducted by the federal departments of education and justice indicate that schools are not more dangerous now than in the past. By comparing responses between different years, the survey indicates that schools have experienced very little change in the level of victimizations (Chandler et al., 1998).

The data clearly indicate that children are safer at school than at home, and they are certainly safer in school than in prison. There is no evidence that levels of violence have increased on school grounds in recent years (Chandler et al., 1998; NCJA, 1998). Only about 14 percent of students report being victimized by violence at school annually, and it is highly likely that a majority of these victimizations were nonserious (Chandler et al., 1998). Property crimes are also relatively rare on school property, with about 11 percent of students reporting this form of victimization in 1995 (Chandler et al., 1998). A survey of school principals indicated that only about 10 percent of public schools experienced a crime of violence in 1996–1997 (NCJA, 1998). In short, there is no evidence to indicate an increase in the level of violence being committed at schools in the United States. There is certainly no evidence to warrant the types of policies that have been implemented as a result of the tragedies that have occurred at schools.

The alleged juvenile crime wave that occurred in the 1990s was short, lasted only 2 years, was based largely on official statistics, and did not impact most of the country. It is important to put into perspective the types of crimes for which children are being victimized by draconian policies. In 2000, law enforcement agencies across the country arrested 1,200 juveniles for homicide, the same number who were arrested for "suspicion" (OJJDP, 2002c). Compare this to 154,700 arrests for curfew and loitering, 159,400 for liquor law violations, and 142,000 for running away from home. According to self-report surveys, the most common offenses committed by juveniles continue to be truancy, drinking alcohol, using a false ID, shoplifting or larceny under $5, fighting, using marijuana, and damaging the property of others (Siegel and Senna, 2000). These numbers hardly indicate a juvenile crime wave. They do not support the efforts of lawmakers to arrest and incarcerate more juveniles than ever before.

9.3 Getting Tough on Juvenile Crime: Reconstructing the Juvenile Justice System

Since the first U.S. juvenile court was established in Illinois in 1899, our society has treated juveniles charged with criminal behavior very differently from adult offenders. The juvenile court system was based on the doctrine of *parens patriae*, or the idea that all adjudications of juveniles should be in the best interest of the child. To facilitate this, juvenile court judges had great discretion in deciding the appropriate disposition of each case. Only the most serious offenders were transferred to the adult court system, and the role of the court was one of protection and rehabilitation of wayward youth (Siegel and Senna, 2000). The language was different from that of adult court. Juveniles, for example, were adjudicated as delinquents, and adults were convicted as criminals. The proceedings were closed to the public, records were expunged upon reaching the age of majority, and names of offenders were not released.

The recent trend to alter the notions of protection and rehabilitation has led to an abundance of legislative and judicial changes impacting the way our society treats delinquent youth (Torbet et al., 1996). These transformations have included lowering age limits for waiver to adult court, the addition of crimes to the lists of offenses for which waiver could occur, and adding provisions that facilitate transfer of a juvenile with a prior record to adult court (Torbet et al., 1996). The process of judicial waiver offers the state many more sentencing options. The juvenile justice system has no death penalty and no life without the possibility of parole. Judicial waivers offer the state more punitive measures and ignore the idea of rehabilitation. This recent trend of juvenile waivers is anathema to the origins of the juvenile justice system. Prior to the 1920s only 10 states permitted juveniles to be tried in adult courts. In the United States today, all 50 states have laws permitting the transfer of juveniles to adult court (Siegel and Senna, 2000, p. 668). In 22 states and the District of Columbia, at least one provision exists for transferring juveniles to adult court for which no minimum age is specified (Sickmund, 1998). It is important to note that a large majority of these changes occurred during the 1990s in the period of the superpredator epidemic (Torbet and Szymanski, 1998).

In addition to making it easier to waive children to the adult court system, the juvenile court system is shifting toward a more punitive approach. In recent years, a dramatic shift in disposition practices has occurred across the United States. These changes involve blending adult and juvenile punishments, relying on mandatory sentences, and extending juvenile court jurisdiction beyond the age of 21 (Torbet et al., 1996). These developments are not only leading to harsher sentences than ever before, but they have limited judicial discretion.

One very troubling change in the juvenile justice system is the new way that information regarding juvenile offenders is handled. Originally, the juvenile court operated to protect the child. One protective measure taken by the court was the sealing of information that could adversely impact the child in adulthood. In the wake of the superpredator epidemic, 42 states now allow the release of an accused juvenile's name, address, and photograph to the media or general public under certain circumstances; 30 states allow or require juvenile hearings to be open to the public in some circumstances; and several states have opened juvenile court records to school officials (Torbet and Szymanski, 1998). Although these measures are designed to protect the public, little attention has been paid to the consequences this will have on affected children. It is doubtful that these new procedures will aid rehabilitation and reintegration into the community.

Feeling that society is not protected enough from its children, some politicians are seeking even harsher policies. The Violent and Repeat Juvenile Offender Act was introduced in the U.S. Senate in 1997 but has not yet been signed into law. This legislation would allow juveniles arrested for both crimes and status offenses to be housed with adults; make juvenile felony arrest records available to colleges, even if the child was not convicted; require up to a 6-month expulsion of teens from school for regular tobacco use; and offer federal prosecutors sole and nonreviewable discretion to try juveniles as adults for all felonies (Schiraldi and Soler, 1998; Kappeler et al., 2000). If made law, this legislation would reverse decades of effort designed to remove children from adult jails, end the hopes of rehabilitation and reintegration, and ensure continued criminality into adulthood. This legislation appears to be based on the chilling notion that children who are charged with criminal offenses in the United States are not worthy of rehabilitation. The provisions in this legislation would almost guarantee an increase in crime in the coming decades. Criminologists have long recognized that restricting legitimate opportunities results in more crime, not less (Messner and Rosenfeld, 1997).

A survey conducted by Schiraldi and Soler (1998) indicates that the public does not support many of the harsh provisions of the Violent and Repeat Juvenile Offender Act. This lack of public support is likely a reason the legislation has not passed. The bill is, however, indicative of the trend to sway the juvenile justice system away from protecting children toward punishing them. The punishment directed at children under this legislation would not be childhood-specific, it would last their entire lives. The provisions of this legislation would create a permanent underclass of uneducated and unemployable people pre-disposed to criminality. Essentially, these lawmakers are calling for the socialization and education of our nation's children to be handled by incarcerated adult criminals and the corrections officials. It is doubtful that many children could grow to be responsible, law-abiding, and properly socialized adults under these conditions.

9.4 Lock 'Em Up and Throw Away the Key: Juveniles in Custody

The superpredator hysteria of the 1990s and the subsequent legislative changes have directly impacted the number of juvenile offenders who are formally processed, tried as adults, and incarcerated. Between 1989 and 1998 the number of formally processed delinquency cases increased 62 percent with formal cases now outnumbering informal cases by 32 percent (OJJDP, 2001a). The number of delinquency cases waived to criminal court also increased during this period. Waivers for public order offenses increased 19 percent and waivers for person offenses increased 28 percent (OJJDP, 2001b). The trend of formally charging and waiving a child to criminal court increased the percentage of juveniles formally detained. Between 1989 and 1998 there was a 63 percent increase in incarceration rates for person offenses, a 55 percent increase in incarceration rates for drug offenses, and a 44 percent increase in detentions for public order cases (OJJDP, 2001c).

The overall rates of juvenile detentions have increased for all races, but the increases for minority youth have been the most dramatic. The number of African American youth detained in correctional facilities increased from 13,752 in 1979 to 43,268 in 1995. The proportion of African Americans housed in juvenile detention facilities grew from 28 percent in 1979 to 40 percent in 1995 (Kappeler et al., 2000; Smith, 1998). Hispanic youth also experienced an increase in detention rates; during the same period this population increased from 9 to 17 percent. In 1998, children were detained at some point in the process in 17 percent of delinquency cases involving white juveniles, 23 percent involving African American youth, and 21 percent involving other races (OJJDP, 2001d). In short, between 1989 and 1998 there were 66,100 more children held in detention in the United States for various offenses (OJJDP, 2001e).

As previously discussed, many politicians and even some social scientists would point to these statistics as proof of a wave of violent crimes committed by juvenile superpredators. It is important, however, to review the types of crimes these children have been charged with and incarcerated for. According to Smith (1998), in 1995 only 31 percent of males and 13 percent of females were detained for violent offenses. Although it is beyond the scope of this chapter to pursue the defining elements of a violent offense, it is clear that the majority of juveniles housed in correctional facilities are not superpredators. Instead, children are being held for being truant, incorrigible, violating drug codes, damaging property, and committing acts of vandalism.

Between 1989 and 1998, a substantial increase in the number of adjudicated juveniles placed on probation or committed to a residential facility occurred. The number of delinquency cases that resulted in formal probation increased 73 percent and residential placement increased 37 percent (OJJDP, 2001c). According to Smith (1998), the proportion of juveniles placed in secure public facilities increased from 68 to 86 percent between 1979 and 1995. At the same time, legislatures across the country cut funding for education, treatment, and rehabilitation for these facilities (Kappeler et al., 2000). This negatively impacts the potential for successful reintegration upon release. Complicating the problem, many of these facilities are operating above their capacities. The overcrowded conditions in these secure residential facilities has worsened in recent years. In 1983, 36 percent of these facilities were overcrowded, but by 1995, 68 percent suffered from overcrowding conditions (Smith, 1998). In short, more children are being incarcerated, are housed in overcrowded facilities that are operating under budget, and are not receiving the level of treatment and care required. This offers little hope for the rehabilitation of these children. This increased rate of incarceration has occurred during a time when self-report surveys indicate a stabilization or reduction in delinquency rates, and official statistics report a decrease in the number of arrests of children (see OJJDP 2002a and c; Bachman and O'Malley, 1996).

9.5 Treating Juveniles as Adults: Does It Work?

As we have previously discussed, one result of the superpredator hysteria of the 1990s was the increased ability of states to waive juvenile offenders to criminal court and charge them as adults. A primary goal of these policies is deterrence, which can be general or specific. General deterrence is the idea that juveniles who are tempted to violate the law will be discouraged from doing so when they witness the tough sanctions experienced by law violators. Specific deterrence involves attempting to decrease recidivism through harsh punishment. The American system of justice is based on the notion of deterrence, and studies have examined the deterrent effect of treating juvenile offenders as adults.

Jensen and Metsger (1994) examined this practice in Idaho. In 1981, Idaho implemented a law that mandated that all offenders between 14 and 18 year old charged with murder, attempted murder, robbery, forcible rape, and aggravated assault be tried in adult court. The state eliminated waiver hearings, automatically transferring these children to criminal court. The researchers reviewed the rates of these offenses and compared them to the rates in Montana and Wyoming. Their analysis indicates that rates of serious juvenile crime increased in the poststatute period only in Idaho. The comparison states both reported decreases in these offenses. In short, Jensen and Metsger (1994, p. 102) concluded: "that the Idaho legislative waiver did not have a deterrent effect on violent juvenile crime."

In an examination of the deterrent effect of treating juveniles as adults in New York, Singer and McDowall (1988) reached similar conclusions. Their research examined the effect of one of the most punitive juvenile statutes in the United States. The law passed in New York in 1978 allowed juveniles as young as 14 to be waived to criminal court for a multitude of offenses. The media was utilized to inform young people of this new legislation. The researchers utilized an interrupted time-series design to assess the general deterrent impact of provisions in the legislation and concluded that the number of juveniles held in secure confinement had increased, so they had not affected the level of juvenile crime in the state.

Another way to test the effectiveness of treating juveniles as adults is to compare recidivism rates of children adjudicated as delinquents to similar cases in which the child was waived to adult court. A study of this nature was conducted in Florida by Bishop et al. (1996). The researchers employed several indicators of recidivism and matched cases based on the seriousness of offense, number of charges, number and severity of prior offenses, age, race, and gender. They concluded that juveniles who had been waived to adult criminal court were more likely to be rearrested; they were rearrested sooner and a greater proportion of the rearrests were for felony offenses (Bishop et al., 1996). In a similar study conducted by Fagan (1995, p. 254), comparing New York and New Jersey, the researcher concluded: "rather than affording greater community protection, the higher recidivism rates for the criminal court cohort suggest that public safety was, in fact, compromised by adjudication in the criminal court." Clearly, this research indicates that treating juvenile offenders as adults will only negatively affect crime rates in the coming years.

Although more research is needed in this area, the studies that have been conducted clearly indicate that treating juveniles as adults is not in the best interest of the child or society. It fails as both a general and specific deterrent, and it has other negative consequences. Juveniles tried and incarcerated as adults carry the lifelong stigma of being a convicted felon, and they lose many rights, including the right to vote. Their ability to participate in the labor market upon release is negatively impacted (Fagan, 1995), and an overwhelming majority of adult prisons do not offer counseling to juveniles housed in those facilities (Reddington and Sapp, 1997). Perhaps most important, young people in prison are the most vulnerable to physical and sexual victimization by older and more experienced inmates (Reddington and Sapp, 1997).

Again, in placing juveniles in these environments, society is allowing convicted adult criminals to be responsible for the socialization of a growing body of young people. According to differential association theory, this exposes these juveniles to values and attitudes that are not conducive to a law-abiding lifestyle upon release (Sutherland and Cressey, 1970). The research of Eisikovits and Baizerman (1983) supports this idea. They surveyed juveniles incarcerated in an adult facility and concluded that "youth who are committed to prison for violent acts become violent youth. Violence becomes a way of life" (p. 16). Glassner (1999, p. 74) indicates that "the youths themselves point out that in adult prisons kids learn to survive by intimidating others. They tend to lose whatever respect they had for authorities and for themselves. Once released, they engage in more and worse crimes." Clearly, these are not the results lawmakers had in mind when they facilitated waiving children to adult court. The preceding examples are only a few of the negative consequences of the policies that were based on the prediction of superpredators roaming our streets.

9.6 Blaming the Victims: Crime against Juveniles

The policies designed to punish juvenile offenders are ill-conceived and ineffective. These policies are based on a crime wave that evidence fails to support. It appears that politicians have failed to see the truth about juveniles and violence. The truth they have missed is that juveniles are far more likely to be victimized by violence than to commit it. The National Crime Victimization Survey (NCVS) provides data on victimization rates for juveniles and adults for all violent offenses except homicide. According to the NCVS, in 1994 juveniles aged 12 to 17 were victimized by crime at a rate nearly three times that of adults. For rape, robbery, and assault, the rate is far higher for juveniles than adults, and they are more likely to experience crime-related injuries (Sickmund, Snyder, and Poe-Yamagata, 1997).

The National Incidence Study of Child Abuse and Neglect measures the rates of various forms of abuse experienced by children in the United States. The data indicate that between 1986 and 1993, the number of children abused or neglected almost doubled (Kappeler et al., 2000). It is estimated that 2 million children were reported abused or neglected in 1994. The subsequent investigations revealed that 37 percent of the allegations were substantiated or reasonable grounds existed to suspect the abuse. This equates to hundreds of thousands of cases of children victimized every year by adults, with over 1000 children dying as a result of maltreatment (Sickmund et al., 1997, pp. 9–10). The problem of childhood victimization is clearly an area that calls for more attention. Perhaps our society would be better served if the media and politicians focused their attention on protecting children rather than fearing them.

Although child abuse is obviously a widespread and serious problem in our society, there is another area of victimization that has directly resulted from the superpredator myth, the children victimized by the policies designed to treat them as monsters. It is impossible to know the true number of children wrongfully convicted or incarcerated under these new statutes; it is, however, possible to point to some of the most egregious cases. For example, in 1998 two boys, aged 7 and 8, were arrested in Chicago for the murder of an 11-year-old girl. Under police questioning the two boys confessed. As Kappeler et al. (2000, p. 193) discuss, the boys were not read their Miranda rights because they were not in custody. It is highly unlikely that these boys understood that they were free to leave. Although the boys were eventually cleared of the crime and an adult male arrested, the public had quickly believed in their guilt.

In Jacksonville (Florida) 15-year-old Brenton Butler was charged with the murder and robbery of 64-year-old tourist Mary Ann Stephens while she and her husband walked to their hotel room. He was arrested walking near the hotel later the same day and identified by the victim's husband as the shooter. During his interrogation, Brenton claims that he was punched in the chest and called racial slurs by Michael Glover, the interviewing officer. He was only allowed to call his parents after signing a confession. At trial, Brenton was acquitted, but was haunted by statements made by prosecutors and sheriff's deputies indicating that he was "wrongfully acquitted." Eventually, Brenton's public defender found evidence of the involvement of two other men in the murder, and they have since been charged. Brenton was issued an apology by the sheriff, and he and his family are now suing the city (Schoettler and Pinkham, 2001; see also *Murder on a Sunday Morning,* HBO Undercover).

Across the country, children are being criminally charged with offenses and tried as adults. They are receiving the harshest of sentences, including life without the possibility of parole, and even the death penalty. Although these children are offered legal counsel for their hearings and trials, law enforcement officers across the country are treating them as adults from the onset of the investigation. This is clearly to the detriment of the children affected by these policies. Legal statutes across the nation protect children from purchasing cigarettes, alcohol, and pornography. Statutes do not allow those under the age of majority to enter into a legal contract, donate their organs, or serve on juries. Most importantly, they are denied voting rights. At the heart of these statutes lies their lack of maturity and ability to exercise sound judgment. Unfortunately, lawmakers assume that children are fully in control of their actions and judgments when they engage in criminal behavior. This is a horrific and illogical contradiction in the law.

9.7 Conclusion

No evidence exists to indicate that the nation is under attack by a violent body of young superpredators. The fear of young people fueled by media accounts of juvenile violence has led to the metamorphosis of our rehabilitative juvenile justice system into a punitive mini-adult system. We are treating more juveniles as adults than ever before, incarcerating them for longer periods of time and housing them with adults. This has all occurred during a time when the juvenile delinquency and crime rate has decreased. It has even occurred during a period when the arrest rate of juveniles has decreased.

Armed with stories of extreme acts of violence committed by very young children, state legislatures across the country reacted by passing tougher laws and building new facilities. One example of this phenomenon is in Illinois. The Illinois General Assembly responded to the threat of juvenile violence by allowing children as young as ten to be sent to a youth prison rather than a residential treatment facility and authorized the construction of a new facility. The construction of the facility was delayed until 1997, "by which time it became obvious that there was no need for one" (Kappeler et al., 2000, p. 194). The original intention of the facility "illustrates the risks of fashioning public policy from political outrage and demonstrates the gap between the perception of juvenile crime and its reality" (Kiernan,1999, p. 1). The experience in Illinois is indicative of the truth of the superpredator myth: "There was never more than a handful of very young kids charged with serious crimes" (Kiernan, 1999, p. 9). Fortunately, Illinois has readdressed this policy and in 1999 the state's attorney recommended that children younger than ten who are accused of crimes be handled in a way that provides intensive social services rather than detention or incarceration. This option is also available to children ages 11 and 12 ("Children's Court," 1999, p. 16).

The experience in Illinois illustrates the pattern of the superpredator myth. Fortunately, the media, lawmakers and social scientists are catching on to the fact that it was a myth. For example, the *Los Angeles Times* in 1996 published an opinion piece by University of California Law Professor Franklin Zimring who argued: "If politicians and analysts can believe in 'superpredators,' they can believe in anything" (Templeton, 1998, p. 1). Robin Templeton (1998), a journalist with Fairness and Accuracy in Reporting, published an article in *FAIR Extra* outlining the myth of the superpredator. The Office of Juvenile Justice and Delinquency Prevention published in their *Juvenile Justice Bulletin* (2000) an article titled "Challenging the Myths," in which it concluded that the superpredator argument cannot explain the increase in violent crime arrests. Even Professor DiIulio began to distance himself from his claims of savage young people running amok when he was interviewed by the *Wall Street Journal* in 1997. He argued that he favors a small-government approach, believing that churches should have responsibility for saving these "godless" children, who should not be punished into submission (see Templeton, 1998). Although this enlightenment may bode well for future juveniles processed under reformed statutes and guidelines, it does not correct the mistakes made in the 1990s. Quite simply, this nation victimized hundreds of thousands of children out of fear. Studies clearly report that juveniles tried as adults are more likely to become repeat offenders. Children are also more likely to be the victims of violence rather than its perpetrators.

In sum, superpredators are a myth. Instead of policies designed to protect our society from this mythical danger, we need policies to protect us from the unintended outcome of society's fears.

References

Arnette, J.L. and Walsleben, M.C. (1998). Combating Fear and Restoring Safety in Schools. Office of Juvenile Justice and Delinquency Prevention. Washington, D.C.

Bachman, J.G. and O'Malley, P.M. (1998). A Continuing Study of American Youth: 12th Grade Survey. Ann Arbor, MI: Institute for Social Research.

Barkan, S. (1997). *Criminology: A Sociological Understanding.* Englewood Cliffs, NJ: Prentice-Hall.

Teens Face Life in Prison before Having a Life of Their Own. (March 1998) *Beat Within.*

Bernard, T.J. (1999). Juvenile crime and the transformation of juvenile justice: is there a juvenile crime wave? *Justice Quarterly.*

Bishop, D.M., Frazier, C.E., Lanza-Kaduce, L., and Winner, L. (1996). The transfer of juveniles to criminal court: does it make a difference? *Crime and Delinquency,* 42(2), 171–191.

Butterfield, F. (January 6, 1996). Experts on Crime Warn of a Ticking Time Bomb. *The New York Times.*

Chandler, K.A., Chapman, C.D., Rand, M.R., and Taylor, B.M. (1998). Student's Reports of School Crime: 1989 and 1995. U.S. Departments of Education and Justice. Washington, D.C.

Children's Court: Back to the Future. (July 25, 1999). *Chicago Tribune,* p. 16.

Departments of Education and Justice (1998). Annual Report on School Safety, Washington, D.C.

DiIulio, J. (1995). Arresting ideas: tougher law enforcement is driving down urban crime. *Policy Review,* Fall: p. 15.

Eisikovits, Z. and Baizerman, M. (1983). "Doin' time." Violent youth in a juvenile facility and in an adult prison. *Journal of Offender Counseling Services and Rehabilitation,* 6(5).

Fagan, J. (1995). Separating the men from the boys. In Howell, J.C., Krisberg, B., Hawkins, J.D., and Wilson, J.J. (Eds.), *Serious, Violent, and Chronic Juvenile Offenders: A Sourcebook.* Thousand Oaks, CA: Sage.

Federal Document Clearing House (April 16, 1997). Remarks made by James Wootton before the subcommittee on Youth Violence of the Senate Committee on the Judiciary.

Glassner, B. (1999). *The Culture of Fear: Why Americans Are Afraid of the Wrong Things.* New York: Basic Books.

Hindelang, M.J., Hirschi, T., and Weis, J.G. (1981). *Measuring Delinquency.* Beverly Hills, CA: Sage.

Huizinga, D.H. and Elliot, D.S. (1981). A Longitudinal Study of Drug Use and Delinquency in a National Sample of Youth: An Assessment of Causal Order. A report of the National Youth Survey. Boulder, CO: Behavioral Research Institute.

Jensen, E.L. and Metsger, L.K. (1994). A test of the deterrent effect of legislative waiver on violent juvenile crime. *Crime and Delinquency*, 40(1), 96–104.

Kappeler, V., Blumberg, M., and Potter, G. (2000). *The Mythology of Crime and Criminal Justice*, 3rd ed. Prospect Heights, IL: Waveland.

Kiernan, L. (August 30, 1999). Doors shut on one theory as youth prison opens. *Chicago Tribune*, pp. 1, 9.

Lotke, E. (1997). Youth homicide: keeping perspective on how many children kill. *Valparaiso Law Review*, 31, 2.

Males, M.A. (April 20, 1998). Five myths and why adults believe they are true. *The New York Times*.

Messner, S. and Rosenfeld, R. (1997). *Crime and the American Dream*, 2nd ed. Belmont, CA: Wadsworth.

Mills, S. (May 2, 1999). On the record: interview with Frank Zimring. *Chicago Tribune*, Sec. 2, p. 3.

National Criminal Justice Association. (1998). School crime not increasing, according to surveys. *Justice Bulletin*, 18(4).

Office of Juvenile Justice and Delinquency Prevention. (September, 1999). *OJJDP Statistical Briefing Book*. Online. http://ojjdp.ncjrs.org/ojstatbb/html/qa092.html.

Office of Juvenile Justice and Delinquency Prevention. (February, 2000). Challenging the Myths. Juvenile Justice Bulletin. Juvenile Justice: A Century of Change. http://www.ncjrs.org/html/ojjdp/jjbul2000_02_2/chal3html.

Office of Juvenile Justice and Delinquency Prevention. (May, 2001a). *OJJDP Statistical Briefing Book*. Online: http://ojjdp.ncjrs.org/ojstatbb/html/qa188.html.

Office of Juvenile Justice and Delinquency Prevention. (May, 2001b). *OJJDP Statistical Briefing Book*. Online: http://ojjdp.ncjrs.org/ojstatbb/html/qa191.html.

Office of Juvenile Justice and Delinquency Prevention. (May, 2001c). *OJJDP Statistical Briefing Book*. Online: http://ojjdp.ncjrs.org/ojstatbb/html/qa185.html.

Office of Juvenile Justice and Delinquency Prevention. (May, 2001d). *OJJDP Statistical Briefing Book*. Online: http://ojjdp.ncjrs.org/ojstatbb/html/qa187.html.

Office of Juvenile Justice and Delinquency Prevention. (May, 2001e). *OJJDP Statistical Briefing Book*. Online: http://ojjdp.ncjrs.org/ojstatbb/html/qa184.html.

Office of Juvenile Justice and Delinquency Prevention. (May, 2001f). *OJJDP Statistical Briefing Book*. Online: http://ojjdp.ncjrs.org/ojstatbb/html/qa190.html.

Office of Juvenile Justice and Delinquency Prevention. (January, 2002a). *OJJDP Statistical Briefing Book*. Online: http://ojjdp.ncjrs.org/ojstatbb/html/qa276.html.

Office of Juvenile Justice and Delinquency Prevention. (January, 2002b). *OJJDP Statistical Briefing Book*. Online: http://ojjdp.ncjrs.org/ojstatbb/html/qa251.html.

Office of Juvenile Justice and Delinquency Prevention. (January, 2002c). *OJJDP Statistical Briefing Book*. Online: http://ojjdp.ncjrs.org/ojstatbb/html/qa250.html.

Osgood, D.W., O'Malley, P., Bachman, J., and Johnston, L. (1989). Time trends and age trends in arrests and self-reported illegal behavior. *Criminology* 27: 389–417.

Reddington, F.P. and Sapp, A.D. (1997). Juveniles in adult prisons: problems and prospects. *Journal of Crime and Justice*, 20(2).

Rouse, B.A., Kozel, N.J., and Richards L.G. (1985). Self-Report Methods of Estimating Drug Use: Meeting Current Challenges to Validity. NIDA Research Monograph 57. Rockville, MD: National Institute on Drug Abuse.

Sarri, R. (1983). Gender issues in juvenile justice. *Crime and Delinquency*, 29: 381–397.

Schiraldi, V., and Soler, M. (1998). The will of the propel? The public's opinion of he violent and repeat juvenile offender act of 1997. *Crime and Delinquency*, 44(4), 590–601.

Schiraldi, V. and Keppelhoff, M. (June 5, 1997). As juvenile crime drops, experts backpedal and public policy pays the price. *Star Tribune*, p. 24A.

Schoettler, J. and Pinkham, P. (February 22, 2001). 2 men linked to murder after teen acquitted. Jacksonville officials apologize to 16 year old. *Florida Times-Union*.

Sickmund, M., Snyder, H.N., and Poe-Yamagata, E. (1997). Juvenile Offenders and Victims: 1997 Update on Violence. Office of Juvenile Justice and Delinquency Prevention: Washington, D.C.

Sickmund, M. (1998). States that changed their transfer laws, 1992–1997. Adapted from Torbet, P. and Szymanski, L. State Legislative Responses to Violent Juvenile Crime: 1996–1997 Update. Washington, D.C.: Office of Juvenile Justice and Delinquency Prevention. *OJJDP Statistical Briefing Book*. Online: http://ojjdp.ncjrs.org/ojstatbb/html/qa091.html.

Siegel, L. and Senna, J. (2000). *Juvenile Delinquency: Theory, Practice, and Law*, 7th ed. Belmont, CA: Wadsworth/Thomson Learning.

Singer, S. and McDowall, D. (1988). Criminalizing delinquency: the deterrent effects of the New York juvenile offender law. *Law and Society Review*, 22, 521–535.

Smith, B. (1998). Children in custody: 20-year trends in juvenile detention, correctional, and shelter facilities. *Crime and Delinquency*, 44(4), 526–543.

Snyder, H. (1998). Juvenile Arrests 1997. Office of Juvenile Justice and Delinquency Prevention. Washington, D.C.

Steinberg, J. (1999). Ideas and Trends: Storm Warning; the Coming Crime Wave is Washed Up. *The New York Times*, Sec. 4, p. 4.

Sutherland, E. H. and Cressey, D. J. (1970). *Criminology*. Philadelphia, PA: Lippincott.

Templeton, R. (1998). Superscapegoating. *FAIR Extra!* January–February 1998.

Thomas, C. (1995). Private Adult Correctional Facility Census, 8th ed. Gainesville, FL. Private Corrections Project. University of Florida.

Torbet, P., Gable, R., Hurst, H., IV, Montgomery, I., Szymanski, L., and Thomas, D. (1996). State Responses to Serious and Violent Juvenile Crime. Office of Juvenile Justice and Delinquency Prevention. Washington, D.C.

Torbet, P. and Szymanski, L. (1998). State Legislative Responses to Violent Juvenile Crime: 1996–1997 Update. Office of Juvenile Justice and Delinquency Prevention. Washington, D,C.

Uniform Crime Reports (1999). *Crime in the United States 1998*. Washington, D.C.: Federal Bureau of Investigation.

Chapter 10

The Emerging Problem of Preppie Gangs in America

Gordon A. Crews, Johnny R. Purvis, and Mary Hjelm

10.1 Introduction

One might initially believe that a gang is a gang is a gang, no matter whether the setting is rural, urban, suburban, or inner city. One might also assume that a gang is a gang is a gang if it is composed of poverty-stricken adolescents from families that have a history of conflicts with law enforcement and not youngsters from affluent, gated communities. In reality, all might be labeled a gang, but there is a vast difference in the culture of traditional gangs (e.g., inner-city street or rural drug-associated) and *Preppie Gangs*, that latter of which are composed of teens from rich, gated communities or upper-middle-class backgrounds. Although law enforcement and community agencies often regard traditional gangs as security threats, most do not classify Preppie Gangs as such, which is extremely erroneous and very symbolic of how deceptively rich Preppie Gangs can present themselves within a community.

The purpose of this chapter is to define and explore the cultural inner workings and structure of these relatively new, nontraditional gangs, which the authors have labeled Preppie Gangs. This term was first used by Dr. Johnny Purvis in the early 1990s to describe a new phenomenon that he discovered while working with law enforcement throughout the Southeast.

10.2 Characteristics of Preppie Gangs

In the early 1990s, youth from affluent, upscale communities began organizing their own "gangs." As with traditional street gangs, it is virtually impossible to determine how many of these types of gangs exist or the extent of their membership. Preppie Gangs generally consist of adolescents from homes considered upper class or upper-middle class in socioeconomic status. This obviously includes the inherent social and political influence that wealth and social status often bring.

As a general rule, adolescents are very intelligent and creative. This does not necessarily mean that Preppie Gangs have developed "street smarts," as a high level of intelligence is not necessarily synonymous with an individual's ability to use one's intellect in a resourceful manner. Nor does it allow for ample reasoning in analyzing the consequences of a person's decisions prior to taking action. This combination of wealth and intelligence is probably the primary reason for their arrogant attitude toward traditional authority and their perceived intellectual superiority over peers of lower economic status.

A myriad of issues surround the phenomena of Preppie Gangs that actually reinforce and encourage the influence of a Preppie Gang. The following is a list of just a few of these related issues:

■ Money
■ Mobility of members within a local community
■ Secrecy between members
■ Intimidation of community residents and leadership
■ Community indifference to gang problems and reluctance to label groups as gangs
■ Intelligence and creativity of preadolescents or adolescents
■ Rebellious attitude and conduct of preadolescents or adolescents in general
■ Lack of adequate community strategies to respond to gangs

In spite of these perceptions, Preppie Gang members are fundamentally "cowards." This does not mean that they cannot be harmful, especially when they believe they have a definite advantage over an individual due to their numbers or when drugs or alcohol provide them with the courage to physically confront another. It also does not mean that Preppie Gang members will not take advantage of another when they have an advantage, vandalize property, or secretly scrawl graffiti on private or public property.

10.3 Types of Preppie Gangs and Member Characteristics

When one begins to investigate the phenomenon of Preppie Gangs, a lack of empirical research will immediately be discovered. Reasons for this are discussed throughout this chapter. Crews and Montgomery (2001) have identified four primary types of Preppie Gangs that should be identified and monitored by parents, educators, community leaders, and law enforcement: "wannabes," delinquent or criminal gangs, ideological gangs, and occult-based/goth groups.

The first type of Preppie Gang, for lack of a better term, is the *wannabe*. The use of this term is very controversial. Some experts believe there is no such thing as a wannabe. They will argue that wannabes are *gonnabes*. An adolescent who thinks he or she is a gang member is in fact one. They desire gang involvement because of the perceived benefits of members' lifestyle and enjoy "playing" as members. However, many of these individuals are no more than imitators. They simply have the strong desire to be "cool" and identify with what they think is the "real thing" or maybe with popular rap music groups they enjoy. In addition, gang lifestyle, dress, and activity have become "fashionable" in American society. Music videos offer an extremely unrealistic view of the money, glamour, and excitement that can come from gang membership. Regrettably, this term is frequently used by officials who try to argue that there are no "pure" gangs (i.e., gangs that are exhibiting what most would see as the traditional view of street gangs) in their area. Such a use gives a false sense of security to a community and minimizes the possible usefulness of the term.

The authors would also agree that labeling youths in this fashion is often insulting and can result in increased antisocial behavior as they try to prove to be what they claim to be. The problem lies in finding an appropriate term to use in describing those upper-middle- to upper-class, generally white, adolescents who mimic the style, dress, and activities of traditional street gangs. In some instances, the use of the term *wannabe* may actually be proper and accurate. This is especially true when it comes to an examination of Preppie Gangs. Inherent in the phenomenon of Preppie Gangs is many, if not all, of the typical characteristics that come to mind when trying to define what a wannabe would be. The vast majority of Preppie Gang members are trying to be, or be perceived as, tough and potentially violent characters. This chosen identity is just that, *chosen*. It is not one that is required for survival, nor learned in their environment. Therefore, this might mean that their behavior can be changed with less drastic crime control types of actions (such as the redirection of interests as opposed to incarceration).

Although research related to Preppie Gangs is sparse at best, there is enough reliable evidence to draw a picture of the typical member as one who is from an affluent neighborhood, comfortable home, and prosperous family. The inner-city life experience is far from what these adolescents are accustomed. Therefore, what they think they know comes from television, magazines, or movies, obviously giving them a very distorted view of gang activities and the gang lifestyle.

Preppie Gangs are real gangs, but the wannabe participant is generally weak in nature except when in a group of like-minded peers. Alcohol and other drugs often enhance this pseudo bravado, especially when the wannabe feels he or she has an advantage over others of lower social or physical status. These youth actually have no idea of what they are doing, but they attempt to mimic what they "think" they are supposed to be doing to be "part of the scene." However, these youth look for things and people with which they can identify and often make the wrong choices.

This is not to say that these individuals should not be considered dangerous. In actuality, this type of individual can sometimes be the most dangerous. Because adolescents have no experience of how to commit a criminal act or react to a violent situation, they often overreact. This overreaction leads to being overly violent or attacking an adult or another juvenile out of fear or panic. Also, their lack of experience often results in their getting hurt or hurting others because they do not know how to handle firearms or illegal narcotics. There are numerous examples of upper-class adolescents accidentally shooting one another while playing with handguns or overdosing while experimenting with drug mixtures of which they have heard.

10.3.1 Delinquent or Criminal Gangs

A second type of Preppie Gang is more closely aligned with the traditional criminal or street gang. It must be remembered that the term *gang* has no fixed legal meaning. Furthermore, definitions of gangs have varied over time, according to the perceptions and interests of the definer, academic fashions, and the changing reality of the gang in society. Once even defined as *play groups* (Crews, 1997), the term *gang* has increasingly taken on pejorative connotations. In the most recent views, gangs are considered more pathological than functional organizations, so that the term has become almost synonymous with violent and criminal groups. Therefore, inherent in most recent definitions of a gang is the idea of criminality in which a group is considered a gang if it has a formal organizational structure, identifiable leadership, identifiable territory, and recurrent interaction and is engaged in serious or violent criminal behavior.

This view of gangs as pathological and criminal underlies many of the initiatives that states and local jurisdictions have adopted over the past decade. Because many acts of juvenile delinquency are committed by groups, the notion of juvenile delinquency has become closely associated with gang activity. Still, without an accepted definition to rely on, state and local jurisdictions have tended to develop their own ideas of what constitutes gang activity.

Less urban areas are no longer safe from the infiltration of gangs and gang violence. Although some of the gangs are branches of quintessential gangs such as Los Angeles' Crips and Bloods, most gangs in midsize or smaller cities both originate locally and form more "grassroots efforts." That is to say, the gangs that exist consist of local juveniles who have never traveled, much less lived, outside the towns in which they were born. In these less urban areas, as discussed repeatedly in this chapter, the members are white, middle-to-upper class, and of higher intelligence. Their criminal activities range, as the more traditional black and Hispanic street gangs, from robbery, burglary, grand theft, vehicle theft, and receiving stolen property to assault, battery, drive-by shootings, and murder. They are also becoming involved in the entrepreneurship of narcotics, designer drugs, heroin, methamphetamine, and marijuana. Frighteningly, some Preppie Gangs' arsenals also include large caches of high-caliber handguns, shotguns, and automatic weapons as their crimes become increasingly violent.

10.3.2 Ideological Gangs

Adolescents are drawn into hate and supremacist groups and so-called "patriot groups" as well as other ideologically based groups through many avenues. The two most popular avenues in the 21st century appear to be through carefully placed and developed propaganda disseminated by the Internet and through racist-type "white power" music. Although the majority of the youth drawn to these groups are those in the working class or lower-middle class, those from comfortable homes and wealthy families are just as susceptible to messages of hate. Also, recent examinations of hate crimes and racist group activity seem to reflect the rise of ethnic nationalism with young people of all races more willing than they have been in decades past to accept separation of the races (Crews, 2001).

Amid huge social changes in American society over the last few decades, a type of suburban youth has emerged that could shape the future of hate groups and hate crime in the United States. These suburban youth possess a potentially dangerous combination of resources and abilities; this, combined with motivation, can be positive or negative. A growing number of white youths, in many cases impacted by extreme social chaos around them, are altering the state of American views of hate. This is evidence that many youths come to the white supremacist movement through no particular personal hardship. They are involved in the movement or activity simply because they *choose* to be, not because they are *pushed* to be. Again, it would be a mistake to state that all racist youth come from deprived circumstances. Although many are alienated, upper-middle class kids who are led to neo-Nazism through hate Web sites or other propaganda, are a far larger and apparently growing number of white supremacist youth who have emerged from American socioeconomic discontent, whether they personally experience it or not (Crews and Tipton, 2000).

As would be expected, it is virtually impossible to determine the true extent of Preppie Gangs and members involved in these types of belief systems in the United States. The only way to get a feel for the extent of the problem is to examine the number of active groups in a particular area of the country. Fortunately, a number of organizations in the country help monitor the activities of those groups that can be identified and evaluate new groups as they emerge. The Internet has allowed extensive dissemination of information from and about these groups and does offer some information about the extent of these groups. The difficulty comes in trying to determine whether a group is actually as large as may be portrayed on the Web or is merely one individual with a modem connection trying to represent himself as a group.

There are a myriad of groups that Preppies relate to, but a few of the major types are the Klan, Neo-Nazis, Skinheads, Christian Identity, and Separatists. As would be expected, many of these groups are migratory in nature and not affiliated with a primary national group, which makes maintaining estimates of their memberships difficult. Most would agree that Skinheads are such an organization. Christian Identity describes a religion that is fundamentally racist and anti-Semitic, stating that whites are the only true people of God. Separatist groups are organizations whose ideologies include tenets of racially based hatred insisting that the races should be kept separate. Another category, called "Other," includes groups and publishing houses endorsing a hodgepodge of hate doctrines (Crews and Montgomery, 2001).

The expression of hate comes in all shapes, sizes, and colors. Preppies are exposed to it through home radios, televisions, and computers in their bedrooms through their family's Internet connection. Still, it is most available in the printed word. The American hate movement has long relied on the power of the printed word to proclaim the superiority of one race or group of people over another. From glossy full-color magazines to crude homemade tabloids, hate literature has played an important role in recruitment, movement building, and the wide dissemination of conspiracy theories.

It has been said that *love* brings people together, but others would argue that it is actually *hatred* of a common enemy that brings them the closest. Hate works. It brings people together, it sells merchandise, it can develop a subculture, and it can provide impetus or energy for a struggling movement. It should, then, be no wonder why it is so popular among Preppies.

10.3.3 Occult-Based/Goth Groups

A final group of Preppie Gangs and gang members are those involved in alternative belief systems and/or lifestyles (Crews, 2003). These groups are being seen on high-school campuses, in shopping malls, and in neighborhoods. This has increasingly caused parents, educators, and law enforcement to deal with adolescents who are self-labeling themselves as goths, Preppies, vampires, wiccans, witches, warlocks, magicians, and satanists. Many of these groups have been around for a very long time, but now they are more prevalent and more comfortable expressing their lifestyles to others. No matter how it manifests itself, the vast majority of belief systems or practices in this type will be occult based.

A central question asked by law enforcement, parents, and educators is whether juveniles involved in such alternative practices are truly a gang. Individuals involved in these activities do travel and gather in groups. They are often seen together in coffee shops, bookstores, school yards, and even cemeteries. Those familiar with traditional gangs will even add that they do exhibit many of the traits that would be expected of a gang, such as wearing of the same colors, dress, and hairstyles. They also may share a similar race and gender, and display uniform behaviors (Crews, 2003).

In actuality, no evidence exists of any typical gang activities involving these juveniles. Initiation to become a member in the groups or wearing of black or unusual clothing is a preference, not a requirement. Some alternative groups have been labeled as gangs because of criminal activity of some of the individuals. Those involved would argue that such criminal behavior is derived from individual choice, not through a leadership structure that requires it. The vast majority of the evidence here supports the idea that any violence is usually caused by some mental instability in an individual, not by simply being part of one of these groups (Crews and Montgomery, 2001).

10.4 Demonstrated Behaviors within a Psychosocial Perspective

From a psychosocial perspective, involvement in a Preppie Gang often provides a number of critical ego and personal enhancing opportunities that are attractive to an adolescent. Preppie Gang affiliation and membership often provide youngsters an opportunity to become involved in a cause that gives them a false sense of being a part of something "bigger than themselves" and, as a result, to take revenge upon those individuals whom they believe have wronged them or treated them unjustly. As a result of their membership, they often acquire a veneer of respect because of their affiliation with a gang and the manner of dress, grooming, jewelry, and slang unique to their circle. Membership also enhances and reinforces their ego and self-esteem and provides them an incentive to continue to engage in more illegal activities. For those who feel alienated from others, membership can fill an actual or perceived void in their lives because of family issues, loss of a loved one, rejection from a peer group, loss of a caregiver, failure of a relationship, not being selected to a particular group or organization, or failure to receive a coveted award or honor.

For those who are seeking fulfillment of something other than socioeconomic success, membership can signify an opportunity to achieve "immortality" due to possible alternative belief systems linked with some occult gangs. This opportunity gives them a chance to fulfill a fantasy regarding activities (e.g., role-playing games, card games, ritual participation fantasies) and to have an outlet to employ and expand their artistic expression and creative talents through the study and "creation" of an alternative belief system. Through these opportunities, they are often able to release tension and anger by committing violent acts owing to the support and encouragement of members in their gang. They can also intimidate and manipulate others because of their reputation, dress and grooming habits, beliefs, connections within the community, political affiliation, and obligations owed to their families by influential individuals and groups. Of course, because Preppie Gangs are indeed gangs, regardless of location, and gangs provide members with the same opportunities for antisocial behavior as do the more traditional gangs. They have to defy, challenge, or ignore society's traditional values and expectations, and they have to provide themselves with additional financial resources to supplement and justify their lifestyle and to secure weapons and ammunition (Crews and Montgomery, 2001).

10.5 Possible Causes of Involvement

There are probably as many causes of involvement in Preppie Gangs as there are Preppie Gang members. Also, there are volumes written dealing with the causes of gang involvement. The purpose of Figure 10.1 is to give a brief overview of the role that the traditional ideas of gang involvement causation play in the development of Preppie Gangs. Figure 10.1 appears to be complex but, in reality, is quite simple. Basically, all youth go through a period of adolescence with its multitude of biological and psychological changes. Exacerbating these changes are vast amounts of emotional and social stress as juveniles try to deal with these changes while moving from childhood to young adulthood.

Elkind (1982) discusses the impact of several concepts that can be relevant to an examination of Preppie Gangs: "adolescent egocentrism," "identity work," "imaginary audiences," and the "invincibility myth," all of which are part of the reasons for Preppie Gang involvement.

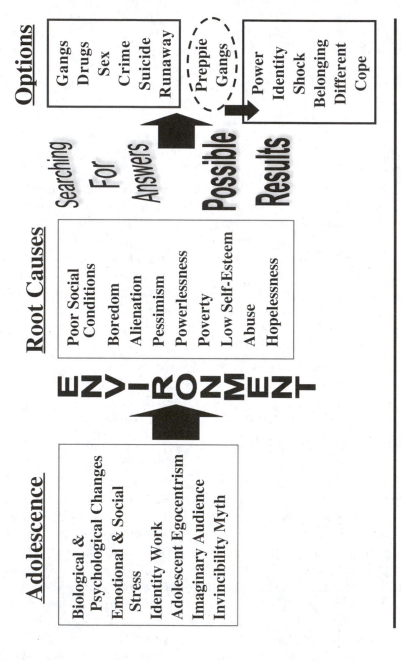

Figure 10.1 Diagram of root causes vs. options. (Developed by Gordon A. Crews.)

These concepts are very relevant when examining youth from comfortable homes in wealthy neighborhoods. Whereas youth in the inner city have to grow up fast to survive, these youth can be children who want the world and expect to receive it. Most are used to having things handed to them; therefore, patience is not a common trait. They do not have to worry about survival, but they do have to worry about what is expected of them by others. With wealth comes certain societal expectations. These individuals are expected to be productive citizens, go to college, and follow in their parents' footsteps.

Adolescent egocentrism (Elkind, 1982) describes the ego of the typical adolescent and its desire for immediate gratification, unrealistic expectations, and immature cognitive reasoning patterns. Typically, juveniles want what they want when they want it. They will most often be unwilling or unable to understand another's perspective of why something may not be immediately possible. Because their thought patterns are not fully developed, they often cannot think through a situation to see all of the possible outcomes of a particular behavior. This idea, combined with youth who are used to not having to wait or have not had to develop this understanding, begins to have its own synergic effect.

Identity work (Elkind, 1982) is typically described as being part of the process as well. Some would argue that juveniles change identities, reinventing themselves over and over again (one semester a juvenile may be the jock, the next, an intellectual). It allows the child to experiment with different objects in order to discover his or her interests, abilities, and strengths. Most of this reinventing of oneself occurs in the child's mind and in front of an imaginary audience. That is to say, most adolescents view themselves in the world as if they were constantly on stage being judged by others, especially their peers. This manifests itself in the child being overly concerned with appearance and the actions of others, particularly, the fear of being embarrassed by parents.

Finally, the characteristic that is of most concern is the *invincibility myth* (Elkind, 1982). Most young people feel they are invincible and that nothing bad will ever happen to them (e.g., they will never become pregnant, they will never acquire AIDS, they will never get killed driving under the influence). They know the dangers that are possible but feel like they are either too smart or too lucky for those things to ever happen to them. The problem is that they do happen to them. Therefore, what one is basically left with is the fear that no one understands youth. No one has ever lived the life that this individual has, nor has anyone had to face the same choices. They see themselves as completely unique individuals who are being forced into molds that do not match anything that they want to be. They, in turn, begin to hate the very thing that most would love to possess: money and power.

The problem is that many do not wish to follow the unwritten expectations of those in the wealthy class; therefore, they rebel against parental and societal expectations. Yet, while these changes are occurring, the child is placed in an environment that may also produce boredom, alienation, and powerlessness, resulting in low self-esteem and hopelessness. These juveniles will naturally begin searching for answers in drugs, sex, crime, suicide, or running away. Not surprisingly, there are many options from which they can choose, and gangs and gang activity provide one. For many of the Preppies, though, that is not enough. They want more.

Very often, the something more that they want is found in becoming involved in such behaviors as goth, satanism, or the occult in general. The inherent behaviors, activities, and clothing are extremely attractive to these Preppies. When they start wearing all black clothes and silver jewelry, dyeing their hair purple, and carrying around the "Satanic Bible," they see an immediate reaction. The immediate resulting shock provides a false sense of power over others. They see that they can have their own identity, and find others with whom to identify. As with most juvenile behavior, this identification is most often simply a way to cope and, therefore, involvement in a Preppie Gang is just another way to cope.

10.6 Attitude of Parents/Guardians

Sociologically speaking, the majority of Preppie Gang members come from affluent, white family households located in neighborhoods that are generally perceived as being safe for families to live and rear their children. The community will generally offer a variety of recreational opportunities for youngsters, and the "breadwinners" are members of professions that require at least a bachelor's degree. Another characteristic of Preppie Gang neighborhoods is that there seems to be an endless parade of houses for sale due to the professional mobility of the residents. But because of the nature of the culture from which Preppie Gangs emerge, parental or guardian attitudes towards gang membership may range from "my child would never do such a thing" to "we gave that kid everything and this is the thanks we get." There may also be expressions of frustration and anger; embarrassment and humiliation; blaming the other parent, school officials, or law enforcement; and condemning print and electronic media, movies, and video games.

Because of their anger, frustration, embarrassment, or need for denial, many Preppies' parents or guardians are very difficult, if not impossible, for officials to work with as partners in any attempt to help their youngsters. In many situations, this is further compounded by parents and guardians deflecting responsibility from themselves and providing excuses for their youngsters rather than recognizing and accepting their youngsters' role in choosing their particular mode of conduct and lifestyle. Yet it is vital that they realize and accept the fact that help is necessary for both their children and themselves to explore any possibility of enabling their children to become positive and productive members of society.

Those who intend to work with the Preppies' parents and guardians must recognize that these people often live in extreme anxiety and fear of their own children. Preppie Gang members' parents and guardians' anxieties can be generated by the fear that their youngsters might physically harm them, commit suicide, reject them as their parents or guardians, destroy their property, harm a family pet, commit a crime, or become addicted to drugs or alcohol. Any one of the preceding fears, let alone a combination of them, can contribute to the improper and unacceptable choices parents or guardians make in their own conduct and the manner in which they seek help for both themselves and their children.

10.7 Reactions of the Law Enforcement Community

The reaction of law enforcement to Preppie Gangs can range from ambivalence, condemnation, and frustration to hope that the issue will go away or failure to recognize, know, or understand the issues involved. Actually, any one of the preceding reactions can reinforce Preppie Gang membership and their corresponding activities within a community. And any of the preceding reactions can compound the issue when it comes to preventing, intervening, and suppressing Preppie Gang activity. For example, if the law enforcement community comes down too hard on Preppies, their parents and guardians will accuse officials of overreacting and singling out their children unjustly. On the other hand, if the law enforcement community overlooks Preppie activity, traditional gang members and other juvenile law violators will declare that Preppies are given preferential treatment, whereas they are being discriminated against. At the same time, Preppie Gang behavior is reinforced because they suffer no consequences for their behavior. Additionally, Preppies often believe they intimidate law enforcement and community officials when they are not held account-able for their behavior, which only further compounds the entire issue.

As a result of the influence of the parents, many law enforcement officials will choose not to arrest and charge the youngsters but only retain the Preppies until their parents or guardians can pick them up at the police station or sheriff's office. This often results in the young-sters' being given a verbal warning to remind them of their conduct and the law or ordinance they violated. In many situations, the responses of the law enforcement community to Preppie Gang mem-bers' activity might be to simply take the youngsters home because they know the children's families, talk to youngsters in a positive manner in an effort to secure their cooperation, or avoid offending them because of the political and economic influence of their families. They may call the youngsters' parents or guardians in an effort to inform them of their children's activities and to secure their cooperation in holding their children accountable, and then tell Preppies that they are "being cut some slack this time" and are not being formally charged. Although probably expedient, this is seldom the right way to handle Preppie Gang members who already believe that they are not account-able for breaking the law.

Unfortunately, there will be times when law enforcement commu-nity officials know, in a given situation, that their integrity will be challenged in ways that may cost them their careers, create much more paperwork and documentation than usual, and subject them to much more scrutiny by their superiors and other influential citizens within the community. All of this is due to a family's ability to secure the best legal representation for their child and the media coverage often achieved when a prominent family's child is arrested and charged with a civil or criminal offense.

10.8 Games Played with the Law Enforcement Community

For many reasons, Preppies can be very frustrating for the authorities that supervise and monitor youngsters. Preppies are very intelligent, creative, and highly skilled in manipulating people's situations. Law enforcement officials must always remember when working with Preppies to do so in such a manner that Preppies do not believe that they have an advantage because of their alibi, intellectual ability, craftiness with both words and body language, or mob conduct.

Some of the creative body language and word games that Preppies employ when confronted by members of the law enforcement community include being disingenuous ("I didn't know that was against the law" or "I didn't know that I was supposed to do that" or "She said it was OK, and so I assumed it was OK"); aggressive ("Everybody else does it, so why single me out?"); begging or bargaining ("Please give me another chance, and I will never do it again" or "Just let get out of here and you will never see me here again" or "Don't tell my mom and dad, because they'll kill me" or "I know the chief, and he knows my mom and dad"); denial ("I don't know how that got there" or "This isn't my car" or "What did I do wrong?"). They will also employ distraction (smiling, flirting, or rearranging clothing to expose more skin), claim to know the officer or something about him or her, or deny everything and admit to nothing.

10.9 Dangers of Preppie Gangs

Most youngsters who become involved in Preppie Gangs grow out of such behavior and associations; however, many youngsters are not so fortunate. Some of the dangers connected with even short-term Preppie Gang membership are drug addiction, alcoholism, sexually transmitted diseases, a criminal record, being drawn into a cult or a deviant group, family conflict, jail or prison time, ruined physical health, lack of ambition or motivation, severe mental and emotional problems, financial drain on themselves and their families and society, suicide, self-mutilation, mistrust of others, lying, difficulty in distinguishing reality from fantasy, drop in academic performance, and loss of friends.

10.9.1 Criminal Activity Associated with Preppie Gangs

There is much debate (Howell and Lynch, 2000) over the extent and characteristics of Preppie Gang–related criminal and antisocial behavior. The common perception is that these groups are plaguing and terrorizing neighborhoods and schools with often bizarre and violent crimes. Because many of the types of activities that these gang members are involved in deal with alternative beliefs and practices, the general public is inclined to believe almost anything, no matter how unusual it is.

As with all discussions about youth involved in alternative belief systems and practices, there is much debate over the extent of the associated criminal activity that they may be involved. Criminal activity commonly associated by the general public with alternative beliefs and practices involves crimes such as abuse of children, kidnapping, murder, and even human sacrifice. Fortunately, there is not much evidence, if any, to support these associations. It is true that crime occurs in connection with some of these activities, but it is much more mundane and commonplace than most would expect (Crews et al., 1996).

Although most people involved in such alternative practices would argue that those involved in any type of criminal behavior are not true practitioners, some crime does in fact occur. Vandalism, trespassing on private property, and desecration of and thefts from churches and cemeteries do occasionally involve some practitioners. These crimes are most often committed by individuals or gangs that may be trying to explore "evil" by practicing what they believe is an alternative belief system. Some of these individuals or groups do go as far as animal mutilations, suicides, and even murder; fortunately, most are very isolated incidents that can be explained by a myriad of factors, not just by the alternative behavior involvement (Crews and Montgomery, 2001).

10.9.2 Preppie Gang-Related Violence

This subsection presents a few examples of recent incidents that have occurred involving adolescents who fit the Preppie Gang definition as offered in this chapter. Inherent in such an application of a definition upon individuals is the fact that this effort is very subjective in nature.

In January 2003, "goths, freaks, and vampires" made headlines in the media which reported the following:

- Growing incidents of business owners with problems of juveniles "hanging out," but different from ever before in their actions and appearance
- Problems with large groups of gothic juveniles hanging out in malls and shopping center parking lots
- Juveniles claiming they are responsible for panhandling, vandalism, assaults, theft, and scaring away customers
- Juveniles claiming they are doing nothing wrong, just talking, shopping, and eating

Primarily, Preppie Gangs as well as gang activity manifest when upper-middle- and upper-class adolescents grow bored by their lifestyles or rebel against those they feel are forcing them into becoming something they do not wish to become. Becoming involved in an alternative lifestyle is a very effective way to shock parents and other adults. It is also a way to express one's individualism or idea of self. What is most interesting about this aspect of the problem is that the juveniles do not have to actually commit an act to cause problems; they just simply need to be seen.

Here is a "snapshot" of the February 1999 "Trench Coat Mafia" incident:

- Columbine High School (Littleton, CO)
- Eric Harris (18) and Dylan Klebold (17)
- A teacher and 12 students killed, 23 wounded
- Teased by "jocks," called "faggots"
- Into Marilyn Manson, video games Doom and Quake
- Hero: Adolf Hitler
- Reportedly into Nazi occultism
- Targeted athletes and minorities

Some would argue that a classic example of possible Preppie Gang activity would be the tragic Columbine school shooting. Although Harris and Klebold did not follow the typical dress code of a Preppie Gang member, they did fit the financial profile. Both came from upper-class families and had the same resources and advantages of other "Preps." For example, they built their bombs in the garage of one parent's estimated $3 million home and drove a brand-new BMW to the school to carry out their plan. They also set up and maintained a Web site detailing their beliefs and interests. This is an example of resources, intelligence, and motivation making a very dangerous combination.

Another example is an incident that occurred in Burlington, Wisconsin, in March 1998, called "Revenge of the Goths":

- Five "goth" juveniles (15 to 16 years of age) planned to kill 15 to 20 people
- Targets included disliked teachers and classmates, the principal, and the "cowboys"
- Caught planning to steal guns, attacking a school, and listing those to kill
- All described as "outcasts"

These juveniles were all from middle- to upper-class homes. Although considered outcasts by others, they were of the same socioeconomic level as those by whom they were being abused. Their behavior is just another example of how such juveniles use their skills and the access they have because of their social class.

Finally, the Tavares, Florida, "vampires" of April 1996 are outlined here:

- Rod Ferrell (17), sentenced to die for beating to death a Florida couple
- Leader of vampire coven from Murray, Kentucky
- Drank blood and indulged in sex rites and animal mutilation rituals
- In November 1996 on a trip to Florida, Ferrell inducted Heather Wendorf (15) and talked his group into killing her parents
- All were described as "outcasts"

The "Vampire Murders," as they eventually became known, are a good example of how the social classes can intermingle. Even though Ferrell, the cult leader, was a member of a lower class, he was able to draw members from other social classes. Heather Wendorf, a recruited member and former acquaintance, came from a very prosperous family and was typical of an adolescent who wanted more from her life than what she felt she was getting. Joining Ferrell's clan gave her the excitement she felt she needed.

These examples demonstrate the variety of activities of what could be labeled Preppie Gangs or of gang members. Unfortunately, some readers may use examples such as these to argue that there is a national epidemic of such behavior. Also, due to the bizarre nature of many of these examples, many will try to generate panic and hysteria in the general public. These individuals may be law enforcement types who wish to share what they believe is accurate information and believe that people will only take action if they are scared enough to move. These individuals may be members of the clergy who feel that behavior such as this is a sign of Satan's existence in the world and must be stopped at any cost. Alternatively, these individuals may be consultants or so-called experts who realize that the larger the problem, the more in demand they are.

10.10 Preppie Gang Migration

As with traditional gangs, migration of individuals is a suspected primary factor in the growth of number of Preppie Gangs in small towns and rural counties across the United States (Crews and Montgomery, 2001).

This perception, as well as the resulting fear, is confirmed by law enforcement and governmental reports. Not surprisingly, most task force and federal reports supporting this idea are at odds with empirically based studies. However, most of the evidence used in local reports of gang problems is anecdotal at best. Recent studies conclude that migrant gang members have less of an impact on the proliferation of gangs than previously believed. For the general public, common perceptions — misperceptions actually — are the cornerstone of what they believe causes gangs or ganglike activity in their neighborhoods. The impact of this is obvious: What they believe the problem to be, and its causes, will dictate the solutions they propose and enact.

Obviously, some migration does occur but, in reality, only to a small extent. Many false common perceptions about gang migration exacerbate the problem, such as that proliferation is directly related to gang migration, that it increases violence by existing gangs, that it is directly related to the increase of gangs in rural areas, and that gangs spread directly through family migration. Because of such misperceptions, it may be difficult for many to believe that migration actually plays a very minor role in overall growth of gangs and ganglike behavior. Most movement of gang members can be attributed to normal residential relocations. This is in stark contrast to the belief that member recruitment, drug market expansion, and fleeing from law enforcement are the primary reasons for movement of gang members in the United States (Crews and Montgomery, 2001). Ironically, most law enforcement agencies, although supporting the idea of gang migration, will (when asked) still describe their gang problem as homegrown with locals involved.

Although research dealing with Preppie Gangs is minimal, empirical studies (Crews and Montgomery, 2001) find the following when it comes to discussing the impact migration has on gangs and gang activity in general:

- Gang migration only minimally affects gang proliferation.
- Indigenous gangs and groups are most often found to be the primary cause of gang problems.
- Most gangs or groups have no outside connections with national groups.
- No convincing evidence exists that metropolitan gangs or groups are branching out to new markets.
- Most gangs and groups originate from neighborhood conflicts influenced by popular culture rather than big-city connections.

Such findings about the lack of impact of gang member migration on current problems allows one to look beyond these standard explanations and seek alternative reasons. This search for alternative explanations led the authors to ask: If not actually because of migration of individuals, how then do gangs spread? Is it possible that the sheer idea or concept of what a gang or gang member is can have that effect? That is, can one choose a totally different lifestyle based simply upon information they receive instead of actually living it?

10.10.1 Member Migration vs. Concept Migration

Debate rages over the idea of gang migration and its impact on the increasing number of gangs, gang members, and gang activity plaguing many American communities. The authors propose, however, that gang member migration has a very small impact on the growing problem of gang activity in the United States.

Most traditional gangs do not have the skills or knowledge to move to other communities in which they would feel out of place and have no base from which to initiate their new gang efforts. Also, there is a big difference between name association and structural links; just because a gang or group claims affiliation with a national group does not mean they actually are connected. Therefore, gang migration cannot be a major culprit in the current problems. This is not to say that the concept of migration is not a factor in the problems being experienced in the country. However, it may be only the migration of concepts and ideas, and not the migration of individuals.

In reality, the authors believe that actual gang member migration does not cause the spread of gang and gang-type activity, but the migration of the idea or concept of how to act is instead the cause. Most often what is seen occurring in neighborhoods is adolescents mimicking what they see others doing, not gang members moving in and creating new gangs. Proponents of the idea that music, movies, books, and the media influence adolescents in general would agree with this opinion. When it comes to Preppie Gangs, this idea of how concepts and ideas can mutate and manifest themselves is quite persuasive (see Figure 10.2).

Although still debatable, most authorities would agree that the vast majority of traditional criminal-type street gangs remain in inner-city areas. One can also safely point out, as shown in Subsection 10.3.1, the general characteristics of typical gang members and gang activity (i.e., black or Hispanic, male, adherence to a street gang structure,

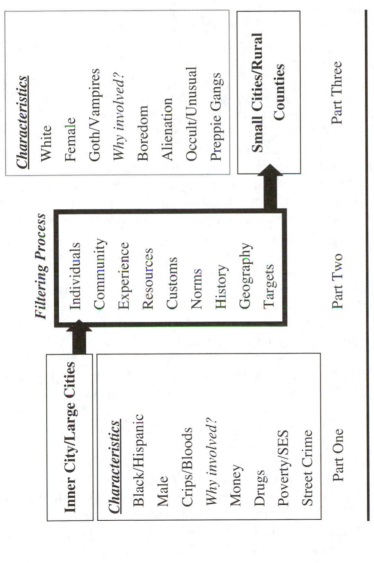

Individual Vs. Concept Migration

Inner City/Large Cities

Characteristics

Black/Hispanic

Male

Crips/Bloods

Why involved?

Money

Drugs

Poverty/SES

Street Crime

Part One

Filtering Process

Individuals

Community

Experience

Resources

Customs

Norms

History

Geography

Targets

Part Two

Characteristics

White

Female

Goth/Vampires

Why involved?

Boredom

Alienation

Occult/Unusual

Preppie Gangs

Small Cities/Rural Counties

Part Three

Figure 10.2   Diagram of member migration vs. concept migration. (Developed by Gordon A. Crews.)

desire for money and drugs, impoverishment, etc.). The reasons for involvement generally focus on the desire for wealth, drugs, recognition, or respect.

Those who would argue for the idea of gang member migration as a causative factor would say that these individuals simply relocate to other areas and continue their gang behavior of recruiting local youth, thereby initiating gangs and ganglike behavior in small cities and rural counties. In reality, ideas and concepts go through a filtering process (Subsection 10.3.2) as they migrate across the country into local suburban neighborhoods long before actual gang members migrate to these new areas. These individuals are in upper-middle- and upper-class neighborhoods, far from the inner city, have their own customs and norms, and will not react as individuals who have lived in gang-filled areas. Even the geography is different, with different resources for new gang members to utilize and different targets for them to attack. Therefore, these migrating ideas and concepts are manifesting themselves in myriad ways (Subsection 10.3.3). In the last several decades, an increasing number of upper-class white youths have become involved in gang-like behavior, not true, traditional, street gang behavior but a mutated version of it.

The mutated version is characterized by an interest in matters such as the occult, satanism, vampirism, and other exotic philosophies (including Preppie Gang involvement). They exhibit typical gang-like behavior, but their belief system, reasons for involvement, and desired outcomes are completely different. Unlike traditional street gangs, their motivation appears to center around boredom, feelings of alienation, and a desire for excitement. Additionally, many feel as if they are being pressured into an undesired career or education path by their parents.

Instead of a desire for money or material goods — they generally already have them — Preppies are more interested in the excitement and shock value derived from their behavior. They cannot relate to having to fight for survival on city streets, so they attempt to carry out these types of behavior (extortion, assaults, and drive-bys) in a bedroom community environment. This sets up an extremely difficult situation for law enforcement, educators, and parents, who simply do not know what to do. Although these concerned individuals are probably familiar with the criminal activity of traditional street gangs (i.e., robbery, drugs, and thefts), they are not familiar with the criminal activities of Preppie Gangs (i.e., cemetery desecrations, trespassing, and dress violations). Their types of behavior are very different and therefore need very different approaches in trying to deal with this problem.

10.11 Responsible and Accountable

On the surface, it may look as though Preppies have everything. Often, the majority of teens who become involved in Preppie Gangs will survive such social experimentation and mature into responsible and productive citizens. However, some children are lost forever as potentially productive and talented individuals owing to the choices they make and actions they take while involved with such groups.

Holding Preppies responsible and accountable requires consistent enforcement among and between agencies and the law enforcement community. Consistency is a very important element in not only holding youngsters accountable but also in sending a message regarding the behavioral norms to which a community holds all its citizens accountable. There are several ways in which the law enforcement community can achieve this goal (Crews, 2003):

1. Consistently enforce all laws, community ordinances, restraining orders, and judicial rulings for everyone in the community.
2. Provide routine and consistent vehicle and foot patrols for monitoring and surveillance of areas in which Preppies and other gangs hang out.
3. Establish and consistently practice positive verbal interaction with Preppies.
4. Be consistent about interviewing Preppies and related groups regarding their concerns and questions, and their expectations concerning behavior.
5. Establish and maintain a coherent and comprehensive strategy for establishing reasonable suspicion as a prerequisite for probable cause prior to interviewing and searching Preppies and their possessions.
6. Contact parents and guardians regarding their children's conduct and the possible consequences related to their behavior.
7. Consistently monitor areas of the community where Preppies and other youngsters hang out.
8. Constantly collect and catalog information (e.g., tattoos, style of clothing, color of clothing, jewelry, hairstyle and color, music, body language, and slang).
9. Consistently respond to and follow up on complaints by home owners, merchants, landowners, family members, and others.
10. Accurately document information obtained by individual law enforcement personnel.

Holding Preppies responsible and accountable is often very costly for law enforcement personnel because of the amount of time required for surveillance and related follow-up activities. However, support of the community's judicial authorities is a critical necessity when law enforcement and other officials attempt to hold Preppies accountable for their conduct. If judicial officials do not support law enforcement, Preppies will immediately conclude that they can get away with their behavior and will be able to manipulate the entire system, continuing to play their potentially deadly games. Always remember that these youngsters are intelligent and learn very quickly how to manipulate those in power to their advantage. Most of them have had years of practice in manipulating their own parents and guardians and can transfer these skills to their immediate community and its leadership rather easily.

Preppies must learn that they are responsible and accountable for their behavior and related repercussions just as other individuals. On the other hand, they should not be held to a higher standard of expectation than others. A consistent enforcement of laws by both law enforcement and judicial officials is vital for all persons and groups, regardless of their socioeconomic and political status. Although this is a very demanding task, community leaders, law enforcement, and the judicial system must constantly strive for impartiality.

10.12 Conclusion

The intent of this chapter was to define and explore the phenomenon of Preppie Gangs in the United States. Youngsters, especially during adolescence, are going to experiment and explore in myriad ways, some good but many bad. However, it is imperative for authority figures within both the home and community to provide guidance, structure, and accountability during this vulnerable time of children's lives. Responsible adults must assist youngsters in realizing that people discipline and hold accountable those whom they are concerned about. After all, discipline does inherently mean teaching and providing structure. As many who work with juveniles would counsel, authority figures should "have one arm around children's necks and at the same time have one foot against their butts." They must demonstrate that they care about teens enough to hold them responsible and accountable for their actions. This means that authority figures will provide the parameters (e.g., policies, regulations, rules, laws, and ordinances) within which teens can safely experiment with various beliefs and out-of-the-mainstream behaviors. Preppie Gang members need to understand, however, that when they attempt to violate the parameters of society, they will be held accountable and will suffer the consequences of their actions.

References

Crews, G.A. (1997). A study of school disturbance in the United States: a twentieth century perspective, part two. *Journal of Security Administration*, 19(2), 63–74.

Crews, G.A. (2001). Shadows in the streets: policing, crime prevention, and street gangs. Deborah M. Robinson, Ed., *Policing and Crime Prevention*. pp. 127–136.

Crews, G.A. (2003). Everyday is Halloween: A goth primer for law enforcement. *Forum: Law Enforcement Execution Journal*, 3(3): 165–182.

Crews, G.A. and Montgomery, R.H., Jr. (2001). *Chasing Shadows: Confronting Juvenile Violence in America*. Upper Saddle River, NJ: Prentice Hall.

Crews, G.A., Montgomery, R.H. Jr., and Garris, W.R. (1996). *Faces of Violence in America*. Needham Heights, MA: Simon and Schuster.

Crews, G.A. and Tipton, J.A. (2000). A comparison of school vs prison security measures: too much of a good thing? *KCI On-line Journal*. Topeka, KS: Koch Crime Institute.

Elkind, D. (1982). *The Hurried Child*. Reading, MA: Addison-Wesley.

Howell, J. and Lynch, J.P. (2000). Youth Gangs in Schools. Washington, D.C.: Office of Juvenile Justice Delinquency Prevention, U.S. Department of Justice.

Chapter 11

Juvenile Cybercrime: An Exploration of Theoretical and Legal Implications

Edward J. Girard

11.1 Introduction

Cybercrime is increasing, resulting in major financial losses to businesses (Swartz, 2002). There were over 8000 computer intrusions in 1999 (Wolf, 2000), and in 2001 reported losses were estimated at approximately $455.8 million, up from $378 million in 2000. Many businesses do not quantify or report their losses, fearing bad publicity or an FBI investigation (Swartz, 2002; Wolf, 2000). Cybercrimes are divided into four categories: trespass, theft, obscenity, and violence (Wall, 1998). Cybertrespass merely involves unauthorized entry into another's computer system. This can range from an intellectual challenge to spying and terrorism. Cybertheft, similar to traditional theft, involves anything from credit-card fraud to piracy. These two categories are most common among juvenile hackers, whereas cyberobscenity and cyberviolence are mostly adult crimes (Demarco, 2001).

Computer crimes have become an increasingly popular alternative to traditional crimes committed by juveniles, but the motivation for committing such crimes may not be significantly different from traditional delinquency (Demarco, 2001; Swartz, 2002). Furthermore, on computers juveniles are able to commit crimes that are "disproportionately serious to their age" (Demarco, 2001, p. 2). For example, a 16-year-old from Miami pleaded guilty and was sentenced to 6 months in a juvenile detention facility for computer crimes that he carried out from August 23, 1999, to October 27, 1999. Using the code name "Comrade," he hacked into the Defense Threat Reduction Agency (DTRA) computer that maintains records concerning the reduction of conventional, nuclear, biological, and chemical threats to the United States and its allies. After gaining access to the computer through a router in Dulles, Virginia, he installed a backdoor to the program that allowed him access to over 3300 electronic messages and over 19 user names and passwords. Comrade was also responsible for accessing 13 National Aeronautics and Space Administration (NASA) computers and downloading proprietary software valued at $1.7 million. Letters of apology to the U.S. Department of Defense and NASA accompanied his 6-month sentence (USDOJ, 2000).

Although this incident marked a defining moment in the manner in which juvenile computer crimes are handled by the federal government, it was not the first such incident. Two years earlier, a juvenile hacker disabled telephone computers serving a Federal Aviation Association control tower at an airport in Worcester, Massachusetts, for 6 hours. He was also responsible for hacking into a Worcester pharmacy and downloading prescriptions filled by the pharmacist to his personal computer, which included customer names, addresses, telephone numbers, and medications. This constituted an invasion of privacy. By accepting a plea agreement, the juvenile had to complete 250 hours of community service, pay restitution to the telephone company, and was placed on 2-year probation during which he could not possess or access a computer modem (USDOJ, 1998). Other less notorious cases also exist. For example, a 16-year-old hacked into a Massachusetts Internet service provider's system, causing $20,000 in damages, and a 13-year-old boy from California made terroristic threats to a 13-year-old girl by creating a Web game with the girl's picture, petitioning for her death (Demarco, 2001).

Title 18, Section 1030 of the U.S. Code identifies fraudulent activities involving computers. They include the public switched network and other major computer network intrusions, network integrity violations, privacy violations, industrial espionage, pirated computer software, and various other crimes involving a computer (U.S. Code Collection, n.d.). Juveniles are more likely to commit computer crimes involving the trading of stolen credit card numbers, fraudulent purchases made using those cards, and the piracy and subsequent trade (usually with other juveniles) of copyrighted software (Demarco, 2001). Given the computer prowess of today's youth, they also have the capability to unleash computer viruses and commit any number of the other illegal activities outlined in the U.S. Code.

An exploration of various criminological theories is required to attempt an explanation of the motivation behind these crimes, especially given the prevalence of computers and their easy accessibility among juveniles. It may once have been said that most children with computers come from more affluent families, but that is no longer the case. The competitive pricing of computers has made them affordable to many more families. Furthermore, almost all children have access to computers, not exclusively at home but in schools, libraries, friends' homes, and computer clubs. Essentially, almost any youth has the opportunity to be a cyberdelinquent and, given the expertise of many in using the technology, has the capability as well. The anonymity of the computer in chat rooms, auction Web sites, and financial Web sites gives them access to an adult world that they could never enjoy in traditional criminal activities (Demarco, 2001). Similarly, the mobility of youth, previously circumscribed, is virtually limitless with a computer, allowing them to commit crimes at great distances and to cavort with other cyberdelinquents (Demarco, 2001).

11.2 A Theoretical Examination of Cybercrime

11.2.1 The Classical Perspective

The origins of modern criminology began with the classical theorists. Although their contributions were the result of a need to reform the corruptive influences of the criminal justice system, theories of criminal behavior emerged (Akers, 1999). Most notable among these theorists was Cesare Beccaria (1775), who noted that laws are created by states to prevent individuals from harming one another. If unchecked, these "passions," as Beccaria called them, will circumvent the greater good in society. Taking this deterrence theory one step further, the rational choice theory explains that crime is roughly a cost–benefit analysis.

An offender first weighs the benefits of the crime against the punishment (if caught), and then decides to commit a particular offense (Cornish and Clarke, 1986).

The rational choice theory assumes that all mentally competent individuals have free will to make appropriate decisions or that all aspects of a delinquent act are weighed in order to reach the conclusion to proceed. Although Grisso (1996) argues that there is little difference in the decision-making capacity of juveniles and adults (as cited in Bartol and Bartol, 1998) in waiving Miranda rights, there are several mitigating circumstances that might affect the process. Grisso cites poor intellect, low socioeconomic statues, cultural characteristics, negative emotion, and stress as influencing factors. The same decision-making processes that are required to waive rights also allow an individual to determine the utility of a particular crime.

There are many factors competing for an adolescent's attention and decision-making abilities. Unlike adults, who are ultimately responsible for their own actions, juveniles are drawn in many directions. Age, then, can certainly be added to the list of explanatory circumstances listed above (Shoemaker, 1996). Some juvenile crimes are based on impulse, others are premeditated. If the crime was premeditated, an argument can be made as to whether or not a child has the ability for competent, rational decision-making with all-important issues.

Juveniles committing cybercrimes may not even consider the pros and cons, and may act on impulse, failing to realize how wrong their decision could be. Most troubling, too, is that children fail to believe that computer crimes are actual crimes (Demarco, 2001). In a recent poll, 48 percent of 47,235 elementary- and middle-school students did not consider hacking a crime (Demarco, 2001). Even at the college undergraduate level, 34 percent admit to illegally copying copyrighted software, and 16 percent admit to hacking systems to exchange or to browse information (Demarco, 2001). College-level individuals no doubt realize they are committing a crime but are willing to take the risk.

11.2.2 The Biopsychosocial Approach

Another early theory was introduced in 1876 when Cesare Lombroso first proposed a biological theory that crime is predetermined by biological deficiencies, arguing that criminals are not as evolved as noncriminals (Lombroso, 1911). His theory states that a large cranial bone, strong canine teeth, long arms, a flat nose, and large eye sockets could distinguish a criminal. Although his theory, which underwent numerous revisions during his lifetime, was refuted, the positivist theory, which he helped establish, remains. Positivist theories rely on biological, sociological, or psychological influences as explanations of crime.

A psychological approach to delinquency involving intelligence quotients can be ruled out. In this theory, a low intelligence quotient is associated with delinquent behavior (Glueck and Glueck, 1950). Glueck and Glueck explain that delinquent youth do not approach problems in a systematic manner and, consequently, fail to consider the repercussions of their behavior. Little empirical evidence supports this theory (Akers, 1999), and the computer is not necessarily the best support mechanism to further it. Although not necessarily difficult to use, the computer does require higher levels of specialized knowledge to operate (Wall, 1998).

Increased hormonal activity cannot be ruled out (Farrington, 1996). Hormones are produced in greater quantities during adolescence than at any other time in human development (Marieb, 1998). Increases in testosterone levels could be an explanation for the overall disproportionate percentage of male criminals between the ages of 15 and 17, but sociological factors at this age might also produce a link. The onset of crime (Hirschi and Gottfredson, 1983) and the onset of puberty coincide almost perfectly, and research indicates that increased hormonal levels may increase one's tendency to disregard legal norms (Akers, 1999). Increases in testosterone, then, may lead to any form of delinquency, including cybercrime.

11.2.3 *The Social Learning Viewpoint*

Sutherland (1947) states that criminal behavior is learned (as cited in Akers, 1999). In addition, he states that delinquency occurs when this learned behavior is rationalized as favorable to the violation of existing laws. Advancing Sutherland's theory, Akers (1985) injected a classical behaviorist approach by adding that delinquency is learned through associations with other delinquent persons, which leads to the social reinforcement of delinquent acts. Juvenile delinquency can be caused by a combination of family, peer, and community influence. Akers (1999) contends that family, peer groups, schools, churches, and other groups can either promote or discourage deviant behavior in individuals. Whether such deviance occurs depends on how the juvenile assimilates the cultural norms unique to his or her social structure.

Given the lack of ethical considerations cited above, some youth rationalize cybercrime as favorable to the violation of Title 18, section 1030 of the U.S. Code. The perpetuation of these acts, however, may be accomplished through differential association, most commonly referred to as peer pressure. Teenagers often learn to manipulate a computer to their benefit through experiences with other teenagers who do the same. Associations with like-minded individuals is not restricted to close contacts but also occurs through on-line associations via the Internet. Continued or increased criminal activity is promoted by reinforcement, regular exposure to delinquent peers, and the lack of restrictions (Akers, 1999).

11.2.4 Social Bonding Approach

Hirschi (1969) explains that there are four major elements to his social bonding theory (as cited in Akers, 1999). The first is *attachment* to others, which he explains by the fact that the less responsive we are to others, the greater the risk of violating social norms. Secondly, *commitment* is an investment one has in the norms of society, either positive or negative. The third is *involvement*, which refers to how occupied one is in everyday activities. The last element is *belief* in the general values and norms in society. A weakening of one or more of these elements or bonds could result in deviance.

As Hirschi's (1969) theory proposes that delinquency results when societal bonds are weakened or broken (as cited in Akers, 1999), could America's morally relativistic society be to blame? Addressing just the belief issue in his theory, the feel-good attitude and increased exposure to questionable stimuli may be causing delinquency. Several areas have normalized deviant or problematic acts while playing down conventional values and norms. Questionable material available on the World Wide Web may also have contributed to a decreased value system. With almost everything available in the virtual world of the computer, all of which can be accessed by youth, Hirschi (1969, p. 26) explains that "the less a person believes he should obey the rules, the more likely he is to violate them." These factors might be responsible for the breakdown of the belief system, but nothing is being done to prevent it. They may also explain the lack of regard for ethical uses of the computer.

Unlike most theories that seek to determine the causes of crime, the social bond theory attempts to find out why people do not commit crime. Hirschi (1969) concluded that the type of bond one establishes determines the path that will be taken. The bond or attachment developed with a parent is the determining factor. The relationship established through the bond forms an emotional link causing those in the bond to care about what the other feels. If the parental bond is strong, a child will be less likely to commit delinquent acts, even when not under direct control of the parent. If the bond with peers, especially delinquent peers, is the stronger of the two, then a child is more likely to commit delinquent acts. One bond may not be more permanent than the other, but the strength of the bond may determine the outcome of a youth's behavior.

11.2.5 Strain and Anomie Theories

One illustration of a biosocial explanation for crime is the strain theory. First developed by Robert Merton, it defines crime as a result of importance society gives to goals such as financial success, while at the same time giving little emphasis to acceptable ways of obtaining success (Bartol and Bartol, 1998; Merton, 1938). This theory emphasizes that criminal behavior is predominant in lower-class citizens, as they are often excluded from achieving these successes.

Cohen (1955) furthered Merton's theory by adding manual laborers to the list of those likely to become involved in crime. He proposed that any goal obstruction that prevents such persons from achieving middle-class status might lead to delinquency. Advancing this theory, Cloward and Ohlin (1959, 1961) drew upon the work of several other theorists and proposed that the criminal behavior outlined by these theorists would not happen without certain learning environments and unlawful opportunities (as cited in Akers, 1999). Agnew (1992) proposed another revision of the strain theory. In his broad approach to the theory, he states that goal achievement is only one aspect of crime and delinquency. The others are the removal of positive stimuli and the presentation of, or inability to escape, negative stimuli (Agnew, 1992; Akers, 1999).

Although the strain theory does not specifically address middle- or upper-class individuals, it could very well extend to offenders in these socioeconomic categories, given certain circumstances. As stated above, Agnew (1992) first projected Merton's original strain theory, which only addressed lower-class individuals, to include those of the middle class. The premise of both of these theories is that the aspiration to obtain a higher standard of living, together with the inability to achieve it, causes frustration leading to strain. Middle- and upper-class individuals would have to experience strain for this theory to apply to them.

Consider some of the middle- and upper-class youth whose parents may be involved in their work or social lives to the exclusion of the youth. This might put strain on the youth as they vie for their parents' attention, without success. Retreating to their computers, these juveniles may rebel against their parents through criminal activity. The computer is a unique learning environment, and children generally excel at its use. In addition, unlawful opportunities present themselves through Web sites and are even posted there by cybercriminals (Demarco, 2001). Cybercrimes are not unique to lower-class citizens, either. Any goal blockage may entice juveniles to commit such crimes. The lack of visible restraints further exacerbates the problem.

Anomie is a term Durkheim gave to the conditions he classified by weak or nonexistent controls (Bartol and Bartol, 1998). America, as a whole, has placed a great deal of value on achievement and has denigrated traditional norms and rules. As a result, some people will utilize any means to achieve their goals, even resorting to crime (Merton, 1938). Merton (1938) believed that the reason some communities have higher crimes than others is because they place a higher emphasis on cultural goals such as making money and less emphasis on the rules for reaching such goals. Some, in order to attain such goals, may resort to crime. Merton (1938) also believed that the strain experienced by those unable to attain these goals through legal means could also make them resort to crime.

The cultural goal of making money is not unique to any particular community nor is it unique to any specific socioeconomic class. The value of money, learned at a very young age, may cause some to resort to computer crime in order to amass wealth. This, however, does not explain computer criminal mischief. Most anomie and strain theories of crime deal with individuals who, through means beyond their control, commit crime in order to survive or reach an elevated status (e.g., Cloward and Ohlin, 1960; Merton, 1938). Some youth, however, commit cybercrimes in order to obtain something that may be well within their families' means but which parents feel is unnecessary for their children. This is not necessarily a social concern created by parents but by a commercial, "must-have" society. Some television commercials, for instance, are directed at children, as opposed to adults, and children may sometimes feel that they must possess the advertised item or service. The onus for delinquency in this case may be on society as a whole and not just on the parents.

11.2.6 *Other Control Theories*

Laws have been used as a means of social control since the United States declared its independence. The emergence of new laws regarding the computer and the Internet may be another form of social control and therefore draws on the works of conflict theorists. Conflict theories draw on the assumption of social control to explain both criminality and its control. In these theories, Marxism among them, economic power holders label certain behaviors as criminal. Therefore, certain acts are criminal only because the state deems them criminal; this is also referred to as the *labeling theory*. Although little empirical validity exists for these theories, they do merit examination to demonstrate historical injustices (Akers, 1999). One such theorist, Richard Quinney (1980), notes that police brutality and civil liberties violations are two such aspects of conflict theories. Historical injustices aside, William Bonger (1969) contends that crime is a result of placing one's own interests above that of others. This latter aspect of the conflict theory may best demonstrate cybercrime, although not to the extent of true conflict theorists.

Bonger (1969) uses the term "egoism," or the belief that self-interest is the just and proper motive for all conduct, to explain crime. He contends that given the right environmental pressures, an individual can act on his or her egoist tendencies and commit criminal acts. As with all true conflict theorists, however, Bonger (1969) blames capitalism for the woes of society. The proletariat, or working man, is at the mercy of capitalists who run the market. Furthermore, ignorance, lack of training, and a lack of culture lead to poor economic and social conditions, which in turn are linked to criminality. Although computer crimes are not unique to any particular class, Bonger's egoist contribution should be noted as relevant to cybercrime.

11.2.7 *Social Disorganization and the Chicago School*

The major facet in the social disorganization theories is the presence or absence of controls, such as self-control, family, and communal institutions. Some individuals give in to a certain lack of controls and succumb to the criminal activities prevalent in some neighborhoods, whereas others overcome the overwhelming influences of crime and rise out of the neighborhood to become conventional, productive members of society. Although computer crimes occur across societal boundaries, these theories are worth exploring.

Although Burgess's concentric circle model represents a general idea of the type of environment indicative of large cities, it in no way speaks for all those living in this environment (as cited in Bartol and Bartol, 1998) nor does it explain crime outside these neighborhoods. Poor or impoverished communities may have a stronger leaning toward criminal activity, but crime also occurs in affluent neighborhoods, albeit to a lesser extent.

Perhaps crime is not a result of strict environmental factors but a social disorganization that spans communities. This disorganization may contain values that sustain crime rather than conventional activities (Shaw and McKay, 1942). Although Shaw and McKay noted that social institutions become weak and give way to crime, their critics assert that delinquency occurs across communities and is common among a wide range of socioeconomic backgrounds. So theorists agree that crime is manifest in all socioeconomic areas.

11.2.8 Developmental Theories

Temporary antisocial behavior or delinquency around the period of adolescent development is characteristic of juveniles with no history of antisocial behavior (Moffitt, 1993). Almost 80 percent of adolescent males have some contact with the police, often caused by mimicking their peers (Moffitt, 1993). Adolescents mimic antisocial behavior in order to obtain a sought-after resource and to gain power and prestige (Moffitt, 1993). Improvements in healthcare have caused early biological development, resulting in a blurred delineation of social adult status and an increase in the duration of adolescence (Moffitt, 1993). Being financially dependant on their parents, adolescents are denied the benefits of adulthood including intimate relationships, material accumulations, and decision making despite their advanced biological and sexual capabilities. Adolescents often turn to peers to satisfy this inconsistency in their lives, many of whom have endured the same problems and then turned to delinquency to cope (Moffitt, 1993).

Other developmental perspectives follow a line of reasoning that focuses on social control, although not as formal as those offered by similar theorists. Sampson and Laub (1993), for example, believe that crime and deviance is a result of a certain trajectory, or life-course dynamic. These pathways can influence such things as work, marriage, self-esteem, or even criminal behaviors. The precursor to these trajectories is transition, which may relate to the age of an individual. The development of an individual, then, is a function of the duration, timing and order of major life events (Sampson and Laub, 1993). It may be that during these crossroads or transitions, the opportunities for cybercrime are nurtured.

11.3 Putting It All Together

No single theory can be used to explain every incident or type of crime. Therefore, some criminologists combine several different theories for a more comprehensive explanation. One noted work combines strain, social control, and social-learning theories (Elliot et al., 1987). In their integrated theory, they start with two socialization outcomes similar to standard strain theories, one involving strong bonds and the other, weak bonds.

Strong bonds offer adolescents a high degree of integration with and commitment to societal norms, thus leading to a low probability of delinquency. Juveniles in this category often associate with conventional peer groups, and are successful within the normal social structures both in the home and in the community. This ultimately leads to integration in traditional activities and roles. Their increased personal commitment to societal norms also results in a positive labeling experience (Elliot et al., 1987).

Weak social bonds involve a low degree of integration with and commitment to societal norms. Failure in conventional social contexts, social isolation, disorganization, and decreased personal commitment may lead adolescents to associate with delinquent peers. This increases the likelihood of delinquent behavior and the related label. While peer associations are an important aspect of both socialization outcomes, delinquent peer associations are central to juvenile delinquency. Also, a severe decrease in once-strong bonds could develop into attenuating circumstances that lead to delinquency (Elliot et al., 1987). Thus, individuals with otherwise strong bonds may have an experience that weakens their control as they fail to achieve certain goals.

This integrated theory may be the most appropriate in explaining cybercrime. Those with weak social bonds are as likely to commit computer crimes as they would conventional crimes, and delinquent peer association increases the likelihood of these crimes. In addition, this theory offers an explanation for those with strong bonds. Therefore, even those from affluent social backgrounds or possessing no apparent antisocial behavior may start with strong societal bonds but may experience something in their lives to weaken those bonds, resulting in delinquent acts such as cybercrime.

11.4 Legal Problems and Implications

The detection and management of cybercrime is difficult as law enforcement agencies and legislators have failed to adequately attack the problem (Wolf, 2000). Both the Federal Bureau of Investigation (FBI) and the Department of Commerce, responsible for cybercrime investigations, do not have sufficient resources to keep up with hackers. The FBI and the Department of Justice both have computer crime components to "patrol" the Internet, but they only catch about 10 percent of those who hack into government computers. Even fewer individuals who hack into private company computers are ever caught (Wolf, 2000). Computer break-ins are virtually undetectable as cybercriminals take the time to cover their entry, thus going unidentified.

The main group of individuals involved in the detection of cyber-crimes is the Internet community. Through the development of software programs, hackers are finding increased difficulty in obtaining access to some sites. In addition to software, some have set up hotlines where unauthorized accesses can be reported. The Internet Rapid Response Team (IRRT) is one such voluntary group that patrols the Internet, seeking out hackers (Wall, 1998).

Where no state or local jurisdictions exist, or when a state or local government lacks adequate programs, juveniles are being prosecuted under federal statues. They are still protected as juveniles under 18 U.S.C. §§ 5031 to 5042, with the exception of acts of violence. Thus, prosecutors must not only have a good knowledge of computer crimes but must also possess a good working knowledge of juvenile law.

Congress and the courts have likewise erred. For instance, the Computer Fraud and Abuse Act duplicates existing laws while believing that computer crimes warrant separate laws (Wolf, 2000). Old laws are created around tangible property, but this new type of crime involves information, and lawmakers cannot decide whether it is categorized as goods, wares, or merchandise. The courts have declared that existing laws cannot support cybercrime. For instance, in *Dowling v. United States*, the Supreme Court held that the Interstate Transportation of Stolen Property statute does not apply to transporting bootlegged albums across state lines because they are not physically identical to the original. Similar court decisions have undermined other existing laws because of the medium involved. Thus, instead of amending existing laws to account for data, files, or other computer media, Congress enacted new laws.

Growing concern over cyberliberties is also brewing. The FBI currently restricts the use of cryptography to effectively patrol the Internet for criminals and terrorists (Strossen, 2000). Encrypted files would protect trade secrets and reduce economic espionage. Some feel that FBI patrol constitutes an invasion of privacy and further limits organizations from protecting themselves against hackers. Constitutional limitations on online injuries are also an issue and must be addressed with regard to the due process clause (Wall, 2000). Some stability in cyberspace is necessary but not at the expense of current ethical considerations (Hauptman, 1996).

11.5 Conclusion

Through the Internet, juveniles have found a new outlet for delinquency. Their uncanny computer abilities have allowed them to deviate from traditional forms of crime and, without departing from the comfort of their homes or other computer access points, they have engaged in trespass, theft, and in rare cases, violence and obscenity. Government agencies and the Internet police are cracking down on all cybercriminals, and juveniles are no exception.

Many theories may be used to explain cyberdelinquency. Social bonding, social learning, and rational choice may be among the most appropriate models, but the integrated model of Elliot et al. (1987) offers the best explanation, considering all levels of societal attachment and socioeconomic groups. This explanation relies on formal theories to ascertain an explanation for cyberdelinquency. A great deal more information must be gathered on the juvenile population and its increasing fascination with the computer as a means of acting out their delinquency.

References

Agnew, R.S. (1992). A general strain theory of crime and delinquency. In Cullen, F.T. and Agnew, R. (Eds.), *Criminological Theory: Past to Present,* 2nd ed. Los Angeles, CA: Roxbury, pp. 208–217.

Akers, R.L. (1999). *Criminological Theories: Introduction and Evaluation,* 2nd ed. Chicago, IL: Fitzroy Dearborn.

Bartol, C.R. and Bartol, A.M. (1998). *Delinquency and Justice: A Psychosocial Approach,* 2nd ed. Englewood Cliffs, NJ: Prentice Hall.

Bonger, W. (1969). Criminality and economic conditions. In Cullen, F.T. and Agnew, R. (Eds.), *Criminological Theory: Past to Present,* 2nd ed. Los Angeles, CA: Roxbury. pp. 343–350.

Beccaria, C. (1775). An essay on crimes and punishments. In Cullen, F.T. and Agnew, R. (Eds.), *Criminological Theory: Past to Present,* 2nd ed. Los Angeles, CA: Roxbury. pp. 20–22.

Cohen, A.K. (1955). Delinquent boys. In Cullen, F.T. and Agnew, R. (Eds.), *Criminological Theory: Past to Present,* 2nd ed. Los Angeles, CA: Roxbury. pp. 186–190.

Cornish, D.B. and Clarke, R.V. (1986). Crime as a rational choice. In Cullen, F.T. and Agnew, R. (Eds.), *Criminological Theory: Past to Present,* 2nd ed. Los Angeles, CA: Roxbury. pp. 278–283.

DeMarco, J.V. (2001). It's not Just Fun and "War Games" — Juveniles and Computer Crime. Retrieved June 5, 2003 from the Justice Department. Web site: http://www.usdoj.gov/criminal/cybercrime/usamay2001_7.htm.

Elliot, D.S., Ageton, S.S., and Canter, R.J. (1979). An integrated theoretical perspective on delinquent behavior. In Cullen, F.T. and Agnew, R. (Eds.), *Criminological Theory: Past to Present,* 2nd ed. Los Angeles, CA: Roxbury. pp. 489–502.

Dowling v. United States, 474 U.S. 207 (1985).

Farrington, D.P. (1996). The explanation and prevention of youthful offending. In J.D. Hawkins (Ed.), *Delinquency and Crime.* New York: Cambridge University Press, pp. 68–148.

Glueck, S. and Glueck, E. (1950). Unraveling juvenile delinquency. In Cullen, F.T. and Agnew, R. (Eds.), *Criminological Theory: Past to Present,* 2nd ed. Los Angeles, CA: Roxbury. pp. 36–47.

Grisso, T. (1996). Society's retributive response to juvenile violence: a developmental perspective. *Law and Human Behavior,* 20, 229–247.

Hauptman, R. (1996). Cyberethics and social stability. *Ethics and Behavior,* 6(2), 161–163.

Hirschi, T. (1969). Social bond theory. In Cullen, F.T. and Agnew, R. (Eds.), *Criminological Theory: Past to Present,* 2nd ed. Los Angeles, CA: Roxbury. pp. 178–185.

Hirschi, T. and Gottfredson, M. (1983). Age and the explanation of crime. *American Journal of Sociology,* 89(3), 552–584.

Lombroso, C. (1911). Criminal man. In Cullen, F.T. and Agnew, R. (Eds.), *Criminological Theory: Past to Present,* 2nd ed. Los Angeles, CA: Roxbury. pp. 23–25.

Marieb, E.N. (1998). *Human Anatomy and Physiology,* 4th ed. Menlo Park, CA: Addison-Wesley Longman.

Merton, R.K. (1938). Social structure and anomie. In Cullen, F.T. and Agnew, R. (Eds.), *Criminological Theory: Past to Present,* 2nd ed. Los Angeles, CA: Roxbury. pp. 450–469.

Moffitt, T.E. (1993). Pathways in the life course to crime. In Cullen, F.T. and Agnew, R. (Eds.), *Criminological Theory: Past to Present,* 2nd ed. Los Angeles, CA: Roxbury. pp. 178–185.

Sampson, R.J. and Laub, J.H. (1993). Crime and the life course. In Cullen, F.T. and Agnew, R. (Eds.), *Criminological Theory: Past to Present,* 2nd ed. Los Angeles, CA: Roxbury. pp. 470–482.

Shaw. C.R. and McKay, H.D. (1942). Juvenile delinquency and urban areas. In Cullen, F.T. and Agnew, R. (Eds.), *Criminological Theory: Past to Present,* 2nd ed. Los Angeles, CA: Roxbury. pp. 104–117.

Shoemaker, D.L. (1996). The classical school: issues of choice and reasoning. In Shoemaker, D.L. (Ed.), *Theories of Delinquency.* New York: Oxford University. pp. 12–20.

Strossen, N. (2000). Cybercrimes v. cyberliberties. *International Review of Law, Computer and Technology,* 14(1), 11–24.

Sutherland, E.H. (1947). *Principles of Criminology,* 4th ed. Philadelphia, PA: J.B. Lippincott.

Swartz, N. (May–June 2002). Cybercrime soars. *Information Management Journal,* 36(3), 6.

Up Front (September–October 2002). The House votes to increase penalties for cybercrime. *Information Management Journal,* 36(5), 12.

United States Department of Justice (September 21, 2000). Juvenile Computer Hacker Sentenced to Six Months in Detention Facility. Retrieved June 5, 2003 from the Justice Department. Web site: http://www.usdoj.gov/comrade.htm.

United States Department of Justice (March 18, 1998). Juvenile Computer Hacker Cuts off FAA Tower at Regional Airport — First Federal Charges brought against a Juvenile for Computer Crime. Retrieved June 5, 2003 from the Justice Department. Web site: http://www.cybercrime.gov/jevenilepld.htm.

U.S. Code Collection. (nd). Retrieved June 5, 2003 from the Legal Institute. Web Site: http://www4.law.cornell.edu/uscode/18/1030.html.

Wall, D.S. (July 1998). Catching cybercriminals: policing the Internet. *International Review of Law, Computer and Technology, 12*(2), 201–219.

Wall, D.S. (2000). Introduction: Cybercrimes, cyberspeech and cyberliberties. *International Review of Law, Computer and Technology,* 14(1), 5–9.

Wolf, J.B. (2000). War games meets the Internet: chasing 21st century cybercriminals with old laws and little money. *American Journal of Criminal Law,* 28, 95–117.

Chapter 12

Juvenile Stalkers: An Introduction

Deborah L. Laufersweiler-Dwyer and
R. Gregg Dwyer

12.1 Introduction

In the study and analysis of stalking by children, several aspects must be examined. This chapter will explore the concept of stalking, the incidence in the general population, the explanations given for stalking in the adult population, and the phenomenon in the juvenile population.

From a clinical and theoretical perspective, a definition depends on the adequate explanation and formulation of terms and concepts (McCann, 2001). In this chapter, stalking will be defined using the technical, legal, and behavioral definitions. This will allow the reader to understand how each of these definitions influences the ways and means of examining stalking behaviors in juveniles.

12.2 Stalking Defined

12.2.1 Technical Definitions

As a technical term, *stalking* has been defined as various types of aggressive actions that are a prelude to violence (Meloy, 1988). These actions can be characterized as coldhearted, calculated, and planned aggression. Such actions often precede violence in which the offender maintains a reality. There is, however, a significant degree of confusion that can be attached to this definition of stalking. Often an informal definition, likening the action to that of the predatory animal stalking its prey, teasing and frightening it, is used in many crimes where such predatory activities occur. Robbers, burglars, and muggers often stalk their victims waiting for just the right opportunity to strike. Burglars are known to survey their targets determining movement patterns, again looking for an opportunity. Thus, a distinction must be made between the idea of lying in wait to "ambush" a victim and the behavior of stalking.

12.2.2 Legal Definitions

Legal definitions begin by creating a distinction between behaviors that are simply part of a criminal's desire to obtain opportunity and those behaviors that the concept of stalking truly encompasses. California was the first state to enact legislation establishing stalking as a criminal act. By 1993, 48 states and the federal government had created some form of antistalking legislation (National Institute of Justice, 1993). All states have now enacted legislation making stalking illegal (Bradfield, 1998).

Most legal definitions have several elements that must be met in order for an act to be classified as stalking. Two chief elements found in most antistalking legislation are threat and criminal intent. Threatening behaviors encompass a variety of acts, including harassment, repeated phone calls or letters, and threats to the victim's family members (McAnaney et al., 1993). These behaviors are most often manifested in the form of trespassing, displaying a weapon, vandalizing the victim's property, making threats of bodily harm, intimidating the victim and his or her family, and surveillance of the victim. Beyond the simple act, most statutes require police to show that the behavior is ongoing or repeated and that these acts also pose a credible threat to the victim.

In establishing a credible case for arrest and prosecution of offenders, criminal justice professionals must establish criminal intent. This aspect of the law is very clear. In order to arrest and prosecute an individual for stalking, it must be shown that the perpetrator's acts meet the standard of intent by being purposeful, intentional, willful, or knowing (National Institute of Justice, 1993).

12.2.3 Behavioral Definitions

The behavioral definitions associated with stalking offer a dissimilar approach in that it is not based on the analysis of the actions as described in the preceding text. In an extensive review of the literature, Meloy (1996) pointed out significant limitations of the term stalking. Most of society has connected the word stalking with the various sensationalized cases that have commanded popular media attention. Meloy and Gothard (1995) proposed the term *obsessional follower* as a clinical corollary of "stalker." This term was developed from clinical studies of individuals who engage in stalking (as per the technical definition) and describes a person who engages in a deviant or long-term pattern of threat or harassment directed toward a specific individual (Meloy, 1996). This definition differs from the legal definition in that it encompasses the abnormal nature of the behavior (McCann, 2001).

Another definition associated with the behavioral model of analyzing stalking is *obsessive relational intrusion,* which is included in the work by Cupach and Spitzberg (1998). It states that "repeated unwanted pursuit and invasion of one's sense of physical or symbolic privacy by another person who desires or presumes an intimate relationship" (pp. 234–235). One key component of this definition is that the goals of the parties are not mutual. In addition, Cupach and Spitzberg (1998) identified grades of relational intrusion by placing the acts along a continuum. This helps provide a subjective boundary between reasonable and unreasonable intrusion in relationships, which is particularly helpful in applying the definitions to the actions of children and adolescents. As will be noted later, many of the behaviors exhibited by children are "normal" adolescent behaviors. The continuum established by Cupach and Spitzberg (1998) helps to differentiate between normal behavior and abnormal or problem behaviors.

12.3 Stalking in Adults

12.3.1 Prevalence

The criminal justice community is still in the initial stages of analyzing stalking. Consequently, statistics for this phenomenon are changing constantly. It is believed that stalking is an extensive problem within our society. Several epidemiological studies have been done to document the prevalence of stalking. Fremouw et al. (1997) revealed that in a sample of 600 undergraduates, 30 percent of females and 17 percent of males reported having been stalked. A survey conducted by the National Institute of Justice and the Centers for Disease Control and Prevention found that one out of every 12 women (8 percent) and one out of every 45 men (2 percent) had been stalked in their lifetimes (1993). The second study limited their definition of stalking to those incidents in which there was a credible threat, meeting the legal definition for stalking as mentioned earlier.

In the most recent study by the Institute of Justice (1997), 94 percent of stalkers identified by female victims were men, and 60 percent of stalkers identified by male victims were men, with 87 percent of stalkers overall being men. In the adult population of stalkers, the median age is 34, indicating that he or she is older than the "average" criminal.

Studies have focused attention on adult perpetrators and victims of stalking. The absence of studies on children and adolescents is frightening. The behavioral science literature shows that behaviors previously believed to occur only in adults are now being observed in children and adolescents (Barbaree et al., 1993). More important is the knowledge that theories designed to explain similar behaviors in adults are not applicable to children and adolescents.

One of the most comprehensive examinations of stalking was done by J. Reid Meloy. In his book *The Psychology of Stalking,* some general characteristics of stalkers were identified. It must be noted that these characteristics were generated from research on adults. It does, however, provide an understanding about the general nature of stalking. The majority of analysis on stalking has concentrated on perpetrator characteristics and has utilized forensic samples of adjudicated stalkers (Meloy, 1996; Zona et al., 1993; Meloy and Gothard, 1995).

The research has reported a variety of descriptors, such as demographic information, personality features, and clinical variables that appear in the forensic samples. Stalkers tended to be males, between the ages of 35 and 40 (Lewis et al., 2001), had never been married, had poor attachments or were currently divorced (Harmon et al., 1995; Schwartz-Watts et al., 1997), and were unemployed or underemployed with unstable work histories. In addition, these offenders were better educated than the average criminal (Kienlen et al., 1997; Meloy, 1996; Meloy and Gothard, 1995; Mullen and Pathe, 1994; Meloy, et al., 2000). These offenders were generally considered intelligent (Schwartz-Watts et al., 1997; Meloy and Gothard, 1995; Zona et al., 1993).

In the research on adult stalkers, there are certain demographic factors identified as having an impact on the development and maintenance of stalking (McCann, 2001). Many of these factors have been identified as behavioral aspects rather than characteristics (Freund et al., 1983; Meloy, 1998). One specific factor is "courtship disorder." In this disorder, the person has a history of failed intimate relationships (Freund et al., 1983; Meloy, 1998). These individuals have extreme feelings of isolation and failure, which contributes to the behaviors associated with stalking. Another behavioral factor identified is the feeling of loss created by immigration to a new country. Cultural differences and inability to understand gestures may result in misinterpretation of cues from people, causing interpersonal problems (Meloy, 1998; Meyers and Meloy, 1994).

The prevalence of mental disorders has also been examined in the population of incarcerated stalkers. Those in the forensic samples have exhibited a wide range of mental disorders suggesting that stalkers are not psychologically healthy. Among the disorders identified were depression, bipolar disorder, substance abuse, schizophrenia, delusional disorder, and organic mental disorders (Harmon et al., 1995; Meloy and Gothard, 1995; Mullen and Pathe, 1994; Schwartz-Watts et al., 1997). Meloy (1998) found that a large percentage of stalking offenders had personality disorders. These consisted of character disturbances with eccentric thought and behavior patterns and anxious or other fearful attachments to others. It should be noted that Meloy (1998) also found that although some of these individuals were psychotic and could be influenced by their delusions, the majority were not actively psychotic at the time of their commiting the offense.

12.3.2 Adult Typologies

A number of behavioral studies have been conducted in an attempt to categorize the different types of stalkers. Although there are a vast number of typologies, only some selected typologies are presented in this chapter. In the initial studies of stalkers, Zona et al. (1993), with the help of the Threat Management Unit of the Los Angeles Police Department, identified three types of adult stalkers. These were the simple obsessional, love obsessional, and erotomanic groups. Under the simple obsessional definition, the offender and victim have most often had some type of prior relationship. These relationships range from marriage and dating to a workplace or professional relationship. Those who fall within the love obsessional category are characterized by the absence of an existing relationship. These are the types that are most often publicized, because their victims are usually celebrities. Many of these offenders suffer from some form of mental illness, with the most common being bipolar disorder and schizophrenia. The erotomanic cases differ from the love obsessional because the stalker delusionally believes that the victim loves him or her.

Harmon et al. (1995) conducted additional research in an attempt to develop a typology of stalkers. In their study, cases were referred to the forensic psychiatric clinic of the Criminal and Supreme Court of New York. Harmon et al. (1995) identified a two-dimensional typology. The first was labeled *affectionate/amorous*, in which the offender wishes a personal relationship with the victim. In the second category, *persecutory/angry*, the offender is in pursuit of the victim for some real or perceived injury. Similar to the simple obsessional category of Zona's typologies, the relationship between the perpetrator and the victim usually originates in the workplace or from some other professional relationship (Harmon et al., 1995).

12.4 Stalking by Children and Adolescents

12.4.1 Prevalence

In the study of stalking by children and adolescents, there are many barriers to obtaining accurate information. The treatment of juveniles within the criminal justice system is based on the concept of rehabilitation and resists strongly the idea of labeling. As a result, many juveniles are diverted, never formally entering the juvenile justice system. Many stalking behaviors are also simply considered nuisance behaviors and may therefore be diverted from formal intervention (McCann, 2001). Secondly, there is the assumption that behaviors associated with stalking are not problematic among children and adolescents. Not only are there barriers to obtaining the information, but there are methodological issues that must be considered as well. Collecting information is difficult, but the problem extends beyond the simple collection of data. There are also problems with conceptualizing the idea of stalking by children and adolescents. One specific problem area is defining appropriate age boundaries. The legal system has created a distinction between being a juvenile and being an adult; however, there is significantly more to examining stalking behaviors than the legal definition of age (Suarez, 1994). The behavioral literature is clear that the development of an individual is a combination of cognitive factors, social relationships, and psychosocial dimensions. Theoretical and clinical concepts such as attachment, identity, and interpersonal relations are used to conceptualize some of the psychodynamics of stalking

(McCann, 2001). These are developed at different stages of childhood and adolescence and at different times for each individual person. Researchers must consider age very carefully when assessing behaviors related, or similar, to those defined as stalking.

In examining the extent of stalking in this population, the majority of the information has come from a review of those studies done on related behaviors such as dating violence, sexual harassment, sexual aggression, and bullying. There is significant data available on these behavioral disturbances and other obsessional forms of harassment in young offenders that are related to or overlap stalking (McCann, 2001).

12.4.2 Obsessional Behaviors

Studies have been done examining obsessional behaviors in high-school students. A study done by the National Victim Center (1995) examined the number of restraining orders requested during a ten-month period. Although this study included all abusive behaviors as well as stalking behaviors, it is clear that stalking, once limited to adults, does occur in the adolescent population. In addition to this limited study on restraining orders, several studies have been conducted examining dating and court-ship violence. One of the most pervasive forms of stalking in the adult population has generally been strongly associated with domestic violence. This form of stalking in the adult population has been an "obsessional man who stalks a prior intimate female partner" (McCann, 2001, p. 37). The violence that occurs in dating and courtship relationships involves obsessional forms of harassment that are closely aligned with the defini-tions (legal and behavioral) of stalking. There is a large amount of data that shows that the prevalence of dating and sexual violence in the adolescent population is comparable to the rate of such violence in adult populations. A number of studies of courtship and dating violence found that a significant proportion of high-school students knew someone who had experienced dating violence (Roscoe and Callahan, 1985; O'Keefe et al., 1986; Bennett and Fineran, 1998; Bergman, 1992). This research reported that the rate of dating and courtship violence did not differ from that of adults. When further analysis was done by Roscoe and Callahan (1985), it was discovered that violence was more likely to occur in short-term rather than long-term dating relationships. These findings are significant in that they lead to a better understanding of stalking and the perceived motivation for violence.

In addition to dating violence, sexual harassment has also been studied in high-school populations. Sexual harassment often involves threatening and harassing behaviors that overlap stalking. Another parallel between the two behaviors involves the issues of control over the victim, exerting power over the victim, and the repetitive nature of sexual harassment (McCann, 2001). In a study done in American high schools (American Association of University Women Education Foundation, 1993), it was found that four out of five students had been the victim of some type of sexual harassment. When younger populations were studied, the results further supported the finding that sexual harassment is common in schools and that a subset of the behavior may involve stalking and obsessional following (Roscoe et al., 1994). In this study, six broad categories of sexual harassment could be distinguished, with obsessive letter writing and telephone calls being common among children and adolescent populations (McCann,1998; Urbach et al., 1992). Even with the filtering of the data to represent only those activities that rise to the level of stalking, these studies suggest that this is a social problem of prominence in school-age children.

The third form of obsessional behaviors involves sexual aggression. Araji (1997) examined the literature on sexually aggressive behavior in children 12 years old and younger. Sexual aggressive behaviors that are manifested in children involve force, coercion, and secrecy, and are patterned acts rather than isolated incidents (Araji, 1997). In examining the relationship between these behaviors and stalking, it is important to note the repetitive nature common to sexually aggressive acts and stalking behaviors. Araji (1997) also noted that these offenders exhibited characteristics that are comparable to those found in the legal and behavioral definitions of stalking.

The literature shows that despite some methodological problems, the analysis of sexual aggression in children provides insight into the nature of stalking because many of the characteristics that have been used to explain sexual aggression have also been found in the stalking literature (McCann, 2001). It was noted that deviant fantasies, dysfunctional and abusive family life, poor attachment patterns, and severe conduct disturbances have been identified as risk factors associated with both sexual acting-out and stalking (Araji, 1997).

The final form of obsessive behavior associated with stalking is bullying. This form of harassment has been associated with childhood for generations. Research on the long-term effects and prevalence of this type of behavior has only recently been conducted. There are significant parallels between the definitions of stalking and bullying. Both require repetitive behavior patterns which instill fear in the victims

(Hazler, 1996; Guy, 1993; McAnaney et al., 1993; Meloy, 1992). The parallels go beyond behavioral similarities. The courts have also noted similarities in behaviors. Two legal cases, *Svendberg v. Stamness* (1994) in America and a case in Leicestershire, England, have used antistalking laws to address instances in which children have been chronically bullied by other children (McCann, 2001).

12.5 Theoretical Explanations and Typologies for Child and Adolescent Stalking

12.5.1 Typologies

The literature on developing typologies for child and adolescent stalkers is limited. The majority of researchers have relied on typologies developed for adults. Their applicability to children and adolescents is questionable. The preponderance of information about stalking perpetrated by children and adolescents has been developed from published case studies and media accounts. Individual case studies provide researchers with the most "accurate" evidence of stalking in the adolescent population. These studies have shown that many of the forms of stalking thought to exist only in adults are present in the adolescent population as well. In analyzing the classification of the child or adolescent stalker, it must be noted that in order to be useful these classification structures must provide a guide to the course and duration of harassment, the risks of escalation of assaultive behaviors, and the most effective strategies for ending stalking behaviors (Mullen et al., 1999).

McCann (1998) utilized those typologies present in the adult literature to separate child and adolescent stalking behaviors into three types. Using the three categories of erotomanic, simple obsessional, and love obsessional, McCann presented a series of case studies showing how child and adolescent stalkers fit into these categories. Although this is helpful in a legal sense in profiling behaviors, it is not helpful as an explanation for the behavior and for identifying the factors that might be used to change obsessional behaviors.

In an article published in 1992, Urbach et al. examined a case of erotomania. *Erotomania* is defined by the *Diagnostic and Statistical Manual for Mental Disorders*, 4th edition, as a delusional disturbance in which a person falsely believes that he or she is loved by another person (APA, 2001). In several additional case studies, examples of obsessional subtypes of stalking were identified. Zona et al. (1993)

found an example of an adolescent with a severe mental disorder who maintained delusional beliefs about several female classmates. This case of love obsessional stalking displays classic signs of mental illness, which are also the classic signs of stalking or of obsessional stalkers.

12.6 Theoretical Models

Several models have been proposed as a method for examining the factors contributing to the deviation of normal relationships among adolescents to behaviors that are assaultive, controlling, or harassing. The models examined in this chapter are the behavioral models, which include the psychodynamic model, the functional analysis model, and the communication theory.

12.6.1 Behavioral Models

There are currently several behavioral models that examine the underlying factors that may contribute to stalking in children and adolescents. It is important to note in any discussion on stalking by children and adolescents that children are progressing through a number of stages of psychological development; disturbances in any one of these stages can trigger the behavioral aspects often associated with stalking.

12.6.2 Psychodynamic Model

One explanatory theory used to analyze stalking behavior is the psychodynamic model, in which behaviors are viewed as a disturbance of attachment. In the psychodynamic model, there is an inability to develop healthy relationships and to cope with rejection. These inabilities are often a result of feelings of inadequacy and a scattered sense of one's own values (Meloy, 1996; Meloy, 1998). This model includes the two key components of attachment pathology and identity disturbances (McCann, 2001).

The first component of the psychodynamic model is attachment disturbances. According to attachment theory, early experiences of infants with their caregivers influence subsequent well-being and behavior through their effect on "working models" of the self and others (Greenberger and McLaughlin, 1998). Stalking has been conceptualized as a disturbance in attachment (Kienlen, 1998; Meloy, 1992, 1996, and 1998). Researchers who attempt to explain obsessional and stalking behaviors in children and adolescents look for how the disruption or severing of these early attachments affect functioning in later life (Hazen and Shaver, 1994). Meloy (1998) described stalkers as individuals who are attempting to protest separation as a means of avoiding feelings of despair and detachment.

The second component of this explanatory model is identity disturbances. Identity is an important component in most theories of personality. When explaining stalking behaviors, identity disturbances have been identified as a key component associated with stalking (Meloy, 1996 and 1998). This is a result of a person's vulnerability to shame and humiliation. These feeling often trigger the defensive behaviors of rage, anger, and controlling behavior (McCann, 2001). In the psychodynamic model presented by Meloy (1998), feelings of shame and rage are the primary dynamic forces that drive a stalker's need to control the behavior of his or her victim.

12.6.3 *Functional Analysis*

A second theoretical approach is functional analysis. This model was set forth by Westrup and Fremouw (1998). Westrup and Fremouw (1998) suggest that the previous explanations are limiting in that they do not adequately capture all stalking behaviors. A functional analysis model uses a classical principle of behavior by relying on the assumption that the function or purposes served by the behavior should be the primary focus of assessment. Westrup and Fremouw (1998) argue that the majority of stalking literature focuses on the behaviors and not the purposes. Understanding and intervention can best be done by an analysis of the function and purpose served by the behavior rather than just the isolated behavior.

12.6.4 *Communications Theory*

The final theoretical approach is communications theory. Cupach and Spizberg (1998) analyzed obsessional relational intrusions. They outlined three important features of obsessive relational intrusions. First, these behaviors ran a spectrum from mild forms to more threatening behaviors. Second, the boundaries of intrusive behavior vs. normal behavior is not clear. Lastly, these behaviors happen in the context of an interpersonal relationship. The utilization of this concept in explaining stalking by young people is the notion that intrusive and harassing behaviors lie along a continuum. In this model, many of the behaviors related to stalking are also in the continuum and part of normal childhood behavior. Teasing, mild bullying, and mild forms of harassment are part of many social interactions in childhood and adolescence. It is only when they reach an extreme that they should be considered in the intrusive category.

Each of these theoretical approaches is in its infancy. Our understanding of juvenile stalkers is limited. Large controlled studies are few in number. Most of what is known is based on case reports, extrapolation from adult stalker research, and studies of similar behavior, such as bullying and dating violence. In order to identify the source of such behavior and address it clinically, more studies on larger clinical samples should be undertaken.

12.7 Conclusion

As this chapter presents, there is still much that needs to be done in the examination of stalking and obsessional behaviors in children and adolescents. Although this chapter has documented that stalking by children and adolescents is a problem that the criminal justice system must address, there is a need for research with larger samples and rigorous methodology. Among the issues that must be addressed are the demographic characteristics of children and adolescents who stalk, the relationship between the threatening behaviors in this population and violence, differences between adults and children who stalk, the risk factors that can be identified in children that may lead to adult stalking, interventions that can be used to stop the behavior in children from continuing into adulthood, and a separate typology for children and adolescents distinct from that of adults.

References

American Association of University Women Education Foundation (1993). Hostile Hallways: The AAUW Survey on Sexual Harassment in America's Schools. Washington, D.C.: Author.

American Psychiatric Association (2001). *Diagnostic and Statistical Manual for Mental Disorders*. 4th ed. Washington, D.C.: Author.

Araji, S.K. (1997). *Sexually Aggressive Children: Coming to Understand Them*. Thousand Oaks, CA: Sage.

Barbaree, H.E., Marshall, W.L., and Hudson, S.M. (1993). The *Juvenile Sex Offender*. New York: Guilford.

Bennett, L. and Fineran, S. (1998). Sexual and severe physical violence among high school students: power beliefs, gender, and relationship. *American Journal of Orthopsychiatry*, 68, 645–652.

Bergman, L. (1992). Dating violence among high school students. *Social Work*, 37, 21–27.

Bradfield, J.L. (1998). Anti-stalking laws: Do they adequately protect stalking victims? *Harvard Women's Law Journal*, 21, 229–266.

Cupach, W.R. and Spitzberg, B.H. (1998). Obsessive relational intrusions and stalking. In Spitzberg, B.H. and Cupach, W.R. (Eds.), *The Dark Side of Close Relationships*. Mahwah, NJ: Lawrence Erlbaum. pp. 233–263.

Fremouw, W.J., Westrup, D., and Penny Packer, J. (1997). Stalking on campus: the prevalence and strategies for coping with stalking. *Journal of Forensic Sciences*, 42, 666–669.

Freund, K., Sher, H., and Hucker, S. (1983). The courtship disorders. *Archives of Sexual Behavior*, 12, 369–379.

Greenberger, E. and McLaughlin, C.S. (1998). Attachment, coping, and explanatory style in late adolescence. *Journal of Youth and Adolescence*, 27, 121–139

Guy, R.A. (1993). The nature and constitutionality of stalking laws. *Vanderbilt Law Review*, 46, 991–1029.

Harmon, R., Rosner, R., and Owens, H. (1995). Obsessional harassment and erotomania in a criminal court population. *Journal of Forensic Sciences*, 40, 188–196

Harmon, R., Rosner, R., and Owens, H. (1998). Sex and violence in a forensic population of obsessional harassers. *Psychology, Public Policy and Law*, 4, 236–249.

Hazler, R.J. (1996). *Breaking the Cycle Of Violence: Interventions for Bullying and Victimization*. Washington, D.C.: Accelerated Development.

Hazen, C. and Shaver, P.R. (1994). Attachment as an organizational framework for research on close relationships. *Psychological Inquiry*, 5, 1–22.

Kienlen, K.K. (1997). Developmental and social antecedents of stalking. In Meloy, J.R. (Ed.), The *Psychology of Stalking: Clinical and Forensic Perspectives*. San Diego, CA: Academic Press. pp. 51–67.

Kienlen, K.K., Birmingham, D.L., Solberg, K.B., O'Regan, J.T., and Meloy, J.R. (1997). A comparative study of psychotic and nonpsychotic stalking. *Journal of American Academy of Psychiatry and the Law*, 25, 317–334.

Lewis, S.F., Fremouw, W.J., Del Ben, K., and Farr, C. (2001). An investigation of the psychological characteristics of stalkers: empathy, problem-solving, attachment and borderline personality features. *Journal of Forensic Sciences*, 46, 80–84.

McAnaney, K.G., Curliss, L.A., and Abeyta-Price, C.E. (1993) From imprudence to crime: anti-stalking laws. *Notre Dame Law Review*, 68, 819–909.

McCann, J.T. (1998). Risk of violence in stalking cases and legal case management. Pennsylvania Bar Association.

McCann, J.T. (2001). *Stalking in Children and Adolescents: The Primitive Bond.* Washington, D.C.: American Psychological Association.

Meloy, J.R. (1998) The psychology of stalking. In Meloy, J.R. (Ed.), *The Psychology of Stalking: Clinical and Forensic Perspectives.* San Diego, CA: Academic Press, pp. 1–23.

Meloy, J.R. (1999). Stalking: an old behavior, a new crime. *Psychiatric Clinics of North America*, 22, 85–99.

Meloy, J.R. and Gothard, S. (1995). A demographic and clinical comparison of obsessional followers and offenders with mental disorders. *American Journal of Psychiatry*, 152, 258–263.

Meloy, J.R., Rivers, L., Siegel, L., Gothard, S., Naimark, D., and Nicolini, R. (2000). A replication study of obsessional followers and offenders with mental disorders. *Journal of Forensic Sciences*, 45, 189–194.

Meloy, J.R. (1992). *Violent Attachments.* Northvale, NJ: Jason Aronson.

Meyers, J. and Meloy, J.R. (1994). Discussion of "A comparative study of erotomania and obsessional subjects in a forensic sample." *Journal of Forensic Sciences*, 39, 906–907.

Mullen, P.E. and Pathe, M. (1994). Stalking and the pathologies of love. *Australian and New Zealand Journal of Psychiatry*, 28, 469–477.

Mullen, P.E., Pathe, M., Purcell, R., and Stuart, G.W. (1999). Study of stalkers. *American Journal of Psychiatry*, 165, 614–623.

National Center for Victims of Crime. (1995). School Crime: K–12. Arlington, VA.

National Institute of Justice. (1993). Projects to Develop a Model Anti-Stalking Code for States (NIJ Publication No. NCJ 144477). Washington, DC; U.S. Government Printing Office.

National Institute of Justice. (1997). The Crime of Stalking: How Big Is the Problem? (NIJ Publication No. FS 000186). Washington, DC; U.S. Government Printing Office.

O'Keefe, N.K., Brockopp, K., and Chew, E. (1986). Teen dating violence. *Social Work*, 31, 465–468.

Roscoe, B. and Callahan, J.E. (1985). Adolescents' self-report of violence in families and dating relations. *Adolescence*, 20, 545–553.

Roscoe, B., Strouse, J.S., and Goodwin, M.P. (1994). Sexual harassment: Early adolescents' self-reports of experiences and acceptance. *Adolescence*, 29, 515–523.

Schwartz-Watts, D., Morgan, D.W., and Barnes, C.W. (1997). Stalkers: the South Carolina experience. *Journal of American Psychiatry and the Law*, 25, 541–545.

Suarez, K.E. (1994). Teenage dating violence: The need for expanded aware-ness and legislation. *California Law Review*, 82, 423–471.

Svedberg v. Stamness, NW2d 678 (N.D. 1994).

Urbach, J.R., Khalily, C., and Mitchell, P.P. (1992). Erotomania in an adolescent: clinical and theoretical considerations. *Journal of Adolescence*, 15, 231–240.

Westrup, D. and Fremouw, W.J. (1998). Stalking behavior: a literature review and suggested functional analytic assessment technology. *Aggression and Violent Behavior*, 3, 255–274.

Zona, M.A., Sharma, K.K., and Lane, J. (1993). A comparative study of erotomanic and obsessional subjects in a forensic sample. *Journal of Forensic Sciences*, 38, 894–903.

Part III Conclusion

DISCUSSION QUESTIONS FOR PART III

1. In Chapter 9, Miller-Potter et al. attempt to dispel the myth of the juvenile "superpredator." Do they accomplish this goal? Explain.
2. Explain how Crews et al. establish the cultural foundation for the development of Preppie Gangs (see Chapter 10). In what type of behaviors do these gangs engage? Briefly discuss the problems, according to these authors, with the community response to preppie gangs.
3. Briefly summarize Girard's (see Chapter 11) theoretical explanations for why young people engage in cybercrime. What are the legal problems and possible implications for dealing with juvenile cybercrime?
4. Compare the technical, legal, and behavioral definitions of stalking as outlined by Laufersweiler-Dwyer and Dwyer in Chapter 12. What do they mean by "obsessional behaviors" that are associated with juvenile stalking?

Part IV

POLICING AND PROSECUTING THE YOUTHFUL OFFENDER

There exists a plethora of issues surrounding the policing and prosecuting of the youthful offender in American society. Children, as has been established earlier in Part I, are viewed as needing special treatment, and this mindset, although chipped away at in the most recent past, is very much alive and well in the juvenile justice system. The next five chapters address problem-solving strategies for local police departments in their dealings with the youthful offender (Chapter 13 by McCluskey et al.), the recent increase in the juvenile curfew and issues associated with those practices (Chapter 14 by Ahmad and Ruiz), issues associated with prosecuting juveniles (Chapter 15 by Owen) as well as juvenile waiver (Chapter 16 by Hemmens and Steiner), and the early history and contemporary policies and programs dealing with status offenders (Chapter 17 by Burton and Tracy).

Chapter 13

Police Organizations and Problem-Solving Strategies for Juvenile Intervention: Identifying Crucial Elements

John D. McCluskey, Timothy S. Bynum,
Sean P. Varano, Beth M. Huebner, Justin W. Patchin,
and Amanda Burgess-Proctor

13.1 Introduction

The implementation of community policing and problem-solving strategies at the start of the 21st century has permeated the institution of policing in the United States such that there is near-universal desire for police managers to be associated with these ideas (Skogan and Hartnett, 1997). Part of the ethos of community policing, by some measures (Bayley, 1994), is that the agency no longer operates alone but builds partnerships to confront problems within the community.

These partnerships can include mental health services, building inspectors, community groups, and other actors focused on particular facets of the community and its problems.

This chapter centers on four departments that confronted the problem of young juvenile delinquents who were at great risk of becoming chronic delinquents. Each agency received a Byrne grant to engage in problem-solving strategies focused on juvenile crime and response development consonant with Eck and Spelman's (1987) scanning, analysis, response, and assessment (SARA) model. In the following text, we first outline the scope of the child delinquency problem in these four cities as well as nationally — which constitutes the scanning and analysis phase of the project. Next, we turn to a broader understanding of the essential elements for building a successful intervention program or developing a response. Finally, we examine the four sites to evaluate their success in implementing interventions with community partners or, more succinctly, whether the programs crafted in each site can be considered an effective use of the problem-solving strategy. To accomplish this, attention is given to five primary characteristics of the program implementation: variety of the program partners, the extent of support within the partnership network, the level of program awareness or knowledge among partners, the complexity of the programmatic response, and the commitment to evaluation of the outcome.

13.2 Early Onset

The work of Loeber and Farrington (2001) and their collaborators on early childhood intervention (see Loeber et al., 1998) has sparked interest both in identifying child delinquents and devising treatment programs for these "early starters." Howell (2001), in particular, argues for outlining comprehensive strategies and partnerships for dealing with child delinquents. This chapter describes the efforts of four police departments in dealing with arrested child delinquents. In 1999, each department was committed to addressing the needs of arrested and adjudicated youths 13 years old and younger through specialized services.

Motor, Lakeside, Central, and Riverside cities, all located in Michigan, engaged in problem-solving efforts (Bynum et al., 2000) that identified youths between the ages of 10 and 13 with a first- or second-time, nonviolent, serious offense as being at a very high risk of becoming a serious and/or chronic delinquent. The results of the problem-solving efforts, coupled with national research from the Office of Juvenile Justice and Delinquency Prevention's (OJJDP) Study Group on Serious and

Chronic Juvenile Offenders were the impetus for implementing a delinquency reduction strategy in each police agency. Analysis of official data as well as anecdotal evidence indicated that youth in this category were often overlooked (Snyder, 1998; Schumacher and Kurz, 2000). For example, interviews with personnel at each site indicated that dismissal of court cases or informal probation was the typical treatment for early offenders because their age and crime seemed trivial.

Recent research, however, indicates that these early starters are in need of special attention (Loeber et al., 1998). Rather than follow the tradition of nonintervention, the sites sought to bring early starters in contact with a variety of services and build a web of support and monitoring around these children. Howell (2001) for example, argues that if one adopts successful interventions that use the early starter as a focal point, then one can expect large yields in terms of recidivism reduction.

Building a varied and extensive program network is an intermediate step toward delivering the intensive programming and monitoring that youth are likely to require for a successful intervention. Another essential component of a network is the degree to which its members agree upon program goals. As noted by Loeber and Farrington (2001), information exchange and integration of services is essential for dealing with child delinquents and, thus, is an appropriate focal point for examining issues of implementation with regard to this target group.

13.3 Essential Elements for Programmatic Innovation

13.3.1 Integration of Key Policymakers (Stakeholders)

Terms such as *stakeholders* and *partners* have, to a large extent, become part of the day-to-day jargon of many program managers. The reliance on partnerships stems partly from the recognition that the synergy of cooperation is necessary to overcome intractable problems. Sadd and Grinc (1994, p. 41) note that " … no police department can do effective and efficient problem solving without the active involvement of other city agencies." This collaborative momentum has also been directly influenced by grant-funding agencies that have placed increasing emphasis on the identification and inclusion of key stakeholders.[1] Implementing successful interventions is not only contingent upon securing resources (e.g., grants) or having a vision for change, but on ensuring collaboration and interlinkage with organizations that sometimes have competing organizational goals (see generally Scott, 1987).

From the perspective of traditional organizational theory, organizations are rational entities that create logical processes to achieve predetermined and agreed-upon outcome measures of success (Denhardt, 1993). In the case of organizations related to the juvenile justice system, the rational model would stipulate that multiple components of the system function to achieve system-level goals. Regardless of the rationale, organizations have a basic interest in cooperating with other agencies in which they have exchange relations (Hall, 1991). Yet, observations of organizations, especially police organizations, clearly indicate that there are often competing goals within and between organizations that thwart unified movements toward collaboration, cooperation, and partnership (Sadd and Grinc, 1994). Thus, integrating key stakeholders into decision-making processes is important to ensure follow-through with agreed-upon decisions. As noted previously, the variety of other organizations that are brought into the stakeholder status is important because child delinquents are likely to have expansive service needs. Additionally, the exchange relationship that develops in interorganizational relationships, especially in terms of resources that grantees can make available, should be considered important for understanding program implementation. Grantees willing to directly subsidize other stakeholders, for example, should be considered as building a stronger stakeholder web.

13.3.2 Communication and Shared Vision

Once the proper policymakers have been brought to the table, the next most important aspect is to ensure that core members have a sense of a shared vision about the fundamental purpose of the program, the causal processes underlying the problem, and the strategies that are most likely to create the intended change. Essentially, the *analysis* and *response* phases of the Eck and Spelman (1987) model must be agreed upon by the participants. The effect of integrating key policymakers who have a shared vision can be a powerful determinant of success. As noted by Klofas et al. (1990), however, law enforcement agencies are typically not effective in generating collaborative communication patterns. In order to create a sense of a shared vision, the planning process must be grounded in a conceptual understanding of the *causes* (analysis) of the problem, and there must be a close connection between these causes and the characteristics of types of treatment strategies (response).

Lack of information sharing tends to be one of the biggest impediments to successful planning and implementation of any program

(Slayton, 2000). At least two types of information sharing must be considered. The first we consider is *definitional* information. This comprises the nature of the problem and the nature of the solution as understood in the local context. Sharing and refining definitional information is essential for building a cooperative, interorganizational response to the problem. The second type of information is *technical* information, including criminal histories, school data, social-service information, and other records collected and maintained by government or private sources.[2]

Obstacles to gathering technical information can thwart the analysis component of an intervention because data are usually protected by federal and state laws and local ordinances. For example, the Family Educational Rights and Privacy Act (FERPA) of 1974 placed strict guidelines over the dissemination of educational information to individuals outside the immediate school or school district. An approach that values the balance of technical information sharing with privacy can be effective in developing information sources. In contrast, an approach proceeding from the starting point that technical information sharing is inherently bad will likely fail. Educational institutions in all but one of the four sites, for example, were not data-sharing partners in the intervention because of broad institutional interpretation of the aforementioned FERPA statute.

Definitional information assembled by the grantees, from the standpoint of these four programs, was fairly similar across sites. The police agencies' problem-solving strategies yielded several "facts" from the analysis of technical data. First, youths aged 13 and under were at an elevated risk for becoming chronic delinquents if arrested for a serious nonviolent offense. Thus, a target group was defined in each city. Second, the definitional information drew upon the literature on the causes and correlates of delinquency, which has consistently demonstrated that early and serious offending is not only developmentally out of sequence, but that early offenders usually experience family, peer, school, and social problems that are considerably worse than those experienced by their peers. Acceptance of that definitional information by stakeholders at each site occurred in various settings with help from the Michigan State University (MSU) technical assistance team.

Developing shared definitions of target populations and approaches to problems is consistent with Hall's (1991) conception of ideological consensus, which is an important environmental factor that influences interorganizational relationships. Specifically, he notes, in the context of police and social welfare agencies:

Ideological issues can involve the compatibility of the goals of the organizations involved, conformity in terms of treatment ideologies in social service organizations, *or compatibility in terms of understanding the nature of the issues faced*. The ideological issue becomes important in practice. For example, police agencies typically have a different ideology toward problem youth than do social welfare agencies. These differences, which can be severe or mild, affect the qualities of interactions among the organizations. (1991, p. 226; italics added for emphasis)

In summary, we argue that the success with which any site was able to communicate and generate agreement about the definition of the problem and its solution across organizational boundaries is an important measure of implementation. The extent to which the analysis and response to the problem are known outside (and, to some extent, inside) the police agency is an important component of building an interorganizational response to child delinquency. Those collaborations in which definitional agreement is weak or nonexistent are unlikely to achieve the comprehensive response that Howell (2001) suggests is vital for handling the problems of child delinquents. In addition to a shared conception of what the problem and response ought to be, the complexity of the response, especially in light of the intricate etiology of child delinquency, should be taken into consideration as a measure of programmatic adequacy. Those programs that have a greater specificity in terms of the problem statement and logic model are likely to be more effective when compared with programs with simplistic notions of the problems that face delinquents.

13.3.3 Assessment and Evaluation

Determining what actually "works" in terms of rehabilitating serious juvenile offenders continues to pose one of the most significant challenges to policymakers. Indeed, as Lipsey and Wilson (1998, p. 314) aptly observed, there is "little systematic attention … given to reviewing the evidence for effectiveness with distinct types of offenders." As such, from a programmatic point of view, the most important challenge is planning for evaluation. Evaluation is, unfortunately, often an afterthought that usually results in insufficient data collection during the life of the program. It is important to stress that evaluation of the program should remain at the forefront of the planning process and at all subsequent stages of the intervention. In short, the viability of any evaluative effort is fundamentally dependent on the quality of the information collected prior to, during, and immediately following the program. Both process and outcome measures must be collected to best understand which methods prove effective.

A primary outcome element of this evaluation was assessed through the collection of detailed information on the individuals involved in the program and their response to the services provided. As noted, the purpose of the intervention project was to provide comprehensive intervention services to young, serious, first- or second-time offenders. As such, the program intended to provide services directed at the most basic causes of the problem (delinquency risk factors) and to inhibit program participants from maturing into more serious and chronic offenders. A comprehensive risk assessment was administered to all participants in the programs at or near intake to determine initial levels for risk. This risk assessment involved a structured interview including standard open- and closed-ended responses that identified constructs theoretically important to the onset and trajectory of delinquency careers (i.e., level of self-control, attitudes toward gangs, beliefs supporting aggression, attitudes toward school, and several measures of the familial bond). Follow-up interviews were also scheduled after 6 months and 12 months to discern any apparent subsequent reductions in risk. Because little is known about the treatment of child delinquency, tracking individual outcomes is truly an essential element of such a program (Loeber and Farrington 2001).

Additionally, each site was trained to collect data about the extent of program services, including frequency and type of contacts with program staff and extent of each juvenile's participation in specific program services. Other data were also collected at each research site from court, social service, and school records.[3]

As mentioned, part of the problem-oriented policing approach is to determine whether interventions worked and what changes might enhance the effectiveness of the program. Agencies that are most committed to problem solving are likely to hold themselves accountable to success measures beyond receiving grant award monies. Thus, we argue that those grantees that provide more information flow about the program population through the facilitation of data collection are likely to keep a successful intervention intact after seed money evaporates. Conversely, agencies that implement programs and pay little attention to outcomes are unlikely to have the capacity to continue efforts once temporary funds are exhausted.

Table 13.1   Site Demographics, Size, and Awards

City	Population (2000)	Poverty Level(%)	Police Department Size	Total Grant (Approximate)
Lakeside	197,800	8.9	366	$775,000
Central City	119,128	14.6	261	$600,000
Motor City	124,943	13.1	321	$500,000
Riverside	61,799	13.9	136	$465,000

Note: The average poverty level for the United States is 12.4 percent.

13.4 Site Descriptions

As discussed earlier, four police departments were invited to participate in the Michigan Juvenile Intervention Initiative (MJII). All of the police departments participating in this program were located in urban areas. A general description of the program models that were implemented in each site is given in the following text. In addition, general descriptive statistics as to the nature of each city and police department are included in Table 13.1.

The city of Lakeside is the largest of the participating sites and, correspondingly, has the largest police department. The city has collaborated with several stakeholders to develop and implement a program model that melds intense supervision and monitoring with comprehensive programming and prosocial activities. The intervention group is unique for this project in that only second-time offenders (between the ages of 10 and 13) who were arrested for a serious, nonviolent offense are enrolled in the program. The intervention program has four main components, including an established partnership with the probation department to provide both intensive monitoring and social services to all participants in the program. In addition, civilian surveillance officers are employed by the grant and are responsible for contacting the juveniles at multiple points during the day. A third component includes attendance at one of two recreational program centers provided by the city (or other suitable programs as determined by the court) as a condition of probation. Finally, an additional officer on the habitual offender team coordinates police activity with the Community Policing and Probation program and provides beat officers with updated information on juvenile offenders. Because of the depth of the programming provided in Lakeside, the site was also eligible to receive the largest amount of funding.

The Central City police department program has also developed from a preexisting partnership between the police department and probation. The staff funded by the grant is responsible for intensive supervision. In addition, the probation officer works to link youth with comprehensive services including drug testing and treatment and psychological counseling. This program is also unique in that a family counseling component is provided to families in need. Finally, the program is intended to create positive change in educational experiences by connecting students to tutoring and mentoring programs available through the local school district.

The Motor City intervention program is police-centered. Juveniles enrolled in this program, unlike those in the other sites, are not formally charged and the program serves as a quasi-diversion program. The program model is centered primarily on services provided through the Motor City Police Athletic League (PAL). Each program participant is expected to participate each day in the after-school programming offered at the PAL office. Three types of programming are provided including general recreation, biweekly group counseling sessions with a psychologist, and life-skills training provided by a local community group.

The Riverside Police Department program, also police-centered, includes both monitoring and service provision. The program is unique in that only males are eligible to participate. Individuals in the program are assigned to a probation officer and are referred to intensive programming services through this department. Programming addresses the problems of substance abuse, negative peer association, and poor educational achievement. The police officers employed by this program are responsible for providing strict monitoring of the enrolled youth.

13.5 Data and Methods

The four research sites have been in regular contact with the research team since the spring of 1999. Interviews were conducted with core staff (primarily grant-funded personnel) during periods of program observation in 2001 and 2002. These staff members acted as informants for key program participants in other agencies. This "snowball" type sample, based on informants, yielded 33 interviews with stakeholders across the four sites. The number of interviews ranged from 6 in Riverside to 11 in Lakeside. Interviews were semistructured and occurred in person and over the telephone. Analysis of the interviews produced measures of the varieties of stakeholders, the level of knowledge about the program that had passed from the police agency to the stakeholders, and the level of financial support that was extended from the grant recipients to other stakeholders. To augment the interviews, we also analyzed the grant applications from each department submitted in the fiscal year 2001 to determine the complexity of the problem definition and response generated by each site. Additionally, several meetings were convened throughout the program period where key personnel from each site were invited to report on progress.

13.5.1 Measures

A measure of the *varieties of stakeholders* indicates the number of different agency types that are partners with the delinquency intervention efforts in each of the cities. This measure is consonant with our first key element, which centers on integrating key stakeholders. Programs with more breadth are likely to be better able to provide for the service needs of child delinquents, which, as noted by Howell (2001), tend to be greater than typical delinquent youths.[4]

Stakeholder funding was coded from the interviews and grant applications and indicated whether the grant resources were used to support the home agency of the stakeholder. This effort indicated that unfunded stakeholders, funded stakeholders, and contractual stakeholders were considered partners with the four sites. Exchange relationships built on a funded interaction are likely to represent higher-quality interactions between agencies and lead to more elaborate analysis of the problem and collaborative solutions.

Stakeholder knowledge was coded as the level of knowledge that the interviewee had about the program. The coding was conducted as follows: 0 indicates that the interviewee was unclear or unfamiliar with the program; 1 indicates that the interviewee knows of the project (e.g., site-specific name) and that the program is focused on child delinquents; 2 indicates that the interviewee knows the target group and some activities that occur with youths; and 3 indicates that the interviewee has knowledge of program goals, target youths, and current activities. Where there is greater ideological consensus, the grantee has achieved greater acceptance of the definition of the problem (assessment) and the treatment strategy (response).

Complexity of the logic model was examined using grantee applications for fiscal years 2000–2002. Grant applications and corresponding problem statements and program models were analyzed for mention of key domains for early intervention. Five domains were examined including antisocial behavior, substance abuse, positive peer association, family problems, and school success. It is important to note that although a program may attempt to address a number of domains, the quality and intensity of the intervention is still likely to have a large impact on the outcome of participants (e.g., Lipsey and Wilson, 1998).

Assessment effort is measured using two sources. First, the total number of youths who received a risk-assessment survey is computed across each site. This was derived from records kept by the MSU research team and is not entirely reliable because it is partially dependent upon the cooperation of program juveniles. Second, and within the control of each department, we measured the completeness of the data collected on individuals at each site. Reasonably complete records, including contact and program information, were considered adequate data collection for evaluation. Overall, sites that are more committed to data collection are more likely to be dedicated to understanding whether and where program failure occurred. As such, one would argue that those sites are more attuned to the SARA model.

13.5.2 Analysis

Analysis of grants from the four sites and interview results yield interesting findings regarding the various dimensions of the problem-solving activity outlined earlier. We found wide variation with respect to the variety of stakeholders and the support that is given to partnerships as one might expect from a SARA approach to early delinquency (see Table 13.2). The approach in Lakeside incorporated a large number of different stakeholders within and outside the police department, including probation, prosecution, and recreation. In addition, the Lakeside Police Department funded the greatest number of partnerships through direct grant funding, including money for court and recreation personnel. The Central City model of problem solving also involved an array of external partnerships. In this city, however, the court was the sole partner funded directly through the grant. All other partnerships were contractual, whereby the grantee paid user fees for services. Neither Motor City nor Riverside had a grant-funded partner, though Motor City had a fair number of external relationships

Table 13.2   Stakeholder Funding and Knowledge of Program

Site/Stakeholders	Number Interviewed	Mean Knowledge	Funding Source
Lakeside			
Police department	3	3.00[c]	Grant-funded
Family court/probation	3	3.00[c]	Grant-funded
Recreation	3	2.33	Grant-funded
Prosecutor	2	0.00[d]	Unfunded
Total nonpolice (external)	8	2.00	Grant-funded (2)
Central City			
Police department	1	3.00[c]	Grant-funded
Family court/probation	1	3.00[c]	Grant-funded
Counseling	3	0.33	Contractual
Community mental health	1	2.00	Contractual
Other[a]	1	0.00[d]	Contractual
Total nonpolice (external)	6	1.00	Grant-funded (1)
Motor City			
Police department	2	2.50	Grant-funded
Family court/probation	1	1.00	Unfunded
Counseling	3	1.33	Contractual
Other[b]	3	1.33	Unfunded
Total nonpolice (external)	7	1.14	Grant-funded (0)
Riverside			
Police department	1	3.00[c]	Grant-funded
Family court/probation	4	1.50	Unfunded
Total nonpolice (external)	4	1.50	Grant-funded (0)

[a] Drug-testing personnel.

[b] One school official and two community leaders (one from Weed and Seed and one from a soup kitchen).

[c] A score of 3.00 indicates that the respondent had a strong knowledge of the program.

[d] A score of 0.00 indicates that the respondent had no knowledge of the program.

developed beyond the family court. Those relationships largely involved counselors who serviced youths on a contract basis.

With respect to levels of program knowledge, we found that most stakeholders we interviewed (outside of the police departments) lacked intimate knowledge of the programs. In terms of the complexity of approach, as measured by the risk factors attended to by the program model, we found that the sites generally took a multifactor approach.

Lakeside clearly led all four sites in effectively communicating the definition of the problem to those outside the immediate police department. On average, the external stakeholders in Lakeside scored a 2.00 on our scale (mean knowledge, Table 13.2), indicating familiarity with the program. Especially encouraging is the fact that those stakeholders from the Lakeside recreation programs who were interviewed scored a 2.33 on that measure. Riverside's external level of knowledge was the next highest at 1.50, which indicates incomplete communication (outside of the police department). It is important to note that Riverside's external interviewees came entirely from the family court where scores indicating complete familiarity with the program among stakeholders had been obtained in Lakeside and Central City. Central City and Motor City had respective scores of 1.00 and 1.14 in communicating their program-model goals and definitions to external stakeholders. It is interesting to note, especially with regard to counselors in contractual relationships, that the communication of the program model was noticeably absent in both sites. In Central City, however, the grant-funded stakeholder in their family court had a score of 3.00 for program familiarity.

Complexity of program model is an indicator of the comprehensive approach that the sites implemented to deal with child delinquency. Central City's program model addressed four of the five risk factors, Riverside and Lakeside three risk factors, and Motor City only addressed peer association and antisocial behavior (see Table 13.3).

The results presented in Table 13.4 indicate that there were large differences in sites' commitment to data collection. Motor City, for example, had a 92 percent completion rate for participant surveys; however, they collected no on-site data for their program. Therefore, program data are not available to determine whether intensity influences outcomes. Conversely, Central City collected contact information for 75 percent of the program participants but only facilitated interviews with 68 percent. At the extremes, Lakeside had high levels of data collection on both measures whereas Riverside had low levels on both, including 41 percent of the surveys completed and 38 percent of the basic on-site information collected.

Table 13.3   Risk Factors for Intervention

	Domains for Intervention				
Site	Antisocial Behavior	Substance Abuse	Positive Peer Association	Family Problems	School Success
Lakeside		×	×		×
Central City	×	×		×	×
Motor City	×		×		
Riverside		×	×		×

Table 13.4   Site Evaluation Efforts

City	Total Number of Juveniles	Completed 1st Interviews[a]	Basic Information Collected[b]	Contact Information Collected[b]	Juveniles Dismissed to Date[c]
Lakeside	84	62 (74%)	77 (92%)	60 (71%)	39 (46%)
Central City	60	41 (68%)	45 (75%)	56 (93%)	24 (40%)
Motor City	26	24 (92%)	0 (0%)	0 (0%)	17 (65%)
Riverside	37	15 (41%)	14 (38%)	19 (51%)	16 (43%)

[a] Although the evaluation team conducted these interviews, program administrators at each site were responsible for ensuring that program youth were available to be interviewed on specified days.

[b] Each individual site is responsible for collecting this information, entering it into an Access database, and forwarding it to the evaluation team.

[c] Dismissed due to program completion or discharged due to a violation of program rules.

Overall, it appears that two sites, Central City and Lakeside, were able to integrate segments of the service community into a complex and varied response to early childhood delinquency. The other two sites, Motor City and Riverside, exemplify agencies that were less able to formulate a solid response to their problem statement, especially with regard to external collaboration. Their approaches recognized the complexity of the situations confronted by childhood delinquents, but they failed to integrate those needs into a multiagency collaboration. Unlike the tactic suggested by Sadd and Grinc (1994), where police agencies must seek to build partnerships outside their agencies, these two sites essentially adopted an independent approach. Both utilized police as mentors to the youths, and neither had sufficiently detailed plans for execution or significant cooperation from agencies experienced in dealing with juveniles (e.g., the courts and probation). Thus, complexity without cooperation or effective communication patterns with external agencies cuts down on the innovation that these two programs can bring to the youths they serve.

From numerous hours of on-site observation, technical assistance, and evaluation research, it appears that innovations that target child delinquents are likely to require preexisting and, perhaps, co-funded relationships between the juvenile court and the police. In Lakeside and Central City, where youths arguably have the greatest exposure to services (both through police funding and through programs that courts may have available for young offenders), the partnership between courts and police has been formalized and is supported by grant money that passes through the police department. It should be noted that the cooperation between these agencies existed prior to the introduction of grant funding, but the problem of child delinquency was not the focus of that interaction. In the latter two sites, the partnership with the courts was informal to nonexistent. By failing to partner successfully with an outside agency, these two sites offer limited breadth of programming for the youth that they serve.

One is likely inclined to argue that we have ordinally ranked four sites on implementation, but we have not spoken of the issue of outcomes for youths in these programs. Given the limited space, we can say that the same ranking holds in terms of services received by youths (McCluskey, 2002). Lakeside and Central City provide high levels of service to their youths, whereas the latter two sites keep minimal records on services provided. In addition, limited data on frequency of contacts indicate that the relationship between program intensity (nearly daily contact in Lakeside and somewhat lower levels in Central City and Riverside) and the web of informed stakeholders also is directly and positively associated. If one accepts the importance of program intensity and comprehensiveness of service for these youths, then these implementation patterns will be important to policy makers and service providers alike. One optimistic observation that we have made is that sites which are likely to effectively implement programs appear willing to expend energy on documenting extensively the actions taken with individual clients (a necessary element of a comprehensive evaluation and program revision).

13.6 Conclusion

In the preceding text, we have outlined several elements that are starting points for building comprehensive partnerships among criminal justice agencies and service providers to deal with child delinquents and their problems. Our observations and interviews reveal that preexisting partnerships among agencies and a shared commitment to the definition of a problem, as well as routes to the solution, are the *sine qua non* of building more comprehensive early juvenile interventions. A more general statement about the funding of innovative programming is suggested. Partnerships that are fashioned from the necessities of grant requirements are unlikely to germinate programs that are problem focused and more likely to result in efforts to maintain funding. Despite the effort of building a coalition through the problem-solving process for 1 year of grant funding, two of the sites were unable to successfully partner with other criminal justice agencies. The two agencies that did successfully incorporate the juvenile court and probation into the program already had a preexisting level of interagency cooperation. Moving across an interagency boundary to address a novel issue such as child delinquency requires an unfunded cooperation, because funding itself does not appear to be useful in encouraging interagency cooperation. This suggests that models such as the Strategic Approaches to Community Safety Initiative (SACSI) built from the Boston and Indianapolis violence-reduction models (Kennedy, 1997; McGarrell et al., 2002), which bring agencies together under an umbrella of problem identification and implementation of a comprehensive solution (e.g., Bynum, 2001), serve as an alternative to the "ready, fire, aim" approach noted by Sherman (2001).

Preliminary analysis of the level and intensity of contacts and varieties of services that individual youth receive in each of these four programs indicates that they are ordinally ranked according to the level of comprehensiveness and goal sharing among stakeholders at each site (McCluskey, 2002). Preliminary analyses of the most integrated site indicate that the Lakeside program has substantially reduced recidivism among youthful offenders (Bynum, 2002; Patchin, 2002).

13.6.1 Future Directions

The initial reaction to these results is that the acquisition of sufficient resources has been erroneously omitted from the analysis. Contrary to common sense, resource availability was not placed on the list of crucial elements. Yet, after 5 years of participation in the MJII program, our collective experiences firmly indicate that resources were, in reality, not as important as many had originally anticipated. More crucial was the inclusion of the key policymakers, a sense of shared vision, and the will to make change happen. Innovation was possible in agencies in which innovation and creativity were fostered as part of the normal routines of the organization. Inter- and intra-agency conflict and failure appeared to be justified on the "lack of resources" thesis. Not surprisingly, two agencies made little to no progress in establishing creative, innovative responses to delinquency even after being provided liberal access to substantial sums of grant dollars and a full research team to assist with implementation issues.

As noted by Loeber and Farrington (2001), there is a need for understanding what does not work just as much as there is a need for finding solutions to problems. Documenting future efforts at early intervention across multiple sites is useful for understanding how programs fail. Had fewer sites been chosen, one might have formed a mistaken impression about how successful police can be in partnering and problem-solving issues such as early juvenile delinquency. Consonant with that conclusion, we argue that greater attention must be paid to the outcomes that youths had in these programs. In a time of scarce grant resources, implementation and outcome measures must be collected to ensure that an effective program is continued and ineffective programming is eliminated (Maxfield, 2001).

References

Bayley, D.H. (1994). *Police for the Future*. New York: Oxford University Press.

Bynum, T.S. (2001). *Using Analysis for Problem-Solving: A Guidebook for Law Enforcement*. Washington, D.C.: Office of Community Oriented Policing Services.

Bynum, T. S. (2002). The Michigan Juvenile Intervention Initiative: Assessing Program Outcomes. Paper presented at the American Society of Criminology, Chicago, IL.

Bynum, T.S., McCluskey, J.D., Huebner, B.M., Varano, S.V., and Patchin, J.W. (2000). Michigan Juvenile Intervention Initiative Fiscal Year 2000 Report on Project Activities. East Lansing, MI: Michigan State University.

Cohen, D. (2001). Problem-Solving Partnerships: Including the Community for a Change. Washington, D.C.: Office of Community Oriented Policing Services (COPS).

Denhardt, R.B. (1993). *Theories of Public Organizations.* Belmont, CA: Wadsworth.

Eck, J. and Spelman, W. (1987). Problem-Solving: Problem Orient Policing in Newport News. Washington D.C.: U.S. Department of Justice, National Institute of Justice.

Hall, R.H. (1991). *Organizations: Structures, Processes, and Outcomes.* Englewood Cliffs, NJ: Prentice Hall.

Howell, J.C. (2001). Juvenile justice programs and strategies. In Loeber, R. and Farrington, D.P. (Eds.), *Child Delinquents: Development, Intervention, and Service Needs.* Thousand Oaks, CA: Sage.

Kennedy, D.M. (1997). *Juvenile Gun Violence and Gun Markets in Boston.* Washington, D.C.: National Institute of Justice.

Klofas, J., Stojkovic, S., and Kalinich, D. (1990). *Criminal Justice Organizations: Administration and Management.* Pacific Grove, CA: Brooks/Cole.

Lipsey, M.W. and Wilson, D.B. (1998). Effective intervention for serious juvenile offenders. In Farrington, D.P. (Ed.), *Serious and Violent Juvenile Offenders* Thousand Oaks, CA: Sage. pp. 313–345.

Loeber, R. and Farrington, D.P. (2001). *Child Delinquents: Development, Intervention, and Service Needs.* Thousand Oaks, CA: Sage.

Loeber, R., Farrington, D.P., and Washbush, D.A. (1998). Serious and violent juvenile offenders. In Farrington, D.P. (Ed.), *Serious and Violent Juvenile Offenders.* Thousand Oaks, CA: Sage. pp. 13–29.

Maxfield, M. (2001). Guide to Frugal Evaluation for Criminal Justice, Final Report. Washington, D.C.: National Institute of Justice.

McCluskey, J.D. (2002). Police Problem-Solving and the Nature of Juvenile Interventions in Four Cities. Paper presented at the American Society of Criminology, Chicago IL.

McGarrell, E.F., Chermak, S., and Weiss, A. (2002). Reducing Gun Violence: Evaluation of the Indianapolis Police Department's Directed Patrol Project. Washington, D.C.: National Institute of Justice.

Patchin, J.W. (2002). Issues in Juvenile Delinquency Programming: Measuring and Assessing Change. Paper presented at the American Society of Criminology, Chicago, IL..

Sadd, S. and Grinc, J. (1994). Innovative neighborhood oriented policing: an evaluation of community policing programs in eight cities. In Rosenbaum, D.P. (Ed.), *The Challenge of Community Policing.* Thousand Oaks, CA: Sage.

Scott, W.R. (1987). *Organizations: Rational, Natural, and Open Systems* 2nd ed. Englewood Cliffs, NJ: Prentice Hall.

Sherman, L.W. (2001). Reducing gun violence. In National Institute of Justice (Ed.). *Perspectives on Crime and Justice: Lecture Series.* Washington, D.C.: National Institute of Justice.

Schumacher, M. and Kurz, G.A. (2000). *The 8% Solution: Preventing Serious, Repeat Juvenile Crime*. Thousand Oaks, CA: Sage.

Skogan, W.G. and Hartnett, S.M. (1997). *Community Policing, Chicago Style*. New York: Oxford University Press.

Slayton, J. (2000). Establishing and Maintaining Interagency Information Sharing (No. NCJ178281). Washington, D.C.: Office of Juvenile Justice and Delinquency Prevention.

Snyder, H.N. (1998). Appendix: serious, violent, and chronic juvenile offenders. In Loeber, R. and Farrington, D.P. (Eds.), *Serious and Violent Juvenile Offenders*. Thousand Oaks: Sage Publications. pp. 428–444.

Notes

1. Many programs funded through the U.S. Department of Justice's grant dissemination agencies make specific requirements or strongly encourage the identification and inclusion of appropriate policymakers in the planning process. For example, many documents distributed by the Office of Community Oriented Policing Services (COPS) intended to assist practitioners in implementing successful programs specifically identify this as a key ingredient to success (Cohen, 2001).

2. The aggregation of this technical information, in the cases of the juvenile intervention projects, is what led to the definitional information about early starters and their problems at the local level. This dichotomy is a device for differentiating agency data (arrests, grades, etc.) from information that is interpreted by the stakeholders. In this case, the data were interpreted to mean that intervention with child delinquents would be warranted.

3. School records proved to be the most difficult data to obtain; we were only able to gain access to this data in one city.

4. It should be noted that, although the initial contact was in the police agency, each respondent was queried for other contacts that serve key roles in dealing with the youth in the program. This ensured that service to youth that might have been "hidden" from the police in terms of daily working of the program would be uncovered by the snowball method.

Chapter 14

Juvenile Curfews: The Recent Increase of Their Use

Janice Ahmad and James Ruiz

14.1 Introduction

Curfews have long been used to control the movement of certain groups of people during specific hours and in certain places. Emergency curfews are often established during times of natural or man-made disasters and are for a short duration until order can be restored. During the early and mid-1800s restrictions were placed on the movement of African Americans to further control slaves as well as those African Americans who had been freed. The hours that juveniles can be on the street or the places they can be present have been restricted by governmental entities for almost 12 decades. These restrictions were established to protect juveniles from becoming victims of crime and to reduce crimes committed by juveniles, including gang members. More recently, states have implemented graduated drivers' licensing programs which, in effect, restrict the times that juveniles can drive and limits their association with their peers, at least while operating a motor vehicle. In this chapter, we discuss the purpose and extent of youth curfews, the arguments that have been put forth in support of and in opposition to juvenile curfews, and the legal issues and research on such laws. We conclude with the role of the police in curfew enforcement and policy issues relating to juvenile curfews.

14.2 Purpose and Extent of Youth Curfews

The main concern with juvenile criminal and deviant behavior has been regard for the future. Shoemaker (1990) noted that, "… the concern over youthful deviance stems from the thought (however accurate) that today's delinquent is tomorrow's criminal, if nothing is done to change the antisocial behavior of the youth" (p. 4). This line of thinking has prompted adults to question the effectiveness of laws and policies regulating juvenile behavior and yet, at the same time, push for more effective and creative solutions to what appears to be a persistent problem. One of these solutions is the passage of juvenile curfew laws by many local jurisdictions, as well as by some state legislatures.

Violation of juvenile curfews falls in the second type of behavior recognized as delinquent acts by the criminal justice community — status offenses. These acts apply only to juveniles, unlike those of the first type, which are considered criminal if committed by an adult. Examples of status offenses include, but are not limited to, school truancy, runaways, youths classified as uncontrollable, underage drinking and smoking, and curfew violations (Lundman, 1993).

Curfews were originally adopted by entities in the United States in the 1890s to check delinquency among immigrant juveniles. During World War II, youth curfews were used to control juvenile behavior, as many parents were occupied in the defense industry (OJJDP, 1997). Curfews reemerged in the 1970s as a means of combating increasing juvenile crime (Henry, 1995) and have continued to make a comeback due to the effort by policymakers to deter juvenile delinquency.

Curfew laws can be viewed as being based on deterrence theory, which reasons that swift, certain, and severe punishment will cause juveniles to consider the repercussions of their actions and engage in less delinquent activity. Youth curfews may also act as deterrent against juvenile and adult victimization (Lundman, 1993; Ruefle et al., 1997). Yet others claim that arresting juveniles for actions that if committed by adults would not be a criminal violation infringes on fundamental constitutional protections, causes unneeded friction between the police and juveniles, and is a poor method of deterring crime (Harvard Law Review Association, 1997).

Another theory that could be used to justify the adoption of curfew laws is the incapacitation theory. According to this theory, the majority of juvenile delinquency is perpetrated by a few whose identity can be ascertained, and their activities constrained. Curfews, it is argued, could be employed to selectively incapacitate only those juveniles identified as recidivists or repeat offenders and need not be applied to all juveniles. Boston's Operation Nightlight incorporated curfews to incapacitate only those juveniles on probation and was declared successful in preventing homicides (Lundman, 1993). This theory may also have support from a study conducted in Largo, FL, in which juveniles who self-reported being picked up by the police for violating the curfew law reported more involvement in other delinquent acts, including running away from home, truancy, burglary, vandalism, theft, assault, and robbery; higher usage of alcohol and other drugs; and higher rates of criminal victimizations than those who reported not being apprehended for curfew violations (Lersch and Sellers, 2000). Therefore, one could argue that apprehending juveniles for violating curfew laws could incapacitate them before they commit additional delinquent or deviant acts or become the victim of a crime. However, Lersch and Sellers' study did not link the time of criminal and deviant acts to curfew times, so the deviant acts reported could have been done during the hours not covered by a curfew.

There are several objectives for curfew laws, such as preventing juvenile delinquency, protecting juveniles from becoming victims of crime, identifying at-risk children, assisting parents to set boundaries for their children, and acting in the parents' place for those parents who abdicate their parental role (O'Brien, 1999; Ruefle and Reynolds, 1995). By requiring that juveniles not be on the street during certain hours, they can be prevented from engaging in crime, and their chances of being victimized during those hours can be decreased. Enforcement of curfew laws may help identify at-risk children who are away from their homes because of abuse, neglect, or criminal behavior by the parent or other siblings, and through the use of curfew centers, identification can be made and resources provided to the child and family. Finally, curfew laws can help parents in setting boundaries and rules regarding when their children should be home at night as the parents now are backed by legal sanctions if juveniles violate curfew.

Those opposed to curfew laws claim that curfew laws should not be passed on legal and practical grounds. The National Council on

Crime and Delinquency (NCCD) claims that curfews are unproductive, and they needlessly "widen the net" to channel nondelinquent youth into an already overburdened criminal justice system. Critics also point to research indicating a lack of empirical evidence on the effectiveness of curfew laws in reducing crime and on the repercussions of curfew enforcement on the overall criminal justice system (Ruefle and Reynolds, 1995). Joseph (1999) argues that curfews are not effective as they may not be enforced at all or be selectively enforced, criminalize status instead of behavior, take away child-rearing responsibility from the parent, and penalize the child in an abusive relationship and not the parents. He also argues that limited governmental resources would be better used in the detection and prevention of criminal behavior, not status offenses.

Although juvenile curfew laws are controversial, with convincing arguments on both sides, curfews have become commonplace in the legislative landscape of most local governments in the United States. Research conducted by the U.S. Conference of Mayors of 1,000 cities with populations over 30,000 found that 70 percent had curfew laws (*Washington Post*, December 26, 1995). More recently, Bannister et al. (2001) surveyed 797 municipal police departments serving jurisdictions of 15,000 or more citizens and found that 68 percent of the 446 responding agencies had a juvenile curfew. Of those with curfew laws, two-thirds had such ordinances in place for over 5 years, whereas less than 5 percent reported passing such a law during the previous year. Interestingly, almost 10 percent had daytime restrictions as well as nighttime ones, allowing police officers to investigate juveniles who were on the street during school hours.

Curfew restrictions differ according to locale, time regulated, age, and penalties assessed. Commonly, juveniles are required to be off the street or out of public places during the hours of 11:00 PM to 6:00 AM, but these hours are sometimes extended on weekends and during summer months when school is not in session. Exceptions are generally made for youths attending or traveling to and from school, religious, and public functions or employment, during emergency situations, traveling with the permission of the parent, if accompanied by an adult, or if married. Some curfew laws target particular areas, such as high-crime areas or commercial areas that may cause juveniles to be victimized or increase the potential of juveniles to be involved in delinquency (OJJDP, 1997). As so many communities have curfew laws in place, we now turn to an examination of some programs that have been put in place to effectively enforce the curfew law and deal with curfew violators.

14.2.1 Examples of Curfew Programs

OJJDP (1996) evaluated curfew enforcement and programs in seven jurisdictions. The jurisdictions reported using one or more programs in an effort to reduce juvenile delinquency and victimization and increase compliance with curfew hours. These programs included a dedicated curfew center to which curfew violators were taken and which was staffed with social service professionals and community volunteers. Several intervention efforts were available, such as referrals to social service providers; counseling for juveniles and their families; recreation, antidrug, antigang, and jobs programs; and hotlines for follow-up services and crisis intervention. For youths who were repeat offenders, different procedures were in place, including fines, counseling, or community service sentences.

A summary of the principal characteristics of juvenile curfew laws for each of the seven jurisdictions in the OJJDP study is provided in Table 14.1 and Table 14.2. It is interesting to compare the different characteristics of, and the exceptions provided by, each ordinance. As you can see, penalties for curfew infractions vary from $50 to hundreds of dollars. In addition, parental responsibility provisions were found in some ordinances, including fines, participation in diversion programs, and even jail sentences (OJJDP, 1996). Some of the cities in this study are clearly concerned about the constitutionality of their ordinance and have provided exceptions to the curfew ordinance in an effort to make it less likely for the curfew law to be ruled unconstitutional.

OJJDP (1996) indicated that all jurisdictions, except Jacksonville, reported decreases in juvenile delinquency. Because Jacksonville's program had been in operation for less than a year, it was deemed too early to determine its impact. However, "[t]he initial evidence offered by the seven communities profiled in this bulletin is that community-based curfew programs that offer a range of services are more easily and effectively enforced, enjoy community support, and provide a greater benefit in preventing juvenile delinquency and victimization" (p. 9). In the section on research, we examine other research concerning the effectiveness of juvenile curfews and their ability to meet their objectives. But before we do that, we look at the legal issues that have surfaced in regard to juvenile curfew laws.

14.3 Legal Issues

The U.S. Supreme Court has denied *certiorari* in three cases concerning the constitutionality of curfew laws (*Bykofsky v. Borough of Middletown*,

Table 14.1   Statutory Provisions of Juvenile Curfew Ordinances in Seven Jurisdictions

Jurisdiction	Age (Years)	Weekday Times	Weekend Times	Parental Fines: Discretionary
Dallas	Under 17	11 PM–6 AM	12 AM–6 AM	Up to $500
Phoenix	15 or under	10 PM–5 AM	10 PM–5 AM	Up to $75
	16 and 17	12 AM–5 AM	12 AM–5 AM	Up to $75
Chicago	Under 17	10:30 PM–6 AM	11 PM–6 AM	$200–$500
New Orleans	Under 17	8 PM–6 AM, September–May	11 PM–6 AM	$500 and/or 60 hours of community
		9 PM–6 AM, June–August		service at discretion of judge,
				$23 court fee per ticket
Denver	Under 18	11 PM–5 AM	12 AM–5 AM	None
N. Little Rock	17 or under	10 PM–6 AM	12 AM–6 AM	Fine for second violation, but
				suspended for 1 year if no more
				violations
Jacksonville	Under 18	11 PM–6 AM	12 AM–6 AM	None

Source: Office of Juvenile Justice and Delinquency Prevention (OJJDP) (1996). *Curfew: An Answer to Juvenile Delinquency and Victimization.* Rockville, MD: U.S. Department of Justice, p. 4.

Table 14.2 Exceptions to Juvenile Curfew Ordinances in Seven Cities

City	Adult Escort	Interstate Commerce, Travel Activities	First Amendment Rights	Travel to or from Work	Emergency, Necessity	Married	Attending School, Religious, or Supervised Activity	Sidewalk Bordering Residence
Dallas	X	X	X	X	X	X	X	
Phoenix	X			X		X	X	
Chicago	X			X		X	X	
New Orleans	X			X			X	
Denver	X	X		X	X		X	X
N. Little Rock	X	X	X	X	X		X	
Jacksonville	X	X	X	X	X		X	X

Source: Office of Juvenile Justice and Delinquency Prevention (OJJDP) (1996). *Curfew: An Answer to Juvenile Delinquency and Victimization.* Rockville, MD: U.S. Department of Justice, p. 5.

1976; *Qutb et al. v. Strauss*, 1994; *Schleifer ex rel. Schleifer v. City of Charlottesville*, 1999). The refusal by the Court to hear such cases has left a mixture of circuit court rulings. Three circuit courts (Third, Fourth, and District of Columbia) have ruled the curfew ordinances they examined as constitutional; whereas the Second, Seventh, and Ninth circuits determined other curfew laws were unconstitutional. The Fifth Circuit ruled in an early case that a curfew law was unconstitutional, but in a later case determined that the appealed curfew law, from a different jurisdiction, was constitutional. These rulings are indicative of the differences in curfew laws, the appellate challenges made, and the level of scrutiny applied by the courts.

The first case to be appealed to a circuit court was *Bykofsky v. Borough of Middletown* (1975). The curfew law in this case, along with those in *Qutb v. City of Dallas* (1993), *Schleifer v. City of Charlottesville* (1998), and *Hutchins v. District of Columbia* (1999) was deemed constitutional, whereas the cases in *Johnson et al. v. City of Opelousas* (1981), *Nunez by Nunez v. City of San Diego* (1997), *Ramos v. Town of Vernon et al.* (2003) and *Hodgkins et al. v. Peterson et al.* (2004) were determined to be unconstitutional. The differences in the rulings appear to be due to the differences in the laws themselves and the bases for implementing them. The curfew laws that were upheld provided several exceptions that allowed minors to participate in First Amendment activities, allowed parents to remain responsible in most child-rearing areas, connected the need for the curfew law to a stated government purpose, and had clear language. The curfews that did not hold up under appeal were weak in one or more of these areas.

Although the circuit courts used different levels of scrutiny (i.e., strict scrutiny, rational basis, or intermediate scrutiny) when reaching their decisions, it appears that this was not the link between statutes that were found constitutional and those that were not. In other words, some courts applied strict scrutiny, in which the law must be narrowly tailored to promote a compelling governmental interest, and found some curfew ordinances constitutional and others not. Several other courts applied intermediate scrutiny, which requires the ordinance be substantially related to important governmental interests and, again, rulings were mixed.

Given this mix of decisions and the different levels of scrutiny that have been applied, U.S. Supreme Court watchers are perplexed as to why the Court has not agreed to hear a case concerning curfew ordinances. Perhaps the reasoning can be found in the decision of another U.S. Supreme Court case in which the Court wrote "the peculiar vulnerability of children; their inability to make critical decisions in an informed, mature manner; and the importance of the parental role in child-rearing" (*Bellotti v. Baird*, 1979, p. 638) justifies, in some cases, more restraints for children than for adults. Given this, the overall question in juvenile curfew laws remains the balance between (1) the government's interest of protecting children and the community from crime and victimization, (2) the least interference with juveniles' freedom of movement and practice of First Amendment rights, and (3) limited interference with parental responsibility of raising their children.

14.4 Research on Curfew Laws and Enforcement

The popularity of youth curfew laws as a means of attempting to control juvenile involvement in crime and potential criminal victimization can be demonstrated by a search of newspaper articles in which cities as varied as Buffalo, New York (Tan, 2002), Chicago, Illinois (Vock, 2003), Houston, Texas (Summa, 2003), Lancaster, Pennsylvania (*Lancaster New Era*, November 8, 2002), Palmdale, California (*Los Angeles Daily News*, October 13, 2002), and Wilmington, North Carolina (Ives, 2002) were highlighted in articles that dealt with the problem of juvenile crime and curfews. In an article by Kawada (2003), the widespread adoption of curfews is further demonstrated in that it was reported that more than 60 municipalities in the state of Washington have similar curfew ordinances. Due to the popularity of juvenile curfews, it is important to review research that has been conducted to determine if these laws are effective and meet their objectives.

In a review of enforcement of curfew ordinances, Ruefle and Reynolds (1995) found that 71 percent of cities with curfew laws used police personnel on regular duty for enforcement and the remaining cities used police personnel on an overtime basis when needed. These additional personnel were employed specifically for sweeps, "zero tolerance," and occasional crackdowns for brief periods. The use of police resources in this manner is expensive and the effectiveness of the expenditure must be considered when implementing such a program.

A study by the Center on Juvenile and Criminal Justice (2002) examined juvenile arrest data from the California Department of Justice's Law Enforcement Information Center covering 1980 to 1996. The study hypothesized that community governments with rigid curfew enforcement would have lower arrests for curfew violations and serious juvenile crime than locales with less curfew restrictions; however, it was found that in "many jurisdictions serious juvenile crime increased at the very time officials were touting the crime reduction effects of strict curfew enforcement" (CJCJ, 2002, p. 9). It was also hypothesized that jurisdictions with strict juvenile curfew enforcement would experience a reduction in juvenile crime when compared to adult crime, but "[o]n virtually every measure, no discernable effect on juvenile crime was observed" (CJCJ, 2002, p. 9). What was found was that adult and juvenile crime rose and fell in unison. That is to say, when adult violent crime rates rose, the rates of juvenile crime rose as well. It was also argued that higher levels of curfew enforcement resulted in more juvenile arrests for status rather than criminal offenses. As such, proactive policing of curfew violations could be considered selective incapacitation in that such a stance would be "detaining youths likely to commit crime" (p. 5).

In another study on the effectiveness of juvenile curfew laws, Reynolds et al. (2000) examined the outcome of curfew enforcement in New Orleans. Using time-series analysis, they compared victimizations and arrests before and after curfew implementation. Contrary to the initial reports of success in the New Orleans program (OJJDP, 1996), the researchers concluded that the New Orleans curfew was ineffective as there was no significant decrease in overall criminal victimizations, juvenile victimizations, and juvenile arrests. It must also be noted that victimizations during noncurfew hours increased after implementation of the curfew law. Based on these findings, the researchers concluded that curfew laws failed to properly implement the theory and research concerning juvenile delinquency, did not significantly change the dominant correlates of delinquency (exposure to delinquent peers, school, and the family), and were grounded on the erroneous assumption that police crackdowns reduce crime. Reynolds et al. (2000) deemed the juvenile curfew laws were ineffective because they failed to include older adolescents and young adults who comprise a large group of crime perpetrators, and the laws, for the most part, did not cover the hours during which juveniles most commonly committed crime.

Washington, D.C. enacted a juvenile curfew law in 1995 that was later declared unconstitutional by the court. In 1999, the curfew was once again put into place when the first court ruling was reversed (Cole, 2003). Cole compared total juvenile arrests before and after each implementation of the curfew law and found, contrary to expectations, that no differences existed in the arrest rate of juveniles after the implementation of the curfew law. Cole speculated that the reasons for this were that juvenile crime occurred at times not covered by the curfew (especially the hours immediately after school), enforcement of curfew violations was not uniform, and the curfew law excluded 17-year-olds, who accounted for almost one-third of all juvenile arrests.

Findings from other research projects echo those of Reynolds et al.'s and Cole's. For example, in a study of Prince George's County, MD, Gouvis and Moore (2003) found that arrests of juveniles under 17 years of age did not decrease during curfew hours after such a law was implemented, nor did the number of calls for service, as was expected.

Research has also been conducted relating to curfew enforcement and gang activity. In an evaluation of the Dallas Police Department's antigang initiative, Fritsch et al. (2003) found that when the police used saturation patrol to enforce the juvenile curfew and truancy laws, greater decreases in gang-related crime were seen in the target areas than in the control beat areas. When comparing both the control and target beats to identified gang crime in the previous year, the saturated patrol beats were associated with decreased, whereas the control beats were associated with increased gang-related activity. To determine if displacement was occurring, the researchers examined gang crime in beats contiguous to the target areas and determined that displacement was minimal, if it occurred at all. However, in the target areas it was also found that reported robbery and auto theft incidents increased, whereas arrests for weapons violations and criminal mischief decreased. This could be explained by the increased presence of police, citizens being more willing to report crimes when they see more police, and that gang members, knowing there are more police in the neighborhood, did not engage publicly in illegal activities. Fritsch et al. (2003) concluded that although saturation patrol and enforcement of curfew violations may not lead to less gang membership, it can "affect the nefarious effects of gangs — crime and violence" (p. 279).

Ruefle and Reynolds (1995) and Lait (1998) also conducted research relating to juvenile curfews and gang activity. Evaluation of the Detroit curfew ordinance, which was intended to deter gang activity, found the curfew to be effective during the hours covered; however, this decrease was accompanied by a corresponding increase in criminal activity in the early afternoon hours prior to curfew, suggesting time displacement (Ruefle and Reynolds, 1995). In Los Angeles, 3600 police officers wrote 4800 curfew violations during a 6-month period (Lait, 1998). This stringent enforcement of the curfew ordinance demonstrated no effect on violent crime by juveniles or crime in general. Yet, aggressive enforcement of curfews in Corpus Christi, Texas, as part of a gang suppression initiative resulted in a substantial drop in the number of curfew violations after the first few weeks of enforcement, indicating that such enforcement has an immediate effect (Bannister et al., 2001). This, however, was anecdotal information concerning curfew violations, and no study of juvenile crime or victimization rates was undertaken.

Curfew violations and the use of public resources to enforce them are not limited to broad curfew ordinances covering all minors under a certain age, but have also been used in an attempt to stop continued delinquent behavior by juveniles already in the criminal justice system. For example, the Florida Department of Juvenile Justice conducted a pilot program that allowed police officers, instead of probation officers, to enforce court-ordered curfews of juveniles sentenced to probation. The data showed juvenile crime was reduced, thus providing positive support for using police officers to supervise juvenile offenders. In addition, both police and parents approved of the program (Jones and Sigler, 2002).

Two research projects undertook analysis of the findings of several studies relating to curfew enforcement and effectiveness. In the first, CJCJ (2002) located 25 studies of the effects of curfew laws nationwide since 1990. They determined that the results of these studies were mixed and frequently contradictory, stating that:

> Statistical analysis provides no support for the proposition that stricter curfew enforcement reduces youth crime either absolutely or relative to adults, by location, by city, or by type of crime. Curfew enforcement generally had no discernible effect on youth crime. In those few instances in which a significant effect was found, it was more likely to be positive (that is, greater curfew enforcement was associated with higher rates of juvenile crime) than negative. (CJCJ, 2002, p. 5)

In a second similar study, Adams (2003) examined the results of ten research projects relating to curfew enforcement and found mixed results. He concluded "[B]y and large, however, the research fails to demonstrate that curfews produced a decrease in juvenile crime" (Adams, 2003, p. 144). Based on the research, we must also conclude that it remains questionable whether the objectives of curfew laws (i.e., to reduce juvenile involvement in crime and decrease their likelihood of becoming crime victims) are being met. Additionally, some of this research may support the argument against youth curfews in that there may be a propensity on the part of law enforcement officials to use curfew laws to stop, question, and arrest certain groups of juveniles but not others.

The mixed results of the research and the different court rulings do not provide clear guidance to government officials, including police managers, regarding effects of the adoption, retention, and enforcement of juvenile curfew laws. Yet, if a curfew ordinance is adopted by a jurisdiction, police have the responsibility to enforce the law. We now discuss the role of the police in the enforcement of curfews.

14.5 The Role of the Police

Lundman (1993) noted that there are three identifiable prevention and control points in the juvenile justice system: "(1) predelinquent intervention, (2) preadjudication intervention, and (3) postadjudication intervention" (p. 17). The police are involved at the predelinquent intervention point in which the prime objective is to prevent delinquency. Under this rubric, it is common to "identify and treat" at-risk juveniles. A second and somewhat more nebulous goal is to identify high-delinquency areas (Lundman, 1993). Police officers operate in both of these domains when enforcing curfew laws.

Police officers have always been the primary frontline responders to crime and disorder. In that role, they have been dubbed the "gatekeepers" of the criminal justice system (Bittner, 1967: Durham et al., 1984; Ruiz, 2002). As such, it can be argued that police officers are the most important decision makers in the chain of the juvenile justice system and have wide discretion to determine whether a juvenile enters that system. For this to happen, police must have initial contact with juveniles. This contact is generated by one of two means. One is the result of a call for service from the public. For example, residents will call the police with a complaint concerning a group of juveniles on the sidewalk being loud and boisterous, and disturbing the residents of the neighborhood. The police are then obliged to respond to this call for service and, as noted by Ericson (1982), to "reproduce order." In other words, police officers are called to deal with "something that ought not be happening and about which someone had better do something now" (Bayley and Bittner, 2001, p. 87).

The second method through which police have contact with juveniles is through police-initiated contact. This contact can be due to an observed violation or a situation that provides the officer(s) with a legal basis to make contact with the youths. These contacts may then lead the police officer to believe that the juvenile had either committed a crime or a status offense. During this initial contact, it is up to the discretion of the police officer whether or not the juvenile enters the criminal justice system. This arrest or intervention may be characterized as the first step in the treatment phase.

As stated earlier, police officers use their discretion to make decisions, which are based on several factors. Often, the demeanor of the juvenile when the initial contact is made by the police officer in the field, or later by the juvenile detectives, will determine how the juvenile will be handled. In fact, it is not uncommon for one-third of those arrested for minor violations to be released if they "were polite in their conversations" (Lundman, 1993, p. 15).

Another factor affecting police discretion is the police officers' perceptions of their occupation. Most police officers view themselves as "law enforcement officers" rather than keepers of the peace or maintainers of order (Ruiz and Treadwell, 2002). By accepting the role of the former, police officers often miss the opportunity to connect with juveniles on an informal basis and instead react to curfew violations as enforcers.

This enforcer role is further played out when police–juvenile encounters take place in areas identified as high-crime or high-delinquency areas or in response to increased criminal and/or gang activity. In some respects, these contacts are all but guaranteed because concentrated police coverage usually occurs in these areas. Police perceptions of juveniles in high-crime or high-delinquency areas make the youths prime targets for police contact even if no status or criminal violation is taking place. This reactive police strategy is often referred to as suppression and involves saturation patrol, intensive crackdowns on criminal activity, and aggressive stop-and-frisk activity in which arrests are prosecuted at a high level (Fritsch et al., 2003).

Another area of police discretion concerning curfew violation enforcement is based on organizational norms or expectations. For example, Bannister et al. (2001) found that 20 percent of the respondents indicated that enforcement of the curfew law was aggressive and ongoing, and another 38 percent reported enforcement to be fairly aggressive. However, almost 42 percent reported that enforcement was sporadic, left to the discretion of individual officers, or only occurred during special circumstances. This indicates that not all jurisdictions that have a curfew ordinance actively promote it, or they may enforce curfew violations with some groups of individuals (i.e., suspected gang members) but not other groups that are viewed in a better light by police officers. As Bannister et al. (2001) state, "[t]his variance in enforcement practices also raises a legal question: If curfew enforcement is sporadic and intentionally targeted to specific groups (i.e., gangs), does this equate to a denial of equal protection or fundamental fairness (due process)?" (p. 237).

Using the same data as CJCJ, Males and Macallair (1999) found that in some jurisdictions, although not all, enforcement was disparate. Whereas curfew laws and their enforcement are to be race and ethnic neutral, the researchers found that juvenile curfew arrest rates of Hispanic and black juveniles were higher than for White or Asian youth. Therefore, the role of police managers is not only to determine the level of enforcement that will be most effective for their agency and jurisdiction and to determine the benefits and costs of endorsing the passage of a curfew law, if none exists, but also to ensure that enforcement of curfew laws is done fairly.

As in the mixed results of the research on juvenile curfew effectiveness, there is disagreement between police managers on the need for, or the enforcement of, such laws, as shown by the results in the study conducted by Bannister et al. (2001). They found that most of the jurisdictions that did not have a juvenile curfew ordinance had no plans to adopt such a law because of a variety of reasons, such as "police do not have the resources to enforce it," "there is no need for it," "it is too difficult to enforce," political leaders do not want a curfew," and "citizens do not want a curfew." But on the flip side, 95 percent of the police agencies that had a curfew law (whether they aggressively enforced it or not) reported that enforcement of the curfew was a wise use of police resources and strongly agreed that curfews were effective at reducing crimes such as vandalism, graffiti, burglary, and gang-related offenses, even though many reported that they did not collect crime statistics to determine the actual effectiveness of curfew violation enforcement.

The police role in enforcing curfew laws varies with the circumstances, from the individual police officer on the street making decisions about contacting groups of juveniles to the police manager concerned with whether to endorse the passage of such a law. These decisions must be based on fundamental fairness and the role of the police in the community they serve.

14.6 Policy Issues and Conclusion

Many policymakers consider curfew legislation a universal remedy for juvenile crime. Although cure-all concepts will generally placate those in favor of such an approach, they have been found to produce little by way of effect (CJCJ, 2002). As demonstrated by the research, simply enforcing curfew ordinances has negligible effects on juvenile criminality and victimization and, therefore, future research and preventive programs should center on multifaceted approaches that engage more agencies than just the criminal justice system and must include prevention, rehabilitation, and sanction-based accountability alternatives.

If juvenile curfew laws are to be adopted, policymakers must continue to be aware that the introduction of new legislation, including juvenile curfews, may have unknown effects on the juvenile justice system as a whole. Indeed, change in one area will often have unintended effects on other programs, services, and budgets. In addition, legislators should be familiar with initiatives that have been successful and those that have not, so that curfew laws are written specifically to fit the community's needs.

When writing a curfew law, policymakers must consider current court rulings as well as the legal challenges that may occur years after enactment of the ordinance. Periodic review of the ordinance must be done to ensure that it reflects current court rulings and is based on up-to-date statistical evidence that juvenile crime and victimization occurs during the time that the curfew is in effect and in the places from which juveniles are restricted.

Two keys to a successful curfew program were consistent enforcement and active participation by the community, marked by long-term commitment, utilization of volunteers, and on-the-spot counseling for parents and juveniles (OJJDP, 1996). Other recommendations included establishing curfew centers to hold violators while they await their parents, providing intervention services for juveniles and their families, creating specific procedures for repeat offenders, and providing a community hotline for questions or problems relating to curfews and juvenile delinquency in general. Curfew centers, away from police stations, and other community programs afford the community an opportunity to provide social and community services as an alternative to formal sanctions, be proactive in the identification and prevention of juvenile delinquency and victimization, and provide resources for prosocial activities (Bannister et al., 2001; Lersch and Sellers, 2000)

One such program is the Mountlake Terrace Neutral Zone, a place where youths safely congregate and participate in a variety of activities on Friday and Saturday nights (Thurman and Mueller, 2003). This crime prevention program provides social intervention and community organization to prevent juvenile involvement in crime and gang-related activities. Observation and interviews with workers, volunteers, and participants revealed that all had benefited from the program. The youths reported their interpersonal skills, tolerance for others, and perception of police officers had improved, and almost two-thirds "claimed that if the Neutral Zone were closed, they would be getting into some kind of trouble" (Thurman and Mueller, 2003, p. 181). In addition, police records revealed that calls for police service and crimes often attributed to juveniles (i.e., assaults, burglaries, vandalism, gang-involved incidents, and graffiti) decreased when the Neutral Zone was in operation.

Based on programs such as the Neutral Zone and research that has been conducted relating to the effectiveness of curfew laws and their enforcement, curfew laws and the enforcement of those laws should be one approach among many that communities use to protect juveniles from criminal victimization, prevent juvenile delinquency and deviance, and to identify juvenile involvement in crime.

References

Adams, K. (2003). The effectiveness of juvenile curfews at crime prevention. *The Annals of the American Academy of Political and Social Sciences, 587*, 136–159.

Bannister, A.J., Carter, D.L., and Schafer, J. (2001). A national police survey on the use of juvenile curfews. *Journal of Criminal Justice, 29*, 233–240.

Bayley, D. and Bittner, E. (2001). Learning the skills of policing. In Dunham, R. and Alpert, G. (Eds.), *Critical Issues in Policing: Contemporary Readings*. Prospect Heights, IL: Waveland. pp. 82–106.

Bittner, E. (1967). Police discretion in emergency apprehension of mentally ill persons. *Social Problems, 14*, 278–292.

Cities with Curfews Trying to Meet Constitutional Test (December 26, 1995). *Washington Post*, p. 1.

Center on Juvenile and Criminal Justice (CJCJ) (2002). The Impact of Juvenile Curfew Laws in California. http://www.cjcj.org/pubs/curfew/curfew.html. (Downloaded from the Internet March 11, 2003.)

Cole, D. (2003). The effect of a curfew law on juvenile crime in Washington, D.C. *American Journal of Criminal Justice, 27*, 217–232.

Curfew sweep in Palmdale nets 38. (October 13, 2002). *Daily News of Los Angeles*, p. AV1.

Daytime curfew is crime-fighting tool. (November 8, 2002). *Lancaster New Era*, p. A-14.

Durham, M., Carr, H., and Pierce, G. (1984). Police involvement and influence in involuntary civil commitment. *Hospital and Community Psychiatry, 35*(6), 580–584.

Ericson, R. (1982). *Reproducing Order: A Study of Police Patrol Work.* Toronto: University of Toronto Press.

Fritsch, E.J., Caeti, T.J., and Taylor, R.W. (2003). Gang suppression through saturation patrol and aggressive curfew and truancy enforcement: a quasi-experimental test of the Dallas anti-gang initiative. In Decker, S.H. (Ed.), *Policing Gangs and Youth Violence.* Belmont, CA: Thomson Wadsworth. pp. 267–284.

Gouvis Roman, C. and Moore, G. (2003). Evaluation of the Youth Curfew in Prince George's County, MD: The Curfew's Impact on Arrests and Calls for Service. Rockville, MD: National Institute of Justice.

Harvard Law Review Association. (1997). Curfews may be ineffective and discriminatory. In Bender, D. and Leone, B. (Eds.), *Juvenile Crime: Opposing Viewpoints.* San Diego, CA: Greenhaven. pp. 193–198.

Henry, T. (April 5, 1995). Curfews attempt to curb teen crime. *USA Today,* p. 1.

Ives, M. (December 18, 2002). Town to begin curfew for teens: boiling spring lakes wants minors inside from 11 p.m. to 5 a.m. *Morning Star,* pp. 1A, 7A.

Jones, M.A. and Sigler, R.T. (2002). Law enforcement partnership in community corrections: an evaluation of juvenile offender curfew checks. *Journal of Criminal Justice, 30,* 245–256.

Joseph, P. (1999). Are juvenile curfews a legal and effective way to reduce juvenile crime? No. In Sewell, J.D. (Ed.), *Controversial Issues in Policing,* Boston, MA: Allyn and Bacon, pp. 62–66.

Kawada, E. (January 21, 2003). Washington State Supreme Court strikes down Sumner's curfew law as too vague. *News Tribune,* p. A1.

Lait, M. (February 10, 1998). Report questions teen curfews. *Los Angeles Times,* p. A15.

Lersch, K.M. and Sellers, C.S. (2000). A comparison of curfew and noncurfew violators using a self-report delinquency survey. *American Journal of Criminal Justice, 24,* 259–269.

Lundman, R. (1993). *Prevention and Control of Juvenile Delinquency.* New York: Oxford University Press.

Males, M.A. and Macallair, D. (1999). An analysis of curfew enforcement and juvenile crime in California. *Western Criminology Review, 1*(2). Online: http://wcr.sonoma.edu/v1n2/males.html.

O'Brien, L.F. (1999). Are juvenile curfews a legal and effective way to reduce juvenile crime? Yes. In Sewell, J.D. (Ed.). *Controversial Issues in Policing.* Boston, MA: Allyn and Bacon. pp. 59–62.

Office of Juvenile Justice and Delinquency Prevention (OJJDP). (1997). Juvenile Justice Reform Initiatives in the States: 1994–1996. http://ojjdp.ncjrs.org/pubs/reform/contents.html. (Downloaded March 11, 2003.)

Office of Juvenile Justice and Delinquency Prevention (OJJDP) (1996). *Curfew: An Answer to Juvenile Delinquency and Victimization.* Rockville, MD: U.S. Department of Justice.

Reynolds, K., Seydlitz, R., and Jenkins, P. (2000). Do juvenile curfew laws work? A time-series analysis of the New Orleans law. *Justice Quarterly, 17*(1), 205–230.

Ruefle, W. and Reynolds, K.M. (1995). Curfews and delinquency in major American cities. *Crime and Delinquency,* 4(1), 355–358.

Ruefle, W., Reynolds, K.M., and Brantley, A. (1997). Curfews can be effective and constitutional. In Bender, D. and Leone, B. (Eds.), *Juvenile Crime: Opposing Viewpoints.* San Diego, CA: Greenhaven. pp. 187–192.

Ruiz, J. (2002). Policing Persons with Mental Illness: The Pennsylvania Experience. Middletown, PA: The Pennsylvania State Data Center.

Ruiz, J. and Treadwell, D. (2002). The perp walk: due process v. freedom of the press. *Criminal Justice Ethics,* Summer/Fall, 21(2), 44–56.

Shoemaker, D. (1990). *Theories of Delinquency: An Examination of Explanations of Delinquent Behavior.* New York: Oxford University Press.

Summa, A. (January 16, 2003). How late teens can stay out depends on the city: curfew laws differ throughout county. *Houston Chronicle,* p. 10.

Tan, S. (October 8, 2002). 10:30 curfew is considered for unsupervised youth. *Buffalo News,* p. B3.

Thurman Q.C. and Mueller, D.G. (2003). Beyond curfews and crackdowns: an overview of the Mountlake Terrace Neutral Zone — AmeriCorps program. In Decker, S.H. (Ed.). *Policing Gangs and Youth Violence,* Belmont, CA: Thomson Wadsworth. pp. 167–187.

Vock, D. (March 4, 2003). Ensure legal rights of juveniles, state justices urged. *Chicago Daily Law Bulletin,* p. 1.

Cases Cited

Bellotti v. Baird, 443 U.S. 622 (1979).

Bykofsky v. Borough of Middletown, 401 F. Supp. 1242 (M.D. Penn. 1975), aff'd without opinion, 535 F.2d 1245 (3rd Cir. 1976), cert. denied 429 U.S. 964 (1976).

Hodgkins, et al. v. Peterson, et al., 355 F.3d 1048 (7th Cir. 2004).

Hutchins v. District of Columbia, 188 F.3d 531 (D.C. Cir. 1999).

Johnson, et al. v. the City of Opelousas, 658 F.2d 1065 (1981).

Nunez by Nunez v. City of San Diego, 114 F.3d 935 (9th Cir. 1997).

Qutb, et al. v. Strauss and City of Dallas, 11 F.3d 488 (5th Cir. 1993), cert. denied 511 U.S. 1127 (1994).

Ramos, et al. v. Town of Vernon, 353 F.3d 171 (2nd Cir. 2003).

Schleifer, a Minor, by Schleifer, et al., v. City of Charlottesville, 159 F.3d 843 (4th Cir. 1998), cert. denied 526 U.S. 1018 (1999).

Chapter 15

Prosecuting Juvenile Offenders

Leanne Owen

15.1 Introduction

Prosecutors are highly influential in determining the outcomes of cases involving juvenile offenders. In a famous speech to U.S. attorneys about ethics in prosecuting, former Attorney General Robert Jackson, who later became a Supreme Court justice, stated on April 1, 1940, that "[t]he prosecutor has more control over life, liberty, and reputation than any other person in America. His discretion is tremendous." This is as true today, if not more so, as it was in the middle of the last century. As one prosecutor has asserted: "Prosecution in the juvenile justice system is a means to an end. How we as a society will live 10 to 15 years from now depends on how well we do with these kids."[1]

Yet the prosecution of juvenile offenders is not a straightforward process. How prosecutors exercise their discretion and how they make decisions about juvenile offenders depend on two primary elements: first, how prosecutors perceive their role (both within the community and within the criminal and juvenile justice framework) and, second, how prosecutors perceive the juvenile offenders in question (specifically with regard to blameworthiness or blamelessness). Therefore, in order to understand the complexities involved in the prosecutorial decision-making process, it is crucial to understand first what the prosecutorial job is, and how doing the job differs from carrying out the perceived prosecutorial role. There is no single way to understand or perceive the prosecutorial role, and prosecutors, in determining their role, are influenced by a number of internal and external factors. These factors include, but are not limited to, the elective nature of the office, feelings of responsibility toward others, notions of guardianship toward juvenile offenders, societal expectations, and institutional values.

Likewise, as there is no single way to interpret the prosecutorial role, so too is there no one way to understand or make sense of juvenile offenders. The law understands juveniles in one particular way based on capacity. By virtue of their chronological age, individuals either fall below or above a particular cut-off point. If they fall below it, they are presumed by law to be incapable of forming criminal intent and, therefore, are not believed to be legally liable for their actions. If they fall above it, they are, in contrast, presumed by law to be capable of forming criminal intent. Therefore, they may be held legally liable for their actions. For example, in Kansas, where the age of responsibility is 10 years, children younger than 10 may not be held legally liable for their actions, regardless of how heinous those actions may be or how devastating the consequences. It is a central tenet of the American legal system that the law must punish only the guilty. It follows that if children who fall below the age of responsibility are presumed to be incapable of a guilty mind, a crucial element of guilt, then surely they must not be placed in a situation in which the State might impose sanctions upon them. Legally, their actions are excused. On the other hand, the reverse is not necessarily true in all scenarios: not all individuals who have attained the age of responsibility will necessarily be held legally liable for their actions. The law merely dictates that they may be, that they are eligible to be so held.

It is in this gray area between the stark contrasts of automatic excusal on the one hand for the very young or automatic prosecution on the other for the "old enough" that prosecutors are empowered to exercise their discretion. For while the law merely distinguishes between individuals on the basis of the presence or absence of certain vital capacities, prosecutors make moral distinctions among juvenile offenders on the basis of how good or bad they are believed to be, how child-like or adult-like their behavior appears to be, and what prospects exist for future behavior modification. Once these distinctions have been made, prosecutors determine what they believe the most appropriate outcome to be.

For example, should an 11-year-old girl with no previous history of misbehavior who has been caught shoplifting be prosecuted, or would a warning and a possible diversion program be more suitable? Should a 16-year-old boy with a record of stealing cars be given another chance at rehabilitation when his latest joyride results in vehicular homicide, or would prosecution and a custodial sentence be more appropriate? Prosecutors make these decisions based on their perceptions of the juvenile offenders in question, and they then seek the most effective legal means to achieve their desired goals.

Prosecutors must always operate within the confines of the law, and they must apply their policies and rules within legal boundaries. However, the decisions they make about juvenile offenders, and how they make sense of them, are driven by their own sense of moral consciousness, their own moral sense of right and wrong. In a nutshell, the process of prosecuting juvenile offenders involves prosecutors making moral decisions about the best way to apply legal principles.

It is this moral aspect underpinning the prosecution of juvenile offenders, its origin and its effects, that will be the concern of this chapter.

15.2 Distinguishing between What Prosecutors Do and Who They (Think They) Are

As mentioned previously, it is imperative that the prosecutorial job and the tasks associated with it not be confounded or in any way misconstrued as the prosecutorial role. A prosecutor's job involves the application of certain legal criteria in deciding, among other things, who should be prosecuted, what charges should be brought against the offender, and what sentence should be sought. This prosecutorial job entails the administration of certain particular legal duties or tasks and the exercise of a broad range of discretionary powers, which the prosecutor is presumed to undertake in a way that is consistent with the standards of professional conduct and legal ethics.

The prosecutorial perception of role, on the other hand, is not dictated by specific legal mandates or professional standards, nor explicitly stated in any job description. Instead, it is the manifestation of a sense of commitment and responsibility that prosecutors have toward their position and toward the people they serve, regardless of whether they ever encounter these individuals face to face. Prosecutors perceive their role in a particular way, and this specific perception of the prosecutorial role is pivotal in formulating their understanding of juvenile offenders and, likewise, of how they are expected to respond to the juvenile crime "problem." Role perceptions indicate to individuals "how they think they are supposed to act in their own roles and how others should act in their roles" (Newstrom and Davis, 1993, p. 52). Consequently, the prosecutorial perception of role refers to how prosecutors understand or make sense of what it is they should be doing, not in the sense of carrying out particular duties but of acting according to an overarching sense of moral consciousness. The basis of the prosecutorial perception of role and its impact on the decision-making processes involving juvenile offenders will be addressed later in this chapter. For now, what is important to recognize is that the job with which prosecutors have been entrusted and the specific duties which they are charged with carrying out must not be confused with the role they perceive themselves as having. It may be useful at this point to explain the origins of the prosecutorial job and the significance its very nature has on the prosecutorial decision-making process.

15.3 The Origins of the Prosecutorial Job

Jacoby (1980), a social researcher who has been examining prosecutorial discretion and decision-making processes since the 1970s, asserts that the American prosecutor is remarkably and distinctly unique. According to Jacoby, while American prosecutors may share some features with their counterparts in other countries, no other prosecuting body has an identical combination of powers, authority, and duties. The American system, unlike its English forerunner, is one of public prosecution: crime is perceived to be a public matter whereby society as a whole, rather than a particular individual, has been victimized. Yet the doctrine of public prosecution as enshrined in the American legal system does not afford the public the right or authority to make decisions in specific cases. Instead, the public elects the prosecutor, whose job it is to ensure that the law is applied consistently and fairly and that appropriate policies are conceived of and utilized in dealing with juvenile offenders.

15.3.1 An Advocate for the Public: The Prosecutor as Elected Official

The office of prosecutor in America has not always been an elective one. It was only during the presidency of Andrew Jackson in the 1820s that the American political process became increasingly democratic.

The effect of this democratization movement was to change the way political officials were viewed, and more public officials began to be popularly elected. With the increase in the number of local elections, elected officials were given greater independence and, eventually, discretionary powers to make decisions they deemed appropriate. As the democratization movement swept through the country in the early 19th century, more judges began to be popularly elected and the local elections of prosecutors soon followed. Today, the majority of local prosecutors (over 95 percent) still hold elected office (Bureau of Justice Statistics, 1992). By the time of the Civil War, the public's perception of the office of prosecutor and the responsibilities it was seen as entailing had changed in a fundamental way. The American prosecutor's new elective status resulted in the public's perception of the office as that of a public advocate.

This public perception of the prosecutor as a public advocate has been instrumental in shaping prosecutors' understanding of their role and their decisions regarding which policies to implement in particular cases involving juvenile offenders. American prosecutors as locally elected officials, it must be acknowledged, may feel an obligation to reflect the values and norms of the community that elected them to office, and this sense of responsibility may be perpetuated and intensified in turn by the public's expectations of prosecutors.

15.3.2 *"Doing More": Ideals of Community Justice and Community Prosecution*

Jacoby (1980, p. 274) has written that the unique position of the American prosecutor necessitates the "[s]traddling of many arenas, the political, legislative, executive, and judicial, [and as a result the prosecutor] often projects a confused image ... that stubbornly defies easy solution or clarification." This is hardly surprising considering many prosecutors' elective status and the expectation that society has that prosecutors may be the most appropriate individuals to deal with certain duties (that may or may not be explicitly mentioned as part of their job description, but may yet comprise a part of their role). In keeping with this societal expectation that prosecutors will fulfill more than their expressed function, the National District Attorneys Association (NDAA) has set out two policy initiatives that seemingly extend the prosecutorial job and encourage prosecutors to interpret their role as it relates to juvenile offenders in a very particular way. These policies are as follows:

> Prosecutors should play an active role in juvenile crime prevention efforts.

> Prosecutors should work with other community leaders to ensure community involvement in crime prevention efforts. (NDAA, 1996, p. 17)

The justification for these policy initiatives is the prevailing belief that the problem of juvenile crime is a multifaceted one and, therefore, that responses to it (as suggested elsewhere in this volume) must originate from different sources and different avenues of expertise. Consequently,

> [E]veryone in the community needs to be involved in these efforts, including parents, teachers, school administrators, faith communities, civic and business leaders, law enforcement officials, prosecutors, local elected officials, and youth themselves. Coupled with effective enforcement and prosecution efforts, crime prevention initiatives are important and necessary. (NDAA, 1996, p. 17)

Prosecutors as representatives of the community, therefore, should seek to uphold "community justice," and their goal should be, among other things, to improve the community and enhance the welfare and safety of the members of that community by partnering with other stakeholders such as schools, businesses, or civic groups. What makes the introduction of community justice coalitions such an urgent necessity at this time is the high levels of juvenile violence and crime that modern communities must cope with. As the nature of the juvenile crime "problem" changes, so too does the role of prosecutors in responding to that problem. Prosecutors are no longer merely the gatekeepers to the juvenile and adult justice systems. Today, they must do more. They must partner with the various stakeholders in the community and strive to prevent juvenile crime before it occurs, rather than simply respond to its effects.

The aim of community prosecution proponents is the encouragement of a shift in role for prosecutors from that of upholder of law and order to something resembling a human resource for the community. The prosecutor would conceivably become the one who helps the victim, the community, and the offender by designing and managing a process in which everyone in the community can become involved. He or she would be seen as not just an individual who is "tough on crime," but also as a leader in education, prevention, and treatment efforts. These policy-driven, community-based ideals may impact significantly upon a prosecutor's working rules. In other words, knowing about community priorities in the prosecution of juvenile offenders may affect the way a prosecutor does the tasks that are part of his or her job.

15.4 "Should We or Shouldn't We?" — The Decision to Charge

One crucial task that is part of the prosecutor's job is the charging decision. As indicated in the introduction to this chapter, the decision to charge is far from automatic. Many prosecutors have indicated that once an individual is brought formally into the criminal or juvenile justice system, it is virtually impossible to withdraw him or her from it. Therefore, it is of paramount importance to prosecutors to ensure that only those persons who are truly deserving of punishment are charged and formally introduced into the system. How prosecutors view the charging decision and what they do once the decision to charge has been made will hinge largely on their prosecutorial value system and their perceptions of the "bottom line." In other words, some prosecutors' offices encourage prosecution if probable cause exists and if the evidence is strong, arguing that all prosecutions are in the public interest. On the other hand, other offices subscribe to the belief that prosecution should only be sought if probable cause exists, if the evidence is strong, and if prosecution is in both the public's and the juvenile's best interest. Naturally, this results in some discrepancies, as identical cases will be handled differently by different prosecutors. Therefore, the charging decision is a stage of the criminal and juvenile justice system that reflects prosecutorial values.

15.4.1 Prosecutorial Constructions of Juvenile Offenders and Their "Just Deserts"

Although there are certain legal criteria that must be adhered to, the charging decision for prosecutors revolves around notions of goals and outcomes, and the very authorities that seek to guide prosecutorial decision-making in this matter recognize that this is, in fact, the case. Chapter 3 of the American Bar Association Standards Relating to the Administration of Criminal Justice sets out explicitly the criteria that must be considered by prosecutors in making the decision to charge

— namely, such factors as probable cause, evidential sufficiency, and the public interest — and discusses the exercise of prosecutorial discretion in making that decision:

> The prosecutor is not obliged to present all charges which the evidence might support. The prosecutor may in some circumstances and for good cause consistent with the public interest decline to prosecute, notwithstanding that sufficient evidence may exist which would support a conviction. (Fisher, 2000, p. 6)

In other words, regardless of evidential sufficiency and probable cause, prosecutors may, for other reasons, make the decision to prosecute or not. This extralegal influence on the decision-making process is particularly relevant with regard to the prosecutorial construction of juvenile offenders and notions of blameworthiness, blamelessness, and just deserts. This notion of prosecutorial construction should not be confused with the process of case construction, whereby prosecutors piece together their policy and choice of strategies, drawing upon their prosecutorial values and perception of role, and even evidence that they have gathered from law enforcement. Rather, prosecutorial construction refers specifically to the way in which, theoretically, prosecutors understand the juvenile offenders they confront.

Whereas case construction might reveal how prosecutors put together their cases in preparing for trial, prosecutorial construction would account for why prosecutors choose a particular policy or strategy over another. Prosecutorial construction of juvenile offenders is fundamental to the prosecutorial decision-making process and suggests possible ways in which prosecutors may make sense of these offenders. Furthermore, the prosecutorial decision to charge is entirely premised upon the idea that there is a particular outcome that prosecutors want to reach or accomplish, and that that outcome can best be achieved by charging an individual juvenile. This ends-based thinking is fundamental to the prosecutorial decision-making process. One prosecutor described it as being tunnel-visioned: "When I look at the report, I tend to be a little tunnel-visioned and I know what I want, and that's what I go after." Upon their initial review of cases, prosecutors develop an immediate sense of who the juvenile offender is and which outcome would be most desirable. In other words, they determine which legal outcome a juvenile offender morally deserves. As stated earlier, the criminal law makes no moral distinctions between offenders, and this creates the risk that those juvenile offenders whom prosecutors have constructed as either deserving or undeserving of punishment will not receive their just deserts. For this reason, prosecutorial constructions of juvenile offenders as deserving or undeserving of punishment intend to secure moral justice by legal means. This prosecutorial construction of juvenile offenders draws largely upon prosecutorial values and their perceived role — as suggested earlier, that of public advocate and community stakeholder — and determines the choice of policy and strategies that they will make. It must not be inferred that the public dictates which outcomes a prosecutor will choose and whether the decision to charge should be made. Rather, a prosecutor is influenced by both internal and external factors in constructing his or her perception of the prosecutorial role, and this role perception influences prosecutors in making general policy decisions and specific decisions regarding the suitability of outcomes and strategies.

In reviewing each case, prosecutors identify those aspects of the case that they deem the most important. They are obligated to determine the appropriate rules of law and procedure that must be invoked in cases involving juvenile offenders and to act in accordance with the formal rules of criminal and procedural law that regulate prosecutorial dealings with juvenile offenders. Similarly, however, they are under a professional imperative to make sense of situations involving juvenile offenders and to determine whether these offenders fall within the jurisdiction of the criminal law and the criminal or juvenile justice system. Individuals who subscribe to the objectivist school of sociology will argue that notions of "making sense" of a situation and indeed of a particular juvenile offender are illogical, as "individuals cannot do anything other than to act out whatever is predetermined by structural constraints" (Munch, 1994, p.176). Contrarily, symbolic interactionists and other subjectivist thinkers will recognize the value in acknowledging that a situation only exists insofar as someone is interpreting a particular social interaction and set of events in a particular way. Prosecutorial actions, therefore, specifically those that govern their decisions regarding juvenile offenders, are the product of a particularly and uniquely subjective view of those offenders.

15.4.2 Prosecutorial Considerations and Formulation of Concepts

In making sense of juvenile offenders, indeed, in formulating their construction of these individuals, prosecutors refer to such factors as the individual circumstances of the offender, including age, previous criminal history, family background, school record, attitude about the offense, or perceived future dangerousness; the specific circumstances of the crime, specifically the level of violence that has been inflicted, the seriousness of the offense, or the number of victims who have been affected; and the rehabilitative aspects of the offender, namely whether or not diversion or treatment programs have anything to offer or whether prosecutors believe the juvenile offender to be beyond redemption. It is hardly surprising that prosecutors consider cases on such an individualized basis if one assumes that their own personal ethical code and notions of compassion, justice, and fairness will influence their perception of their role and their subsequent decisions about juvenile offenders. Prosecutors' sense of moral justice, as determined by their role perceptions, by society's expectations of them, and by prosecutorial and personal values, and their pursuit of legal justice are very closely intertwined. The way in which they regard a particular case and a particular juvenile offender will almost certainly affect the way in which they attempt to see that legal justice is done.

Understanding concepts as constructs that are grouped or defined in a particular way so as to help individuals make sense of and interpret commonly used everyday language is especially relevant in appreciating prosecutorial constructions of juvenile offenders. Prosecutors use everyday vernacular such as "evil," "sophisticated," "just a kid," or "serious" to describe juvenile offenders. Consider the following example from a local prosecutor: "I think most 10-year-olds today are fairly sophisticated ... they are computer-literate, their organizational skills tend to be pretty good, they are addressing issues in school that we wouldn't have addressed."

To prosecutors, those words and phrases — such as "sophisticated" — are indicative of particular concepts within a particular conceptual framework they have created to assist them in making sense of juvenile offenders. In other words, they may say that a juvenile offender is "sophisticated," but they mean something else, something that is crucial to their understanding and construction of that offender and, subsequently, to the decisions they make about that offender. What that particular prosecutor went on to explain is that viewing a child as "sophisticated" translates into "a factor in whether or not to pursue charges, not juvenile charges but adult charges."

Prosecutors, as both individuals and as members of the prosecutorial groups, may have a preconceived conception of various crimes and juvenile offenders. The remainder of this chapter is concerned with six such concepts, and with the way this specific prosecutorial construction of the offender impacts on prosecutorial perceptions of and decisions about offender accountability. The six prosecutorial conceptions of juvenile offenders have to do with the offender's past history ("goodness" or "badness"), his or her maturity level (adulticism and infanticism), and rehabilitative prospects (salvageability or disposability). Before introducing these concepts in any great detail, these moral assessments about juvenile offenders must be understood within their unique prosecutorial context. In other words, concepts such as "good" or "bad" may appear to have a generally agreed upon meaning in everyday discourse. However, when utilized in the context of prosecutorial constructions of juvenile offenders, they are designated in a very specific way in order to convey particular prosecutorial notions and meanings of what constitutes "good" or "bad" characteristics and what the legal and moral implications of these meanings may be. What one person may view as "good" or "bad" may not coincide with a prosecutorial understanding of "good" or "bad" with regard to decision-making about juvenile offenders.

15.4.3 Goodness and Badness: Considering the Juvenile's Behavior

A prosecutorial construction of a "good" or "bad" juvenile offender revolves around that offender's previous behavior. Prosecutors can only glean what they know about juvenile offenders from information they are given about those offenders from such sources as law enforcement, juvenile intake officers, school and education officials, relatives, other members of the community, and, in the case of prosecutors operating in a small jurisdiction, their own personal acquaintanceship with the offender. In addition to these sources that suggest to the prosecutor what the juvenile offender may have been like in the past, prosecutors may also have the opportunity to observe offenders and to make determinations based not upon other people's descriptions of them, but upon their own assessments of such factors as attitude, remorse, or maturity level. A good kid, for instance, would be the following:

> A child who has never been in trouble before, and it's a misdemeanor. We can put them in several different types of diversion programs, and that's where we use a lot more of our discretion. Those first contacts, we try to get them in a program right away so hopefully they don't come back a second time.

A bad kid, on the other hand, is usually one who has caused trouble before:

> What's a bad guy? Well, that's when you say society has to be protected. We have this person who is extremely violent and whatever age he is we have to make sure he does not inflict this violence on somebody again. I mean, it's not unusual to see a guy who did a violent crime when he was fifteen, and he was sent to some juvenile home for a year and he gets out and does it again. So you've got to recognize that you've got those kinds of people.

Three things must be understood with regard to these notions. First, that a prosecutorial construction of a juvenile offender as "good" or "bad" will influence how that prosecutor understands the offender in question with regard to being deserving or undeserving of punishment, and how decisions about that offender will be made. For instance, a juvenile offender who is constructed as "good" will be expected to be considered for diversion or other informal means of resolving the case more than a "bad" kid, and conversely, a "bad" offender will be more likely to be charged. Second, that these prosecutorial constructions of "good" or "bad" are largely informed by the data with which prosecutors are presented. Prosecutors can only make sense of a juvenile offender based on what they know about them. Third, prosecutorial constructions of "good" or "bad" are unique and specific. If the father of a juvenile offender describes his son as a "good" kid, this does not necessarily mean that the individual will meet the prosecutorial criteria for what constitutes a "good" kid.

15.4.4 Adulticism and Infanticism: Considerations of Maturity

The second distinction that prosecutors make in constructing juvenile offenders as deserving or undeserving of punishment (and, consequently, of being charged or not) is one of maturity. Thomas Szasz, an American psychiatrist who has written extensively on law and mental illness (see Watkins, 1998) has argued that modern propensities to treat children as if they are adults have resulted in a heightened maturity level for children of younger ages. He coined the word *adulticism* to refer to the adult-like behavior of children. Adulticism is that behavior which may indicate that children are "older than their years." Prosecutorial assessments of adulticism, as with their evaluations of goodness or badness, are informed by what they know about juvenile offenders. Older juveniles may be viewed as more adulticistic than younger offenders, as may those who hold down a job, have visible responsibilities, or have left the formal schooling system. Moreover, those juvenile offenders who are constructed as adulticistic by prosecutors may be deemed more deserving of punishment, because their adult-like behavior suggests that they know better and are therefore more accountable for their actions. In other words, if they act like adults, they should be treated or punished as adults. As one prosecutor described: "Are they living like an adult? Some of them have jobs, aren't going to school, things of that nature; so you treat them more like one."

Consequently, adulticistic juvenile offenders are more likely to be charged than those juvenile offenders who are not so constructed.

The opposite of adulticistic behavior is that behavior which implies that a juvenile offender is "younger than his or her years," that he or she is immature and incapable of making rational decisions about the consequences of "bad" behavior, and is therefore undeserving of punishment. That type of behavior, and indeed the juvenile offender who displays that type of behavior, may be constructed as *infanticistic*. Prosecutorial notions of infanticism may be tied in to the philosophy of *parens patriae* which, as explored Chapter 2, underpins the juvenile justice system. In keeping with the paternalistic notion of *parens patriae,* it is more likely that prosecutors will seek to deal with juvenile offenders whom they construct as infanticistic in informal ways, rather than by charging them for their actions. Infanticistic juveniles will be constructed as such by prosecutors who believe that because they know no better, they are undeserving of punishment and, instead, should be treated informally.

15.4.5 Salvageability and Disposability: Rehabilitative Prospects

The final aspect of juvenile offenders that prosecutors must make sense of before they can make any particular decisions about policy and strategy has to do with the rehabilitative prospects of the juvenile offender. When the first juvenile court was established in Cook County, Illinois, in 1899, its proponents, subscribing to the doctrine of *parens patriae,* believed that it should have a different objective from the criminal court. Whereas the criminal justice system may seek to punish, the juvenile court would seek to treat and to rehabilitate. Yet judges and lawmakers recognized that not all juvenile offenders would be amenable to treatment and to rehabilitation, and this recognition resulted in the creation of waiver provisions (discussed in Chapter 16) to have some juvenile offenders transferred to the adult criminal court. In making sense of juvenile offenders and in making decisions about their just deserts, prosecutors consider whether or not they will be likely to be rehabilitated and whether they will be amenable to treatment, or whether they will simply revert to their unlawful behavior if and when released.

Those juvenile offenders constructed as "salvageable" may be deemed undeserving of punishment, and prosecutors may attempt to deal with them informally through diversion programs. One prosecutor explained his feelings on the matter:

> Generally speaking, this is by definition a population that should be rehabilitated or susceptible to being rehabilitated. It's not like they've got forty years of a criminal lifestyle and drug abuse under their belts. Now, they may need to have 2 or 3 years of it, but they should be susceptible to treatment and that sort of thing. So what should be looked at as the first alternative is how we can make sure this kid gets on to being a productive adult.

On the other hand, those juvenile offenders whom prosecutors construct as being "disposable" may be perceived as being beyond redemption. As one prosecutor described the concept of disposability: "Are you willing to say that this is a person who is disposable? Is this person never going to have any use for society again?"

If prosecutors believe there is nothing the juvenile justice system or informal means such as diversion may offer these disposable juveniles by way of rehabilitation, they may be charged and, in due course, waivers may be sought to have them tried as adults for their crimes. In determining whether juvenile offenders have strong rehabilitative prospects or whether sending them to treatment or rehabilitation programs would be nothing short of a waste of time and resources, prosecutors consider such factors as the offenders' ages (believing that younger offenders have a better likelihood of rehabilitation) and their prior records (arguing that if opportunities for rehabilitation afforded them in the past have failed, this time should prove no different). In the words of one prosecutor: "What possible reason do we have of giving them a break when we know that they haven't taken advantage of any of the other breaks they got? If they haven't learned their lesson yet, why would this be different?"

And so the decision is made to charge.

15.5 Conclusion

These prosecutorial constructions of juvenile offenders as "good" or "bad," infanticistic or adulticistic, and salvageable or disposable, and, therefore, respectively undeserving or deserving of punishment, are uniquely subjective. Moreover, the way that prosecutors understand and make sense of these juvenile offenders will determine what they decide on as the most desirable outcome and how they will work to secure that outcome, both in terms of general prosecutorial policy and specific strategies. As predominantly elected officials, prosecutors feel duty bound and responsible to both their office and the community that elected them to that office. Their interest in dealing with juvenile offenders is to seek justice — not merely legal justice that might be measured by the number of convictions obtained, but moral justice. Individual prosecutors' senses of moral justice, of what constitutes just action in a particular juvenile's case, will differ. Yet as professionals in a larger institution, one with a shared history and shared core values, the possibilities for role perceptions, for the functions they believe they should fulfill, are not infinite. As such, they can be expected to act in whichever way they believe to be in the best interests of the public, the juvenile, and indeed, in the best interests of the law. The juvenile justice system has struggled for centuries to devise the most appropriate methods for dealing with juvenile offenders. It comes then as no surprise that prosecutors have struggled as well.

References

Bureau of Justice Statistics (1992). Prosecutors in State Courts 1990. Washington, D.C.: Department of Justice, Bureau of Justice Statistics.

Fisher, G. (2000). Prosecutorial Ethics. Supplemental material for course at Harvard Law School.

Jacoby, J.E.(1980). *The American Prosecutor: A Search for Identity.* Washington, D.C.: The Free Press.

Munch, R.(1994). *Sociological Theory,* Vol. 3. Chicago, IL: Nelson-Hall.

National District Attorneys Association.(1996). *National Prosecution Standards,* 2nd ed. Alexandria, VA: NDAA.

Newstrom, J.W. and Davis, K.(1993). *Organizational Behavior — Human Behavior at Work*. New York: McGraw-Hill.

Watkins, J.C., Jr. (1998). *The Juvenile Justice Century: A Sociolegal Commentary on American Juvenile Courts*. Durham, NC: Carolina Academic Press.

Notes

1. Statements from local prosecutors were gathered in the course of the author's doctoral research during 1999–2001.

Chapter 16

Issues Associated with Juvenile Waiver

Craig Hemmens and Benjamin Steiner

16.1 Introduction

The juvenile court was created in the early part of the 20th century for the purpose of providing an alternate method of dealing with juveniles who ran afoul of the law. Early juvenile court advocates argued that juveniles, because of their tender age, were less culpable than adult offenders and, thus, should be dealt with differently. Dealing with juveniles in a separate court would allow for more attention to the individual needs of the juvenile; the motto of the juvenile court quickly became *in the best interests of the child* (Feld, 1987). This approach differed radically from the punishment-oriented approach of the criminal court system. By the latter part of the 20th century, however, a number of constituencies had become disenchanted with the juvenile court. Conservatives argued that it allowed juveniles who had committed serious crimes to escape with little or no punishment; liberals argued that the juvenile court disregarded the constitutional rights of juvenile offenders. The result was an increase in the use of juvenile waiver. Juvenile waiver is the mechanism by which a juvenile court's jurisdiction is waived, and a juvenile offender is transferred to the jurisdiction of the criminal court. This allows for the imposition of different (and generally greater) sanctions on the juvenile, should he or she be convicted in criminal court.

This chapter provides an overview of the history of the juvenile court system and the practice of juvenile waiver, as well as a review of the current status of waiver in the 50 states.

16.2 The Juvenile Court

At common law, only children under the age of 7 were considered incapable of felonious intent. Children between the ages of 7 and 14 were considered similarly incapable unless it could be established that the child was able to understand the consequences of his or her actions. Persons over the age of 14 were considered fully responsible for their actions. This was known as the *infancy defense* (Gardner, 1997). At common law, juvenile offenders received the same punishment as adult offenders and were usually housed in the same facilities. Before the establishment of New York's House of Refuge in 1825, no state bothered to separate children from adults in prison. In 1847, other state reform schools and industrial schools were opened. In 1869, Massachusetts began to use probation, and in 1870, separate trials for juveniles were established. In 1877, separate dockets and records were established for juveniles, and in 1880, the first separate probation system utilized for juveniles was instituted. By 1899, there were 65 facilities for juveniles in the United States, but juvenile offenders still received the same punishment as adults. In 1898, children under the age of 16 awaiting trial were segregated (Drowns and Hess, 2000).

Several events contributed to the creation of a separate juvenile justice system. The Industrial Revolution of the late 19th century transformed the United States from a rural country to an urban nation. The number of children living in cities increased rapidly, and juvenile delinquency became a problem in many cities. Progressive era reformers became concerned about the welfare of these urban children, whereas others became concerned that the increase in immigrants from Europe was creating social disorganization. The Progressive movement combined these concerns to produce wide-ranging social reforms, including the creation of a separate juvenile court system. Proponents of a separate juvenile justice system believed that juveniles lacked the maturity and level of culpability that traditional criminal sanctions presupposed, and that juvenile offenders should, therefore, not only be treated as less blameworthy but also as more amenable to treatment and rehabilitation than hardened adult criminals. The primary justification for creating a separate juvenile justice system was the distinction between punishment and treatment. The criminal justice system at the turn of the century emphasized the classical school's belief in punishment and deterrence as proper goals. Separating juvenile offenders from adult criminals would allow the juveniles to be treated instead of punished (Fritsch and Hemmens, 1995).

In 1899, the first juvenile court was established in Illinois, marking the formal beginning of a separate juvenile justice system. Other states quickly followed Illinois' lead. Within 12 years, 22 states had adopted some form of juvenile court system. By 1920, all but three states had juvenile courts, and by 1932, all but two states had enacted juvenile codes. By 1945, every state had a juvenile court system (Thomas and Bilchik, 1985).

The juvenile court system in most states was organized as an entity entirely distinct from the adult court system. Juvenile proceedings were held in their own courtrooms, with judges who heard only juvenile cases. Juvenile court procedure was markedly different from that of the general jurisdiction court. Hearings were private and informal in nature. Juvenile court judges enjoyed enormous discretionary power. Juvenile court jurisdiction was classified as civil rather than criminal. A whole new vocabulary sought to differentiate juvenile court activities from adult criminal court activities. Juveniles were not arrested; they were "taken into custody." Instead of indicting a juvenile, prosecutors "petitioned the juvenile court." Juveniles were not convicted; they were "adjudicated delinquent." Juvenile court sanctions were not referred to as sentences, but as "dispositions." Juveniles were not sent to prisons; they were sent to "training schools" (Fritsch and Hemmens, 1995). The belief that the juvenile court's primary purpose was to help the child remained a cornerstone of the U.S. juvenile justice system for decades. As late as the 1960s, most state statutes still declared that the purpose of the juvenile justice system was to help rather than punish the child (Hemmens et al., 1997). In 1967, the President's Commission on Law Enforcement and Administration of Justice recommended maintaining separate juvenile and adult court systems, even while admitting that the juvenile justice system had so far failed in its task of rehabilitating juvenile offenders.

16.3 Challenges to the Juvenile Court

The juvenile justice system continued to grow in size and power well into the 1960s, when several U.S. Supreme Court decisions forced a change in the form of the juvenile court system, and the rising crime rate caused many to reexamine the role of the criminal justice system, including the juvenile court. In *Kent v. United States* (1966), the Supreme Court for the first time directly addressed juvenile court procedures. *Kent* extended several due process rights to juveniles involved in waiver hearings. The Court said that the decision whether to transfer a juvenile to an adult court required a full hearing. The Court also established the juvenile's right to have counsel present at the waiver hearing. One year after *Kent* was decided, the Supreme Court again examined juvenile court procedures. *In re Gault* (1967) held that whenever a juvenile was charged with an act that could result in his or her being sent to a state institution, be it a prison or a reform school, he or she must be accorded due process. Rights guaranteed the juvenile under the rubric of due process included the right to counsel, the right to confront one's accusers and cross-examine witnesses, and the right not to incriminate oneself.

At the same time, the Supreme Court was forcing juvenile courts to undergo massive internal changes, American society was experiencing a dramatic increase in the juvenile crime rate, which increased by almost 250 percent between 1960 and 1980 (Hamparian et al., 1982). Between 1960 and 1975, juvenile arrests increased over 140 percent, whereas adult arrests during this time increased less than 13 percent (Thomas and Bilchik, 1985). Gang activity became a major problem in some large urban areas, and much of the gang activity involved extreme violence. Both criminal justice professionals and the public sensed that the juvenile justice system was failing to control juvenile delinquency and offenses.

Some began to blame the juvenile justice system's emphasis on rehabilitation and treatment for the failure to halt the growth of crime. These "crime control conservatives" believed that the emphasis on treatment was thwarting the effectiveness of the criminal law, and they called for revision of the methods of handling juvenile offenders (van den Haag, 1975). Chief among the complaints was the criticism of the juvenile courts' perceived leniency toward juveniles charged with serious crimes.

State legislatures began to respond to the criticisms of the existing juvenile justice system and the calls to "get tough" on juvenile offenders. Many states amended their statutes to emphasize that punishment should either replace, or at least be a coequal concern in the juvenile court's decision making process (Hemmens et al., 1997). For example, when Washington changed its legislation regarding juveniles, the objectives of the juvenile justice system were rewritten to include "making the juvenile accountable for his criminal behavior" and to "provide punishment commensurate with the age, crime, and criminal history of the juvenile offender."

One of the most common methods employed to increase the punitive nature of the juvenile justice system was to permit increased use of the waiver process. Waiver involves removing a juvenile offender from the juvenile court jurisdiction and processing him or her as an adult in the general jurisdiction criminal court. This process is most commonly referred to *as waiver of jurisdiction* or *transfer*, although it is sometimes referred to as *determination of fitness*, *certification*, *reference*, *decline*, or *remand*. The two reasons most commonly given for making it easier to transfer juvenile offenders to adult court are the following: (1) the juvenile justice system has failed to control these juveniles, and (2) these juveniles have demonstrated, either by the seriousness of their offense or by the frequency of their appearances in the juvenile justice system, that they are not amenable to the sort of treatment the system provides (Feld, 1987).

16.4 Public Support for Juvenile Waiver

The decision to transfer juveniles to criminal court is one that is generally supported by the public. Wu (2000) and Mears (2001) both examined data from the 1995 National Opinion Survey of Crime and Justice and found that most of the public supports transferring juveniles to criminal court. More than two-thirds of the public support the transfer of juveniles who commit violent, property- and drug-related offenses. However, the level of support declines when violent crime is separated from the two other categories and when the juvenile is younger (Wu, 2000). Mears (2001) discovered that marital status and philosophy of punishment are consistently associated with support for sanctioning youth as adults when the offense involves selling illegal drugs, committing property crime, or committing violent crime (Mears, 2001).

Bouley and Wells (2001) found that most people surveyed believed juveniles should be tried as adults for serious property crimes, selling illegal drugs, and serious violent crime. Furthermore, the decision to try juveniles as adults was significantly related to income and the respondent's opinion of the purpose of sentencing. The majority of the individuals surveyed reported that they felt the primary objective of sentencing was to discourage others from committing crime (Bouley and Wells, 2001).

Feiler and Sheley (1999) found that the public supports the waiver of juveniles who commit violent acts, especially those involving weapons. However, public support lessened when age was taken into account. The public did not take into account prior record, but relied on offense seriousness and age (Feiler and Sheley, 1999).

16.5 Effects of Juvenile Waiver

The effects of the changes to state waiver statutes can best be described as conflicting. Research conducted to date has examined the consequences of waiving juveniles to criminal court in several domains. In examining the effectiveness of sentencing and correctional policy, several goals typically emerge: punishment, deterrence, incapacitation, retribution and rehabilitation. It has been hypothesized that by transferring a juvenile to criminal court, a harsher penalty will be imposed, thereby satisfying the punishment, incapacitation, and retribution goals of the system. However, some research (Bortner, 1986; Champion, 1989; Merlo et al., 1997) seems to support the contrary notion that transferred juveniles are actually being sentenced to probation more often than incarceration. In contrast to this are other studies (Fritsch et al., 1996; Podkopacz and Feld, 1996; Strom and Smith, 1998) that determined that transferred juveniles were imprisoned more often and longer when sentenced in the criminal court.

Some research controlled for offense type examined sentence severity for a matched cohort of juveniles who were transferred, against those who were retained. Barnes and Franz (1989) found juveniles who were transferred for property offenses received lighter sentences than they would have in the juvenile court, whereas those waived for person-related offenses were sentenced more severely. Podkopacz and Feld (1996) found those juveniles transferred for nonviolent offenses served less time than they would have had they been retained in the juvenile system.

In addition to sentence severity, some research has examined recidivism rates of transferred youth in an effort to measure the deterrent effects of the process. Fagan (1995) found the recidivism rates for juveniles convicted of robbery in the criminal court was nearly 50 percent higher than youth who were adjudicated for robbery and retained in the juvenile court. However, when burglary offenders were examined, no significant differences were found (Fagan, 1995). Podkopacz and Feld (1996) found a larger proportion of youth who were transferred reoffended within a 2-year follow-up period than those who remained in the juvenile system. Winner et al. (1997) examined recidivism in Florida and found that transferred youth reoffended more quickly than those juveniles dealt with in the juvenile system. However, when the rearrest data were examined several years later, the nontransferred youth caught up in terms of prevalence of arrest. In addition, the transferred youth were rearrested more often than the nontransferred youth who reoffended, regardless of the offenses for which they were prosecuted (Winner et al., 1997).

Several other studies have attempted to measure the general deterrent effects of waiver legislation on juvenile crime rates. Singer and Mcdowall (1988) found no appreciable difference in the juvenile crime rates for serious and violent crimes after the New York juvenile offender law was enacted. Jensen and Metsger (1994) found the arrest rates for serious and violent crime actually increased 18 percent after Idaho enacted its legislative waiver provision. Similar results were found in Georgia (Risler et al., 1998).

16.6 Forms of Juvenile Waiver

There are several different forms of waiver. These include judicial, prosecutorial, and legislative. Judicial waiver is the oldest and most common form of waiver, but both prosecutorial and legislative waiver have increased in recent years. Most states employ more than one form of waiver (Griffin et al., 1998). Judicial waiver is the process by which the juvenile judge may waive jurisdiction of the juvenile, and he or she is transferred to the criminal court. Prosecutorial discretion, or direct file, is the means by which prosecutors are given the authority to file certain cases in either juvenile or criminal court under concurrent jurisdiction status. Legislative waiver, or statutory exclusion, is the method by which state legislatures have excluded certain offenses from being handled in juvenile court.

Additionally, 23 states allow for reverse waiver, in which a juvenile being prosecuted as an adult may petition to have the case returned to juvenile court. In addition, 31 states have a "once an adult always an adult" provision. This means that if a juvenile is waived to criminal court, any subsequent accusations are also handled in criminal court (Griffin et al., 1998).

16.6.1 Prosecutorial Waiver

Fourteen states and the District of Columbia have prosecutorial waiver. It is sometimes referred to as *concurrent jurisdiction* or *direct file*. The prosecutor has the option of filing charges against juvenile offenders in either juvenile or adult court. This method of transfer is perhaps the most controversial because it vests considerable discretion in the prosecutor, whose primary duty is to secure convictions and who is traditionally more concerned with retribution than with rehabilitation. Prosecutorial waiver is the least-utilized form of waiver.

16.6.2 Judicial Waiver

The most common method of waiver, and the one that has the longest history, is judicial waiver. Originally, this was the only means of transferring juveniles to adult criminal court. The juvenile court judge uses his or her discretionary authority to waive jurisdiction and send the case to the adult court. A juvenile court may decide on its own motion to transfer a juvenile to adult court. Alternatively, the prosecutor may move to transfer, and the juvenile court judge must decide the motion. Judicial waiver is the most popular form of waiver, receiving general support from scholars, criminal justice professionals, and professional organizations such as the American Bar Association and the National Advisory Committee on Criminal Justice Standards and Goals. At present, 48 states and the District of Columbia allow for discretionary waiver by juvenile court judges. These states must conduct a hearing in which the parties are allowed to present evidence on the waiver issue, but the judge makes the ultimate decision.

In the past 20 years, a number of states have modified the judicial waiver process, either by lowering the age at which a juvenile is eligible for waiver or by increasing the number of offenses eligible for judicial waiver. Although most states had always permitted some use of juvenile waiver, it was quite rare until the late 1960s. Early-waiver statutes gave the juvenile court complete authority and discretion to transfer a juvenile offender to criminal court. The burden of proof was on the official attempting to have the juvenile transferred to adult criminal court. Table 16.1 provides a summary of current judicial waiver statutes.

There have been numerous modifications of judicial waiver statutes in the 50 states in the past quarter century. Between 1979 and 1995, 18 states modified their judicial waiver statutes (Fritsch and Hemmens, 1995). The nature of these modifications varies. Some states have lowered the age at which a juvenile is eligible for judicial waiver,

Table 16.1   Judicial Waiver

State	Eligibility for Judicial Waiver	
	Age (years)	*Crimes*
Alabama	14 and older	Felony offense, any offense if previously committed as a delinquent
Alaska	Any age	Any offense
Arizona	Any age	Any offense
Arkansas	15 and older	Any offense
	14 and older	Murder, first degree kidnapping, aggravated robbery, aggravated sexual assault, first degree battery, aggravated assault with a deadly weapon, possession of a handgun on school property
	16 and older	Felony offense
California	16 and older	Any offense
	14 and 15	Murder, kidnapping, aggravated sexual assault, aggravated assault, aggravated burglary, drug sales
Colorado	14 and older	Felony offense
	12 and older	Class 1 or 2 felony or a crime of violence
Connecticut	14 and older	Any felony, serious juvenile offense if second
Delaware	14 and older	Any offense if juvenile is determined not amenable to treatment
District of Columbia	15 and older	Felony offense
	16 and older	Any offense if already committed as delinquent
	Any age	Illegal possession or control of a firearm at school or school event
Florida	14 and older	Any offense
	Any age	Any offense punishable by death or life imprisonment
Georgia	15 and older	Any offense

Table 16.1 Judicial Waiver (continued)

| State | Eligibility for Judicial Waiver | |
	Age (years)	Crimes
	14 and older	Murder, voluntary manslaughter, aggravated assault or battery committed while confined in a juvenile facility
	13 and older	Any offense punishable by death or life imprisonment
Hawaii	16 and older	Felony offense
	14 and older	Felony that results in serious bodily injury or Class A felony, or if the juvenile offender has one or more prior adjudications for a felony
	Any age	First or second degree murder or attempted murder
Idaho	14 and older	Any offense
Illinois	13 and older	Any offense
Indiana	10 and older	Murder
	14 and older	Heinous or aggravated act, any offense if part of pattern of delinquent acts
	16 and older	Felony offense
Iowa	14 and older	Any offense
Kansas	Any age	Any offense
Kentucky	14 and older	Capital offense, Class A or B felony
	16 and older	Class C or D felony and one prior felony adjudication
Louisiana	14 and older	Murder, aggravated kidnapping, aggravated sexual assault, aggravated battery
Maine	Any age	First or second degree murder, Class A, B, or C offense
Maryland	15 and older	Any offense
	Any age	Any offense punishable by death or life imprisonment

Table 16.1 Judicial Waiver (continued)

State	Eligibility for Judicial Waiver	
	Age (years)	*Crimes*
Massachussetts	14 and older	Any violent offense, or felony offense and prior delinquency commitment
Michigan	14 and older	Felony offense
Minnesota	14 and older	Any felony
Mississippi	13 and older	Any offense
Missouri	12 and older	Felony offense
Montana	16 and older	Murder, negligent homicide, arson, aggravated assault, sexual assault, robbery, burglary, aggravated kidnapping, sale or manufacture of drugs, possession of explosives
	12 and older	Murder, sexual assault, assault on a peace officer or judicial officer, attempted deliberate homicide
Nebraska		No provision for judicial waiver
Nevada	14 and older	Felony offense
New Hampshire	Any age	Felony offense
New Jersey	14 and older	Murder, manslaughter, treason, kidnapping, unlawful possession of a weapon, arson, conspiracy, distribution of a controlled substance within 1000 ft of school property, any offense if previous adjudicated or convicted for waivable offense
New Mexico	16 and older	Felony offense
	15 and older	Murder, assault, kidnapping, aggravated battery, sexual assault, robbery, aggravated burglary, aggravated arson, any felony if three prior felony adjudications within the last 2 years

Table 16.1   Judicial Waiver (continued)

State	Eligibility for Judicial Waiver	
	Age (years)	Crimes
	14 and older	Murder, assault with intent to commit a violent felony, kidnapping, aggravated battery, shooting at an occupied building or shooting at or from a motor vehicle, dangerous use of explosives, sexual assault, robbery, aggravated burglary, aggravated arson, abuse of a child that results in great bodily harm or death, any felony if previously adjudicated for three separate felony offenses within the last 3 years
New York		No provision for judicial waiver
North Carolina	13 and older	Felony offense
North Dakota	16 and older	Any offense
	14 and older	Violent felony
Ohio	15 and older	Felony offense
Oklahoma	Any age	Felony offense
Oregon	Any age	Murder, first degree manslaughter, first degree assault, first degree sexual assault, first degree robbery
	16 and older	Any offense
	15 and older	Class A or B felony, selected Class C felony
Pennsylvania	14 and older	Felony offense
Rhode Island	16 and older	Any offense
	Any age	Any felony
South Carolina	Any age	Murder, sexual assault
	14 and older	Class A, B, C, or D felony punishable by 15 years or more in prison
South Dakota	Any age	Any felony
Tennessee	Any age	Murder, manslaughter, aggravated sexual assault, aggravated robbery, aggravated kidnapping

Table 16.1   Judicial Waiver (continued)

State	Eligibility for Judicial Waiver	
	Age (years)	Crimes
	16 and older	Any offense
Texas	15 and older	Second or third degree felony or a state jail felony
	14 and older	First degree felony
Utah	Any age	Felony offense
Vermont	10–13	Murder, manslaughter, aggravated assault, armed robbery, kidnapping, sexual assault, aggravated burglary, maiming
Virginia	14 and older	Felony
Washington	17 and older	Second degree assault, first degree extortion, second degree kidnapping, second degree sexual assault, second degree robbery, indecent liberties
	15 and older	Class A felony or attempt to commit such felony
West Virginia	Any age	Violent felony if previously adjudicated for violent felony, felony if previously adjudicated for a felony twice
	14 and older	Treason, murder, robbery, kidnapping, arson, sexual assault in the first degree, violent felony, felony if also previously adjudged a felon or if a firearm was used during the commission of said felony, drug crimes
Wisconsin	15 and older	Any offense
	14 and older	First or second degree murder, first degree sexual assault, kidnapping, burglary, drug offenses, any felony offense if committed in furtherance of organized gang activity
Wyoming	Any age	Any offense

whereas some went even further, doing away with the age limit altogether. Other states modified their judicial waiver statutes by adding offenses to the list of crimes eligible for judicial waiver. Still other states modified their judicial waiver statutes by not only lowering the age at which some offenders could be transferred, but by combining this change in age eligibility with an increase in the number of offenses eligible for transfer. Other states actually raised the age limit for some offenses eligible for waiver while lowering it for others.

There have been numerous additional modifications of judicial waiver statutes in the 50 states between 1995 and 2002. Twenty-seven states have modified their judicial waiver statutes. The nature of these modifications varies. Ten states have lowered the age at which a juvenile is eligible for judicial waiver. For example, Delaware lowered the age at which a juvenile could be waived for any offense from 16 to 14 years provided it was determined he or she was not amenable to treatment. Colorado modified its statute to allow for the waiver of 12-year-olds charged with a Class 1 or Class 2 felony or a crime of violence. This was in addition to the provision of the previous statute that allowed for the transfer of any juveniles 14 years and older charged with a felony.

Fourteen states modified their judicial waiver statutes by adding offenses to the list of crimes eligible for judicial waiver. Vermont added more offenses juveniles could be waived for, such as arson causing death, assault or robbery causing serious bodily injury, unlawful restraint, maiming, sexual assault, and burglary. Wisconsin modified its law so than juveniles 15 years and older could be waived for any offense.

Other states clarified their statutes by limiting offenses for which juveniles of certain ages could be waived. For example, Indiana changed its statute, which used to allow waiver for any felony if the juvenile was 16 years or older, to only allow waiver if the youth was charged with a Class A or Class B felony or involuntary manslaughter or reckless homicide if charged as a Class C felony. Texas modified its statute, which had allowed for the waiver of any juvenile 14 years and older, to provide for it only in the case of those juveniles 14 years and older charged with a capital offense, first-degree felony, or aggravated controlled substance offense, as well as those youths 15 years or older who are charged with a second- or third-degree or state jail felony.

16.6.3 Legislative Waiver

Another form of waiver, and the one that has received the most attention in recent years, is legislative waiver. Legislative waiver is sometimes referred to as *automatic waiver* because juvenile court jurisdiction is removed automatically without a motion by the prosecutor or a decision by the juvenile court judge. Statutes exclude specified offenses or offenders from juvenile court jurisdiction. Generally, this exclusion is reserved for the most serious offenses or for repeat offenders. There are two types of legislative waiver. One, referred to as *offense exclusion*, excludes some offenses from juvenile court jurisdiction. These are usually serious, violent crimes such as murder, rape, and aggravated assault. The reason for excluding juveniles charged with such offenses from the juvenile justice system is that juvenile courts cannot impose sufficiently severe sanctions for such offenses. A second type of legislative waiver excludes from juvenile court those juveniles who possess a particular combination of prior record and present offense. This form of waiver is directed at juvenile offenders who have failed to desist from criminal activity despite previous contact with the juvenile justice system. Legislative waiver is found in 31 states.

In the past 25 years, states have made increasing use of legislative waiver, primarily by adding offenses that are excluded from juvenile court jurisdiction or by enacting a waiver statute where none previously existed. Table 16.2 provides a summary of current judicial waiver statutes.

Examination of Table 16.2 makes it clear that the most serious crimes are the ones most commonly excluded from juvenile court jurisdiction, as one would expect. Several states, however, exclude all felonies, including some relatively minor, nonviolent offenses. In 1979, 14 states had some form of legislative waiver. Today, 33 states utilize some form of legislative waiver.

Legislative waiver gained in popularity during the 1980s. States that adopted legislative waiver during this period often limited its use to the most serious offenses. On the other hand, some other states adopted legislative waiver during this period not merely for serious offenses but also for repeat offenders.

In 1995, 21 states had some form of legislative waiver. Between 1995 and 2002, 12 states enacted legislative waiver statutes, whereas 16 states amended existing statutes. Four states lowered the age at which a juvenile could be legislatively waived into criminal court. For example, Illinois now mandates that juveniles 13 years and older charged with first-degree murder committed during the course of a sexual assault or aggravated kidnapping be transferred immediately to criminal court. Indiana decreed that a juvenile of any age be automatically transferred if charged with murder, kidnapping, rape, or robbery

Table 16.2 Legislative Waiver

| State | Eligibility for Legislative Waiver | |
	Age (years)	Crimes
Alabama	16 and older	Capital offenses, Class A felony, felony involving the use of a deadly weapon, felony causing serious physical injury, trafficking in drugs
Alaska	16 and older	Unclassified felony or Class A felony against person, arson in first degree, Class B felony against person in which the minor is alleged to have used a deadly weapon and the minor was previously adjudicated of an offense that involved an offense against a person with the use of a deadly weapon
Colorado		No legislative waiver
Connecticut	14 and older	Murder, Class A or B felony
Delaware	Any age	First or second degree murder, sexual assault, kidnapping
	16 or older	Previously convicted of a felony and alleged to have committed conspiracy in the first degree, rape in third degree, assault in first degree, arson in first degree, burglary in first degree, robbery in first degree, trafficking in illegal drugs
District of Columbia	16 and older	Murder, sexual assault, first degree burglary, armed robbery
Florida	16 and older	When the child has previously been adjudicated for murder, sexual battery, armed robbery, carjacking, aggravated assault and a subsequent offense of this type is alleged, a forcible felony if previously adjudicated of a felony in the past 45 d, possession of a firearm or destructive device, discharge of a firearm or destructive device
	Any age	Stealing a motor vehicle and inflicting serious bodily injury or death

Table 16.2   Legislative Waiver (continued)

State	Age (years)	Crimes
		Eligibility for Legislative Waiver
Georgia	13 and older	Murder, manslaughter, rape, aggravated sodomy, aggravated child molestation, aggravated sexual battery, aggravated robbery if committed with a firearm
	15 and older	Burglary, if three prior burglary adjudications
Hawaii		No legislative waiver provision
Idaho	14 and older	Murder, attempted murder, sexual assault, assault or battery with intent to commit a serious felony, first degree arson, robbery, mayhem, illegal possession of drugs or firearms near school or school event
Illinois	15 and older	First degree murder, aggravated sexual assault, armed robbery, possession or sale of drugs at school or school event, if prior felony adjudication and forcible felony in furtherance of organized gang activity; or if prior forcible felony adjudication and felony in furtherance of organized gang activity
	13 or older	First degree murder committed during the course of either sexual assault or aggravated kidnapping
Indiana	16 and older	Carjacking, criminal gang activity, possession of firearm, any misdemeanor or felony if prior felony or misdemeanor conviction
	Any age	Murder, kidnapping, rape, armed robbery
Iowa	16 or older	Any felony
Kansas		No legislative waiver
Kentucky	14 or older	Any felony in which a firearm was used
Louisiana	15 and older	Murder, manslaughter, aggravated sexual assault, aggravated kidnapping

Table 16.2   Legislative Waiver (continued)

	Eligibility for Legislative Waiver	
State	Age (years)	Crimes
	16 and older	Armed robbery, aggravated burglary
Maine (provisions added)	Any age	Murder, manslaughter, elevated aggravated assault, arson that recklessly endangers a person, robbery, sexual assault

if committed with a deadly weapon or resulting in serious bodily injury. In addition, 12 states added legislatively excluded offenses to their existing statutes. Idaho added assault or battery with intent to commit a serious felony and first-degree arson. Maryland added second- and third-degree sexual offenses, possession of a firearm in relation to drug trafficking, carjacking, and assault in first degree to their existing statue for juveniles 16 years and older.

16.7 Conclusion

In recent years, the "get tough on crime" clamor has filtered into the juvenile justice system. Liberals decry the system's occasional disregard for due process and the ease with which the state may intervene in the lives of juveniles. Conservatives complain that the juvenile justice system is too easy on young criminals, and that this failure to adequately punish juvenile offenders leads not only to a setback in preventing future criminal activity, but also to a failure in adequately addressing society's right to punish persons who violate its laws. The result of this attack on the juvenile justice system has been a tremendous change in the use and applicability of juvenile waiver in all its forms. Numerous state legislatures have either lowered the judicial waiver age or have added offenses eligible for judicial waiver to general jurisdiction court. In addition, numerous states have enacted legislative waiver statutes that automatically send an offender to adult court for prosecution based on the offense committed. Although the 1980s saw a tremendous increase in the use of waiver at a time when the juvenile crime rate was increasing, this trend has not slowed as the juvenile crime rate has slowed. The increased use of both discretionary and mandatory waiver suggests a continued infatuation with the "get tough" approach to juvenile crime in the face of crime statistics and research that suggests the practice is not achieving its intended goals.

References

Barnes, C. and Franz, R. (1989). Questionably adult: determinants and effects on the juvenile waiver decision. *Justice Quarterly* 6(1): 117–135.

Bouley, E. and Wells, T. (2001). Attitudes of citizens in a southern rural county toward Juvenile crime and justice issues. *Journal of Contemporary Criminal Justice* 17(1): 60–70.

Bortner, M.A. (1986). Traditional rhetoric, organizational realities: remand of juveniles to adult court. *Crime and Delinquency* 32(1): 53–73.

Champion, D. (1989). Teenage felons and waiver hearings: some recent trends, 1980–1988. *Crime and Delinquency* 35(4): 577–585.

Drowns, R. and Hess, K. (2000). *Juvenile Justice.* 3rd ed. Belmont, CA: Wadsworth.

Feld, B. (1987). The juvenile court meets the principle of the offense: legislative changes in juvenile waiver statutes. *The Journal of Criminal Law and Criminology* 78(3): 471–533.

Fritsch, E. and Hemmens, C. (1995). Juvenile waiver in the United States 1979–1995: a comparison and analysis of state waiver statutes. *Juvenile and Family Court Journal* 46(3): 17–35.

Fritsch, E., Caeti, T., and Hemmens, C. (1996). Spare the needle but not the punishment: the incarceration of waived youth in Texas prisons. *Crime and Delinquency* 42(4): 593–609.

Gardner, M. (1997). *Understanding Juvenile Law.* New York: Matthew Bender.

Griffin, P., Torbet, P., and Szymanski, L. (1998). Trying Juveniles as Adults in Criminal Court. Washington, D.C.: Office of Juvenile Justice and Delinquency Prevention.

Hamparian, D., Estep, L., Muntean, S., Priestino, R., Swisher, R., Wallace, P., and White, J. (1982). Youth in Adult Courts: Between Two Worlds. Washington, D.C.: Office of Juvenile Justice and Delinquency Prevention.

Hemmens, C. Fritsch, E., and Caeti, J. (1997). Juvenile justice code purpose clauses: the power of words. *Criminal Justice Policy Review* 8(2): 221–240.

Jensen, E. and Metsger, L. (1994). A test of the deterrent effect of legislative waiver on violent juvenile crime. *Crime and Delinquency* 40(1): 96–104.

Mears, D. (2001). Getting tougher with juvenile offenders. *Criminal Justice and Behavior* 28(2): 206–226.

Merlo, A., Benekos, P., and Cook, W. (1997). Waiver and juvenile justice reform: widening the punitive net. *Criminal Justice Policy Review* 8(2–3): 145–168.

Podkopacz, M. and Feld, B. (1996). The end of the line: an empirical study of judicial waiver. *The Journal of Criminal Law and Criminology* 86(2): 449–492.

Risler, E., Sweatman, T., and Nackerud, L. (1998). Evaluating the Georgia legislative waiver's effectiveness in deterring juvenile crime. *Research on Social Work Practice* 8(6): 657–667.

Singer, S. and McDowall, D. (1988). Criminalizing delinquency: the deterrent effects of the New York juvenile offender law. *Law and Society Review* 22(3): 521–535.

Strom, K., and Smith, S. (1998). Juvenile Felony Defendants in Criminal Courts. Washington, D.C.: Department of Justice, Office of Justice Programs.

Thomas, C., and Bilchik, S. (1985). Prosecuting juveniles in criminal courts: a legal and empirical analysis. *The Journal of Criminal Law and Criminology* 76(2): 439–479.

Van den Haag, E. (1975). *Punishing Criminals*. New York: The Free Press.

Wu, B. (2000). Determinants of public opinion toward juvenile waiver decisions. *Juvenile and Family Court Journal* 51(1): 9–20.

Winner, L., Lanza-Kaduce, L., Bishop, D., and Frazier, C. (1997). The transfer of juveniles to criminal court: reexamining recidivism over the long term. *Crime and Delinquency* 43(4): 548–563.

Cases Cited

Kent v. U.S., 383 U.S. 541 (1966).
In re Gault, 387 U.S. 1. (1967).

Chapter 17

Status Offenders: Early History and Contemporary Policies and Programs

Catherine E. Burton and Sharon K. Tracy

17.1 Introduction

The term *juvenile* appeared in 1899 when the first American juvenile court was established in the state of Illinois (Whitehead and Lab, 1999). Since this time, there has been constant debate over how juveniles who commit age-related minor offenses should be treated. This chapter explores such age-related (juvenile status) offenses. Included in this exploration are discussions of the history of status offenses, how the courts have dealt with status offenses over the years, and the impact of the Juvenile Justice and Delinquency Prevention Act (JJDPA) of 1974. The chapter will conclude with a discussion of more recent programs developed to deal with status offending.

17.2 Background

Under the law, a juvenile is any person under the legal age of adulthood in a given jurisdiction. This age varies from state to state, but in most states, the District of Columbia, and in all federal districts, any person age 18 or younger is considered a juvenile. In several states such as New York, Connecticut, and North Carolina, a juvenile is age 16 or less, and in Georgia, Illinois, Louisiana, Massachusetts, Michigan, Missouri, New Hampshire, South Carolina, Texas, and Wisconsin, a juvenile is age 17 or less. Wyoming is the only state that has established the age of juveniles to be 19 or younger (Whitehead and Lab, 1999).

In addition to upper age limits, status or juvenile jurisdictions also have lower age limits. Such lower age limits refer to the age at which a child is thought to form *mens rea*, criminal intent, and also the age at which children are unable to tell what is right from what is wrong, *dolci incapax*. This age is usually about 6 or 7 years but is not fixed by statute (Agnew, 2001).

In juvenile jurisdictions, the age of the offender refers to the age at the time the offense was committed, but in some states, age refers to the offender's age at the time of apprehension. This distinction allows for the sometimes-lengthy periods it takes to investigate and clear a case (Champion, 2003).

Once the courts were divided into adult and juvenile jurisdictions (see Chapter 1 and Chapter 2), there were a number of activities that were deemed offenses for juveniles, because they were thought to be harmful to minors. These activities are called *status offenses* simply because of the age status of the offender. Examples of status offenses are truancy, possession and consumption of alcohol, incorrigibility, curfew violations, and purchase of cigarettes. If someone over the age of 21 commits any of these same acts, the action is not a criminal offense (Calhoun and Chapple, 2003).

17.3 The Impact of the Juvenile Justice and Delinquency Act of 1974 on Status Offenders

In 1966, the National Council on Crime and Delinquency (NCCD) was commissioned to study state and local juvenile institutions that confined juvenile nonviolent offenders. The results of this study indicated that more than 50 percent of juveniles confined were being held for status offenses. Often, the conditions at these facilities were less than ideal (Crank, 1995). Later on, studies revealed that juvenile suicide rates;

physical, mental, and sexual assaults, and antisocial behavior were linked to confinement in juvenile facilities (Calhoun and Chapple, 2003).

In response to the NCCD's findings, the Juvenile Justice and Delinquency Preventions Act (JJDPA) of 1974 was proposed and passed. Included in the act were provisions for the formula grant program, the establishment of the Office of Juvenile Justice and Delinquency Prevention (OJJDP), the separation of juvenile and adult detainees, and guidelines for deinstitutionalization of status offenses. Although there had been a push for deinstitutionalization of status offenses during the late 1960s, the movement was cemented by the 1974 Federal Juvenile Delinquency Act (Dryfoos, 1990). Deinstitution-alization meant that juveniles who committed status offenses were diverted from the juvenile justice system to agencies outside the juvenile court's jurisdiction. The county or district attorney was given the authority to divert an offender, and this decision was usually made before a petition was filed and sometimes prior to arrest. After diversion, juveniles who were adjudicated for status offenses were often classified as "children in need of supervision" (CHINS), "persons in need of supervision" (PINS), "minors in need of supervision" (MINS), and "minors requiring authoritative intervention" (MRAI) (Whitehead and Lab, 1999).

The main rationale behind diversion was the fact that many legis-lators felt that status offenses were minor, and juveniles were better off having their families or some other agency deal with the matter as opposed to being formally processed by the justice system. Formal processing of status offenses was also linked to labeling and secondary delinquent acts, negating the whole purpose of the juvenile justice system (Agnew, 2001).

The JJDPA consists of four major components. The first component is deinstitutionalization. The act mandates that a juvenile status offender cannot be held in secure detention or confinement. However, the formula grants program allows juvenile status offenders to be held temporarily for up to 24 hours in a detention center, excluding week-ends and holidays, for purposes of identification; notifying parents; or transfer to court, another jurisdiction, or another facility. A second 24-h period may be granted after a juvenile has made a court appearance. The other exception to the confinement policy is that juveniles charged with violations of the Federal Handgun Safety Act or other similar firearms legislation may be confined (Loeber and Farrington, 2000).

The second component of the JJDPA is the separation mandate. This facet of the act specifies that adults and juveniles who are incarcerated will have no contact with each other. This includes all areas of the facility, such as entry and booking areas, hallways, sleeping areas, dining and recreation areas, educational facilities, etc. The third and fourth components of the JJDPA address nonsecure custody criteria and disproportionate minority confinement, neither of which is relevant to status offenders (Loeber and Farrington, 2000).

During the 1970s, one status offense that received much attention was incorrigibility. Juveniles who do not obey their parents are deemed *incorrigible* or incapable of parental correction. With *parens patriae* still in force at this time, many juveniles were confined for this offense. Critics argued that almost all children disobey their parents at some point, and such behavior did not warrant the state's intervention. A number of studies conducted by the Department of Justice (DOJ) indicated that incarcerating status offenders actually exposed juveniles to much more severe criminality and sometimes even sexual and physical abuse. Basically, juveniles came out of the system less socialized than when they went into the system (see Agnew, 2001 and Whitehead and Lab, 1999 for discussions).

In 1980, Congress amended the JJDPA to allow states to exclude reporting confinement of juveniles who had violated a court order (Berger, 1996). This amendment had a large impact on status offenders as many status offenders could then be confined for failure to comply with the terms in their diversion agreement. In a study of Illinois juvenile court judges, Beger (1994) found that this amendment allowed judges to incarcerate juvenile status offenders more frequently as the less punitive options did not have to be exhausted in order to comply with the amended JJDPA.

17.4 Contemporary Status Offenses and Status Offender Programs: An Examination of Curfew Violations and Truancy

Even though status offenders were deinstitutionalized during the 1970s, the recent trend in juvenile crime policy has been to get tough on juvenile crime, including juvenile status offenses. In 1996, DOJ estimated that the juvenile courts around the United States formally disposed of 162,000 status offenses, of which 44,800 were liquor law violations (Puzzanchera et al., 1998). Informal disposition has not been estimated.

In recent years, there are two modern status offenses for which juvenile jurisdictions have become quite punitive. The first is violation of curfew and the second is truancy. The subsequent discussion will examine both of these status offenses and will evaluate programs that have been developed to combat them.

Many states, including Georgia, Ohio, and Tennessee, as well as Washington, D.C., have passed legislation allowing local jurisdictions to enforce curfew laws. Most often, curfew requires persons under the age of 17 to be off the streets between the hours of 11 PM and 6 AM. Such a law was passed by Hawaii at the state level and is enforced statewide. Any teenager found violating this curfew is held at a police-designated truancy center until a parent or guardian claims him or her. Parents who are determined to be aiding and abetting curfew violators are also subject to fines and community service (Catalano et al., 1998).

Curfew laws have existed since the 1890s and were originally designed to lower crime rates among immigrant youth who were poor and had taken mainly to property crime for survival (Agnew, 2001; Snyder and Sickmund, 1995). During World War II, curfew laws were enacted as a way for parents to concentrate on the war effort. In the late 1970s, however, curfew laws were adopted in response to rising juvenile crime rates. Today, curfew laws are designed to keep juvenile crime rates low and also to prevent juvenile victimization. Some curfew laws even target specific areas that are known as high-crime spots. For example, in Austin, Texas, curfew laws were adopted in the nightclub area of the city and laws specified that juveniles could not be in the area after 10 pm (Ruefle and Reynolds, 1995).

Curfew laws have been challenged on the grounds that they violate the First Amendment by prohibiting a juvenile's right to free association. In *Qutb v. Strauss* (1993), the U.S. Court of Appeals held that curfew laws were not unconstitutional because they are designed to protect the community as well as the juvenile. Other critics have argued that we are getting back to the *parens patriae* doctrine, as the State is once again acting as a parent (Agnew, 2001; Dryfoos, 1990; Hawkins and Catalano, 1995; Whitehead and Lab, 1999).

The connection between curfew and juvenile delinquency has been studied extensively and for long periods of time. Studies conducted by the OJJDP indicate that juvenile delinquency increases between the ages of 10 and 16. Furthermore, the most likely time for murders of and by juveniles is between 10 PM and 1 AM, and the most frequent place for these murders were alleyways, streets, and car parking lots. Aggravated assaults are most likely to take place between the hours of 11 pm and 1 am, and rapes are most likely to occur between 1 am and 3 am. Again, these crimes occur most frequently on public streets and highways (Dryfoos, 1990; Hawkins and Catalano, 1995; Ruefle and Reynolds, 1995; Whitehead and Lab, 1999).

Although violation of curfew is a status offense and, therefore, falls under the JJDPA, offenders should be diverted. Many curfew violators, however, are confined for up to 24 hours under the exception rule. In an analysis of seven major cities, the OJJDP compared sanctions for curfew violations and the effectiveness of the curfew laws by examining crime rates prior to the curfew and 3 months after the curfew laws were enacted. During the study, the officers enforced the curfew rigorously by writing tickets and confining repeat offenders as well as parents. Results from the different cities highlighted successes in different areas. For example, in Dallas juvenile victimization rates fell 17.7 percent after just 3 months. Juvenile arrest rates also decreased about 15 percent during the same period.

In Phoenix, juvenile arrests for violent crimes decreased by 10 percent after the curfew program was implemented. In addition, the city implemented a number of other crime prevention programs such as community policing, weapon laws, and police-led programs in elementary and secondary schools. In Chicago there was a decrease in serious, violent, juvenile crime and also some property crimes, such as auto theft and theft.

In New Orleans, the curfew program was implemented along with a summer jobs program and recreation programs. As a result of all three programs, juvenile crime decreased by 27 percent, with armed robbery decreasing 33 percent and auto theft decreasing by 42 percent. In Little Rock, the curfew program was associated with a 12 percent decrease in violent crimes and a 10 percent reduction in burglaries (Ruefle and Reynolds, 1994).

The OJJDP generally advocates that curfew programs be implemented along with other programs for juveniles, such as recreation programs and summer job programs. Thus, there is a community partnership that strives to keep juvenile crime rates and juvenile victimization rates low (OJJDP, 2001).

The second status offense that has been adopted by many jurisdictions is truancy or excessive unexcused absences from school. Truancy has been associated with serious delinquent activity in youth and also negative behavior in adults (see Bell et al., 1994; Dryfoos, 1990; and Garry, 1996), in addition to its being a precursor of dropping out of school permanently. Further, truancy has also been associated with substance abuse, gang activity, and property crime among juveniles (Baker, 2000; Rohrman, 1993). Thus, the main rationale behind enforcement of truancy laws is to decrease crime among juveniles and also decrease antisocial and other negative behavior among future adults.

The ages at which students must be in school vary by jurisdiction; for example, Pennsylvania mandates that juveniles attend school from age 8 to age 17, whereas Illinois mandates school attendance from ages 7 to 16. The number of days that a student can be truant also varies by jurisdiction. Typically, the state sets guidelines and then school districts take those guidelines and tighten them considerably (Calhoun and Chapple, 2003). In most cases, a juvenile is deemed truant after the fourth or fifth absence when the absences occur in the same month. If caught being truant, juveniles may be processed in juvenile court, or processed informally. In some states such as Virginia and Arizona, parents can also be held accountable for their children's truancy and may be fined or jailed (Calhoun and Chapple, 2003).

Similar to curfew violations, truancy is a status offense and should technically not be handled by the juvenile court system. Instead, it is usually handled either in the schools or by the parents of the young person. The final stop is juvenile court. However, OJJDP estimates that in 1998, 26 percent of all formally handled status offenses were truancy cases, which is an 85 percent increase from 1989. Interestingly, the gender split for truancy is about even, which is rare for juvenile offenses (OJJDP, 2001)

A number of programs have been implemented to try to decrease truancy. One such program is Abolish Chronic Truancy (ACT) Now. This program was developed by the Pima County Attorney's Office in Arizona and was designed to be an alternative to adjudication. The truancy rates in Pima County were among the highest in the state between 1991 and 1995. In response to these rates, a program was developed that emphasized enforcement of mandatory school attendance through (1) holding parents accountable, (2) provision of a program that examined the root causes for truancy and offered services to remedy those causes, and (3) sanctions for both youth and parents if truancy became chronic. This program is a community partnership that requires the participation of numerous agencies and organizations including the school, police, community agencies, social services agencies, and other organizations that provide services to youth and their families (OJJDP, 2001).

Several steps are outlined in the ACT Now program. After a student's first unexcused absence, a letter is mailed to parents outlining what sanctions may be enforced if truancy continues. After the third unexcused absence, data on the offender and the offense are sent to the Center for Juvenile Alternatives (CJA), a nonprofit organization that provides services for juveniles. Parents and juveniles are referred to CJA and are told they can be prosecuted or they can enroll in the diversion program. Most families opt for the diversion program and sign a contract outlining their commitment. During the program, counseling for both the juvenile and parents is offered, parenting-skills classes are given, and the root causes of truancy are examined (OJJDP, 2001).

The American Prosecutors Research Institute evaluated the ACT Now program during the 1997–1998 school year and concluded that this measure was reducing status offenses. Results from the evaluation indicated that truancy levels decreased significantly, and the threat of prosecution of parents or guardians significantly increased the numbers of families involved in the ACT Now program. Further, dropout rates also significantly decreased (OJJDP, 2001). This program has since been used as a model for other similar programs around the country.

Another meritorious program attempting to combat truancy is a special unit located within the probation division of the Juvenile Court Services in Las Vegas. This unit focuses on middle school and younger high school students (first and second years) and is partially funded by OJJDP (salary for one probation officer). Nevada's Habitual Truant Act provision requires that upon the third unexcused absence, school officials must contact the parents of the truant juvenile. Three contacts or attempted contacts must be made, and if attendance does not improve, the dean of the school refers the youth to Clark County (Las Vegas) Juvenile Court Services officers. In this instance, there is a truancy citation issued by the police that includes documentation of the absences and the parental contacts, and a date for juvenile court appearance is noted (Ellis, 2003).

At this juncture, the youth meets with the Truancy Unit officers or their assistants and is Mirandized and informed that this citation could mean a court appearance. If the youth admits to the truancies, he or she is referred to diversionary programs and school attendances are monitored. If attendance improves over the subsequent 60 to 90 d, the citation is held; if attendance continues to decline, or if the truant is a younger individual, that truant is referred to social skills/education classes. For older high school students, there is a 2- to 3-h mandatory truancy intervention class that emphasizes the value of education and offers alternative suggestions for getting high-school credit.

If another citation occurs or the student is totally noncompliant, the youth goes to truancy court conducted by truancy masters (licensed attorneys), where a petition is filed. At this point, the individual may admit to the truancies or deny them and go to trial in the juvenile court. If the latter occurs, sanctions may be imposed, parents can be fined, and the youth will be monitored. The court can detain for a brief time under the federal guidelines if it so desires.

Usually, the youth admits to the truancy citation and is referred to mandatory community service programs. Some of these diversion programs include skills courses such as the following: (1) courses offered in-house by the Center for Independent Living for Truants (SOAR); (2) courses jointly offered by the juvenile court services agency and the Nevada National Guard (1-d and weekend camps in the mountains, offering challenges to the youth, such as ropes courses); (3) Saints in Services, offered by Lutheran Social Services (a 5-week program, meeting once a week and conducting some positive community service); and (4) referrals to counseling agencies, especially for the families of these youth (Ellis, 2003).

Clark County Juvenile Court Services received 2171 referrals for truancy for the period of January 1 to December 31, 2002 (for the first three quarters of this fiscal year, beginning July 1, 2002, there were 1244 referrals). This agency has met its objective — the diversion of youth from the juvenile court system. Interestingly, during this term, 70 percent of youth supervised by this court were truancy offenders, and 70 percent of them were diverted from the truancy courts. For ages 13 to 15, males and females were nearly equal in truancy offenses; but at age 17, females accounted for double the truancy offenses over those of males. Of the 1244 referrals, 221 were male Caucasians, 225 female Caucasians, 499 Hispanic (only 158 males), 212 black, and 39 Asian (Ellis, 2003).

Additional community programs for at-risk youth are the Big Brothers/Big Sisters Program, in which an adult mentor is assigned to a youth; and the Boys Clubs/Girls Clubs Program, providing after-school activities such as tutoring, music lessons, art lessons, and sports. These programs are touted as two of the more successful prevention and diversion programs in the country. Although most of the programs we have cited have evidenced at least a modicum of success, many jurisdictions enjoy neither adequate funding nor the community resources to maintain or to continue most status offender diversion programs.

17.5 Conclusion

The treatment of juvenile status offenders has had a circuitous history in the United States, with the current trends appearing to diminish the strength and authority of the age-based status offender exception.

When the juvenile justice system was first initiated more than a century ago, the state had a great deal of influence over juveniles' lives. Both delinquent and status offenders often received punitive sentences from the courts. After the JJDPA of 1974, many status offenses were decriminalized and offenders were diverted from the justice system in an attempt to avoid negative labeling of youth who are not delinquent. The separation of status and delinquent offenders also aided in preventing associations with undesirables and criminal influences in the penal institutions.

The removal of status offenders from the juvenile courts has been an appealing decision from a constitutional perspective as well. Bynum and Thompson (1999) argue that the lack of clear definitions of delinquent conduct, coupled with age parameters, has led to local police and juvenile agencies using subjective interpretations of behavior, which has often led to capricious adjudications.

Chesney-Lind and Shelden (1998) argue against the entire concept of a status offender, noting that status offender laws have violated 8th Amendment rights, as "punishment ensues from status rather than behavior," and that these laws "deny equal protection because the laws apply only to children." They suggest further that the status offenders are "denied due process in that they are deprived of liberty in the name of treatment."

There are critics who call attention to a substantial "downside" of the reform efforts provided by the JJDPA. Sharp and Hancock (1998) believe that the diversion programs, purportedly created in response to the act and attempting to limit the "arm of the courts," actually may have created a "widening of the net" effect. Others view deinstitutionalization of status offenders as in fact creating a gap in providing services to troubled youth.

As a result of substantial criticisms as well as other factors, gradually the JJDPA has been amended until there are more and more exceptions to the diversion rule. Although there are some promising programs for status offenders being implemented in some jurisdictions, they are limited in number, in funding resources and, most importantly, in support from community members. Whether the offense is status or delinquent, most individuals believe that these "crimes" are due to a juvenile court system that is far too lenient. As a result, more juveniles are beginning to be formally processed for status offenses, particularly truancy and curfew violations. If the trend continues, it is likely to result in patterns similar to those of the late 1960s, when many juvenile offenders were confined for status offenses alone.

Even more ominously, a number of states are selectively eliminating the status exception for particular criminal cases, murder being the most common, in order to make juveniles eligible for adult punishment, including the death penalty. These changes in the definition of the status offender, and the jurisdiction of the adult and juvenile courts, are increasing the inconsistency and incompatibility of sentencing and incarceration on a state-by-state basis, leading many critics to maintain that there exists a considerable degree of unequal enforcement in the state courts for juvenile offenders in the United States.

References

Agnew, R. (2001). *Juvenile Delinquency: Causes and Controls*. Boston, MA: Roxbury.

Baker, M.L. (2000). Evaluation of the Truancy Reduction Demonstration Program: Interim Report. Denver, CO: Colorado Foundation for Families and Children.

Beger, R.R. (1994). Illinois juvenile justice: An emerging dual system. *Crime and Delinquency*, 40(1): 54–68.

Berger, R. (1996). *The Sociology of Juvenile Delinquency*, 2nd ed. Belmont, CA: Wadsworth.

Bell, A.J., Rosen, L.A., and Dynlacht, D. (1994). Truancy intervention. *The Journal of Research and Development in Education* 57(3): 203–211.

Bynum, J.E. and Thompson, W. (1999). *Juvenile Delinquency: A Sociological Approach,* 4th ed. Boston, MA: Allyn Bacon.

Calhoun, T.C. and Chapple, C.L. (2003). *Readings in Juvenile Delinquency and Juvenile Justice*. Upper Saddle River, NJ: Prentice Hall.

Champion, D. (2003). *The Juvenile Justice System: Delinquency, Processing, and the Law*, 4th ed. Upper Saddle River, NJ: Prentice Hall.

Chesney-Lind, M. and Shelden, R.G. (1998). *Trends in Delinquency and Gang Membership*. Pacific Grove, CA: Brooks/Cole.

Catalano, F.R., Arthur, M.W., Hawkins, J.D., Berglund, L., and Olson, J.J. (1998).Comprehensive community- and school-based interventions to prevent antisocial behavior. In *Serious and Violent Juvenile Offenders: Risk Factors and Successful Interventions,* Loeber, R. and Farrington, D. (Eds.), Thousand Oaks, CA: Sage.

Crank, K.K. (1995). The JDDP act mandates: Rationale and summary. *OJJDP Fact Sheet #22*. U.S. Department of Justice, Office of Juvenile Justice and Delinquency Prevention.

Dryfoos, J.G. (1990). *Adolescents at Risk: Prevalence and Prevention*. New York: Oxford University Press.

Ellis, J. (June 2003). Personal interview.

Garry, E.M. (1996). Truancy: First Step to a Lifetime of Problems. Bulletin. Washington, D.C. U.S. Department of Justice, Office of Justice Programs, Office of Juvenile Justice and Delinquency Prevention.

Hawkins, J.D. and Catalano, R. (1995). Risk Focused Prevention: Using the Social Development Strategy. Seattle, WA: Developmental Research and Programs.

Loeber, R. and Farrington, D. (2000). Young children who commit crime: epidemiology, developmental origins, risk factors, early interventions, and policy implications. *Development and Psychopathology* 12(4): 737–762.

Office of Juvenile Justice and Delinquency Prevention (September, 2001). Truancy reduction: Keeping Students in School. *Juvenile Justice Bulletin.* Washington D.C.: U.S. Department of Justice.

Puzzanchera, C., Stahl, A., Finnegan, T., Snyder, H., Poole, R., and Tierney, N. (1998). Juvenile Court Statistics 1998. Report. Washington, D.C.: U.S. Department of Justice, Office of Justice Programs, Office of Juvenile Justice and Delinquency Prevention.

Ruefle, W. and Reynolds, K.M (1995). Curfews and delinquency in major american cities, *Crime and Delinquency* 41: 347–363.

Rohrman, D. (1993). Combating truancy in our schools — a community effort. *NASSP (National Association of Secondary School Principals) Bulletin* 76(549): 40–51.

Sharp, P. and Hancock, B. (1998). *Juvenile Delinquency Historical, Theoretical, and Societal Reactions to Youth,* 2nd ed. Upper Saddle River, NJ: Prentice Hall.

Sigmon, J.N., Nugent, M.E., and Engelhardt-Greer, S. (1999). Abolish Chronic Truancy Now Diversion Program: Evaluation Report. Alexandria, VA: American Prosecutors Research Institute.

Snyder, H.N. and Sickmund, M. (1995). *Juvenile Offenders and Victims: A National Report.* Washington, D.C.: U.S. Department of Justice, Office of Justice Programs, Office of Juvenile Justice and Delinquency Prevention.

Whitehead, J.T. and Lab, S.P. (1999). *Juvenile Justice: An Introduction,* 3rd ed. Cincinnati, OH: Anderson.

Cases Cited

Commonwealth v. Fisher, 213 Pa. 48 (1905).
Ex parte Crouse, 4 Whart. 9 (Pa. 1938).
In re Gault, 387 U.S. 1 (1967).
Kent v. U.S., 383 U.S. 541 (1966).
People v. Turner, 55 Ill. 280 (1870).
Qutb v. Strauss, 11 F.3d 488 (5th Cir. 1993), cert. denied.

Part IV Conclusion

DISCUSSION QUESTIONS FOR PART IV

1. In Chapter 13, McCluskey and his colleagues discuss four police departments that were involved in their study titled "The Juvenile Intervention Initiative." What is the basic foundation for this type of approach to policing juveniles? What are the major implications of the authors' findings?

2. According to Ahmad and Ruiz (Chapter 14), what are juvenile curfew laws supposed to accomplish? What effects do these laws have on juvenile delinquency according to these authors?

3. Owen (Chapter 15) outlines the nature of the juvenile prosecutorial process. Briefly describe that process and discuss what factors might influence a prosecutor when deciding to charge or not to charge a juvenile defendant.

4. In Chapter 16, Hemmens and Steiner outline the evolution of the use of juvenile waiver into the adult criminal justice system. Briefly discuss the use of waiver from a historical perspective. According to these authors, what are the consequences of waiver?

5. Burton and Tracy (Chapter 17) describe several programs established to deal with status offenders. First, define what they mean by the term *status offender*, and then give an overview of the major argument they are making in this chapter.

Part V

SPECIAL JUVENILE POPULATIONS

The term "special" in relation to juveniles discussed in the next seven chapters is by no means used in a derogatory manner. Rather, this term is often used in the literature and in the field to describe unique problems with which practitioners are confronted. Collectively, these chapters address issues associated with physical and mental challenges sometimes faced by youthful offenders (Chapter 18 by Preston), the juvenile sex offender (Chapter 19 by Dwyer and Laufersweiler-Dwyer, Chapter 20 by Veneziano and Veneziano, and Chapter 21 by Weinberg et al.), juvenile justice among America's Indian population (Chapter 22 by Bond-Maupin), gang affiliations among Mexican American adolescent females (Chapter 23 by Petersen and Olveda), and substance-addicted juveniles (Chapter 24 by Cowles and Lanphierd).

Chapter 18

The Disabled Juvenile Offender

Pamela Preston

18.1 Statement of the Problem

The Americans with Disabilities Act (ADA) of 1990 was intended to improve access and opportunities to Americans with a wide range of disabilities (Preston, 2003). Although some may debate its applicability to persons in the custody of the criminal justice system, the Supreme Court, on June 15, 1998, ruled that states were required to make a reasonable effort to accommodate the needs of disabled inmates (*Pennsylvania Department of Corrections et al., petitioners v. Ronald R. Yeskey.* No. 97, June 15, 1998). Despite some contention, the decision stands. Other suits have focused on law enforcement practices involving disabled offenders and issues relating to legal representation. The impact of the ADA is being felt throughout the criminal justice system, especially as it is estimated that upwards of 6 percent of adult inmates experience some form of mental disability, and the percentage experiencing physical difficulties will only rise with the aging of the prison population. The impact will be even stronger within the juvenile offender population, as estimates put the percentage of the learning-disabled-only juvenile offender population at 50 to 80 percent (Jacobson, 1976). This figure does not include those with physical disabilities or mental illness.

One of the problems facing organizations as they attempt to comply with the ADA is the definition of disability. Although the ADA does not include descriptions of all the disabilities that it covers, it does define a disability as an impairment (physical or mental) that significantly interferes with normal activity and includes those who at one time had the said impairment as defined under the ADA. Additionally, whether an individual self-defines himself or herself as disabled is irrelevant; only if an individual is defined by others as disabled (and not self-labeled) is he or she covered under the ADA (Mears and Aron, 2003). In spite of this rather broad definition, there is disagreement as to classification of disabilities, particularly in the juvenile population where nonsynonymous terms such as *disorder*, *impairment*, and *handicap* are used simultaneously and/or inter-changeably (Mears and Aron, 2003; Mulford et al., 2004).

Institutional programming in line with ADA guidelines is also severely lacking within the criminal justice system. Many suits brought by inmates (Preston, 2003) focused on unequal access to programs such as boot camps and work programs that could have significantly reduced time served. Other suits have focused on accessibility issues within both prisons and other institutions of the criminal justice system; for example, visually impaired and deaf inmates and defendants have sued, claiming restricted access to facilities and counsel (Preston, 1999). The disabled juvenile offender is also entitled to equal access under the ADA. Given the high percentage of learning disabled (LD) youth in the juvenile justice system (many of whom suffer multiple disabil-ities), special education programs become especially critical.

Politicians like to claim that "no child will be left behind." Under the ADA this applies to disabled youth, inside or outside the juvenile justice system. This chapter will discuss the types and definitions of disabilities found within the juvenile population, the prevalence of disability among juvenile offenders, and related programming issues that face juvenile justice professionals.

18.2 Types of Disability

Early legislation directed at issues facing disabled juveniles included the Education for All Handicapped Children Act of 1975, which was later reinvented as the Individuals with Disabilities Education Act (IDEA). Although IDEA is more applicable to educational institutions than to the juvenile justice system, it is useful to understand how IDEA conceptualizes disability in order to better understand the range of disabilities encountered by practitioners in the juvenile justice system. Although the specifics may vary from state to state, the list of disabilities addressed by IDEA generally includes the following: speech, language, visual, or hearing impairment, mental retardation, brain injury, autism, specific learning disabilities (SLD), orthopedic impairment, and emotional disturbance (Burrell and Warboys, 2000; Jacobson, 1976).

Disabilities most commonly found within the juvenile justice system include SLD and emotional disturbance (ED). SLD is an umbrella term for a number of conditions that result in a compromised ability to think, speak, read, write, spell, listen, or perform mathematical functions. It is important to note that SLD is not the result of disadvantage but, rather, has a physiological cause such as brain injury or dysfunction, perceptual difficulties, dyslexia, etc. (Burrell and Warboys, 2000).

One of the problems with this definition of SLD is that it seems to be a catch-all term that could describe roughly 80 percent of American schoolchildren (Mears and Aron, 2003). Additionally, there are no specific, standardized tests or criteria available at present that can be used to detect the presence or absence or many of these disabilities (Mears and Aron, 2003). It is also important to note that although the number of children with all other learning disabilities has increased by 13 percent over the past 30 years, the number of students diagnosed with SLDs has increased by 233 percent (Mears and Aron, 2003). It seems unlikely that the bulk of this increase is due to anything more than changing definitions of learning disability; hence, it is natural to assume that this will be the most commonly found disability within the juvenile justice system. Still, it must be pointed out that research has indicated a significant similarity between delinquent youth and LD youth (Reilly et al., 1985), which suggests that the effect of learning disability on delinquency, or the presence of some relationship between the two, cannot be ignored.

ED includes a number of conditions; however, in order to be classified as ED these conditions must occur over a long period of time and adversely affect the child's educational performance. It includes inability to form and maintain social relationships, schizophrenia, inappropriate behavior, unhappiness or depression, the development of physical reactions to problems in or out of school, and learning difficulties that cannot be explained by health, sensory, or intellectual causes (Burrell and Warboys, 2000). Juveniles suffering from ED may be assigned differing diagnoses depending on the agency involved; for example, the same youth may be diagnosed as behaviorally–emotionally handicapped

(BEH), severely emotionally disturbed (SED), or behavior disordered (BD) (Mears and Aron, 2003). These changes in terminology across time and across agencies compound the difficulty of treating the emotionally disturbed juvenile inside or outside the criminal justice system.

SLD and ED are believed to be the most common disabilities found within the juvenile justice system. However, as pointed out by Mears and Aron (2003), this information should be approached with caution. There are a number of factors that may bias these results. The most common problem is, again, that of definition. Institutions and researchers use many different terms to describe the same or similar behavior; as such, estimates of disability within this population will be just that — estimates. Some studies may underreport the incidence of ED, reporting ED, BEH, SED, and BD separately. Conversely, behavior disorder (conduct disorder) is not the same as SED, and, perhaps, should not be included under the umbrella term of ED. Another factor affecting the accuracy of reports on disability in the juvenile justice system is that studies focus on incarcerated youth and, as such, the results are not generalizable to all youth caught up in the juvenile justice system, as those who are incarcerated tend to be the most serious offenders. A final concern is that studies of disabled youth in the system focus mostly on LD (probably due to the impact of IDEA) and ED (given the popularity of psychological explanations of delinquent behavior and the apparent popularity of a treatment model within the juvenile justice system).

18.3 The Prevalence of Disability in the Juvenile Offender Population

As pointed out by Mears and Aron (2003), data on disabled youth in the juvenile justice system tend to focus on incarcerated youths. Additionally, estimates within this population vary due to definitional and screening issues. Learning disabilities and mental health issues are the most common disabilities within this population. The following are estimates of the prevalence of different types of disabilities within the institutionalized juvenile population:

■ Institutionalized youth experience mental illness rates 2 to 4 times that of the general population (Cocozza and Skowyra, 2000).
■ More than 50 percent suffer from ED, and as many as 20 percent suffer from severe ED (Mears and Aron, 2003).

- Up to 80 percent suffer from conduct disorder (Cocozza and Skowyra, 2000) and from 20 to 50 percent are attention-deficit hyperactivity disorder (ADHD) (Mears and Aron, 2003).
- About 1 in 5 youths have serious mental health problems (Cocozza and Skowyra, 2000).
- About 50 percent of the youth receiving mental health treatment in the general population have co-occurring substance abuse problems; this is likely higher in the institutionalized population (Cocozza and Skowyra, 2000).
- Half of the youth in the general population diagnosed with mental illness experience co-occurring mental illness; it is reasonable to assume that this number is higher in the incarcerated population (Cocozza and Skowyra, 2000).
- Whereas only 6 percent of all students are arrested at least once before they leave school, 1 in 5 mentally ill students are arrested before they leave school (Burrell and Warboys, 2000).
- Within 5 years of leaving school, nearly 60 percent are arrested. (Burrell and Warboys, 2000).
- Between 30 to 50 percent have special education needs (compared to only 1 in 10 in the general population), and as many as 12 percent can be classified as mentally retarded (Mears and Aron, 2003).
- From 10 to 36 percent of incarcerated youth suffer from SLDs. (Mears and Aron, 2003).
- Of all youth with learning disabilities, by the time they have been out of school for 5 years, nearly 1 in 3 have been arrested (Burrell and Warboys, 2000).

Past research has found that the most common form of disability found within the juvenile offender population is learning disability; however, physical and mental disabilities and illness are not uncommon. Cook and Perry (1990) found that the IQ scores for Louisiana-adjudicated youth on the verbal- and full-scales fell at the upper end of the below-average range. Sawicki and Schaeffer (1979) found that out of 125 adjudicated youth in their study, only 7 percent were not at least mildly LD. Similar patterns were found in Cheek's 1983 study of incarcerated juvenile females, with slightly over 60 percent of the subjects having been diagnosed as LD, mentally disabled, or emotionally disturbed. It is important to note, however, that quite often the mentally disabled offender is an accomplice, rather than a principal, in an offense (Weber and Spears, 1975); it may also be the case that he or she is more likely, due to his or her disability, to be caught. There has also been research linking the severity of learning disability with the severity of offense (Sawicki and Schaeffer, 1979).

18.4 Programming

A study of the California Department of Corrections (Petersilia, 1997) found that inmates (adults and juveniles) who suffer from mental retardation (an estimated 4 percent of all persons in custody) are generally neither identified nor steered toward appropriate programming with the system. Although statistics show that the mentally retarded offender is treated more harshly at every stage of the criminal justice system, he or she tends to remain unidentified and unrehabilitated despite the requirements of the ADA.

It is no different within the juvenile justice system, particularly within the incarcerated population. Problems encountered include lack of clarity as to who is responsible for the provision of services to youth within the system, lack of proper assessment, and lack of training and staffing for program delivery (Cocozza and Skowyra, 2000). Given that the two main disabilities found within the incarcerated juvenile population are SLD and ED, this section will focus on both special education programming and mental health treatment. It will conclude with a discussion of facilities modifications that the juvenile justice system should consider in order to be in compliance with the ADA and order to accommodate those youth with physical disabilities that cannot be defined as learning disabilities or mental disturbances.

An early program, described by Sawicki and Schaeffer (1979), points to the St. Louis Project LEARN as a prototype for programming for LD youth within the juvenile justice system. This program focused on the identification and treatment of LD youth within the St. Louis juvenile justice system and was funded by the Bureau of Education for the Handicapped. Under this program all youths detained 6 d or more were automatically screened for LD; additionally, juvenile officials could recommend screening for any youth under their jurisdiction who were out of school or failing in school. When a positive diagnosis of learning disability was made, a multidisciplinary team sketched out an educational plan, encompassing educational, vocational, counseling, and social programming. At the end of the 12-week training period the LD youth were placed in community-based educational or vocational programs.

LEARN is a multidisciplinary program designed not only to improve education for the LD juvenile offender, but also to address social and familial issues. Burrell and Warboys (2000) place emphasis on the importance of education, stating that "education may be the single most important service the juvenile justice system can offer young offenders in its efforts to rehabilitate them and equip them for success." They then point out that although success in school may not by itself prevent future delinquency, the absence of appropriate education will make success much more difficult.

In order to understand the issues surrounding special education in the juvenile justice system, it is necessary to understand IDEA, 1997. LD youth are more likely to be disruptive or dangerous in the schools than non-LD youth; however, federal law requires that these youth remain in their current educational settings until the end of proceedings or appeals (Burrell and Warboys, 2000). This is referred to as the "stay-put" rule. This enables the LD juvenile to continue his or her educational program until adjudicated. This is problematic in that it made it difficult for schools to remove the dangerous or exceptionally disruptive youth; however, youth can be removed for weapons or drug violations, as well as in situations where others (or the youth himself or herself) are in danger. IDEA does allow for suspension of LD youth for up to 10 school days, assuming that the same suspension would be given a non-LD student. Schools may remove a child to an alternative educational setting for up to 45 d in cases of drug use or sale and weapons violations. Hearing officers may also change a youth's educational placement for up to 45 d if it is determined that the child poses a danger to himself or others; however, the placement must enable the youth to continue to meet the goals identified in the IEP (individualized educational program) established at the beginning of the school year. Under IDEA, as soon as a decision is made to remove an LD youth from school for more than 10 d, the IEP team (consisting of the child's parents, regular teacher if the youth was enrolled in regular classes, special education teacher, someone who can interpret the institutional implications of the results, a representative of the LEA [local educational agency], and the child himself or herself). At this stage the team evaluates the child's original placement, consistency of services provided, whether the youth's disability was a function of his or her inability to understand the consequences of his or her actions, and if the disability interfered with the youth's ability to control his behavior. If the youth's behavior was a result of the disability, the LEA is required to remedy any deficiencies in the IEP and to place the youth in an alternative educational setting.

These general guidelines set by IDEA could be useful to juvenile justice professionals. Burrell and Warboys (2000) describe how these guidelines could be implemented at various stages in the process.

Given the speed with which youth are moved through the juvenile courts, they recommend that juvenile justice professionals prepare to recognize signs of disability by contacting LEA to gather legal definitions of the different types of disabilities; they must also obtain screening instruments. Under IDEA, whenever a crime is committed by a juvenile with a disability, school officials are required to provide the youth's records, both educational and disciplinary, to the authorities. They recommend that standard operating procedure by the juvenile justice system should include, immediately upon intake, coordinating court proceedings with the IEP team, interviewing parents and the juvenile, gathering educational records [permitted by the Family Educational Rights and Privacy Act (FERPA) only when parents give written consent], and coordinating court proceedings with the IEP team.

Protections granted disabled youth by IDEA do not negate juvenile court authority over school-related crimes. Under IDEA, schools still have the responsibility to conform to special educational requirements, even when a youth enters the juvenile justice system; however, in many cases, it is decided that the most appropriate course of action is to dismiss court cases involving disabled juveniles or at least defer the case. Burrell and Warboys (2000) state that because of learning disabilities, these youth may be unable to succeed in programs geared toward the minor offender, resulting in a longer-than-anticipated stay, which decreases his or her chance of success upon release. Instead, they suggest three alternatives:

1. Deferring the prosecution, pending the outcome of a due process hearing designed to determine whether or not the incident is a result of the disability or of other factors. It may be that the issue can be resolved within the special education system.
2. Steering these youth into diversion or community programs. This can allow for the completion of special education programs and, at the same time, include a greater degree of supervision. It may include counseling, regular school attendance, curfews, and community service programs. Obviously, this is only appropriate for less serious offenses.
3. In cases in which there is disability so pronounced that the youth would be unable to comply with court orders (due to severe mental illness or mental retardation), the case may be dismissed.

One concern is that disabled youth are overrepresented in the juvenile justice system (Leone et al., 1995); this may be more a function of the inability of these youth to make a positive impression on juvenile justice authorities. Behavior that is simply symptomatic of the disability may be misinterpreted as inappropriate. To this end, most experts recommend moves away from institutionalization and toward home confinement or other community-based programming, especially as most juvenile facilities are not set up to provide special education programming.

When cases involving disabled juveniles go to court, documentation of the youth's disabilities may affect trial outcome. It is important to bring records of disability to the court as this may affect outcome. Records of disability (such as special education evaluations) may be proof that the disability so alters the juvenile's functioning that he or she may be declared legally insane under state law. This could prove especially important in cases involving serious offenses, particularly those in which waiver to adult criminal court is a possibility. Obviously, in cases of severe brain injury, a waiver to adult court would not be appropriate. Youth with communication, memory, and perceptual difficulties may, based on information about his or her disability, be declared incompetent for adjudication (Grisso, 1997). Similarly, youths with low levels of mental functioning may lack criminal intent, and information about the disability may contribute to the courts' determining that there was no criminal intent (Burrell and Warboys, 2000). Confessions may also be ruled inadmissible if there is reason to believe that, because of the disability, the juvenile's waiver of *Miranda* rights cannot be considered voluntary.

Burrell and Warboys (2000) also address the issue of placement of disabled youth, emphasizing the importance of the courts' taking into consideration the impact of the youth's disability on his or her behavior; for example, the juveniles with attention-deficit disorder (ADD) may be treated more harshly in the system simply owing to the characteristics of the disorder, which include impulsive behavior, inability to anticipate consequences of one's actions, tendency to gravitate toward dangerous activities, limited ability to cope with frustration, and having trouble following instructions, all of which are contrary to the expectations of juvenile justice practitioners.

Whether in an adult or juvenile facility, a very high proportion of the institutionalized population lacks basic survival skills. It is estimated that about one-third are unable to master the skills necessary for finding a job (locating a street address on a map or filling out an application). Another one-third cannot enter information on a automobile maintenance form or write up an explanation of a billing error. Only 5 percent can use a bus schedule (U.S. Department of Education, Office of Special Education Programs, 1997). Legally, under IDEA, all State and local juvenile correctional facilities are required to provide special education to juveniles who have been identified as disabled. Those who do not are subject to class-action and individual lawsuits, administrative proceedings, consent decrees, and other measures to bring them into compliance.

Experts also recommend diverting youths suffering from mental health disorders away from the juvenile justice systems. Cocozza and Skowyra (2000) point to the Wraparound Milwaukee program as a community alternative to inpatient or institutionalized treatment. This program provides care to youth from both the child welfare and juvenile justice systems and, similar to the earlier LEARN program, has a holistic approach to treatment, involving not only the children, but their families as well. Ohio's PAIR (Project for Adolescent Intervention and Rehabilitation) works with probationary youth after their first offense (any offense); after screening them for mental health problems and substance abuse, they develop a treatment plan, which is supervised by a team including the probation officers, case managers, and treatment providers.

Both Wraparound Milwaukee and PAIR were local-level programs and multidisciplinary in nature. Successful programs need to be interdisciplinary and collaborative, with justice and treatment personnel working in tandem to deliver the full range of necessary programs to the emotionally disturbed juvenile offender. This general model can be adapted for statewide application. One successful statewide program is New York's PINS (Persons in Need of Supervision) program. Developed in the mid-1980s, it was created to moderate court contact in cases where it may have been inappropriate. Counties are required to create a strategy for diversion of mentally ill youth from court and offer, as an alternative, community-based programs. Although individual communities develop treatment plans on their own, the State holds final approval, giving the counties the authority to divert juveniles and their families to appropriate programming.

Programming for the LD and emotionally disturbed juvenile offender focuses, whenever possible, on community treatment. As pointed out, the chances of success through incarceration are particularly low for this population. In the case of the LD juvenile, incarceration or institutionalization will most likely disrupt the educational process; it is preferable to continue the IEP within the school setting. However, when institutionalization is necessary the juvenile justice system needs to act quickly to reimplement the IEP within the placement facility. The emotionally disturbed youth is also better served within the community. Diversion is preferred as both LD and emotionally disturbed juveniles suffer from disabilities that make it unlikely that they will do well.

18.5 Conclusion

As with the adult prison population, a high percentage of youth in the juvenile justice system suffers from disabilities, most commonly a learning disability or a mental-health issue. As many as 50 percent suffer from co-occurring disability. The juvenile justice system was created more than 100 years ago, in part, to reclaim and rehabilitate youths. Even when programming is available, many juveniles, whether because of cognitive and perceptual issues, conduct disorders, mental illness, or other disabilities, are literally unable to successfully participate in programming that is not designed for special-needs populations. Alternative methods, such as diversion away from the juvenile justice system, community placement, or retention in the same educational environment may offer these youth their best chances for success. New York's PINS program allows for greater supervision of these youth, while allowing them to remain in their communities.

Despite the current trend toward more punitive sentencing measures, including treating juveniles as adults, recent legislation requires that all agencies address the needs of their disabled populations. Despite attempts by some lawmakers to exclude prisons from compliance with the ADA, most courts have ruled that the ADA is applicable to all State and federal agencies. Criminal justice agencies have been ordered by the courts to assist hearing-impaired inmates and suspects, restructure facilities to accommodate physically disabled inmates, provide American sign language interpreters in the courts and for hearing-impaired defendants working with counsel, and make programs such as boot camps and work-release programs accessible to inmates with a wide range of physical disabilities, ranging from hypertension to visual impairment.

The juvenile justice system was originally developed to help steer youths, considered a special-needs population, away from the adult criminal justice system and to ultimately place them back into society. Disabled youths can be viewed as a double-special-needs population. As discussed earlier in this chapter, most experts recommend community placement, particularly in the case of the LD youth. As the LD and emotionally disturbed youth may not be in control of his or her actions, or understand the consequences of these actions, programs such as LEARN and PINS should be considered as appropriate alternatives for the intake and processing of these youth. These programs would address the needs of this group as required by both the ADA and by IDEA.

References

Burrell, S. and Loren, W. (July 2000). Special Education and the Juvenile Justice System. Juvenile Justice Bulletin.

Cheek, M.C. (1983). The Educational and Sociological Status of Handicapped and Non-handicapped Incarcerated Female Adolescents. Ann Arbor, MI: University Microfilms International.

Cocozza, J.J. and Kathleen R.S. (2000). Youth with mental health disorders: issues and emerging responses. *Juvenile Justice* Vol. 7(1), 3–13.

Cook, J.M. and Hill G.P. (1990). Preplacement characteristics and educational status of handicapped and non-handicapped youthful offenders. *Journal of Correctional Education* 41(4), 194–198

Grisso, T. (1997). The competence of adolescents as trial defendants. *Psychology, Public Policy, and Law* 3(1), 3–32.

Jacobson, F.N. (1976). The Juvenile Court Judge and Learning Disabilities. Reno, NV: National Council of Juvenile Court Judges.

Leone, P.E., Zaremba, B.A., Chapin, M.S., and Iseli, C. (1995) Understanding the overrepresentation of youths with disabilities in juvenile detention. *District of Columbia Law Review* 3(Fall), 389–401.

Mears, D.P. and Laudan Y.A. (2003). Addressing the Needs of Youth with Disabilities in the Juvenile Justice System: The Current State of Knowledge.

Mulford, C.F., Reppucci, N.D., Mulvey, E.P., Woolard, L., and Portwood, S.L. (2004). Legal issues affecting mentally disordered and developmentally delayed youth in the justice system. *International Journal of Forensic Mental Health* 3(1), 3–22.

Petersilia, Joan. (1997). Justice for all? Offenders with mental retardation and the California corrections system. *Prison Journal* 77(4), pp. 358–380.

Preston, P. (1999). Explaining Criminality in the Older Adult Population: A Formulation and Test of a Strain/Control Model of Older Adult Criminality. Dissertation. University of California, Riverside.

Preston, P. (2003). Should there be separate justice systems for special needs populations? Results from the Penn state public opinion poll. *Criminal Justice Policy Review* 4(3), 322–338.

Reilly, T.F., Wheeler, L.J, and Leonard E.E. (June 1985). Intelligence versus academic achievement: a comparison of juvenile delinquents and special education classifications. *Criminal Justice and Behavior* 12(2), 193–208.

Sawicki, D. and Beatrix, S. (1979). An affirmative approach to the LD/JD link. *Juvenile and Family Court Journal* 30(2), 11–16. Reno, NV.

Weber, R.E. and Catherine E.S. (1975). The Naïve Juvenile Offender: Mental Retardation as Learning Disablement. Trenton, NJ.

Chapter 19

Juvenile Sex Offenders: An Overview

R. Gregg Dwyer and Deborah L. Laufersweiler-Dwyer

19.1 Introduction

This chapter provides an overview of the literature regarding typologies of juvenile sex offenders, including information about their victims, offenses, and motivations. Although it was once thought that only adults commit serious sex crimes, it is now an accepted fact that children commit them as well (Barbaree, Hudson et al., 1993). The majority of research into juvenile sexual offending has been conducted relatively recently and studies are few in number (Barbaree, Hudson et al., 1993). Research on sex offenders and associated matters have more often than not focused on adults and, although their offenses are often indistinguishable from those of adults, juveniles are not just miniature versions of adults (Barbaree, Marshall et al., 1993; Cashwell and Caruso, 1997).

Given the limited research foundation, the content of this chapter was organized with the goal of providing a broad perspective in terms of both history and disciplines. Consequently, a few dated references are included to give readers a historical context from which to view more current theories. Additionally, sources from several fields of study, including criminology, counseling, psychiatry, psychology, and sociology, are included to provide the perspective from various schools of thought on this topic. The content is arranged under major headings to facilitate use as a reference. Given the limitations of space in a text designed to provide a broad treatment of a topic while maintaining utility, the depth of coverage has been attenuated, but the references provide excellent resources for further exploration.

19.2 Definitions

For the purposes of this chapter, *sex offender* is defined, based on the American Psychiatric Association (APA) Task Force definition, as a person who purposely commits an act of sexual contact against another person by physical or verbal force or other forms of coercion (APA Task Force report, 1999). *Juvenile* is defined in this chapter as a person under the age of 18, unless otherwise specified by an author cited herein.

19.2.1 Offenders

There have been several attempts to develop a system of profiling juvenile sex offenders, with none being universally accepted and implemented as yet. Therefore, this chapter provides a broad descriptive approach rather than describing each system of classification or singling out only one. In the following text is a description of offenders, which addresses the characteristics of age, gender, psychiatric illness, abuse history, and socialization.

Although they are not uncommon (Shaw et al., 1993), juvenile sex offenders do not readily lend themselves to a concise description. By all accounts, they are a heterogeneous population (APA Task Force report, 1999; Cashwell and Caruso, 1997; Kavoussi et al., 1988; Knight and Prentky, 1993; Martin and Pruett, 1998; Righthand and Welch, 2001; Shaw et al., 1993; Smith et al., 1987; Zolondek et al., 2002). As Shaw et al. (1999) noted, there are no tests that can definitively identify or diagnose sex offenders. Despite this, we can provide some demographic descriptors and a few perspectives on victimization, substance use, and less tangible characteristics, such as socialization.

19.2.2 Gender

Juvenile sex offenders are typically male (Davis and Leitenberg, 1987; Gilby et al., 1989; MacHovec and Wieckowski, 1992; Vinogradov et al.,

1988). Righthand and Welch (2001), as well as others, noted that although female juvenile sex offenders have been studied, the research is minimal and infrequent. Barbaree, Hudson et al. (1993) noted that it is not clear how many juvenile females commit sex offenses. Consequently, the majority of the information cited herein relates to male offenders, except in those studies which are identified as including female offenders.

19.2.3 Age

No specific age range has been consistently given as typical for juvenile sexual offenders. The age cited in the studies reviewed ranged from a minimum of 5 years to a maximum of 21 years (Ryan et al., 1996). Weinhouse (1992) reported rapes by teenagers and preteens alike. Shaw et al. (1999) reported that most adolescent offenders begin offending before they are 15 years old. In Zolondek et al.'s (2002) study, the typical age of offenders was 14 to 15, with offending starting at 13 to 14. In Shaw et al.'s (1993) study, the average age of the first offense was 9 years old. Davis and Leitenberg (1987) stated that a large percentage of adolescent offenders continue offending into adulthood. It must be kept in mind that these figures, similar to most crime statistics, are based on reported offenses and how well they represent actual occurrences is unknown. Although adolescents are more often the subjects of scientific inquiry, younger children engage in criminal sexual activity too.

19.2.4 Socioeconomic Status

Socioeconomic status was not frequently addressed. This may have been a function of available data, as when Barbaree, Hudson et al. (1993) noted that socioeconomic status was not clear. When it was described, there did not seem to be a consensus as illustrated in the following examples. In their study of adolescent rapists, Vinogradov et al. (1988) reported that offenders were most commonly from low socioeconomic levels. Ryan et al. (1996) noted that sex offenders were comparable to the population as a whole. In a study comparing adolescent sex offenders and adolescent non-sex offenders, socioeconomic level did not show significant variation, but it was noted that data for this characteristic was not complete, thus implying an inadequate evaluation (Butler and Seto, 2002). A related characteristic, urban vs. rural settings, was also not consistently reported. Vinogradov et al. (1988) and Kavoussi et al. (1988) reported the urban setting as most common. Ryan et al. (1996) again stated that there was no significant difference between sex offenders and the nonoffending population in terms of urban vs. rural setting. This does not appear to be a distinguishing characteristic at this time.

19.2.5 Psychiatric Diagnosis

The psychological functioning of sex offenders is an obvious choice for examination, given the nature of the offenses. The presence of psychiatric illness was found to be commonplace among juvenile sex offenders (Barbaree, Hudson et al., 1993; Kavoussi et al., 1988; Shaw et al., 1993; Shaw et al., 1999). Conduct disorder was typically the most frequently reported diagnosis (Kavoussi et al., 1988; Losada-Paisey, 1998; Shaw et al., 1993; Zolondek et al., 2002), along with associated problems in behavior, development, and emotional response (Shaw et al., 1993). Other mental illnesses were identified by researchers as follows: In a study of twenty-six 9- to 14-year-old boys at a treatment facility in Florida, identified psychiatric illnesses included anxiety disorder, major depression, dysthymia, and posttraumatic stress disorder (Shaw et al., 1993). In their study of 58 outpatient male adolescent sex offenders, Kavoussi et al. (1988) found that 48 percent had a diagnosis of conduct disorder based on the *Diagnostic and Statistical Manual of Mental Disorders* (DSM)-III criteria, 19 percent had no diagnosis, 10 percent had a marijuana abuse diagnosis, and less than 10 percent had the following various diagnoses: alcohol abuse, adjustment disorder with depressed mood, attention deficit disorder, and social phobia. They noted that the offenders could have lied about more serious symptoms and substance abuse and that personality disorders were not assessed (Kavoussi et al., 1988), the implication being that their findings might not be a true representation, with either an under- or an overestimation of mental illness among sex offenders.

A study using an instrument designed to assess psychopathology found some interesting distinctions between sexual and nonsexual adolescent offenders. Losada-Paisey (1998) stated that there is no specific adolescent-sex-offender profile, but she did find subgroups when using the Minnesota Multiphasic Personality Inventory–Adolescent as a discriminating tool. The study was focused on 21 adolescent male sex offenders and 30 adolescents with non-sex offenses, ranging in age from 13 to 17, during 1994 and 1995 (Losada-Paisey, 1998). She found "antisocial personality" and "cognitive disorganization" scales most relevant for sex offending adolescents and "hysterical" and "anxiety" disorder scales most associated with non-sex offending juveniles (Losada-Paisey, 1998). Conversely, when evaluating for the presence of a paraphilia, Saunders and Awad (1988) found that most adolescent sex offenders in their study of 100 male sex offenders did not meet the requirements of the DSM-III-Revised for a diagnosis of paraphilia.

19.2.6 Socialization

Given that appropriate sexual behavior is often a part of healthy intimate social interactions, the socialization of offenders is another source of information. Juvenile sex offenders are frequently labeled as being socially immature (Davis and Leitenberg, 1987; Gilby et al., 1989; Knight and Prentky, 1993; Saunders and Awad, 1988; Shaw et al., 1999; Smith et al., 1987). In their study of 262 primarily nonincarcerated and, therefore, presumably less violent, male sex offenders in Washington state, Smith et al. (1987) identified four personality groupings. The first was composed of those lacking appropriate social skills and having limited peer interaction; the next included those who were socially adequate with appropriate peer interaction but were "overcontrolled"; the third consisted of those who were impulsive; the fourth was composed of the "overtly emotionally disturbed" (Smith et al., 1987). All four groups represent a poor foundation for healthy social inter-actions. Interestingly, they also found that with regard to general adaptive functioning, the offenders were more similar to adolescents in general than adult sex offenders or nonsexual juvenile offenders (Smith et al., 1987).

The reported data is not consistent across studies as illustrated by the following works: Davis and Leitenberg (1987) suggested that the lack of social graces may not be specifically related to sexual offending. They referenced two studies in which adult sex offenders were com-pared to non-sex offending adult prisoners and no differences were found related to social interactions (Davis and Leitenberg, 1987). Butler and Seto (2002) studied 114 male offenders composed of sex offenders only, sex offenders with other non-sex offenses, and nonsexual offend-ers in Toronto, Canada, between 1994 and 1997. They found no differences between sex offenders and non-sex offenders relative to "early childhood conduct problems, current behavior adjustment, and postcriminal attitudes and beliefs" (Butler and Seto, 2002). Those offenders who only had sex offenses were less likely to have behavior problems, more likely to have "prosocial attitudes and beliefs," and less likely to reoffend than the sex offenders with histories of other crimes (Butler and Seto, 2002). Dalton (1996) assessed 20 males with an average age of 10.1 years old who were accused of sexually aggressive behavior with child victims, using the Behavior Assessment System for Children (BASC) self-report of personality, and found no atypical scores. Scales on the BASC that are particularly relevant to this topic include social stress, anxiety, depression, feeling inadequate, attitudes toward school and teachers, self-esteem, and interpersonal relationships (Dalton, 1996).

A related finding by Ryan et al. (1996) noted that offenders have been described as having lower levels of accurate sexual knowledge and assertiveness than their nonoffending cohort members, whereas Gilby et al. (1989) found that offenders claim more sexual experience, including consensual, than nonoffenders.

19.2.7 Abuse History

A history of having been victimized sexually or physically is often present in juvenile sex offenders as reported in the following studies. Ryan et al. (1996) studied data from 1000 males and females ranging in age from 5 to 21 years old and found a consistent history of trauma, including physical abuse, sexual abuse, neglect, and witnessing domestic violence. Shaw et al. (1993) also found a large percentage (65 percent) of offenders who had a history of being victims of sexual abuse. The APA Task Force report (1999) and Martin and Pruett (1998) noted a prevalence among offenders of those who had been victims of physical or sexual abuse or neglect. In a study by Knight and Prentky (1993), there was limited evidence that the more coercive offenders were more likely to have been victims of sexual abuse. Davis and Leitenberg (1987) noted that male offenders have generally been victims of sexual abuse. Chorn and Parekh's (1997) study subjects had experienced "severe physical and/or emotional abuse."

A unique finding of Shaw et al. (1999) was that the younger the children are when they offend, the greater the likelihood that they have been victimized earlier in their lives. Not all researchers came to the same conclusion; Knight and Prentky (1993) noted more physical abuse and neglect but found that greater sexual abuse was not as evident. Although this point will be addressed later in this chapter, it should be stressed that not all victims of physical and/or sexual abuse become perpetrators.

19.2.8 School Difficulties

The existence of school problems is another matter that has been reported, but not universally defined. What are school problems? Given the frequency of the psychiatric diagnosis of conduct disorder, some difficulty in the school setting is likely. Whether it is a separate factor or merely the consequence of a covariable is unclear. Shaw et al. (1999) found that 50 to 80 percent of offenders had school problems, including repeating grades and learning disabilities. According to Davis and Leitenberg (1987), a history of school problems is evident but not necessarily a distinguishing factor among adolescent offenders in general. On a related issue, Gilby et al. (1989) found inconclusive evidence regarding differences in intelligence. This is certainly an area worthy of better understanding, given that schools might afford an avenue for preventative programs.

19.2.9 Family Functioning

Family dysfunction is a reported characteristic of offenders. But again, it does not lend itself well to a common definition and reports are contradictory. Certainly physical and sexual abuse and neglect can be family problems, but authors vary on whether these are included under the heading of family problem or as a separate category. Knight and Prentky (1993) found that poorly functioning family environments contribute to offending. Kourany et al. (1979) stated that lack of parental influence was usually present in cases of adolescent sexual activity. Chorn and Parekh (1997) noted that all 7 of the adolescent sex offenders in their qualitative study had some form of family difficulty. On the other hand, in Saunders and Awad's (1988) study of 100 male sex offenders aged 12 to 16 years old, a subgroup was identified who had no other offenses and did not have major family problems. Similar to school problems, family issues may be the result of another covariable of a more global factor, such as conduct disorder or an antisocial behavior pattern, and warrant additional study before conclusions may be drawn.

19.2.10 Substance Abuse

The use of alcohol and illicit substances by juvenile sex offenders is another intuitively logical element to suspect when considering the offenses, but again it has not been consistently described. Davis and Leitenberg (1987) reported that there is no evidence to discern what percentage of adolescent sex offenders have alcohol or drug abuse problems. Lightfoot and Barbaree (1993) suggested that the degree of use and abuse is probably variable. It does appear that adolescent offenders are not typically under the influence when they offend, but claims of such are employed as an excuse for offending, according to Davis and Leitenberg (1987). Zolondek et al. (2002) also found substance abuse problems to be infrequent. Although not always, substance abuse was a factor for many of the offenders, according to Morris et al. (2002). Unless tested following commission of the offense, substance use during the offense cannot be objectively determined. General use is also questionable given that not all substances can be detected by blood and/or urine analysis several hours to days after these were last consumed. The presence of a substance abuse diagnosis in conjunction with offending can be important with regard to prevention, identification of motivating factors, and treatment.

19.3 Victims

Although this chapter focuses on juvenile sex offenders, having at least some basic knowledge about their victims adds to the understanding of the perpetrators. Based on published data, the victims are slightly more readily describable, but no specific profile is available. The following demographic data provides a brief outline of victims.

19.3.1 Gender

Victims are usually female (Gilby et al., 1989; Ryan et al., 1996; Vinogradov et al., 1988; Zolondek et al., 2002). This applies to the entire population of victims. A variation was noted when victims were children. According to Gilby et al. (1989) and Davis and Leitenberg (1987), when victims are children, they are more likely to be male.

19.3.2 Age

There was a variable range of ages for victims. They are typically younger than the offender (Barbaree, Hudson et al., 1993; Gilby et al., 1989; Davis and Leitenberg, 1987; Saunders and Awad, 1988), at least in those cases in which both the perpetrator and victim are juveniles

(Zolondek et al., 2002). Ryan et al. (1996) identified the typical age range as 3 to 16 years old, and Shaw et al. (1999) found the majority to be under 9 years of age. According to Shaw et al. (1993), victims range from age 6 months to 15 years old, with the average being 7 years old. In Vinogradov et al.'s (1988) study of adolescent rapists, victims ranged in age from 15 to 29 years old. Weinhouse (1992) reported that juvenile offenders typically victimize other children. Based on these studies, victims range from the infant age group to young adults, with the preteens being common. Identifying an age range could prove useful in developing and implementing prevention programs, but the range appears to be quite broad.

19.3.3 Relationship to Offender

What, if any, relationship exists between sex offenders and their victims prior to the offense? Again, this is a useful question to answer relative to prevention and intervention. Juvenile sex offenders usually victimize people they know (Barbaree, Hudson et al., 1993; Davis and Leitenberg, 1987; Morris et al., 2002; Saunders and Awad, 1988; Zolondek et al., 2002) or the child they are babysitting (Saunders and Awad, 1988).

The opposite was also reported in the context of extent of criminal behavior and a specific type of offense. Butler and Seto (2002) found that sex offenders who also committed other crimes were more likely than those with only sex offense histories to target victims they did not know. Rape victims of juvenile offenders are also less likely to know their offenders (Vinogadov et al., 1988).

19.4 Offenses

What type of sex crimes do juveniles commit? Are they unique to juveniles? These questions, along with the use of force during commission of the offenses, are addressed in this section. Consistent with other aspects of the general topic of juvenile sexual offending, there is no single accepted list or hierarchy of offenses that applies to all offenders.

Barbaree, Hudson et al. (1993) reported that juvenile offenders commit the same types of offenses as adults. Righthand and Welch (2001) reported that offenses ranged from no physical contact to penetration. The APA Task Force report (1999) documented that most cases included penetration vaginally or anally and/or oral sex. Zolondek et al.'s (2002) study of 485 adolescent boys in the United States and Canada identified the following sex offenses: exhibitionism, fetishism, voyeurism, zoophilia, obscene phone calls, frottage, child molestation, and rape. According to Gilby et al. (1989), adolescent offenders commit acts of sexual assault, "child molestation, exhibitionism, voyeurism, making obscene phone calls, buggery, bestiality, and stealing women's underwear." Ryan et al. (1996) listed offenses of genital to vaginal, anal, and oral contact, exhibitionism, voyeurism, obscene phone calls, and stealing underwear. Shaw et al. (1993) reported that offenders commit a variety of acts, including rape, sodomy, fondling, fellatio, cunnilingus, and pedophilia. Shaw et al. (1999) listed offenses including obscene phone calls, exhibitionism, voyeurism, frottage, sodomy, fondling, and penetrative acts. An interesting finding by Shaw et al. (1999) was that offenders who have been victims in the past are more likely to commit more serious sexual offenses.

Use of force and the amount employed varied with the reporting source. Ryan et al. (1996) found the use of force in over 30 percent of their studied cases, even in those cases in which it was not needed to get victims to submit. Shaw et al. (1993) reported that force was often used. Davis and Leitenberg (1987) reported that perpetrators claim less use of force than their victims report. The opposite finding was also documented several times. According to Zolondek et al. (2002), offenders used verbal manipulation rather than physical force to overpower their victims. Less force is used when victims are younger than their offenders (Davis and Leitenberg, 1987). Shaw et al. (1999) reported that juvenile offenders are less likely to harm victims.

Offenders will typically lie about offending, downplay its significance (Shaw et al., 1999; Becker, 1990), or claim mutual consent (Shaw et al., 1999). These responses obviously make collection of accurate data difficult to impossible. Nevertheless, the type of offenses clearly span the range of sex offenses committed by adults and use of force in some form is employed by juveniles, although to what degree and frequency is less clear and less likely to ever be objectively assessed.

19.5 Causes for Offending

There is no unifying paradigm to explain why juveniles commit sex crimes. Obviously, the reason for this void is, at least in part, a function of the source of the answer being elusive and the causes being most likely multifactorial and probably of multiple etiologies. In the following text are several suggested explanations for why juveniles commit sex offenses. All have some degree of face validity, but definitive controlled studies are lacking.

19.5.1 Sexual Victimization

Being sexually victimized has been implicated as a factor in becoming a juvenile sexual offender (Cashwell and Caruso, 1997; Davis and Lietenberg, 1987; Martin and Pruett, 1998; Morris et al., 2002; Muster, 1992; Shaw et al., 1993; Shaw et al., 1999; Weinhouse, 1992). Shaw et al. (1999) suggested a link between being a sexual assault victim and becoming a victimizer but pointed out that this is clearly not a direct causation nor a guaranteed result, given that most victims do not become perpetrators. Cashwell and Caruso (1997) and Martin and Pruett (1998) also noted that sex offending can be a response to being physically and sexually victimized, although not all victims become offenders.

Muster (1992) described the "'sexually reactive" child, who engages in a variety of behaviors in response to having been abused. These behaviors can include touching peers and adults, pretending to engage in sex acts with peers, abusing animals, masturbating at times and in places that are considered unacceptable, and developing sexual relationships at an early age (Muster, 1992). Several of these can obviously be defined as sexual offending when committed by adolescents (Muster, 1992). Shaw et al. (1993) suggested that although not causative, sexual abuse early in life may contribute to future sexual offending and to the seriousness of the actual offenses.

Morris et al. (2002) suggested that being victims of physical and sexual violence can lead to the person becoming violent in general toward others and thus can include sexual offending.

19.5.2 Psychiatric Diagnosis

Another perspective views sexual offending as a component of a larger behavior pattern, with a foundation in a psychiatric diagnosis, such as conduct disorder, or antisocial traits. Kavoussi et al. (1988) suggested that given the high prevalence of the conduct disorder diagnosis, offenses might be secondary to impaired control of impulses and antisocial activity. Becker (1990) identified the following categories of reasons for committing sex offenses: It may be just one of many antisocial offenses in the perpetrator's general behavior, abnormal sexual fantasies and paraphilias, inadequate control of impulses, and the role of psychiatric illness. He noted that none of these reasons have research evidence to support them as being the exclusive model (Becker, 1990).

Shaw et al. (1993) speculated that within the population of adolescent sex offenders, a subgroup of offenders with antisocial traits commit the most serious offenses. Zolondek et al. (2002) also viewed offending as a component of a more global antisocial behavior pattern. MacHovec and Wieckowski (1992) reported that reasons for offending are not clear but considered one possibility: that it is a compulsive and opportunistic act. Saunders and Awad (1988) reported that some mental health professionals believe offenders commit offenses as a result of "cognitive distortions."

19.5.3 Substance Abuse

Substance abuse has been suggested as being a factor in sexual offending (Becker, 1990; Lightfoot and Barbaree, 1993). In their study of adolescent rapes committed by 63 males between 1973 and 1977 in California, Vinogradov et al. (1988) reported the offenses as being related to drug use and impulsiveness. It should be noted that their study only included rapists and excluded statutory rape, homosexual sodomy, pedophilia, persons with severe psychiatric illnesses, and high-security-risk offenders (Vinogradov et al., 1988). Conversely, substance use was not found to be a cause of sex offending by other researchers (Righthand and Welch, 2001). Clearly, there is yet to be a consensus on the role of substance use in sexual offending.

19.5.4 Developmental Factors

Another area of speculation relates to early development. Shaw et al. (1999) described juvenile sexuality as developing based on early experiences. Similar to other conditioned responses, aggressive behavior may become linked with sexual arousal during early development (Shaw et al., 1999). The result could then be a desire for an aggressive and/or coercive element when seeking sexual gratification (Shaw et al., 1999). MacHovec and Wieckowski (1992) also noted that offending can be secondary to a conditioned response, albeit an inappropriate act or fantasy. Kourany et al. (1979) stated that trial-and-error adolescent sexual expression ideally results in healthy relationships, but advised that the winner in the risks vs. gains was not clear. They further advised that too early an involvement in sexual activity could result in acting out "unresolved neurotic problems," including "aggression, control, and dependency" (Kourany et al., 1979).

Also in keeping with the developmental origin of the problem is the notion that poor mother–child bonding contributes to offending (APA Task Force report, 1999). Ryan et al. (1996) found less sexually aggressive behavior with increased mother–child bonding. In addition, the modeling theory of behavior has been implicated as a factor in offending (APA Task Force report, 1999; Davis and Lietenberg, 1987; Martin and Pruett, 1998; Morris et al., 2002).

19.5.5 Socialization

Social inadequacy was already reported as a common characteristic of juvenile sex offenders. Elements of this facet have been implicated as a cause of offending. Noting that research evidence is lacking, Davis and Lietenberg (1987) identified the characteristics of offenders that might contribute to their offending as including poor self-esteem, deviant fantasies, feelings of inadequacy, and fear of rejection by females. It has been speculated that some offenders seek younger children out of fear that peers will not accept them (MacHovec and Wieckowski, 1992). Barbaree, Hudson et al. (1993) suggested that poor social skills may contribute to the cause of sexual offending.

The idea that offending is an expression of anger has been postulated. According to Ryan et al. (1996), offenders viewed sex as a means to "hurt/degrade/punish," "dissipate anger," and "control/feel powerful," with only approximately one-third describing sex as an expression of love or a demonstration of positive feelings for another. Davis and Lietenberg (1987) included anger directed toward females in their list of offender characteristics that might contribute to sexual offending. When describing why juveniles commit rape, Weinhouse (1992) stated that they are expressing anger toward women, trying to prove their masculinity, or acting as part of a group.

19.6 Summary

Juvenile sex offenders are not a population that allows a concise description. They are a heterogeneous grouping with few readily identifiable distinguishing or consistent characteristics based on studies to date. A review of the literature reveals that most are male, many have been sexually and/or physically victimized themselves, and their social development appears to be delayed. Their victims are typically female (unless they are children, in which case the victims are usually male), younger than their offenders, and known to their offenders. As a population, the offenders commit the same types of acts as adult sex offenders, including obscene phone calls, exhibitionism, voyeurism, frottage, child molestation, and rape.

Other issues such as intelligence and socioeconomic status of offenders, use of force during the commission of sexual offending, and reasons for offending, are addressed less often and with less objective data from controlled studies. Although no single model exists to explain why juvenile sex offending occurs, there are several commonly hypothesized reasons, including the idea that (1) offenders exhibit a constellation of behavioral problems in conjunction with psychiatric illness, and sexual offending is but one manifestation, (2) past victimization leads to future victimizing, (3) poor social skills result in inappropriate, dysfunctional, and criminal interactions; and (4) sexual behavior is used as an expression of anger.

Further study of this topic may aid in preventing the offenses, helping victims, and identifying and treating offenders. The nature of the offenses and society's view of them, the impact on the victims, and the potential causative factors all contribute to making it a difficult area to explore in a scientific and reproducible manner. Nonetheless, we must make every effort to learn more about juveniles who sexually offend.

References

American Psychiatric Association Task Force on Sexually Dangerous Offenders (1999). Dangerous Sex Offenders A Task Force Report of the American Psychiatric Association. Washington, D.C: American Psychiatric Association.

Barbaree, H.E., Hudson, S.M., and Seto, M.C. (1993) Sexual assault in society: the role of the juvenile offender. In Barbaree, H.E., Marshall, W.L., and Hudson, S.M. (Eds.), *The Juvenile Sex Offender*. New York: The Guilford Press. pp. 1–24.

Barbaree, H.E., Marshall, W.L., and Hudson, S.M. (1993). *The Juvenile Sex Offender*. New York: The Guilford Press.

Becker, J.V. (1990). Treating adolescent sex offenders. *Professional Psychology: Research and Practice*, 21(5): 362–365.

Butler, S.M. and Seto, M.C. (2002). Distinguishing two types of adolescent sex offenders. *Journal of the Academy of Child and Adolescent Psychiatry*, 41(1): 83–90.

Cashwell, C.S. and Caruso, M.E. (1997). Adolescent sex offenders: identification and intervention strategies. *Journal of Mental Health Counseling*, 19(4): 336–348.

Chorn, R. and Parekh, A. (1997). Adolescent sexual offenders: a self-psychological perspective. *American Journal of Psychotherapy*, 51(2): 210–228.

Dalton, J.E. (1996). Juvenile male sex offenders: mean scores on the basic self-report of personality. *Psychological Reports*, 79, 634.

Davis, G.E. and Leitenberg, H. (1987). Adolescent sex offenders. *Psychological Bulletin*, 101(3): 417–427.

Gilby, R., Wolf, L., and Goldberg, B. (1989). Mentally retarded adolescent sex offenders. a survey and pilot study. *Canadian Journal of Psychiatry*, 34(6): 542–548.

Kavoussi, R.J., Kaplan, M., and Becker, J.V. (1988). Psychiatric diagnoses in adolescent sex offenders. *Journal of the American Academy of Child and Adolescent Psychiatry*, 27(2): 241–243.

Knight, R.A. and Prentky, R.A. (1993). Exploring characteristics for classifying juvenile sex offenders. In Barbaree, H.E., Marshall, W.L., and Hudson, S.M. (Eds.), *The Juvenile Sex Offender*. New York: The Guilford Press. pp. 45–83.

Kourany, R.F.C., Martin, J.E., and Armstrong, S.H. (1979). Sexual experimentation by adolescents while babysitting. *Adolescence*, 14(54): 283–288.

Lightfoot, L.O. and Barbaree, H.E. (1993). The relationship between substance use and abuse and sexual offending in adolescents. In Barbaree, H.E., Marshall, W.L., and Hudson, S.M. (Eds.), *The Juvenile Sex Offender*. New York: The Guilford Press. pp. 203–224.

Losada-Paisey, G. (1998). Use of the MMPI-A to assess personality of juvenile male delinquents who are sex offenders and nonsex offenders. *Psychological Reports*, 83: 115–122.

MacHovec, F. and Wieckowski, E. (1992).The 10FC ten-factor continua of classification and treatment criteria for male and female sex offenders. *Medical Psychotherapy*, 5: 53–64.

Martin, E.F. and Pruett, M.K. (1998). The juvenile sex offender and the juvenile justice system. *The American Criminal Law Review*, 35(2): 279–332.

Morris, R.E., Anderson, M.M., and Knox, G.W. (2002). Incarcerated adolescents' experiences as perpetrators of sexual assault. *Archives of Pediatrics and Adolescent Medicine*, 156: 831–835.

Muster, N.J. (1992). Treating the adolescent victim-turned-offender. *Adolescence*, 27(106): 441–450.

Righthand, S. and Welch, C. (2001). Juveniles Who Have Sexually Offended a Review of the Professional Literature. Washington, D.C.: Office of Juvenile Justice and Delinquency Prevention.

Ryan, G., Miyoshi, T.J., Metzner, J.L., Krugman, R.D., and Fryer, G.E. (1996). Trends in a national sample of sexually abusive youths. *Journal of the American Academy of Child and Adolescent Psychiatry*, 35(1): 17–25.

Saunders, E.B. and Awad, G.A. (1988). Assessment, management, and treatment planning for male adolescent sexual offenders. *American Journal of Orthopsychiatry*, 58(4): 571–579.

Shaw, J.A. and The Work Group on Quality Issues (1999). Practice parameters for the assessment and treatment of children and adolescents who are sexually abusive of others. *Journal of the American Academy of Child and Adolescent Psychiatry*, 38(Suppl. 12): 55S–76S.

Shaw, J.A., Campo-Bowen, A.E., Applegate, B., Perez, D., Antoine, L.B., Hart, E.L., Lahey, B.B., Testa, R.J., and Devaney, A. (1993).Young Boys who commit serious sexual offenses: demographics, psychometrics, and phenomenology. *Bulletin of the American Academy of Psychiatry and the Law*, 21(4): 399–408.

Smith, W.R., Monastersky, C., and Deisher, R.M. (1987). MMPI-based personality types among juvenile sexual offenders. *Journal of Clinical Psychology*, 43(4): 422–430.

Vinogradov, S., Dishotsky, N.I., Doty, A.K., and Tinklenberg, J.R. (1988). Patterns of behavior in adolescent rape. *American Journal of Orthopsychiatry*, 58(2): 179–187.

Weinhouse, B. (1992). The number of rapes committed by youths has increased. In Biskup, M.D. and Cozic, C.P. (Eds.), *Youth Violence*. San Diego, CA: Greenhaven Press. pp. 37–43.

Zolondek, S.C., Abel, G.G., Northey, W.F., Jr., and Jordan, A.D. (2002). The self-reported behaviors of juvenile sexual offenders. In Holmes, R.M. and Holmes, S.T. (Eds.), *Current Perspectives on Sex Crimes*. Thousand Oaks, CA: Sage. pp. 153–161.

Chapter 20

The Treatment of Adolescent Sex Offenders

Louis Veneziano and Carol Veneziano

20.1 The Epidemiology of Juvenile Sex Offending

Until approximately 20 years ago, adolescents who committed sex offenses received little attention in the research literature. Their behavior was often explained as normal experimentation, and the focus of investigation of deviant sexual behavior was on adult sexual offenders. However, crime reports and surveys have indicated that adolescents are responsible for about 20 percent of rapes and 30 to 50 percent of cases of child sexual abuse (Davis and Leitenberg, 1987; Groth and Loredo, 1981). Current estimates suggest that more than 70,000 boys and 110,000 girls are victims of adolescent sex offenders each year (Ryan and Lane, 1997). Such estimates may be conservative because of the reluctance to report adolescent offenders (Kempton and Forehand, 1992). Thus, the phenomenon of adolescents and children as perpetrators of sex offenders against younger children has become increasingly recognized (Cashwell and Caruso, 1997; Straus, 1994).

These figures probably underestimate the actual number of juvenile sexual offenders, because many of these incidents go unreported

(Groth and Loredo, 1981). Studies of adult sexual offenders indicate that about half of adult offenders report that their first sexual offense occurred as a juvenile, and their offenses often escalated in frequency and severity over time (Becker and Abel, 1985). These findings have led to increased efforts to identify and treat juvenile sex offenders and to the recognition of this group as a distinct population for study (Hunter and Becker, 1994; Veneziano et al., 2000).

Research indicates that juvenile sexual offenders are a heterogeneous population with varying characteristics and treatment needs (Hunter and Becker, 1994; Ryan and Lane, 1997; Veneziano et al., 2000; Hunter et al., 2000). For example, whereas some juveniles may begin their behaviors with the onset of puberty, some begin at very young ages (Cantwell, 1988; Friedrich and Luecke, 1988; Johnson, 1988). They vary in terms of the ages of their victims and whether their offenses involve psychological coercion, violence, or both.

Prior sexual victimization of sex offenders has been a consistent finding across both the adult and juvenile literature, despite considerable differences in sample selection and data collection (Veneziano et al., 2000; Ford and Linney, 1995; Langevin et al., 1989). In samples of adolescent sex offenders undergoing treatment, 40 percent to 70 percent of the adolescent sexual offenders were known to have been sexually abused (Ryan et al., 1996; Veneziano et al., 2000). A study of very young perpetrators suggested that at least 49 percent had been sexually abused (Johnson, 1988). Other studies have found even higher rates of sexual victimization (Friedrich and Luecke, 1988). Widom (2000) found a variety of negative outcomes, including sexual perpetration, as a result of physical or sexual abuse and neglect.

Several studies have examined the victimization behaviors and the characteristics of the victims of juvenile sexual offenders. Ryan et al., (1996) found that 35 percent had engaged in vaginal or anal penetration, 14.7 percent in oral–genital contact, and 17.9 percent in both types of contact; thus about two-thirds involved one or both of these behaviors. A study on a national sample reported that twice as many victims were female than male (Ryan et al., 1996). Most other studies support these findings for juvenile sexual offenders, with females constituting approximately 70 percent of the victims (Worling, 1995). When the victim was a child, the proportion of male victims increased, up to 63 percent (Davis and Leitenberg, 1987).

The literature indicates that adolescent males who commit child molestation offenses tend to select young victims (Davis and Leitenberg, 1987). The majority (more than 60 percent) of the victims were under 12 years old, and 40 percent were less than 6 years old (Fehrenbach et al., 1986). In a national sample, 63 percent were younger than 9 years old, and the modal age was 6 years old (Ryan et al., 1996). Adolescent male rapists, however, are more likely to select victims their own age or older.

Studies indicate that often adolescent sexual offenders know their victims (Johnson, 1988). In one study the victims were blood relations in 38.8 percent of the cases (Ryan et al., 1996), and in another sample of young perpetrators about 46 percent involved family members (Johnson, 1988). A study comparing incest vs. nonincest cases found that sibling offenders were more likely to have assaulted younger children than nonsibling offenders (Worling, 1995).

The relationship between early sexual victimization and later sexual offending is not well understood. The reasons some victimized youths later perpetrate and others do not have yet to be fully explored. Mechanisms thought to contribute to a "cycle of abuse" include a reenactment of the abuse and an attempt to achieve mastery over resulting conflicts (Watkins and Bentovin, 1992) and the subsequent conditioning of sexual arousal to assaultive fantasies (Hunter and Becker, 1994). Rasmussen et al. (1992) argued that prior trauma might be one of a number of precursors to sexual perpetration, with other predisposing factors including social inadequacy, lack of intimacy, and impulsiveness.

Some researchers have advocated and used direct measurement of sexual arousal through phallometric assessment (Weinrott et al., 1997). Research in this area suggests that sexual interests and sexual arousal of juveniles is less fixated than those of older adult offenders. Results reflect greater fluidity in the offense patterns of the juvenile offenders and generally less correspondence between measured arousal and offense histories than has been cited for adults (Hunter et al., 1994; Kaemingk et al., 1995). The behavior of many adolescent sex offenders might be more concerned with abuse rather than with sexual deviance.

20.2 Characteristics of Juvenile Sex Offenders

Several studies describing the backgrounds of juvenile male sexual offenders have found overlaps among adolescent sexual offenders, juvenile delinquents, boys from abusive and neglectful families, and socially isolated boys (Righthand and Welch, 2001). Although the studies are only partially comparable, the following characteristics of adolescent sexual offenders have been repeatedly described: a history of severe family problems, separation from parents and placement away from home, experience of sexual abuse, neglect or physical abuse, social awkwardness or isolation, academic and behavioral problems at school, and psychopathology (Veneziano and Veneziano, 2002).

Research on juvenile sexual offenders suggests that they may be different from their adult counterparts in several ways. For example, early developmental trauma and familial dysfunction appear to be more common and severe in the histories of youth with sexual behavior problems than in those of adult sexual offenders (Hunter and Becker, 1994; Hunter and Figueredo, 1999). Such histories are particularly seen in prepubescent sex offenders, who tend to display a variety of psychiatric, behavioral, social, and educational disturbances that appear to be related to their abuse histories, exposure to violence, and familial dysfunction (Gray et al., 1997; Caputo and Frick, 1999). Marshall and Mazzucco (1995) argue that attachment problems, characterized by neglectful or rejecting parenting, make youths susceptible to becoming sex offenders.

The percentages of juvenile sex offenders who experienced physical abuse as children range from 25 to 50 percent (Becker and Hunter, 1997). In addition, factors such as family instability, disorganization, and violence appear to be common among youths who engage in sexually abusive behavior (Morenz and Becker, 1995; Kobayashi et al., 1995). Research on family communication styles have found that supportive communication is limited in the families of both juvenile sex offenders and violent offenders, whereas negative communication, such as aggressive statements and interruptions, is frequent (Henggeler et al., 1998). Inadequate support and supervision are common in the families of these juveniles (Hunter and Figueredo, 1999).

Research also documents that juveniles with sexual behavior problems often have significant deficits in social competence (Knight and Prentky, 1993). Inadequate social skills, poor peer relationships, and social isolation are some of the difficulties identified (Fehrenach et al., 1986; Katz, 1990; Miner and Crimmins, 1995). Juveniles who had committed child molestation offenses were more socially maladjusted than other sex offenders or delinquents (Katz, 1990).

Juvenile sex offenders have been noted to have poor impulse control, judgment, and problem-solving skills (Prentky et al., 2000). They appear to have less empathy for others and more difficulty recognizing and accurately identifying emotions in others (Knight and Prentky, 1993). Cognitive distortions, such as blaming the victim, have been associated with increased rates of sexual reoffending among juveniles who committed sexual offenses (Kahn and Chambers, 1991; Ward et al., 1995).

Juveniles who sexually offend typically have experienced difficulties in the school setting, including disruptive behavior, truancy, or a learning disability (Fehrenbach et al., 1986; Kahn and Chambers, 1991; Bourke and Donahue, 1996; O'Callaghan, 1998). Kahn and Chambers (1991) found that 50 percent of the juveniles in their study had behaved disruptively at school, 30 percent had been truant, and 39 percent had been diagnosed with a learning disability. Studies indicate that 30 to 60 percent of juvenile sex offenders had symptoms of an attention deficit disorder (Kavoussi et al., 1988; Ferrara and McDonald, 1996).

Studies have indicated that juvenile sex offenders' average IQ scores tended to be in the low-average range, and they scored more poorly on verbal subtests, similar to other groups of delinquents (Jacobs et al., 1997; Ferrara and McDonald, 1996). Juvenile sex offenders with lower IQ scores showed significantly more inappropriate sexual behaviors than did those with higher scores (McCurry et al., 1998). Neuropsychological impairments were found at higher rates in groups of juvenile sex offenders and juvenile violent non-sex offenders, including difficulties with executive functions (planning skills and impulse control) and deficits with respect to verbal skills, and between one-fourth and one-third of the samples demonstrate some degree of neuropsychological impairment (Ferrera and McDonald, 1996).

Overall, juveniles who commit sex offenses and juveniles who commit other types of offenses share many characteristics. They tend to come from dysfunctional families, and they are more likely to have been abused and to have received inadequate support and supervision. Both groups tend to have poor verbal skills, more behavioral problems at school, lower academic achievement, and higher rates of learning disabilities. They tend to have poorer social skills and, perhaps, have higher rates of neuropsychological difficulties, especially in areas related to planning and impulse control.

Follow-up studies of juvenile sex offenders have indicated that recidivism rates hover around 50 percent and consist of both sexual and nonsexual offenses. Recidivism in terms of sexual offenses is not particularly high. For example, recidivism rates for sexual offenses have ranged from 8 to over 30 percent, with most studies indicating ranges from 10 to 15 percent (Righthand and Welch, 2001). Recidivism rates reflecting nonsexual offenses are higher, ranging from 16 (Sipe et al., 1998) to 54 percent (Rasmussen, 1999). Worling (2001) found that more pathological subgroups were most likely to be charged with a subsequent violent (sexual or nonsexual) or nonviolent offense.

These findings suggest that when a longitudinal perspective is used, sexual offending among juveniles is often part of a pattern of general delinquency. The data concerning recidivism indicate that juveniles who commit sexual offenses are more at risk for subsequent nonsexual delinquency than sexual recidivism and are more similar to other juvenile delinquents than adult sex offenders. The research concerning sexual arousal of adolescent sex offenders, which indicates that their sexual interests and arousal are less fixated and more fluid, would appear to support this conclusion.

20.3 Typologies of Juvenile Sex Offenders

The general consensus among researchers is that juveniles who have committed sex offenses are a heterogeneous group. Consequently, there is a need to develop reliable and valid typologies. The first typologies were offense driven (e.g., rapists, child molesters), whereas others were personality driven (e.g., disturbed impulsive, pseudosocialized).

An example of an offense-driven typology can be seen in the classification developed by Graves et al. (1996). This classification consisted of three categories: pedophilic, sexual assaultive, and undifferentiated. Pedophilic juveniles tended to lack social competence and to be socially isolated; they molested children, usually girls, at least 3 years younger than themselves. The sexual-assaultive group typically assaulted peers or older females. The undifferentiated group committed a variety of offenses, and the ages of their victims varied considerably.

O'Brien and Bera (1986) developed a seven-category classification scheme for juvenile sex offenders that is used by many residential facilities. These categories include: (1) naive experimenters, (2) undersocialized child exploiters, (3) sexual aggressives, (4) sexual compulsives, (5) disturbed impulsives, (6) group-influenced, and (7) pseudosocialized. Although these categories appear to have superficial validity, there has not been any systematic investigation of their reliability and validity.

The most promising empirically derived typologies are in the process of development. Prentky et al. (2000) have developed a protocol for risk assessment, the juvenile sex offender assessment protocol (JSOAP). Kaufman et al. (1998) focus on the pattern of behaviors that perpetrators display in the periods leading to and following sexual contact — the *modus operandi*. Subgroups of offenders differed significantly in the strategies used (Kaufman et al., 1998).

Worling (2001) has used the California Psychological Inventory to establish groups. Cluster analysis revealed four personality-based subgroups: antisocial/impulsive, unusual/isolated, overcontrolled/reserved, and confident/aggressive. Significant differences were observed in his initial study with respect to such variables as physical status, parental marital status, residence, and disposition of their cases.

Progress in the field will be significantly enhanced once reliable and empirically validated typologies emerge. Typologies based on combining type of offense with individual personality characteristics would appear to hold the most promise. The use of multivariate statistical techniques and hierarchical cluster analysis is likely to be beneficial in this regard.

20.4 Assessment of Juvenile Sex Offenders for Treatment

Because of the heterogeneous nature of juveniles who have committed sex offenses, a comprehensive clinical assessment should be performed on each client for the development and implementation of an individualized treatment plan. Based upon the research literature, such assessment should identify strengths and weaknesses in the following areas: (1) intellectual and neuropsychological, (2) personality and psychopathological, (3) social and behavioral, (4) sexual, (5) history of victimization, and (6) substance usage.

Recent research focuses on risk and protective factors. The Clinical Assessment Package for Assessing Client Risks and Strengths (CASPARS), for example, is a newly developed set of instruments that gives equal consideration to client strengths and weaknesses, yielding a risk score and an asset score. This information may be useful for assessment intervention and the evaluation of the effects of treatment (Gilgun et al., 1999).

It can also be noted that several research studies have concluded that labeling juveniles as sex offenders has potentially negative consequences and should be avoided (Ryan and Lane, 1997; Hunter et al., 2000). This is particularly important because it appears that juveniles are at lower risk for sexual recidivism and are more amenable to change than is believed to be the case for adult offenders.

20.5 Treatment of Adolescent Sexual Offenders

In the past, most treatment programs for juveniles who committed sex offenses were long-term (12 to 24 months) residential programs. More recently, however, the majority of juvenile sex offenders are being treated in the community (Ryan and Lane, 1997; Hunter et al., 2000; Worling and Curwen, 2000). Research is being conducted to determine the effectiveness of particular treatment programs and interventions for juveniles who have committed sex offenses. Traditionally, treatment programs were modeled after programs used with adult sex offenders, but it has not been established whether such programs are in fact effective with juveniles (Marshall and Barbee, 1990).

At the present time, many treatment programs for juveniles who have committed sex offenses utilize cognitive–behavioral techniques conducted in groups. Target areas for treatment typically include the following: (1) decreasing cognitive distortions, (2) increasing empathy, (3) enhancing problem-solving skills, (4) decreasing deviant sexual arousal, (5) enhancing age-appropriate social skills, including dating skills, (6) resolution of traumatic consequences associated with being victimized, and (7) enhancing management of emotions such as anger (Becker and Hunter, 1997; Hunter and Figuerdo, 1999; NAPN, 1993).

However, there is considerable ongoing research evaluating program models for juveniles. Such programs are more holistic and comprehensive than earlier models. Newer programs are being influenced by the research on delinquency, psychiatric disorders, and the research on risk and asset models (Swenson et al., 1998; Borduin, 1999; Marshall, 1996). The applications of risk and protective factors have led researchers to recommend continuous reassessments of juveniles for both strengths and risks to keep pace with the changes occurring in adolescence (Gilgun et al., 1999). These juvenile programs differ from those of adults because the research now indicates that juveniles are more changeable than adults. They are also more at risk in terms of global functioning than adults and at lower risk for sexual recidivism than was initially assumed (Worling and Curwen, 2000; Prentky et al., 2000).

Some researchers have argued that programs designed to focus only on sex-offending behavior are limited and that, given the other problems many juvenile sex offenders also experience, a more holistic approach is needed. Thus, treatment should include strategies to enhance impulse control and good judgment (Becker and Hunter, 1997). Family interventions and the facilitation of positive school attachments are recommended as treatment goals (Miner and Crimmins, 1995). As truancy is empirically correlated to juvenile recidivism (Jenkins, 1997; Gottfredson, 2000), treatment should target school performance. Bourke and Donohue (1996) emphasized the development of dating skills as a treatment component.

Perhaps the most promising holistic approach is multisystemic therapy (MST), a flexible and individualized treatment approach that addresses the multiple determinants of antisocial behavior in the youth's natural ecology. The youth's family, school, work, peers, and neighborhoods are viewed as interconnected systems with reciprocal influences, and all are addressed in MST (Henggeler et al., 1998; Swenson et al., 1998). More assessment and intervention in the social contexts of these youths is employed, as opposed to the traditional therapies used with adults. This technique has demonstrated long-term reduction in criminal activity and violence in high-risk violent youth (Henggeler et al., 1998; Borduin, 1999). MST was found to be more effective than individual therapy in improving important family and peer correlates of antisocial behavior and in preventing future criminal behavior (Borduin et al., 1995). Recent research indicates promise for MST with young sexual offenders (Swenson et al., 1998; Borduin, 1999).

A particularly problematic issue in the treatment of juveniles who have committed sex offenses is the selection of an intervention designed to decrease deviant sexual arousal (NAPN, 1993). The effectiveness of covert sensitization and masturbatory conditioning with juveniles has not been adequately empirically demonstrated (Hunter and Lexier, 1998). A promising intervention is vicarious sensitization, in which juveniles are exposed to a taped crime scenario designed to stimulate arousal, and then, immediately afterwards, they view an aversive video that presents the negative social, emotional, and legal consequences of sexually abusive behavior (Weinrott et al., 1997). However, the effectiveness of vicarious sensitization needs to be empirically established (Hunter and Lexier, 1998). Advocates of MST argue that enhancing competencies, ecological supports, and normalizing experiences are more relevant than decreasing deviant arousal, which their research suggests is less often the source of the sexual offending behavior (Swenson et al., 1998; Borduin, 1999).

Most treatment programs also incorporate a relapse-prevention component. Relapse prevention was initially designed to help substance abusers deal with and prevent the reoccurrence of drug abuse. When used with juveniles, this program requires that the adolescents learn to identify factors associated with an increased risk of sex offending and use strategies to avoid high-risk situations or effectively manage them when they occur. For example, if a youth's offending behavior occurred while babysitting, it would be prudent for him to avoid such jobs. When relapse prevention is applied to children and adolescents, greater emphasis is placed on external supervision to prevent further problems (Gray et al., 1997). The incorporation of a relapse-prevention component to the treatment protocol for adolescent sex offenders appears to be promising conceptually. Although theoretically sound, empirical studies investigating the effectiveness of using this approach with juveniles who have committed sex offenses have yet to be conducted (Gray and Pithers, 1993).

Noting the similarities between juveniles who commit general delinquent nonsexual acts and juveniles who commit sex offenses, several researchers have argued that relevant empirically based treatment interventions for juvenile delinquents be used with those who commit sex offenses whenever the interventions appear to be indicated. MST, applied to violent offenders, appears to have considerable promise for sexual offenders (Borduin et al., 1995; Borduin, 1999).

20.6 Conclusions: A Practical Orientation

At a secondary-prevention level, prevention efforts should be aimed at high-risk children, particularly those from dysfunctional families who are experiencing other academic and behavioral difficulties. Children who are physically and sexually abused are at heightened risk for sexual perpetration and should receive specialized treatment in order to avoid the cycle of abuse in which they become perpetrators themselves.

The research literature indicates that juveniles who have committed sex offenses are a heterogeneous group who are likely to have a number of special needs related to their families, schools, and social competencies, in addition to the special risks posed by their sexually abusive behaviors toward others. Juvenile sexual offenders should be assessed in a variety of areas, given the findings of the research, so that appropriate treatment plans may be established. Programs that target the specific problems of the individual offender would seem more likely to be effective, rather than attempts to apply "canned" programs to all juvenile offenders who have been found to have committed sexual abuse.

Cognitive–behavioral techniques and MST have been the most promising techniques used with juvenile delinquents. Given that juvenile sexual offenders share many of their characteristics with other delinquents, research should perhaps focus on those programs found to be effective with delinquents, in addition to programs that have been used with adult sex offenders. Relapse-prevention approaches would also appear logically to be techniques that might prove to be effective with juvenile sexual offenders. Further research into classification, assessment, and treatment of this population is much needed.

References

Becker, J.V. and Abel, G.G. (1985). Methodological and ethical issues in evaluating and treatment adolescent sex offenders. In Otey, E.M. and Ryan, G.D. (Eds.), *Adolescent Sex Offenders: Issues in Research and Treatment.* Rockville, MD: USDHHS. pp. 109–129.

Becker, J.V. and Hunter, J.A. (1997). Understanding and treating child and adolescent sex offenders. In Ollendick, T.H. and Prinz, R.J. (Eds.), *Advances in Clinical Child Psychology.* New York: Plenum Press, 177–197.

Borduin, C.M. (1999). Multisystemic treatment of criminality and violence in adolescents. *Journal of the American Academy of Child and Adolescent Psychiatry,* 38, 242–249.

Borduin, C.M., Mann, B.J., Cone, L.T., Henggeler, S.W. (1995). Multisystemic treatment of serious juvenile offenders: long-term prevention of criminality and violence. *Journal of Consulting and Clinical Psychology,* 63, 569–578.

Bourke, M.L. and Donohue, B. (1996). Assessment and treatment of juvenile sex offenders: an empirical review. *Journal of Child Sexual Abuse,* 5, 47–70.

Cantwell, H.B. (1988). Child sexual abuse: very young perpetrators. *Child Abuse and Neglect,* 12, 579–582.

Caputo, A.A. and Frick, P.J. (1999). Family violence and juvenile sex offending. *Criminal Justice and Behavior,* 26, 338–356.

Cashwell, C.S. and Caruso, M.E. (1997). Adolescent sex offenders: identification and intervention strategies. *Journal of Mental Health Counseling,* 19, 336–348.

Davis, G.E. and Leitenberg, H. (1987). Adolescent sex offenders. *Psychological Bulletin,* 101, 417–427.

Fehrenbach, P.A., Smith, W., Monastersky, C., and Deisher, R.W. (1986). Adolescent sex offenders: Offenders and offense characteristics. *American Journal of Orthopsychiatry,* 56, 225–233.

Ferrara, M.L. and McDonald, S. (1996). *Treatment of the Juvenile Sex Offender: Neurological and Psychiatric Impairments.* Northvale, NJ: Jason Aronson.

Ford, M.E. and Linney, J.A. (1995). Comparative analysis of juvenile sex offenders, violent nonsexual offenders, and status offenders. *Journal of Interpersonal Violence,* 10, 56–69.

Friedrich, W.N. and Luecke, W.J. (1988). Young school-age sexually aggressive children. *Professional Psychology: Research and Practice,* 2, 155–164.

Gilgun, J.F., Keskinen, S., Marti, D.J., and Rice, K. (1999). Clinical applications of the CASPARS instruments: boys who act out sexually. *Families in Society,* 80, 629–641.

Gottfredson, D.C. (2000). *Schools and Delinquency.* New York: Cambridge University Press.

Graves, R.B., Openshaw, D.K., Ascione, F.R., and Ericksen, S.L. (1996). Demographic and parental characteristics of youthful sexual offenders. *International Journal of Offender Therapy and Comparative Criminology*, 40, 300–317.

Gray, A., Busconi, A., Houchens, P., and Pithers, W.D. (1997). Children with sexual behavioral problems and their caregivers: demographics, functioning and clinical patterns. *Sexual Abuse: A Journal of Research and Treatment*, 9, 267–290.

Gray, A.S. and Pithers, W.D. (1993). Replace prevention with sexually aggressive adolescents and children: expanding treatment and supervision. In Barbee, H.E., Marshall, W.L., and Hudson, S.M. (Eds.), *The Juvenile Sex Offender*. New York: Guilford Press, pp. 289–319.

Groth, A.N. and Loredo, C.M. (1981). Juvenile sexual offenders: guidelines for assessment. *International Journal of Offender Therapy and Comparative Criminology*, 25, 31–39.

Henggeler, S.W., Schoenwald, S.K., Borduin, C.M., Rowland, M.D., and Cunningham, P.E. (1998). *Multisystemic Treatment of Antisocial Behavior in Children and Adolescents*. New York: Guilford Press.

Hunter, J.A. and Becker, J.V. (1994). The role of deviant sexual arousal in juvenile sexual offending. *Criminal Justice and Behavior*, 21, 132–149.

Hunter, J.A. and Figueredo, A.J. (1999). Factors associated with treatment compliance in a population of juvenile sexual offenders. *Sexual Abuse: A Journal of Research and Treatment*, 11, 49–67.

Hunter, J.A., Goodwin, D.W., and Becker, J.V. (1994). The relationship between phallometrically measured deviant sexual arousal and clinical characteristics in juvenile sexual offenders. *Behavior Research and Therapy*, 32, 533–538.

Hunter, J.A., Hazelwood, R.R., and Slesinger, D. (2000). Juvenile-perpetrated sex crimes: Patterns of offending and predictors of violence. *Journal of Family Violence*, 15, 81–93.

Hunter, J.A. and Lexier, L.J. (1998). Ethical and legal issues in the assessment and treatment of juvenile sex offenders. *Child Maltreatment*, 3, 339–348.

Jacobs, W.L., Kennedy, W.A., and Meyer, J.B. (1997). A between group comparison study of sexual and nonsexual offenders. *Sexual Abuse: A Journal of Research and Treatment*, 9, 201–207.

Jenkins, P.H. (1997). School delinquency and the social bond. *Journal of Research in Crime and Delinquency*, 34, 337–367.

Johnson, T.C. (1988). Child perpetrators — children who molest other children: preliminary findings. *Child Abuse and Neglect*, 12, 219–229.

Kaemingk, K.L., Koselka, M., Becker, J.V., and Kaplan, M.S. (1995). Age and adolescent sexual offender arousal. *Sexual Abuse: Journal of Research and Treatment*, 7, 249–257.

Kahn, T.J. and Chambers, H.J. (1991). Assessing re-offense risk with juvenile sex offenders. *Child Welfare*, LXX, 333–345.

Katz, R.C. (1990). Psychosocial adjustment in adolescent child molesters. *Child Abuse and Neglect*, 14, 567–575.

Kaufman, K.L., Holberg, J.K., Orts, K.A., McCrady, F.E., Rotzien, A.L., Daleiden, E.L., Hilliker, D.R. (1998). Factors influencing sexual offenders' modus operandi: an examination of victim-offender relatedness and age. *Child Maltreatment*, 3, 349–361.

Kavoussi, R.J., Kaplan, M., and Becker, J.V. (1988). Psychiatric diagnoses in adolescent sex offenders. *Journal of the American Academy of Child and Adolescent Psychiatry*, 27, 241–243.

Kempton, T. and Forehand, R.L. (1992). Suicide attempts among juvenile delinquents: the contribution of mental health factors. *Behavioral Research and Therapy*, 30, 537–541.

Knight, R.A. and Prentky, R.A. (1993). Exploring characteristics for classifying juvenile sex offenders. In Barbaree, H.E., Marshall, W.L., and Hudson, S.M. (Eds.), *The Juvenile Sex Offender*. New York: Guilford Press. pp. 45–83.

Kobayashi, J., Sales, B.D., Becker, J.V., Figueredo, A.J., and Kaplan, M.S. (1995). Perceived parental deviance, parent-child bonding, child and abuse and child sexual aggression. *Sexual Abuse: A Journal of Research and Treatment*, 7, 25–43.

Langevin, R., Wright, P., and Handy, L. (1989). Characteristics of sex offenders who were sexually victimized as children. *Annals of Sex Research*, 2, 227–253.

Marshall, W.L. (1996). Assessment, treatment, and theorizing about sex offenders: developments during the past twenty years and future directions. *Criminal Justice and Behavior*, 23, 162–199.

Marshall, W.L. and Barbee, H.E. (1990). Outcome of comprehensive cognitive-behavioral treatment programs. In Marshall, W.L., Laws, D.R., and Barbee, H.E. (Eds.), *Handbook of Sexual Assault: Issues, Theories and Treatment of the Offender*. New York: Plenum Press. pp. 363–385.

Marshall, W.L. and Mazzucco, A. (1995). Self-esteem and parental attachments in child molesters. *Sexual Abuse: Journal of Research and Treatment*, 7, 279–285.

McCurry, C., McClellan, J., Adams, J., Norrei, M., Storck, M., Eisner, A., and Breiger, D. (1998). Sexual behavior associated with low verbal IQ in youth who have severe mental illness. *Mental Retardation*, 36, 23–30.

Miner, M.H. and Crimmins, C.L.S. (1995). Adolescent sex offenders: issues of etiology and risk factors. In Schwartz, B.K. and Cellini, H.R. (Eds.), *The Sex Offender, Vol 1. Corrections, Treatment and Legal Practice*. Kingston, NJ: Civic Research Institute. pp. 9.1–9.15.

Morenz, B. and Becker, J. (1995). The treatment of youthful sex offenders. *Applied and Preventive Psychology*, 4, 247–256.

National Adolescent Perpetrator Network (1993). The revised report from the National Task Force on juvenile sexual offending. *Juvenile and Family Court Journal*, 44, 1–120.

O'Brien, M. and Bera, W.H. (1986). The PHASE Typology of Adolescent Sex Offenders. The Oregon report on juvenile sex offenders. Salem, OR: Children's Services, Department of Human Resources.

O'Callaghan, D. (1998). Practice issues in working with young abusers who have learning disabilities. *Child Abuse Review*, 7, 435–448.

Prentky, R., Harris, B., Frizell, K., and Righthand, S. (2000). An actuarial procedure for assessing risk in juvenile sex offenders. *Sexual Abuse: A Journal of Research and Treatment*, 12, 71–93.

Rasmussen, L.A. (1999). Factors related to recidivism among juvenile sexual offenders. *Sexual Abuse: A Journal of Research and Treatment*, 11, 69–85.

Rasmussen, L.A., Burton, J.E., and Christopherson, B.J. (1992). Precursors to offending and the trauma outcome process in sexually reactive children. *Journal of Child Sexual Abuse*, 1, 33–47.

Righthand, S. and Welch, C. (2001). Juveniles Who Have Sexually Offended. Washington, D.C.: Office of Juvenile Justice and Delinquency Prevention.

Ryan, G.D. and Lane, S.L. (1997). *Juvenile Sex Offending: Causes, Consequences, and Corrections* (new and revised ed.). San Francisco, CA: Jossey-Bass.

Ryan, G., Miyoshi, T.J., Metzner, J.L., Krugman, R.D., and Fryer, G.E. (1996). Trends in a national sample of sexually abusive youths. *Journal of the American Academy of Child and Adolescent Psychiatry*, 33, 17–25.

Sipe, R., Jensen, E.L., and Everett, R.S. (1998). Adolescent sexual offenders grown up: Recidivism in young adulthood. *Criminal Justice and Behavior*, 25, 109–124.

Straus, M.B. (1994). *Violence in the Lives of Adolescents*. New York: W.W. Norton.

Swenson, C.C., Henggeler, S.W., Schoenwald, S.K., Kaufman, K.L., and Randall, J. (1998). Changing the social ecologies of adolescent sexual offenders: implications of the success of multisystemic therapy in treating serious antisocial behavior in adolescents. *Child Maltreatment*, 3, 330–338.

Veneziano, L. and Veneziano, C. (2002). Juvenile sex offenders. In *Encyclopedia of Juvenile Justice*. Williams, F. and McShane, M. (Eds.). Thousand Oaks, CA: Sage Publications, 346–349.

Veneziano, C. Veneziano, L., and Legrand, S. (2000). The relationship between adolescent sex offender behaviors and victim characteristics with prior victimization. *Journal of Interpersonal Violence*, 15, 363–374.

Ward, T., Hudson, S.M., and Marshall, W.L. (1995). Cognitive distortions and affective deficits in sex offenders: a cognitive deconstructionist interpretation. *Sexual Abuse: Journal of Research and Treatment*, 7, 67–83.

Watkins, B. and Bentovin, A. (1992). The sexual abuse of male children and adolescents: a review of current research. *Journal of Child Psychology and Psychiatry*, 33, 197–248.

Weinrott, M., Riggan, M., and Frothingham, S. (1997). Reducing deviant arousal in juvenile sex offenders using vicarious sensitization. *Journal of Interpersonal Violence*, 12, 704–728.

Widom, C.S. (2000). Child abuse and neglect. In White, S. (Ed.), *Handbook of Youth and Justice*. New York: Kluwer Academic. pp. 31–47.

Worling, J.R. (1995). Adolescent sibling incest offenders: differences in family and individual functioning when compared to adolescent nonsibling sex offenders. *Child Abuse and Neglect*, 19, 633–643.

Worling, J.R. (2001). Personality-based typology of adolescent male sexual offenders: differences in recidivism rates, victim-selection characteristics, and personal victimization histories. *Sexual Abuse: Journal of Research and Treatment*, 13, 149–166.

Worling, J.R. and Curwen, T. (2000). Adolescent sexual offender recidivism: success of specialized treatment and implications for risk prediction. *Child Abuse and Neglect*, 24, 965–982.

Chapter 21

Utilizing Applied Behavior Analysis with Juvenile Sexual Offenders

Scott LeGrand, Michael Weinberg, and E. K. McIntyre

Abstract

The increase in the population of juvenile sexual offenders in the last two decades has created a challenge for the juvenile justice system to provide treatment for the offenders while ensuring community safety. Due to current pressures on the system there is a need to further develop effective and empirical models that utilize integrated approaches for assessment and treatment. This chapter will present an applied behavior analysis (ABA) perspective to the treatment of juvenile sexual offenders. One such approach that we are advocating is the use of positive behavioral support (PBS) as a service delivery model based on a functional assessment of the juvenile's sexual or challenging behaviors. This chapter also presents a theoretical model based on approaches from clinical behavior analysis relating to the development of challenging behaviors of juvenile sexual offenders who have been sexually abused and a framework to complete a functional assessment. The goal is to present an integrated system for the assessment process and treatment of juvenile sexual offenders within the community setting.

21.1 Introduction

There are a number of approaches that are currently utilized in the treatment of juvenile sexual offenders. Many individual treatment approaches have a cognitive or behavioral perspective and focus on individual changes to provide successful outcomes. Although many provide sound methodology, they do not provide a systematic method to integrate assessment process and treatment with the juvenile and involved external sources (i.e., family, school, and community). A review of the sexual abuse cycle, relapse-prevention model, and aversive conditioning and satiation behavioral treatment will lay the foundation for reasons to have a more integrated assessment process and treatment approach that deals with the treatment of juvenile sexual offenders in the community.

One approach in treating juvenile sexual offenders is using the sexual abuse cycle to help juveniles to develop an understanding of their sexually abusive patterns and identify problematic areas for treatment (Lane, 1997). Juveniles work on defining their cycle and the factors that trigger their progression through a series of steps that lead to their sexual offending. Each step of the cycle is defined by cognitive and affective responses that result in a behavioral reaction. If a juvenile distorts his or her cognitive process and displays maladaptive coping, he or she is at risk of committing a sexual offense. Offense-specific interventions focus on the pattern of fantasy, planning, victim selection, grooming, access and opportunity, sexual arousal and reinforcement, distortions and rationalizations, decision making, secrecy, and denial (Ryan, 1999). Through this process, juveniles are able to develop strategies to prevent themselves from progressing in their cycle, thus preventing further sexual offenses.

The disadvantage of the sexual abuse cycle is that it relies on the self-report of the juvenile to identify triggers and their cognitive and affective responses. If the juvenile presents distorted or incorrect information this could lead to the misidentification of his or her cycle and result in relapse for the juvenile. Also, juveniles who are impulsive or have cognitive delays may not be able to process the information to prevent triggers or stop themselves from progressing in the cycle.

Interventions are developed based on past offenses and may not account for all external or internal factors relating to the juvenile's offense cycle. External supports for the individual are limited in their treatment involvement, and social and other skills are developed to enhance normalization of interactions in relation only to the deviant sexual behavior pattern.

The relapse-prevention (Laws, 1989; Pithers et al., 1988) approach is similar to the sexual abuse cycle in that both agree that a sequential process leads the juvenile to commit a sexual offense. In the relapse-prevention approach the premise is that juveniles make a series of lapses through seemingly unimportant decisions (SUDs) that place them in higher-risk situations and could lead to reoffense or relapse. In the relapse process the initial precursors are emotional, i.e., boredom, social or sexual embarrassment, anger, fear of rejection, and numbness (Stickrod Gray and Pithers, 1993). This initial precursor leads to maladaptive coping in the form of increased frequency and strength of abusive sexual fantasies. During this lapse, the juvenile experiences a conflict of self-image as a person who can manage his or her behaviors and as a person who has self-doubts about his or her treatment and thoughts of failure (abstinence violation effect [AVE]). If juveniles are unable to display adaptive coping responses they progress or lapse further in the process through the development of cognitive distortions that are maladaptive psychological defenses. The possibility of relapse becomes the greatest when the juvenile's cognitive distortions are combined with his or her focus on the positive payoff of committing the sexual offense along with limited concern over the consequences (problems of immediate gratification [PIG]). Identification and monitoring of the precursors is an essential part of treatment in the relapse-prevention approach. The juvenile, his family, therapist, and other external support systems monitor changes and address them in order to help prevent the juvenile from progressing to the point of relapse.

As in the sexual abuse cycle the relapse-prevention approach focuses on identifying factors that cause the juvenile to reoffend. Preventive cognitive strategies are then developed to prevent lapses and relapses through enhanced self-management skills, development of coping skills, and external supervision. A primary concern in this approach is the need for understanding that juveniles can relapse at any point and that they are never "cured" of their sexual offending behaviors. Unlike other conduct and behavioral problems that a juvenile may display, the juvenile sexual offender is forever labeled with this behavioral issue. Also, this approach tends to focus on avoidance as a method to prevent relapse (i.e., the juvenile avoids coming in contact with young children) rather than encouragement of social activities with juveniles of the same age to promote social development and skills. External supports (families, therapists, juvenile officers, and schools) are used primarily for monitoring in the treatment process and not as resources for further development of skills or socialization.

A major controversy in the treatment of juvenile sexual offenders has been in the area of aversive conditioning and satiation. These treatment techniques can include vicarious or covert sensitization, verbal or masturbatory satiation, and olfactory or faradic conditioning. The primary objectives of these interventions are to help reduce deviant sexual urges, thoughts, fantasies, and masturbatory behaviors, which 90 percent of juvenile sexual offender programs support (Knopp et al., 1986). Initially, the juvenile is introduced to deviant sexual stimulation that relates to their behavioral pattern via script, audio, or videotape, or self-induced fantasies. This induces arousal to the deviant sexual act and, at this point, the aversive stimulus is presented to deter this deviant arousal. This type of approach requires repetitive exposure to the aversive stimulus prior to completion of treatment.

Although treatment providers dealing with the juvenile sexual offender support the objectives of reducing deviant sexual urges, thoughts, fantasies, and masturbatory behaviors, there is much concern over the use of this treatment with juvenile sexual offenders and other populations with challenging behaviors (Horner et al., 1990). A solution to this controversy is through the development of nonaversive techniques, which can address specific challenging behaviors related to juvenile sexual offenders. Also, further emphasis is needed on developing more adaptive skills through socially acceptable methods, which will enhance socialization and help deal with deviant sexual behaviors.

In the presentation of the sexual abuse cycle, relapse-prevention model, and the aversive conditioning and satiation behavioral treatment approach there is some form of integration with the cognitive and the behavioral perspective in the treatment of juvenile sexual offenders. Although these methodologies provide sound principles of treatment, there is still a need for an integrated assessment process and treatment approach that systematically involves the juvenile sexual offenders, their families, and other external sources in the community.

To address these issues an ABA perspective is being presented to define a sound system of care that integrates the assessment process and treatment and utilizes external sources in socialization and skill development. The delivery system will be outlined through the use of PBSs. The assessment process will initially present a model relating to the development of deviant sexual behavior patterns resulting from childhood sexual abuse. It then presents a functional assessment format based upon functional analytic psychotherapy (Kohlenberg et al., 1993; Kohlenberg and Tsai, 1991) that can be utilized in determining treatment interventions for juvenile sexual offenders in the community. Recommendations for further developments and research in this approach will be presented to encourage continuation of services for juvenile sexual offenders.

21.2 PBS: A Service Delivery Model

Conceptually, PBS presents an appealing approach for the treatment of juvenile sexual offending. Shifting away from traditional pathology-based models of care, PBS endorses a pathology-free model of care that emphasizes the role of maladaptive learning patterns and problematic environmental conditions, rather than latent dysfunction processes, to explain aberrant behavior (Carr et al., 1999 and 2002; Koegel et al., 1996). PBS is an applied science that uses instructional methods for improving adaptive functioning skills along with methods of systems change, targeting ecological factors that promote and maintain the newly acquired adaptive skills (Carr et al., 2002; Koegel et al., 1996). Essentially an empirically driven approach to problem solving (Scotti and Meyer, 1999), PBS looks to apply behavioral principles in environmental contexts in order to diminish problem behaviors and build socially appropriate behaviors that result in lasting change and lead to more enriched lifestyles (Carr et al., 1999).

The establishment of PBS has grown out of the demands of families, teachers, and clinicians wanting effective methods of treating challenging behaviors such as aggression, self-injury, and property destruction — behaviors that function as impediments to successful experiences in educational, societal, and vocational settings (Meyer et al., 1991). Having been used almost exclusively on individuals with developmental disabilities, PBS has recently begun receiving greater attention with regard to its use on individuals with emotional and behavioral disorders (Kern et al., 1994). Although debate currently focuses on whether PBS should be categorized as an applied science or as a method of service delivery (Wacker and Berg, 2002), the more important point to note is the positive outcomes that continue to be achieved by using PBS on extremely challenging clinical populations (Knoster and McCurdy, 2002). To build the case that PBS presents a legitimate treatment paradigm and service-delivery model for juvenile sexual offenders, PBS is examined from its conceptual framework and theoretical underpinnings. A PBS service-delivery model for the juvenile sexual offending population is presented thereafter as a means to exemplify how a PBS approach to treating juvenile sexual offenders might look.

21.3 Origin of PBS

PBS can be viewed as a blend of science and philosophy, originating from three major sources: (1) ABA, (2) inclusion/normalization, (3) and person-centered planning (Carr et al., 2002). Having a scientific basis, ABA is the systematic application of behavioral principles to problems and issues holding social relevance (Baer et al., 1968). As a science, ABA provides procedures that can be tested and refuted through processes of experimentation (Wacker and Berg, 2002). Functionally, ABA has made two major contributions to PBS. First, ABA offers a framework that is relevant to socially meaningful behavior change. Second, it has provided a scientific method for assessment, intervention, and outcome evaluation (Carr et al., 2002). Inclusion/normalization represents a philosophical position that individuals with disabilities should have the same opportunities and accesses as those without disabilities. Historically linked to individuals with developmental disabilities, this philosophical position can easily be extended to several clinical populations, as they are often ostracized by society as a whole. Person-centered planning refers to the process of learning how a person wants to live and then describing what needs to be done to assist that person in moving toward his or her goal (Smull and Harrison, 1992). Although person-centered planning is rooted in the values, goals, and outcomes that are important to the person, it also takes into account other critical factors that have an impact on the individual's life, including family and agency views, funding issues, and the person's disability and community (Lyle O'Brien et al., 1997).

21.4 Goals of PBS

The ultimate goal of PBS is to assist individuals in positively changing their lifestyles so that all relevant stakeholders have the opportunity to perceive and enjoy the quality-of-life improvements that result (Carr et al., 2002). To bring about this ultimate goal, two intermediate goals are perceived to be necessary. First, prosocial behaviors and support systems (that maximize or make possible these prosocial behaviors) have to be formally integrated into the individual's behavioral repertoire and his or her environment, respectively. Second, problematic behaviors have to be systematically reduced to the point where they no longer serve as the maintaining agents that they originally were. By simultaneously increasing these prosocial behaviors and creating contextual systems for change and reducing pre-existing challenging behaviors, socially meaningful behaviors begin to effectively replace previous problematic behaviors as functional equivalence is achieved.

21.5 Assumptions and Characteristic of PBS

Four assumptions and five characteristics underlie PBS as a treatment modality and are essential to its effective application on all clinical populations (Bambara and Knoster, 1998). The first assumption is that all challenging behaviors serve a function. Although some debate exists on the number of functions that exist, three are commonly identified throughout the literature in this area of study. These functions include gaining attention, avoiding aversives, and attaining regulation. The second assumption is that challenging behaviors are context-related. In other words, functional determinants such as establishing events or setting events, antecedents, and consequences affect behavior. The third assumption is that effective interventions are based upon thorough understanding of the challenging behaviors. Functionally derived interventions are the product of knowing the determinants that are maintaining the challenging behaviors. The fourth assumption is that a strong value base should guide behavior support plans. In determining the appropriateness of an intervention, its effectiveness and its social acceptability should be considered by way of a cost–benefit analysis.

The first characteristic of PBS is that it is assessment-based and hypothesis-driven. As an applied science, functional assessment and hypotheses are critical for establishing an experimental premise for understanding the challenging behaviors. Second, PBS emphasizes skill building and environmental engineering as major strategies for interventions. Both are viewed as critical for maintaining the desired outcomes in the environmental context of the individual. Third, PBS treatment plans are comprehensive, usually involving multiple intervention components; this stands to reason, as challenging behaviors are viewed to be multidimensional in their etiology. Fourth, PBS holds a broad view of intervention success, looking at the meaningfulness of success in addition to the outcome of success. Fifth, PBS is process-oriented, focusing on long-term solutions and not temporary fixes. From this point of view, PBS is a commitment to a process of change, rather than simply an intervention of time-limited duration.

21.6 PBS: A Service-Delivery Model

As a service-delivery model for juvenile sexual offenders, PBS should follow the conceptual underpinnings outlined above. Using the PBS model as a framework for treatment, at the outset, a multistakeholder collaboration should identify the goals of treatment for the juvenile sexual offender. These goals would be socially relevant, based upon values that are person-centered, and designed to ultimately achieve normalization/inclusion. Next, a functional assessment should be conducted on the challenging behavior (i.e., sexual offending) that is effectively barring the individual from adaptively functioning in social settings. This functional assessment would look at the multiple contexts in which the sexual offending behavior occurs and operate to systematically identify the functional determinants maintaining its manifestation. As an outcome of the functional assessment, contextually related hypotheses regarding the functional(s) of the sexual offending behavior would be generated and prioritized and used to develop a comprehensive behavior-support plan designed to the specific needs of the individual.

This behavior-support plan would systematically outline the interventions and environmental supports needed to develop a lifestyle change for the individual, wherein prosocial behaviors would functionally serve to replace the sexual offending behavior. These interventions would be contextually derived and based upon the unique needs of the individual and would include all the skills needed to increase the likelihood of success and personal satisfaction in normative academic, occupational, social, recreational, and community settings. The environmental components of this behavior-support plan would include all those instructional methods that could be used to teach, strengthen, and expand positive behavior and the system-change methods that could be used to maximize the opportunities for these prosocial behaviors to be exhibited (Carr et al., 2002). Although PBS presents a comprehensive service-delivery model for juvenile sexual offenders, a behavior analytic formulation and assessment process is required to completely implement the approaches.

21.7 Victim to Victimizer: A Behavioral Analytic Formulation

There are very few behaviorally based explanations in the literature for understanding the effects of sexual abuse of children as well as behavioral treatment approaches. One behavior analyst has conducted research on the treatment of children identified as "sexually reactive" and with sexual predators (Lutzker, 1998). A behavior analytic understanding of the effects of sexual abuse involves understanding the traumatic nature of the abuse and the potential Pavlovian sequelae. When a child is repeatedly abused, virtually any stimulus component in the immediate environment can serve as a conditioned stimulus (CS) to elicit the emotional responses that are paired with the abuse, the unconditioned stimulus (US) (Estes and Skinner, 1941). Much of the behavior of children who are said to be "reactive" has to do with the effects of experiencing these aversive events. Certainly the emotional components of these behaviors can be attributed to reexperiencing the CS. The operant ("Skinnerian") component of the behaviors, which is expressed in a wide range of possible behaviors, from running away, aggression, property destruction, sexual predation, or even becoming a willing victim for others, can be attributed to serving as an escape function. Another possibility is that even though the behaviors may have originated as escape behaviors, they may later be reinforced and strengthened because the child may be able to exert control over others by engaging in these behaviors. The ultimate outcome of the child controlling the sexual scenario would serve as a powerful reinforcer. Such reinforcement (strengthening of behavior) would then replace the original escape-based motivation for the behavior and account for such behaviors lasting many years following the abuse and even into adulthood. This analysis would also account for the development of sexual predatory behaviors, as well as explain why it is extremely difficult to provide effective treatment and more socially acceptable replacement behaviors for these individuals.

One of the behavioral explanations for problem behaviors, and for symptoms of post–traumatic stress disorder (PTSD) in particular, is based upon the Pavlovian model in which stimuli present during the incident are paired with the abuse itself, as well as with control dimensions, being physically assaulted, fear, and the abuser (Rescorla and Wagner, 1972). The effects of the environmental stimuli as a CS, acting as the culprits in later behavior, are potentially problematic and need further analysis. The potential limitations of such an argument are that later exposure to such stimuli, or related stimuli in new environments, are as follows: (1) In order for the stimuli to continue to function as CS in new environments, stimulus generalization needs to take place and (2) continued effects of such CS over long periods of time is questionable because of the likely extinction effects that would take place as the CS is no longer paired with US (the abuse, being controlled and/or battered, fear, and the abuser). Some potential answers to these problems include the following: (1) It is possible that the stimuli in new settings may be similar enough to those in the setting where the abuse took place such that stimulus generalization may be likely; and (2) if the abuse took place in more than one setting and with more than one abuser, the possibility for generalization to take place would greatly increase. It would be helpful to provide a more expanded explanation of possible continued US effects. One possible reason for claiming that the US is continuing to be paired with the CS in the new environment is that the child continues thinking about the abuse and the abuser when exposed to the CS in new settings and, further, these events serve to elicit conditioned emotional responses (CERs), which are termed in traditional clinical terms as PTSD symptoms. A second reason could be that these stimuli serve as an operant cue (discriminative stimulus or SD) to engage in either (1) escape behavior to eliminate the thoughts of the abuse and abuser or (2) controlling or predatory behavior as a means of overcoming the thoughts of the abuse as well as the emotional effects. Such an explanation is plausible, given current knowledge of operant and Pavlovian effects, but has not been extensively applied to the effects of sexual abuse in particular in the literature. Hence, what is being proposed is a relatively novel synthesis of concepts from the field of behavior analysis. Clearly, research is needed to provide accurate behavioral accounts of the effects of sexual abuse, which can then be used to assist in more effective treatment approaches.

21.8 Relational Frame Theory

Another explanatory approach from the field of behavior analysis utilizes a relatively new theory in the field known as *relational frame theory* (RFT) (Hayes, 1991 and 1994; Healy et al., 2000, Roche and Barnes, 1997; Stewart et al., 2001). An RFT approach to the understanding of the behaviors of sexually abused children does not require the presence of an ongoing US to account for trauma-based behaviors following abuse and in new environments. Instead, the RFT approach expands upon a behavioral model known as *stimulus equivalence* (Sidman, 1992 and 1994). Stimulus equivalence is a model for understanding human abstraction abilities, in which one is capable of forming "equivalences" among a variety of items, activities, events, etc. For example, our ability to relate the printed word "baseball" to an actual baseball, a photo of one, a drawing of one, and even someone else saying the word "baseball," involves such equivalence sets. The concept, based on transitivity, can be stated in the form of: If a = b and b = c, then a = c. In RFT, the concept has been taken a step further to form such "abstractions" or "relational frames" among nonequivalent stimulus sets, such as one's knowledge that a person's height is represented by a particular number of feet and inches on a ruler or yardstick. Our ability to readily equate any measure we are given in such a way is not an "equivalence set," because the measures vary, and the points corresponding to the measure on a ruler or scale are not equivalent. Such generality and variety of possible relations is encompassed within RFT. In addition, RFT is being used as a means of constructing a behavior-analytic view of social psychology and "community belongingness" (Roche et al., 2002).

An RFT account of the effects of sexual abuse would refer to the relationship between the events of the abuse and related dimensions as discussed above (control, assault, fear, and the abuser). A relational frame would then evolve between these events, and later behavior with respect to exposure to these stimuli or subvocal or covert experiences (i.e., "cognitions") about these events would be adequate to maintain the relational frames. Corresponding behaviors, such as "reactivity," "emotional reactions or PTSD symptoms," and/or predation or victimization, would be accounted for by the experiencing of these relational frames. To the extent that there were Pavlovian processes that occurred during the abuse and that related emotional and escape behaviors occurred, one can account for the continuation of these behaviors in new environments and over long periods of time (unless treated) due to the relational frames that were developed among these classes of events or stimuli. Thus, the absence of Pavlovian or operant extinction would not require explanation in the RFT model because the behaviors are a result of relational frames that evolved and not current effects of Pavlovian CS and US. As with the more traditional Pavlovian and operant models, more research is needed to clarify the roles of these events and to develop treatment approaches.

21.9 Assessment Process and Treatment Issues: Functional Assessment

A major focus for determining treatment in the field of ABA is the use of functional assessment/analysis that leads to the identification of functionally equivalent replacement behaviors (Iwata et al., 1982; O'Neill and Horner, 1991; O'Neill et al., 1996). In this approach, one needs to identify the specific function of the behavior for the person. The behavior analyst would first specify and obtain agreement on the behaviors to be observed and then addressed in treatment. Next, a functional assessment would be conducted, which may require paper-and-pencil interviews, direct observation of the child (always recommended), and perhaps conducting various tests in a controlled setting to determine the functions of the behavior. The various functions of behavior are in four general categories: for attention, seeking tangible items or events, for escape or avoidance, and "automaticity" (i.e., feedback from the behavior itself serves to reinforce it). Such an assessment can take several days or even many weeks to clearly and conclusively identify the functions of the behavior. Once one is relatively confident that the function has been correctly identified, a treatment plan can be developed that ensures linking the treatment approach to the function. This allows for more effective and efficient treatment because the behavior analyst can more precisely identify what the person was seeking to obtain or accomplish via the functional assessment and can now identify an appropriate replacement behavior. The thinking in modern views of behavior analysis treatment, particularly in the subdiscipline known as positive behavioral support (PBS) (Turnbull et al., 1999) is to either (1) alter the environment or ecological variables to promote more desirable behavior or (2) teach the person new skills or behaviors that allows the individual to obtain the desired outcome. This approach differs from what is now considered an outdated approach of attempting to teach the child to engage in the behavior we wish to see the child engaging in and to utilize another reinforcer in the situation to promote the behavior we want to see. This approach has resulted in both failure for the child and those who are in the presence of the child such as teachers, parents, the behavior analyst, and so on. The failure is generally due to the fact that in such an approach, the child feels forced into doing something he or she does not wish to do and, in addition, is expected to like or desire the reinforcer we choose to provide instead of making what the child wants in that situation available to him or her. The older behavior-modification approach does not appear to be logical, nor does it respect the wishes or needs of the person whose behavior is to be changed.

21.10 Clinical Behavior Analysis

In a more recent approach now under development in the field of ABA is a subdiscipline being referred to as *clinical behavior analysis* (Dougher, 2000). This approach is being specifically developed to address treatment issues for more traditional client populations presenting with mental-health issues (Dougher and Hayes, 2000), and this includes the population of adjudicated sexual offenders being addressed in this volume. This approach incorporates components of behavior analysis, cognitive behavioral approaches, and functional assessment methods known as *functional analytic psychotherapy* (FAP) (Kohlenberg and Tsai, 1991). FAP is a variation of the functional assessment methods that have been briefly reviewed earlier and are geared toward more typical therapeutic interventions that may be utilized in an outpatient therapy setting in which the client can benefit from "talk therapy" approaches. Given that those who opt for therapy tend to be capable of speech, can benefit from various therapeutic modalities, and include those who can form abstractions and relate effects of past and present events, a different approach to functional assessment is warranted. Assessment using FAP methodology involves interviewing the client, utilizing questions targeted at obtaining specific types of information about the person's perceptions and feelings about present and past events that appear to lead to the person's current problems. The questions are not geared toward ascertaining DSM-IV diagnostic information for the purposes of a formal diagnosis; instead, the information sought helps the therapist understand the issues and situations for that individual, which will provide an aid to devising optimal treatment strategies. Behavior analysis emphasizes the behavior of individuals and that each individual has a unique background history of events, punishers, reinforcers, and various other influences that have resulted in how the person interacts, thinks, and feels; it also influences the various behavioral styles and, of course, behavior problems at any particular point in the person's life. For example, a young child who is never acknowledged for his or her accomplishments by his or her parents and who is never told that he or she has done a good job, and perhaps is even told that he or she is "worthless," may come to believe that this is true and develop what is typically referred to as *low self-worth* or *low self-esteem*. The consequences of this in adolescence, as we know, can be devastating and may lead to self-incriminating statements, not seeking higher education to be able to get a good job that pays well, or perhaps to self-injurious acts, drug and/or alcohol abuse, and constant feelings of worthlessness, depression, or helplessness and hopelessness. Other consequences of such early life experiences could be an anxiety disorder that the person is unable to change without outside intervention. Hence, understanding the circumstances that may have led to such depression, feelings of worthlessness, and perhaps to substance abuse, and even sexual and physical assault, would require a structured interview that can assist in answering key questions. During the functional assessment interview, the interviewer is seeking particular types of information but, of course, permits the client to lead the way in discussing issues, past events, feelings, and possible associations that are relevant to them. The role of the therapist during the interview is to ask relevant questions in a careful manner so as not to blame or unduly upset the client or challenge him or her. It is important at this point to seek clarification and pose questions that will shed light on what may have contributed to the client's current thinking and feelings, as well as the behaviors that brought him or her to treatment.

Generally there are three dimensions on which the therapist attempts to ascertain information from the client. These are: (1) global vs. specific instances (i.e., does the situation or problem appear to occur in all situations or with all people, or only in some situations or with certain people?); (2) internal vs. external locus (i.e., is the problem coming from within the person or is the problem perceived as coming from outside or environmental influences or circum-stances?); and (3) acute vs. chronic (i.e., is the problem or feeling only recent or does it occur only for a short time, or has it been going on for a relatively long period of time [usually resulting in long-term suffering or distress?). For example, in depression or helplessness, the dimensions are usually (1) global (the feeling is present every-where, with every one, and all the time); (2) internal (statements such as "it's my fault, I can't do anything right," etc.); and (3) chronic (usually the person indicates that she or he has been experiencing these feelings of depression and helplessness or hopelessness for a long time) (Follette et al., 2000). Behavior analysts are also interested in the bases for current specific behavior patterns that may result in reactivity, distancing behaviors, aggression, self-injury, and a host of other problems. One distinction is that between behaviors that may have been shaped by their consequences over time, or what is referred to as *rule-governed behavior* (Skinner, 1957). Knowledge about the function of the behavior and the likely way in which the behavior evolved for a given client is then used to address the person's presenting problems, including his or her self-concept and feelings, in the therapy sessions. This approach is embodied in a treatment method referred to as *functional analytic psychotherapy-enhanced cognitive therapy* (FECT) (Bolling et al., 2000; Kohlenberg et al., 1993).

Application of the three dimensions that are the focus of the functional assessment interview to anxiety disorders, for example, would lead to a different pattern. For instance, "panic disorder could be seen as abrupt psychophysiological responses to a general class of internal sensations, whereas specific phobias and PTSD would represent abrupt psychophysiological responses to either specific or more generalized classes of environmental events" (Forsyth, 2000).

Applying the modern approach to behavior change for children who have been victims of sexual abuse will similarly require that a functional assessment be completed with some degree of confidence that the correct function can be identified. For example, if the function of the aggressive and predatory behavior of an 11-year-old child who was the victim of sexual and physical abuse is to escape the horrors that she experienced and keeps reexperiencing in her thoughts, then an approach that uses systematic desensitization, combined with teaching more appropriate replacement behaviors that will serve to escape such emotionally laden thoughts, could be very effective. One would hope that systematic desensitization will result in lessening or hopefully eliminating the unpleasant thoughts by the process of Pavlovian extinction, and teaching replacement behaviors to accomplish avoidance of such thoughts could be a powerful treatment package for this child. The usefulness of the current PBS model for treatment of problem behaviors in children who have been sexually abused has yet to be researched directly and explicitly. In our view, applying available technology from the field of ABA to this specific problem will result in a useful and highly effective treatment approach, and we hope that this chapter will serve to prompt those in this area of work, as well as behavior analysts who are not yet working on the problem of child sexual abuse, to conduct such research.

21.11 Conclusion

This chapter has presented the juvenile justice system with an effective and empirical model that utilizes integrated approaches for assessment and treatment of juvenile sexual offenders. In this model, PBS is the overarching delivery system that would lead to day-to-day intervention to promote prosocial behaviors. The focus is on the development and acquisition of skills that foster socialization and integration in natural community settings. Also, systems changes would be made to support these newly acquired skills and to promote lifestyle change in order to prevent recidivism. Outcome efficacy of this model needs to evaluate behavior change, long-term changes, community safety, and reduction of recidivism rates.

This comprehensive model proposed for the juvenile justice system offers it the opportunity to revise its current punitive image and shift to a perceived role of a provider of caring and positive treatment services. Administrators and policy decision makers need to strongly consider the function of the juvenile justice system and consider the development of new trends for the 21st century.

References

Baer, D.M., Wolf, M.M., and Risley, T.R. (1968). Some current dimensions of applied behavior analysis. *Journal of Applied Behavior Analysis*, 1, 91–97.

Bambara, L. and Knoster, T. (1998). Designing positive behavior support plans. *Innovations,* 13. Washington, D.C.: American Association on Mental Retardation.

Bolling, M., Kohlenberg, R.J., and Parker, C. (2000). Depression: a radical behavioral analysis and treatment approach. In Dougher, M. (Ed.), *Clinical Behavior Analytic Approach to Treatment.* Reno, NV: Context Press.

Carr, E.G., Dunlap, G., Horner, R.H., Koegel, R.L., Turnbull, A.P., Sailor, W., Anderson, J.L., Albin, R.W., Koegel, L.K., and Fox, L. (2002). Positive behavior support: evolution of an applied science. *Journal of Positive Behavior Interventions*, 4(1), 4–15, 20.

Carr, E.G., Horner, R.H., Turnbull, A.P., Marquis, J., Magito-McLaughlin, D., McAtee, M.L., Smith, C.E., Anderson-Ryan, K., Ruef, M.B., and Doolabh, A. (1999). Positive Behavior Support for People with Developmental Disabilities: A Research Synthesis. Washington, D.C.: American Association on Mental Retardation.

Dougher, M.J. (Ed.) (2000). *Clinical Behavior Analysis.* Reno, NV: Context Press.

Dougher, M.J. and Hayes, S.C. (2000). Clinical behavior analysis. In Dougher, M. (Ed.), *Clinical Behavior Analytic Approach to Treatment.* Reno, NV: Context Press.

Estes, W.K. and Skinner, B.F. (1941). Some quantitative properties of anxiety. *Journal of Experimental Psychology*, 29, 390–400.

Follette, W.V., Naugle, A.E., and Linneroth, P.J. (2000). Functional alternatives to traditional assessment and diagnosis. In Dougher, M. (Ed.), *Clinical Behavior Analytic Approach to Treatment.* Reno, NV: Context Press.

Forsyth, J.P. (2000). A process-oriented approach to the etiology, maintenance and treatment of anxiety disorders. In Dougher, M. (Ed.), *Clinical Behavior Analytic Approach to Treatment.* Reno, NV: Context Press.

Hayes, S.C. (1991). A relational control theory of stimulus equivalence. In Hayes, L.J. and Chase, P.N. (Eds.), *Dialogues on Verbal Behavior: Proceedings on the 1st International Institute on Verbal Relations.* Reno, NV: Context Press.

Hayes, S.C. (1994). Relational Frame Theory: A functional approach to verbal events. In Hayes, S.C. and Hayes, L.J. (Eds.), *Behavior Analysis of Language and Cognition.* Reno, NV: Context Press. pp. 9–30.

Healy, O., Barnes-Holmes, D., and Smeets, P.M. (2000). Derived relational responding as generalized operant behavior. *Journal of the Experimental Analysis of Behavior,* 74, 207–227.

Horner, R.H., Dunlap, G., Koegel, R.L., Carr, E.G., Sailor, W., Anderson, J., Albin, R.W., and O'Neill, R.E. (1990). Toward a technology of "nonaversive" behavioral support. *Journal of the Association for Persons with Severe Handicaps,* 15(3), 125–132.

Iwata, B.A., Dorsey, M.F., Slifer, K.J., Bauman, K.E., and Richman, G.S. (1982). Towards a functional analysis of self-injury. *Analysis and Intervention in Developmental Disabilities,* 2, 3–20.

Kern, L., Childs, K.E., Dunlap, G., Clarke, S., and Falk, G.D. (1994). Using assessment-based curricular intervention to improve the classroom behavior of a student with emotional and behavioral challenges. *Journal of Applied Behavior Analysis,* 27, 7–19.

Koegel, L.K., Koegel, R.L., and Dunlap, G. (1996). *Positive Behavior Support.* Baltimore, MD: Brookes.

Kohlenberg, R.J. and Tsai, M. (1991). Functional analytic psychotherapy: creating intense and curative therapeutic relationships. New York: Plenum Press.

Kohlenberg, R.J., Tsai, M., and Dougher, M.J. (1993). The dimensions of clinical behavior analysis. *The Behavior Analyst,* 271–282.

Knopp, F.H., Rosenberg, J., and Stevenson, W. (1986). Report on Nationwide Survey of Juvenile and Adult Sex-Offender Treatment Programs and Providers. Orwell, VT: Safer Society Press.

Knoster, T.P. and McCurdy, B.L. (2002). Best practices in functional behavioral assessment. In Thomas, A. and Grimes, J. (Eds.), *Best Practices in School Psychology IV.* Washington, D.C.: The National Association of School Psychologist.

Lane, S. (1997). The sexual abuse cycle. In G. Ryan and S. Lane (Eds.), *Juvenile Sexual Offenders: Causes, Consequences and Correction.* San Francisco, CA: Jossey-Bass. pp. 77–121.

Laws, D.R. (Ed.) (1989). *Relapse Prevention with Sex Offenders.* New York: The Guilford Press.

Lyle O'Brien, C., O'Brien, J., and Mount, B. (1997). Person-centered planning has arrived ... or has it? *Mental Retardation,* 35, 480–484.

Lutzker, J.R. (Ed.) (1998). *Child Abuse: A Handbook of Theory, Research and Treatment.* New York: Plenum Press.

Meyer, L.H., Peck, C.A., and Brown, L. (Eds.) (1991). *Critical Issues in the Lives Of People with Severe Disabilities.* Baltimore, MD: Paul Brookes.

O'Neill, R.E. and Horner, R.H. (1991). Generalized reduction of difficult behaviors: analysis and intervention in a competing behaviors framework. *Journal of Developmental and Physical Disabilities,* 3(1), 5–21.

O'Neill, R.E., Horner, R.H., Albin, R.W., Spraque, J.R., Storey, K., and Newton, J.S. (1996). *Functional Assessment and Program Development for Problem Behavior* 2nd ed. Pacific Grove, CA: Brooks/Cole.

Pithers, W.D., Kashima, K.M., Cumming, G.F., and Beal, L.S. (1988). Relapse prevention: a method of enhancing maintenance of change in sex offenders. In Salter, A.C. (Ed.), *Treating Child Sex Offenders and Victims: A Practical Guide.* Newbury Park, CA: Sage. pp. 131–170.

Rescorla, R.A. and Wagner, A.R. (1972). A theory of Pavlovian conditioning: variations in the effectiveness of reinforcement and nonreinforcement. In Black, A.H. and Prokasy, W.F. (Eds.), *Classical Conditioning II: Current Research and Theory.* New York: Appleton-Century-Crofts. pp. 64–99.

Roche, B. and Barnes, D. (1997). A transformation of respondently conditioned stimulus function in accordance with arbitrarily applicable relations. *Journal of Experimental Analysis of Behavior,* 67, 275–301.

Roche, B., Barnes-Holmes, Y., Barnes-Holmes, D., Stewart, I., and O'Hora, D. (2002). Relational frame theory: a new paradigm for the analysis of social behavior. *The Behavior Analyst,* 25(1), 75–91.

Ryan, G. (1999). Treatment of sexually abusive youth: The evolving consensus. *Journal of Interpersonal Violence,* 14(4), 422–436.

Scotti, J.R. and Meyer, L.H. (1999). *Behavioral Intervention: Principles, Models, and Practices.* Baltimore, MD: Brookes.

Sidman, M. (1992). Equivalence relations: Some basic considerations. In Hayes, S.C. and Hayes, L.J. (Eds.), *Understanding Verbal Relations.* Reno, NV: Context Press. pp. 15-27.

Sidman, M. (1994). *Equivalence Relations and Behavior: A Research Story.* Boston, MA: Authors Cooperative.

Skinner, B.F. (1957). *Verbal Behavior.* New York: Appleton-Century-Crofts.

Smull, M.W. and Harrison, S.B. (1992). Supporting People with Severe Retardation in the Community. Alexandria, VA: National Association of State Mental Retardation Program Directors.

Stewart, I., Barnes-Holmes, D., Roche, B., and Smeets, P.M. (2001). Generating derived relational networks via the abstraction of common physical properties: A possible model of analogical reasoning. *The Psychological Record,* 51(3).

Stickrod Gray, A. and Pithers, W. (1993). Relapse prevention with sexually aggressive adolescents and children: expanding treatment and supervision. In Barbaree, H.E., Marshall, W.L., and Hudson, S.M. (Eds.), *The Juvenile Sex Offender.* New York: The Guilford Press. pp. 289–319.

Turnbull, A.P., Turnbull, H.R., Shank, M., and Leal, D. (1999). *Exceptional Lives: Special Education in Today's Schools.* 2nd ed. Upper Saddle River, NJ: Merril/Prentice Hall.

Wacker, D.P. and Berg, W.K. (2002). PBS as a service delivery system. *Journal of Positive Behavior Interventions,* 4(1), 25–28.

Chapter 22

The Complexities of Juvenile Justice and Delinquency Research in American Indian Communities

Lisa Bond-Maupin

22.1 Introduction

According to the 2000 U.S. census, there are 2.4 million American Indians in the United States, and about half of this population lives on or adjacent to reservation communities. The American Indian population in the United States is relatively young. Almost half (43 percent) of American Indians are under the age of 20 (Coalition for Juvenile Justice, 2000). They represent 558 sovereign tribes or nations, each with a unique history, culture, and relationship to state and federal government. These factors combine to make discussions of American Indian delinquency and juvenile justice both important and complex.

Juvenile justice as it is understood in the larger culture is a relatively new idea in American Indian communities. The indigenous tribal peoples of what is now the United States had elaborate and strong systems of law and social control based on shared cultural values and beliefs and a strong sense of identification with one another. Through a series of federal policies, the U.S. government worked at supplanting these systems, first with direct federal control, and later by providing tribal leaders with incentives to model their legal systems after those found throughout the United States. Until relatively recently, the legal status and treatment of juveniles was not necessarily distinguishable from those of adults in these formal systems of justice. As the result of centuries of resistance and persistence on the part of Indian peoples, many tribal governments today control most aspects of their juvenile and criminal justice systems and are investing new-found resources in the development of culturally relevant and meaningful approaches to delinquency and justice.

American Indian youth experience disproportionate rates of victimization by violence and arrest in communities off reservations. On and near reservation communities, American Indian youth crisscross into multiple legal jurisdictions and may be simultaneously under the surveillance of tribal, federal, municipal, county, and state legal authorities, resulting in higher rates of contact with the police. Because of the legacy of inadequate federal support and limited tribal resources within some reservation communities, they may still experience the inadequate services and programs that plague rural communities throughout the United States, resulting in relatively high rates of detention and placement away from their homes. In other reservation communities, detention is relatively rare, and tribal members are creating a range of services designed to keep youth at home. The story of delinquency and juvenile justice for American Indian youths is as complex and varied as these young people and their diverse communities.

This chapter provides an overview of some of the key legal and political actions that have given form to the sometimes perplexing jurisdictional and justice issues facing American Indian communities today. It also includes a review of the state of the research literature on delinquency and juvenile justice processing of American Indian youths, and a discussion of the implications of the limitations of this research for future inquiry. The chapter ends with a brief discussion of what tribes and nations are struggling with and accomplishing as they work to strengthen their sovereign status and create policies and programs to meet the needs of the families and youth of their communities.

22.2 Policy and Legal Context for Understanding Jurisdiction and Juvenile Justice in American Indian Communities

22.2.1 Introduction

Throughout history, U.S. Indian policy has sought to remake Indian communities in the image of the states of the union, each with elected officials, majority rule, and systems of formal law that were superseded by federal mandate (Deloria and Lytle, 1983; Peak, 1989). The aboriginal peoples of North America were viewed by U.S. policymakers as lawless and in need of the "civilizing" effects of law (Peak, 1989). As Chief Justice Marshall of the U.S. Supreme Court wrote in 1823, it was assumed by citizens of the United States that Indian people, as is customary in conquest, would be "incorporated with the victorious nation, and become subjects or citizens of the government with which they are connected" (Prucha, 1990, p. 37). Each period of U.S. Indian policy has included legislation and high court rulings designed to transplant Western legal structures to Indian communities.

Most contemporary Indian communities have legal codes, police forces, jails, and courts closely resembling those found in any municipality or county in the United States. These formal systems of social control are very different from the traditional systems that existed among Indian peoples. Yet, in spite of the pervasiveness of these Anglo-American institutions, some tribes have managed to sustain much of their strong and rich tradition (Strickland, 1975; Chaudhuri, 1982). Many tribes and nations are investing in their youth and juvenile justice systems by developing alternative approaches to delinquency based on more traditional approaches to social control. "In one way or another, American Indians have resisted the political and cultural intrusions of colonizing Western societies ... [in order to] maintain control over territory and to preserve political and cultural autonomy" (Champagne, 1989, p. 1).

The story of criminal and juvenile justice in American Indian nations is one of simultaneous imposition of and resistance to Western ideologies and corresponding legal structures. Issues related to delinquency and juvenile justice in American Indian communities today can best be understood in this context of federal control, resistance, and ongoing work to preserve and strengthen the tribal sovereignty established early on through treaties.

22.2.2 The Transformation of Legal Forms and Structures in Indian Nations

Indian nations were viewed by early U.S. policymakers as possessing no legal system or formal system of social control (Deloria and Lytle, 1983). In 1869, one of the U.S. Army officers stationed in "Indian Territory" wrote to federal officials that Indian leaders had no real authority because "there is no code in any tribe which enables a chief to exercise authority, nor is there any system of punishment to compel obedience" (Fritz, 1963, p. 22). U.S. leaders often failed to "give the Indians credit for following a higher and more sophisticated under-standing of the mechanisms of human social interaction" (Deloria and Lytle, 1984, p. 27). They did not acknowledge the elaborate and ageless law of the indigenous people nor the devastation to traditional social organization caused by Anglo encroachment.

At the close of the 18th century, the newly formed U.S. government began to institute a series of policies that would result in the supplant-ing of traditional Indian ways of self-government and decision making. Indian tribes were redefined in U.S. courts as possessing only limited sovereignty, and official policy focused on remaking traditional com-munities in the image of the states of the new union.

Western legal philosophy and form was progressively imposed through the following mechanisms: The General Crimes Act, Indian police forces, courts of Indian offenses, The Major Crimes Act, The Dawes Act, The Indian Reorganization Act, termination and tribal court autonomy, The Indian Civil Rights Act, The Indian Self-Determination and Education Assistance Act, and *Oliphant v. Suquamish*. The legal status of Indian people on reservations and the complex nature of juvenile and criminal jurisdiction in "Indian country" today are best understood in the context of this history of federal policy.

The General Crimes Act of 1817 dictated that offenses committed on Indian land were to be defined and processed as those committed anywhere else in the United States. Both state and federal courts were given jurisdiction to try these cases (Peak, 1989, p. 394). This policy marked the beginning of attempts to replace traditional Indian systems of self-government and living law with federal control and Western approaches to social control.

Following the Civil War in the United States, the westward move-ment of U.S. citizens gained momentum and Indian reservations were created. This "inception of reservation life ... brought extensive sur-veillance of [the actions of Indian people] by the U.S. Army and the Bureau of Indian Affairs (BIA). During this time, federal attempts began in earnest to provide reservation justice and order maintenance via an Indian criminal justice system" (Peak, 1989, p. 396).

In 1869, Commissioner of Indian Affairs Parker argued that Indians "have been falsely impressed with the notion of national independence. It is time that this idea should be dispelled and the government cease the cruel farce of this dealing with its helpless and ignorant wards" (Peak, 1989, p. 396). The imposition of Western European notions of criminal "justice" upon Indians was one of the first Congressional attempts to "civilize" them. Formal law, along with the imposition of Anglo conformity on children through forced boarding school attendance, were seen as "gifts" given in hopes of creating "legitimate" Indian societies and members.

Without formal mechanisms for the enforcement of law, however, federal Indian agents were not able to exercise its full power. In 1877, Commissioner of Indian Affairs Hayt begged for further help from Congress and described reservation life in this way: "Civilization has loosened ... this evil continues unabated. Women are beaten and outraged, men murdered in cold blood, children are molested on their way to school. It is a disgrace to our land ... as long as by the absence of law Indian society is left without a base" (Peak, 1989, p. 396).

Around the same time that Hayt pleaded for help, Indian police forces were being created by individual Indian agents, without official Congressional approval or funding, to keep Indian people contained on the reservation. "Agent John L. Smith, among the Oto and Missouri in Nebraska, in 1866 appointed a police force of six [Indian men] to see that everything was 'kep strate'" (Fritz, 1963, p. 24). These first forces proved to be the "bulwark of the government in the administration of justice and in the preservation of order on the reservation" (Peak, 1989, p. 399).

In 1879, Congress appropriated $30,000 for 480 new Indian police officers on reservations. They were required to dress and behave as the white man and were given the following duties:

> Removal of squatters' stakes; driving out cattle, horse, and timber thieves; escorting survey parties; stopping bootleggers; keeping agents informed of deaths, births, and strangers in town; making arrests for wife-beating and drunkenness; and serving as guards at ration and annuity distributions. Some assignments were certain to create enmity with fellow tribesmen, such as determining whether people were working hard enough to merit rations of sugar, coffee, and tobacco. (Peak, 1989, p. 397)

Indian police officers were also eventually charged with enforcing the federal policy of mandatory day or boarding school attendance and in many communities were active in apprehending "truants" and returning them to school.

In 1880, Congress authorized 800 police officers, and, by 1881, 72 percent of all Indian reservations had Indian police forces. Law enforcement activity into the late 1800s and early 1900s focused on violations of laws prohibiting alcohol on the reservation. In fact, a BIA Liquor Suppression Office was created to lend support to the efforts of the Indian police (Peak, 1989, p. 400). Liquor suppression laws resulted in incredible rates of arrest for Indian people on the reservations. In 1942, these rates of arrest were three times higher than in white society and over half of all Indian people had been convicted of liquor violations. By 1978, "most tribal court proceedings involved minor alcohol-related charges" (Peak, 1989, p. 401–403). The criminalization of alcohol legally prohibited Indian people from integrating the white man's intoxicants into their communities or developing their own regulations regarding alcohol consumption. "Most reservation and urban Indian populations still do not have a culturally relative perspective on alcohol" (French, 1982, p. 127).

Courts of Indian Offenses were established in 1882 "to formulate rules for the suppression of certain practices considered a hindrance to the civilization of the tribes" such as "sun dancing, medicine making, polygamy, and the sale of wives" (Peak, 1989, p. 398). These courts, although they had no basis in federal statute, were also charged by the secretary of the interior with promoting acculturation (Fritz, 1963; Peak, 1989). A federal court judge described these courts as "educational and disciplinary instrumentalities by which the government is endeavoring to improve and elevate the condition of these dependent tribes to whom it sustains the relation of guardian" (Peak, 1989, p. 399).

The Major Crimes Act passed in 1885 brought the contrasting characteristics of Indian and Anglo-American law into the public light, offending the "sensibilities" of "proper" white people (Peak, 1989, p. 398). The Major Crimes Act gave the federal government exclusive power to try and punish Indian people living on reservations for seven serious offenses. Since then, the number of offenses on reservations under federal jurisdiction has increased to include the following: murder, manslaughter, maiming, rape, involuntary sodomy, felonious sexual molestation of a minor, assault with intent to kill, arson, burglary, larceny, kidnapping, carnal knowledge of any female (not his wife) under 16 years old, assault with attempt to commit rape, incest, assault with a dangerous weapon, assault resulting in serious bodily injury, and robbery. Indian people of all ages charged with one of these fourteen offenses are tried in federal courts and serve their sentences under federal supervision. "The Act also brought federal law enforcement officers into the reservation and forbade tribal governments from using traditional punishments for criminal acts" (Peak, 1989, p. 399). The constitutionality of the Major Crimes Act was challenged shortly after its enactment. The U.S. Supreme Court ruling upholding its constitutionality (*United States v. Kagama*, 1886) provided official affirmation for assimilationist federal Indian policy and paved the way for the Dawes Act (Fritz, 1963, p. 217).

The Dawes Act of 1887 called for the allotment of reservation land in small parcels to Indian family heads to "encourage" the development of family farms. This policy officially imposed the foreign concept of private ownership and the corresponding property rights central to Anglo-American law. Ostensibly, under this policy, once Indian people learned to succeed at farming, they would become full and independent citizens of the United States under the jurisdiction of the states in which they resided (with the exception of the major crimes).

The Indian Reorganization Act of 1934 represented a policy shift back toward tribal "self-government." Under the provisions of this act, "tribes were to draft their own laws and constitutions, establish their own traditional court system, and revitalize their old customs" (Peak, 1989, p. 400). Indian people were placed under the legislative and adjudicatory powers of the reorganized tribal governments. Although the federal government retained jurisdiction over major crimes committed on reservations, tribes created their own legal codes defining those offenses under tribal court jurisdiction, outlining court procedures and appropriate sanctions. Secretary-of-the-interior approval of tribal constitutions served the organizational maintenance requirements of the BIA. The act actually increased the scope of federal intrusion and power over tribal affairs in that "processes and problems that had formerly been handled by community consensus were now formalized and required tribal resolutions and secretarial approval" (Deloria and Lytle, 1983, p. 102).

In 1953, the federal policy of termination gave criminal and civil jurisdiction of Indian lands to state court systems in five states and parts of other states. However, in the late 1950s tribal court authority and autonomy was reaffirmed (Peak, 1989, p. 402). In federal court cases continuing into the 1970s, "deference was given to the judgment of tribal courts, thus requiring exhaustion of tribal remedies before redress could be sought in the federal court system and precluding action by the state involving activities on the reservation" (Peak, 1989, p. 402). In 1968, presidential candidate Richard Nixon introduced the concept of Indian "self-determination" into Indian policy rhetoric. These developments, coupled with studies on "Indian criminality" that found the Indian arrest rate to be up to ten times that of whites (Reasons, 1972), contributed to $2.5 million being given to Indian criminal justice agencies through the Omnibus Crime Control and Safe Streets Act of 1968 to "fight crime" on the reservations (Peak, 1989, p. 402).

Also in 1968, the Indian Civil Rights Act (ICRA) was passed. The ICRA was "billed as a measure for the furtherance of self-determination, …. In reality it constrained the workings of the tribal courts, which were held under the act to much tighter due process standards" (Peak, 1989, p. 402). In addition, the act profoundly limited the sanctions available to tribal courts. It read: "(1) no tribe shall imprison a convicted offender in excess of six months or exact a fine of over $500 and (2) habeas corpus is available to any Indian who wants to test (in federal courts) the legality of his detention by a tribe" (Brakel, 1982, p. 148). The ICRA constrained the autonomy of tribal courts and introduced the foreign concept of rights against tribal governments. The results of a 1978 survey of the tribal courts on 23 reservations included the following illustrations of the failings of these federally constituted courts:

> Often, Congressional funds earmarked for tribal courts — after being tapped at the BIA level — were diverted to the police …. There was a high rate of guilty pleas … and in most courts surveyed, attorneys appeared less than ten times per year, and some had never had an attorney present at trial ….The collection of evidence by police was often done casually; only three reservations had formal rules of evidence, and hearsay was admitted in all courts surveyed …. Fines were the most common form of punishment, traditional forms of justice being used only rarely. (Peak, 1989, p. 403)

In the 1970s, several federal court decisions attempted to articulate the Congressional intent in the Indian Civil Rights Act. In *Lohnes v. Cloud* (1973) the judge ruled that "While [the ICRA] has indeed encroached upon, and redefined tribal sovereignty, it is clear that the act is not meant to substitute a federal forum for the tribal court" (Peak, 1989, p. 403). *Ortiz-Barraza v. U.S.* (1975) reaffirmed that a tribe has full criminal jurisdiction over its members on the reservations, "subordinate only to the expressed limitations of federal law" (Peak, 1989, p. 403). In 1977, the U.S. Supreme Court in *Oliphant v. Suquamish* (1977) ruled "that tribal courts lacked inherent jurisdiction to try and punish non-Indian criminal offenders [who offend in their communities]" (Peak, 1989, p. 404). In this case, the majority justices held that Indian tribes fall under the "authority" of the United States and that "by submitting to the overriding sovereignty of the United States, Indian tribes therefore necessarily give up their power to try non-Indian citizens of the United States, except in a manner acceptable to Congress" (Peak, 1989, p. 404). Today, tribal courts have no jurisdiction over non-Indians who commit offenses on reservations.

The Indian Self-Determination and Education Assistance Act of 1975 provided that tribes could contract with the federal government, through the BIA, to operate programs or functions, including criminal justice entities such as police forces, jails, and juvenile detention facilities. The BIA remained responsible for approving these contracts, the budgets involved, and for monitoring and evaluating the "effectiveness and efficiency" of these tribal operations. In fact, according to Nelson and Sheley (1982, p. 77), during the years since the enactment of this act, "the BIA has maintained and increased its dominance over Indians through (1) a planning orientation suited more to its bureaucratic needs than to tribal needs and (2) the conversion of tribes themselves to a bureaucratic planning orientation."

In 1978, the Indian Child Welfare Act (ICWA) was ratified. This act primarily reestablished tribal control and jurisdiction in cases involving the removal of Indian children from their homes. It also provided for tribal representatives to have input into the cases involving the termination of parental rights for American Indian children in state courts. Youths charged with running away or truancy are also protected under ICWA and have a right to have these cases heard in a tribal court. If the child lives off the reservation, under ICWA, the tribe retains concurrent jurisdiction with the state court. In 1983, the National Indian Child Welfare Association was established and began providing technical assistance and training to child welfare workers on and off reservations.

As what has been called the "self-determination" era of federal policy toward American Indians began in the 1970s, many tribes expanded existing tribal legal codes to include children's codes, and tribal courts began hearing juvenile cases in a manner distinct from adult cases. Tribal social service and child welfare agencies developed under contract with the BIA. Most of the codes and the structure of these new tribal departments were modeled after the children's codes and social services systems of the states in closest proximity to the tribe.

In 1986, tribal governments began successfully asserting concurrent jurisdiction over those major crimes that were under federal jurisdiction, and tribal sanctions allowed by the federal government for adults and juveniles were increased to a maximum of 1-year confinement or $1000 fine. Juveniles in American Indian reservation communities may be (and are) adjudicated and sentenced in both tribal and federal court for major crimes. American Indian youth on reservations are the only category of youth in the United States not protected from this unique form of double jeopardy by the U.S. Constitution or the Indian Civil Rights Act. Into the 1980s, through the BIA Law Enforcement Division, funding was made available to tribal governments to build detention centers and adult jails on reservations. Other nations eventually used gaming and other revenues to create their own tribal detention centers independent of federal oversight. Prior to this, the BIA was operating what have been described as "iron box"–style jails built decades before, perhaps with a designated cell for juveniles. Also during this decade, many tribal governments assumed control of their police forces, further minimizing the role of the BIA in their criminal and juvenile justice systems.

In 1988, the Native American Pass-Through Program was established by amendment to the Juvenile Justice and Delinquency Prevention Act of 1974. Under the state formula grant program, states are required to make grant money available to tribes:

> The amount that must be made available is based on the ratio of the number of Indian juveniles within a state's boundaries compared to the total number of juveniles within that state. Funding under the pass-through program may go toward a variety of areas such as prevention control or reduction of juvenile delinquency, apprehension efforts, and activities of adult and juvenile corrections, probation, and parole authorities. (Nighthorse, 1997)

Into the 1990s many American Indian nations focused on economic development, self-government, and the expansion and improvement of tribal programs. Those tribes that were receiving revenues from gaming operations and other sources created tribal justice complexes or centers, further reclaiming juvenile and criminal justice systems in their communities. Some tribal government officials resisted grant monies passed through the state, identifying this as a threat to their sovereignty.

Representatives of tribal governments spoke out during U.S. Senate hearings about their ongoing struggles to develop meaningful, comprehensive, and effective approaches to dealing with what they were experiencing as a growing problem with juvenile delinquency. These representatives urged federal officials to provide designated money directly to tribal governments rather than giving state governments control over its distribution (Senate Oversight Hearing, April 1997). The Office of Juvenile Justice and Delinquency Prevention (OJJDP) of the U.S. Department of Justice responded to this pressure by tribal representatives by increasing direct funds for tribal juvenile justice initiatives and American Indian juvenile delinquency and justice research.

In the 1990s the Department of Justice and OJJDP created a variety of initiatives designed to fund juvenile justice system improvement efforts among tribes, and in 1999 implemented the Tribal Youth Program through OJJDP, awarding nearly $8 million that year to tribal entities in the form of grants for initiatives to prevent and control juvenile delinquency. The Tribal Youth Program includes funding for research on delinquency and juvenile justice issues in Indian communities. In part due to recognition of the profound limitations of Uniform Crime Report (UCR) data for understanding juvenile delinquency in Indian communities, and at the encouragement of American Indian scholars and tribal representatives, OJJDP provides funding not only for research across Indian communities, but also for tribal-specific research that involves and has the potential to be of use to tribal officials themselves. "This recent shift in policy seeks to empower tribes to combat crime at the local level by enhancing programs designed to better their own justice systems, just as the department does with state and local government" ([Araujo, cited in] Baca, 2001).

22.3 Resisting Generalization

When discussing the development of contemporary criminal and juvenile justice systems in Indian communities, it is important to note that there are varying degrees of "legal acculturation" among tribes across the United States, partly attributed to the relative geographic and social isolation of a given community (Lujan, 1991). Also, there are differences in legal jurisdiction across Indian communities (Chaudhuri, 1982). For example, "In 1978, when Congress created a new reservation for the Pascua Yaquis near Tucson, AZ, it did not extend ordinary law enforcement powers in nonfelonious contexts to the tribe but maintained the enforcement jurisdiction of the state enforcement agencies" (Chaudhuri, 1982, p. 11).

Despite the overwhelming force leveled by the federal government, many Indian communities continue to utilize more traditional forms of intratribal dispute resolution, apparently preferring to avoid the dominant system (Peak, 1989, p. 398). Some of these communities still "place a great emphasis on tolerance of other peoples' wrongdoing as a way to avoid employing more formal methods of social control" (Lujan, 1991, p. 13). As Chaudhuri so aptly puts it:

> [T]he evolution, adaptation, and persistence of Indian customary relationships, in spite of the overwhelming nature of Anglo-American law, illustrate the great distance between formal legal prescription and Indian behavior .... The normative suppositions of Indian "living law" and American Indian "positive" law continue to be quite different. (Chaudhuri, 1982, p. 10)

The 558 federally recognized tribes vary profoundly in the extent to which they rely on traditional systems of social control. Traditional forms of conflict resolution and responses to deviance vary greatly across Indian nations. Reliance on traditional forms of dispute or conflict resolution is more common among isolated groups on larger reservations, but takes varying forms (Zatz, et al., 1991, p. 102). In addition, not all Indian people view formal, Western law and judicial practices as just or relevant. The extent to which members of Indian communities relate to law enforcement and the courts as "foreign" will also impact reliance on these mechanisms of control, reflected in varying rates of reporting crime (Zatz et al., 1991, p. 104).

Additional factors making generalizations about crime and justice very difficult include the size of the reservation, the extent to which Indian youth and adults are subject to multiple jurisdictions and police forces, the economic stability of a tribe and its relative resources, and the proximity of the Indian community to an urban area. In addition, depending on their proximity to nonreservation communities and their relationship with the state and federal governments, some reservation residents are subject to surveillance by tribal, federal, city, and state law enforcement, whereas others are subjected only to tribal and federal law enforcement. Indian communities also vary in the operation of law as applied to bingo and casino establishments and revenues from settlements in disputes with states and the federal government over land and other natural resources.

22.4 Research on American Indian Delinquency and Juvenile Justice

22.4.1 Introduction

On the cover of the recent Bureau of Justice Statistics (BJS) report entitled *American Indians and Crime* (Greenfeld and Smith, 1999) is a graph depicting that American Indians over 12 years of age are twice as likely to be victims of violent crime than members of all other racial or ethnic categories combined. This report has been widely cited in recent newspaper articles and federal announcements as evidence that crime among Indians is escalating. Often excluded from summaries of this report is the additional and startling finding that when American Indians are the victims of violent crime, it is most often non-Indians who are the perpetrators, and the highest rates of violence are in urban settings (Greenfeld and Smith, 1999):

> While it is important to recognize the significance and scope of this report, it is limited by the fact that about two-thirds of American Indian people live on or adjacent to largely rural reservations (Armstrong et al., 1992), candidates for the small population subgroups that the federal surveys used for this report likely do not measure (Greenfield and Smith, 1999, p. 36). In addition, because the median age for American Indians is eight years younger than the median age for the United States population in general, there is a need for more specific information on youth and crime in reservation communities.

22.4.2 Review of the Literature

There are two published studies of delinquency and American Indians, supplementing federal arrest data with tribal data (Minnis, 1963; Peak and Spencer, 1987). Minnis (1963) examined arrest rates from 1934 to 1960 using tribal law enforcement data to supplement the UCR. Comparing the United States with tribal data, the author found lower rates of arrest among Indian people for all but three categories of offense: "personal demoralization (drunkenness, vagrancy, disorderly conduct, etc.)," offenses related to the operation of a motor vehicle ("driving while drunk, traffic, etc."), and juvenile status offenses ("truancy, juvenile mischief, incorrigible") (Minnis, 1963, p. 401).

Peak and Spencer (1987) examined both UCR data from 1976 to 1985, and BIA arrest figures for 207 reservations in 1983. Using the UCR, they noted a rise in illegal activity among Indian juveniles off the reservation from 1976 to 1980 and a decline from 1980 to 1985. Although the authors blur adult and juvenile statistics in their discussion of on-reservation findings, their study is one of the most recent and extensive examinations of arrests on reservations. They found that "69% of the actual offenses that were investigated in 1982 involved the use of alcohol or drugs" with public intoxication accounting for almost one-third of all arrests (Peak and Spencer, 1987, p. 401). Arrests for disorderly conduct were the most frequent (45 percent), followed by drunkenness.

In a more recent study using UCR data, Flowers (1988) found that American Indian youths were arrested at a rate slightly higher than their representation in the U.S. population. This disproportionate representation in arrest for American Indian youths was also found in O'Brien's (1977) study of juvenile arrests in Oregon. In Oregon this overrepresentation was explained mostly by higher rates of arrest for status offenses and victimless crimes among Indian youths. These disparities were found by Poupart (1995) to carry through the juvenile justice process when American Indian youths are arrested in off-reservation communities. In her study of one rural county in Wisconsin, "American Indian youths were more likely to receive the more severe outcome" at multiple decision points. "The greatest disparity occurred at the [decision to prosecute]. White juveniles were significantly more likely to have their cases closed or resolved informally, whereas American Indian juveniles were more likely to have their cases referred to a prosecutor for additional handling" (Poupart, 1995, p. 197).

Other research on Indian delinquency utilizes self-report or survey data from youth living on reservations. Forslund and Cranston (1975) collected self-report data on delinquency from Indian and Anglo high school students on the Wind River reservation in Wyoming. This self-report study was a follow-up to Forslund and Meyers' (1974) article in which the authors concluded that "the officially recorded delinquency rate of Indian youth from [this reservation] is relatively high compared to that of the general American population" (Forslund and Cranston, 1975, p. 193). In their self-report study "delinquency" included 29 acts, primarily status, minor, and property offenses, and were mostly school related. In comparing self-reported delinquency between Indian and Anglo youths, they found that school-based offenses (truancy, theft from desks and lockers, fighting) and drug use were most common among Indian youths, and that Indian girls were more likely to have run away from home or committed minor theft or vandalism than Anglo girls. A higher proportion of Anglo males reported drinking alcohol and making anonymous telephone calls.

> In a ten-year study involving over fifty Indian reservations, Oetting and Beauvais (1985) surveyed all seventh through twelfth graders in reservation schools regarding their use of alcohol and drugs. Comparing the prevalence of use data on Indian youth with results from a "moderate sized, Western non-Indian community," the authors found that "a greater percentage of Indian than non-Indian youth are getting drunk" and reporting having blacked out on three or more occasions (Oetting & Beauvais, 1985, p. 5, 13). They found that "for nearly every category of drug, Indian youth have higher use rates." (Oetting and Beauvais, 1985, p. 17)

In her study of three Seminole reservation communities, Robbins (1985) found that self-reported delinquency was least common on the most rural or isolated reservation. Robbins used a measure of delinquency that included mostly property offenses ranging from theft of something worth less than $5 to taking someone's car without permission. She also included "physically hurting someone on purpose." Although she does not delineate which acts youths reported involvement in, Robbins reports that an average of 21 percent of respondents had done one of these things, and 52 percent had done more than one of these things. She concluded that these reservations had "high rates" of delinquency and that on all three "it is only a minority of youth who are *not* delinquent" [emphasis added] (Robbins, 1985, p. 60).

Using tribal arrest and detention data, Bond-Maupin et al. (1995) examined the arrest and detention of youths by law enforcement in one southwestern reservation community. They found that although all youths arrested were jailed prior to a hearing, the pervasive use of detention did not reflect the severity of the offenses for which they were charged. In this community, "74% of the charges for which youths were arrested and jailed were minor delinquency and status offenses" (Bond-Maupin et al., 1995, p. 7). In this community, "less than 11 percent of the charges ... involved serious felonies [sexual conduct with a minor was the most serious charge] ... and close to one-third of the 'offenses' ... were nondelinquency charges" (Bond-Maupin et al., 1995, p. 7).

In a second study, Bond-Maupin (1996) analyzed arrest and detention in the same community after the tribal government assumed control of the detention center under the provisions of the Indian Self Determination and Education Assistance Act. She found that even though the tribe had initiated juvenile justice system reform, all charged youths were detained regardless of the severity of their charges. During this study period, serious felonies accounted for about 10 percent (sexual assault was the most serious charge) of the arrests, whereas almost half of detained youths were charged with status offenses.

According to Andrews (2000), violent crime arrest rates for American Indian youths fell 20 percent between 1995 and 1998. However, the number of American Indian youths adjudicated and confined by federal courts rose during this period. American Indian youths comprise 60 to 70 percent of the juveniles adjudicated in federal court who are confined by the Federal Bureau of Prisons (Scalia, 1997; Andrews, 2000). "Since the federal government does not own or operate any juvenile correctional facilities, American Indian youth are often shipped to public and private facilities hundreds of miles from their homes" (Coalition for Juvenile Justice, 2000). At the close of 2000, a reported total of 189 American Indian juveniles were confined in state correctional facilities under contract with the Federal Bureau of Prisons. Using 1994 data, the BJS reports that 81 percent of the 75 American Indian youths confined by the federal government in that year were adjudicated for an offense against a person: sex offenses 32 percent, assault 28 percent, negligent manslaughter 20 percent, and robbery 1 percent (Scalia, 1997, p. 3).

These BJS reports are limited as sources of information in that they do not identify the tribal affiliation of confined youths and do not specify what percentage of those youths whose cases were dismissed or adjudicated in federal court are American Indian. These reports make it impossible to determine whether American Indian youths are more likely to be confined than their non-Indian counterparts in the federal system and to understand their delinquency in the context of a particular community. However, it is these and violent victimization data from off reservations that have prompted federal officials to come to the conclusion that violence among youths in "Indian country" is on the rise.

Some existing research on delinquency in Indian communities contradicts the notion of a serious juvenile crime wave among Indian youths. Recent longitudinal research in one reservation community in the four-corner area found no increase in the arrests of tribal youths on the reservation over an 11-year period and supported earlier research findings that most of their arrests were for the underage consumption of alcohol or related offenses (Bond-Maupin et al., 2002).

Generalizations about Indian delinquency are premature as there are profound differences across Indian peoples and too few studies accounting for too few of those differences. Armstrong et al., in their 1992 report to the OJJDP, note this "relative lack of general information and specific research findings on the causes, nature, and extent of ... delinquency among Native Americans" (p. 2). Although they propose that "the disproportionate extent to which Indian adolescents are involved in criminal and delinquent activities" is a serious problem in Indian communities, they acknowledge that the diversity of language, culture, customs, traditions, and relationship to state and local governments make generalizations difficult (Armstrong et al., 1992, p. 2). Zatz et al. (1991) also make this point in their chapter on the complexities of studying crime in Indian communities. Not only are intertribal comparisons difficult, but "research on a specific Indian population cannot be generalized to members of other tribes" (Zatz et al., 1991, p. 111).

22.4.3 Limitations of Prior Research and Implications for Ongoing Research

Because many American Indian youths living off or adjacent to reservation communities reside in rural communities, our understanding of the dynamics of their delinquency and the legal processing of youths in state systems is limited by the urban focus of the literature on racial disparity and minority overrepresentation.

> Besides diverting empirical attention away from Native Americans and other understudied groups which may be subjected to unequal treatment, the urban focus of research addressing race disparities in the juvenile justice processing serves to deflect attention from ways in which decisions may be conditioned by the particular minorities involved and/or by characteristics of the communities in which they live (Parry, 1996, p. 125).

The usefulness of urban-based or aggregate federal data is also limited owing to the relatively small percentage of American Indian youths in the general population and the corresponding tendency to identify their racial or ethnic identity as "other."

Most prior research based in reservation communities provides little to no information on the legal processing of youths beyond arrest. This profoundly limits our understanding of the juvenile justice process in Indian communities. This lack of information on juvenile justice precludes an understanding of both the formal and informal, or more traditional approaches to delinquency prevention and intervention occurring in Indian communities. Although Bond-Maupin et al. (1995) and Bond-Maupin (1996) address more informal mechanisms of social control in the community they studied, this area of inquiry is underdeveloped.

In most research using arrest statistics, the arrest is the unit of analysis. In addition, the earliest research equated arrests of any type with "criminality." These methodological limitations resulted in the harmful and misleading conclusion that Indians were the most "criminal" group in society. Research using the individual as the unit of analysis will contribute to a greater understanding of delinquency in a given community. In addition, owing to the limitations of self-report data on relatively minor offenses and a failure to distinguish among types of arrests in some prior research, there is a need for data that will account for the full range of illegal activity in which youths are involved.

Community-based research must account for the impact of the availability of services and programs on rates and types of delinquency. Bond-Maupin (1996) found that referrals to the tribal children's court tripled during the year that juvenile detention beds became available. This analysis of the changes in resources in the community should include the impact of tribes' assuming operation of legal and social service programs through contracts with the BIA. In addition, research should be able to take into account the impact of a casino on delinquency and community resources.

Research accounting for changes in communities must be longitudinal. Much prior research on delinquency among Indian youths provides a "snapshot" at a particular point in time. Research over time will make it possible to determine the extent to which the idea made popular in newspaper headlines and bylines that juvenile crime among Indians is on the rise applies in a community.

The relevance, validity, and utility of future research will depend on the involvement of Indian peoples at all stages in the research process. Community members should be involved in the development of research questions and in the design, implementation, and analysis of the implications of research. To more fully understand the informal and formal mechanisms of control in operation in an Indian community, researchers must be willing to talk with community members.

Little prior research builds upon the knowledge of tribal members about delinquency and juvenile justice in their communities. Interview and participant observation data can also provide information regarding the ways that multiple legal jurisdictions are negotiated in a given community, including the ways that concurrent and competing jurisdictions impact the arrests and legal processing of youths.

22.5 The Future of Juvenile Justice for American Indian Youths

American Indian tribes and nations continue to recognize the importance of federal funding for the ongoing development of their juvenile justice systems. Many are taking advantage of training and technical assistance and direct service funding through OJJDP. OJJDP has recently been responsive to the recommendations of tribal leaders that funding should be granted directly to tribal governments for community- and culture-specific research and intervention related to delinquency and juvenile justice. An ongoing commitment by OJJDP to funding community-specific research on delinquency and justice will provide tribal leaders with the information required to design and implement relevant and effective interventions in their communities.

Representatives of tribal social-service, law-enforcement, and mental-health agencies face the same challenges in coordinating their services as do these agencies off reservation. Some have developed or are in the process of developing interagency prevention and intervention teams to streamline services to families and youth. In addition, when reservation communities border towns and cities, tribal officials must work to collaborate with law enforcement and juvenile justice officials off reservation. Lately, this collaboration has resulted in some tribes' assuming the responsibility, through intergovernmental agreement, for intervention with or supervision of community youths charged with offenses off the reservation. When reservation communities or portions of reservation communities are relatively geographically isolated, tribal officials face the same challenges of vast distances and few local resources that rural off-reservation communities face. Some tribes have developed alternatives to police and court intervention based more closely on village or band leadership and social-control structures across relatively isolated areas of their reservations.

Newly developed economic resources have also made it possible for some tribes to develop prevention and intervention programs independent of federal priorities and beyond those modeled in off-reservation systems. These programs emphasize strengthening tribal youths' identification with their larger community, teaching traditional language, addressing the generational and cultural gap between elders and youth, and engaging youth in art, craft, fishing, farming, and other activities that are unique and important to their communities. Other tribes continue to struggle with unemployment rates that are triple those in the surrounding states, dependence on too little federal funding, legal battles to preserve their autonomy and survival, and racism in surrounding communities. Many tribes struggle with the impact of alcoholism and the use of drugs and alcohol by young people. Tribal members and their leaders understand that any meaningful work to prevent and control delinquency depends on solutions to the larger social and economic problems they face.

The direction of approaches to juvenile justice for Indian youth in reservation communities is increasingly in the hands of the leaders of their tribes and nations. These tribes and nations have resisted federal control and dominance for centuries and continue to be involved in simultaneously advocating for federal support and strengthening tribal sovereignty. Meaningful future research and policy will be shaped by Indian people themselves drawing on the best practices outside their communities as they create services and programs that meet the unique needs of the youth of their communities.

References

Andrews, C. (2000). OJJDP tribal youth program. *Juvenile Justice Journal*, VII(2).

Araujo, T. (April 2001). Cited in Kim Baca. The changing federal role in Indian country. *National Institute of Justice Journal*, 13.

Armstrong, T.L., Guilfoyle, M.H., and Melton, A.P. (1992). Native American Delinquency: An Overview of Prevalence, Causes, and Correlates, and Promising Tradition-Based Approaches to Sanctioning. Rockville, MD: National Criminal Justice Reference Service.

Bond-Maupin, L., Chiago Lujan, C., and Bortner, M.A. (1995). Jailing of American Indian adolescents. *Crime, Law and Social Change*, 23: 1–16.

Bond-Maupin, L. (1996). Who made the code in the first place?: delinquency and justice in an American Indian community. *Crime, Law and Social Change*, 25: 133–152.

Bond-Maupin, L., Maupin, J., and GoodTracks, T. (2002). Research on Native American Delinquency and Juvenile Justice: A Longitudinal Study of Delinquency and Juvenile Justice in the Southern Ute Nation. Final Report to Office of Juvenile Justice and Delinquency Prevention.

Brakel, S. (1982). American Indian tribal courts. In L. French (Ed.), *American Indians and Criminal Justice.* Totowa, New York: Allan Held, Osmun and Co. pp. 147–162.

Champagne, D. (1989). American Indian societies: strategies and conditions of political and cultural survival. Cambridge, MA: Cultural Survival.

Chaudhuri, J. (1982). American Indian policy: an overview of the legal complexities, controversies, and dilemmas. *The Social Science Journal, 19*(3), 10–21.

Coalition for Juvenile Justice (2000). Enlarging the Healing Circle: Ensuring Justice for American Indian Children, Report on the 5th Annual Ethnic and Cultural Diversity Training Workshop.

Deloria, V., Jr. and Lytle, C. (1983). *American Indians, American Justice.* Austin, TX: University of Texas Press.

Deloria, V., Jr. and Lytle, C. (1984). *The Nations within: The Past and Future of American Indian policy.* New York: Pantheon Books.

Flowers, R.B. (Ed.). (1988). *Minorities and Criminality.* New York: Greenwood.

Forslund, M.A. and Cranston, V.A. (1975). A self-report comparison of Indian and Anglo delinquency in Wyoming. *Criminology, 13*(2), 193–197.

Forslund, M.A. and Meyers, R.E. (1974). Delinquency among wind river Indian reservation youth. *Criminology, 12*(1), 97–106.

French, L. (Ed.). (1982). *Indians and Criminal Justice.* Totowa, NJ: Allan Held, Osmun and Co. pp. 19–23.

Fritz, H.E. (1963). *The Movement for Indian Assimilation, 1860–1890.* Westport, CN: Greenwood Press.

Greenfeld, L.A. and S.K. Smith, (1999). American Indians and Crime. Washington D.C.: U.S. Department of Justice, Office of Justice Programs.

Lohnes v. Cloud, 366 F. Supp. 619 (D.N.D. 1973).

Lujan, C. (1991). American Indians and imposed law: the impact of social integration on legal perceptions among two southwestern tribes [unpublished manuscript]. Arizona State University.

Minnis, M.S. (1963). The relationship of the social structure of Indian community to adult and juvenile delinquency. *Social Forces, 41,* 395–403.

Nelson, R.A. and Sheley, J.F. (1982). Current BIA influence on Indian self-determination: a criminal justice planning illustration. *The Social Science Journal, 19*(3), 73–85.

Nighthorse, B. In *Juvenile Justice in Indian Country,* Hearing before the Committee on Indian Affairs of the United States Senate, April 8, 1997, Washington, D.C. (S.Hrg. 105–140).

O'Brien, M. (1977). Indian juveniles in the state and tribal courts of Oregon. *American Indian Review,* 5: 343–367.

Oetting, E.R. and Beauvais, F. (1985). Epidemiology and correlates of alcohol use among Indian adolescents living on reservations [unpublished manuscript].

Oliphant v. Suquamash, 431 U.S. 964 (1977).

Ortiz v. Barraza, 512 F.2d 1176 (1975).

Parry, D., (1996). Race and community in juvenile justice decision making: native Americans and the convergence of minority status and rural residence. *Social Pathology*, 2(2).

Peak, K. (1989). Criminal justice, law and policy in Indian country: a historical perspective. *Journal of Criminal Justice, 17*, 393–407.

Peak, K. and Spencer, J. (1987). Crime in Indian country: another trail of tears. *Journal of Criminal Justice, 15*, 485–494.

Poupart, L.M. (1995). Juvenile justice processing of American Indian youths: disparity in one rural county. In Leonard, K.K., Pope, C.E., and Feyerherm, W.H. (Eds.), *Minorities in Juvenile Justice*. Thousand Oaks, CA: Sage.

Prucha, F.P. (1990). *Documents of United States Indian Policy*. Lincoln, NE: University of Nebraska Press.

Reasons, C. (1972). Crime and the American Indian. In Bahr, H.M., Chadwick, B.A., and Day, R.C. (Eds.), *Native Americans Today: Sociological Perspectives*. New York: Harper and Row. pp. 319–326.

Robbins, S. (1985). Commitment, belief, and Native American delinquency. *Human Organization*, 44(1): 57–62.

Scalia, John. (1997). Juvenile Delinquents in the Federal Criminal Justice System, Bureau of Justice Statistics Special Report, February (NCJ-163066).

Strickland, R. (1975). *Fire and the Spirits: Cherokee Law from Clan to Court*. Norman, OK: University of Oklahoma Press.

United States v. Kagama, 118 U.S. 375 (1886).

Zatz, M.S., Lujan, C.C., and Snyder-Joy, Z.K. (1991). American Indians and criminal justice: some conceptual and methodological considerations. In Lynch M.J. and Patterson, E.B. (Eds.), *Race and Criminal Justice*. New York: Harrow and Henton. pp. 100–112.

Chapter 23

Using Culture and Social Structure to Predict Gang Affiliation among Mexican American Adolescent Females

Rebecca D. Petersen and David Olveda

23.1 Introduction

Many in the field of criminal justice have acknowledged the rarity of studies in which females, either individually or collectively, have been the subject. Historically, the role of females in crime, especially in regard to gangs, has relegated them to nothing more than bystanders or "the other" sex. However, recent trends include more research focused on females without such pejorative and inaccurate portrayals (Campbell, 1991; Chesney-Lind and Pasko, 2003; Curry, 1998; Deschenes and Esbensen, 1999a, 1999b; Esbensen and Deschenes, 1998; Fleisher, 1998; Joe and Chesney-Lind, 1995; Miller, 1998; Miller and Decker,

2001; Moore, 1991; Petersen, 2000a, 2000b). This chapter addresses this concern by examining gang affiliation among Mexican American adolescent females.

Gang-affiliated females are neither official members of a male or female gang nor do they claim to be. Instead, they associate or affiliate with one or more gang members, usually a boyfriend, a good friend, or a family member, with some regularity and frequency. By virtue of her relationships with such individuals, she associates with gang members. Typically, research has referred to this population of young women as *auxiliaries* to or *affiliates* of male gangs.

Furthermore, exploring gang affiliation among Mexican Americans is critical given that they represent over 60 percent of all U.S. Hispanics and are experiencing consistent rapid growth (U.S. Bureau of the Census, 2000). By examining their ethnic identity, as measured by the Multigroup Ethnic Identity Measure (MEIM), and stress levels, as measured by the Hispanic Stress Inventory (HSI), this research addresses how the principles of the general strain theory (GST) might demonstrate a predictive relationship among Mexican American adolescent females, stressors, and gang affiliation.

Using GST, female gang affiliation is examined to explore how cultural variables, such as ethnic identity and stress, invoke frustration in adolescent girls that may predispose them to gang affiliation. Because GST attempts to explain delinquency and other behaviors by listing categories of strain that influence the probability of delinquent behavior, gang affiliation is observed in this context (Mazerolle, 1998).

Drawing upon previous works (Gray-Ray and Ray, 1990; Hagedorn, 1988; Vigil, 1988), links between "environmental" social factors, such as poverty and single-parent households, and ethnicity or race and gang membership, have been shown. Gang affiliation has been attributed to other social endemics, such as poverty, single-parent households or unemployment, and as such, is detrimental to society (Adams et al., 1994).

Our research examines the extent to which stress and culture, combined with environmental factors of poverty and nonintact households, may produce strain toward gang affiliation and/or if that strain predisposes them to not effectively countering affiliation through the use of two psychometric instruments, HSI and MEIM, respectively. Furthermore, is there a difference in the levels of MEIM, HSI, poverty, and nonintact households between those affiliated with gangs and those not? For the purposes of testing this hypothesis, a scale measuring Hispanic stress is used to demonstrate how stress within an individual may produce anomic conditions. Furthermore, ethnic identity is used to demonstrate how identification with one's ethnic culture, combined with stress, makes gang affiliation more predictable. It is assumed that greater Hispanic stress combined with a weak ethnic identity, compounded with income inequality and nonintact familial structures, will predict gang affiliation among Mexican American adolescent females. Moreover, it is also assumed that poverty, nonintact families, high HSI, and a weak MEIM is more prevalent among gang affiliates than non-gang members.

23.2 Review of the Literature

Females and gangs usually have been categorized into three types based largely on Miller's (1975) threefold typology. The first and most common are young women affiliated with a male gang as a result of a relationship (sister, cousin, boyfriend, or good friend) to one or more members of the male gang rather than a primary desire to be a gang member. Their involvement with the gang results from whom they know in the gang, and they, typically, do not engage in serious or frequent illegal gang activity. The duration of their affiliation often lasts as long as their relationship does. For example, a young woman with a brother in a gang most likely has associated with that gang for a longer period of time than a young woman with solely a boyfriend in the gang.

Another type of category proposed by Miller (1975) is the female member of a mixed-gender or coed gang. Such young women often go through initiations and rituals of getting into the gang, i.e., "rolled-in," "jumped-in," or "sexed-in," and are official gang members. They may participate in illegal gang activities similar to those of males in their gang but, overall, play a lesser role in gang-related activities.

A final type of gang involvement is with the all-female independent gang, comprised solely of girls not subordinate to any male gang. They may "hang out" with male gang members and participate in illegal and legal activities with them, but these young men are not part of their gang. To date, independent all-female gangs are still the exception rather than the rule.

Although some research has examined violence and delinquency among females in mixed-gender gangs or among female gang members (Campbell, 1991; Chesney-Lind and Pasko, 2003; Curry, 1998; Deschenes and Esbensen, 1999a, 1999b; Esbensen and Deschenes, 1998; Fleisher, 1998; Joe and Chesney-Lind, 1995; Miller, 1998; Miller and Decker, 2001; Moore, 1991), studies have not adequately examined delinquency for gang-affiliated females, who may account for a greater number of girls than those of the all-female independent gangs and the mixed-gender gangs combined.

Moreover, cultural identity or Hispanic stressors have attracted little attention, with respect to testing GST. Typically, the theory is applied and intended to relate cross-culturally regardless of sex or ethnicity. The lack of consideration of ethnic issues or other stressors related to ethnicity, which has also been criticized, has limited the usefulness of the theory with regard to a heterogeneous society. These reasons, first, justify testing the theory. Moreover, Hispanic stress and ethnic identity are not exclusively mentioned in any of the literature proposed by GST or its predecessors. This, in turn, leads to the second justification, which lies in the fact that Mexican Americans are quickly becoming the greatest aggregate of minorities (U.S. Bureau of the Census, 2000). Understanding their culture will make a longstanding social ill much easier to counter without the symptom-related remedy of jail.

The basis of GST is found in Merton's strain theory. Following his contention, strain theory purports that conditions inducing gang affiliation are expressions of structural forces contributing to delinquency. At its macro roots, strain theory is usually described as a socio-structural theory that refers to the inability of groups or communities to realize collective goals, including the goal of crime control (Moyer, 2001). Because structural tenets are largely based on culture and social structure, they provide valuable insights about the dimension from which gangs arise (Messner and Rosenfeld, 2001).

In the strictest sense at the individual level, Merton proposes, as does GST, too, that strain results from negative experiences, especially goal frustration, associated with the discrepancy between an individual's aspirations, on one hand, and achievements or expectations, on the other (Moyer, 2001). Because of "dissociation between culturally prescribed aspirations and socially structured avenues for realizing these aspirations," a strain or anomic condition is induced (Moyer, 2001, p. 60). However, under GST, the negative experience is brought about by negative stimuli, for instance, stress or poverty.

From a microlevel perspective, GST argues that youths high in emotionality and low in self-control are more likely to react to strain with delinquency (Agnew et al., 2002). For example, the first category of strain results when individuals fail to achieve positively valued goals. A second source of strain is based on the recognition that aversive situations may arise when individuals lose something they value. Based on this value principle, ethnic identity is used to comply with this second source. GST's third source of strain occurs when negative or harmful stimuli are present, i.e., gang members. HSI is further employed to parallel this latter principle.

According to the GST, individuals who experience strain are prone to developing negative affective states, such as anger, anxiety, depression, or frustration, which may contribute to acting out adversely (Mazzerole, 1998). More to the point, Agnew et al. (2002: 44) state:

> GST predicts … factors that condition the effect of strain on delinquency, these factors [include] the ability to engage in criminal versus non-criminal coping, the costs of criminal versus noncriminal coping, and the disposition for criminal versus noncriminal coping. Also, such factors include the importance attached to the goals, values, or identities that are threatened; coping skills; coping resources like money, self-esteem, and self-efficacy, family attachment, moral beliefs, association with peers [and in this particular case, ethnic identity and stress specific to Hispanics].

These conditioning effects then become destabilizers that remove the ability to counter stress.

23.3 Measurements

Because of the complexity of stress, the range of stressors can be unique to populations (Petersen and Valdez, 2004). For these purposes, a clearer picture of stress is formulated so that it is more indicative of a particular population. For example, the HSI is computed so as to "assess the conflict resulting from changes in traditional culture (acculturation, loss of traditional morals and norms) and problems within the family structures such as divorces, separations, and family arguments" (Center for Drug and Social Policy Research, 1999). Through a series of questions, four sub-scales (marital, occupational or economic, parental, and family or cultural stress) are compared to six symptomatolgy scales (Center for Epidemiological Studies Depression Scale, Symptom Checklist-90-Revised [depression, anxiety, somatization], Rosenberg Self-Esteem Inventory and Personal Competence Inventory) to evaluate stress levels (Cervantes et al., 1991). Thus, HSI draws its strength from its distinctiveness as a vast measurement of stressors unique to the Hispanic experience.

As with stress, identity may also be a relevant factor of ethnicity. Multigroup ethnic identity is a complex construct that includes "a commitment and a sense of belonging to one's ethnic group, positive evaluation of the group, interest in and knowledge about the group and involvement in activities and traditions of the group" (Phinney, 1990, p. 508). According to Phinney (1993), ethnic identity is achieved through a progression of identity stages. In the first stage, a child or adolescent achieves identity through acceptance of the values and attitudes present in his or her environment. At this stage, it is quite possible to receive a positive identity image, from within the group, or a negative identity image from stereotypes largely from the wider society. The subsequent stage is characterized as a state of search or immersion of ethnic identity, during which individuals become deeply interested in knowing more about their group. The final stage is presented as the period in which individuals "develop a secure, confident sense of themselves as members of their group" (Phinney, 1993, p. 146). This stage marks the point in which an individual realizes the possibility of intergroup relations or relationships with people who possess similar identities or the point at which one can become disillusioned with the majority and minorities' coexistence. Therefore, as GST would propose, disillusionment would provide for negative stimuli to induce strain conditions, and in this case, gang affiliation.

Furthermore, economic deprivation and nonintact households have long been seen as sources of crime and delinquency (Bursik and Gramsick, 1993). The extent to which these factors are related to delinquency and gang affiliation and the nature of the relationship are noteworthy. As youth face "molding" through their immediate surroundings, these variables are instrumental in showing how they may relate to gang affiliation.

23.4 Methods and Setting

This research involved life-history-related interviews with 150 gang-affiliated and 150 non-gang-affiliated Mexican American adolescent females aged 14 to 18, from fall 1998 through summer 2001 in San Antonio, Texas. The city of San Antonio has a metropolitan population of approximately 1.3 million residents with a high concentration of Hispanics. According to the U.S. Census (2000), nearly 60 percent of San Antonio is Hispanic, the majority of whom are of Mexican descent, compared to 12.5 percent of the national population. Although the Mexican American population resides throughout the entire city, most live in the western, eastern, or southern parts, which are more economically disadvantaged than areas in the north.

First, we discuss sampling methods for the gang-affiliated young women.[1] This sample is particularly unique and innovative in that it did not use already existing populations, i.e., youth arrested, incarcerated/detained or in school, as potential subjects, which often results in numerous sampling biases (Moore and Hagedorn, 2001) and external and internal validity limitations. Those included in this study were obtained from community-based methods.

For a young woman to be considered a potential subject in this research study, she needed to: (a) be Mexican American, (b) be between the ages of 14 and 18, and (c) know of a good friend or relative in one of the 26 male gangs identified in a previous National Institute of Drug Abuse study on drug-related gang violence among Mexican American males in South Texas (see Yin et al., 1996). For this study it was speculated that a large number of girls "knew" gang members but may not actually associate with them. Therefore, it was decided that a young woman would be included in the study only if she knew a good friend or close family relative in a gang.

The study respondents were actively recruited using snowball recruitment and sampling techniques that have been known to work well with hidden populations (see, for example, Valdez and Kaplan, 1999; Wright and Decker, 1997; Wright et al., 1992). The snowball method involved identifying potential subjects by asking known gang members (see Yin et al., 1996), youth on the streets and "gatekeepers" (see Valdez and Kaplan, 1999, Burgess, 1991; Shaffir, 1991) to identify those who might fit the inclusion criteria. These three field-based research techniques continued throughout the 3-year duration of the study and were used extensively to compile a universe of 519 gang-affiliated females (Petersen, 2002).

Stratified random sampling was used to obtain a randomized list of 150 young women from an original list of 519 names. This method was chosen to ensure a proportionate representation of all 26 represented gangs whom the young women affiliated with. The 519 identified young women were placed in a list for each of the 26 gangs, and then 150 were randomly selected from each stratum.[2] This was done via http://www.randomizer.org. Each individual was then contacted to participate in the interview. If they could not be contacted or located, a randomizer replacement was used. We anticipated that this population would be difficult to locate and, thus, devised a system to allow for a randomized replacement if one of the original 150 could not be located or refused an interview.

To obtain a parallel number of girls not affiliated with gangs for comparison, several independent school districts in the San Antonio area were contacted. All declined our request. We speculated that this was due to the sensitive nature of the study and also because the largest school district was in the midst of a lawsuit pertaining to parental consent that appeared to echo all across the news and within the various school districts.

Therefore, we contacted all the Catholic high schools in the target area to see if they might be interested in the study. Three of them agreed. Contrary to public perception, all of these were located within the same areas where the gang-affiliated youth lived and, as such, represented the social and economic conditions of the area. In other words, these parochial schools were not oozing with wealth and white youth. From these three schools, we obtained a list of 150 young women between the ages of 14 and 18 who did not affiliate with gangs or know of a good friend or relative in a gang and were Mexican Americans living in the target area.

23.5 Analysis

In testing the hypothesis that a high HSI score and a weak MEIM compounded with poverty (as measured by respondents receiving Aid for Family with Dependent Children [AFDC]) and nonintact households (respondents living with only one parent), a hierarchical multiple linear regression or nested regression was used. Descriptive analyses were conducted on all variables (HSI, MEIM, poverty, and nonnuclear households) to determine their statistical means and standard deviations. The HSI was computed from 13 variables, whereas the MEIM composite comprised 12 variables. Poverty was measured by federal standards determining to whom AFDC was awarded. Nonintact households were measured by the number of youths living with one parent.[3] Moreover, because nonintact family structure and poverty variables were dichotomous, they were recoded into dummy variables for compatibility in the multiple nested ordinary least squares (OLS) regression.

OLS regression models are used to predict a dependent variable; in this case, this would be gang affiliation. Using a nested OLS regression is preferable given the need for observation of predictability among the variables. The basic unit, beta, is the average amount gang affiliation increases when one independent variable (poverty, nonintact households, MEIM, or HSI) increases while others stay constant.

A multiple nested model refers to entering multiple independent variables (HSI, MEIM, poverty, and nonnuclear households) at separate times of the equation so that the variables would not adversely impact each other. OLS regression nested was run using each gang status as a dependent variable. The HSI variables used were the intensity variables distinguished by the HSI qualifier variables in the form of time. For qualifiers, a stress question was asked to determine if it had occurred recently, i.e., sometime within the last 3 months. Alternatively, HSI intensity questions asked how much these stressors worried the respondents. Lastly, ANOVA tests, correlation distribution tables, model summaries to explain variance, collinearity diagnostics, and coefficient distributions were provided.

23.6 Findings

Table 23.1 indicates that the average age of the respondents was 16. Regarding frequencies of the demographics, 122 (40.7 percent) reported living with both parents, whereas 178 (59.3 percent) reported not living with both parents. As for respondents receiving AFDC, 96 (32 percent) answered affirmatively, 199 (66.3 percent) negatively, and 5 (1.7 percent) claimed that they did not know. Under the GST hypothesis, the research yielded results that some respondents in the survey experienced stress from either single-parent households or poor households.

As shown in Table 23.1, independent variables, HSI and multigroup ethnic identity, proved to be reliable. That is, because a number of questions comprise the scale of HSI or MEIM, the questions were joined. The fact that the HSI's alpha (measurement) of 0.82 and MEIM's 0.87 were each close to one demonstrated their reliability and, as such, appropriateness for the model.

Of the 300 respondents, 295 qualified for inclusion in the multiple nested OLS regression model. Because the nested regression relies on two parts, the first part is the demographic model (which includes poverty and nonintact households), which is then followed by the inclusive model (the demographic model in tandem with MEIM and HSI). As for the demographic variables (poverty and nonintact families), respondents who replied affirmatively or positively to either poverty or nonintact households were included in the analyses. Therefore, everyone included in the analysis was afflicted with a demographic condition (poverty or a nonnuclear household).

The demographic model, in this instance, proved to be significantly legitimate because its significance level as reported by the ANOVA table stood at 0.000, which is less than the 0.01 standard. The second model, or the inclusive model (which included the demographic variables as

Table 23.1 Frequencies, Descriptives, and Reliability

Variable	a	Mean (SD)	N	Percentage	Item #
Age		16 (1.43)	300		
Status		1.37 (0.69)	263		
Non-gang member			150	50	
Gang affiliate			150	50	
Demographic variables					
Poverty (as set by AFDC)		0.67 (0.47)	295		
Yes			96	32.5	
No			199	67.5	
Nonintact households		0.59 (0.49)	300		
Yes			122	40.7	
No			178	59.3	
Independent variables					
Multigroup Ethnic Identity Measure (MEIM)	0.87	1.84 (0.52)	295		12
Hispanic Stress Inventory (HSI)	0.82	1.56 (0.60)	295		13

Note: SD = Standard deviation; N = number.

well as the independent variables, MEIM and HSI), proved to be significant at 0.000.

Having ensured that the models were reliable, a correlation matrix was employed to indicate correlations between the independent variables (poverty, nonintact households, HSI, and MEIM) and the dependent variable (gang affiliation).[4] As demonstrated in Table 23.2, all predictors (nonintact familial structure, poverty, MEIM, and HIS) collectively had weak correlations, meaning that they mildly correlated to gang affiliation. The strongest positive correlation significantly indicated that the more nonintact a family, the stronger the relationship with gang affiliation. Similarly, another correlation indicated that a greater poverty level is related with less gang affiliation. Interestingly, HSI was positively correlated, which means that higher stress increases

Table 23.2 Predicting Gang Affiliation: Partial Tests of Strain and Differential Association Using an OLS Regression, Inclusive Model

Variable	B	(SE)	Beta	r
Demographics				
Poverty	0.199*	(.058)	0.187*	0.268*
Nonintact households	0.284*	(.056)	0.279*	0.353*
Multigroup Ethnic Identity (MEIM)	0.0083	(.051)	0.088	0.101*
Hispanic Stress Inventory (HSI)	0.118*	(.045)	0.141*	0.213*
R^2	0.187			
Adjusted R^2	0.176			
R^2	0.026			
F-ratio	16.712			
N	295			

Note: Dependent variable: gang affiliation; B = B coefficient; SE = standard error; r = coefficient of correlation.

* $p < 0.05$

the relationship with gang affiliation. As for multigroup ethnic identity, it was found that the stronger the ethnic identity, that is, the more closely an individual is to his or her culture, the greater the relationship to gang affiliation. One caveat concerning the weak correlation could be the small sample size.

The next concern in the model is to see how the coefficients or variables change when the constant (dependent variable or gang affiliation) changes. The B coefficients (unstandardized regression coefficients) for each of the variables indicates the amount of change expected in gang affiliation given a one-unit change in the value of that variable while all other variables in the model are held constant. Beta coefficients (standardized regression coefficients) compare the relative strength of various predictors within the model. Whereas B coefficients are measured in units, Beta coefficients are measured in standard deviation for comparison. That is, an OLS has a linear relationship to each variable.

Referring again to Table 23.2, the demographic model showed that nonintact families and poorer families significantly predict gang affiliation.

Table 23.3   Testing Means between Gang Affiliates and Non-Gang Members

Variable	t-Test	Mean (SD)	N
Demographics			
Poverty	−4.770*		
Gang affiliates		1.55(0.50)	150
Non-gang members		1.80(0.40)	150
Nonintact households	6.510*		
Gang affiliates		1.77(0.42)	149
Non-gang members		1.42(0.50)	146
Multigroup Ethnic Identity Measure (MEIM)	1.894		
Gang affiliates		1.90(0.567)	150
Non-gang members		1.78(0.467)	150
Hispanic Stress Inventory (HSI)	3.768*		
Gang affiliates		1.68(0.637)	150
Non-gang members		1.43(0.522)	150

Note: SD = Standard deviation; N = number.

* $p < 0.05$

Similarly, poverty and nonintact families followed by HSI were found to significantly predict gang affiliation. In essence, the more a family is poor, nonintact, and has higher stress, the greater the chance of gang affiliation. Thus, the cases of poverty, nonintact families, and HSI rejected the null hypotheses (that there is no significant relationship between the independent variables and gang affiliation). However, the lone exception to predicting gang affiliation was MEIM, which was not a statistically significant predictor of gang affiliation. Therefore, the conclusion drawn is that stressors from poverty, nonintact households, and those in the HSI (marital, occupational or economic, parental, and family or cultural stress) produce strain toward gang affiliation.

Once the predictive power of the variables was confirmed, the research proceeded by testing means between both dependent groups (affiliates and nonmembers) and each of the independent variables (MEIM and HSI). Thus, as shown in Table 23.3, *t*-tests concluded that multigroup ethnic identity was not statistically significant for either group. The difference between both groups with regard to HSI illustrated that gang affiliates tended to be more stressed than their nongang counterparts. In keeping with GST, the research shows that HSI as a stressor significantly predicts gang affiliation. As such, HSI is related to gang affiliates and gang affiliation. As for poverty and nonintact households, gang-affiliated girls tested affirmatively for both independent variables in comparison to both groups.

Following GST's two strain sources, all findings indicate that "strain is based on the recognition that adverse situations may arise when individuals lose something they value," which in this case is ethnic identity (Mazerolle, 1998, p. 67). Hence, although ethnic identity did not predict gang affiliation, a relationship does (as demonstrated by Pearson's R) exist. However, this was not the case with HSI. That is, all tests indicated that Hispanic stress does have a relationship to gang affiliation in predicting it, with such stress being higher among affiliates than non-gang members. Moreover, GST's third source of strain, the type of stress that occurs when individuals are exposed to various adverse situations or experiences (i.e., negative or harmful stimuli), helps to explain how HSI predicts and correlates with gang affiliation.

23.7 Summary and Conclusion

The implicit purpose of the research was to find and emphasize the problems that surround Mexican American adolescent females and gangs. Findings indicate that stress is related to gang affiliation. Stress found in the family and acculturation, coupled with poverty and nonintact families, was shown to be detrimental to these females. Although ethnic identity was not a statistically significant predictor of gang affiliation, the findings showed that stronger identity is correlated to gang affiliation. Hence, the next questions were whether demography combined with ethnic identity and Hispanic stress was related to gang affiliation and to investigate if differences existed between the two groups (affiliates and non-gang members) with respect to "amounts" of identity or stress. To that extent, our research found that (a) these variables were related to gang affiliates, and (b) there were statistically significant differences in amounts between both groups.

As the analysis (OLS regression) showed, general stressors (demographic and sociopsychometric) were correlated with gang affiliation. As with the other three correlations (nonintact households, MEIM, or HSI), the results illustrated that they were, indeed, positively correlated with gang affiliation. Except for MEIM, the predictive power of these variables showed them to be significant predictors of gang affiliation. In addition, a comparison among both groups demonstrated a statistically significant difference in his.

Couple these findings with other research (Petersen, 2002; Miller, 1998; Nurge and Shively, 2003), and there is cause for concern. For example, some studies have found that gangs may not be reluctant to physically and sexually violate their own members (Jankowski, 1991; Knox, 1996; Spergel, 1995). Additionally, a study by Valdez et al. (2002) found the existence of antisocial behaviors, such as destructive or violent temperaments, among Mexican American gang members. Other deviant behaviors among gang members include murders, carjacking incidents, assaults, senseless violence, and other vices (Rosenthal, 2000).

Finally, without understanding cultural diversity, policy is rendered useless. For instance, stressors unique to Hispanics seem to have predictive powers in terms of gang affiliation (Petersen, 2002). Understanding the roles of distinct identity and stress of particular groups helps create awareness based on empirical evidence and not stereotypical images.

Acknowledgments

This work was supported by a grant from the Centers for Disease Control and Prevention (grant R49/CCR615627-01). Opinions expressed are those of the authors and do not necessarily reflect those of the funding agency.

The authors wish to thank Avelardo Valdez, University of Houston Graduate School of Social Work, but for whom this research would not have been possible, and most importantly, the young women who participated in this study, we thank you.

References

Adams, G.R., Gullotta, T.P., and Markstrom-Adams, C. (1994). *Adolescent Life Experiences* (3rd ed.). Pacific Grove, CA: Brooks/Cole.

Agnew, R., Brezina, T., Wright, J.P., and Cullen, F.T. (2002). Strain, personality, traits, and delinquency: extending general strain theory. *Criminology, 40*(1), 43–71.

Burgess, R.G. (1991). Sponsors, gatekeepers, members, and friends: access in educational settings. In Shaffir, W.B. and Stebbins, R.B. (Eds.), *Experiencing Fieldwork: An Inside View of Qualitative Research.* Newbury Park, CA: Sage. pp. 43–52.

Bursik, R.J. and Gramsick, H.G. (1993). Neighborhoods and crime: the dimensions of effective community control. New York: Lexington.

Campbell, A. (1991). *The Girls in the Gang* (2nd ed.). Oxford: Basil Blackwell.

Center for Drug and Social Policy Research (1999). Socio-Psychometric Scales for the CDC Study. San Antonio, TX: University of Texas at San Antonio.

Cervantes, R. C., Padilla, A. M., and Salgado de Snyder, N. (1991). The Hispanic stress inventory: a culturally relevant approach to psychosocial assessment. *Psychological Assessment, 3*(3), 438–447.

Chesney-Lind, M. and Pasko, L. (2003). *The Female Offender: Girls, Women, and Crime,* 2nd Edition. Thousand Oaks, CA: Sage.

Curry, G.D. (1998). Female gang involvement. *Journal of Research in Crime and Delinquency, 35,* 100–118.

Deschenes, E.P. and Esbensen, F.A. (1999a). Violence among girls: does gang membership make a difference? In Chesney-Lind, M. and Hagedorn, J.M. (Eds.), *Female Gangs in America.* Chicago: Lakeview. pp. 277–294.

Deschenes, E.P. and Esbensen, F.A. (1999b). Violence in gangs: gender differences in perceptions and behavior. *Journal of Quantitative Criminology, 15,* 63–96.

Esbensen, F.A. and Deschenes, E.P. (1998). A multisite examination of youth gang membership: does gender matter? *Criminology, 36,* 799–828.

Fleisher, M. (1998). *Dead End kids: Gang Girls and the Boys They Know.* Madison: University of Wisconsin Press.

Gray-Ray, P. and Ray, M.C. (1990). Juvenile delinquency in the black community. *Youth and Society, 22,* 67–84.

Hagedorn, J.M. (1988). *People and folks: Gangs, crime and the underclass in a rust belt city.* Chicago, IL: Lake View.

Jankowski, M.S. (1991). *Islands in the Street: Gangs and American Urban Society.* Berkeley, CA: University of California Press.

Joe, K.A. and Chesney-Lind, M. (1995). Just every mother's angel: an analysis of gender and ethnic variations in youth gang membership. *Gender and Society, 9,* 408–430.

Knox, G.W. (1996). Gang profile: the black disciples. *Journal of Gang Research, 3,* 45–65.

Mazerolle, P. (1998). Gender, general strain, and delinquency: empirical examination. *Justice Quarterly, 15*(1), 65–91.

Messner, S.F. and Rosenfeld R., (2001). *Crime and the American Dream* (3rd ed.). Belmont, CA: Wadsworth.

Miller, J. (1998). Gender and risk of victimization among young women in gangs. *Journal of Research in Crime and Delinquency, 35,* 429–453.

Miller, W.B. (1975). Violence by Youth Gangs and Youth Groups as a Crime Problem in Major American Cities. Washington, D.C.

Miller, W. (1958). Lower class culture as a generality of milieu of gang delinquency. *Journal of Social Issues. 3,* 5–19.

Moore, J. (1991). *Going Down to the Barrio: Homeboys and Homegirls.* Philadelphia, PA: Temple Press.

Moore, J. and Hagedorn, J. (2001). Female Gangs: A Focus on Research. (Grant No. NCJ 986159). Washington, D.C.: U.S. Department of Justice.

Moyer, I.L. (2001). *Criminological theories: Traditional and Nontraditional Voices and Themes.* Thousand Oaks, CA: Sage.

Nurge, D.M. and Shively, M. (2003). The role of victimization in criminal offending of female youth gangs. In Sgarzi, J.M. and McDevitt, J. (Eds.), *Victimology: A Study of Crime Victims and Their Roles.* Upper Saddle River, NJ: Prentice Hall. pp. 101–116.

Petersen, R.D. (November 2002). Understanding Gang-Affiliated Adolescent Females: Developing a Typology. American Society of Criminology. Chicago, IL.

Petersen, R.D. (2000a). Definition of a gang and impacts on public policy. *Journal of Criminal Justice, 28,* 139–149.

Petersen, R.D. (2000b). Gang subcultures and prison gangs of female youth. *Free Inquiry in Creative Sociology, 28,* 27–42.

Petersen, R.D. and Valdez, A. (2004). Intimate partner violence among Hispanic females. *Journal of Ethnicity in Criminal Justice,* 2(1/2), 67–89.

Petersen, R.D. and Valdez, A. (2005). Using snowball-based methods in hidden populations to generate a randomized community sample of gang-affiliated adolescents. *Youth Violence and Juvenile Justice,* 3(2), 151–167.

Phinney, J.S. (1990). Ethnic identity in adolescents and adults: review of research. *Psychological Bulletin, 108,* 499–514.

Phinney, J.S. (1993). A three-stage model of ethnic identity development. In Bernal, M.E. and Knight, G. (Eds.). *Ethnic Identity: Formation and Transmission among Hispanics and other Minorities.* Albany, New York: State University of New York Press.

Phinney, J.S. (1996). Understanding ethnic diversity. *The American Behavioral Scientist, 40*(2), 143–152.

Rosenthal, L. (2000). Gang loitering and race. *Journal of Criminal Law and Criminology, 91*(1), 99–160.

Shaffir, W.B. (1991). Managing a convincing self-presentation: some personal reflections on entering the field. In Shaffir, W.B. and Stebbins, R.B. (Eds.), *Experiencing Fieldwork: An Inside View of Qualitative Research.* Newbury Park, CA: Sage. pp. 72–81.

Spergel, I.A. (1995). *The Youth Gang Problem: A Community Approach.* New York: Oxford University Press.

U.S. Bureau of the Census. (2000). http://www.census.gov/main/www/cen2000.html.

Valdez, A. and Kaplan, C.D. (1999). Reducing selection bias in the use of focus groups to investigate hidden populations: the case of Mexican-American gang members from South Texas. *Drugs and Society, 14,* 209–224.

Valdez, A., Kaplan, C.D., and Codina, E. (2000). Psychopathy among Mexican American gang member: a comparative study. *International Journal of Offender Therapy and Comparative Criminology, 44*(1), 46–58.

Vigil, D. (1988). *Barrio gangs: Street Life and Identity in Southern California*. Austin, TX: University of Texas Press.

Wright, R.T. and Decker, S.H. (1997). *Armed Robbers in Action*. Boston, MA: Northeastern University Press.

Wright, R., Decker, S.H., Redfern, A.K., and Smith, D.L. (1992). A snowball's chance in hell: doing fieldwork with active residential burglars. *Journal of Research in Crime and Delinquency, 29,* 148–161.

Yin, Z., Valdez, A., Mata, A.G., and Kaplan, C. (1996). Developing a field-intensive methodology for generating a randomized sample for gang research. *Free Inquiry in Creative Sociology, 24,* 195–204.

Notes

1. For a detailed description of the methods used, see Petersen and Valdez, 2005.
2. For a more detailed description of this type of sampling, see Yin et al., 1996.
3. It should be noted, however, that living with only one parent was the only criterion for nonnuclear households; therefore, as an example, youths having one parent and a stepparent were not considered a traditional nuclear family (i.e., two parents and child) for this study.
4. The scale for the Pearson's R correlation ranges from 0 (no correlation) to ±1 (a perfect correlation); in essence, the greater the correlation to ±1, the stronger the relationship.

Chapter 24

Understanding and Treating the Substance-Addicted Juvenile

Ernest L. Cowles and Rebekah J. Lanphierd

24.1 Introduction

The world of adolescent substance abuse is complex. Despite advances in understanding the causes of abuse behavior, many dark corners still exist, particularly in those areas that serve as the bridges between "nature" and "nurture" factors. As a result of this void, the treatment of adolescent substance abuse is uncertain at best, and is often driven more by philosophical and political agendas than by knowledge-based approaches. Nowhere is this more evident than in the juvenile justice system.

In this chapter, we attempt to provide insight into this problem by extracting some of the more important factors that shape responses to juvenile substance abuse prevention and treatment. We begin by providing an important legal–clinical context that sets the stage for much of the confusion about how juveniles with substance abuse problems are handled by the justice system. From there, we review some of the major findings regarding the etiology of adolescent substance abuse. The underlying complexity revealed in this section may help in understanding the difficulties in establishing and delivering effective treatment programs. In the final portion of the discussion, we turn our attention to highlighting what we believe are the major issues facing adolescent substance abuse prevention and treatment, particularly within the juvenile justice system.

24.1.1 The Treatment Context

The two most conflicting and influential forces shaping both perspectives of substance use and abuse, and substance abuse treatment, are those created by two very different definitional sets: clinical and legal. The first of these, the clinical definition, arises from the study of the physical and psychological mechanisms that determine behavior and the behavioral adaptation of the individual to the environment. The clinical orientation assumes there are normal physical and behavioral states that form a baseline upon which behavior and the behavioral adaptation of the individual to the environment can be viewed. Variations from this baseline can then be assessed and described (i.e., diagnosed). Extreme or prolonged variation can be described as *pathological*.

Following this notion, in order to medically diagnose an individual's substance abuse problems, the clinical community (those who assess and treat substance abuse) examines the extent to which an individual uses substances in conjunction with the individual's dependence on substances. Once such a diagnosis is made, the clinician can then prescribe the appropriate treatment.

In contrast, the second definitional framework is centered on an individual's personal responsibility to uphold the law. Descriptions of prohibited behavior and penalties for engaging in such behavior form the framework for legal definitions. Within our current legal framework, statutory definitions ignore the issues of substance use or dependence within the individual. Rather, the severity of the use and abuse problem is implied by the range of penalties available under the law, which can be imposed on individuals for possessing and providing illegal drugs to others.

The problems stemming from the forced marriage of these clinical and legal perspectives on substance use and abuse are most noticeable in the juvenile justice arena, where standards of legal responsibility are softened or, perhaps more accurately, blurred to accommodate what is perceived as a minor's lesser ability to make rational judgments and greater potential for changing inappropriate behavior. This approach to handling of illicit substance use by juveniles has its roots in the long-standing *parens patriae* doctrine of the juvenile court. As a result of this, the juvenile legal system's proscriptions are inconsistent; simultaneously being more severe and more lenient than the adult legal system. For example, while adults can legally possess and use tobacco and alcohol, these products become unlawful substances in the hands of adolescents. By contrast, a juvenile found guilty of selling a particular illegal substance would generally face a much less severe sentence than would an adult engaging in the same behavior. The focus of the judicial decision making in the adult system is on a punishment to fit the crime that is significantly different from the juvenile system, in which the primary goal of legal sanctions is to treat the juvenile offender so that the individual may overcome problems and later become a productive citizen. Philosophically, few would disagree with this rationale, yet when translated into practice, the dual elements of the juvenile justice approach impart a schizophrenic quality to treatment, often emphasizing style over substance.

24.2 What Do We Need to Treat?

24.2.1 Risk and Protective Factors

A vast amount of research from various disciplines has been conducted to identify factors that cause substance use and abuse; however, the research on drug use and addiction in children and adolescents is much more limited (Doweiko, 1990). Explanations and accompanying research perspectives generally have focused on three arenas. At the individual level, the focus has been on looking at the physical mechanisms of substance use and abuse or at the development of personality characteristics that promote substance use and abuse. At the second level, attention has centered on the broader environment in which the individual lives, most particularly the social interactions that foster use and abuse. The third level, which has been the target of much recent research, looks to the interaction between the individual and environmental domains.

Today, much of the research concentrates on risk and protective factors within these areas. Risk factors are personal characteristics or social settings that increase the probability of substance use, whereas protective factors are seen to decrease the likelihood of substance use (Gerstein et al., 1997). To date, research (see, for example, National Institute on Drug Abuse, 1985; Jessor et al., 1986; Newcomb and Bentler,

1989; Bentler, 1992; Spooner, 1999; Lane et al., 2001) has identified a multitude of factors that appear to either enhance or reduce the likelihood of use and abuse of substances by juveniles. However, the relationship between risk and protective factors appears to be a dynamic rather than static concept. That is, evidence suggests that different patterns of drug use at different developmental stages have different precursors (Kandel, 1982). During the maturation of an individual from childhood through adolescence and into adulthood, the impact of various risk and protective factors changes. Equally important, the likelihood of future drug use and abuse is more dependent on the number of risk factors than on the presence or absence of any individual factor (Newcomb et al., 1986). Spooner (1999) sums up the dynamics of risk and protective factors thus: "… a variable that is associated with drug abuse could be a risk factor, a protective factor, a correlate and/or a consequence; and that relationship can change over time" (p. 454).

It is beyond the scope of this discussion to provide a comprehensive review of the research of juvenile substance use and abuse. Rather, in the following section we attempt to point out some of the central themes in the complex picture regarding the elements that promote and insulate juveniles from illegal substance use and abuse.

24.2.2 Key Factors in the Developmental Approach

24.2.2.1 Genetics and Personality

One of the unanswered questions in substance abuse research is whether risk factors that lead to substance abuse are caused by genetics or environment. To date, studies seeking to isolate a specific gene that causes substance abuse have not found evidence of a "magic genetic bullet." Rather, research suggests a moderate role for genetic influences, most likely occurring in an indirect fashion. For example, Weinberg (2001) supports the notion of an indirect genetic influence that shapes personality features and, in turn, raises individuals' susceptibility to substance use. An example of the notion of this genetic and environmental interaction is reflected in the linkage between gender and juvenile substance abuse. Whereas an individual's sex is genetically determined, the manifestation of gender differences in adolescents is both genetically and culturally based. This combination makes understanding the specific role gender plays in substance use and abuse difficult. For example, research indicates that male adolescents use a greater amount of drugs and use a greater variety of drugs than female adolescents (Johnston et al., 2001). However, this disparity between male and female drug use develops as adolescents age. The differences between male and female adolescent drug use in the 8th and 10th grade are slight, but as the adolescents grow older (and frequently use more drugs), the gender gap between male and female drug use widens. By the time individuals reach the age of high school seniors, college students, and young adults, a significant gender gap is seen (Johnston et al., 2001), with male adolescents using a greater percentage of illicit substances in comparison to female adolescents (Miller et al., 2000).

24.2.2.2 Personality and Self-Medication

Another aspect of the interaction between genetic predisposition and individual development focuses on the idea that an individual's genetic composition and psychological makeup can create a personality that is more susceptible to substance use. Curran et al. (2000) have shown how personality variations might push certain individuals differently in regard to the types and amount of substances used. These investigators concentrate on the interaction of certain types of personalities that make people more prone to drug use when they are immersed in reinforcing the social network of substance users. In this framework, adjustment disorders such as depression may make an adolescent more susceptible to problem drug use. Curran and his associates (2000) maintain that some adolescents who have psychological problems use illegal substances as a method of self-medication. According to Curran et al., when adolescents with depression-based personality disorders are in environments with peer groups that advocate drug use as an acceptable way to deal with problems, there is a greater likelihood that they will develop problem drug use. Similarly, adolescents suffering from social anxiety may regard alcohol as an effective way of "loosening up" in order to overcome their inhibitions in social situations. Conversely, adolescents under extreme stress may use a drug such as marijuana as a way to "calm down."

Unfortunately, the list of identified personality risk factors found in childhood is extensive: high anger, high depressive mood and low achievement (which contribute to high rebelliousness), high aggression, poor emotional control, unconventionality, low ego-control, impulsivity, aggression, inability to delay gratification, low social confidence, assertiveness, and self-efficacy (Curran et al., 2000; Kandel, 2002). The breadth of these risk factors does not lend much focus in terms of a treatment approach. However, if the self-medication hypothesis is valid, it is easy to see how the variety of licit and illicit drugs available to juveniles could become abused as the juvenile seeks to overcome perceived inadequacies and objectionable moods.

24.2.2.3 The Gateway Hypothesis

Today, one of the popular theories driving current policy on juvenile substance use and abuse is the *gateway hypothesis*. In general, this hypothesis asserts that the use of certain drugs acts as a gateway into harder drug use. The theory posits that cigarettes and alcohol serve as a gateway to marijuana use which, in turn, acts as a gateway into harder illicit drug use (Kandel, 2002).

Much of the research on drug gateways in adolescent substance abuse has focused on early use of alcohol and tobacco. For example, most adolescents use alcohol and tobacco before using marijuana or hard drugs (Hawkins et al., 2002). Similarly, studies on marijuana (e.g., Fergusson and Horwood, 2000; Perkonigg and Lieb, 1999) have indicated that marijuana use appears to be a precursor to other illicit drug use. The explanation of why substances such as alcohol and marijuana may serve as a gateway varies. Some believe if a juvenile has a positive experience with one type of drug, say alcohol, the youth will tend to think the same positive experience will occur with a more potent drug like marijuana (Willner, 2001). Others believe these gateways exist not because of effect, but owing to opportunity. That is, those juveniles who have access to alcohol find it easier to access marijuana, and those who have access to marijuana find it easier to access harder drugs. As the adolescent's opportunity to use illegal drugs decreases, the likelihood of the adolescent using drugs also decreases. Further, if adolescents do not smoke cigarettes or drink alcohol, there is a decrease in the quantity of illegal drugs they will be offered (Strang, 2001).

Another dimension in the gateway from experimentation to addiction is found in the age of onset of drug use. The age when the juvenile first tries licit drugs (alcohol and cigarettes) has a significant impact on later illegal drug use, and the age when the juvenile first tries illegal drugs is a significant factor in later substance abuse. Further, early use of drugs by a juvenile, followed by consistent use, is a significant factor in predicting a substance use disorder. Research has shown that the longevity of an adolescent's marijuana use is often based on the amount and frequency of marijuana used when the youth first began using marijuana. The more marijuana is used at onset, the more likely the adolescent will continue with marijuana use and increase its use (Perkonigg and Lieb, 1999). Additionally, the gateway hypothesis seems to be supported by research indicating that the early onset of cigarettes, alcohol, and marijuana use increases adolescent involvement with harder drugs (Fergusson and Horwood, 2000). However, although such connections appear valid during adolescent years, other research shows that these factors are not significant in predicting adolescent drug use escalating into an adult substance use disorder (Kandel, 2002). A study by Zimmer and Morgan (1997; based upon the U.S. Department of Health and Human Services, Substance Abuse and Mental Health Services Administration National Household Survey on Drug Abuse) revealed that for every 100 people who tried marijuana, only one was a current cocaine user. A similar analysis of the same NHSDA data by Golub and Johnson (2001) also casts further doubt on the youth-to-adult gateway connection. Finally, in one of the most thorough examinations of linkages between early and later usage, Kandel's (2002) well-documented review of the gateway hypothesis led her to reject the drug causality proposition of the hypothesis, i.e., that earlier drug use in the developmental sequence, such as alcohol or drugs, causes later drug use of other drugs, such as marijuana. Similar studies have led individuals such as Rosenbaum to flatly assert, "There is no credible research evidence demonstrating that using one drug causes the use of another" (2002, p. 11).

24.2.2.4 *Environmental Factors*

Whereas some risk or preventative factors may originate within the individual, others clearly have their genesis in the environment in which the youth is found. As noted earlier, the relative impact of such factors changes as the individual matures. Research (e.g., Jones and Battjes, 1985; Roger et al., 1987) seems to indicate that family influences are the most important determinants of substance use and abuse in childhood or early adolescence, whereas community and peer influences dominate in later adolescence and as the individual enters into adulthood.

Families in which parents and children have detached relationships, in which parents themselves are drug users, or in which discipline is lacking or inconsistent may foster drug use (Bureau of Justice Statistics, 1992). Kandel (1982) indicates that there are three parental factors that correspond with juvenile initiation into drug use: parent drug-using behaviors, parental attitudes about drugs, and parent–child interactions. Along these lines, Stephenson and Henry (1996) have identified a number of family characteristics impacting adolescent substance use, including family interaction patterns, the upkeep of family traditions, internal family strength and durability, hardiness of individual family members, family coherence, ability of family to deal with stress, adolescent satisfaction with family life, and family consistency with times and routines. In a similar vein, Hoffman (2002) has identified additional causes such as parent–child relations, differences in family income, residential mobility, single-parent homes, and having a step-parent as being related to adolescent substance abuse. These effects may be due in part to the fact that juveniles who do not have stable or secure home environments may be more susceptible to acute stressors, e.g., moving, change in family structure, etc., and seek refuge in illegal substance use. Thornberry et al. (1999) found that the more transitions a juvenile experiences, the more likely the youth is to engage in delinquent activity and drug use. Hoffman and Johnson (1998) similarly concluded that the more residential moves adolescents undergo, the more likely they are to use marijuana. Interestingly, living with a single biological father, or a biological father and a stepmother, is a greater risk factor for juvenile drug use than living with the biological mother in the same situations (Stephenson and Henry, 1996). Adolescents who live in father-only, father–stepmother, and relative-only families also are more mobile which, as indicated previously, is a factor increasing the likelihood for juvenile substance use (Hoffman and Johnson, 1998). Adolescents who live in stepfamilies are more likely than adolescents in intact families to experiment with gateway drugs such as cigarettes, marijuana, beer, wine coolers, and liquor. Additionally, adolescents from stepfamilies also are more likely to associate with peers who have significantly less disapproval for drug use than the peers of adolescents from intact families (Jenkins and Zunguze, 1998). Moreover, adolescents who report less parental attachment or poor parental relationships generally report a higher rate of drug use (Hoffman, 2002). Conversely, adolescents who see their family as strong and durable report lower amounts of substance use. In addition, adolescents who feel their family can handle stress by working together are less likely to turn to drugs in order to cope with stress (Stephenson and Henry, 1996).

Beyond the connectedness that the juvenile has with family, additional factors related to attitude and belief systems may serve to strengthen or weaken the social bonds between an individual and conventional norms. Such bonds have been identified as inhibiting delinquency and drug use (e.g., Hirshi, 1969). Among the factors that have been identified as reducing the likelihood of drug involvement are religiosity, commitment to school and education, and prosocial values (Hawkins et al., 1985). Similarly, an adolescent's expectancies for legal and illegal drugs also appear to mediate use. Research by Lee et al. (1998) found that an adolescent's risk perception of marijuana was responsible for 21 percent of the variation in risk-taking behavior of marijuana use. Essentially, if an adolescent perceives alcoholic parties and carousing in bars as enjoyable and participates in these activities, there is an increased likelihood of that individual using marijuana. Their research also has shown that adolescents tend to have more positive expectancies of marijuana and alcohol if they expect to use these substances again (1998). Further, there is an increase in positive expectations of alcohol and marijuana use as the adolescent ages.

Associating with drug-using peers has been shown to be a factor for adolescent drug use among all age levels (Jenkins, 1996); however, as youths mature, the peer group of an adolescent becomes the predominant source of influence on substance use. In fact, Kandel's research (1978) suggests that drug behavior and drug attitudes by peers are among the strongest predictors of drug involvement. The fact that other perceived risk factors for juvenile substance use, such as community, family, academics, and socioeconomic status, interact with one another in establishing an adolescent's peer groups probably strengthens this relationship. Often, adolescents whose peers do not use drugs themselves do not use drugs; whereas adolescents whose peers do use drugs, often begin to use drugs as well. Likewise, adolescents who use drugs tend to associate with other drug-using adolescents. In addition, adolescents who are high risk-takers have a tendency to associate with other risk-takers, which also heightens the likelihood of risky behavior such as drug use among that social group (Pearson and Michell, 2000). Jessor et al. (1980) found that certain social–environmental factors, such as friends modeling drug use behavior, accounted for twice the variance in drug use as compared to personality factors.

24.2.3 The Relationship between Delinquency and Substance Use

As noted at the beginning of this chapter, legal and clinical definitions create an ambiguous landscape for juvenile substance abuse treatment. This results in delinquency being seen as both a cause of juvenile substance use and a result of it, creating a chicken-or-egg dilemma. Adolescents who are in the juvenile justice system are even more likely to use drugs than those who are not. In a study of more than 1800 adolescents in the juvenile justice system, Teplin found that 46 percent of these adolescents, evaluated with the Diagnostic Interview Schedule for Children, met clinical criteria for substance abuse and dependence (Callahan and Patrick, 2001). Similarly, Winter (1998) indicated that half of the juveniles in the criminal justice system have used drugs. It is significant, however, that most juveniles who use drugs had engaged in delinquent acts before they tried illegal drugs (Brunelle et al., 2000). Nurco et al. (1999) explain that a high level of early delinquency in a juvenile often leads to associations with deviant peers, a negative perception of home atmosphere, and later adolescent drug use. This cycle of association caused by a high level of early juvenile delinquency can often lead to later drug addiction and incarceration as a young adult. Additionally, factors such as childhood aggression contribute to both delinquency and drug use (Brook and Whiteman, 1992), making it difficult to disentangle the cause-and-effect relationship. Parenthetically, juveniles who start early with antisocial behavior are more likely to associate with antisocial peers and have certain psychological characteristics that make them more susceptible to substance dependence (Taylor et al., 2002).

Studies suggest that different types and use levels of substances are correlated with levels of delinquent behavior. Generally, legal drugs (specifically the use of alcohol; Dawkins, 1997) are more likely to be used by delinquents than illegal drugs — an exception being the use of marijuana. Whereas juveniles who commit minor acts of delinquency are likely to use only alcohol or to be non–drug users, juveniles with a higher level of drug use have sizably higher rates of delinquency (Taylor et al., 2002). Interestingly, while juveniles with a higher level of drug use have significantly higher rates of delinquency than delinquent non-drug-using juveniles, most juveniles who commit delinquent acts and who use drugs do not commit delinquent acts in order to obtain drugs (Johnson et al., 1991); nor do substance-using juveniles frequently commit delinquent acts to obtain assets to buy drugs (Otero-Lopez and Luengo-Martin, 1994).

In summary, there is evidence of both "nature" and "nurture" components in the development of adolescent substance use and abuse. Most likely, it is some combination of factors, variously enhanced or diminished by risk and protective factors over the course of the youth's development, which shapes the level, type, and duration of drug involvement. Armed with this knowledge, it would appear that substance abuse juvenile prevention and treatment interventions must be capable of addressing a considerable amount of individual differences between adolescents, as well as changes within individuals as they develop.

24.3 Prevention and Treatment

The complexity of the development of substance use and abuse in youth results in a frequent disconnect between what causes the problem and what is done to prevent and treat it. The disconnect is often seen in how prevention and treatment programs are developed, who they serve, and the type of treatment they provide. Further, a lack of resources frequently intensifies the effects of this divide.

One of the most pervasive problems in this regard is the lack of clarity regarding the clinical relevance and theoretical basis of the treatment provided (see Andrews et al., 1990). Which begs the question, is the therapeutic approach of treatment appropriate for the specific substance abuse problem and does it tie to an established (i.e., valid) explanation for the abusing behavior? This is particularly true of treatment occurring in criminal justice settings such as residential facilities in which treatment programs offered at different locations often claim that they are offering the same treatment elements, and that they are based on same theoretical underpinning (yet in reality they are remarkably different). To illustrate, take the findings of a study of substance abuse treatment in correctional "boot camps" conducted by this chapter's lead author and his colleagues (Cowles et al., 1995). In a survey of boot camp facilities, all of the responding facilities that provided substance abuse treatment stated they used an Alcoholics Anonymous (AA) 12-step program, a common self-help treatment approach. However, the vast majority of facilities having 12-step programs also indicated use of reality therapy and stress management as specific treatment interventions. In fact, across the surveyed facilities, on average (mean), 7.41 different types of substance abuse treatment were offered at each facility. (The number of treatment types ranged from 1 to 15.) Moreover, these programs were delivered within a variety of treatment approaches or modalities, including group counseling, individual counseling, milieu, and self-help regimes at these facilities. This "everything but the kitchen sink" (Cowles et al., 1995, p. 64) situation may be due to a misidentification of the treatment approach or lack of precision in defining a therapy model. However, it also may be reflective of a more serious problem in that popular treatment approaches are simply copied from one setting to the next with little consideration of the treatment environment or the population being treated. Ultimately, this process can result in layered or multiple interventions (some with little relevance to the target population) being combined into a mishmash of treatment activities lacking coherence or grounding.

A parallel problem lies in the fact that programs often are designed for adults rather than juveniles. There are significant differences between adolescent and adult substance abusers. Adolescents tend to have used drugs for a shorter amount of time than adult addicts; they also tend to be involved more with alcohol and cannabis and less involved with opiates (Winter et al., 2000). Adolescents also are more likely to partake in binge drinking and polydrug abuse (Winter et al., 2000). However, despite these differences, many common treatment programs designed specifically for adults have only been slightly changed for use with adolescents (Rounds-Bryant et al., 1999). In order for adolescent drug treatment to be successful, the treatment program should include a constellation of elements relevant to the underlying causes of juvenile use and abuse and take note of differences between adolescents and adults. Research suggests that elements in adolescent substance abuse treatment should include family participation in therapy; elements tailored to encourage an adolescent's participation in treatment until completion; treatment services that incorporate educational, vocational, psychological, and legal concerns; staff familiar with adolescent issues; strong aftercare programs; and parental and peer support for the adolescent's abstinence from drugs. Unfortunately, most adolescent treatment programs contain some, but not all of these recommended components (Drug Strategies, 2003).

Additionally, the research on adolescent use and abuse suggests that juvenile programs must provide for a high degree of individualization. Risk and protective factors differ among individuals, and programs must be sensitive to this variation. For example, research suggests that the type of treatment should be matched to the different levels of substance use (e.g., Cowles et al., 1995; Nissen, 2003). A juvenile whose involvement has been at the experimentation level will not require the same intensity or duration of intervention as an individual who is psychologically and physiologically addicted to narcotics. The gateway hypothesis further suggests that there are optimal times to prevent or intervene in the progression of adolescent substance use and abuse. Because susceptibility to drug abuse varies over the course of a youth's development, a "one-size-fits-all" approach likely will only show occasional success and be cost-inefficient.

There are a number of successful targeted-prevention programs, such as the Westchester Student Assistance Program (SAP) in Westchester County (New York). SAP offers counseling to students on a voluntary and confidential basis at school and throughout the day. Versions of the Westchester SAP have been replicated in 20 other states across the United States. In 1992, a nationwide study showed that SAP was one of the most effective drug programs for high-risk adolescents, because SAP dealt with drugs and alcohol within the broader context of adolescence as a whole. Another prevention program, Smart Moves, is specifically targeted toward high-risk inner-city children. Smart Moves was based on social influences models and is specially tailored for Boys and Girls

Clubs in inner-city neighborhoods (Falco, 1992). Even broad-based media campaigns seem to benefit from specificity. Antidrug televised campaigns with a high reach and frequency, specifically designed to target high-sensation-seeking adolescents, have been found to signifi-cantly reduce adolescent substance use (Palmgreen et al., 2001).

Finally, both historically and currently, most drug policies in the United States are based on the *rational choice* model, a view that MacCoun (1993) and MacCoun and Caulkins (1996) indicate is "analytically attractive but psychologically implausible" (1996, p. 177). Yet, as noted at the beginning of this chapter, this perspective serves as an underpinning for a criminal justice response to drug use and abuse. However, even the general public, with isolated exceptions, accepts the fact that juveniles do not have the same capacity as adults for weighing con-sequences and then making rational choices. It is therefore ironic that much of our youth prevention and treatment effort is aimed at drug education, for such education is premised on the notion that providing children and adolescents with information about the harm and dangers of using such substances will provide them with knowledge that would serve as an effective deterrent or treatment.[1] From this approach come overly simplistic "just-say-no"–type programs.

The problem is that the vast majority of these education programs involve self-control and social competency training but do not use cog-nitive–behavioral or behavioral methods. A meta-analysis by Gottfredson et al. (2002) of school-based prevention programs found these instruc-tional intervention programs to have low effectiveness. Included in this group is the very high profile Drug Abuse Resistance Education (D.A.R.E) program, which Gottfredson et al. analyzed separately because it is the most popular school-based prevention program. The researchers' eval-uation of D.A.R.E. (involving 12 treatment contrasts) revealed an overall average effect near zero (average effect size = 0.02). Gottfredson and her colleagues noted that even in the best-case scenario, the likely effect of D.A.R.E. is not enough to justify its costs.[2] These findings, including those on D.A.R.E., are now added to a substantial amount of research (e.g., Botvin, 1999; Botvin, G.J and Botvin, E.M., 1992; Schinke et al., 1991) that shows simple instructional approaches without a cogni-tive–behavioral component are not effective.

Given the evidence supporting the need for substance abuse pre-vention and treatment programs that are tailored to juveniles, individu-alized, and based in comprehensive strategies, the question is why do we continue to replicate simple generic programs that may be largely ineffective? A major portion of the answer is likely rooted in society's unwillingness to provide the needed funding for these types of programs.

In the mid-1980s, federal funding for the drug problem was nearly equally split between supply (enforcement) and demand (prevention and treatment) programs. Recent budgets now have more than two-thirds of federal drug control budget earmarked for supply reduction. Not only has this likely had the impact of bringing more juveniles into the criminal justice system, but there are very real treatment and prevention impacts as well. For example, in 2000, 1.1 million adolescents (ages 12 to 17) were in need of substance abuse treatment, which is 4.6 percent of the age group's population (Office of Applied Studies, 2002). Of these 1.1 million adolescents in need of treatment, only 11.4 percent (0.1 million persons) actually received it (Office of Applied Studies, 2002).

The lack of available treatment is caused by several factors: the high cost of treatment, limited insurance coverage to meet the cost of treatment, lack of access to appropriate treatment centers, lack of adolescents who desire treatment, and degrading social stigma attached to adolescents who undergo drug treatment (Sindelar and Fiellin, 2001). In 1999, 15.9 percent of children under the age of 22 had no health insurance. It was especially difficult for these uninsured children to receive treatment for substance abuse problems. In order to receive government assistance for substance abuse, these families must meet low-income restrictions, and the child must evidence severe emotional disturbances before qualifying for assistance (American Academy of Pediatrics, 2001).

The 65.4 percent of children covered by private insurance do not fare much better at finding help for drug addictions (American Academy of Pediatrics, 2001). Private insurance generally does not cover substance abuse assessment, early intervention, relapse prevention, crisis intervention, partial hospitalization, or day treatment. Furthermore, inpatient substance abuse services are generally not completely covered by insurance, unless the treatment is for a short period of time for detoxification purposes (American Academy of Pediatrics, 2001).

Given this situation, it is perhaps not surprising that the criminal justice system is the major source of referrals to substance abuse treatment, particularly for adolescents and young adults. In 2002, for example, the percentage of those under 18 admitted to treatment from criminal justice sources was double the percentage admitted from all other sources (Substance Abuse and Mental Health Services Administration, 2002). And although research indicates that correctional drug treatment programs can have a substantial effect on the behavior of chronic drug abusers (Anglin and Hser, 1990), within the criminal justice milieu, treatment efforts must compete for resources with other programs and security needs. Given that among the various treatment modalities, research has shown that long-term residential programs, such as therapeutic communities, are the most effective (for example, see Wexler et al., 1990; MacKenzie, 1997), the resource issue becomes even more problematic. That is, for substance abuse treatment programs to be effective, they must be of sufficient scope and duration to bring about major lifestyle changes in the abuser, rather than narrowly focusing on abuse as an isolated issue. Further, the aftercare component of treatment is critical: "The high rate of drug abuse among juvenile offenders and these high relapse rates indicate a need for aftercare treatment services to reinforce skills and behaviors learned during treatment" (Sealock et al., 1997, p. 212). Thus, the most successful approaches are those requiring a great commitment of resources and a well-designed and integrated approach that includes lengthy involvement in a structured program. Such programs often fall victim to the budget ax, leaving behind less thorough programs that show little real effectiveness but are cheaper and easier to implement.

It is not a particularly flattering comment on our society that for many of today's poorer youth, treatment availability will not become a reality until they have reached a level of drug involvement that brings them into the criminal justice system. Moreover, once in the criminal justice system, they are likely to find treatment programs poorly tailored to individual needs and lacking resources to provide the rigorous intervention and follow-up needed to remain drug free. Regrettably, the larger social and budgetary costs of failing to provide effective substance abuse prevention and treatment will be seen in youth crime, wasted potential, and the cyclical problem of drug involvement.

References

American Academy of Pediatrics. (2001). Improving substance abuse prevention, assessment, and treatment financing for children and adolescents. *Pediatrics*, 108(4), 1025–1029.

Andrews, D.A., Zinger, I., Hoge, R..D., Bonta, J., Gendreau, P., and Cullen, F.T. (1990). Does correctional treatment work? A clinically relevant and psychologically informed meta-analysis. *Criminology* 29(3), 369–404.

Anglin, M.D. and Hser, Y. (1990). Treatment and drug abuse. In Tonry, M. and Wilson, J.Q. (Eds.), *Drugs and Crime*. Chicago, IL: University of Chicago Press. pp. 393–460.

Bentler, P.M. (1992). Etiologies and consequences of adolescent drug use: implications for prevention. *Journal of Addictive Diseases* 11(3), 47–61.

Botvin,. G.J. (1999). Adolescent drug prevention: current findings and future directions. In Hartel, C.R. and Glantz, M.D. (Eds.), *Drug Abuse: Origins and Interventions*. Washington, D.C.: APA Books. pp. 285–308.

Botvin, G.J. and Botvin, E.M. (1992). Adolescent tobacco, alcohol, and drug abuse: prevention strategies, empirical findings, and assessment issues. *Journal of Developmental and Behavioral Pediatrics*, 13, 290–301.

Brook, J.S. and Whiteman, M.M. (1992). Childhood aggression, adolescent delinquency and drug use: a longitudinal study. *Journal of Genetic Psychology*, 153(4), 369–373.

Brunelle, N., Brochu, S., and Cousineau, M.M. (2000). Drug-crime relations among drug-consuming juvenile delinquents: a tripartite model and more. *Contemporary Drug Problems*, 27, 835–865.

Bureau of Justice Statistics. (1992). *Drugs, Crime and the Justice System: A National Report from the Bureau of Justice Statistics*. Washington, D.C.: Author.

Callahan, J. and Patrick, F. (2001). *Adolescent Portable Therapy (APT) for the Juvenile Justice System*. (1/7/2003). www.vera.org/publication_pdf/aptplan.pdf.

Cooper, M.H. (1988). The business of illicit drugs. *Congressional Quarterly's Editorial Research Reports*, 1(19), 257–271.

Cowles, E.L., Castellano, T.C., and Gransky, L.A. (1995). *"Boot Camp" Drug Treatment and Aftercare Intervention: An Evaluation Review*. Washington D.C.: U.S. Department of Justice.

Curran, G.M., White, H.R., and Hansell, S. (2000). Personality, environment, and problem drug use. *Journal of Drug Issues*, 30(2), 375–405.

Dawkins, M.P. (1997). Drug use and violent crime among adolescents. *Adolescence*, 32(126), 395–405.

Doweiko, H.E. (1990). *Concepts of Chemical Dependency*. Pacific Grove, CA: Brooks/Cole.

Drug Strategies. (2003). *Treating Teens: A Guide to Adolescent Drug Problems*. Washington D.C.: Drug Strategies.

Falco, M. (1992). *The Making Of A Drug-Free America: Programs That Work*. New York: Times Book, a division of Random House, Inc.

Fergusson, D.M. and Horwood, L.J. (2000). Does cannabis use encourage other forms of illicit drug use? *Addiction*, 95(4), 505–520.

Gerstein, D., Lane, J., Huang, L., and Wright, D. (1997). *Risk and Protective Factors for Adolescent Drug Use: Findings from the 1997 National Household Survey on Drug Abuse*. (6/21/2002) www.samhsa.gov/oas/NHSDA/NAC97/HIGHLIGHTS.HTM.

Golub, A. and Johnson, B. (2001). Variation in youthful risks of progression from alcohol/tobacco to marijuana and to hard drugs across generation. *American Journal of Public Health*, 23(3), 225–232.

Gottfredson, D.C., Wison, D.B., and Najaka, S.S. (2002). The schools. In Wison, J.Q. and Petersilia, J. (Eds.). *Crime: Public Policies for Crime Control*. Oakland, CA: Institute for Contemporary Studies. pp. 149–189.

Hawkins, J.D., Lishner, D.M., and Catalano, R.F. (1985). Childhood predictors and the prevention of adolescent substance abuse. In Jones, C.L. and Battjes, R.J. (Eds.), *Etiology of Drug Abuse: Implications for Prevention*. (NIDA Research Monograph #56). Rockville, MD: Department of Health and Human Services, National Institute on Drug Abuse.

Hawkins, D.F., Hill, K.G., Guo, F., and Battin-Pearson, S.R. (2002). Substance use norms and transitions in substance use: implications for the gateway hypothesis. In Kandel, D.B. (Ed.), *Stages and Pathways of Drug Involvement: Examining the Gateway Hypothesis.* New York: Cambridge University Press.

Hirshi, T. (1969). *The Causes of Delinquency.* Berkley, CA: University of California Press.

Hoffmann, J.P. and Johnson, R.A. (1998). A national portrait of family structure and adolescent drug use. *Journal of Marriage and the Family,* 60(3), 633–645.

Hoffmann, J.P. and Johnson, R.A. (2002). The community context of family structure and adolescent drug use. *Journal of Marriage, and Family* 64(2): 314–330.

Jenkins, J.E. and Zunguze, S.T. (1998). The relationship of family structure to adolescent drug use, peer affiliation, and perception of peer acceptance of drug use. *Adolescence,* 33(132), 811–822.

Jenkins, J.E. and Zunguze, S.T. (1996). The influence of peer affiliation and student activities on drug involvement. *Adolescence,* 31(122), 297–305.

Jessor, R., Chase, J.A., and Donovan, J.E. (1980). Psychosocial correlates of marijuana use and problem drinking in a national sample of adolescents. *American Journal of Public Health,* 70, 604–613.

Jessor, R., Chase, J.A., and Donovan, J.E., and Costa, F. (1986). Psychosocial correlates of marijuana use in adolescence and young adulthood: the past as prologue. *Alcohol, Drugs and Driving* 2(2–3), 31–49.

Johnson, B.D., Wish, E.D., Schmeidler, J., and Huizinga, D. (1991). Concentration of Delinquent Offending: Serious Drug Involvement and High Delinquency Rates. *Journal of Drug Issues,* 21(2), 205–228.

Johnston, L.D., O'Malley, P.M., and Bachman, J.G. (1996). *National Survey Results on Drug Use From the Monitoring the Future Study, 1975–1995; Volume Secondary School Students.* Rockville, MD: National Institute on Drug Abuse. NCADI#BKD213.

Johnston, L.D., O'Malley, P.M., and Bachman, J.G. (2001). *Monitoring the Future National Survey Results on Drug Use, 1975–2000. Volume I: Secondary School Students.* (NIH Publication No. 01-4924). Bethesda, MD: National Institute on Drug Abuse.

Jones, C.L., and Battjes, R.J. (Eds.). (1985). *Etiology of Drug Abuse* (NIDA, Research Monograph Series #56). Rockville, MD: U.S. Department of Health and Human Services, National Institute on Drug Abuse.

Kandel, D.B. (1978). *Longitudinal Research on Drug Use: Empirical Findings and Methodological Issues.* New York: John Wiley & Sons.

Kandel, D.B. (1982). Epidemiological and psychosocial perspectives on adolescent drug use. *Journal of the American Academy of Clinical Psychiatry,* 21(4), 328–347.

Kandel, D.B. (Ed.). (2002). *Stages and Pathways of Drug Involvement: Examining the Gateway Hypothesis.* New York: Cambridge University Press.

Lane, J., Gerstein, D., Huang, L., and Wright, D. (February 2001). *Risk and Protective Factors for Adolescent Drug Use: Findings from the 1997 National Household Survey on Drug Abuse*. (1/10/2003). www.samhsa.gov/oas/ NHSDA/NAC97/Table_of_Contents.htm.

Lee, C.F., Yang, S., and Hazard, B.P. (1998). The contingent effects of risk perception on risk-taking behavior: adolescent participative orientation and marijuana use. *Journal of Youth and Adolescence*, 27(1), 17–27.

Lipton, D.S., Falkin, G.P., and Wexler, H.K. (1992). Correctional drug abuse treatment in the United States: an Overview. In Leukefled, C. and Tims, F. (Eds.), *Drug Abuse Treatment in Prisons and Jails*. (NIDA Research Monograph No. 118, pp. 8–31). Rockville, MD: U.S. Department of Health and Human Services, National Institute on Drug Abuse.

MacCoun, R.J. (1993). Drugs and the law: a psychological analysis of drug prohibition. *Psychological Bulletin*, 113, 497–512.

MacCoun, R.J. and Caulkins, J. (1996). Examining the behavioral assumptions of the national drug control strategies. In Bickel, W.K. and DeGrandpre, R.J. (Eds.), *Drug Policy and Human Nature: Psychological Perspectives on the Prevention, Management, and Treatment of Illicit Drug Abuse*. New York: Plenum Press. pp. 177–197.

MacKenzie, J. (1997). Glen Parva therapeutic community — an obituary. *Prison Service Journal*, No. 111, 26.

Miller, M.A., Alberts, J.K., Hecht, M.L., Trost, M.R., and Krizek, R.L. (2000). *Adolescent Relationships and Drug Use*. Mahwah, NJ: Lawrence Erlbaum Associates.

National Institute on Drug Abuse. (1985). *Etiology of Drug Abuse* (NIDA, Research Monograph Series #56). Rockville, MD: U.S. Department of Health and Human Services.

Newcomb, M.D. and Bentler, P.M. (1989). Substance use and abuse among chidren and teenagers. *American Psychologist*, 44(2), 242–248.

Newcomb, M.D., Maddahian, E., and Bentler, P.M. (1986). Risk factors for drug use among adolescents: concurrent and longitudinal analyses. *American Journal of Public Health*, 76, 525–531.

Nissen, L. (2003). *Interpreting the Key Elements Within a Juvenile Justice Setting*. (2/12/2003). http://www.drugstrategies.com/teens/juvjustice.html.

Nurco, D.N., Blatchley, R.J., Hanlon, T.E., and O'Grady, K.E. (1999). Early deviance and related risk factors in the children of narcotic addicts. *American Journal of Drug and Alcohol Abuse*, 25:1, 25-45.

Office of Applied Studies. (2002). *National and State Estimates of the Drug Abuse Treatment Gap: 2000 National Household Survey on Drug Abuse* (NHSDA Series H-14, DHHS Publication No. SMA 02-3640). Rockville, MD: Substance Abuse and Mental Health Services Administration.

Otero-Lopez, J.M. and Luengo-Martin, A. (1994). An empirical study of the relations between drug abuse and delinquency among adolescents. *British Journal of Criminology*, 34(4), 459–478.

Palmgreen, P., Donohew, L., Lorch, E.P., Hoyle, R.H., and Stephenson, M.T. (2001). Television campaigns and adolescent marijuana use: test of sensation seeking targeting. *American Journal of Public Health*, 91(2), 292–296.

Pearson, M. and Michell, L. (2000). Smoke rings: social network analysis of friendship groups, smoking and drug-taking. *Drugs: Education Prevention and Policy*, 7(1), 21–37.

Perkonigg, A. and Lieb, R. (1999). Patterns of cannabis use, abuse, and dependence over time: incidence, progression, and stability in a sample of 1228 adolescents. *Addiction*, 94(11), 1663–1678.

Peters, R. (1993). Drug treatment in jails and detention settings. In Inciardi, J. (Ed.), *Drug Treatment in Criminal Justice*. Newbury Park, CA: Sage, pp. 44–80.

Rogers, P.D., Harris, J., and Jarmuskewicz, J. (1987). Alcohol and adolescence. *The Pediatric Clinics of North America*, 34(2), 289–303.

Rosenbuam. M. (2002). *Safety First: A Reality-Based Approach to Teens, Drugs, and Drug Education*. San Francisco, CA: Drug Policy Alliance.

Rounds-Bryant, J.L., Kristiansen, P.L., and Hubbard, R.L. (1999). Drug abuse treatment outcome study of adolescents: a comparison of client characteristics and pretreatment behaviors in three treatment modalities. *American Journal of Drug and Alcohol Abuse*, 25(4), 573–592.

Schinke, S., Botvin, G.J., and Orlandi, M. (1991). *Substance Abuse in Children and Adolescents*. Newburg Park, CA: Sage

Sealock, M.D., Gottfredson, D.C., and Gallagher, C.A. (1997). Drug treatment for juvenile offenders: some good and bad news. *Journal of Research in Crime and Delinquency,* 34(2), 210–236.

Sindelar, J. and Fiellin, D.A. (2001). Innovations in treatment for drug abuse: Solutions to a Public Health Problem. *Annual Review of Public Health*, 22(1), 249–272.

Spooner, C. (1999). Causes and correlates of adolescent drug abuse and implications for treatment. *Drug and Alcohol Review*, 18, 453–474.

Stephenson, A.L. and Henry, C.S. (1996). Family characteristics and adolescent substance use. *Adolescence*, 31(121), 59–78.

Strang, J. (2001). Drug use in adolescence: the relationship between opportunity, initial use and continuation of use of four illicit drugs in a cohort of 14–16-year-olds in south London. *Drugs: Education, Prevention, and Policy*, 8(4), 397–405.

Substance Abuse and Mental Health Services Administration. (May 10, 2002). *Drug and Alcohol Treatment in Juvenile Correctional Facilities. The DASIS Report*. (1/7/2002). www.samhsa.gov/oas/2k2/YouthJusticeTX/YouthJusticeTX.pdf.

Taylor, J, Malone, I.S., and McGue, W.G. (2002). Development of substance dependence in two delinquency subgroups and non-delinquents from a male twin sample. *Journal of the American Academy of Child and Adolescent Psychiatry*, 41(4), 386–393.

Thornberry, T.P., Smith, C.A., Rivera, C., Huizinga, D., and Stouthamer-Loeber, M. (September 1999). Family disruption and delinquency. *Juvenile Justice Bulletin*. Office of Juvenile Justice and Delinquency Programs. Washington, D.C.: U.S. Department of Justice, Office of Justice Programs. NCJ 178285.

Weinberg, N.Z. (2001). Risk factors for adolescent substance abuse. *Journal of Learning Disabilities*, 34(4), 343–351.

Wexler, H.K., Falkin, G.P., and Lipton, D.S. (1990). Outcome evaluation of a prison therapeutic community for substance abuse treatment. *Criminal Justice and Behavior* 17(1), 71–92.

Willner, P. (2001). A view through the gateway: expectancies as a possible pathway from alcohol to cannabis. *Addiction*, 96(5), 691–704.

Winter, K.C., Stinchfield, R.D., Opland, E., Weller, C., and Latimer, W.W. (April 2000). The effectiveness of the Minnesota model approach in the treatment of adolescent drug abusers. *Addiction*, 95(4), 601–613.

Winter, K.C. (1998). Kids and drugs. *Corrections Today*, 60(6), 118–123.

Zimmer, L. and Morgan, J.P. (1997) *Marijuana Myths, Marijuana Facts: A Review of the Scientific Evidence*. New York: The Lindsmith Center.

Notes

1. Many maintain that substance abuse education or programs that provide information about drugs and drug use do not represent treatment (e.g., Lipton et al., 1992). Yet it is a commonly found element in self-help approaches (e.g., Alcoholics Anonymous and Narcotics Anonymous), and what Peters (1993) refers to as psychoeducational approaches.
2. Interestingly, Gottfredson et al. found a similar lack of effect for D.A.R.E. programs with regard to their modifying general delinquent and problem behavior of school-age children and youth (2002, p. 169).

Part V Conclusion

DISCUSSION QUESTIONS FOR PART V

1. One of the most common disabilities found in the juvenile offender population is learning disability (LD). What is the recommended course of action when an LD youth comes in contact with the juvenile justice system? What is the second most common disability and the recommended course of action? (See Chapter 18.)
2. Dwyer and Laufersweiler-Dwyer (Chapter 19) outline several possible reasons for why young people engage in sexual offending. What are they?
3. Describe the characteristics of juvenile sex offenders as suggested by Veneziano and Veneziano (see Chapter 20). Describe what these authors mean by a "practical orientation" in the prevention of offenses of this nature among juveniles.
4. Chapter 21 presents an applied behavior analysis perspective as an alternative treatment for juvenile sex offenders, offering it as an alternative to the sexual abuse cycle, relapse prevention model, and aversive conditioning. Discuss the major shortcomings of each of these three programs. What reasons are given by the authors for a child who is sexually victimized eventually victimizing a child himself or herself?

5. Bond-Maupin (see Chapter 22) suggests that high rates of police contact with American Indians, including American Indian youth, may be a function of the many layers of jurisdiction common to reservation lands. What are these layers? How did the Indian Reorganization Act of 1934 and subsequent legislation affect the legal structure of American Indian reservations? Describe how the 1978 Indian Child Welfare Act affected juvenile justice for American Indian youth.

6. How does the gang-affiliated female differ from a female gang member as discussed in Chapter 23? In this study, what factors are associated with gang affilation for Mexican American females?

7. How do Cowles and Lanphierd (see Chapter 24) describe the context of treatment in general for people who abuse substances? Discuss briefly the explanations they give for substance abuse by juveniles as well as the type of prevention and treatment programs now being used with this population.

Part VI

JUVENILE CORRECTIONS

The outcomes of cases involving juveniles have long-lasting implications for the youthful offender. Theoretically, diversion programs are encouraged for the less serious adjudicated juvenile offender, but this is not always the case. Chapter 25 through Chapter 28 tackle some of the more salient and critical issues involving juvenile corrections, including diversion programs (Chapter 25 by Marsh and Patrick), placement and programming (Chapter 26 by King and Settles), restorative justice programming (Chapter 27 by White), and capital punishment for juveniles (Chapter 28 by Patenaude and Reynolds). An equally important issue in juvenile corrections is the working environment for those who function within those systems. Minor and his colleagues address this issue in Chapter 29.

Chapter 25

Juvenile Diversion Programs

Robert L. Marsh and Steven B. Patrick

25.1 Introduction

The dilemma of dealing with youth culture has been an age-old cultural concern. The process of socializing the young and dealing with their positive and negative behaviors has concerned societies and governments as diverse as the ancient Romans and Greeks and modern Americans. In the American colonies, children occupied a low status and, as such, were treated harshly. Societies have employed a number of methods to control and teach correct behavior to the young. Most policies concentrated on some type of punishment. The public policies for youthful misbehavior in both England and its former colonies often included trial in an adult court and adult punishments.

The concept of the juvenile court was developed in the midst of improved attitudes toward child welfare. The establishment of the first juvenile court in Cook County, Illinois, in 1899 provided a different focus to the American court system that treated the young like adults. Under the *parens patriae* power of the state, the needs of children and youth were to be the primary concern of the government and court. To achieve these ends courts were to act to diagnose, guide, and treat juveniles, and not to adjudicate guilt and punish them. The doctrine of *parens patriae* changed the role of the state and court from one of seeking justice to seeking the course of action that was in the best interests of the child so that they would eventually become productive adults (Pogrebin et al., 1984).

The creation of the juvenile court was obviously an idea whose time had come. From its beginnings in Cook County in 1899, the juvenile court concept had spread to every state by 1945. The court's mandate was to act in the best interests of the child. To achieve that end, the proceedings were informal and based on a rehabilitative model rather than on a due process model. Judges had wide latitude to make decisions in the best interests of the child and the community.

The development and expansion of the juvenile court happened at a time when probation programs for juveniles were also expanding. By 1927, juvenile probation programs existed in most states. The development of a system of juvenile probation reinforced the concept of guiding and rehabilitating the young, rather than a punitive approach. Interestingly, this new philosophy and focus on the young had a powerful impact on public attitudes toward youthful misbehavior, both legal and illegal. The concept of child welfare was given a great impetus by the "child-saving movement" that rapidly gained popularity during that time (Platt, 1969). During the late 19th and early 20th century, a number of conditions regarding child welfare dramatically changed. In addition to a more benevolent attitude of society toward the young, a clear philosophical distinction was being made between the young and adults. Importantly, this related to the concept of child and adolescent development, and the concept of responsibility or *mens rea*. That is, the young were treated differently because of the lack of criminal intent in their actions or the conditions in which they were raised. The state began to focus on the concept that parents, as well as the state, had the responsibility to raise and care for the young.

Slowly, over the course of the last century, a distinction was created between adults, who are capable of being responsible for their actions, and juveniles who may not be able to differentiate between right and wrong. Juveniles came to be seen as different from adults with regard to crime, and different methods were developed and utilized to deal with underage crime. In an attempt to guide the young, juvenile law has expanded into areas in which many activities that are legal for adults are prohibited for juveniles. In attempting to care for the young, a much broader area of juvenile court intervention has been created that provides for legal intervention in their lives. This has been related to a broad area of youthful behavior known as "status" offenses, behaviors that are denied to anyone under age 21.

Juveniles are capable of committing and do commit the full spectrum of crimes but, until the last few decades, the vast majority have been treated very differently from adults committing the same crimes, except for some violent juvenile offenders transferred to adult courts. This separate system has been created to adjudicate juvenile offenders.

This process has also reduced the rights held by juveniles. While adults are assumed innocent and have a right to trial by jury, juveniles have lost these rights in the process of the system's attempts to protect them. While the punishment of juveniles is often less severe than that of adults, the punishment of juveniles is often more swift and sure. While juveniles retain the right to admit or deny their crime, their judgment is often based solely on the perceptions of a single judge (Binder and Binder, 1982).

There is little debate that older juveniles should be held accountable for serious adult felonies if they are old enough and have the capacity to understand (*mens rea)* their actions. The difficulty in the juvenile justice system has been the wide variety of status offenders who have to be processed by the system and need supervision, hence the programs Children in Need of Supervision (CHINS) and Persons in Need of Supervision (PINS). These are the young who are drawn into the system under the guise they are beyond control of their parents and need guidance to grow and develop in the right manner.

In effect, the discretion of the juvenile court has encouraged it to act with the child's best interests in mind in the area of status offenses. Furthermore, the court has justified its discretionary decision making and the absence of due process procedural safeguards because their actions were "in the best interests of the child" (Platt, 1977).

Much of the subsequent criticism of the court has centered on two specific issues. First of all, the juvenile court has been criticized for its perceived leniency on serious offenders under the guise of rehabilitation. That has led to an increased number of transfers of serious juvenile offenders to adult courts to enhance sentencing options. The second major criticism of the juvenile court has centered on the fact that the court, in using its broad discretion to "act in the best interests of the child," has failed in rehabilitation. In effect, many of the children it has sought to help have become worse by being drawn ever more deeply into the criminal justice system, even becoming institutionalized. It is outside the scope of chapter to discuss the first criticism but we will discuss the second, namely, the broad discretion of the system and the response of the system in addressing this issue.

25.2 Juvenile Court Discretion

The juvenile court controversy reached one of the highest levels when juvenile crime and crime in general were soaring in the United States during the 1960s. The first large federal intervention occurred when legislation was passed to fund a number of programs to address local crime. These federal programs had a number of important impacts on the criminal justice system. In fact, the programs and funding stimulated so many reforms it became known as the beginning of the modern criminal justice era. Juvenile delinquency and criminology played an important part in providing "answers" or, at least, theories to what was wrong with society and the system, and appropriate ways to respond.

Policy makers and experts in the justice system discussed many perspectives to address those issues. It is important to review some of the prominent theories related to the juvenile court system that ultimately led to the diversion programs established in the country. Some even see these changes in the treatment of juveniles as revolutionary (Hellum, 1979).

25.3 Theories of Diversion

25.3.1 The Social Learning Theory

The social learning theory is a general theory in social psychology arguing that humans learn behavior greatly through the observation of others. Albert Bandura (1962) believed, through a process of "behavioral modeling," that juveniles model new behavior by a process of observational learning. If juveniles see themselves and others punished for deviant behavior, they will learn not to commit these actions to avoid punishment. On the other hand, if they associate with law or rule breakers, they may learn inappropriate behavior from these associations.

25.3.2 The Labeling Theory

Diverting juvenile offenders from the traditional juvenile justice system has been influenced by various theories but most prominently by the labeling and differential association theories. The differential association theory's basic premise is that through association with deviant groups individuals are more likely to become deviant themselves. Juveniles incarcerated with other juvenile offenders will interact with and are more likely to join deviant groups.

The rise of juvenile diversion is in large part attributable to the popularity of the labeling theory during the 1960s (Osgood and Weichselbaum, 1984, p. 35). The labeling theory continues to be the most powerful force for diversion from the justice system. It hypothesizes that the delinquent behavior (primary deviance) and the act of being negatively labeled by powerful authority figures in society will strongly influence juveniles to believe themselves to be deviant and create secondary deviance (Klein, 1986). This, in turn, creates a self-fulfilling prophecy and a higher potential for a life of crime (Schur, 1973).

Diversion programs are intended keep juvenile offenders out of the criminal justice system from the beginning and thus reduce their interaction with other, possibly more serious, deviant groups. By keeping juveniles out of the system, the labeling impact of courts and judges will be reduced. Juveniles will also develop less of the secondary deviance patterns that result from being labeled by the system as delinquent.

The labeling theory was particularly influential when status offenders were incarcerated in the juvenile justice system. Their behavior, which was not criminal, gave them exposure to persons who had committed criminal acts and also labeled them as delinquent because of their association with the juvenile court. This, in turn, created images of delinquency in persons who had committed status offenses, giving a powerful opportunity for status offenders to adopt the behavior of primary deviance learned from their association with more serious juvenile offenders. In effect, status offenders, according to theory, became worse because we tried to "help" them (Frazier and Cochran, 1986).

25.3.3 The Social Control Theory

Hirschi (1969), in the 1960s, argued that deviance is the norm in juveniles and that only through attachment to conventional ideas and others can youth be molded into upstanding citizens. The idea of the control theory as it relates to diversion is that through attachment (i.e., diversion) to conventional activities, deviant behavior can be replaced by socially responsible behavior.

25.3.4 The Differential Association Theory

Sutherland (1992), in the 1930s, developed a perspective related to the learning theory that juveniles learn criminal behavior from their close peer associations. The old saying "birds of a feather flock together" holds here. The basic idea of diversion is to break these peer associations and replace them with more socially desirable peer relationships.

25.4 The Rationale of Diversion Programs

The concept of diversion became very popular during the 1960s when various sociologists, federal policy makers, and juvenile justice practitioners looked for innovative ways to address the problems of crime among youth. There was special concern that in the attempt to act paternalistically toward youth, they were actually drawing too many into the system under the guise of helping them (Minor et al., 1997; Rose, 1997; Rausch, 1983). The labeling theory provided a very timely approach in attempting to stop nondelinquent youth from penetrating further into the system after contact because of a status offense. The arguments and theories of Lemert and Schur provided much of the theoretical rationale for handling certain youth in a new way. Lemert's arguments of both primary and secondary deviance provided much of the rationale that society's attempts to "guide status offenders onto the right pathway" actually had greater potential to introduce them to a life of primary deviance. Lemert's theories on deviance were influential in the arguments of Schur (1973), who proposed a policy of "radical nonintervention" especially as it related to status offenders. In effect, those persons who had not committed crimes and were in the juvenile justice system because of a status offense should not be drawn further into the system. In effect, the "help" that the juvenile justice system provided would actually make them worse. Schur's (1973) suggestion that juveniles should be restrained from penetrating too far into the system was adopted as a policy approach.

These arguments and the increased activism (i.e., federal funds) of the federal government into the areas of both adult and juvenile crime policy gave the concept of diversion the needed impetus to develop into a respected approach to addressing the problems of the young. The initial programs funded by the Office of Juvenile Justice and Delinquency Prevention (OJJDP) served to provide the funding and policy initiative that created numerous types of diversion programs. The funding and the interest in keeping certain types of offenders out of the system were firmly established during this time.

25.5 Types of Diversion Programs

25.5.1 Group Homes

A variety of diversion programs have developed over the last 30 years. The intention to stop juveniles, especially status offenders, from entering the system has been interpreted in a number of ways. Very simply some offenders were left in their current living arrangement. Others, because of more serious problems, were removed from their parents. Quite often these juveniles were sent to group homes rather than to detention centers. This kept them from being exposed to the juvenile justice system, and they received help in a place that did not label them juvenile offenders.

25.5.2 Behavioral Contracts

A number of programs utilized the concept of setting up a separate agreement with juveniles to, hopefully, change their behavior without formal processing through the juvenile court. Often, in addition to the agreement, the juveniles attend group counseling sessions with diversion workers. A variety of other services, both educational and counseling, can also be provided if their problems deserve that type of attention.

25.5.3 Scared Straight Programs

An early effort to divert juveniles from the path of criminal activity was based partly on the idea of deterrence. If youth show signs of taking the wrong path, they can be diverted from the ultimate outcome of this path by a preview of what prison is like. The Scared Straight Program brought groups of youth to local jails and prisons where inmates told them their stories of how they started as small-time juvenile delinquents and ended as long-term prisoners.

25.5.4 Public Service

Public service is a treatment-oriented approach for dealing with juvenile crime, which many youth who are detached from society become involved in. They are old enough to be seen in many ways as adults but are still shackled with the label of youth. In a real sense, young people often have too much time on their hands and few organized activities. This can result in a lack of bonding to conventional society. When these juveniles became involved in crime, it was hoped that they could be diverted from bonding to a criminal lifestyle by being encouraged to bond with their community through conventional activities performed as public service. "Volunteering" (actually forced community service) was believed to allow young offenders the chance to repay their violation through community service. Young offenders were placed with agencies — mostly public agencies — and put to work removing graffiti from walls or cleaning parks, among other activities.

Community or public service was often the most common form of deterrence. Offenders were assigned to a variable number of hours serving the public good as punishment for minor crimes. The services provided were limited only by the program coordinator's imagination. Community service was based on a complex theoretical foundation. Through productive service it was hoped that youthful offenders would become attached to socially positive activities. This attachment to social positive activities was based partly on the control theory. Additionally, the service was to be presented to the offender not as a punishment but as an alternative and, if completed, the criminal violation would be removed from the record. It is hoped that service would label the offending juvenile as a positive, helpful individual and not as a criminal. Finally, the agencies that coordinated the service were designed to be positive role models for the juveniles.

25.5.5 Education

Education was another old attempt to divert juveniles from crime. DARE programs attempted to educate children on the dangers of drugs. Commercials were run on television, during programs watched by juveniles in an attempt to instruct them on the dangers of many socially unacceptable behaviors. These educational programs were based partly on the rational choice theory and partly on social learning perspectives. It is hoped that the negative consequences of smoking or doing drugs would outweigh the positive aspects. Also, many of the programs were designed to appeal to the youth culture through the use of popular cultural symbols providing them with positive role models.

25.5.6 Restitution

Restitution was a diversion program designed to assist the victims as much as the offenders and to hold offenders responsible for their actions (Shichor and Binder, 1982; Staples, 1986). A mediator works with the two parties involved to come to both an emotional and financial agreement for closure over the issue of restitution. Victims were in need of closure, and offenders need to be made aware that they have violated an individual's rights. This perspective was based on symbolic interaction. In symbolic interaction, the shared meaning or definition of the situation was the key. Offenders were believed not to take the role of "the other" in their actions. The mediation process was partly designed to bring the two parties together and come to a shared definition. In this way, the victim came to see that the violation was not his or her fault, and the offenders came to see that they hurt a real person. The two parties, with the assistance of the mediator, came to a mutual agreement to resolve the problem. Of course, this type of diversion was most useful in the case of property crimes. Status offenses have no specific victim, and violent offenses were often too personal to the victim to be mediated. As with all types of diversion, the purpose of restitution is to hold juvenile offenders liable for their actions without labeling the juvenile as a delinquent (Levi, 1982).

25.6 Summary of Research on Diversion Programs

Research on diversion is very broad, and includes public service and education (Campbell and Retzlaff, 2000). The results have been mixed at best (Osgood, 1983; Reker and Peacock, 1980). Early research showed promise with reported reductions of more than 25 percent in recidivism, but these early reports had many methodological problems (Regoli et al., 1985: Lipsey et al., 1981; Palmer and Lewis, 1980; Quay and Love, 1977; Gibbons and Blake, 1976). Most of the more recent research has been unsupportive of these programs, reducing recidivism (Kammer et al., 1997; Severy and Whitaker, 1982; Sleke, 1982; Rojek and Erickson, 1981). In any case, most research strongly suggests that these programs are not quick fixes and that extensive aftercare is most likely the key to any reductions that may be gained. Some programs showed positive results (Myers et al., 2000), and others showed some short-term lowering of recidivism for first-time offenders (Emshoff and Blakely, 1983) but not all of these were scientific studies. Others show the need for longitudinal analysis (Polk, 1984). While there are many different kinds of diversion, they tend to be used in combination. Education takes place in group homes, and behavioral contracts usually involve community service.

Group homes are seen as a diversion tactic for youth with a troubled home life. These troubles are often manifested in the form of running away from home. Juveniles who run away from home are at much greater risk of committing many other crimes and even of being the victim of crimes. While removing the troubled youth from a disruptive home environment can be seen as a solution, most research points to the need to extensive therapeutic treatment in group homes (Moses, 1978).

Youth courts may be capable of handling more serious offenses (Seyfrit et al., 1987), although more control empirical research is needed to confirm this.

Most diversion programs involve some form of education designed to change the offender's attitudes (Fox et al., 1994).

A subset of diversion research focuses on restitution. The research in this area also does not support reductions in recidivism but does point to positive results for victims of crime. Restitution has been utilized as a method of diversion for over 20 years. Research shows that restitution does not reduce recidivism in most cases (Sudipto, 1995; Sudipto, 1993). Some research indicates that restitution may reduce recidivism for early stage offenders but only if face-to-face offender–victim mediation occurs, and/or community service is part of the restitution process. Additionally, victims often find restitution more satisfying than traditional punishments (Umbreit, 1993, 1994).

25.7 Conclusions of Past Research

Ultimately, it was hoped that most diversion programs would save money and reduce recidivism (Binder, 1985). This does not seem to be the case. While no one is giving up on diversion programs, the research focus has changed to a call for more extensive aftercare (Blechman et al., 2001). Social psychological research shows that dramatic changes can be made to individuals in a short time, but without reinforcement more individuals will return to their former patterns of behavior (Goffman, 1962). Reinforcement can produce long-term change.

25.7.1 One Example of a Longitudinal Study

In 1999, the City of Boise, Idaho, a midsized urban community located in the intermountain West, began a new diversion program with federal grant funding. The main goal of the program was to reduce the backlog of juvenile cases in the magistrate's court and evaluate different program options. In order to conduct this evaluation and assess options, an experimental design was chosen with a control group and three experimental groups. The groups were:

1. A new diversion program
2. An established youth court
3. The traditional magistrate's court
4. An educational court group

For a period of 1 year, all first-time status offenders for tobacco and alcohol were randomly assigned to each of the four groups. At the end of the first year of data collection, the groups were analyzed and found to be statistically the same. Approximately 400 first-time offenders were followed for the next 2 years, analyzing the recidivism rates for each of the four groups. The final analysis shows that there was no significant statistical difference in the recidivism rates among the four groups.

A new diversion program (called Juvenile Accountability) was a program run by the City Attorney's Office with assistance from volunteer high school students and the involvement of parents. Those juvenile offenders referred to the program took part in an intake interview. Based on this interview and discussions with offenders' parents, the juveniles were assigned educational counseling and public service. If the juvenile did not recidivate for 1 year, his or her record was to be cleared.

The established youth court operates as a mock trial with volunteer high school students serving as defense, prosecution, and jury. The sanctions involved both community service and educational programs.

The traditional magistrate's court usually involved the payment of a fine established by city or state code. In this case, the punishment involves a monetary fine and a black mark on the juvenile's permanent record. The fine was $50.

The educational control group was made to undergo an intake interview by the diversion program staff, offered educational counseling, and told that if they did not recidivate for 1 year, their records would be cleared.

25.8 Demographics: Who Are These First-Time Offenders?

25.8.1 Ethnicity

For those whose ethnicity is known, the percentages of first-time offenders closely match the percentage composition of the population. Whites made up 91.4 percent of the sample; Hispanics, 5.6 percent; Asians, 2.1 percent;

Table 25.1   Recidivism among the Four Groups

	Juvenile Accountability Group	Youth Control Group	Magistrate's Court Group	Educational Control Group
No recidivism	44 (62%)	43 (57%)	45 (57%)	34 (50%)
Yes recidivism	27 (38%)	32 (43%)	34 (43%)	34 (50%)
Chi-square two-tailed significance	.56			

and blacks, less than 1 percent (.9 percent) of the sample. These percentages were very close to the population percentages in the county.

25.8.2 Age

The age range for this study was from 12 to 18. The lower boundary was set by the actual behavior of the offenders. A 12-year-old was the youngest offender caught. The upper boundary was set by the legal age for tobacco use of 18. Although 19- to 21-year-olds are prohibited from drinking alcohol, it was decided to include only those who were juveniles. Please see Table 25.1 for the age of actual frequencies. The more or less normal distribution can be partly accounted for by degree of mobility. Younger children have less mobility to commit crimes, and older teens often had cars to escape arrest. Those in the middle were most likely to be caught as they were able to be absent from home but were without their own vehicles.

25.8.3 Gender

Males slightly outnumbered females, 160 to 133. This was likely due to the fact that males smoke more than females and also because males are somewhat more likely to be seen out in public when engaging in illegal activities.

25.8.4 Outcomes

Interestingly, over 3 years, 56.7 percent of these first-time offenders did not recidivate at all. Of those that did recidivate the most, 32.4 percent recidivated 3 times or less. More than 1 percent recidivated 10 times or more during this time.

25.8.4.1 Tobacco or Alcohol

For the 127 juveniles that did recidivate over the 3-year period, more recidivated for the same offenses than for any other. Ninety-six (75.6 percent) were cited again for tobacco or alcohol problems whereas 31 (24.4 percent) were not. It is interesting that almost 25 percent were not caught again for tobacco or alcohol offenses. More specifically, 46 (36.2 percent) were caught smoking again, and 61 (48.0 percent) were caught drinking again. Those caught drinking also included DUI traffic offenses.

25.8.4.2 Recidivated for Drugs

Of those who recidivated, 22 (17.1 percent) were caught committing drug-related offenses. It seemed that tobacco and alcohol were not the gateway drugs some people believe them to be. Less than 10 percent of the total sample was caught using drugs.

25.8.4.3 Recidivated for Non-Alcohol-Related Traffic Offenses

Of those that did recidivate, 41 (31.8 percent) committed various traffic offenses. We believe that this number was so low because most 12- to 15-year-olds (over 38 percent of the sample) did not drive.

25.8.4.4 Recidivated for Violent Crimes

It was encouraging to see that only 9 of these 293 first-time offenders recidivated for violent crimes over the 3-year study period. This is only 6.9 percent of those that recidivated and 3.1 percent of the total sample.

25.8.4.5 Recidivated for Property Crimes

Recidivism for property crime was more common than all others except recidivism, and 16.9 percent of those that recidivated did so for property-related crimes. This accounted for 7.5 percent of the total sample.

25.8.4.6 Recidivism for Running Away from Home

A small number of juvenile offenses were for running away from home (N = 9).

25.8.5 Bivariate Findings

No major differences among the four different groups were found in this analysis. Whether first-time offenders were sent to the new diversion program, the established youth court, or the traditional magistrate's court, or placed in the control group, recidivism rates were not statistically different.

Additionally, the groups did not differ significantly in any of the demographic characteristics measured, such as ethnicity, gender, or age. This basically shows that doing nothing to curb such behavior will work as effectively as doing something to (or diverting) them. Of course, the current social environment does not permit doing nothing, so another way of looking at the research is that diversion works as well as traditional punishment. Additionally, diversion programs are often less costly and always provide more services to youth (Gavazzi et al., 2000).

25.9 Summary

This work is moving in the right direction after several years of tracking the assignment of offenders at random and the use of a control group. To confirm these results, this basic system needs to be applied to different kinds of offenders in various parts of the country. The agency that supported this research is moving to expand this program to minor offenders who are not first-time offenders. Although this is a move in the right direction, more research is needed.

25.10 The Future of Diversion

With the average yearly cost of housing an adult inmate in prison rising above $34,000, there is a strong desire to reduce incarceration rates. If even a small percentage of future adult criminals can be diverted from a life of crime while still juveniles, then cost savings can be achieved (Schwartz, 1984; Weibush, 1993).

Additionally, reducing recidivism may not be the ultimate goal of diversion (Wilderman, 1984). Many — maybe most — juvenile crimes are minor offenses or status crimes that will be outgrown. In the past, these offenses were dealt with informally or off the record but changes in public opinion over the past several decades have moved them to the formal bureaucracy of the juvenile justice system (Vanagunas, 1979;

Fuller and Norton, 1993; Ezell, 1989; Osgood, 1984). Juveniles must be held accountable for crime, but this has created a large, expensive legal system, not fully funded despite the fact that budgets have grown. Diversion programs are seen as a way to reduce costs while still doing something about juvenile crime. Even if none of the juvenile diversion programs work, they are less costly and satisfy public opinion (Binder and Geis, 1984). Until public opinion changes, these programs will be necessary, and even then, we as a society will continue to seek solutions to juvenile crime.

References

Bandura, A. 1962. *Social Learning through Imitation*. Lincoln, NE: University of Nebraska Press.

Binder, A and Geis, G. 1984. *Ad populum* argumentation in criminology: juvenile diversion as rhetoric. *Crime and Delinquency* 30(2), 309–333.

Binder, A. and Binder, V. Juvenile diversion and the constitution. *Journal of Criminal Justice* 10(1), 1–24.

Binder, A. 1985. A diversion program for the 80's. *Federal Probation* 49(1), 4–12.

Blechman, E., Hile, M., and Fishman, D. 2001. Restorative justice and prosocial communities solution. *Youth and Society* 33(2), 273–295.

Calaway, B. 1988. Crime victim and offender mediation as a social work strategy. *The Social Service Review* 62(4), 668–683.

Emshoff, J. and Blakely, C. The diversion of delinquent youth: family-focused intervention. *Children and Youth Services Review* 5(4), 343–356.

Ezell, M. 1989. Juvenile arbitration: net widening and other unintended consequences. *Journal of Research in Crime and Delinquency* 26(4), 358–377.

Fox, J., Minor, K., and Pelkey, W. 1994. The relationship between law-related education diversion and juvenile offender's social and self perceptions. *American Journal of Criminal Justice* 19(1), 61–77.

Frazier, C. and J. Cochran. 1986. Official interventions, diversion from the juvenile justice system, and dynamics of human services work: effects of a reform goal based on labeling theory. *Crime and Delinquency* 32(2), 157–176.

Fuller, J. and Norton, W. 1993. Juvenile diversion: the impact of program philosophy on net widening. *Journal of Crime and Justice* 16(1), 29–45.

Gavazzi, S., Wasserman, D., and Partidge, C. 2000. The growing up fast diversion program: an example of juvenile justice program development for outcome evaluation. *Aggression and Violent Behavior* 5(2), 159–175.

Gibbons, D. and Blake, G. 1976. Evaluating the impact of juvenile diversion programs. *Crime and Delinquency* 22(4), 411–420.

Goffman, I. 1962. *Asylums*. Chicago, IL: Aldine.

Hirschi, T. 1969. *Causes of Delinquency*. Berkeley, CA: University of California Press.

Hellum, F. 1979. Juvenile justice: the second revolution. *Crime and Delinquency* 25(3), 299–317.

Kammer, J., Minor, K., and Wells J., 1997. An outcome study of the diversion plus program for juvenile offenders. *Federal Probation* 61(2), 51–56.

Levi, K. 1982. Relative redemption: labeling in juvenile restitution. *Juvenile and Family Court Journal* 33(1), 3–13.

Lipsey, M., Cordray, D., and Berger, D. 1981. Evaluation of a juvenile program using multiple lines of evidence. *Evaluation Review* 5(3), 283–306.

Minor, K., Hartmann, D., and Terry, S. 1997. Predictors of juvenile court actions and recidivism. *Crime and Delinquency* 43(3), 328–344.

Moses, A. 1978. The runaway youth act: Paradoxes of reform. *The Social Service Review* 52(2), 227–243.

Myers, W., Burton, P., Sanders, P. 2000. Project back-on-track at 1 year: a delinquency treatment program for early-career juvenile offenders. *Journal of the American Academy of Child and Adolescent Psychiatry* 39(9), 1127–1134.

Osgood, D. 1983. Offense history and juvenile diversion. *Evaluation Review* 7(6), 793–806.

Osgood, D. 1984. Juvenile diversion: when practice matches theory. *Journal of Research in Crime and Delinquency* 21(1), 33–56.

Osgood, W. and Weichselbaum, H. 1984. Juvenile diversion: When practice matches theory. *Journal of Research in Crime and Delinquency* 21(2), 33–56.

Palmer, T. and Lewis, R. 1980. A differentiated approach to juvenile diversion. *Journal of Research in Crime and Delinquency* 17(2), 209–229.

Platt, A. 1977. *The Child Savers: The Invention of Delinquency*, 2nd ed. Chicago, IL: University of Chicago Press.

Pogrebin, M., Poole, E., and Regoli, R. 1984. Constructing and implementing a model juvenile diversion program. *Youth and Society* 15(3), 305–324.

Polk, K. 1984. Juvenile diversion: a look at the record. *Crime and Delinquency* 30(4), 648–659.

Quay, H. and Love, C. 1977. The effect of a juvenile diversion program on rearrests. *Criminal Justice and Behavior* 4(4), 377–396.

Rausch, S. 1983. Court processing versus diversion of status offenders. *Journal of Research in Crime and Delinquency* 20(1), 39–54.

Reker, G. and Peacock, E. 1980. Juvenile diversion: conceptual issues and program effectiveness. *Canadian Journal of Criminology* 22(1). 36–50.

Regoli, R., Wilderman, E., and Pogrebin, M. 1985. Using an alternative evaluation measure for assessing juvenile diversion programs. *Children and Youth Services Review* 7(1), 21–38.

Rojek, D. and M. Erickson. 1981. Reforming the juvenile justice system: the diversion of status offenders. *Law and Society Review* 16(2), 241–264.

Rose, S. 1997. Analysis of a juvenile court diversion program. *Journal of Offender Rehabilitation* 24(34), 153–161.

Schur, E.M. 1973. *Radical Non-Intervention*. Englewood Cliffs, NJ: Prentice Hall.

Schwartz, I. 1984. Getting tough with juveniles: is it working. *Public Welfare* 42(3), 40–41.

Selke, W. 1982. Diversion and crime prevention: a time series analysis. *Criminology* 20(3–4), 395–406.

Severy, L. and Whitaker, M. 1982. Juvenile diversion: an experimental analysis of effectiveness. *Evaluation Review* 6(6), 753–774.

Seyfrit, C., Reichel, P., and Stutts, B. 1987. Peer juries as a juvenile justice diversion technique. *Youth and Society* 18(3), 302–316.

Shichor, D. and Binder, A. 1982. Community restitution for juveniles: an approach and preliminary evaluation. *Criminal Justice Review* 7(2), 46–50.

Staples, W. 1986. Restitution as a sanction in juvenile court. *Crime and Delinquency* 32(2), 177–185.

Sudipto, R. 1995. Juvenile restitution and recidivism in a Midwestern county. *Federal Probation* 59(1), 55–62.

Sudipto, R. 1993. Two types of juvenile restitution programs in two Midwestern counties: a comparative study. *Federal Probation* 57(4), 48–53.

Sutherland, E. 1992. *Principles of Criminology*. Dix Hills, New York: General Hall.

Umbreit, M. 1994. Crime victims confront their offenders: the impact of a Minneapolis mediation program. *Research on Social Work Practice* 4(4), 436–447.

Umbreit, M. 1993. Cross-site analysis of victim-offender mediation in four states. *Crime and Delinquency* 39(4), 565–585.

Vanagunas, S. 1979. Police diversion of juvenile offenders: an ambiguous state of the art. *Federal Probation* 43(3), 48–52.

Wiebush, R. 1993. Juvenile intensive supervision: the impact of felony offenders diverted from institutional placement. *Crime and Delinquency.* 39(1), 68–89.

Wilderman, E. 1984. Juvenile diversion: from politics to policy. *New England Journal of Human Services* 3(3), 19–23.

Chapter 26

Juvenile Placement and Programming

Kate King and Sarah Settles

26.1 Introduction

When a young person is found to be delinquent or in need of supervision by a juvenile court judge, a placement decision must be made. Dispositional alternatives include sending the juvenile home or to foster care, forestry camps, group homes, reception centers, boot camps, and training schools. The quality of life and opportunities provided vary enormously depending on placement. In some states, training schools are simply referred to as "juvenile prisons" (Housewright, 2000).

Virtually all juvenile institutions offer some kind of treatment program. The programs tend to vary by type of institution, which may be privately or publicly funded. The most serious violators who are deemed delinquent can be committed to the state department of corrections and placed in a secure facility. This is typically a last resort and is used to protect society (Cox et al., 2003).

Juvenile placement in residential programs has steadily increased over the last decade. Studies reveal there were nearly 93,732 children in custody in 1991 (Moone, 1993a, 1993b), 125,805 in 1997 (Gallagher, 1999), and 134,011 in 1999 (Sickmund, 2002). In addition, more and more juveniles are being waived to criminal courts and placed in adult institutions. Although there are twice as many privately operated juvenile facilities in this country, they hold less than half as many offenders as public facilities (Snyder and Sickmund, 1999).

The purpose of this chapter is to discuss both private and public juvenile holding facilities, types of treatment programs for juveniles in these facilities, and some of the issues associated with juveniles with special needs (e.g., substance abuse, HIV/AIDS, etc.).

26.2 Private Juvenile Facilities

Many private programs for juveniles are based in the community. These agencies enter into contracts with the State to provide services to juveniles. Examples of community-based private programs include day treatment centers, group homes, and wilderness programs. Private facilities are generally individually owned and operated. These programs provide alternatives to incarceration. Bartollas (2002) points out that privately funded community programs can serve as short-term placement for juveniles either "halfway in" or "halfway out." Those who are halfway in may be having trouble complying with the terms of probation; those halfway out may be transitioning from a locked facility.

Studies reveal the ratio of female juvenile offenders (38 percent) held in private facilities is greater than that of male juvenile offenders (26 percent) (Sickmund, 2000). This may be due to the fact that female offenders are processed more often for status offenses such as running away or truancy than males. Although private facilities house more female juveniles than public facilities, this does not mean there are more female offenders overall in private facilities. Sickmund (2000) notes there were 24,024 male and 5,430 female offenders in private facilities in 1997.

Private facilities tend to house juveniles who commit less serious offenses. Juveniles charged with crimes against persons make up a larger share of the delinquent population in public facilities (37 percent) than in private ones (33 percent) (Snyder and Sickmund, 1999). In addition, more minorities are sent to public institutions. According to Sickmund (2000), only 24 percent of the youth held in private facilities are minorities.

Private facilities such as group homes, forestry camps, and ranches primarily rely on staff to control access to and from the facility. These facilities allow youth greater access to the community (Moone, 1993a). This can be both positive and negative. Although youth may feel more comfortable not being locked behind a gate, they may also decide to leave. Escapes are a constant problem in less secure environments.

Juveniles may also be sent to private institutions known as training schools. Admissions to training schools have increased over the past two decades. Maguire and Pastore (1994) reported that in 1991, in private training schools 23 percent of the juveniles were being held for crimes against persons, 35 percent for property crimes, and 21 percent for drug offenses. The cost of housing an ever-increasing number of juveniles in training schools is rising rapidly. Sickmund et al. (1997) reported that in private facilities the annual cost per resident increased from 1975 ($21,215) to 1995 ($45,710).

Privately administered programs are often better known to the public because they may advertise to solicit funds or host fund-raising activities. Proponents claim there are many benefits to private institutions, including selective admission, better trained staff, lower staff–client ratios, and more innovative and flexible programming (Bartollas, 2002). Some studies support these claims (Greenwood, et al., 1989), whereas others do not. Shichor and Bartollas (1990) found that in Southern California, hard-core offenders placed in private programs were frequently not separated from those who had committed minor offenses. In general, however, private facilities house fewer delinquents, are less custody oriented, and provide programs aimed at modifying antisocial behavior in a relatively short period of time (Cox et al., 2003).

26.3 Public Institutions

Public institutions are owned and operated by the government and fall under many different categories. These consist of detention centers, training schools, shelters, reception centers, halfway houses, camps, ranches, or farms (Moone, 1993b). These facilities range in their programming, capacity, and the stage of sentencing time served by the juvenile. A publicly funded halfway house may hold youth who have already served time in another facility. The goal of the halfway house is the reintegration of the youth into the community.

Detention centers are designed to determine which treatment plan in which facility will best serve the needs of the juvenile. This process typically takes about 1 month. Psychologists, social workers, and medical and dental staff conduct an evaluation of the youth and then choose their destinations. Unfortunately, as with adults, juvenile placements are often decided by which institution is less crowded rather than by individual needs and programs.

Publicly funded ranches and camps are typically reserved for minor offenders. The residents do hard physical work maintaining the facilities, picking up trash on roads, cutting weeds in state parks, and so forth. More serious offenders are committed to juvenile training schools. Of those held in public training schools in 1991, 32 percent were there for offenses against persons, 36 percent for property offenses, and 10 percent for drug offenses (Maguire and Pastore, 1994). Juvenile training schools can be minimum, medium, or maximum security institutions. At institutions with higher levels of security, greater emphasis is placed on custody and security than on treatment or rehabilitation.

Public juvenile facilities face many problems today. Most are badly overcrowded. Nearly 70 percent of public facilities were operating above their design capacity on February 15, 1995 (Snyder and Sickmund, 1999). Due to overcrowding, juveniles are often put on a waiting list for placement. Sometimes, minor offenders are placed with more serious offenders while awaiting a different placement. One of the largest problems with public facilities is the overrepresentation of minority youth. There were almost twice as many minorities (50,142) than whites (26,193) in public facilities in 1997 (Sickmund, 2000).

In addition, young people sent to institutions tend to be extremely isolated, making reintegration into the community difficult. They also face intense peer pressure, and some juvenile facilities are rife with gang-related activities. Cox et al. (2003) point out that a subculture of delinquency is frequently found in juvenile institutions. This subculture allows dominance and exploitation by the strong over the weak. Forced homosexuality, physical violence, and drug abuse does not prepare the juvenile to return to society as a productive citizen. Solitary confinement, mutual distrust between staff and residents, and harsh discipline are also aspects of some juvenile institutions which can offset any attempts at treatment or rehabilitation. In addition, the use of force and mechanical restraints has increased.

Not all public institutions experience these problems. Some certainly do create environments that are conducive to rehabilitation. Bartollas (2003) states that the programs offered in some training schools are excellent. He notes that juveniles receive medical and dental care, educational opportunities, vocational training, recreation, and religious services. College preparatory classes are also offered in some training schools, as well as special education classes. Unfortunately, these cannot counteract the dangerous living conditions in many training schools.

Private and public juvenile facilities have both positive and negative aspects. Due to the steady increase of juvenile offenders, many incarcerated juveniles will not have a choice of private or public placement. One must simply rely on what is available at the time of adjudication.

26.4 Types of Programs

26.4.1 Treatment

Several treatment methods are commonly used with juvenile delinquents. Some of the more popular treatment modalities are individual counseling, transactional analysis, reality therapy, behavior modification, group therapy, positive peer culture, and multisystemic therapy. Each of these treatment methods utilizes different techniques to approach juvenile offenders and their problems.

Individual counseling is one of the most frequently used treatments, and nearly all juvenile institutions use it. Individual counseling does not try to change a young person's personality but, rather, to help him or her deal with adjustment problems (Siegel, 2002).

Transactional analysis, created by Eric Berne, is centered on the evaluation and interpretation of interpersonal relationships. This therapy can be conducted in either a group or individual therapy unit. Transactional analysis focuses on improving the relationship between juveniles and those with whom they interact. There are three "ego states" identified in this therapy (Berne, 1961). The child ego state is a relic of the juvenile's past. The parent ego state is an identification of the parental role. The adult ego state is the mature and responsible individual (Berne, 1961). Through the juvenile's voice, gestures, demeanor, and vocabulary, the transactional analysis therapist tries to pinpoint the juvenile's reactionary state. Once this state is identified, the therapist will try to move the individual away from the child or parent state and enforce the adult ego state (Berne, 1961).

Reality therapy, developed by William Glasser, focuses on irresponsible behavior stemming from an individual's not being able to fulfill needs. Glasser identifies the strength of reality and accepting responsibility. Reality therapy involves three stages. In the first stage, the therapist and offender form an honest personal relationship. Next, the youth is made to feel accepted although the therapist rejects negative behavior. Last, the offenders are taught to fulfill their needs with appropriate measures (Bartollas, 2001). The goal of reality therapy is to get the juvenile to accept responsibility in everyday situations.

Behavior modification is practiced in many juvenile institutions. Based on the work of Skinner (1953) this treatment approach is founded on the premise that all behavior is learned and can be shaped by punishments and rewards. Contracts are often used, wherein the therapist and the youth agree to certain behaviors and consequences. Seigel (2002) points out, however, that although this may be effective in a structured setting, when the juvenile is released this approach becomes difficult to use successfully.

Some form of group therapy is found in virtually all institutional placements. Therapists work with several individuals at a time, using the group as a tool to channel behavior. Relationships in group therapy tend to be intense, and the group is used to help solve problems, deal with conflict, and teach one another empathy (Siegel, 2002).

Positive peer culture is founded on the concepts originally promoted by Guided Group Interaction (GGI), a common method of group therapy that originated in the 1950s (Bartollas, 2003). Based on the idea that peers have enormous influence over one another, positive peer culture programs use that influence to encourage and enforce pro-social behavior. This is accomplished by teaching the members of the group to care for one another and want what is best for that person (Wicks, 1974).

Multisystemic therapy is a family-based treatment method. In multisystemic therapy, the goal is to reduce the risk factors by building juvenile and family strengths on a highly individualized and comprehensive basis (Henggeler, 2001). The first step in multisystemic therapy is to identify both strengths and weaknesses of the youth and the family situation (Henggeler, 2001). A treatment plan is created for the individual youth and the family. Treatment lasts approximately 4 months. Some aims of multisystemic therapy are to improve caregiver discipline practices, decrease deviant peer associations, and improve educational or vocational performance (Henggeler, 2001). Obviously, this approach is difficult to employ successfully in a high security institution and is more appropriate to community-based programs.

26.4.2 Educational or Vocational Programs

The focus of most educational or vocational programs is to increase education levels and attainment of future career opportunities, to prepare and train juveniles for successful employment, and to teach juveniles to become productive citizens. There are several programs that target the educational or vocational needs of juveniles. In addition to basic reading, writing, and mathematics classes, creative and cooperative ventures between the institutions and the community have been developed.

Some examples of these programs are Law-Related Education, Project Craft, Culinary Education, Training for At-Risk Youth (CETARY), and Quantum Opportunities. Each of these programs provides educational and/or vocational training to divert juveniles away from the criminal justice system.

Law-related education is an educational program designed to promote the development of characteristics that lead to healthy behavior (Bartollas, 2001). Youth are taught different aspects of the law and the criminal justice process. Youth enjoy field experiences such as court tours, internships, and police ride-alongs. They experience cocurricular activities such as mock trials. When properly conducted, law-related education programs may reduce tendencies toward delinquent behavior and improve a range of attitudes related to responsible citizenship (Bartollas, 2001).

Project Craft is a vocational program that focuses on juvenile crime, unemployment, and reducing recidivism. Project Craft can be conducted with juveniles in detention or as a community-based program (Hamilton and McKinney, 1999). This program was created by the Home Builders Institute and is sponsored by the home builders' industry. Juveniles referred to the program are offered pre-apprenticeship training and job placement in the home-building industry. Project Craft has a high rate of job placement after graduation. Project Craft has also been shown to reduce the recidivism rate for active participants (Hamilton and McKinney, 1999).

CETARY focuses on providing juveniles with education and training in food preparation. CETARY is both an educational and vocational program. The aim of the program is to help juveniles reach their goals and become productive citizens. The General Equivalency Degree (GED) is offered along with personal and professional development courses (Brunson and Smith, 2001). CETARY provides financial assistance to those juveniles who wish to further their education with a 2-year associate's degree in culinary arts.

Quantum Opportunities is an educational program that targets small groups of disadvantaged teens. The goal of the program is to help high-risk juveniles from low-income families graduate from high school and continue with college courses (Henggeler, 2001). Financial assistance is provided to those who participate and complete the program. Pilot tests conducted for this program showed that participants were less likely to be arrested during their juvenile years, more likely to graduate from high school, and more likely to enroll in higher education or training (Henggeler, 2001).

Educational programs in institutions are usually accredited and thus may grant either a general equivalency diploma (GED) or a high school diploma. Although the results of these programs are encouraging, it must be remembered that juvenile institutions face many problems. Students are typically behind in their studies; they may dislike school and pose disciplinary problems. Lack of funding can also limit the offerings. Training schools, because of their size, offer more programs, including remedial reading, tutoring services, and computer skills.

Vocational programs have been the mainstay of juvenile institutions for decades. Many offer training in food services, auto repair, carpentry, printing, electrical trade, data processing, cosmetology, and secretarial training. Unfortunately, the programs offered typically follow sex role stereotypes (Seigel, 2002). In addition, many juveniles face difficulties in securing employment after release because of their history.

26.5 Juveniles with Special Needs

Youth in the juvenile system, like adults in the criminal system, have disproportionately high rates of drug and alcohol abuse, engage in risky sexual practices, and suffer emotional and mental health problems. Many juveniles face multiple challenges. Interventions must be designed to address all of a juvenile's problems in order to be effective.

26.5.1 Substance Abuse

The Federal Bureau of Investigation's (FBI's) Uniform Crime Report (1999) revealed approximately 150,000 arrests of juveniles for illegal drug usage. In addition, a growing number of juveniles are institutionalized for drug-related crimes. Arrests represent a fraction of illegal activity, and most of the juveniles who are arrested do not go further into the system (Cox et al., 2003). It is clear that substance abuse is a serious problem among juveniles. Winters (1998) found evidence that the termination of delinquent behavior during adolescence is associated with a reduction in substance abuse. Thus, treatment programs are essential, for if the addiction and its underlying causes are not addressed, recidivism is almost certain.

Various programs address substance abuse, including multisystemic treatment, wilderness programs, and group therapy. Group leaders work to give juveniles personal skills and a support system that can help them resist using drugs. These programs are typically based on the Alcoholics Anonymous (AA) approach. Juveniles who are addicted to drugs often require residential treatment programs where they are detoxified and then treated with hypnosis, aversion therapy, or bio-feedback (Siegel, 2002).

26.5.2 HIV/AIDS

HIV/AIDS is a serious problem with which juvenile institutions must cope. Many juveniles engage in risky sexual behavior and/or use drugs intravenously before their entrance into the juvenile justice system. To juveniles on the streets, particularly those who have run away from home, prostitution may seem like their only survival option. Hersch (1988) reports that teenagers are used for sexual recreation by adult men. O'Brien (1983) claims it is easy for desperate children to turn to pornography and prostitution to support themselves. Although most young people are aware of AIDS, Roscoe and Kruger (1990) report that many believe that it will not affect them, and so they continue their risky sexual behavior.

Treating HIV/AIDS is not easy. It is expensive and controversial. Drug "cocktails" must be taken several times each day, interrupting the daily routine and placing additional burdens on staff. Privacy is also an issue; being infected with HIV can cause stigma or abuse by other juveniles. In addition, based on the principle of least eligibility, incarcerated youth may be denied access to advanced diagnostic techniques and drug therapies (Vaughn and Carroll, 1998).

26.5.3 Mental Illness

Some youth placed in juvenile facilities are mentally handicapped or mentally ill. These youth present special challenges to staff. Lack of training for employees can lead to frustration, neglect, and possibly abuse. Difficulty in adjusting to the institutional routine and following rules makes the placement of youth with mental health issues problematic. Their safety and the safety of others may be compromised.

Mentally handicapped youth require special services and protection, as do those who are mentally ill. Both groups may be mistreated by other youth or sexually assaulted. They may be manipulated into giving up any possessions they have or be tricked into breaking rules. They may not understand the norms of the institution and can find themselves in difficulty (Silverman, 2001). Those who are mentally ill often have trouble complying with their treatment programs or face unpleasant side effects from their medications. Refusing medication can lead to serious consequences as their condition deteriorates.

26.5.4 Violent Recidivists

Juveniles who are serious, violent recidivists have caught the attention of the public and their legislative representatives. Many states have made their juvenile systems more punitive and have added punishment to the purpose of their juvenile codes (Hamparian, 1980). These youth are typically sent to training schools where they are thrust into an inmate society that promotes predatory behavior and is rife with power struggles for dominance between rivals. Bartollas et al. (cited in Bartollas, 2002) stated in 1976 that the training school receives the worst of the worst, the toughest and most brutal youth who manipulate and control the other residents. In a 15-year follow-up study, they found that a negative youth culture still exists wherein the strong victimize the weak. Because of the brutalizing effect possible in training schools, youth with special needs, if at all possible, should be treated in less restrictive settings. Unfortunately, many high-risk juveniles are simply incarcerated. The National Institute of Justice (1988) reports that providing effective treatment for incarcerated youth is difficult due to the unavailability of special correctional programs that meet the needs of serious habitual offenders. In addition, secure institutions are frequently understaffed. The focus in secure institutions is custody and although the official goal may be treatment or rehabilitation, monitoring residents and controlling their behavior often takes precedence over treatment.

Juveniles who have committed serious offenses are sometimes treated in day treatment centers and wilderness programs. Project New Pride, in Denver, Colorado, is a day treatment center which offers intensive treatment for the first 3 months and then follows up with individualized programming for 9 more months. Services provided include academic and vocational training, counseling, and cultural sensitivity courses. Youth with learning disabilities are separated from other youth and given appropriate assistance. Project New Pride (1985) has four major goals that relate to working with this particular kind of juvenile: reducing recidivism, school reintegration, job placement, and remediation of academic and learning disabilities.

26.6 What Works?

In 1993, the Office of Juvenile Justice and Delinquency Prevention (OJJDP) found that most delinquency efforts had been unsuccessful because of their negative approach to juveniles' misbehavior. The OJJDP instead recommended positive approaches that emphasize healthy social, physical, and mental development.

Shepard (1995) states that the most successful programs are those that focus on improving self-control, interpersonal skills, and academic achievement. These programs must be intensive in nature and duration. The most effective treatment programs use a variety of techniques, are comprehensive, address issues relating to peers, school, work, and the larger community, and build on the juvenile's personal strengths (Siegel, 2002). The American Psychological Association (APA) states that effective intervention programs have two primary characteristics: (1) they are founded on our understanding of the developmental and sociocultural risk factors that lead to antisocial behavior, and (2) they use theory-based intervention strategies known to change behavior, as well as tested programs and validated measurement techniques to assess outcome.

Other important factors mentioned by the APA include early intervention to interrupt the "trajectory towards violence"; addressing aggression as one of many antisocial behaviors involving family, peers, school, and the community; and taking advantage of windows of opportunity that arise. Adolescence is a time when children begin to test limits and act out. Programs that help them prepare for this difficult time are especially useful.

Gendreau (1996) examined a significant body of evidence that convinced him that some programs do reduce juveniles' likelihood of reoffending. He states that successful interventions share the same common components:

1. A social learning approach which assumes that attitudes and behavior can change if noncriminal attitudes and behaviors are introduced and reinforced.
2. Clear, consistent rules and sanctions.
3. The illustration and support of noncriminal attitudes and behaviors.
4. Practical problem-solving skills.
5. Positive links between the community and program resources.
6. Open, warm relationships between juvenile offenders and staff.
7. Staff who function as advocates for juveniles within the community.
8. The use of ex-offenders who have made it as role models.

9. The degree of an offender's involvement with the design of specific interventions.
10. Staff focus on positive and pro-social behavior rather than negative behavior.
11. Offender peer groups that are directed toward reinforcing pro-social behavior.
12. Sound, theoretical knowledge and adequate resources to apply these principles of effectiveness.
13. Multiple methods of intervention, i.e., anger management, job skills, counseling, etc.
14. Emphasis on relapse prevention and self-sufficiency.
15. Matching individual offenders with appropriate interventions.

Sherman et al. (1997) reported that family therapy and parent training work with delinquents and at-risk adolescents. They found that factors for delinquency such as hyperactivity and aggression can be successfully addressed through these methods. Improving social competency in programs such as Life Skills Training, which teaches youth such skills as stress management, problem solving, and self-control also works. Training in developing thinking skills using behavior modification or rewards and punishments can be successful in reducing substance abuse (Sherman et al., 1997).

Lipsey and Wilson (1998) evaluated more than 200 delinquency intervention programs, categorizing them by their effectiveness. They found that individual counseling in a noninstitutional setting showed consistently positive effects, reducing recidivism. In addition, behavioral programs in noninstitutional settings were effective. Teaching family, home, and interpersonal skills in institutional settings also showed consistent, positive reductions in recidivism.

Although less consistent, restitution, probation, and parole services in the community showed some positive reductions in recidivism (Lipsey and Wilson, 1998). In general, the most effective programs provide structure, emphasize basic social skills, and provide individual counseling that directly addresses the perceptions, attitudes, and behaviors of juveniles (Altschuler, 1998). In addition, community-based interventions are superior to institutional treatment settings. It is also very important that family members be involved in the treatment and rehabilitation of their children (Sherman et al., 1997). Should children be involved in more than the juvenile justice system, coordinated services are essential. Research shows a reduction of up to 61 percent in the number of crimes committed by juveniles on probation whose families receive coordinated services (Center for Mental Health

Studies, 1998). An example of this continuum of care is provided by the Idaho Youth Ranch. This nonprofit organization works in conjunction with federal and state authorities including law enforcement, the juvenile court, schools, social services, and the community to provide an interactive network of services for youth and their families. The Idaho Youth Ranch monitors juveniles from their initial interaction with the justice system and maintains a flow of services through aftercare designed to provide rehabilitation.

26.7 What Does Not Work?

Many studies have found that simple punishment does not reduce recidivism in the long run (Gendreau and Goggin, 1996). Sherman et al. (1997) report that summer jobs and subsidized work programs for at-risk youth do not have the desired result. Neither do short-term, nonresidential training programs, diversion from court to job training as a condition of case dismissal, or rehabilitation programs with vague, unstructured counseling. They also state that correctional boot camps, which use basic military training procedures, do not reduce recidivism or prevent crime. Scared Straight programs that expose minor juvenile offenders to adult prisons, shock probation, shock parole, or split sentences that use jail time with probation are ineffective. Further, home detention with electronic monitoring, intensive supervision when the offender is on probation or parole, and wilderness or survival programs have no apparent effect in preventing delinquency or recidivism (Sherman et al., 1997).

26.8 What Is Promising?

Juvenile programs are increasingly being evaluated. Several agencies are keeping track of the success rate of juvenile programs. *Blueprints for Violence Prevention* is a series of documents that provides a listing of both model programs and those that are promising. The list includes type of program, target population, evidence of effectiveness, cost–benefit analysis, and sustained effect. The following are examples of promising programs from *Blueprints*.

The Good Behavior Game is a behavior modification program that includes both students and teachers. Disruptive behaviors are focused on and worked on through game playing. The target group is children between first and sixth grade. Grade six males who showed early aggressive behavior patterns had positive outcomes (Center for the Study and Prevention of Violence, 2002). Although this program targets a younger age group, it is important to address problems before they become serious.

Preventive Intervention (PI) is a school-based program focused on high-risk junior high school students from suburban areas. The program deals with problem areas such as juvenile delinquency, substance abuse, and school failure. Students engage in role-playing activities and are rewarded for their monitored behaviors. Both short- and long-term effects have proved positive. Youth who were involved in the program showed grade standings higher than those who did not participate. Youth who finished the program also had fewer court records 5 years later than those who did not complete it (Center for the Study and Prevention of Violence, 2002).

Project Northland is a program that involves many members of the youth's community. This program aims to reduce alcohol use among adolescents. Project Northland is a 3-year program that spans the youth's sixth, seventh, and eighth grade years in middle school. Each year, the student is approached with different activities and expectations. Findings after the third year have revealed that youth who participated had lower alcohol-use scores, had reduced alcohol use in the past week and month, and talked to parents more frequently about the effects of drinking (Center for the Study and Prevention of Violence, 2002).

Sherman et al. (1997) state that the monitoring of gangs by community workers, probation, and police officers may decrease gang violence. Community-based mentoring and after-school recreation programs are also promising. Training in thinking skills may reduce delinquency and substance abuse, whereas residential training programs such as Job Corps may reduce felonies and increase earnings and educational attainment. Although intensive supervision alone does not work, providing aftercare increases the chances of effectiveness. More research is needed on these promising approaches.

26.8.1 Aftercare

Aftercare is defined by Siegel (2002) as transitional assistance to help juveniles successfully adjust to community life. Aftercare is the equivalent of parole in the adult justice system. Aftercare is typically administered by the executive branch of state governments although, in a few states, this service falls under the auspices of the probation department (Torbet, 1988). Juveniles who are released from institutions are often placed on parole or in aftercare facilities to assist them in transitioning from confinement to the free world. Three major factors are considered before releasing a juvenile from an institution to aftercare: institutional adjustment, length of stay and general attitude, and the likelihood of success in the community (Siegel, 2002).

As in the case of parole, aftercare involves adhering to a set of restrictions that have been agreed upon and supervision by a parole officer. Conditions of parole for juveniles are based on risk assessment and include such things as attending school or work, curfew, drug testing, reporting to the supervising officer at specified times, and attending programs.

Altschuler and Armstrong (1994) state that successful aftercare programs should focus on preparing juveniles for increased responsibility and freedom in the community. They should also work with youth and their families, peers, schools, and employers to help identify the qualities necessary for success. They should develop resources and support where needed, and assist juveniles and the community in developing positive (continuously monitored) interactions.

Intensive Aftercare Programs (IAP) created by Altschuler and Armstrong are based on the assumption that serious, repeat delinquency stems from weak controls created by social disorganization, inadequate socialization, and strain. An important aspect of these programs is cooperation and communication between institutional staff and aftercare staff. Youth placed in IAP begin to receive services shortly after adjudication and placement in an institution, which include early aftercare planning, visits by the parole officer to the juvenile in the institution, prerelease visits for the juvenile into the community, and prerelease overnight or weekend furloughs (Wiebush et al., 2000).

This supervised interaction between the youth and the community is essential for a successful transition. Juveniles who have been institutionalized may find it difficult to make decisions or resist peer pressure. In addition, the community may react negatively to the youth, causing adjustment problems. The IAPs stress a mix of intensive surveillance and services with graduated incentives and consequences. These programs offer realistic conditions and attainable goals to enable youth released from institutions to succeed in the community.

26.9 Conclusion

The purpose of the juvenile court is treatment and rehabilitation. Since its creation in 1899, juvenile court judges have struggled to find the right program for each juvenile. Decisions range from dismissing the case and sending the juvenile home to institutionalization in a prison setting. Judges today have a myriad of options open to them. As the number of dispositions in the juvenile court increases, resources are strained. This makes every decision by the judge regarding the use of those resources an important one. In addition, the lives of children and the safety of society are at stake.

Research has shown which approaches do not work and those that are promising. Community-based placements have been shown to be more effective than those provided by secure institutions. Most importantly, service providers must be able to match the programs offered to the specific needs of each juvenile and address all of the problems youth bring with them into the system.

References

Altschuler, D. (1998). Intensive Aftercare for High-Risk Juvenile Parolees: Overview. Washington, D.C.: OJJDP.

Altschuler, D. and Armstrong, T. (1994). Intensive Aftercare for High Risk Juveniles: A Community Care Model. Washington, D.C.: OJJDP.

Bartollas, C. (2002). *Invitation to Corrections*. Boston, MA: Allyn and Bacon.

Bartollas, C. (2003). *Juvenile Delinquency*, 6th ed. Boston, MA: Allyn and Bacon.

Bartollas, C., Miller, S., and Dinitz, S. (1976). *Juvenile Victimization: The Institutional Paradox*. New York: Halstead Press.

Bartollas, C. and Miller, S. (2001). *Juvenile Justice in America*, 3rd ed. Upper Saddle River, NJ: Prentice Hall.

Berne, E. (1961). *Transactional Analysis in Psychotherapy*. New York: Grove Press. Blueprints for Violence Prevention. University of Boulder, CO. Center for the study and prevention of violence. http://www.colorado.edu/cspv/blueprints/.

Brunson, S. and Smith, E. (2001). Culinary Education and Training Program for At-Risk Youth. Office of Juvenile Justice and Delinquency Prevention. Fact Sheet. Washington, D.C.

Center for Mental Health Studies. (1998). Ten Key Findings. Family Matters. Summer. Washington, D.C.

Cox, S.M., Conrad, J.J., and Allen, J.M. (2003). *Juvenile Justice: A Guide to Theory and Practice*, 5th ed. New York: McGraw-Hill.

Federal Bureau of Investigation. (1999). *Crime in the United States 1998*. Washington, D.C.

Gallagher, C. (1999). Juvenile Offenders in Residential Placement, 1997. Office of Juvenile Justice and Delinquency Prevention. Fact Sheet. Washington, D.C.

Gendreau, P. (1996). The principles of effective intervention with offenders. In Harland, A. Ed., *Choosing Correctional Options That Work.* Thousand Oaks, CA: Sage.

Gendreau, P. and Goggin, C. (1996) Principles of effective correctional programming. *Forum on Correctional Research*, 3, 1–6.

Greenwood, P., Turner, S., and Rosenblatt, K. (1989). Evaluation of Paint Creek Youth Center: Preliminary results. Santa Monica, CA: Rand.

Hamilton, R. and McKinney, K. (1999). Job training for Juveniles: Project CRAFT.

Hamparian, D. (1980). *The Violent Few: A Study of Dangerous Juvenile Offenders.* Lexington, MA: Lexington Books.

Henggeler, S. (2001). *Blueprints for Violence Prevention.* Greeley, CO: Kendall.

Hersch, P. (January 1988). Coming of age on city streets. *Psychology Today* 22, 28–37.

Housewright, E. (January 4, 2000). Hard time for kids. *Dallas Morning News*, 1A, 6A.

Lipsey, M. and Wilson, D. (1998). Effective intervention for serious juvenile offenders: a synthesis of research. In Loever, R. and Farrington, D. Eds., *Serious and Violent Juvenile Offenders: Risk Factors and Successful Interventions.* London: Sage.

Maguire, K. and Pastore, A., Eds. (1994). Sourcebook of Criminal Justice Statistics. Washington D.C.

Moone, J. (1993a). Children in Custody 1991: Private facilities. Office of Juvenile Justice and Delinquency Prevention. Fact Sheet. Washington, D.C.

Moone, J. (1993b). Children in Custody 1991: Public juvenile facilities. Office of Juvenile Justice and Delinquency Prevention. Fact Sheet. Washington, D.C.

National Institute of Justice. (September–October 1988). Targeting Serious Juvenile Offenders for Prosecution Can Make a Difference. NIJ Reports, Washington, D.C.

O'Brien, S. (1983). *Child Pornography.* Dubuque, IA: Kendall and Hunt.

OJJDP (1985). *Project New Pride.* Washington, D.C.

OJJDP (November 3–5, 1993). Strategy for juvenile offenders seeks early intervention. *NCJA Justice Bulletin.*

Roscoe, B. and Kruger, T. (1990). AIDS: late adolescents' knowledge and its influence on sexual behavior. *Adolescence* XXV, Spring, 39–48.

Shepard, J., Jr. (1995). State pen or playpen? Is prevention 'pork' or simply good sense? *American Bar Association Journal of Criminal Justice* 10: 34–37.

Sherman, L., Gottfredson, D., Mackenzie, D., Eck, J., Reuter, P., and Bushway, S. (1997). What Works, What Doesn't, What's Promising? A Report to the United States Congress. National Institute of Justice. Washington, D.C.

Shichor, D. and Bartollas, C. (April 1990). Private and public placements: is there a difference? *Crime and Delinquency*, 36, 286–299.

Sickmund, M. (2000). Census of Juveniles in Residential Placement 1997. Pittsburgh, PA: National Center for Juvenile Justice.

Sickmund, M. (2002). Juvenile Offenders in Residential Placement: 1997–1999. Office of Juvenile Justice and Delinquency Prevention. Fact Sheet. Washington, D.C.

Sickmund, M., Snyder, H., and Poe-Yamagata, E. (1997). Juvenile Offenders and Victims: 1997 Update on Violence. Washington, D.C.

Siegel, L. (2002). *Juvenile Delinquency: The Core*. Belmont, CA. Wadsworth/ Thomson Learning.

Silverman, I. (2001). *Corrections: A Comprehensive View*, 2nd ed. Belmont, CA. Wadsworth/Thomson Learning.

Skinner, B.F. (1953). *Science and Human Behavior*. New York. Macmillan.

Snyder, H. and Sickmund, M. (1999). Juvenile Offenders and Victims: 1999 National Report. Washington. D.C.: Office of Juvenile Justice and Delinquency Prevention.

Torbet, P. (1988). Organization and Administration of Juvenile Services: Probation, Aftercare, and State Delinquent Institutions. Pittsburgh, PA: National Center for Juvenile Justice.

Vaughn, M. and Carroll, L. (March 1998). Separate and unequal: prison versus free world medical care. *Justice Quarterly*, 15(1), 3–40.

Wicks, R.J. (1974). *Correctional Psychology: Themes and Problems in Correcting the Offender*. San Francisco, CA: Canfield Press.

Wiebush, R., McNulty, B., and Le, T. (2000). Implementation of the Intensive Community Based Aftercare Program. Washington, D.C. OJJDP.

Winters, K. (October 1998). Kids and drugs: treatment recognized link between delinquency and substance abuse. *Corrections Today*. 118–121.

Chapter 27

Restorative Justice Programming

Karan Kell White

27.1 Introduction

Grounded in religious and indigenous traditions, restorative justice is an ancient concept that has dealt with criminal behavior in ways that are responsive to the offender, the victim, and the community as a whole (Lucas, 2001). The adage "crime wounds ... justice heals" has been at the heart of the American criminal justice system for centuries, focusing on crime as a violation of the law and offering punishment as the appropriate remedy. By limiting reparation to the punishment of the offender, the system has neglected to take into account the needs of the victim, thereby ignoring one of the most important aspects of the justice system (Shenk, 2001).

According to Braithwaite (1999), the core values of restorative justice are assisting both the victim and the perpetrator to heal rather than continue hurting, allowing the perpetrator to engage in a respectful dialogue with his or her victim, and invoking in the perpetrator a sense of responsibility for his or her actions followed by forgiveness by the local community. In short, restorative justice is a process and is not always perfectly linear. It brings together the individuals who have been affected by an offense, and it attempts to have all parties agree as to a reasonable and acceptable outcome. In this way, all parties can be assured that the end result is just (Howarth, 2000).

27.2 Restorative Justice: A Balanced Approach

The concept of restorative justice holds that when a crime is committed, the offender incurs an obligation to restore the victim and, by extension, the community to the state of well-being that existed before the offense. The principle of balance as it relates to restorative justice for juveniles comes from the balanced approach concept, which suggests that the juvenile justice system should give equal weight to ensuring community safety, holding offenders accountable to victims, and providing competency development for offenders in the system (Bilchik, 1996).

In restorative justice principles, both the victim and the offender are necessary participants in the process of making amends, which puts restorative justice, a system that strives to construct common ground, directly at odds with the traditional adversarial system (Howarth, 2000).

27.2.1 History

The American criminal justice system can appropriately be described as retributive, measuring justice by the punishment inflicted upon the offender. Punishments, although often conceivably just, cannot achieve results that aid in restoring or repairing the actual harm done to the crime victim. Punishment does not restore victims' losses, answer their questions, relieve their fears, or heal their wounds. The traditional criminal justice system rarely gives victims the opportunity to explain their needs, let alone provide any input into how the case might be resolved. The traditional system has done an effective job of keeping victims, the community, and offenders from contributing any input regarding how society will respond to crime (Shenk, 2001).

In recent years there has been a trend developing in criminal justice to put the needs of victims before the interests of the system. This changing mentality is symbolized by the move toward restorative justice.

27.2.2 *Traditional Justice*

The traditional means of ensuring justice and the current criminal justice system make it difficult for the community to achieve the type of justice needed to repair and rebuild. Punishment has traditionally been used to as a means of conveying the message that justice has been done; however, and according to Shenk (2001), merely punishing an offender does little to convince him or her that it is in his or her best interest to become a contributing member of the community. Punishment is merely a passive act that does nothing to encourage offenders to be accountable for their actions. Restorative justice provides offenders with an opportunity to become accountable to their victims and to become responsible for repairing the harm they have caused (Shenk, 2001).

27.2.3 *Restorative Justice*

Restorative justice has several potential advantages over traditional criminal justice practices. Restorative justice builds on an offender's positive qualities and abilities rather than focusing only on the offense, encourages offender accountability, and provides him or her with an understanding of the consequences of his or her criminal behavior. The restorative approach is not based strictly on punishment, but can be regarded as an experiential method for helping offenders learn social skills, positive values, empathy, and anticipation of conse- quences. Offenses are treated as teachable moments rather than actions only requiring punishment or retribution (Halstead, 1999).

The restorative justice philosophy has created an alternative to the traditional criminal justice mind-set by suggesting a new way of think- ing about crime, community, and working together for the future (Shenk, 2001). With this philosophy of restorative justice comes a vision in which victims play a central role in crime resolution and the type of reparation for harm incurred.

Restorative justice places upon the victim, the community, and the offender an obligation to right the wrong that has been done, and creates a sense of accountability for the offender to accept responsibility and an obligation to work to repair the harm (Shenk, 2001). Restorative justice increases the likelihood that a youth may ultimately be reac- cepted in the community by performing acts of reparation that will benefit the community as a whole. By confronting the youthful offender, victims are often able to convey their outrage and pain, and can begin to heal the harm caused by the crime (Lucas, 2001).

27.2.4 The Legislative Basis — Federal Law

27.2.4.1 Juvenile Justice and Delinquency Prevention Act of 1974

The Juvenile Justice and Delinquency Prevention Act (JJDPA) was enacted by Congress in 1974 to provide the resources, leadership, and coordination necessary to develop and administer effective programs for prevention of delinquency, divert juveniles from the traditional juvenile justice system, and provide critically needed alternatives to institutionalization (Lucas, 2001). The JJDPA focused primarily on programmatic concerns rather than on individual legal rights, with an overall philosophy of providing states and localities considerable leeway in designing their own programs. The act established the Office of Juvenile Justice and Delinquency Prevention (OJJDP) to research and disseminate information, and provide training and technical assistance to the states in the implementation of juvenile justice programs. Under the JJDPA, states were authorized to allocate federal funds to local governments that adopted proactive programs for dealing with juveniles.

27.2.4.2 Victim's Rights and Restitution Act

The Victim's Rights and Restitution Act of 1990 provided an equally important incentive for Victim Offender Mediation (VOM), and had the potential to provide victims a greater opportunity for participation in juvenile justice proceedings. The Victim's Rights and Restitution Act was enacted to increase sensitivity to victims who had been left out of the justice process. Legislators clearly saw victims playing more of a role in determining an offender's disposition. The essential and active involvement of the victim makes VOM unique in the disposition of juvenile crime. Crime victims who have participated in VOM programs have expressed a high degree of satisfaction with their involvement in the process as well as a reduction in their fear and anxiety over the event. Participation in VOM ultimately gave victims a greater sense of control over circumstances that in the past might have left them feeling vulnerable and powerless (Lucas, 2001).

27.2.4.3 Balanced and Restorative Justice Project

The Balanced and Restorative Justice Project (BARJ) was among the programs established under the auspices of the OJJDP (Lucas, 2001). The BARJ Project began as a national initiative of the OJJDP in 1993 through a grant to Florida Atlantic University (FAU). FAU developed a partnership agreement with the Center for Restorative Justice and Mediation through a subcontract with the University of Minnesota. The goals were to provide training and technical assistance and develop a number of written materials pertinent to the balanced approach mission and restorative justice (ojjdp.ncjrs.org/pubs/implementing/about.html).

The three-dimensional agenda for a community justice response to juvenile crime, the Balanced and Restorative Justice mission, provided a means to help address community crime, control needs and expectations by holding juvenile offenders accountable to individual victims and the community by enabling offenders to function as productive citizens, and make juvenile agencies a resource for enhancing public safety (Bilchik, 1996).

27.2.5 Accountability-Based Sanctions for Juveniles

Community-based sanctioning programs promote accountability more effectively, strengthening rather than severing damaged bonds between the offender and the victimized community. A system of sanctions cannot effectively hold juvenile offenders accountable unless it is timely and consistent with a continuum of sanctions appropriate for different types of offenders and offenses. Sanctions must be graduated, and escalate as offenses recur and become more serious (Griffin, 1999).

27.2.5.1 Criticisms of Victim Offender Mediation for Juveniles

Due process or procedural concerns arise when constitutionally protected rights of offenders are waived for VOM participation. Critics assert that informal dispositions of youthful crimes such as VOM may stand on constitutionally questionable grounds because they pressure juveniles to waive their rights without the requisite knowledge of legal advice. There is nothing inherent in the VOM process, however, that would preclude their seeking the advice of counsel before undertaking the procedure. VOM also provides an opportunity to confront the accuser/victim in a less rigid, nonthreatening setting, which can enable a mutual understanding that would be impossible to achieve in a family court proceeding. In regard to the problem of self-incrimination, maintaining the confidentiality of statements made during mediation sessions is not an insurmountable obstacle, and is consistent with the private nature of the VOM process (Lucas, 2001).

27.2.5.2 Net Widening

Net widening often results in more youths entering the criminal justice system. Some critics refer to the wider net of social control that might inevitably result from the broad use of VOM. Rather than providing youths an opportunity to escape or avoid the traditional juvenile justice system, VOM might actually bring more juveniles into the system. Youths who failed to fulfill their restitution agreements might run the risk of being placed in a secure facility for an offense that would not have resulted in incarceration if it had been processed through traditional channels.

Any discussion of net widening must address the special circumstances of status offenders, those juveniles found guilty of behavior that would not be criminal for an adult but pertain only to youth custody issues such as truancy, curfew breaking, incorrigibility, and loitering. Although incarceration is widely considered an excessive disposition for status offenders, a significant number are being placed out of the home. Although many status offenses are *victimless*, they may lend themselves to family group conferences, where juveniles engage in mediation with parents and other family members.

VOM may be a suitable option for low- or no-risk youth as a relatively inexpensive way of keeping them out of the system, and in light of the mandate of the JJDPA, VOM should be viewed as serving a preventive rather than a punitive function. Potential risks involved with net widening may be outweighed by the unique opportunities presented by VOM for dealing with low-level offenders. Because VOM is minimally intrusive and informal, and not limited by strict procedural rules, it may be the best alternative available among diversionary programs (Lucas, 2001).

27.2.5.3 Fairness and Adequacy of Punishment

VOM raises concerns about the inevitability of different outcomes for offenders committing similar crimes. As pointed out by Lucas (2001), while it is widely accepted in the criminal justice system that there are bound to be disparities because it cannot be avoided, the system can try to ensure that such disparities are not a function of either the background characteristics of offenders or victims or the local political landscape in local communities. Sentencing disparities are already a very real part of the juvenile justice system, which makes having a spectrum of diversions and dispositions, especially less intrusive ones, more viable. Family court judges have wide discretion in sentencing youthful offenders, usually with a preference for the least restrictive available alternative, and although two crimes may seem identical on the surface, no two outcomes are the same (Lucas, 2001).

Advocates as well as detractors of VOM stress the importance of adequate training and standards for mediators that would seem to be even more critical when dealing with juveniles. Practitioners of mediation require high levels of skill in order to use it properly, especially in light of the need to incur "minimal additional trauma" when intervening in cases of juvenile misconduct. Community-based mediation programs that employ volunteer mediators must provide intensive training to help these mediators deal with the ethical dilemmas and interpersonal dynamics they will face. The National Conference of Commissioners on Uniform State Laws has undertaken the task to establish certification and standards for VOM mediators.

A serious concern with VOM used with juveniles is the disparity in the bargaining power between the adult victim and the youthful offender. Mediation's unique system leaves either party free to walk away from the process without reaching an agreement. Although the VOM process may only proceed with the consent of both parties, the participation of the youthful offender is not always voluntary. The offender has the choice of either settling or suffering the unsure consequences of the traditional system.

27.3 Restorative Justice Project: Louisiana Department of Public Safety and Corrections

27.3.1 Initiative #7 for the Eight-Year Document

The Restorative Justice Project was proposed as a cooperative effort with the Louisiana Department of Corrections, the District Attorney's Victim Assistance Coordinator's Office, and the Department of Corrections Victims Services Bureau. Important components of the department's current restorative justice initiative include the Crime Victim's Services Bureau, victim awareness programming for inmates, restorative justice education and information for staff, and victim-initiated victim–offender dialog.

The project moved forward in December 2000 when the Louisiana Department of Corrections Secretary invited the Director of the Ohio Department of Rehabilitation and Corrections to spend 2 d with senior staff, reviewing Ohio's restorative justice programs and their possible applications for Louisiana corrections. A Restorative Justice Task Force was formed to propose and guide the restorative justice initiatives, drawing on the experience and support of Louisiana State University's Office of Social Service Research and Development, victim advocacy groups, and a technical assistance grant from the National Institute of Corrections.

The purpose of the Restorative Justice Project was to introduce the concept and philosophy of restorative justice into the corrections environment. The project was developed to work with offenders in small groups to sensitize them to the issues of victimization and the impact of crime on its victims. Offenders were given the opportunity to examine their own history of victimization, and to consider avenues of addressing the harm caused by their crimes.

Based on the governor's challenge to make Louisiana a better place for its citizens, the Department of Corrections joined national efforts to define and honor the rights of crime victims as legitimate participants in the justice system and to incorporate the restorative justice philosophy into agency operations.

The program objectives stated by the task force were to (1) increase offender sensitivity to the impact of victimization, (2) increase offenders' awareness of the consequences of their actions, (3) provide offenders the means to take personal responsibility for their crimes, and (4) enable offenders, victims, and victims' advocates to understand crime in the context of restorative justice.

In drafting the Victim Impact Program, the task force utilized information from a variety of sources. The California Youth Authority restorative justice program was used as the primary model in adapting the program for use with juveniles in secure custody in the State of Louisiana. The task force recognized that the program would have to have some flexibility in the structure in order to serve the diverse populations within the system. Although secure placement limits some options for promoting accountability among juvenile offenders, especially in the areas involving service and interaction within the community, a number of creative possibilities remain, as seen in the successes of the Impact of Crime on Victims program, the California Youth Authority program, and The Capitol Offender Program at the Texas Youth Commission's Giddings State Home and School (Griffin, 1999).

In a climate in which restorative justice may be seen as something other than a framework and a philosophy to be modified and used to suit the particular needs of different populations, some objections were encountered. Although a general consensus enabled a wide range of players who had never joined in a shared spirit of teamwork to be brought to the table, the inevitable stumbling block was the fragile illusion of shared understanding that began to fall apart as we moved to put our pilot program into operation, a phenomenon shared by other programs at their inception (Boyes-Watson, 2000). In order to overcome possible obstacles, the initial group was set up in a modified format utilizing journaling, sharing, victim panels, and letter writing in an effort to empower and encourage youths to take responsibility for their actions.

27.3.2 *California Youth Authority Program*

Over the past 50 years, the California Youth Authority has been recognized as a national leader in juvenile corrections in the area of innovative offender programming. In the early 1980s, a group of professionals led by Deputy Sharon English of the Office of Prevention and Victim Services asserted that it was of no value to the community to teach offenders to read or give them a vocational skill if they were not instilled with respect for other people's lives or property (Umbreit et al., 1993). The program combined an educational curriculum of 35 to 60 hours of experiential learning over 6 to 12 weeks conducted by specially trained instructors, with personal presentations from crime victims and victims' advocates. The classroom component consisted of readings, audiovisual materials, and interactive teaching strategies covering a number of crime-specific topics. In-person visits from crime victims, survivors, and victims advocates were frequently vivid and emotional (Umbreit et al., 1993).

The Impact of Crime on Victims program was overseen by the California Youth Authority's highly active Victim Services Division, which performed a number of services essential to the operation of a victim-sensitive accountability-based juvenile justice system, including direct victim notification, education, outreach, and maintenance of a centralized database to track confidential victim information (Griffin, 1999).

27.4 Conclusion

Restorative justice deals with crime and the people and the injuries involved, and shifts the focus away from the formal processes of traditional law. Risks are high, but the current juvenile justice systems do not address the interests of the victims, the communities, and the offenders. Restorative justice offers the possibility that by working together, "We, the People, can do better" (Howarth, 2000).

Juvenile offenders and victims caught up in the criminal justice system are more likely to be poor than nonvictims and nonoffenders, and a restorative justice strategy that successfully empowers both victims and offenders has progressive implications for social justice. Conversely, the retributive justice system, which responds to the hurt on one side by inflicting hurt to the other side, is regressive in its impact.

For some the restorative justice model presents itself as a "win–win" alternative to the traditional values and practices of the criminal justice process, but in the final analysis, as with other social and moral phenomena, we may find that there are multiple values and interests at stake, and that we may have to make choices among them (Dzur and Wertheimer, 2002).

According to Tracy (1998), criminologists and criminal justice practitioners should strive to make sure that the emerging vision of restorative justice includes not only an image of a more humanistic form of justice, but also a worldview that minimizes social inequities and injustices by working diligently to stop the war against the powerless and to reverse the harmful consequences of hundreds of years of retributive justice and its legacy of oppression.

References

Beauregard, S.A. (1998). Court-connected juvenile victim-offender mediation: an appealing alternative for Ohio's juvenile delinquents. *Ohio State Journal on Dispute Resolution*. 13, 1005, 1–10.

Boyes-Watson, C. (2000). Reflections on the purist and maximalist models of restorative justice. *Contemporary Justice Review* 3(4), 441–450.

Braithwaite, John. (1999). Restorative justice: assessing optimistic and pessimistic accounts. *The University of Chicago Crime and Justice* 25, 1–7.

Dzur, A.W. and Wertheimer, A. (2002). The practice of restorative justice. *Criminal Justice Ethics* 21, 3–20.

Griffin, P. (1999). Developing and administering accountability-based sanctions for juveniles. *JAIBG Bulletin*.

Halstead, S. (September 1999). Educational discipline using the principles of restorative justice. *JCE* 50(2), 42–46.

Howarth, J.W. (2000). Toward the restorative justice critique of anti-gang public nuisance injunctions. *Hastings Constitutional Law Quarterly* 27, 1–5.

Lucas, Nancy (2001). Note: Restitution, rehabilitation, prevention, and transformation: victim-offender mediation for first-time non-violent youthful offenders. *Hofstra Law Review* 29, 1–10.

Shenk, A.A. (2001). Victim-offender mediation: the road to repairing hate crime injustice. *Ohio State Journal on Dispute Resolution* 17, 185, 1–7.

Tracy, C. (December 1998). The promises and perils of restorative justice. *International Journal of Offender Therapy and Comparative Criminology.*

Umbreit, M.S. and Coates, R.B. (1993). Cross-site analysis of victim-offender mediation in four states. *Crime and Delinquency* 39(4), 565–585.

Chapter 28

Capital Punishment and Juveniles

Allan L. Patenaude and Megan Reynolds

28.1 Introduction

Cohen (1972) defined a moral panic as an episode that emerges as a threat to the established social values, based on its intense presentation by the popular media over a generally short period of time. A moral panic currently exists in the United States concerning the rates of violent juvenile crime, including homicide. Debates over how to deal effectively with chronic and violent juvenile offenders have tended to focus more on the horrific nature of the criminal event than on the characteristics of the criminal actor. Indeed, many television and radio talk shows have had guests who have spoken out in favor of capital punishment for capital crimes, regardless of the age of the offender.

By the end of 2001, 75 of 194 nations had abolished capital punishment. An additional 14 nations had abolished it for all ordinary crimes during peacetime, but retained the death penalty for crimes committed during wartime or while in military service (Hood, 2002, p. 14). There remain 105 nations that continue to employ capital punishment. The execution of persons under the age of 18 is prohibited under the International Covenant on Civil and Human Rights (1989) and other United Nations resolutions. Only 16 nations have yet to ratify or register their reservations about this agreement, including the United States, which has chosen the latter route.

This chapter examines the debate over capital punishment for juveniles in the United States from two opposing viewpoints: the doctrines of *parens patriae* and social defense. Indeed, this chapter will explore whether the notions of rehabilitation and treatment (with the State acting in best interests of the juvenile) can be reconciled with the notions of deterrence, moral correctness, retribution, and proportionality in the best interests of social defense, using capital punishment as its metaphorical straw man. Finally, this chapter will seek to understand whether capital punishment for juvenile offenders is merely political rhetoric or sound juvenile justice policy.

28.2 Juveniles and Capital Punishment

As mentioned previously, there are only 16 nations worldwide that continue to execute juveniles. Whereas the International Covenant on Civil and Human Rights (1989) defines a *juvenile* as any person who has not yet attained his or her 18th birthday, there remain a number of nations in which that is not the age of majority (ranging from 16 to 21 years old). The age at which a person becomes fully responsible for one's criminal actions varies from country to country as well as between states within a single country. The age of criminal responsibility in the United States serves as an example of the latter. On the one hand, children under the age of 10 or 12 (depending on the state) receive full immunity from criminal responsibility under the common law beliefs that their levels of development and dependency make them incapable of forming criminal intent and/or understanding the consequences of their actions. On the other hand, limited immunity from criminal responsibility is granted to juveniles aged 10 to 18 for similar reasons, whereas offenders over that age are considered adults with full criminal responsibility for their actions, although this distinction has not always been in place in the United States (see Chapter 1). A *juvenile* is defined as any person who has attained his or her 12th but not 18th birthday for the purposes of this chapter.

The history of capital punishment for crimes committed by juveniles in the United States has been, for the most part, indistinguishable from the nation's history of capital punishment for adults. Streib (2002) noted that of the approximately 20,000 individuals executed in the American colonies and the United States since 1642, 365 of these executions were for crimes committed as a juvenile. Such crimes included arson, assault, bestiality, manslaughter, murder, and rape (Bohm, 1999; Johnson, 1998; Streib, 1993, 2002; Vito et al., 1998). The number of death sentences imposed upon juvenile offenders remains low, as seen in Table 28.1. Indeed, whereas the percentage of juveniles sentenced to death rose to a high of 8.8 percent of the total number of death sentences imposed during 1977, they have averaged only 3 percent since 1973.

By the end of 2001, statisticians Tracey Snell and Laura Maruschak noted that 2.3 percent (77 of 3311) of the inmates on death row at that time were 17 or younger when they committed the crime (Snell and Maruschak, 2002). This figure had changed by less than 0.5 percent from the figures for 1995, which indicates both the rarity of capital punishment and lack of change among this population.

Prior to the 1980s, public gaze has scarcely fallen upon the execution of juveniles, mainly because of the rarity of such events; it has done so only in those instances in which the crime was particularly heinous or was the subject of a Supreme Court decision. An example of the former may be seen in the 1959 execution of Charles Raymond Starkweather for a murder spree that left 11 people dead (Leyton, 1996), whereas the latter is typified by the decision in *Thompson v. Oklahoma*, 487 U.S. 815 (1988), which imposed a ban on execution of persons under 16 years of age at the time the offense was committed. During the past 23 years, however, both the Supreme Court and lower appellate courts have shown interest in the death penalty as a criminal sanction and its applicability to juvenile offenders (Streib, 2002). Similar interest has also emerged through an increase of public opinion surveys on the topic (see Skovron et al., 1989).

There are currently 39 civil jurisdictions within the United States (38 states and the federal government) that impose the death penalty. Among these same jurisdictions, according to Snell and Maruschak (2002), the age at which the death penalty can be imposed varies between 16 years or less (13 states), 17 years (4 states), and 18 years (14 states and the federal government). It is also interesting to note that seven states do not have statutory provisions that specify a minimum age at which a court is authorized to impose the death penalty on a juvenile who is convicted of a capital crime.

28.3 The Juvenile Death Penalty vs. Evolving Standards of Decency

Although American society can accept a war on crime or a war on drugs, it is not yet prepared to pursue a similar war against its own youth. Rather, it has adopted a "get-tough" approach to dealing with

Table 28.1   Number of U.S. Juvenile Death Sentences

Year	Total Death Sentences	Juvenile Death Sentences	Percentage of Juvenile Death Sentences
2001	155	7	4.5
2000	229	7	3.1
1999	282	15	5.3
1998	303	11	3.6
1997	277	8	2.9
1996	319	12	3.8
1995	318	13	4.1
1994	317	17	5.3
1993	288	7	2.4
1992	287	6	2.1
1991	266	5	1.9
1990	253	9	3.6
1989	259	1	0.4
1988	291	5	1.7
1987	289	2	0.7
1986	300	9	3
1985	267	6	2.2
1984	285	6	2.1
1983	253	8	3.2
1982	266	14	5.3
1981	224	8	3.6
1980	173	6	3.5
1979	151	3	2
1978	185	6	3.2
1977	137	12	8.8
1976	233	3	1.3
1975	298	11	3.7
1974	149	3	2
1973	42	0	0
Total	**7200**	**220**	**3.1**

violent and serious juvenile crime (see Chapter 1). Legislation has been enacted that increases penalties for violent offenders, permits the "blending" of juvenile and adult sentences, and eases the transfer of juveniles to the adult criminal justice system.

Ancel (1954), founder of the New Social Defense Movement, noted that such state-level actions are consistent with a State that develops juvenile justice policy on the basis of social reaction rather than one taking the scientific approach to crime. Such an approach presupposes an inherent sense of fault that each individual is believed to possess and acts solely to protect society from crime and delinquency. Ancel (1954) also argued that there existed the need for preventive actions (eliminating or changing the conditions conducive to crime) and security measures to neutralize the offender (castration for rapists, suspension of driving privileges for impaired drivers, closure of liquor stores that sell liquor to minors, confiscation of all weapons if a weapon is used in crime, and so forth). Again, it would seem that numerous states have already taken such measures in reactive attempts to achieve their version of social harmony.

Although "getting tough" on juvenile offenders may be part of an evolving standard of decency, the question emerges, "Is the imposition of capital punishment on juveniles also part of that same standard at the dawn of the 21st century"? The execution of juveniles has been decried in the international arena as evidenced by: (a) the number of states that have ceased to execute offenders whose crimes occurred when they were juveniles and (b) the number of states which had ratified international covenants prohibiting such executions. Only the Democratic Republic of Congo, Iran, Nigeria, Pakistan, Saudi Arabia, Yemen, and the United States have reported the execution of juveniles since 1990, although both Pakistan and Yemen have since discontinued this practice (Hood, 2002). This fact has been argued by Brewer et al. (2002) as *de facto* evidence of an international consensus on the standard of decency with regard to the execution of persons who were under 18 years of age at the time of their offense.

Shelden and Hussong (2003) dispute the claim that an evolving standard of decency exists in the juvenile justice system in the United States. They argued, instead, that juvenile justice is cyclical in nature, although the metaphor of a pendulum is a more accurate descriptor, and echoed Bernard's (1992) earlier claim that juvenile justice policy fluctuates from "acting in the 'best interests of the child' or rehabilitation (based upon the *parens patriae* doctrine) to an emphasis on upholding certain rights that also apply to adults, along with their corresponding punishments" (Shelden and Hussong, 2003, p. 23). Bernard (1992),

Shelden and Hussong (2003), and Zimring (2003) each argue that the best interests of the child are often best served through the *parens patriae*-oriented juvenile court, but that the child needs to be protected from the abuse of the State.

The notion of a cyclical standard is also partially supported by Zimring (2003). There are a number of contradictions in retaining capital punishment in the face of an evolving consensus on standards of decency that apply to juvenile executions in the United States. Zimring (2003) noted that differences in regional culture, temperament, and history are contributing to a new, more palatable image of capital punishment. Although he noted that public sentiment holds that capital punishment is appropriate for murder, most citizens distrust the mechanisms by which individuals are selected to receive a death sentence. Zimring (2003) noted that whereas public support for capital punishment has been dropping since the 1980s and remains evenly distributed across the United States, the practice of executions is clustered in the South. Finally, the American history of having sentenced both adults and juveniles to death has been accepted as fact while discontent has been expressed over prosecutorial discretion and other factors affecting who receives the ultimate sanction.

Representatives from the United States have registered reservations about international covenants on the execution of adult and juvenile offenders (effectively a nonratification). They have argued, on its behalf, that it is a State's right to punish offenders as it sees fit (Hood, 2002). Interestingly, both the number of states that execute offenders for murders committed prior to their 18th birthday and the number of executions of such offenders have decreased since the U.S. Supreme Court's decision in *Thompson v. Oklahoma* (1988). However, the increased attention paid to appellate court decisions involving violent juvenile offenders may contribute to a further review of the evolving standard of decency and the creation of more punitive juvenile justice policy and a lowering of the age at which juveniles might receive adult sentences, including capital punishment, for their offenses.

28.4 Recent Legal History on the Death Penalty for Juvenile Offenders

Similar to other nations with a common law system, the United States judicial process is ruled by the principle of *stare decisis* (abiding by authorities or cases already adjudicated). Such a system has precedents for both sides of the capital punishment argument when applied to juveniles who kill. Juveniles have been executed throughout the history of the United States, according to Bohm (1999, 2003). Indeed, he noted that whereas the 1642 execution of 16-year-old Thomas Graunger may have been the first recorded execution of a juvenile, 12-year-old Ocunish Hannah's execution in 1786 places her as the youngest juvenile executed in American history.

A number of appellate court decisions have dealt with the issue of capital punishment for persons who were under the age of 18 years at the commission of their offense, including:

- *Eddings v. Oklahoma*, 445 U.S. 104 (1982)
- *Thompson v. Oklahoma*, 487 U.S. 815 (1988)
- *Stanford v. Kentucky*, 492 U.S. 361 (1989)
- *Missouri v. Wilkins*, 492 U.S. 361 (1989)
- *Graham v. Collins*, 506 U.S. 461 (1993)
- *Johnson v. Texas*, 509 U.S. (1993)

As these cases and their relative impact on capital punishment for juveniles are discussed in chronological order, it is possible to perceive the evolving consensus among members of the American appellate courts. Interestingly, these cases deal with the issues that Bernard (1992) and Shelden and Hussong (2003) discuss as the maintenance of rights/punishment for juveniles in line with those same rights and punishments accorded to adults.

In *Eddings v. Oklahoma* (1982), 16-year-old Monty Lee Eddings entered a plea of *nolo contendere* (no contest) to the charge of murder in the shotgun slaying of an Oklahoma Highway Patrol officer; the charges were heard in an adult criminal court rather than a juvenile court. Eddings was convicted and sentenced to death. In passing sentence, the trial judge stated that the prosecution had proved beyond a reasonable doubt each of the three aggravating circumstances required under Oklahoma's death penalty statute and that, as a matter of law, he could not consider any mitigating circumstances other than the defendant's age. The conviction and sentence were upheld in Oklahoma's Court of Criminal Appeals and the case was appealed to the Supreme Court of the United States. The high court ruled 5 to 4 that the lower courts failed to consider all of the mitigating factors as required by its earlier decision in *Lockett v. Ohio* (1978) and vacated Eddings' death penalty.[1]

Four years later, the Supreme Court ruled on the case of William Wayne Thompson. At the age of 15, Thompson was one of four individuals charged and convicted in adult court for the murder of his brother-in-law; he received the death penalty. In *Thompson v. Oklahoma* (1988), the Supreme Court ruled on the narrow issue of whether it was unconstitutional, under the cruel and unusual provisions of the Eighth Amendment and Fourteenth Amendment, to execute someone who was under 16 years of age at the time of his or her offense. Here, the Supreme Court set aside the original sentence citing three concerns:

1. The evolving standards of decency in determining why a state would accept or reject the death penalty for a person younger than 16 years of age
2. The relevant statutes of 18 states that execute offenders which point toward a consensus of 16 as the minimum age for the imposition of the death penalty
3. The reduced moral culpability of juveniles as a class of offenders and the fact that such executions did not contribute to the goals of either retribution or general deterrence (*Thompson v. Oklahoma*, 1988)

Although this decision applied only to those states that did not specify a minimum age for the death penalty, it is nonetheless significant for this chapter as it has identified the issue of moral development vis-à-vis culpability in the imposition of the death penalty for juveniles.

One year later, the Supreme Court ruled that it was not cruel and unusual to execute a juvenile for a murder committed after he or she had attained his or her 16th birthday when it considered *Standford v. Kentucky* (1989) and *Missouri v. Wilkins* (1989). Seventeen-year-old Kevin Standford was convicted and sentenced to death for the rape and murder of a female service station attendant in 1981. Sixteen-year-old Heath Wilkins was convicted and sentenced to death for the robbing and killing of a store owner for $450 in cash, liquor, and cigarettes. The high court explored the constitutionality of these two sentences using the tests of whether the punishment would have been declared unconstitutional by the framers at the time that the Bill of Rights was ratified and a consensus on an evolving standard of decency. Employing an objective standard based on the age permitted by the majority of state and federal capital punishment legislations, the Supreme Court decided that the execution of 16- and 17-year-olds did not violate the Eighth Amendment and Fourteenth Amendment.

Following the reinstatement of the death penalty in 1976, the Texas state legislature enacted a special instruction clause in its death penalty law. The special instruction required that the sentencing jury agree on all three points contained within it, namely: (1) Was the conduct deliberate? (2) Was there a reasonable expectation that death would result from the conduct? and (3) Was there an expectation of future dangerousness (particularly violence) on the part of the convicted party? This clause was put to the test in *Graham v. Collins* (1993) and *Johnson v. Texas* (1993). In *Graham v. Collins* (1993), 17-year-old Gary Graham shot and killed a man during a botched armed robbery in the parking lot of a local grocery store. The Supreme Court was asked to decide whether the special instructions were unconstitutional under the Eighth Amendment. It ruled that although the special instructions restricted the class of persons eligible to receive the death penalty, it did not restrict the introduction of mitigating factors to the jury during the sentencing phase.

Although not a juvenile case *per se* (as the appellant was 19 years of age at the time), *Johnson v. Texas* (1993) illustrated the rationales that continued to underlie both the Texas statute and the Supreme Court's views on age as a mitigating factor in sentencing. Nineteen-year-old Dorsie Johnson and a companion were convicted for having robbed and killed a convenience store clerk and sentenced to death. In keeping with Texas law, the special instruction was given to the jury. The Supreme Court was asked to decide whether the Texas special instructions to death-qualified juries precluded them from specifically considering age as a mitigating factor. In keeping with its earlier decisions in *Lockett v. Ohio* (1978), *Eddings v. Oklahoma* (1982), and *Graham v. Collins* (1993), the Supreme Court ruled that the Texas special instructions violated neither the Eighth Amendment nor the Fourteenth Amendment because they permitted the sentencing jury to explore the appellant's current age as a mitigating factor in the third instruction that dealt with the future dangerousness of the offender.[2]

28.5 Does a Juvenile's Moral Development Correspond to an Adult's Mental Retardation?

Throughout the previous century, for example, the penal standard for juvenile offenders has been that while they should be held responsible for their actions, such responsibility should be less than that to which an adult would be held, because of their levels of moral development and dependency. Indeed, the entire juvenile justice system in the United States is premised on that philosophical notion. Juveniles were regarded as vulnerable because of their levels of moral development and diverted from the adult criminal justice system and, later, from formal processing within the juvenile justice system whenever practical.

However, violent juvenile offenders, as well as the media coverage of their offenses, such as the schoolyard shootings from Jonesboro, Arkansas, to Columbine, Colorado, and the Washington, D.C. area, continue to capture the eyes and ears of the American public. This attention contributes to the swinging of the evolving standard of decency toward more punitive measures rather than less punitive ones while ignoring the levels of maturity and moral culpability of the juvenile offender.

There also exists an interrelationship between the issues of moral development and mental retardation when discussing culpability in capital cases involving juveniles, which needs to be explored. This interrelationship has both legal and ethical aspects.

Under common law, there exists a legal principle that the insane must be granted absolute immunity from prosecution and are, therefore, held nonculpable for their actions. From an ethical standpoint, this approach is morally correct if we, as a society, believe in the principles of cognitive free will and moral reasoning. If an insane person cannot understand and process information in the same manner as others in society, employ abstract logic, control his or her actions, and learn from the reactions of others to his or her behavior, they are granted absolute immunity from prosecution for their actions. In the United States, this principle was extended to death row inmates who were sane at the time of sentencing but subsequently went insane as the result of their conditions of confinement on death row. In *Ford v. Wainwright*, 447 U.S. 399 (1986), the Supreme Court ruled that it was a cruel and unusual punishment to execute an insane prisoner because he or she could not appreciate the application of the punishment.

This principle has been modified and applied to the mentally retarded offender. Here, although the same mental inabilities mentioned in the previous paragraph are germane, the moral and legal issues shift from immunity from prosecution to a reduced level of culpability. For instance, 22-year-old Johnny Paul Penry was convicted of the rape and murder of a young woman during 1979. It was introduced during the trial that Penry possessed an IQ of 54 as well as a mental age of $6^1/_2$ years and the social maturity of a 10-year old. The court was shown that although retarded, Johnny Penry had the ability to reason and learn, albeit to a diminished level. In *Penry v. Lynaugh*, 492 U.S. 302 (1989), the Supreme Court ruled that two primary principles in sentencing, retribution and deterrence, were not applicable to the same degree in mentally retarded offenders as they were to normal offenders, and that mentally retarded offenders who demonstrated a capacity to reason were liable to receive the death penalty.

In *Atkins v. Virginia*, 122 S.Ct. 2242 (2002), the Supreme Court ruled that the execution of mentally retarded individuals was cruel and unusual within the meaning of the Eighth Amendment and Fourteenth Amendment. Eighteen-year-old Daryl Renard Atkins was convicted of abduction, armed robbery, and capital murder and sentenced to death during 1996. He was evaluated by a forensic psychologist who concluded that his IQ of 59 placed him in the mildly retarded range and assessed his mental age as that of a child between 9 and 12 years of age. The appellant in *Atkins v. Virginia* (2002) attempted to sway the high court towards linking clinical definitions of mental retardation with clinical evidence that pointed towards the limited intellectual functioning and adaptive skills of juveniles compared to those found in adults. Although cognitive impairments may reduce the level of moral culpability, the high court ruled, it did not grant immunity from prosecution to mentally retarded offenders. Although the Supreme Court noted the national consensus against the execution of the mentally retarded, it remained silent on the definition of retardation even though the majority decision quoted examples from the American Association of Mental Retardation and the American Psychiatric Association.

In *Simmons v. Missouri*, Missouri SC 84454 (2002), for example, the appellant's attorneys sought to apply the Supreme Court's decision in *Atkins v. Virginia* (2002) to their client. Christopher Simmons was convicted of murder in the 1993 kidnapping of a young woman from a nearby trailer (eventually killing her), and sentenced to death during 1994; he was 17 years of age at the time of the offense. Simmons' attorneys introduced similar clinical studies from the United States and abroad (notably Canada) that identified the lack of physical development in those areas of the brain, coupled with rapid physical changes occurring during adolescence, as the basis for poor impulse control and decision making among juveniles. These physical conditions, they argued, resulted in cognitive and emotional deficiencies as well as the destructive and short-sighted behavior commonly found among both criminal and noncriminal adolescents. Their goal was to convince the Missouri Supreme Court that not only did the principles in *Atkins v. Virginia* (2002) apply in this case, but that the same common law jurisprudence that prohibits the execution of the mentally retarded applies to juvenile death penalty cases.[3]

28.5.1 The U.S. Supreme Court Bans the Execution of Juveniles

In a 5 to 4 decision on March 1, 2005, the U.S. Supreme Court ruled that the Eighth Amendment prohibits capital punishment for offenders who commit murder before their 18th birthday. In *Roper v. Simmons* the Court applied some of the reasoning from *Atkins v. Virginia* in which it proclaimed that the execution of the mentally retarded is a cruel and unusual punishment. The issue comes down to culpability and the fact that young people simply are not as mentally developed as adults. This does not mean that they do not know the difference between right and wrong; rather, they are less culpable than adults because they are not as mentally developed as their adult counterparts. They are easily influenced by their peers and their culture and can quite easily lapse into inappropriate behaviors. Thus, deterrence and retribution cannot be the punishment goals when it comes to juvenile offenders.

The Court also used the evolving standards of decency by arguing that there is a national consensus now in existence against executing juveniles. They relied on facts such as these: (1) Thirty states prohibit the death penalty for juveniles, (2) twelve states have rejected the death penalty for adults and juveniles, (3) juries seldom use the death penalty at the sentencing phase in a juvenile capital murder case, and (4) the execution of juveniles is rare.

Upsetting dissenting justices, Justice Kennedy, writing for the majority, also used (although to a lesser extent) an argument that the death penalty for juveniles was frowned upon by the international community. The United States, in continuing to allow capital punishment in juvenile cases, was in violation of the United Nations Convention on the Rights of the Child and the International Covenant on Civil and Political Rights. Justice Scalia, a dissenting justice, wrote, "Acknowledgement of foreign approval has no place in the legal opinion of this Court" (see www.deathpenaltyinfo.org). Nevertheless, the majority did consider international opinion, but only minimally. The overriding rationale in *Roper v. Simmons* was grounded in the diminished mental capacity of the adolescent along with a growing concern among the public, legislatures, and judges that to impose the death penalty on an individual under the age of 18 was, in fact, in violation of the Eighth Amendment.

28.6 Conclusion

Since the colonial days when England's so-called Bloody Code (due to the high number of offenses for which death was the penalty) ruled, Americans have had a strong moral thread woven through the fabric of their nation. The notion that swift and harsh punishment is equivalent to justice has often been present within American jurisprudence, even for juveniles who have killed another person.

The debate on whether to impose capital punishment on an individual who committed the crime while a juvenile continues throughout the United States. Indeed, the public rhetoric, "get tough on crime," and the moral panic caused by those few juveniles who kill are likely to keep this debate alive for many years, if not decades, to come. At present, however, capital punishment for juveniles has been banished by the U.S. Supreme Court. This does not, however, rule out the possibility that some future Court will reconsider the arguments made in the cases discussed here.

References

Ancel, Marc. 1954. *La défense sociale nouvelle: un mouvement de politique criminelle humaniste*. Paris, France: Cujas.

Bernard, Thomas J. 1992. *The Cycle of Juvenile Justice*. Oxford: Oxford University Press.

Bohm, Robert M. 2003. Death penalty. In Marilyn McShane and Frank Williams, III (Eds.), *Encyclopedia of Juvenile Justice*. Thousand Oaks, CA: Sage. pp. 109–114.

Bohm, Robert M. 1999. *Deathquest: An Introduction to the Theory and Practice of Capital Punishment in the United States*. Cincinnati, OH: Anderson.

Brewer, Jennifer, Patrick J. Berrigan, and Caryn P. Tatelli. 2002. *Petition for a Commutation of, or Reprieve of, a Sentence of Death in the Matter of Christopher Lee Simmons*. St. Louis, MO: Missouri Supreme Court.

Cohen, Stanley. 1972. *Folk Devils and Moral Panics: The Creation of the Mods and Rockers*. London: MacGibbon and Kee.

Hood, Roger. 2002. *The Death Penalty: A Worldwide Perspective*. Oxford: Oxford University Press.

Johnson, Robert. 1998. *Death Work: A Study of the Modern Execution Process*. 2nd ed. Belmont, CA: Wadsworth.

Leyton, Elliott. 1996. *Compulsive Killers: The Story of Modern Multiple Murder*. New York: Washington Mews.

Shelden, Randall G. and Michelle Hussong. 2003. Juvenile crime, adult adjudication, and the death penalty: draconian policies revisited. *Justice Policy Journal*, 1(2), 21–40.

Skovron, Sandra E., Joseph E. Scott, and Francis T. Cullen. 1989. The death penalty for juveniles: an assessment of public support. *Crime and Delinquency*, 35, 546–561.

Snell, Tracy L. and Laura M. Maruschak. 2002. *Capital Punishment, 2001*. Washington, D.C.: Bureau of Justice Statistics.

Streib, Victor L. 2002. Juvenile Death Penalty Today: Death Sentences and Executions for Juvenile Crimes, January 1, 1973–December 31, 2002. Online document. Available at http://www.law.onu.edu/faculty/streib/juvdeath.htm. Accessed: January 28, 2003. Ada, OH: Ohio Northern University.

Streib, Victor L. (Ed.). 1993. *A Capital Punishment Anthology.* Cincinnati, OH: Anderson.

United Nations 1990. International Covenant on Civil and Human Rights. Economic and Social Council Resolution 1989/64.

Vito, Gennaro F., Richard, Tewksbury, and Deborah G. Wilson. 1998. *The Juvenile Justice System: Concepts and Issues.* Prospect Heights, IL: Waveland Press.

Watkins, John C., Jr., 1998. *The Juvenile Justice Century: A Sociolegal Commentary on American Juvenile Courts.* Durham, NC: Carolina Academic Press.

Zimring, Franklin E., 2003. *The Contradictions of American Capital Punishment.* Oxford: Oxford University Press.

Cases Cited:

Atkins v. Virginia, 122 S.Ct. 2242 (2002).

Eddings v. Oklahoma, 445 U.S. 104 (1982).

Ford v. Wainwright (1986) 477 U.S. 399 (1986).

Graham v. Collins, 506 U.S. 461 (1993).

Johnson v. Texas, 509 U.S. (1993).

Lockett v. Ohio, 438 U.S. 586 (1978).

Missouri v. Wilkins, 492 U.S. 361 (1989).

Penry v. Lynaugh, 492 U.S. 302 (1989).

Roper v. Simmons, 543 U.S. 633 (2005).

Simmons v. Missouri, Missouri SC 84454 (2002).

Stanford v. Kentucky, 492 U.S. 361 (1989).

Thompson v. Oklahoma, 487 U.S. 815 (1988).

Tuilaepa v. California, 512 U.S. (1994).

Notes

1. In *Lockett v. Ohio*, 438 U.S. 586, 98 S. Ct. 2954, 57 L. Ed. 2d 973 (1978), the Supreme Court ruled that although the state must enumerate all aggravating factors in its death penalty statutes, it was bound to consider any and all mitigating factors offered in a juvenile death penalty case.
2. California's special instructions to juries in death penalty cases also came under the scrutiny of the Supreme Court in *Tuilaepa v. California*, 512 U.S. (1994), in which another young adult was convicted of murder and sentenced to death. In this case, the high court noted that whereas the jury must consider any mitigating factors (such as age) presented, the trial judge was under no obligation to tell the jury how to weigh those same factors.

3. The Missouri Supreme Court rejected the appellant's argument in *Simmons v. Missouri* (2002). This case was referred to the governor of Missouri for reprieve of the death penalty, which was denied. As of December 31, 2002, Simmons was on death row awaiting execution.

Chapter 29

Job Satisfaction and Organizational Commitment among Staff of Juvenile Correctional Facilities

Kevin I. Minor, James B. Wells, and Earl Angel

29.1 Introduction and Literature Overview

In comparison to research on the residents of juvenile institutions, little has been conducted on the staff. Extant literature on staff focuses on such areas as the treatment role (e.g., Grissom and Dubnov, 1989), strategies of maintaining control over youth (e.g., Polsky, 1977), and staff attitudes and perceptions and corresponding organizational variables (e.g., Gordon, 1999; Minor et al., 2004; Wells et al., 2000). Two key and interrelated variables in the latter area include staff job satisfaction and their level of commitment to the organization for which they work.

Studies in adult corrections and other fields have established that staff members who are more satisfied with their jobs and have greater levels of organizational commitment tend to exhibit more positive job performance (see Lambert et al., 1999 for an excellent synthesis of these studies). Specifically, job satisfaction appears to be an important precursor to organizational commitment, and in turn, commitment seems to be directly related to performance. That is, organizational commitment mediates between job satisfaction on the one hand and job performance on the other. This topic has not been investigated very thoroughly in juvenile corrections. Hence, the present study analyzes the variables predictive of job satisfaction as well as the relationship of job satisfaction to organizational commitment among staff employed in juvenile correctional facilities administered by the Kentucky Department of Juvenile Justice.

Krueger and his colleagues conducted some of the first investigations of job satisfaction and organizational commitment levels among child and youth care staff (Krueger, 1985; Krueger et al., 1986, 1987). Job satisfaction and commitment were found to be associated with such organizational variables as provisions for staff involvement in agency decision making and promotional systems. Education was the only demographic variable of significance; it was negatively related to organizational commitment and unrelated to satisfaction (Krueger et al., 1987). Additionally, job satisfaction and commitment were reciprocally related.

More recently, Wright (1993) reported low to moderate levels of job satisfaction among a sample of juvenile detention center staff. He also found a negative relationship between satisfaction and employee turnover. Mitchell et al. (2000) reported very similar results in their study of juvenile institution staff. Neither of these studies focused on the predictors of job satisfaction, nor did they include organizational commitment. In later research, Mitchell et al. (2001) analyzed a number of variables and discovered an inverse relationship between education and job satisfaction. Wells et al. (2000) reported moderate to positive levels of job satisfaction among staff working in juvenile institutions and identified five significant predictors of satisfaction. Satisfaction was greater among personnel employed at rural (vs. urban) facilities, females, older employees, supervisory personnel, and staff members not involved in the direct care of youth.

In adult corrections, where research is more plentiful, the balance of findings suggests no relationship of job satisfaction to either race or gender; the evidence is mixed with respect to education and age (Lambert et al., 2002). According to Lambert et al., personal characteristics like these have a considerably weaker relationship to job satisfaction than such work-environment variables as job stress, job autonomy, and employee participation in decision making. This statement is consistent with the findings of Krueger and associates, discussed earlier.

Even in the adult corrections literature, however, organizational commitment has seldom been studied. This is unfortunate, as research on organizations in other fields consistently shows that commitment functions as a mediating link between job satisfaction and employee behavior (Lambert et al., 1999). The present study addresses this void in the literature.

29.2 Method

29.2.1 Participants

The data set used in this study was collected as part of a wider, systematic research effort to evaluate the staff training program operated by the Kentucky Department of Juvenile Justice (DJJ). Employees must complete this 10-week program which consists of 6 weeks of academy training and 4 weeks of on-the-job training prior to undertaking full responsibilities at a residential facility administered by DJJ.

Job satisfaction and organizational commitment data were gathered through two separate administrations of a mail survey using a procedure developed by Dillman (1978) for each administration. The first administration resulted in 49 (62.0 percent) of 79 surveys being returned by academy graduates, whereas 91 (42.9 percent) of 212 surveys were returned in the second administration. Of the total 140 surveys returned, 97 (69.3 percent) contained complete data on both job satisfaction and organizational commitment and could thus be included in this study. As an additional criterion for inclusion in the study, an employee had to be on the job for at least a 6-month period following academy graduation so as to ensure reasonable exposure to the job.

More of the 97 employees than not were male (87.6 percent), white (80.4 percent), and married (59.8 percent). Their ages ranged from 20 to 57, with 31.9 as the median age. In addition, most (88.7 percent) were high school graduates, 12.4 percent held associate degrees, and 19.6 percent held bachelor's degrees.

29.2.2 Data

Most data for this study were collected either from DJJ records or, in the case of job satisfaction and organizational commitment data, via mail survey. In addition to the standard demographic variables mentioned above, data were collected on other variables thought to be possible predictors of JDI measures. These included the following:

1. Whether the employee was born in an urban or rural area
2. Whether the employee was born in Kentucky or another state
3. Whether the employee had children and, if so, the number
4. Whether the employee resided in an urban or rural area and whether the employee worked at a facility located in a rural, urban, or suburban area
5. Whether the employee had attempted to complete an associate degree or a bachelor degree
6. Whether the employee had graduated from a specialized (e.g., trade) school
7. Whether the employee had prior correctional, military, or social service work experience
8. Whether the employee had prior experience serving as a volunteer in human services
9. Security rating of facility (ranging from a low of 1 to a high of 4)
10. Gender of facility residents (males, females, or both)
11. Average unemployment rate of the county in which the facility is located and the rate in the employee's county of residence[1]
12. Facility bed capacity
13. Square footage of facility
14. Whether the current mission of the facility (e.g., sex offender treatment) differed from the facility's original mission at the time it opened
15. Suitability level of facility (ranging from 1 to 5)
16. Condition level of facility (ranging from 1 or poor to 4 or excellent)
17. Counselor turnover
18. Whether a facility's staff underwent academy training on-site at the facility
19. Whether the employee participated in mentoring

Variables 9 through 18 reference the particular facility at which any given staff member was employed. Except for the last five, the variables in this list are largely self-explanatory. Facility suitability (variable 15) refers to a rating by staff working at a given facility as to how well the physical plant suits or fits the population currently housed there; higher ratings were indicative of better fit in this study. Facility condition refers to a rating assigned to a given facility by DJJ for insurance purposes (should the facility be damaged or destroyed); higher ratings indicated better conditions. Counselor turnover was defined as the number of counselors who left a given facility between calendar years 1997 and 2001 divided by the number hired during that time frame. Variable 18 refers to whether the staff members of a given facility underwent their academy training on-site as a single class or whether a given staff member completed the centrally located academy training as part of a class comprised of staff from various facilities. Finally, as our study included staff who completed the academy training between early October 1998 and late September 2000, and as DJJ did not implement a systematic program of mentoring newly trained staff by experienced staff until July 2000, it was possible to control for whether each staff member in this study was exposed to the mentoring program.

29.2.2.1 Job Satisfaction Data

Job satisfaction was measured with the Job Descriptive Index (JDI), a multifaceted instrument developed and standardized by Blazer et al. (1997). The JDI is designed to measure employee satisfaction with various facets of a job, including: (1) the work itself, (2) pay, (3) promotion opportunities, (4) supervision, (5) coworkers, and (6) the job in general. On each subscale, the respondent marks "yes," "no," or "cannot decide" for a list of descriptive words or phrases. The developers of the instrument recommend that the subscales be scored and analyzed separately from one another rather than being combined to form one global score. The possible point range on each subscale is 0 to 54, with higher scores indicative of greater satisfaction. Each scale demonstrated high internal reliability in this study.[2]

29.2.2.2 Organizational Commitment Data

Organizational commitment was measured through use of the Organizational Commitment Questionnaire (OCQ) developed by Mowday et al. (1979, 1982). The OCQ requires respondents to rate 15 statements concerning their views toward a particular organization. Each rating is made on a seven-point scale ranging from "strongly disagree" (scored as 1) to "strongly agree" (scored as 7). One derives an overall score for each respondent by computing the mean item score across the 15 responses, so that scores closer to seven indicate greater commitment. This instrument also displayed high internal reliability in the present study (coefficient alpha = 0.89).

Table 29.1   Job Satisfaction and Organizational Commitment Scores

Measure	Mean	SD	Point Range
JDI — Work	42.1	10.5	0–54
JDI — Pay	12.9	12.8	0–54
JDI — Promotion opportunities	29.3	16.6	0–54
JDI — Supervision	40.6	16.4	0–54
JDI — Coworkers	40.7	13.4	0–54
JDI — Job in general	43.0	12.3	0–54
Organizational commitment	5.3	1.1	1–7

29.3 Results

Table 29.1 provides means and standard deviation data for the JDI scales and the OCQ. Blazer et al. (1997) consider JDI scale scores of 32 to 54 to be indicative of job satisfaction, scores of 22 or less to be indicative of dissatisfaction, and scores 23 to 31 to be neutral. Using these guidelines, it can be seen that the DJJ employees exhibited satisfaction on all scales except for promotion, where the mean is in the neutral range, and pay, where the score is exceptionally low. In addition, the mean organizational commitment score is moderate to high.

The next step was to analyze the bivariate relationships between each of the potential predictor variables listed earlier and the measures of job satisfaction and organizational commitment. This was done using t-tests for categorical variables and Pearson correlations for continuous-level variables. The statistically significant findings are presented in Table 29.2 in which data for each of the various measures are summarized in a separate panel. Panel A of Table 29.2 indicates that mean work satisfaction scores were significantly higher among staff members who (1) had not attempted an associate degree and (2) had attempted or received a bachelor degree. Similarly, pay satisfaction mean scores (Panel B) were significantly higher among employees who (1) lacked prior work experience in social services, (2) were not employed at a facility located in an urban area, (3) were older, (4) underwent training

Table 29.2 Significant Bivariate Relationships

	Mean	SD	t	r	df	p
Panel A: JDI — Work						
Associate degree attempted			2.83	—	95	0.006
Yes	38.6	11.8				
No	44.5	8.9				
Bachelor degree attempted[a]			2.57	—	94.3	0.012
Yes	45.3	7.5				
No	40.3	11.7				
Bachelor degree received			2.48	—	34	0.018
Yes	48.0	5.8				
No	42.2	8.1				
Panel B: JDI — Pay						
Prior social service experience[a]			2.39	—	13.7	0.032
Yes	7.3	6.1				
No	13.4	13.1				
Employed at facility in urban area[a]			3.35	—	90.8	0.001
Yes	7.8	8.7				
No	15.5	13.8				
Employee age	—	—	—	.30	—	0.003
Was training on-site[a]			2.23	—	38.3	0.031
Yes	18.0	11.4				
No	10.9	14.9				
Did training include mentoring[a]			2.19	—	24.1	0.038
Yes	7.7	8.8				
No	13.8	13.2				

Table 29.2 Significant Bivariate Relationships (continued)

	Mean	SD	t	r	df	p
Panel C: JDI — Promotion						
Associate degree received			2.21	—	37	0.003
Yes	18.3	15.0				
No	29.8	14.9				
Graduate of specialized school			2.14	—	95	0.035
Yes	25.3	16.6				
No	32.5	16.0				
Prior volunteer experience			2.46	—	95	0.016
Yes	20.3	15.4				
No	31.1	16.3				
Panel D: JDI — Supervision						
Bachelor degree received[a]			2.69	—	34	0.009
Yes	48.8	7.2				
No	38.2	14.8				
Prior social service experience[a]			2.50	—	13.6	0.026
Yes	48.3	7.9				
No	39.9	16.8				
Panel E: JDI — Co-Workers						
Employed at facility in rural area[a]			2.09	—	89.2	0.039
Yes	44.1	11.3				
No	38.6	14.3				
Panel F: Organizational Commitment						
Prior volunteer experience			2.76	—	95	0.007
Yes	4.7	1.4				
No	5.5	1.0				

Table 29.2   Significant Bivariate Relationships (continued)

	Mean	SD	t	r	df	p
Prior social service experience[a]	2.16	—	17.9	0.044		
Yes	5.0	0.4				
No	5.4	1.2				
JDI measures						
Work scale	—	—	—	.71	—	0.000
Pay scale	—	—	—	.38	—	0.000
Promotion scale	—	—	—	.42	—	0.000
Supervision scale	—	—	—	.61	—	0.000
Coworkers scale	—	—	—	.43	—	0.000
Job in general scale	—	—	—	.85	—	0.000

[a] *T*-test results corrected for unequal variances based on Levene's test.

on-site, and (5) were not involved in the staff mentoring program. Satisfaction with promotion opportunities afforded by the job (Panel C) was higher among those who had not received an associate degree, not graduated from a trade or other type of specialized school, and not gained experience working as a volunteer. Satisfaction with supervisors (Panel D) was significantly higher among persons having bachelor degrees and those with prior experience in social services. Satisfaction with coworkers (Panel E) was significantly greater among persons employed at facilities located in rural areas, as opposed to facilities located in suburban and urban areas. None of the variables were significantly related to the satisfaction measure pertaining to the job in general.

Mean organizational commitment scores (Panel F of Table 29.2) were significantly higher for staff without past volunteer experience and those without past social service experience. Additionally, Table 29.2 shows significant positive correlations between each JDI scale and organizational commitment; higher levels of job satisfaction were consistently related to higher levels of organizational commitment.

We used stepwise multiple regression to examine the effect of each of the significant variables shown in Table 29.2, while holding constant all the other variables that were significantly related to a given measure.[3] The significant multivariate findings are summarized in Table 29.3. The directions of the relationships shown in Table 29.3 are the same as the directions in Table 29.2.[4]

Only two of the three significant bivariate predictors of work satisfaction from Table 29.2 are significant in the regression model for work satisfaction shown in Table 29.3. With the other two variables (associate degree attempted and bachelor degree attempted) held constant, the bachelor-degree-received variable exerted the strongest effect (Beta = −0.255); individuals holding these degrees displayed greater work satisfaction. However, the associate-degree-attempted variable also significantly contributed to accounting for variation; those who had attempted the associate degree had lower work satisfaction. As the R^2 indicates, in combination these two significant predictors accounted for 11.4 percent of the total variance in the measure of work satisfaction but left almost 89 percent of the variation unexplained.

The other regression models in Table 29.3 are interpreted in like fashion. Older employees, those who had received their academy training on-site, and those not employed at urban facilities exhibited greater pay satisfaction. Similarly, employees not holding associate degrees and those not having past experience at volunteer work displayed greater satisfaction with promotion opportunities. On the other hand, those holding bachelor degrees showed greater satisfaction with their supervisors than those without such degrees. The three variables comprising the pay model accounted for over 19 percent of the variance in that JDI scale, but both of the other two models accounted for less than 9 percent of total variability.

In contrast, the five variables making up the regression model for the organizational commitment measure explained two-thirds of the variance in that measure, an unusually high proportion by social science standards. As Table 29.3 shows, this is mostly due to the positive effects of four of the six JDI scales on organizational commitment. In addition, employees who lacked past experience working in social service agencies displayed higher levels of organizational commitment.

29.4 Discussion

The concepts of job satisfaction and organizational commitment are critical from the standpoint of developing juvenile justice policy, managing juvenile justice agencies, and engaging in effective practice. It

Table 29.3   Summary of Significant Multiple Regression Results

	Beta	p	R^2	F	df	p
Panel A: JDI — Work						
Overall model			.114	7.11	2, 93	.001
Bachelor degree received	−.255	.012				
Associate degree attempted	.206	.042				
Panel B: JDI — Pay						
Overall model			.191	8.57	3, 93	.000
Age	.293	.002				
Was training on-site	.249	.008				
Employed at facility in urban area	−.252	.008				
Panel C: JDI — Promotion						
Overall model			.085	5.48	2, 94	.006
Associate degree received	−.215	.033				
Prior volunteer experience	−.208	.039				
Panel D: JDI — Supervision						
Overall model			.030	4.02	1, 95	.048
Bachelor degree received	−.201	.048				
Panel E: organizational commitment						
Overall model			.663	38.70	5, 91	.000
JDI — job in general	.440	.000				
JDI — supervision	.270	.000				
JDI — work	.193	.012				
JDI — pay	−.147	.025				
Prior social service experience	.133	.030				

is very important for a correctional organization to have staff members who are generally satisfied with the various aspects of their jobs and committed to the organization and its goals. Literature on effective correctional intervention (e.g., Gendreau and Ross, 1979, 1983; Minor, 1988) suggests that effective programming is unlikely to occur without staff being committed to underlying goals. In addition, the staff turnover associated with low job satisfaction (cf. Mitchell et al., 2000; Wright, 1993) can result in two negative consequences. The first of these is inefficient use of the scarce resources available for staff training and correctional services. The second is instability of agency operations; organizations with consistently high staff turnover tend to be volatile and anomic.

The juvenile correctional employees we surveyed exhibited reasonably good satisfaction with the work, supervision, and coworker facets of their jobs, as well as with their jobs generally. These employees also exhibited moderate to high levels of commitment to the organization for which they worked. They were neutral toward the opportunities they saw their jobs affording for promotion, and they exhibited considerable dissatisfaction with their pay levels.

These findings imply that even though many staff in juvenile justice agencies may receive low pay (something quite pervasive in the United States) and be dissatisfied in that regard as a group, they can still be satisfied with other facets of their jobs and reasonably well committed to their employer organizations. There is no evidence in our data that widespread dissatisfaction with pay is associated with widespread disdain for other features of the job or the organization in general. This finding should not be taken as an excuse for maintaining the low pay levels typical of far too many juvenile correctional agencies; those levels represent a travesty, and every effort needs to be made to prioritize increases when budget decisions are made. But the finding does challenge presuppositions that low pay is at the root of all, or even most, staff-related problems in juvenile justice.

Research conducted outside juvenile justice shows that job satisfaction fosters organizational commitment which, in turn, is linked to positive job performance (Lambert et al., 1999). For its part, job satisfaction seems to be more a function of organizational variables than personal background variables (Krueger et al., 1987; Lambert et al., 2002; Wells et al., 2000). The findings of the present study are largely consistent with these patterns.

The regression model of organizational commitment (Panel E of Table 29.3) accounted for a substantial proportion (66.3 percent) of the variation in commitment scores. Most of this variation was explained by job satisfaction variables. Organizational commitment was greater among persons who were satisfied with their jobs generally and, more particularly, among persons who were satisfied with the supervision, work, and pay features of the job. On the other hand, levels of satisfaction with promotion opportunities and coworkers were not predictive of organizational commitment. This underscores the importance of distinguishing various dimensions of job satisfaction and suggests that it may not be necessary to give all aspects of job satisfaction equal emphasis in order to foster commitment to an organization.

Out of the several factors we studied, other than the measures of job satisfaction, the only one that predicted greater organizational commitment was the absence of a prior background related to working in social service contexts. The effect of this variable was not really strong, but it was statistically significant. One conceivable interpretation is that staff members who worked in social services prior to assuming their present jobs may have had occasion to grow more cynical toward these types of agencies. Interestingly enough, this variable was not significantly related to any of the job satisfaction measures.

Compared to their utility for predicting organizational commitment, the variables we studied had far less utility for predicting job satisfaction. The one exception to this is the regression model of pay satisfaction (Panel B of Table 29.3), where over 19 percent of the variation was explained by three variables. Pay satisfaction was greater among (1) older employees, (2) those who had gotten academy training on-site at their facilities, and (3) those working at facilities located in rural or suburban communities.

A possible interpretation for the age effect is that older employees were actually earning higher salaries than younger ones, something we could not examine due to an absence of data on individuals' salaries. Even were this not true, another interpretation is that some older employees, given their longevity in the workforce, may have grown more accustomed to, or content with, earnings that younger employees perceived as excessively low.

It is difficult to interpret why employees who were trained on-site displayed higher pay satisfaction than those who were trained at the central academy. The former group was probably more culturally and socioeconomically homogeneous; almost 60 percent of staff who trained on-site came from facilities located in rural areas. Still, the effect of this variable was significant with the facility-location variable held constant. For its part, the facility-location effect can be interpreted by bearing in mind that pay satisfaction is a subjective and relative construct. We suspect that many people in this study assessed their pay level vis-à-vis pay offered by other jobs for which they might conceivably qualify in the neighborhood. Compared with suburban and especially rural Kentucky communities, urban areas (both Louisville and the greater Cincinnati area in this study) offer a broader range of jobs at levels of pay that exceed the pay scales in juvenile justice.

The regression models for the JDI supervision and promotion measures accounted for low proportions of variance, and the model for the work scale explained only 11.4 percent. Consistent with some previous research (see Lambert et al., 2002), the education variable exerted mixed effects across these models. Persons holding bachelor degrees displayed greater satisfaction with their work and their supervision than those without these degrees. At the same time, persons having associate degrees displayed lower satisfaction with promotion opportunities than those lacking these degrees, whereas persons who had attempted but not finished associate degrees had lower work satisfaction than persons who had never attempted these degrees. Again, this mixed pattern of findings for education is consistent with the literature.

The main limitation of this study is that only one-third of the surveys sent out initially were returned in complete-enough form to allow data analysis. However, the design of the study did permit us to compare the characteristics of those who provided complete data and those who did not, thereby allowing identification of the variables most likely to be affected by data attrition.[5] Only two such variables, age and whether the person had earned a bachelor's degree, emerged as significant in the multivariate models appearing in Table 29.3. Of course, there is no way to estimate whether any of these variables would have shown as significant predictors, had all persons surveyed provided complete data. Furthermore, since this research did not employ probability sampling, caution in generalizing results is warranted, irrespective of the survey return rate. Although the findings can be generalized only to the degree that juvenile correctional staff members working in other contexts have characteristics similar to the staff members who participated in this study, there is no a priori reason to suppose that substantial differences exist in this regard.

Our findings imply the need to analyze factors other than those studied here in order to understand the correlates of job satisfaction among juvenile correctional staff, especially as regards satisfaction with work, promotion prospects, supervision, and coworkers. This holds true despite the fact that we examined a rather wide range of both organizational and personal background variables. Previous research suggests that it would be fruitful to focus on such factors as job stress, worker autonomy, and participation in decision making, items not measured in this study. At the same time, our study is among the first to empirically link higher job satisfaction to higher organizational commitment among staff members in the field of juvenile corrections. Research from other fields implies that organizational commitment is likely to be related directly to positive job performance in juvenile corrections. Therefore, it is important for juvenile justice policymakers and managers to continue trying to improve job satisfaction and organizational commitment among staff.

References

Blazer, W.K., Kihm, J.A., Smith, P.C., Irwin, J.L., Bachiochi, P.D., Robie, C., Sinar, E.F., and Parra, L.F. (1997). *Users' Manual for the Job Descriptive Index (JDI: 1997 revision) and the Job in General (JIG) Scales.* Bowling Green, OH: Bowling Green State University.

Dillman, D.A. (1978). *Mail and Telephone Surveys: The Total Design Method.* New York: John Wiley & Sons.

Gendreau, P. and Ross, B. (1979). Effective correctional treatment: bibliotherapy for cynics. *Crime and Delinquency,* 25, 463–489.

Gendreau, P. and Ross, R.R. (1983). Correctional treatment: some recommendations for effective intervention. *Juvenile and Family Court Journal,* 34, 31–39.

Gordon, J.A. (1999). Do staff attitudes vary by position?: a look at one juvenile correctional center. *American Journal of Criminal Justice,* 24, 81–93.

Grissom, G.R. and Dubnov, W.L. (1989). *Without Locks and Bars: Reforming our Reform Schools.* New York: Praeger.

Krueger, M.A. (1985). Job satisfaction and organizational commitment among child and youth care workers. *Journal of Child Care,* 2, 17–24.

Krueger, M.A., Lauerman, R., Becker, J., Savicki, V., Parry, P., and Powell, N.W. (1987). Professional child and youth care work in the United States and Canada: a report of the NOCCWA research and study committee. *Journal of Child and Youth Care Work,* 3, 17–31.

Krueger, M.A., Lauerman, R., Graham, M., and Powell, N.W. (1986). Characteristics and organizational commitment of child and youth care workers. *Child Care Quarterly,* 15, 60–73.

Lambert, E.G., Barton, S.M., and Hogan, N.L. (1999). The missing link between job satisfaction and correctional staff behavior: the issue of organizational commitment. *American Journal of Criminal Justice,* 24, 95–116.

Lambert, E.G., Hogan, N.L., and Barton, S.M. (2002). Satisfied correctional staff: a review of the literature on the correlates of correctional staff job satisfaction. *Criminal Justice and Behavior,* 29, 115–143.

Minor, K.I. (1988). An Evaluation of an Intervention Program for Juvenile Probationers. Ph.D. dissertation, Western Michigan University, Kalamazoo, MI.

Minor, K.I., Wells, J.B., and Jones, B. (2004). Staff perceptions of the work
environment in juvenile group home settings: a study of social climate.
Journal of Offender Rehabilitation, 38, 17–30.

Mitchell, O., MacKenzie, D.L., Styve, G.J., and Gover, A.R. (2000). The impact
of individual, organizational, and environmental attributes on voluntary
turnover among juvenile correctional staff members. *Justice Quarterly*,
17, 333–357.

Mitchell, O., MacKenzie, D.L., Gover, A.R., and Styve, G.J. (2001). The influences of personal background on perceptions of juvenile correctional
environments. *Journal of Criminal Justice*, 29, 67–76.

Mowday, R.T., Porter, L., and Steers, R.M. (1982). Employee-organization
linkages: the psychology of commitment, absenteeism and turnover.
In Warr, P. (Ed.), *Organizational and Occupational Psychology*. New
York: Academic Press. pp. 219–229.

Mowday, R.T., Steers, R.M., and Porter, L. (1979). The measurement of organizational commitment. *Journal of Vocational Behavior*, 14, 224–247.

Polsky, H.W. (1977). *Cottage Six: The Social System of Delinquent Boys in
Residential Treatment*. Malabar, FL: Krieger.

Tabachnick, B.G. and Fidell, L.S. (1996). *Using Multivariate Statistics*, 3rd ed.
New York: Harper Collins.

Wells, J.B., Minor, K.I., Woofter, S.L., and Black-Dennis, K. (2000). The social
climate of juvenile institutions: staff perceptions of work environment
and the relationship to demographic and other status characteristics.
Journal for Juvenile Justice and Detention Services, 15, 47–66.

Wright, T.A. (1993). Correctional employee turnover: a longitudinal study.
Journal of Criminal Justice, 21, 131–142.

Notes

1. Unemployment averages were calculated from U.S. Census data for the
   1997 to 2000 time frame.
2. Internal reliability analyses conducted with the JDI data yielded
   alpha coefficients of 0.87, 0.85, 0.90, 0.95, 0.92, and 0.93 for the
   work, pay, promotion, supervision, coworkers, and job-in-general
   subscales respectively.
3. Standard diagnostics were performed prior to estimation of the regression models. We tested for multicollinearity by computing zero-order
   correlations, tolerance coefficients, and variance-inflation factors.
   Results showed that none of the predictor variables were highly inter-
   correlated. Additional tests were conducted for univariate and multivariate outliers, and no cases were eliminated on this basis. However,
   scores on all of the scales except pay and promotion were moderately

to substantially skewed in the negative direction, so scores were "reflexed" prior to square root or log transformations (Tabachnick and Fidell, 1996); this meant that interpretations of results associated with these variables had to be reversed. The pay measure was moderately positively skewed; the promotion measure had no skewness present. Following data transformations, histograms of standardized residuals and plots of observed vs. expected residuals were inspected for each scale, and no significant departures from normality were evident. Standardized residuals were plotted against standardized predicted values, and no evidence was found of violation of equality of variance assumptions. Finally, residual plots showed no outliers that might substantially impact findings.

4. Some of the betas in Table 29.3 have negative values because some measures were reflexed to correct for skewness, and other betas are negative due to the direction of data coding. Nevertheless, the effects' directions are interpreted identically to those in Table 29.2.

5. Chi-square tests revealed that a significantly greater proportion of respondents (n = 97) than nonrespondents (n = 194): had attempted to complete bachelor degrees (χ^2 = 4.40, 1, p = .036); had received bachelor degrees (χ^2 = 4.80, 1, p = .029); were married (χ^2 = 6.61, 1, p = .01); had prior military experience (χ^2 = 7.28, 1, p = .007); worked in facilities that served either males or females, vs. cocorrectional facilities (χ^2 = 9.13, 1, p = .003); and worked in facilities with bed capacities less than or equal to the average for the sample (χ^2 = 16.69, 1, p = .000) as well as in high (vs. low) security facilities (χ^2 = 17.55, 3, p = .001). Additionally, respondents had a significantly higher mean age (M = 34.36, SD = 9.50) than nonrespondents (M = 30.80, SD = 8.00), t (166) = 3.17, p = .002.

Part VI Conclusion

DISCUSSION QUESTIONS FOR PART VI

1. According to Marsh and Patrick (Chapter 25), how does diversion work from a theoretical perspective (e.g., social learning, labeling, social control and social disorganization theories of delinquency)? Compare the six types of diversion programs presented in this chapter.
2. Increasingly, placing "special needs" juveniles for supervision and treatment is problematic. What are some of the critical issues associated with this topic, according to King and Settles (Chapter 26), and what appears to work best?
3. What is the major purpose of restorative justice programming according to White (Chapter 27)?
4. In Chapter 28, Patenaude and Reynolds discuss the evolution of Supreme Court decisions involving capital punishment for juveniles. How has the stance of the court changed over time and what is the major rationale associated with those changes? Explain.
5. What do you think are the major implications of the findings of Minor et al. in Chapter 29? How might these findings be used by juvenile correctional administrators?

Part VII

OTHER CRITICAL ISSUES IN JUVENILE JUSTICE

This last section can be thought of as a potpourri of chapters that address current issues that are quickly gaining much attention in the public's eye or are being hotly debated among academics. The issue of school violence is addressed in Chapter 20 by Hutchinson Wallace and again in Chapter 31 by Schreck and his colleagues. Penn, in Chapter 32, evaluates the ever-present problem of disproportionality when it comes to the handling of African American or black youthful offenders in the modern-day juvenile justice system. Mueller (Chapter 33) presents the evidence and controversy surrounding the continued use of DARE programs in local schools. To conclude, Caeti and Fritsch (Chapter 34) take up the controversy over whether it is time to abolish the separate system for juveniles altogether, bringing us full circle from where we first began in Chapter 1.

Chapter 30

Increases in School Violence: Myth or Reality?

Lisa Hutchinson Wallace

30.1 History of the Socialization of Children

The social reality of children has undergone tremendous change within the last few decades. These changes have permeated all aspects of children's lives. Societal expectations of children, specifically those related to family and school, have seen marked transformations resulting in greater behavioral expectations with decreased support systems. The purpose of this chapter is to explore the impact of these changes on the social reality of children, especially those transformations occurring in the family, society, and schools, as well as their influence on school violence. The various explanations of school violence, such as individual, family, peer, school, and community-related influences, will also be discussed. In conclusion, the responses to the incidents of school violence will be examined and their effectiveness investigated.

30.2 Changing Roles of Adolescents in the Family

Although the primary function of the family is to provide for a child's physical well-being, their most influential role is that of socialization. During the early years of a child's life, personalities and values are influenced heavily by his or her family. One of the most important influences involves the development of a child's morality (Regoli and Hewitt, 1997). While it has historically been the family's responsibility to develop morality; during the last 25 years, the family unit has undergone a tremendous change; a change, which has made this task more difficult. The number of children living in single-parent families has increased. In 1997 only 35 percent of African American and 74 percent of Caucasian children lived with two parents (Lugaila, 1998). While these numbers reached 12 million in 2000 (Fields and Casper, 2001). Further, it is estimated that one out of every two children will live in a single-parent family at some point during their childhood (Children's Defense Fund, 2000). The restructuring of the family is further compounded by divorce. For every 60 children, one will see their parents divorce each year (Children's Defense Fund, 2000). The impact of divorce is not strictly a matter of separation. Divorce impacts children in numerous ways, such as custody battles, issues of support, as well as the physical separation from parents (Regoli and Hewitt, 2003). To complicate matters even further, one out of 24 children do not even live with their parents (Children's Defense Fund, 2000).

The family has also become a more violent place. Many children's lives are affected by violence, which most often occurs in their home. Research indicates that incidents of child maltreatment are on the rise (OJJDP, 2000; Widom and Maxfield, 2001), with some studies claiming increases as high as 142 percent between 1975 and 1983 (American Humane Association, 1983). Shockingly, many of these children are being victimized by the very people who are supposed to provide for their basic needs. A 2002 report from OJJDP found that of the three million child maltreatment cases reported to authorities in 1996, 80 percent involved parents as the perpetrators. Further, researchers agree that child victimization is highly underreported to authorities (OJJDP, 2000) and that it continues to occur at an alarming rate (Osofsky, 2001), making the actual estimation of violence in the family difficult to accurately assess.

30.3 Changing Roles of Adolescents in Society

Society provides no relief from the violent world many children face at home as it, too, has undergone tremendous change. Homicide rates for juveniles peaked in the 1980s, and although they have seen a decrease in recent years, they remain at an exceptionally high level (Centers for Disease Control, 1999). In fact, the United States has a homicide rate at least four times higher than any other industrialized nation (Fingerhut and Kleinman, 1990). If children are fortunate enough not to personally experience violence, they will undoubtedly be exposed to it through the media. By the time a child leaves elementary school, he or she will have seen approximately 8000 murders on television (UCLA, Center for Communication Policy 1995) children's lives have become so saturated with violence in the media, in movies, and in video games that some people suggest that we live in a culture of violence, which breeds aggression (Eron and Huesmann, 1984). With children facing so much violence, the question begs to be asked whether such violence affects their behavior, especially their propensity to commit violence. The answer is mixed. Some individuals claim that adolescents themselves have become more violent, whereas others argue that youth violence is not on the rise (Cook and Laub, 1986; Siegel and Senna, 1991). Research, however, has supported the idea that violence among youth has decreased, with some studies citing a 50 percent decrease in the commission of violent crimes in 1993 (Annie E. Casey Foundation, 2000). While the commission of violence by juveniles has decreased, the belief that juveniles continue to commit large numbers of violent acts has not.

Largely in response to the perceived rise in juvenile violence, children have seen a marked decrease in the freedom they enjoy in society. During the 1960s and 1970s the U. S. Supreme Court bestowed several fundamental rights on juveniles, such as freedom from double jeopardy, proof beyond a reasonable doubt, transfer hearings, fundamental due process rights, and voluntary confessions (*Breed v. Jones,* 1975; *In re Gault,* 1967; *In re Winship,* 1970; *Kent v. U.S.,* 1966; *Miranda v. Arizona,* 1966). As Hurst (1998), however, notes, the juvenile justice system has shifted backward during the last decade, causing the rights of juveniles to suffer severe blows. Specifically, the juvenile justice system has been the scene of several changes that have dramatically reduced a juvenile's rights with regard to the underlying rehabilitative philosophy of the system. Such changes include a loss of discretion for judges, the lowering of the minimum age for transfer, an increased number of statutory exclusions for transfer, and the loss of confidentiality for juvenile offenders (Hurst, 1998).

The restriction of the rights of juveniles continues today with the overwhelming support of many adults. For instance, in a 1999 poll conducted by Public Agenda, a majority of adults expressed agreement with the statement that what kids needed were "stern values, sermons,

and tough discipline." This desire to control is often based on preconceived notions that children are unruly, out of control, and wildly
delinquent, notions that are often highly erroneous, but nonetheless
found to exist throughout the United States. In a 1999 survey conducted
by Public Agenda the majority of Americans used negative descriptions
to portray our current generation of youth with approximately 50 percent
of adults surveyed saying youth today were "lazy and spoiled." During
the research for his book, *Scapegoat Generation: America's War on
Adolescents*, Males (1996) also found that an overwhelming majority of
adults he interviewed reported beliefs about juvenile crime and mental
disorders that were highly exaggerated when compared with "objective
measures" (p. 274). A 1999 survey revealed that two-thirds of the adults
surveyed believed that juvenile crime was on the rise despite the wealth
of statistical information detailing otherwise (Schiraldi and Ziedenberg,
1999). Males (1996) cites the reckless misrepresentation of youth by the
media, as well as several other influential agencies, as a key factor in
inflaming adult disdain for today's youth.

30.4 Changing World of Schools

The most dramatic transformation on the social world of children has
occurred within the school setting. Violence in schools is not new, as
incidents of school violence, primarily in urban schools, can be traced
back to the 1950s. Even in 1975, the Safe School Report noted an
increase in behaviors associated with "school violence" such as violent
offenses and weapons, and drug use (Crews and Montgomery, 2001).
Incidents of fatal school violence occurred throughout the 1970s and
1980s. The manner in which society, especially the schools, have
responded to school violence, however, has changed. The 1990s were
witness to several horrific and widely publicized incidents of violence
within our nation's schools.[1] These highly publicized incidents, especially Columbine, have created an unforgettable picture in the minds
of many Americans; a picture that has evoked a very real sense of
fear about the safety of our nation's schoolchildren. In fact, many
people consider the safety of our nation's schoolchildren to be the
foremost concern facing schools (Elam and Rose, 1995; Elam, Rose,
and Gallup, 1994, 1996; Kaufman et al., 2000; Rose and Gallup, 1999,
2000; U.S. Departments of Education and Justice, 2000).

What exactly does school violence encompass? There is a lack of
consensus regarding what constitutes school violence (Small and
Tetrick, 2001). However, school violence usually refers to incidents of

physical and emotional victimization. School violence, according to Astor et al. (1999), "covers a wide range of intentional or reckless behaviors that include physical harm, psychological harm, and property damage" (p. 140). The media frenzy regarding school violence has focused primarily on incidents of violent school deaths. One must question whether incidents of serious school violence have increased so dramatically in the last few years. Recent data reveal that serious school crime, including school-associated deaths, is not on the rise. The reported incidents of deaths in school are rare and have continued to decrease in recent years (Brooks et al., 2000; Schiraldi and Ziedenberg, 1999; Centers for Disease Control, 1996; Crosse et al., 2002; Crosse et al., 2001; Hyman and Perone, 1998; *Indicators of School Crime and Safety,* 2002; U.S. Departments of Education and Justice, 2000). During the 1998–1999 school year, in fact, there were only 26 school-associated deaths reported, even though the Columbine incident occurred during this time frame (Schiraldi and Ziedenberg, 1999). Research continues to show that violence in the schools, including violent deaths, nonfatal crimes, fighting, and weapon carrying, has decreased during the last decade, especially during the late 1990s (Centers for Disease Control, 1999; Kaufman et al., 1999; Kaufman et al., 2000; Schiraldi and Ziedenberg, 1999; Small and Tetrick, 2001). In fact, most crime that exists in schools is theft related (*Indicators of School Crime and Safety,* 2002).

Despite the statistical evidence of a decrease in school crime and victimization, the relatively few, highly publicized incidents of violent school-associated deaths have led to a distorted view of our nation's youth. Adults view youth today as lazy, spoiled, mentally unstable, and crime-prone individuals. They have even used the term *superpredators* to describe our current generation of youth (Public Agenda, 1999; Schiraldi and Ziedenberg, 1999; Males, 1996). This mass hysteria among adults has had a profound impact on the right of juveniles. First, students have seen an increased use of direct controls including metal detectors, video cameras, weapon detectors, etc. (Green, 1999), and security measures such as clear backpacks, video cameras, locker searches, removal of lockers, and scanners (Brooks, Schiraldi, and Ziedenberg, 2000; Green, 1999; Vera Institute of Justice, 1999; Harrington-Lueker, 1992). Students today have also witnessed an increased presence of law enforcement officers on school grounds, including the placement of full-time school resource officers and specialized school response SWAT teams (Brooks, Schiraldi, and Ziedenberg, 2000; Harrington-Lueker, 1992). Second, the highly publicized school violence episodes resulted in a mass production of programmatic recommendations, including physical design models for safe schools, threat assessment manuals, as well as social skills building and prevention curricula for classroom instruction (O'Toole, 2000; Green, 1999; Vera Institute of Justice, 1999; Dusenbury et al., 1997).

Many of the programmatic responses to serious school violence call for the imposition of severe restrictions on the rights of juveniles. With the birth of zero-tolerance policies, harsh rules have been imposed on students across the United States limiting actions once considered non-threatening and dismissed as the antics of playful youth (Brooks et al., 2000; Zinnecker, 1998). Zero-tolerance policies are those that "mandate predetermined consequences or punishments for specific offenses" (Kaufman et al., 2000). The Gun Free Schools Act of 1990 made it a crime to possess a firearm in a school zone, although it was found to be unconstitutional in *U.S. v. Lopez* (1995). Zero-tolerance policies found their strength in The Gun Free Schools Act of 1994, signed into law by President Clinton in 1994. This act requires a 1-year expulsion for possession of a weapon, and also allows for reporting of the weapon possession to the appropriate justice system, and for the school's chief officer of school districts to modify expulsion on a "case by case basis." This act resulted in zero-tolerance becoming a sort of "national policy" (Skiba, 2000).

By October of 1995, all 50 states were in compliance with this act (Yell and Rotalszki, 2000). This compliance with zero-tolerance policies has resulted in an increase in the number of students who have been expelled or suspended in school during the last several years (Brady, 20001). During 1998–1999 alone, 3523 students were expelled for possessing of weapons at school (*Report on the State Implementation of the Gun-Free Schools Act: School Year 1998–1999, 2000*). Brooks et al. (2000) cite examples of suspensions, such as a 17-year-old who "shot a paper clip with a rubber band at a classmate, missed, and broke the skin of a cafeteria worker," and the suspension of another student for carrying a key chain with an attached can of pepper spray, deemed necessary by the definitions of zero-tolerance policies but representing seemingly unintended harmless actions by students (Brooks et al., 2000).

The behaviors that are the focus of zero-tolerance policies, however, occur "infrequently" (Brady, 2001; Skiba et al., 1997; Heaviside et al., 1998). Despite the low occurrence of such behaviors, these policies continue to be utilized in a majority of our nation's schools (Heaviside et al., 1998), with overwhelming support from school administrators (National Association of Elementary School Principals, 1997). In recent years, these policies have been broadened to include acts not related to the behaviors originally prohibited in the Gun Free Schools Act of 1994. Designed to eliminate gangs, drugs, and weapons from schools, this act has now been expanded in many school systems to include vandalism, threatening behavior, swearing, sexual harassment, and the illegal use of pagers and laser pointers (Borsuk and Murphy, 1999; Brady, 2001; Crosse et al., 2001; Graham Tebo, 2000; Kumar, 1999; Petrillo, 1997; Nancrede, 1998; Skiba, 2000). Some states have even gone so far as to increase the civil liability of parents whose children violate zero-tolerance policies (Brooks et al., 2000). Brady (2001) notes that the broadening of the behaviors defined under The Gun Free Schools Act of 1994 occurs despite the fact that it is "outside the legislative intent of the Act" (p. 161).

Even more troubling is the fact that many of the zero-tolerance policies currently in place do not provide for exceptions to the rules (Graham Tebo, 2000; Skiba, 2000; Yell and Rotalszki, 2000). As a result, students are being kicked out of school for wanting to harm individuals, such as the Spice Girls and Barney, the purple dinosaur (Donahue et al., 1998). The Individuals with Disabilities Education Act Amendments of 1997 allows schools to utilize alternative education for students who possess a weapon at school. However, many of the schools fail to provide an education to students who were suspended or expelled as a result of these policies. The result is that students are expelled for seemingly trivial offenses and, ultimately, denied their right to an education. Even more disturbing is the fact that this loss of student rights continues despite the fact that students are actually statistically safer inside schools than out (Mulvey and Cauffman, 2001; Schiraldi, 1998).

30.5 The Sensationalism of School Violence

If children are safe in schools, then why have their rights been systematically taken away? Why do the expulsions and suspensions of children continue at an alarming rate when school violence has not increased? What has fueled the focus on students' behaviors? The increased focus by the media on violent school shootings has led to a belief that school violence is on the rise, despite the statistical data refuting that belief (Hancock, 2001; Lester, 1998). Because research has shown that sensational and violent crimes get the most media attention (Maguire et al., 2002), it is no surprise that the violent incidents in schools have gripped the nation's attention, especially that of the media. Backed by the interests of certain "self-serving" groups such as the media and politicians (Elliot, 1998), this intense media focus only serves to exacerbate the problem (Kotinsky et al., 2001; Security Research Center, 1999).

The media portrayal of these events has lead to a "climate of fear." Critics have argued that the intense media focus on school shootings has inflamed the public's fear regarding the safety of our schools to the point that a "moral panic" has emerged (Burns and Crawford, 1999; Fishman et al., 2002; Verlinden et al., 2000). As a direct result of the media's portrayal of school violence as a pervasive problem, schools are approaching school violence from a law enforcement rather than an educational standpoint (Hyman and Perone, 1998). The increased focus on and concern about school violence has impacted the school's ability to hire and retain quality staff, the physical design of schools, and the "openness" of their campuses. For students, the impact has been a loss of privacy and a detrimental effect on the learning environment as well as on their personal sense of well-being (Elliot et al., 1998; Verliden et al., 2000). The "recklessness" of the media in creating this climate of fear has led some advocates to call for the media to present a more balanced perspective of school violence. They argue that the public should receive information on the entire spectrum of school violence (such as its decline) rather than just the sensationalized incidents of death, which are atypical (Donahue et al., 1998; Wood, 2001).

30.6 Explaining School Violence

Previous studies of school violence have identified numerous risk factors associated with youth violence. Such factors are numerous, ranging from individual and biological characteristics of youth to influences such as the family, schools, peers, and the community (Harpold and Band, 1998; Hawkins et al., 2000; National Consortium on Violence Research, 1998). This section will focus on five categories of risk factors: specifically, individual, family, peer-related, school, and community influences will be discussed. The focus will be on risk factors for delinquency and violence with specific attention given to factors associated with the commission of school violence.[2]

30.6.1 Individual Explanations

Certain individual characteristics of children have been identified as precursors to violence. Many of these risk factors involve psychological and biological explanations, as well as personality characteristics. Biological explanations are numerous and have linked the propensity for future aggressive or violent behaviors to traumatic births (Kandel and

Mednick, 1991; Mednick and Kandel, 1988) and a low resting pulse (Loeber and Stouthamer-Loeber, 1998; Raine and Jones, 1987; Wadsworth, 1976). Attention deficit disorder has been shown to increase antisocial behavior (Moffitt, 1990; Offord et al., 1979), aggression (Lipsey and Derzon, 1998; Loeber and Stouthamer-Loeber, 1998), and impulsiveness (Klinteberg, Magnusson, and Schalling, 1989). Researchers have found that children with learning disabilities are more likely to be arrested (Zimmermann et al., 1981) and labeled (Post, 1981), which often leads to increased delinquent activity. The role of learning disabilities in the production of delinquency is not without its critics (Pasternack and Lyon, 1982). Finally, although highly controversial, many people have linked delinquent behaviors to low levels of intelligence (Goddard, 1920; Gordon, 1987; Hirschi and Hindelang, 1977; Kirkegaard-Sorenson and Mednick, 1977; Moffitt et al., 1985; West and Farrington, 1973; Wilson and Herrnstein, 1985). Such relationships, however, are treated with skepticism at best by many researchers (Menard and Morse, 1984; Rosenbaum, 1976; Simons, 1978).

Individual choices that children make also influence delinquency. The use of alcohol and drugs has been linked to delinquency. Specifically, the higher an adolescent's rate of delinquency, the more serious their drug and alcohol use (Farrington, 1995; Loeber and Farrington, 1998). The use of alcohol and drugs increases violent behavior (Elliot et al., 1998). The effect of drugs and alcohol on violent behaviors is more severe for certain personality types (McCardle and Fishbein, 1989), and often depends on environmental conditions (Fishbein, 1990). The relationship between delinquency and increased alcohol and drug use is complex, leaving many researchers to caution that the directional effect is hard to identify. Underlying social and personal characteristics may be more likely to account for delinquency than alcohol and drug use (Loeber and Stouthamer-Loeber, 1998), or delinquency and drug use may serve to reinforce one another (Smith and Thornberry, 1995). Others claim that there has been no clearly identifiable link between delinquency and drug use (Huizinga et al., 1994). The newest approach to investigating the influence of individual choices on delinquency involves the issue of diet, which has recently been linked to delinquency, especially increased consumption of sugar (Schoenthaler and Doraz, 1983).

The relationship between delinquency and personality traits has long been of interest to delinquency researchers. Personality characteristics have been linked to delinquency, aggression, and even violence. A *difficult temperament* has been linked to aggression (Kingston and Prior, 1995). Delinquents exhibit more hostile, suspicious, and impulsive behaviors than nondelinquents (Conger and Miller, 1966; Glueck and Glueck, 1950). A relationship between impulsivity and violence has also been established (Farrington, 1989; Loeber and Stouthamer-Loeber, 1998). The role of self-esteem in delinquency has also been a topic of great interest. This relationship, however, is seen by most researchers as an inverse one. Specifically, youth who exhibit lower levels of self-esteem are more likely to engage in delinquent activities (Heaven, 1996; Jensen, 1973; Nye, 1958; Reckless, 1953; Rosenberg et al., 1989). Other researchers posit that the commission of delinquent acts is believed to increase self-esteem (Gold and Mann, 1982; Jang and Thornberry, 1998; Kaplan, 1975; Wells, 1989; Wells and Rankin, 1983). Self-esteem has also been linked to alienation (Miller, 1996). Not all violent or delinquent actions are related to issues of low self-esteem. In fact, Bushman and Baumeister (1999) found a link between narcissistic attitudes and aggression.

Perhaps one of the most influential predictors of violence is anger. Many studies have recognized the role of anger in youth violence (Dwyer et al., 1998; Fleming et al., 2000; Hawkins et al., 2000). The degree of anger experienced by children is also important; higher levels make them more liable to inflict violence (Mazerolle et al., 2000). Anger has also been identified as a precursor to serious incidents of school violence, such as the events at Columbine High School in Littleton, Colorado, in 1999 (Ericson, 2001). The strict controls utilized in schools have been identified as a likely precursor to anger in children (Regoli and Hewitt, 1997; Welsh, 1978). The most likely explanation for the increase in anger and aggression as a result of increased direct control measures stems from the blockage of the child's inherent quest for autonomy (Agnew, 1985; Agnew and White, 1992). Interestingly enough, however, the targets of anger within the school setting are the adults rather than the peers (Centers for Disease Control, 1999). Further, anger has even been linked to an increase in the student's likelihood of victimization (Fishman et al., 2002; Wallace, 2001). The context of anger in students' lives is also significant. Specifically, the more negative relationships a student experiences at home, school, and with peers, the more likely it is that the student will experience anger (Fryxell, 2000). Finally, aggressive tendencies in youth have been linked to future violent behavior (Hawkins, Herrenkohl et al., 1998; Meadows, 2001).

Measuring the effect of external factors in the creation of anger, however, does not address students' individual characteristics, which may also play a role in the creation of anger. Feelings, such as those of rejection, isolation, inferiority, and social withdrawal, have been found to predict anger in youth (Dwyer et al., 1998; Smith, Mullis, Kern, and Brack, 1999). Although many researchers have investigated the role of anger in violence, less attention has been paid to the role of frustration. Frustration and alienation have been shown to be precursors to delinquency (Benda and Corwyn, 2002). The literature also suggests that any negativity causes frustration, which increases an individual's aggressive tendencies (Berkowitz, 1989; Felson, 1992). Children, specifically, tend to become aggressive when they do not get what they want (Berkowitz, 1989). The role of frustration in school violence has received even less attention. Greenberg (1978) views the constant focus on school rules by teachers and administrators as factors associated with school violence. Such a prolonged imposition of authority causes frustration among students, resulting in their rebellion. Although his findings were not specific to incidents of school violence, Felson (1992) found that the presence of frustration often produces a desire to avenge any perceived grievances, usually through an aggressive act.

30.6.2 Family Explanations

Arguably the most influential aspect of a child's life revolves around the family. The primary responsibility of parents is to oversee the socialization of their children. Specifically, families are supposed to instill moral values, as well as provide emotional security for their children (Regoli and Hewitt, 1997). The family has long been identified as a possible source for influencing delinquency and violence. The aspects of the family that increase a child's propensity to commit violence can be divided into four spheres: violence in the family, family management styles, the quality of the parent–child relationship, and parental characteristics.

One of the most detrimental influences of the family on children involves violence. Violence within the family is twofold: Children are affected not only by exposure to violence between their parents, but also by maltreatment at the hands of their parents. The exposure of children to family violence has been linked to general delinquency (Geller and Ford-Sonoma, 1984; Nye, 1958; Osofsky, 2001), as well as the commission of violent acts (Widom and Maxfield, 2001; Elliott et al., 1998; Fagan and Wexler, 1987; Farrington, 1995; Hartstone and Hansen, 1984). There is a substantial amount of literature on the "cycle of violence," which asserts that children who are frequently subjected to or witness familial violence are at an increased risk of becoming delinquent (Widom and Maxfield, 2001). Conflict between parents has even been found to be more influential on delinquent behaviors than broken homes (Nye, 1958).

The relationship between childhood maltreatment and youth violence has been well established in the literature (Alfaro, 1981; Bagley, 1999; Dwyer et al., 1998; Geller and Ford-Sonoma, 1984; Hawkins, Herrenkohl et al., 1998; Jones, 1998; Laub and Lauritsen, 1998; McCord, 1983; Thornberry, 1994; Widom and Maxfield, 2001). The overwhelming majority of child maltreatment is committed by parents (Administration on Children, Youth and Families, 1999; OJJDP, 2000). Much of the literature identifying this link, however, been criticized because of methodological issues (Zingraff et al., 1993), leading many people to discount the claim of an established link between physical abuse and delinquency (Doerner, 1987). Although not considered as heinous a crime as physical abuse, parental neglect of children can also have a profound impact upon children. Studies suggest that neglected children are more likely to become delinquent (Goldman, 1963; Widom and Maxfield, 2001).

Family management styles, or the manner of communication and interaction between children and their parents, have also been found to be linked to delinquency in youth (Baumrind, 1991; Christle et al., 2000; Laub and Laurisen, 1998;). Parents who employ coercive or harsh disciplinary measures, exhibit poor monitoring practices, set inconsistent rules, and are not involved in their children's lives are more likely to produce children who are delinquent (Baumrind, 1991; Christle, Jolivette, and Nelson, 2000; Elliot, 1994; Forgatch and Patterson, 1998; Patterson et al., 1992; Patterson and Yoerger, 1997; Pulkkinen, 1982; Strong and DeVault, 1986). Children who freely and openly communicate with their parents are less delinquent (Barnes et al., 1994; Cernkovich and Giordano, 1987; Conger, 1976; Dentler and Monroe, 1961; Denton and Kampfe, 1994; Gold, 1970; Hirschi, 1969; Kafka and London, 1991; Nye, 1958; Peterson et al., 1994). Whatever the parental styles used, research has identified the likelihood that students who are raised by parents with ineffective parenting styles will become socially inept and experience a higher level of social rejection and failure, which leads to a reduction in their bond to schools (McEvoy and Welker, 2000).

The quality of family relationships is also important, and has been found to produce more of an effect on delinquent behavior than family structure (Cernkovich and Giordano, 1987). Attachment to the family has been found to reduce delinquency (Agnew, 1985; Burton et al., 1995; Elliot et al., 1985; Hindelang, 1973; Hirschi, 1969). However, a child's attachment to his or her parents has been highly criticized as a more accurate means of predicting minor forms of delinquency (Krohn and Massey, 1980) and a less effective predictor of delinquency. Other factors, such as time spent with family, have been found to suppress delinquency more than attachment to the family (Warr, 1993). The quality of the family relationship not only comprises attachment to or time spent with parents, but also includes emotional components. The rejection of children by their parents has been linked to delinquent behaviors (Kaplan et al., 1982; Nye, 1958; Jones, 1998; Simons et al., 1989; Wright and Wright, 1994). When both parents and children reject one another, it is even more of a detrimental influence (Nye, 1958). Finally, according to the differential oppression theory, delinquency is the product of an oppressive process that adolescents experience with adults, specifically parents and teachers, from the time they are born (Regoli and Hewitt, 1997). The role of the family in the production of delinquency and violence is complex, with numerous family variables having been linked to delinquency. Research into the role of the family should recognize and address that complexity (Seydlitz, 1993).

Parental characteristics have also been identified as influences on the delinquent and violent behaviors of their children. Several factors, such as parental criminal behavior, child abuse, parental approval of substance abuse, parental substance abuse, low bonding, and parental separation from children have been identified as significant predictors of violence (Bagley, 1999; Fryxell, 2000; Hawkins et al., 2000; McGaha and Leoni, 1995; Tremlow et al., 2002). Further, parental substance abuse increases child abuse (McGaha and Leoni, 1995), which has been linked to delinquency and violence (Alfaro, 1981; Bagley, 1999; Dwyer et al., 1998; Geller and Ford-Sonoma, 1984; Hawkins, et al., 1998b; Jones, 1998; Laub and Lauritsen, 1998; McCord, 1983; Thornberry, 1994; Welsh, 1985; Widom and Maxfield, 2001), as well as delinquency (McGaha and Leoni, 1995; Zucker, 1987).

30.6.3 Peer-Related Explanations

Peer influence on delinquency has been the most widely studied aspect of juvenile delinquency (Seydlitz and Jenkins, 1998). The ways in which delinquent peers influence an individual's propensity to delinquency, however, are varied. Association with delinquent peers, victimization by peers, and involvement with groups of delinquent peers have all been found to indicate future delinquency. This subsection will explore the various ways in which peers can influence delinquent, violent, and aggressive behaviors.

Children who associate with delinquent peers are more likely to commit delinquent acts (Conger, 1976; Elliot et al., 1985, Erickson and Jensen, 1977; Messner and Krohn, 1990; Richards, 1979; Thompson et al., 1984). Males are more susceptible to peer delinquent influence than females (Fagan and Wexler, 1987; Hindelang, 1973; Hindelang et al., 1981; Hirschi, 1969; Jensen, 1972; Johnson, 1979; Matsueda, 1982; Messner and Krohn, 1990; Patterson and Dishion, 1985; Poole and Regoli, 1979; White et al., 1987). The influence of peers on delinquent behavior increases if children have low attachment to their families (Agnew, 1991; Conger, 1976; Jensen, 1972; Poole and Regoli, 1979) or if their parents utilize ineffective monitoring practices (Elliot, 1994). Adolescents who have delinquent peers are more prone to violence (Hawkins, Herrenkohl et al., 1998).

There is a significant amount of literature that suggests that children are more likely to commit delinquent acts in groups (Ericson and Jensen, 1977; Giordano, 1978; Giordano and Cernkovich, 1979; Gold, 1970; Howell, 1997; West, 1973). Specifically, involvement in gangs has been linked to the commission of more serious delinquency and violence (Bjerregaard and Lizotte, 1995; Shely and Wright, 1993). Male adolescents are more likely to join gangs, which has been linked to increased levels of delinquency when compared to their nongang counterparts (Esbensen and Huzinga, 1993; Fagan, 1989). Gang influences on crime in schools have not gone unnoticed. Spergel (1990) notes that busing and student transfers can lead to transfer of gangs, as well as the associated crime and violence, from one school to another. Bagley (1999) suggests that gang membership is a precursor to school violence.

Although peer associations can have a negative effect on delinquency, victimization at the hands of peers has also been found to be influential. There is a substantial amount of literature that recognizes the existence of peer-related bullying and intimidation as pervasive forms of school violence (Dwyer et al., 1998; Nofzinger, 2001; Olweus, 1991). In fact, some researchers believe it is the most influential precursor of school violence, largely because of its prevalence in today's schools (Tremlow et al., 2002; Whitney and Smith, 1993). A 2001 study found that found that 30 percent of students are involved in bullying, including 13 percent as the bullies and 11 percent as the victims (Nansel et al., 2001). Bullying has been linked to decreased self-esteem (Boulton and Underwood, 1992), which has been linked to delinquency (Heaven, 1996; Jensen, 1973; Nye, 1958; Reckless, 1958; Rosenberg et al., 1989). Further, bullying has been found to lead to alienation and isolation, which had been linked to delinquency (Dwyer et al., 1998; Johnson and Johnson, 1995). With regard to the commission of school violence, bullying has been identified as a precipitating factor in such events (U.S. Secret Service and Department of Education, 2002). In fact, several perpetrators of serious school violence episodes have indicated the significant role that bullying and harassment by peers played in their actions (American Psychological Association, 1999; Garbarino, 1999; Harpold and Band, 1998).

30.6.4 School-Related Explanations

Perhaps the most logical explanations of school violence are based on factors arising from the school setting. During the last several years, school violence has been linked to physical and social characteristics of the school, as well as individual characteristics of the students (Crews and Montgomery, 2000; Lawrence, 1998). This section will explore the role of students' individual characteristics in the commission of delinquency and violence. Specifically, a student's dedication to and success in the educational process as it affects delinquent and violent behaviors will be discussed. The relationship between the school environment, including physical and social characteristics, and the commission of delinquent and violent acts has also been established, and will also be examined.

Certain characteristics of a student's relationship to the educational process may influence delinquency. One of the most important aspects of a student's relationship to this process involves the commitment of that individual to school. Students who are not committed to school and the educational process, in general, are more prone to delinquency (Catalano and Hawkins, 1999; Conger, 1976; Elliot and Voss, 1974; Hirschi, 1969; Jenkins, 1995; Krohn and Massey, 1980; Polk and Burkett, 1972; Polk and Halferty, 1966; Schafer and Polk, 1972a; Thomas and Hyman, 1978; White et al., 1987). A high level of commitment to school also decreases a student's chances of associating with delinquent peers (Thornberry, 1987). The student's success in the educational process has also been indicative of delinquency. Academic failure has been associated with delinquent and antisocial behavior (Dwyer et al., 1998; Hawkins, Farrington et al., 1998; Gold, 1970; Herrenkohl et al., 1998; Huizinga and Jakob-Chien, 1998; Lipsey and Derzon, 1998; Maguin and Loeber, 1996; West, 1973; Verdugo and Schneider, 1999). Students who are committed to education and seek to attain higher levels of education are less likely to become delinquent (Hirschi, 1969; Polk and Burkett, 1972; White et al., 1987). Also, students who exhibit a low level of attachment to school and little interest in the educational process are more prone to delinquency (Conger, 1976; Frease, 1973; Gold, 1963; Hindelang, 1973; Hirschi, 1969; Johnson, 1979; Polk and Burkett, 1972; Polk and Halferty, 1966; Rankin, 1980) and school violence (Dwyer et al., 1998).

Physical and social characteristics of the school are also influential factors for delinquency, antisocial behavior, and violence. Numerous social characteristics of schools have been investigated as possible sources of school violence. One body of research, school climate, has looked at the social characteristics of schools as the possible source for school violence. Whereas some of this research has addressed the broad climate of education, other studies have focused on specific social relationships within the school environment that influence delinquency. Generally, schools have been found to facilitate academic failure (Schafer and Polk, 1972b) through the utilization of practices such as tracking (Kelly, 1974; Kelly and Pink, 1982; Polk, 1969) and the singling and pushing out of at-risk or undesirable students (Bowditch, 1993; Elliott and Voss, 1974; McEvoy and Welker, 2000).

The school climate literature has also examined the treatment of students by administrators and teachers, as well as the severe restriction of their rights within the school, as possible causes of school violence. The treatment of students by adults can increase the propensity to commit antisocial acts (McEvoy and Welker, 2000). The treatment of children by adults is even more significant in the educational system, though the type of treatment that is seen as predictive of school violence is debatable. Some researchers argue that school violence has been associated with the direct result of the loss of teacher authority (Copperman, 1980) and that teachers should exert more authority and regain control of the classroom (Jackson, 1998). Rubel (1979) even linked school violence to the court's recognition of rights of students in schools during the 1960s and 1970s. Some have gone so far as to argue that school discipline is lacking because students do not want to be in school, so the most effective approach to prevent the resulting school violence is to kick those students out of the educational system (Jackson, 1998).

Many other theorists, however, argue that the increased authority of schools and emphasis by teachers on control have led to such violence (Brooks et al., 2000; Greenberg, 1978; Pepinsky, 2001; Noguera, 1995; Regoli and Hewitt, 1997). The treatment of students by teachers has been found to be an influential component of antisocial behaviors (Pink, 1982). The relationship between students and teachers involves aspects of attitudes, behaviors, and interactions. Because of the inherent power differential between teachers and students, much of the research that exists is rooted in conflict theory, specifically oppression. Fryxell (2000) identified a link between teacher attitudes, specifically those of a negative nature, and school violence. Freire (1990) argues that teachers merely mimic the adult emphasis on control that children experience in the home. Teachers make the rules, teachers talk, students listen, and students are forced to abide by the desires of the teacher. Research has failed to recognize that student victimization by staff (e.g., expulsions, suspensions, etc.) is a possible factor in students' anger and aggression levels that has been linked to school violence (Hyman and Perone, 1998).

In keeping with the oppression approach to delinquency, Regoli and Hewitt (1991) offered differential oppression theory as a relatively new approach to delinquency. Specifically, the theory is predicated upon the belief that adults and children have an antagonistic relationship with one another. This relationship is characterized by an adult-based increased emphasis on order and control of children. Such control can exist in any relationship children have with adults, thus permeating nearly every aspect of their lives. When children respond to control negatively or refuse to comply with the demands of adults, they are likely to become delinquent (Regoli and Hewitt, 1997). Differential oppression, specifically its application to school violence, has not undergone substantial empirical research (Miller, 1996; Regoli and Hewitt, 1997; Wallace, 2001).

Although the social characteristics of schools seemingly produce a profound effect on delinquency and violence, the physical characteristics are not without impact. Several physical characteristics of schools have been found to be correlated with delinquency and violence. Specifically, schools that are overcrowded, have poor physical designs, and utilize portable classrooms, and whose student-to-teacher ratio is extremely high, are more likely to experience delinquency and violence (Meadows, 2001). Physical barriers to effective supervision have been linked to the significant increase of school crime and violence at the beginning and end of the school day, as well as during the lunch and between-classes breaks (National Consortium on Violence Research, 1998).

30.6.5 *Community Explanations*

Although a rather debatable explanation owing to the difficulty in determining direct causal effects, the role of the community in the production of delinquency, violence, and antisocial behaviors has been well researched. Crime in the schools has been linked to crime in the community (Gold and Moles, 1978; Gottfredson and Gottfredson, 1985; McDermott, 1983; Menacker et al., 1990; National Institute of Education, 1978). Specifically, social disorder and disorganization, when present in neighborhoods, has been found to increase delinquent activity among youth (Bursik, 1988; Bursik and Grasmick, 1993; Jensen, 1972). Such disorganization has been found to differ significantly across geographical areas (Cohen, 1998). A child's perception of the level of disorder in his or her neighborhoods has also been found to be correlated with delinquency in males (Jensen, 1972). Social disorganization has been shown to increase risk factors associated with delinquency (Matseuda and Heimer, 1987), as well as result in increased levels of gang activity (Sampson and Lauritsen, 1993). Certain characteristics within communities, especially those experiencing social disorder, are predictive of violence. Specifically, communities that have increased levels of low socioeconomic status, transient residents, and housing density have been associated with higher incidents of violence (Laub and Lauritsen, 1998). The role of socioeconomic status in the creation of delinquency is controversial. A substantial body of literature suggests the presence of a link (Cernkovich and Giordano, 1987; Elliot and Ageton, 1980; Gold, 1970; Polk, 1967), whereas some reports have indicated the lack of such a relationship (Joseph, 1995; Tittle and Meier, 1990). Further, low-income areas foster an atmosphere that is not conducive to the formation of formal and informal mechanisms of social control (Garbarino, 1999).

Individuals who experience higher levels of commitment and attachment to social institutions such as the community are found to commit less delinquency (Hirschi, 1969; Nye, 1958). Juveniles who are employed tend to have higher levels of commitment to their community (Friday and Hage, 1976). Commitment has, in fact, been found to be a more significant predictor of delinquency than attachment or belief (Krohn and Massey, 1980). Adolescents who exhibit a higher level of belief in the laws and rules of the community are less likely to become delinquent (Agnew, 1985; Hindelang, 1973; Hirschi, 1969; Johnson, 1979; Matsueda, 1982; Nye, 1958; Thomas and Hyman, 1978). The actual magnitude of the effect that the community has on delinquency is hard to identify. Because community factors are themselves influenced greatly by peer, family, and individual characteristics, the relationship becomes increasingly complex, making it almost impossible to determine the exact causal factors of delinquency (Conger et al., 1991; Laub and Sampson, 1988; Sampson and Laub, 1994).

30.7 Responses to School Violence

School violence has elicited numerous responses from parents, the community, and, most importantly, schools. Many of these responses have proved to be effective (Office of Educational Research and Improvement, 2001). Others, however, have had little or no effect on school violence (Dedman, 2000; Leone et al., 2000; Mayer and Leone, 1999). The various responses that have emerged range from broad-based community efforts to specific programmatic recommendations targeting behaviors associated with school violence (National School Safety Center, 1999). Primary responses have called for the community, parents, and the school to unite to confront the problem of school violence. These broad-based strategies seek to organize and motivate the various components of the community to formulate a strategic, comprehensive response to the issue of school safety (National Parent Teacher Association, 1998; National School Safety Center, 1999). General guidelines have emerged covering topics ranging from the effective ways to control "disruptive students" (Stephens, 1996) to plans for designing the safe school (Green, 1999) to providing advice for legal liabilities in crisis situations (Survey Research Center, 1999). These responses have reached epidemic proportions with many critics arguing that they are merely a reaction to the sensationalism of school violence by the media, the result of a moral panic (Burns and Crawford, 1999; Fishman et al., 2002; Verliden et al., J., 2000). Indeed, many of these responses have been hasty, and a substantial number are not based on empirical research (Crosse et al., 2002).

30.7.1 Current Responses

Indeed, the most common response to school violence has been the implementation of prevention curriculum and instruction (Crosse et al., 2002). These programmatic responses are quite diverse. Further, they can be general, focusing on prevention of school violence and utilizing programs that are administered to the entire student body, or they may target individual behaviors in children or risk factors within the school environment (Crosse et al., 2002). Many responses involve peer mediation, counseling, conflict resolution, character education, and even physical education components (Crosse et al., 2002; Zivin et al., 2001). Other programmatic and regulatory practices have focused on physical control of students to eliminate school violence (Astor et al., 2002; (Dedman, 2000; McEvoy and Welker, 2000).

Generally, schools utilize praise and recognition as the most frequent responses to "desirable" behavior (Crosse et al., 2002). The recognition of such behaviors is the most utilized approach to school violence. In a similar vein, many schools employ conflict resolution programs in an effort to avoid school violence. Conflict resolution assumes that violence is a learned behavior. Thus, the programs seek to teach students the skills needed to adequately and effectively resolve conflictual situations (Lawrence, 1998). The ultimate goal of conflict resolution and a focus on desirable behaviors is to improve the school environment. As discussed previously in this chapter, the climate of the school can exert significant influence on students' behaviors. Thus, many of the efforts that have been utilized are based, at least partially, on this premise.

Not all responses have been as proactive as those designed to promote a peaceful environment. Since the well-publicized school violence events, government and nonprofit agencies have responded with threat assessment guidelines, profiles of "likely" offenders, crisis planning and management recommendations, and legal guidelines. Many responses target individuals at risk for committing school violence, focusing solely on those individuals and their removal from the school environment. A plethora of guidelines and recommendations have been developed and promulgated throughout the nation regarding this issue (O'Toole, 2000; Survey Research Center, 1999; Tremlow et al., 2002). Many of these recommendations identify certain risk factors that make threats more real. Such factors include access to guns, peer-related victimization, expressed concern about the individual by parents or students, influence of media on copycat actions, extreme changes in emotions, and a lack of family attachment and concern (Tremlow et al., 2002). These assessments appeal to school personnel in that their desire to identify students at risk for committing acts of school violence ranked as one of the top three concerns for safety training (Walko-Frankovic and Williard, 2002). Schools have instituted zero-tolerance policies, increased utilization of suspensions and expulsions, placed full-time law enforcement officers on campus, and instituted the use of stringent measures of control.

Recently, many of the measures that have been enacted in response to school crime have required the community to become involved in addressing violence (National Parent Teacher Association, 1998; National School Safety Center, 1999). Most of these measures are prevention-based and target the broader aspects of school crime and prevention. Primarily, community assistance has been sought in the development of a comprehensive prevention plan to address school violence (Crosse et al., 2002). Some programs seek support from the community by formulating an appropriate action plan for preventing and responding to school violence (Zins et al., 1994), whereas others seek resources from the community, such as for after-school programs (Chaiken, 1998) or for general participation in the lives of students through mentoring (Tremlow, Fonagy and Sacco, 2002).

30.8 What Works

The efforts to prevent and reduce school crime and violence have enjoyed some success. Generally, some of the more promising components of effective prevention efforts are the following: (1) an increase in the positive interaction between teachers and students, (2) the implementation of a schoolwide approach to improving the school climate, (3) a continued review and revision of ineffective prevention practices, especially when conducted by a communitywide group, and (4) the use of assessment tools (in moderation) for the sole purpose of early identification and treatment of individual students (Crosse et al., 2002; McEvoy and Welker, 2000; Zinns et al., 1994). The success of the response is, however, contingent on a number of factors, such as school environment, community characteristics, societal influences, quality of responses, frequency of response, length of response, and geographical location. The focus of the prevention effort has also been linked to its success. For instance, Crosse et al. (2002) found that general programs that aimed to influence the school or classroom environment were more successful than those targeted at individual characteristics of students. The location of the school has been shown to influence the quality of the programs utilized. Specifically, urban areas tend to employ higher-quality programmatic responses than do their rural counterparts (Crosse et al., 2002).

Specific types of programs have also enjoyed some success. Although not considered by many adults to be a serious problem, bullying has been linked to school violence (Tremlow et al., 2002; Whitney and Smith, 1993). Although not all antibullying programs have been deemed successful, there has been some success (Astor et al., 2002; Dedman, 2000; Indiana Education Policy Center, 2002; Tremlow et al., 2001). Soskis (2001) found that successful antibullying programs are those that focus on the school as a whole and do not "demonize" or isolate perpetrators. Programs that utilize zero tolerance for bullying, direct victimization, and passive observation of such victimization have also been linked to decreased risk factors (Tremlow et al., 2001).

Perhaps some of the most successful school-based programs are those that seek to address the climate of the school rather than target individual behaviors. Those were found to be higher-quality programs (Crosse et al., 2002; Dedman, 2000). The scope of such programs is vast, yet their success has been linked to certain characteristics. According to Astor et al. (2002) successful school climate programs have the following characteristics in common: They (1) foster an awareness of school violence behaviors among students and teachers while creating and delineating the guidelines for appropriate behavior throughout the school, (2) target all social systems of the school in outlining appropriate procedures for dealing with violent events, (3) involve students, staff, and parents in the program efforts, (4) are easily incorporated into the school system, and (5) utilize more intensive monitoring and supervision practices in areas outside the classroom. Baker (1998) suggests that programs that utilize character development rather than behavior management strategies are more successful.

Programs that incorporate conflict resolution have enjoyed limited success. Primarily owing to their broad focus, many of these programs have been identified as ineffective (Regoli and Hewitt, 1997). Johnson and Johnson (1995) found that the use of conflict resolution in combination with violence prevention is more effective. Specifically, programs that seek to maintain a cooperative atmosphere, increase student learning, develop skills for constructive conflict resolution, and do not attempt to eliminate *all* types of conflict are more effective in the reduction of school crime and violence (Johnson and Johnson, 1995).

There is also room for physical fitness in the fight against school crime. Programs that incorporate a component of physical education have been found to reduce risk factors for violence and delinquency (Tremlow et al., 2001; Zivin et al., 2001). However, the research is limited, and its effectiveness has only been tested on males (Zivin et al., 2001).

Many programs that incorporate the community as a whole, or at least members of the community, have been found to effectively reduce school violence or its associated risk factors. Specifically, programs that incorporate modeling and mentoring components have been found to reduce disciplinary referrals, an identified risk factor (Tremlow et al., 2001). Programs such as youth or teen courts, wraparound sessions, mentoring, and community-based restorative justice programs such as "circles" have been found to effectively address delinquency in general, as well as school violence (Indiana Education Policy Center, 2002).

Indeed, the success of many violence prevention programs has been linked to the involvement of the community (Zinns et al., 1994). Bowen et al. (2002) call for the inclusion of programs that focus on community and neighborhood characteristics as an essential component of any effective school violence prevention effort. Such success, however, is contingent on the community in which the efforts are situated. As Crosse et al. (2002) point out, communities that experience high levels of disorganization or problems are less likely to be an effective component of violence prevention.

30.9 What Does Not Work

There are numerous reasons for why school violence programs fail. Many of these programs have been criticized for being too broad and failing to provide adequate measures for program implementation (Johnson and Johnson, 1995); others, for targeting only one aspect of the problem and not addressing the root causes of the problem (Astor et al., 2002). Programs that fail to provide the requisite frequency and duration necessary for positive results to be achieved are less likely to have an effect (Crosse et al., 2002; Zinns et al., 1994). The application of broad, generic programs to individual schools has also been criticized for its failure to recognize the social and geographical influences upon risk factors. Johnson and Johnson (1995) note that many of the programs currently being utilized within schools were originally intended for use within a neighborhood or community setting. These programs have been implemented in the school setting without any curricular revisions. Finally, many programs are psychologically based, seeking to elicit changes within individual students. Such responses are usually not effective unless utilized in conjunction with programs that target the psychological climate of the school as a whole (Astor et al., 2002).

Programs that target certain aspects of student behavior or school environment have also been shown to be ineffective. The most widely criticized of these measures involves the use of direct controls within the school setting. Most evaluations of school violence programs have failed to measure the effectiveness of direct control measures, such as metal detectors, uniforms, zero-tolerance policies, suspensions, expulsions, and increased presence of law enforcement personnel in schools (Astor et al., 2002). These restrictive measures being implemented in classrooms around the nation have not been proved to be effective. In fact, many law enforcement experts and actual perpetrators of school violence warn that they do little to protect students from everyday occurrences of school violence (Dedman, 2000). In fact, Mayer and Leone (1999) found that such measures may increase victimization. Their research revealed that students who attend schools that utilized "secure-building" policies (metal detectors and searches of lockers) were more likely to be victimized and afraid than students who attended schools that did not utilize such policies (Mayer and Leone, 1999). Although some of the literature suggests that zero-tolerance policies are effective (Burke and Herbert, 1996; Holmes and Murrell, 1995; Schreiner, 1996), much of this research is not empirically based and is subjective in nature (Brady, 2001; Skiba, 2000). Further, such approaches have been found to be ineffective (Dedman, 2000; McEvoy and Welker, 2000). Perhaps the most disturbing aspect of the increased use of zero-tolerance policies is that they have been shown to be disproportionately applied to minority and male students (Skiba et al., 2000; Walker et al., 1996).

The highly publicized events of serious school violence led to a mass production of profiles and threat assessments, tools that have become increasingly common within schools. The demonstrated effectiveness of these instruments, however, is weak. These assessments are condemned as harmful to the school environment, as well as to the children (Mulvey and Cauffman, 2001) because of the atmosphere of distrust that they foster. Practices such as the utilization of direct control measures and threat assessments, these individuals argue, exacerbate the problem by fostering an environment of mistrust, by placing educators in the role of enforcer rather than educator, and by inflicting emotional damage on students (Hyman and Perone, 1998; Jones, 1998; Lockwood, 1997; Shely and Wright, 1998).

The criticisms of direct control measures hinge on the belief that they foster an extremely restrictive atmosphere in which student rights are constantly eroded. Critics argue that the restrictive measures being implemented in classrooms around the nation fail to address the underlying causes of violence (Johnson and Johnson, 1995), while others argue that they are simply ineffective (Dedman, 2000; McEvoy and Welker, 2000; Leone et al., 2000; Mayer and Leone, 1999). Furthermore, the impact of these regulations leaves many students feeling oppressed to the point that they equate the process of going to school with that of serving time in a correctional facility (Brooks et al., 2000). Not only are these "get-tough" measures often ineffective, but as Noguera (1995) argues, they also defeat their intended purpose. By restricting students' rights, the atmosphere of learning is inhibited and suspicion becomes the norm. The constant presence of this suspicion can ultimately lead to defiance by students, either through overt actions or by the mere formulation of attitudes regarding the restrictive environment (Noguera, 1995; Regoli and Hewitt, 1997). The current measures being used to address school violence, both fatal and nonfatal, are based strictly on issues of control. Such strict measures, while not only failing to address the underlying social causes of violence in our schools, result in a severe restriction or oppression of our nation's young people within the very structure entrusted with nurturing and producing self-reliant adolescents. Yet, they continue with overwhelming support (*USA Today*, 1998).

30.10 Recommendations for Future Responses

Efforts to address school crime and violence continue without a lot of guidance from empirical research (Crosse et al., 2002). Many of these efforts not only fail to adequately address the problem of school violence but also seem to exacerbate it. Schools and communities rely more on anecdotal information gained from community meetings than on empirical research in their selection of prevention efforts (Crosse et al., 2002). Such reliance seems unnecessary given the amount of attention and research that has been conducted on school violence. There is an abundance of research that seeks to address the risk factors associated with school violence. Given the plethora of available information, it seems as though any effective response should incorporate knowledge gained from empirical research. In many instances, however, school-specific data are not available regarding risk factors for school violence (Astor et al., 2002). Effective prevention requires that such risk factors be identified and understood. Because each school faces a unique set of factors that influence school violence, it is important that attempts to obtain such data be made. Perhaps the collection of school-specific data would be an appropriate time to engage the community's involvement.

Although the causal factors of school violence have received a lot of attention, researchers have given less attention to the effectiveness of programs. Future empirical research endeavors should address this deficiency in the literature. Specifically, researchers should seek to explore the community's role in prevention more fully. As Astor et al. (2002) note, there is a lack of data at the school and district levels. Effective prevention programs must be based on community-specific information. Efforts should also include attempts to establish a baseline of activity prior to program implementation to more accurately assess its effectiveness. Finally, it is imperative that research into risk factors, as well as effective school violence programs, look into the complex relationships between families, peers, schools, and the community. Such relationships must be more fully explored before effective prevention programs can be created.

Based on the empirical research that is available regarding program effectiveness, several policy recommendations can be made. First, the literature has shown that some programs are effective in reducing school violence. There is also an abundance of literature that points to the ineffectiveness of other programs. Schools should peruse the literature concerning successful programmatic responses. Efforts to address school crime and violence should incorporate those aspects that have been shown to be effective, as well as those that are ineffective. The implementation of such programs should, however, be implemented with caution. As Crosse and his colleagues (2002) caution, the effectiveness of a program depends largely on certain geographical, social, and physical characteristics of the school and the community in which it is located. Such extraneous factors must also be taken into account during the selection of a programmatic response.

Finally, we will continue to fail in our efforts to address the school violence problem until we focus on the real culprit: society. Our society has changed dramatically within the last several decades. Violence permeates society, the family unit has eroded, child maltreatment is epidemic, and the rights of adolescents have been severely restricted. Yet we continue to respond to juvenile delinquency and school violence based on traditional approaches; approaches that have failed to recognize that the social world of adolescents has changed. Until we focus on those changes and recognize their real or potential impact, we will never effectively deal with the problem. Continuing to rely on measures of direct controls will only exacerbate this problem. The roots of school violence are embedded within various aspects of our society, such as peers, families, individuals, and schools. We must look at the complex relationship among these factors for an effective resolution to the problem. Continued reliance on stringent measures of direct control that seek to coerce and repress students will only exacerbate the problem. Instead, we must employ the use of programs designed to recognize and account for the factors associated with violence, such as family and peer victimization; programs that seek to address the whole problem.

References

Administration on Children, Youth and Families. (1999). *Child Maltreatment, 1999*. Retrieved October 8, 2001, from http://www.acf.dhhs.gov/programs/cb.

Agnew, R. (1985). A revised strain theory of delinquency. *Social Forces, 64*, 151–167.

Agnew, R. and White, H.R. (1992). An empirical test of general strain theory. *Criminology, 30*, 475–499.

Alfaro, J. (1981). Report on the relationship between child abuse and neglect and later social deviant behavior. In Hunner, R. and Walker, Y. (Eds.), *Exploring the Relationship between Child Abuse and Delinquency*. Montclair, NJ: Allenheld and Osmun.

American Humane Society. (1983). Highlights of Official Child Neglect and Abuse Reporting. Denver, CO: Author.

American Psychological Association. (1999). Warning Signs of Youth Violence. Bulletins for Family. Retrieved April 16, 2001, from www.apa.org.

Annie E. Casey Foundation. (2000). America's Children: Key National Indicators of Well-Being, 2000. Retrieved October 1, 2002 from http://www.childstates.gov/ac2000.

Astor, R.A., Pitner, R.O., Benbenishtry, R., and Meyer, H. (2002). Public concern and focus on school violence. In Rapp-Paglicci, L.A., Roberts, A.R., and Wodarski, J.S. (Eds.), *Handbook of Violence*. New York: John Wiley & Sons. pp. 262–302.

Astor, R.A., Varas, L.A., Pitner, R.O., and Meyer, H.A. (1999). School violence: research, theory, and practice. In Jenson, J.M. and Howard, M.O. (Eds.), *Youth Violence: Current Research and Recent Practice Innovations*. Springfield, VA: Sheridan Books. pp. 139–172.

Bagley, S. (May 3, 1999). Why the young kill. *Newsweek*, 32–35.

Baker, J.A. (1998). Are we missing the forest for the tress? Considering the social context of school violence. *Journal of School Psychology, 36*, 29–44.

Barnes, G.M., Farrell, M.P., and Banerjee, S. (1994). Family influences on alcohol abuse and other problem behaviors among black and white adolescents in a general population sample. *Journal of Research on Adolescence, 4*, 183–201.

Baumrind, D. (1991). Parenting styles and adolescent development. In Richard Lerner, Anne Petersen, and Jeanne Brooks-Gunn (Eds.), *Encyclopedia of Adolescence*. New York: Garland.

Benda, B.B. and Corwyn, R.F. (2002). The effect of abuse in childhood and in adolescence on violence among adolescence. *Youth and Society, 33*, 339–365.

Berkowitz, L. (1989). Situational influences on aggression. In Groebel, J. and Hinde, R. (Eds.), *Aggression and War: Their Biological and Social Bases*. New York: Cambridge University Press. pp. 91–100.

Bjerregaard, B. and Lizotte, A.J. (1995). Gun ownership and gang membership. *The Journal of Criminal Law and Criminology, 86,* 37–58.

Borsuk, A.J. and Murphy, M.B. (April 30, 1999). Idle or otherwise, threats bring severe discipline: where area students once faced a principal, now they face the police. *Milwaukee Journal Sentinel,* p. 8.

Boulton, M.J. and Underwood, K. (1992). Bully/victim problems among middle schoolchildren. *British Journal of Educational Psychology, 62,* 73–87.

Bowditch, C. (1993). Getting rid of troublemakers: high school discipline procedures and the production of dropouts. *Social Problems, 40,* 493–509.

Bowen, G.L., Bowen, N.K., Richman, J.M., and Woolley, M.E. (2002). Reducing school violence: a social capacity framework. In Rapp-Paglicci, L.A., Roberts, A.R., and Wodarski, J.S. (Eds.), *Handbook of Violence.* New York: John Wiley & Sons. pp. 303–325.

Brady, K.P. (2001). Zero tolerance or (in)tolerance policies? Weaponless school violence, due process, and the law of student suspensions and expulsions: an examination of Fuller v. Decatur Public School Board of Education School District. *Brigham Young University Education and Law Journal, 1,* 159–210.

Breed v. Jones. (1975). 421 U.S. 519.

Brooks, K., Schiraldi, V., and Ziedenberg, J. (2000). School House Hype: Two Years Later. Washington, D.C.: Justice Policy Institute.

Burke, E. and Herbert, D. (1996). Zero tolerance policy: combating violence in schools. *NASSP Bulletin, 80,* 49–54.

Burns, R. and Crawford, C. (1999). School shootings, the media, and public fear: Ingredients for a moral panic. *Crime, Law and Social Change, 32,* 147–168.

Bursik, R. (1988). Social disorganization and theories of crime and delinquency: problems and prospects. *Criminology, 26,* 519–552.

Bursik, R. and Grasmick, H. (1993). *Neighborhoods and Crime: The Dimensions of Effective Community Control.* New York: Lexington.

Burton, V., Cullen, F., Evans, T.D., Dunaway, R.G., Kethinene, S., and Payne, G. (1995). The impact of parental control on delinquency. *Journal of Criminal Justice, 23*(1), 111–126.

Bushman, B.J. and Baumeister, R.F. (1999). Threatened egotism, narcissism, self-esteem, and direct and displaced aggression: does self-love lead to violence? *Journal of Personality and Social Psychology, 75,* 219–229.

Catalano, R. and Hawkins, J. (1999). *The Social Development Model: A Theory of Antisocial Behavior.* New York: Springer-Verlag.

Centers for Disease Control. (1999). Facts about violence among youth and violence in schools. *Media Relations, 404.*

Cernkovich, S. and Giordano, D. (1987). Family relationships and delinquency: a partial replication and extension. *Social Problems, 20,* 471–487.

Chaiken, M.R. (1998). Tailoring established after-school programs to meet urban realities. In Eliot, D.S., Hamburg, B.A., and Williams, K.R. (Eds.), *Violence in American Schools: A New Perspective.* Cambridge, MA: Cambridge University Press. pp. 348–378.

Children's Defense Fund. (2000). *The State of America's Children, Yearbook 2000*. Washington, D.C.

Christle, C.A., Jolivette, K., and Nelson, C.N. (2000). *Youth Aggression and Violence: Risk, Resilience, and Prevention*. Arlington, VA: ERIC Clearinghouse on Disabilities and Gifted Education.

Cohen, D. (1998). Culture, social organization and patterns of violence. *Journal of Personality and Social Psychology, 75*, 408–419.

Conger, R.D. (1976). Social control and social learning models of delinquent behavior: a synthesis. *Criminology, 14*, 17–40.

Conger, R.D., Lorenz, F.O., Elder, G.H., Jr., Melby, J.N., Simons, R.L., and Conger, K.J. (1991). A process model of family economic pressure and early adolescent alcohol use. *Journal of Early Adolescence, 11*, 430–449.

Conger, J.J. and Miller, W.C. (1966). *Personality, Social Class, and Delinquency*. New York: John Wiley & Sons.

Cook, P. and Laub, J. (1986). The surprising stability of youth crime. *Journal of Quantitative Criminology, 2*, 265–277.

Copperman, P. (1980). *The Literacy Hoax*. New York: Morrow.

Crews, G.A. and Montgomery, R.H., Jr. (2000). *Chasing Shadows: Confronting Juvenile Violence in America*. Upper Saddle River, NJ: Prentice Hall.

Crosse, S., Burr, M., Cantor, D., Hagen, C.A., and Hantman, I. (2001). Wide Scope, Questionable Quality: Drug and Violence Prevention Efforts in American Schools. Report on the Study of School Violence and Prevention. Washington, D.C.: U.S. Department of Education, Planning and Evaluation Service.

Crosse, S., Cantor, D., Burr, M., Hagen, C.A., Hantman, I., Mason, M.J., Siler, A.J., von Glatz, A., and Wright, M.M. (2002). Wide Scope, Questionable Quality: Three Reports from the Study of School Violence and Prevention. Washington, D.C.: U.S. Department of Education, Planning and Evaluation Service.

Dedman, B. (October 15, 2000). Deadly lessons: School shooters tell why. *Chicago Sun-Times*. Chicago, IL.

Dentler, R.A. and Monroe, L.J. (1961). Social correlates of early adolescent theft. *American Sociological Review, 26*, 733–743.

Denton, R.E. and Kampfe, C.M. (1994). The relationship between family variables and adolescent substance abuse: a literature review. *Adolescence, 29*, 475–495.

Doerner, W.J. (1987). Child maltreatment seriousness and juvenile delinquency. *Youth and Society, 19*(1), 197–224.

Donahue, E., Schiraldi, V., and Zeidenberg, J. (1998) School House Hype: The School Shootings, and the Real Risks Kids Face in America.

Dusenbury, L., Falco, M., Lake, A., Brannigan, R., and Bosworth, K. (1997). Nine critical elements of promising violence prevention programs. *Journal of School Health, 67*, 409–415.

Dwyer, K., Osher, D., and Wagner, C. (1998). Early Warning, Timely Response: A Guide to Safe Schools. Washington, D.C.: U.S. Department of Education.

Elam, S., Rose, L., and Gallup, A. (1996). The 28th annual Phi Delta Kappa/Gallup poll of the public's attitudes toward the public schools. *Phi Delta Kappan, 78,* 41–59.

Elam, S. and Rose, L. (1995). The 27th annual Phi Delta Kappa/Gallup poll of the public's attitudes toward the public schools. *Phi Delta Kappan, 77,* 41–56.

Elam, S., Rose, L., and Gallup, A. (1994). The 26th annual Phi Delta Kappa/Gallup poll of the public's attitudes toward the public schools. *Phi Delta Kappan, 76,* 41–56.

Elliot, D. (June 21, 1994). What's triggering youth violence? Guns set off volatile mix of problems. *Denver Post,* p. F1.

Elliot, D., Hamburg, B., and Williams, K. (1998). *Violence in American schools.* Cambridge, CA: Cambridge University Press.

Elliot, D., Huizinga, D., and Ageton, S. (1985). *Explaining Delinquency and Drug Use.* Beverly Hills, CA: Sage.

Elliot, D. and Voss, H.L. (1974). *Delinquency and Dropout.* Lexington, MA: D.C. Heath.

Ericson, M.L. and Jensen, G.F. (1977). Delinquency is still group behavior: toward revitalizing the group premise in the sociology of deviance. *Journal of Criminal Law and Criminology, 68,* 262–277.

Ericson, N. (2001). Addressing the Problem of Juvenile Bullying. OJJDP Fact Sheet #27. Washington, D.C.

Eron, I. and Huesmann, I. (1984). Cognitive processes and the persistence of aggressive behavior. *Aggressive Behavior, 10,* 243–251.

Esbensen, F.A. and Huizinga, D. (1993). Gangs, drugs, and delinquency in a survey of urban youth. *Criminology, 31,* 565–587.

Fagan, J. (1989). The social organization of drug use and drug dealing among urban gangs. *Criminology, 27,* 633–669.

Fagan, J. and Wexler, S. (1987). Family origin of violent delinquents. *Criminology, 25,* 643–669.

Farrington, D.P. (1989). Early predictors of adolescent aggression and adult violence. *Violence and Victims, 4,* 79–100.

Farrington, D.P. (1995). Development of offending and antisocial behavior. *Journal of Child Psychology and Psychiatry, 36,* 929–963.

Felson, R. (1992). Kick' em when they're down: explanations of the relationship between stress and interpersonal aggression and violence. *Sociological Quarterly, 33*(1), 1–16.

Fields, J. and Casper, L.M. (2001). Current Population Reports. U.S. Census Bureau. Washington, D.C.

Fingerhut, L.A. and Kleinman, J.C. (1990). International and instate comparisons of homicide among young males. *Journal of American Medical Association, 263,* 3292–3294.

Fishbein, D. (1990). Biological perspectives in criminology. *Criminology, 28,* 27–72.

Fishman, G., Gustavo, S.M., and Eisikovits, Z. (2002). Variables affecting adolescent victimization: findings from a National Youth Survey. *Western Criminology Review, 3,* [Online]. Retrieved December 2, 2002 from http://wcr.sonoma.edu/v3n2/fishman.html.

Fleming, T., Barner, C., Hudson, B., and Rosignon-Carmouche, L.A. (2000). Anger, violence, and academic performance: A study of troubled minority youth. *Urban Education, 35*(2), 195–205.

Forgatch, M.S. and Patterson, G.R. (1998). Behavioral family therapy. In Dattilio, F.M. (Ed.), *Case Studies in Couple and Family Therapy: Systematic and Cognitive Perspectives.* New York: Guilford Press. pp. 85–107.

Frease, D.E. (1973). Delinquency, social class, and the schools. *Sociology and Social Research, 57,* 443–459.

Freire, P. (1990). *Pedagogy of the Oppressed.* New York: Continuum.

Friday, P.C. and Hage, J. (1976). Youth crime in postindustrial societies. *Criminology, 14,* 347–367.

Fryxell, D. (2000). Personal, social and family characteristics of angry students. *Professional School Counseling, 4,* 86–95.

Garbarino, J. (1999). *The Last Boys: Why Our Sons Turned Violent and How We Can Save Them.* New York: The Free Press.

Geller, M. and Ford-Sonoma, L. (1984). *Violent Homes, Violent Children.* Trenton, NJ: New Jersey State Department of Corrections.

Giordano, P.C. (1978). Girls, guys, and gangs: the changing social context of female delinquency. *Journal of Criminal Law and Criminology, 69,* 126–132.

Giordano, P.C. and Cernkovich, S.A. (1979). On complicating the relationship between liberation and delinquency. *Social Problems, 26,* 467–481.

Glueck, S. and Glueck, E. (1950). *Unraveling Juvenile Delinquency.* Cambridge, MA: Harvard University Press.

Goddard, H. (1920). *Efficiency and Levels of Intelligence.* Princeton, NJ: Princeton University Press.

Gold, M. (1970). Status Forces in Delinquent Boys. Ann Arbor, MI: University of Michigan, Institute for Social Research.

Gold, M. and Mann, D. (1982). Delinquency as defense. *American Journal of Orthopsychiatry, 42,* 463–479.

Gold, M. and Moles, O. (1978). Delinquency and violent in schools and the community. In Inciardi, J. and Pottieger, A. (Eds.), *Violent Crime: Historical and Contemporary Issues.* Beverly Hills, CA: Sage. pp. 111–124.

Goldman, N. (1963). *The Differential Selection of Juvenile Offenders for Court Appearance.* New York: National Council on Crime and Delinquency.

Gordon, R.A. (1987). SES versus IQ in the Race-IQ-delinquency model. *International Journal of Sociology and Social Policy, 7,* 30–96.

Gottfredson, G. and Gottfredson, D. (1985). *Victimization in Schools.* New York: Plenum.

Graham Tebo, M. (2000). Zero tolerance, zero sense. *ABA Journal*, 86, 40–46.

Green, M.W. (1999). The Appropriate and Effective Use of Security Technologies in United States Schools: A Guide for Schools and Law Enforcement Agencies (NIJ # 178265). Washington, D.C.: United States Department of Justice.

Greenberg, D. (1978). Delinquency and the age structure of society. *Contemporary Crises, 1,* 189–224.

Gun-Free School Zones Act (1990). 18 U.S.C., § 922(q)(1)(a).

Gun-Free Schools Act (1994). 20 U.S.C., § 8921.

Hancock, L. (2001). The school shootings: why context counts. *Columbia Journalism Review, 40,* 76–78.

Harpold, J.A. and Band, S.R. (1998). Lessons Learned: An FBI Perspective: School Violence Summit. Little Rock, AR: Behavioral Science Unit, FBI Academy.

Harrington-Lueker, D. (1992). Blown away by school violence. *Education Digest*, 58(1), 50–54.

Hartstone, E. and Hansen, K. (1984). The violent juvenile offenders. In Robert Mathias (Ed.), *Violent Juvenile Offenders*. San Francisco: National Council on Crime and Delinquency.

Hawkins, J.D., Farrington, D.P., and Catalano, R.F. (1998a). Reducing violence through the schools. In Eliot, D.S., Hamburg, B.A., and Williams, K.R. (Eds.), *Violence in American Schools: A New Perspective* Cambridge, MA: Cambridge University Press. pp. 188–216.

Hawkins, J.D., Herrenkohl, T.I., Farrington, D.P., Brewer, D., Catalano, R.F., and Harachi, T.W. (1998b). A review of predictors of youth violence. In Loeber, E. and Farrington, D.P. (Ed.), *Serious and Violent Juvenile Offenders*. Thousand Oaks, CA: Sage. pp. 106–147.

Hawkins, J.D., Herrenkohl, T.I., Farrington, D.P., Brewer, D., Catalano, R.F., Harachi, T.W., and Cothern, L. (2000). *Predictors of Youth Violence*. Washington, D.C.: U.S. Department of Justice.

Heaven, P.C. (1996). Personality and self-reported delinquency: a longitudinal analysis. *Journal of Child Psychology and Psychiatry, 37,* 747–751.

Heaviside, S., Rowand, C., Williams, C., and Farris, E. (1998). Violence and Discipline Problems in U. S. Public Schools: 1996-1997 (NCES 98-030). Washington, D.C.: United States Department of Education.

Herrenkohl, T., Maguin, E., Hill, K., Hawkins, J., Abbott, R., and Catalano, R. (1998). Childhood and Adolescent Predictor's of Youth Violence. Seattle: University of Washington, Seattle Social Development Project.

Hindelang, M. (1973). Causes of Delinquency. *Social Problems, 20,* 471-487.

Hindelang, M., Hirschi, T., and Weis, J. (1981). *Measuring Delinquency*. Beverly Hills, CA: Sage.

Hirschi, T. (1969). *Causes of Delinquency*. Berkeley, CA: University of California Press.

Hirschi, T. and Hindelang, M. (1977). Intelligence and delinquency: a revisionist review. *American Sociological Review, 42,* 471–486.

Holmes, T.R. and Murrell, J. (1995). Schools, discipline, and the uniformed police officer. *NASSP Bulletin, 79*, 60–64.

Howell, J.C. (1997). *Juvenile Justice and Youth*. Thousand Oaks, CA: Sage.

Huizinga, D. and Jakob-Chien, C. (1998). The contemporaneous co-occurrence of serious and violent juvenile offenders and other problem behaviors. In Loeber, R. and Farrington, D. (Eds.), *Serious and Violent Juvenile Offenders: Risk factors and Successful Interventions*. Thousand Oaks, CA: Sage. pp. 47–67.

Huizinga, D., Loeber, R., and Thornberry, T. (1994). Urban Delinquency and Substance Abuse: Initial Findings. Washington, D.C.: Office of Juvenile Justice and Delinquency Prevention.

Hurst, H. (1998). Juvenile Court As We Enter the Millennium. *Juvenile and Family Court Journal*. Vol. 50.

Hyman, I.A. and Perone, D.C. (1998). The other side of school violence: educator policies and practices that may contribute to student misbehavior. *Journal of School Psychology, 36*, 7–27. Indiana Education Policy Center. (2001). *Zero Tolerance*. Bloomington, Indiana, Indiana University.

In re Gault. (1967). 387 U.S. 1.

In re Winship. (1970). 397 U.S. 358.

Indiana Education Policy Center (2002). What Works in Preventing School Violence. Retrieved November 20, 2002, from www.indiana.edu/~safeschl.

Indicators of School Crime and Safety. (2002). United States Departments of Education and Justice. Washington, D.C.

Individuals with Disabilities Education Act Amendment (1997). 20 U.S.C. §1400 et seq.

Jackson, T. (1998). Getting serious about school discipline. *The Public Interest, 133*, 68–83.

Jang, S.J. and Thornberry, T.P. (1998). Self-esteem, delinquent peers and delinquency: a test of the self-enhancement thesis. *American Sociological Review, 63*, 586–598.

Jenkins, P.H. (1995). School delinquency and school commitment. *Sociology of Education, 68*, 221–239.

Jensen, G.F. (1972). Parents, peers, and delinquent action: a test of the differential association perspective. *American Journal of Sociology, 78*, 562–575.

Jensen, G.F. (1973). Inner containment and delinquency. *Journal of Criminal Law and Criminology, 64*, 464–470.

Johnson, R.E. (1979). *Juvenile Delinquency and Its Origins*. New York: Cambridge University Press.

Johnson, D.W. and Johnson, R.T. (1995). Why violence prevention programs don't work-and what does. *Educational Leadership, 52*, 63–69.

Jones, C.A. (November 1998). Preventing School Violence: A Review of the Literature. Paper presented at the annual meeting of the Mid-South Educational Research Association, New Orleans, LA.

Kafka, R.R. and London, P. (1991). Communication in relationships and adolescent substance use: the influence of parents and friends. *Adolescence, 26,* 567–598.

Kandel, E. and Mednick, S.A. (1991). Perinatal complications predict violent offending. *Criminology, 29,* 515–524.

Kaplan, H.B. (1975). Increase in self-rejection as an antecedent of deviant responses. *Journal of Youth and Adolescence, 4,* 281–292.

Kaplan, H.B., Martin, S.S., and Robbins, C. (1982). Application of a general theory of deviant behavior: self-derogation and adolescent drug use. *Journal of Health and Social Behavior, 23,* 274–294.

Kaufman, P., Chen, X., Choy, S., Ruddy, S., Miller, A., Fleury, J. et al. (2000). Indicators of School Crime and Safety, 2000 (NCES 2001-017/NCJ-184176). Washington, D.C.: U.S. Departments of Education and Justice.

Kaufman, P., Ruddy, S.A., Chandler, K.A., and Rand, M.R. (1999). *Indicators of School Crime and Safety, 1999.* U.S. Department of Education and Justice. NCES 98-251/NCJ-172215. Washington, D.C.

Kelly, D.H. (1974). Track position and delinquent involvement: a preliminary analysis. *Sociology and Social Research, 58,* 380–386.

Kelly, D.H. and Pink, W.T. (1982). School crime and individual responsibility: the perpetuation of a myth? *Urban Review, 14,* 47–63.

Kent v. United States (1966). 383 U.S. 541.

Kingston, L. and Prior, M. (1995). The development of stable, transient, and school-age onset aggressive behavior in young children. *Journal of the Academy of Child and Adolescent Psychiatry, 34,* 348–358.

Kirkegaard-Sorenson, L. and Mednick, S.A. (1977). A prospective study of predictors of criminality: intelligence. In Mednick, S.A. and Christiansen, K.O. (Eds.), *Biosocial Basis of Criminal Behavior.* New York: Gardner.

Klinteberg, B.A., Magnusson, D., and Schalling, D. (1989). Hyperactive behavior in childhood and adult impulsivity: a longitudinal study of male subjects. *Personality and Individual Differences, 10,* 43–49.

Kotinsky, S., Bixler, E.O., and Ketti, P.A. (2001). Threats of school violence in Pennsylvania after media coverage of the Columbine high school massacre: examining the role of imitation, *Pediatric Adolescent Medicine, 155,* 994–1001.

Krohn, M. and Massey, H. (1980). Social control and delinquent behavior. *Sociological Quarterly, 21,* 529–543.

Kumar, A. (December 28, 1999). Suit fights schools alcohol policy. *St. Petersburg Times,* p. 3B.

Laub, J.H. and Lauritsen, J.L. (1998). The interdependence of school violence with neighborhood and family conditions. In Elliot, D.S., Hamburg, B., and Williams, K.R. (Eds.), *Violence in American Schools: A New Perspective.* New York: Cambridge University Press. pp. 127–155.

Laub, J.H. and Sampson, R.J. (1988). Unraveling families and delinquency: a re-analysis of the Gluecks' data. *Criminology, 26,* 355–380.

Lawrence, R. (1998). *School Crime and Juvenile Justice.* Oxford: Oxford University Press.

Leone, P.E., Mayer, M.J., Malmgren, K., and Misel, S.M. (2000). School violence and disruption: rhetoric, reality, and reasonable balance. *Focus on Exceptional Children 33*(1), 1–20.

Lester, W. (July 30, 1998). School gun deaths decline: Rural incidents drew attention. *The New Orleans Times-Picayune.* p. A8.

Lipsey, M.W. and Derzon, J. (1998). Predictors of violent of serious delinquent in adolescent early adulthood: a synthesis of longitudinal research. In Loeber, R. and Farrington, D. (Eds.), *Serious and Violent Juvenile Offenders: Risk factors and Successful Interventions.* Thousand Oaks, CA: Sage. pp. 86–105.

Lockwood, D. (October 1997). *Violence Among Middle School and High School Students: Analysis and Implications for Prevention.* National Institute of Justice Research in Brief. Washington, D.C.: United States Department of Justice.

Loeber, R. and Farrington, D. (1998). *Executive Summary: Serious and Violent Juvenile Offenders.* Thousand Oaks, CA: Sage.

Loeber, R. and Stouthamer-Loeber, M. (1998). Development of juvenile aggression and violence: Some common misconceptions and controversies. *American Psychologist, 53,* 242–259.

Lugaila, T. (1998). Marital Status and Living Arrangements. U.S. Census Bureau Current Population Survey Report. Washington, D.C.

Maguin, E. and Loeber, R. (1996). Academic performance and delinquency. In Tonry, M. (Ed.), *Crime and Justice: A Review of Research.* Chicago, IL: University of Chicago Press. pp. 145–264.

Maguire, B., Weatherby, G.A., and Mathers, R.A. (2002). Network news coverage of school shootings. *The Social Science Journal, 39,* 465–470.

Males, M.A. (1996). *Scapegoat Generation.* Monroe, ME: Common Courage Press.

Matsueda, R.L. (1982). Testing control theory and differential association: a causal modeling approach. *American Sociological Review, 47,* 489–504.

Matseuda, R.L. and Heimer, K. (1987). Race, family structure, and delinquency: a test of differential association and social control theories. *American Sociological Review, 52,* 826–840.

Mayer, M.J. and Leone, P.E. (1999). A structural analysis of school violence and disruption: implications for creating safer schools, *Education and Treatment of Children, 22,* 333–356.

Mazerolle, P., Burton, V.S., Cullen, F.T., Evans, T.D., and Payne, G.L. (2000). Strain, anger, and delinquent adaptations: specifying general strain theory. *Journal of Criminal Justice, 28*(1), 89–101.

McCardle, L. and Fishbein, D. (1989). The self-reported effects of PCP on human aggression. *Addictive Behaviors, 4,* 465–472.

McCord, J. (1983). A forty-year perspective on effects of child abuse and neglect. *Child Abuse and Neglect, 7*(1), 265–270.

McDermott, J. (1983). Crime in the school and in the community: offenders, victims, and fearful youths. *Crime and Delinquency, 29*, 270–282.

McEvoy, A. and Welker, R. (2000). Antisocial behavior, academic failure, and school climate: a critical review. *Journal of Emotional and Behavioral Disorders, 8*, 130–141.

McGaha, J. and Leoni, E. (1995). Family violence, abuse, and related family issues of incarcerated delinquents with alcoholic parents compared to those with nonalcoholic parents. *Adolescence, 30*, 473–483.

Meadows, R.J. (2001). School violence and victimization. *Understanding Violence and Victimization.* Upper Saddle River, NJ: Prentice Hall. pp. 153–176.

Mednick, S.A. and Kandel, E.S. (1988). Congenital determinants of violence. *Bulletin of the American Academy of Psychiatry and Law, 16*, 101–109.

Menacker, J., Weldon, W., and Hurwitz, E. (1990). Community influences on school crime and violence. *Urban Education, 25*, 68–80.

Menard, S. and Morse, B.J. (1984). A structuralist critique of the IQ-delinquency hypothesis: theory and evidence. *American Journal of Sociology, 89*, 1347–1378.

Messner, S.F. and Krohn, M.D. (1990). Class, compliance structures, and delinquency: assessing integrated structural-Marxist theory. *American Journal of Sociology, 96*, 300–328.

Miller, W.J. (1996). Differential Oppression, Alienation and Edgework: Keys to understanding juvenile delinquency. Dissertation Abstracts International, Unpublished doctoral dissertation, University of Nevada, Las Vegas.

Miranda v. Arizona. (1966). 384 U.S. 436.

Moffitt, T.E. (1990). Juvenile delinquency and attention deficit disorder: boys' developmental trajectories from age 3 to age 15. *Child Development, 61*, 893–910.

Moffitt, T.E., Gabrielli, W.F., Mednick, S.A., and Schulsinger, F. (1985). Socio-economic status, IQ, and delinquency. *Journal of Abnormal Psychology, 90*, 152–156.

Mulvey, E.P. and Cauffman, E. (2001). The inherent limits of predicting school violence. *The American Psychologist, 56*, 797–802.

Nancrede, S.F. (August 20, 1998). School to take foul mouths to task: Southport high will institute zero-tolerance policy on profanity. *Indianapolis Star*, p. A1.

Nansel, T., Overpeck, M., Pilla, R., Ruan, W., Simons-Morton, B., and Scheidt, P. (2001). Bullying behaviors among U.S. youth: prevalence and association with psychosocial adjustment. *Journal of the American Medical Association, 285*(16), 2094–2100.

National Association of Elementary School Principals (NAESP) (1997). NAESP National Poll. Retrieved June 6, 2001 from www.naesp.org.

National Consortium on Violence Research (1998). Violence in the Schools. Pittsburgh, PA: Carnegie Mellon University.

National Institute of Education (1978). Violent School-Safe Schools: The Safe School Study Report to the Congress. Washington, D.C.

National Parent Teacher Association (1998). *Community Violence Prevention Kit*. Chicago, IL: Author.

National School Safety Center (1999). *Working Together to Create Safe Schools*. Westlake Village, CA: Author.

Nofzinger, S. (2001). *Bullies, Fights, and Guns: Testing Self-Control Theory with Juveniles*. New York: LFB Scholarly Publishing.

Noguera, P.A. (1995). Preventing and producing violence: a critical analysis of responses to school violence. *Harvard Educational Review, 65*, 189–210.

Nye, F.I. (1958). *Family Relationships and Delinquent Behavior*. New York: John Wiley & Sons.

Office of Educational Research and Improvement (2000). Safe, Disciplined, and Drug-Free Schools Expert Panel Promising Programs 2001. Retrieved January 15, 2003 from www.ed.gov/offices/OSDFS.

Office of Juvenile Justice and Delinquency Prevention (OJJDP) (May 2000). *Children as Victims*. Office of Juvenile Justice and Delinquency Prevention Bulletin. Washington, D.C.: U.S. Department of Justice.

Offord, D.R., Sullivan, K., Allen, N., and Abrams, N. (1979). Delinquency and hyperactivity. *Journal of Nervous and Mental Disease, 167*, 734–741.

Olweus, D. (1991). Bully/victim problems among schoolchildren: basic facts and effects of a school-based intervention program. In Rubin, I. and Pepler, D. (Eds.), *The Development and Treatment of Childhood Aggression*. Hillsdale, NJ: Erlbaum.

Osofsky, J.S. (October 2001). Addressing Youth Victimization. Washington, D.C.: U.S. Department of Justice.

O'Toole, M.E. (2000). The School Shooter: A Threat Assessment Perspective. Quantico, VA: Federal Bureau of Investigation.

Pasternack, R. and Lyon, R. (1982). Clinical and empirical identification of learning disabled juvenile delinquents. *Journal of Correctional Education, 33*, 7–13.

Patterson, G.R. and Dishion, T.J. (1985). Contribution of families and peers to delinquency. *Criminology, 23*, 63–79.

Patterson, G.R., Reid, J., and Dishion, T. (1992). *Antisocial Boys*. Eugene, OR: Castalia.

Patterson, G.R. and Yoerger, K. (1997). A developmental model for late-onset delinquency. In Osgood, D.W. (Ed.), *Nebraska Symposium on Motivation and Delinquency*. Lincoln, NE: University of Nebraska Press. pp. 119–177.

Pepkinsky, H. (2000). Educating for peace. *The Annals of the American Academy of Political and Social Sciences, 567*, 157–169.

Peterson, P.L., Hawkins, J.D., Abbott, R.D., and Catalano, R.F. (1994). Disentangling the effects of parental drinking, family management, and parental alcohol norms on current drinking by black and white adolescents. *Journal of Research on Adolescence, 4*, 203–227.

Petrillo, L. (October 29, 1997). Eight-year old may be expelled under zero-tolerance code. *San Diego Union-Tribune*, p. B-1.

Pink, W.T. (1982). Academic failure, student social conflict, and delinquent behavior. *Urban Review, 14,* 141–180.

Polk, K. (1967). Class strain and rebellion among adolescents. *Social Problems, 17,* 214–224.

Polk, K. and Burkett, S.R. (1972). School pressures toward deviance: A cross-cultural comparison. In Polk, K. and Schafer, W. (Eds.), *School Delinquency.* Englewood Cliffs, NJ: Prentice Hall. pp. 129–145.

Polk, K. and Halferty, D. (1966). Adolescents, commitment, and delinquency. *Journal of Research in Crime and Delinquency, 3,* 82–96.

Poole, E.D. and Regoli, R.M. (1979). Parental support, delinquent friends, and delinquency: a test of interaction effects. *Journal of Criminal Law and Criminology, 70,* 188–194.

Post, C.H. (1981). The link between learning disabilities and juvenile delinquency: cause, effect and present solutions. *Juvenile and Family Court Journal, 31,* 58–68.

Public Agenda (1999). Kids These Days '99: What Americans Really Think about the Next Generation. Retrieved on August 2, 2000 from www.publicagenda.org.

Pulkkinen, L. (1982). Self-control and continuity from childhood to adolescence. In Baltes, P. and Brim, O. (Eds.), *Life-Span Development and Behavior.* New York: Academic Press.

Raine, A. and Jones, F. (1987). Attention, autonomic arousal, and personality in behaviorally disordered children. *Journal of Abnormal Child Psychology, 15,* 583–599.

Rankin, J.H. (1980). School factors and delinquency: Interactions by age and sex. *Sociology and Social Research, 64,* 420–435.

Reckless, W. (1958). The Etiology of Delinquent and Criminal Behavior. Social Science Research Council No. 50. New York: Social Science Research Council.

Regoli, R. and Hewitt, J. (1991). *Delinquency in Society,* 2nd ed. New York: McGraw-Hill.

Regoli, R. and Hewitt, J. (1997). *Delinquency in Society,* 3rd ed. New York: McGraw-Hill.

Regoli, R. and Hewitt, J. (2003). *Delinquency in Society,* 5th ed. New York: McGraw-Hill.

Report on the State Implementation of the Gun-Free Schools Act: School Year 1998–1999 (2000). United States Department of Education. Washington, D.C.

Richards, P. (1979). Middle-class vandalism and age-status conflict. *Social Problems, 26,* 482–497.

Rose, L.C. and Gallup A.M. (1999). The 31st annual Phi Delta Kappa/Gallup poll of the public's attitudes toward the public schools. *Phi Delta Kappa, 81*(1), 41–57.

Rose, L.C. and Gallup, A.M. (2000). *The 32nd Annual Phi Delta Kappa/Gallup Poll of the Public's Attitudes toward the Public Schools.*

Rosenbaum, J.E. (1976). *Making Inequality: The Hidden Curriculum of the High School.* New York: John Wiley & Sons.

Rosenberg, M., Schooler, C., and Schoenbach, C. (1989). Self-esteem and adolescent problems: modeling reciprocal effect. *American Sociological Review, 4,* 1004–1018.

Rubel, R.J. (1979). The relationship between students victories in the courts and student violence in the schools. *Contemporary Education, 50,* 226–230.

Safe and Drug Free Schools and Communities Act (1994). 20 U.S.C. § 7107 et seq.

Sampson, R.J. and Laub, J.H. (1994). Urban poverty and the family context of delinquency: a look at structure and process in a class study. *Child Development, 65,* 523–540.

Sampson, R.J. and Lauritsen, J. (1993). Violent victimization and offending: individual, situational, and community-level risk factors. In Reiss, A.J., Jr. and Roth, J.A. (Eds.), *Understanding and Preventing Violence, Vol. 3, Social Influences.* Washington, D.C.: National Academy Press. pp. 1–114.

Schafer, W.E. and Polk, K. (1972a). School career and delinquency. In Polk, K. and Schafer, W. (Eds.), *School and Delinquency,* Englewood Cliffs, NJ: Prentice Hall. pp. 165–181.

Schafer, W.E. and Polk, K. (1972b). School conditions contributing to delinquency. In Polk, K. and Schafer, W. (Eds.), *School and Delinquency.* Englewood Cliffs, NJ: Prentice Hall. pp. 182–239.

Schiraldi, V. (August 25, 1998). Hyping school violence. *The Washington Post.*

Schiraldi, V. and Ziedenberg, J. (1999). School House Hype: Two Years Later. Washington, D.C.: Justice Policy Institute.

Schoenthaler, S. and Doraz, W. (1983). Types of offenses which can be reduced in an institutional setting using nutritional intervention. *International Journal of Biosocial Research, 4,* 74–84.

Schreiner, M.E. (1996). Bold steps build safe havens. *School Business Affairs, 62,* 44–46.

Security Research Center (1999). Guide for Preventing and Responding to School Violence. Alexandria, VA: International Association of Chiefs of Police.

Seydlitz, R. (1993). Complexity in the relationships among direct and indirect parental controls and delinquency. *Youth and Society, 24,* 243–275.

Seydlitz, R. and Jenkins, P. (1998). The Influence of Families, Friends, Schools, and Community on Delinquent Behavior. In Gullota, T.P., Adams, G.R., and Montemayor, R. (Eds.), *Delinquent Violent Youth: Theory and Interventions.* Thousand Oaks, CA: Sage. pp. 53–91.

Shely, J.F. and Wright, J.D. (1993). Gun Acquisition and Possession in Selected Juvenile Samples. Washington, D.C.: U.S. Department of Justice, National Institute of Justice, Office of Juvenile Justice and Delinquency Prevention.

Shely, J.F. and Wright, J.D. (October 1998). High school youths, weapons and violence: a national survey. *National Institute of Justice: Research in Brief, 81,* 1–7.

Siegel, L.J. and Senna, J.J. (1991). *Juvenile Delinquency,* 4th ed. St. Paul, MN: West Publishing Company.

Simons, R.L. (1978). The meaning of the IQ-Delinquency relationship. *American Sociological Review, 43,* 268–270.

Simons, R.L., Robertson, J.F., and Downs, W.R. (1989). The nature of the association between parental rejection and delinquent behavior. *Journal of Youth and Adolescence, 18,* 297–310.

Skiba, R.J. (2000). Zero Tolerance, Zero Evidence: An Analysis of School Disciplinary Practice (Policy Report #SRS2). Indianapolis, IN: Indiana University, Indiana Education Policy Center.

Skiba, R.J., Michael, R., Nardo, A.C., and Peterson, R. (2000). The Color of Discipline: Sources of Racial and Gender Disproportionality in School Punishment (Policy Research Report # SRS1). Indianapolis, IN: Indiana University, Indiana Education Policy Center.

Skiba, R.J., Peterson, R.L., and Williams, T. (1997). Office referrals and suspension: disciplinary intervention in middle schools. *Education and Treatment of Children, 20,* 295–315.

Small, M. and Tetrick, K.D. (2001). School violence: an overview. *Juvenile Justice 8,* 3–12.

Smith, S., Mullis, F., Kem, R.M., and Brack, G. (1999). An Adlerian model of the etiology of aggression in adjudicated adolescents. *Family Journal, 7*(2), 135–148.

Smith, C. and Thornberry, T.P. (1995). The relationship between child maltreatment and adolescent involvement in delinquency. *Criminology, 33,* 451–477.

Soskis, B. (May 14, 2001). How America learned to hate bullies. *The New Republic.* pp. 25–27.

Spergel, I.A. (1990). Youth gangs: continuity and change. In Tonry, M. and Morris, N. (Eds.), *Crime and Justice* Chicago, IL: University of Chicago Press. pp. 171–275.

Stephens, R.D. (1996). The Art of Safe School Planning: 40 Ways to Manage and Control Student Disruptions. American Association of School Administrators. Retrieved July 31, 2000 from www.aasa.org.

Strong, B. and DeVault, C. (1986). Societal change in family violence from 1975 to 1985 as revealed by two national surveys. *Journal of Marriage and Family Therapy, 48*(4), 465–479.

Survey Research Center (1999). *School Safety and Security.* Berkeley, CA: University of California, Berkeley Press.

Thomas, C.W. and Hyman, J.M. (1978). Compliance theory, control theory, and juvenile delinquency. In Krohn, M. and Akers, R.L. (Eds.), *Crime, Law, and Sanctions.* Beverly Hills, CA: Sage. pp. 73–91.

Thompson, W., Mitchell, J., and Dodder, R.A. (1984). An empirical test of Hirschi's control theory of delinquency. *Deviant Behavior, 5,* 11–22.

Thornberry, T.P. (1987). Toward an interactional theory of delinquency. *Criminology, 25*(4), 863–891.

Thornberry, T.P., Moore, M., and Christensen, R.L. (1985). The effect of dropping out of high school on subsequent criminal behavior. *Criminology, 23,* 3–18.

Tittle, C.R. and Meier, R.F. (1991). Specifying the SESI delinquency relationship by social characteristics of context. *Journal of Research in Crime and Delinquency, 28*(4), 430–456.

Tremlow, S.W., Fonagy, P., and Sacco, F.C. (2002). Premeditate mass shootings in schools: threat assessment. *Journal of the American Academy of Child and Adolescent Psychiatry, 41,* 475–482.

Tremlow, S.W., Fonagy, P.S., Gies, F.C., and Martin, L. (2001). Creating a peaceful school learning environment: a controlled study of an elementary school intervention to reduce violence. *American Journal of Psychiatry, 158,* 808–810.

UCLA Center for Communication Policy. (1995). Television Monitoring Project. Los Angeles, CA: University of California Press.

USA Today (September 8, 1998). School metal detectors favored, A3.

U.S. Departments of Education and Justice. (2000). 2000 Annual Report on School Safety. Washington, D.C.: Author.

U.S. Secret Service and U.S. Department of Education. (2002). The Final Report and Findings of the Safe School Initiative. Washington, D.C.

U.S. v. Lopez. (1995). 115 S. Ct. 1624.

Vera Institute of Justice. (1999). Approaches to School Safety in America's Largest Cities. Retrieved November 10, 1999, from http://www.vera.org/Publications.

Verdugo, R. and Schneider, J. (1999). Quality Schools, safe schools: a theoretical and empirical discussion. *Education and Urban Society, 31,* 286–308.

Verliden, S., Hersen, M., and Thomas, J. (2000). Risk factors in school shootings. *Clinical Psychology Review, 20,* 3–56.

Wadsworth, M. E. (1976). Delinquency, pulse rates, and early environmental deprivation. *Journal of Criminology, 16,* 245–256.

Walko-Frankovic, D. and Williard, T.B. (2002). School Safety Training Needs Assessment: Report on Findings. Department of Criminal Justice Services, Criminal Justice Research Center Evaluation Unit. Virginia Department of Criminal Justice Services. Available: www.dcjs.state.va.us.

Walker, H.M., Hoerner, R.J., Sugai, G., Bullis, M., Sprague, J.R., Bricker, D., and Kaufman, M.J. (1996). Integrated approached to preventing anti-social behavior patters among school-age children and youth. *Journal of Emotional and Behavioral Disorders, 4,* 194–209.

Wallace, L. (2001). Reports from rural Mississippi: a look at school violence. *Journal of Security Administration, 24*(2), 15–32.

Warr, M. (1993). Parents, peers, and delinquency. *Social Forces, 71*(1), 247–264.

Wells, L.E. (1989). Self-enhancement through delinquency: a conditional test of self-derogation theory. *Journal of Research in Crime and Delinquency, 26,* 226–252.

Wells, L.E. and Rankin, J.H. (1983). Self-concept as a mediating factor in delinquency. *Social Psychology Quarterly, 46,* 11–22.

West, D.J. (1973). *Who Becomes Delinquent?* London: Heinemann.

White, H.R., Pandina, R.J., and LaGrange, R.L. (1987). Longitudinal predictors of serious substance use and delinquency. *Criminology, 25,* 715–740.

Whitney, I. and Smith, P.K. (1993). A survey of the nature and extent of bullying in junior/middle and secondary schools. *Educational Research, 35*(1), 38–47.

Widom, C.S. and Maxfield, M.G. (2001). An Update on the Cycle of Violence. Research in Brief. Washington, D.C.: U.S. Department of Justice, National Institute of Justice.

Wilson, J.Q. and Herrnstein, R.J. (1985). *Crime and Human Nature.* New York: Simon and Schuster.

Wright, K.N. and Wright, K.E. (1994). Family Life, Delinquency and Crime: A Policy Maker's Guide. Washington, D.C.

Wood, D.B. (2001). Are media acting as a publicity machine for shooters? *Christian Science Monitor, 93,* p. 2.

Yell, M.L. and Rotalszki, M.E. (2000). Searching for safe schools: legal issues in the prevention of school violence. *Journal of Emotional and Behavioral Disorders, 8,* 187–209.

Zimmerman, J., Rich, W., Keilitz, I., and Broder. P. (1981). Some observations on the link between learning disabilities and juvenile delinquency. *Journal of Criminal Justice, 9,* 9–17.

Zingraff, M., Lester, T., Myers, K., and Johnsen, M. (1993). Child Maltreatment and youthful problem behavior. *Criminology, 31*(1), 173–202.

Zinnecker, J. (1998). Perpetrators of school violence: a longitudinal study of bullying in German schools. *Cross-Cultural Perspectives on Youth and Violence.* Stanford, CT: JAI Press, pp. 187–203.

Zins, J.A., Travis, L., Brown, M., and Knighton, A. (1994). Schools and prevention of interpersonal violence: mobilizing and coordinating community resources. *Special Services in the Schools, 8,* 1–11.

Zivin, G., Hassan, N.R., and De Paula, G.F. (2001). An effective approach to violence prevention: traditional martial arts in middle school. *Adolescence, 36,* 443–459.

Zucker, R.A. (1987). The four alcoholisms: a developmental account of the etiologic process. In Rivers, P.C. (Ed.), *Nebraska Symposium on Motivation, Vol. 34; Alcohol and Addictive Behaviors.* Lincoln, NE: University of Nebraska Press.

Notes

1. Since the incident in Pearl, other episodes of fatal school violence in Bethel, Alaska, Pearl, Mississippi, Paducah, Kentucky, Jonesboro, Arkansas, Edinboro, Pennsylvania, Springfield, Oregon, Richmond, Virginia, Littleton, Colorado, Conyers, Georgia, Flint, Michigan, Fort Gibson, Oklahoma, and Santee, California, have left numerous people dead and even more wounded.

2. A more thorough discussion of the theoretical explanations of juvenile delinquency can be found in Chapter 4.

Chapter 31

The Adolescent Victim of School Violence: Social and Situational Risk Factors

Christopher J. Schreck, Thomas Ellsworth,
John E. Shutt, and J. Mitchell Miller

31.1 Introduction

There is apparently a common and persistent belief that crime at school is widespread and that any student has a good chance of becoming a victim (e.g., Gottfredson and Gottfredson, 1985; Juvonen, 2001; Tucker, 2001). In response to this concern, schools have implemented costly law-and-order approaches, such as hiring new police officers, as well as installing security devices and putting zero-tolerance policies into practice (Casella, 2001; Juvonen, 2001). These approaches annually receive millions of dollars in federal financial support through the 1994 Safe Schools Act. Clearly, the problem of victimization in schools is visible and has drawn attention from the legislature as well as the public.

In view of the high priority given to efforts to make schools safer, researchers have also begun to show a great interest in learning more about school crime (e.g., Gottfredson and Gottfredson, 1985; Schreck et al., 2003; Welsh, 2001). However, researchers know much more about the characteristics of high-crime schools and violence-prone students than they do about the risk factors that may enhance the chances of individual students falling victim to crime at school. We believe that this focus on offenders is of limited utility in that it does not usually target victims in a random fashion (see Felson, 1998). Our objective is to identify correlates of school victimization and thus help researchers and policymakers better understand who the victims of school crime typically are. We begin by discussing patterns and trends in victimization at school and the theoretical origins of victimization, and then investigate how well school-relevant variables relate to student victimization among a representative sample of tenth-grade American students.

31.2 Trends and Patterns in School Victimization

Contrary to public opinion, the typical student is not likely to fall victim to crime at school. Paralleling nationwide crime trends, the rate of crime at school decreased between 1993 and 2000 (Davoe et al., 2002; Snyder and Sickmund, 1999). Total victimization reported during 2000 (with approximately 74 incidents per 1000 students) was less than half the level of victimization reported during 1993 (152 incidents per 1000 students), and comparisons with National Crime and Victimization Survey data reveal that the rate of victimization of children at school is hardly different from the rate away from school (see Davoe et al., 2002, p. 7). The rate of serious violence at school, however, is much less than serious violence taking place away from school. In short, victimization happens at school, but the typical student during the 2000 school year was extremely unlikely to be the victim of serious violence (about 5 incidents of serious violence victimization per 1000 students). Although these patterns may suggest optimism, millions of occurrences of the victimization of students take place annually at school (Davoe et al., 2002).

Descriptive data also indicate that victimization is not indiscriminate; clearly, some students are more likely to become victims. Victims of violent crime tend to be younger students, male, and black (Davoe et al., 2002). Identification of such demographic characteristics, however, says little about *why* students become victims. Researchers have undertaken to explain patterns in victimization and to identify a broader range of risk factors.

31.3 Theoretical Framework

31.3.1 Routine Activities

Victimization research frequently employs elements of lifestyle and routine activity theories to explain victimization patterns (Hindelang et al., 1978; Cohen and Felson, 1979; Garofalo, 1987). According to these frameworks, the occurrence of victimization depends on the convergence, in time and space, of a motivated offender and a worthwhile and poorly protected target (Cohen and Felson, 1979; Felson, 1992). The daily routines of offenders and victims determine how often this convergence occurs. The routine activity of some individuals places them in situations where they lack guardianship and risk exposure to offenders (such as by staying out late at night among strangers). Such individuals, on average, should experience more victimization. Thus, the fact that black students tend to experience more frequent victimization should be a consequence of their proximity with other blacks who, as a group, have higher levels of offending behavior (see Hindelang et al., 1978; Sampson and Wooldredge, 1987).

The routine activity theory has garnered empirical support in non-school contexts (see, for example, Copes, 1999, for crime-specific context of motor vehicle theft; Beki et al., 1999, for violent crimes; Tremblay and Tremblay, 1998, for victimization during travel; Nelsen and Huff, 1998, for elderly homicide victimization; McElrath et al., 1997, for drug user victimization; Madriz, 1996, for the workplace; Thompson and Fisher, 1996, for household victimization; Kelley, 1993, for marital victimization and family homicide; Lynch, 1987, for workplace victimization). Researchers have only recently concentrated on the school setting (e.g., Wallace, 2001; Welsh, 2001; Welsh et al., 1999, 2000). The routine activity theory has demonstrated predictive power in educational settings, though this research has largely been confined to college campuses (e.g., Tewksbury and Mustaine, 2000; Fisher et al., 1998; Mustaine and Tewksbury, 1998). Put differently, there is still much to learn about how daily routines and lifestyle activities at school dovetail with victimization risk. In particular, demographic patterns in victimization have persisted in spite of controls for measures of lifestyle (e.g., Miethe, Stafford, and Long, 1987).

Having described the basic theoretical framework, we will now consider how routine activity or lifestyle risk factors apply to the school setting.

31.3.1.1 Exposure Factors

Students who are in proximity to delinquents should have a greater risk of victimization. For instance, individuals attending schools with high levels of crime and disorder tend to experience more frequent victimization (Schreck et al., 2003). Research also indicates that spending time with delinquent friends enhances victimization risk (Jensen and Brownfield, 1986; Mustaine and Tewksbury, 1998; Sampson and Lauritsen, 1990; Schreck et al., 2002). One rationale for this correlation is that much victimization occurs within the peer group; supposed friends provide criminal opportunities and temptation for each other. Moreover, delinquent peer groups imply a social network for transmitting information about criminal opportunities involving others in the network. Consequently, students who have delinquent friends should be more likely to experience victimization.

31.3.1.2 Target Attractiveness Factors

Students who have either tangible or symbolic reasons for being worthwhile targets should experience more frequent victimization. The family income of the student may reflect tangible attractiveness, but results for this as a risk factor are mixed. In a general population study, Miethe and Meier (1994) found that income predicted violent victimization but not theft, whereas, in a college campus study, Fisher et al. (1998) found that income predicted theft but not violent victimization. The delinquent activity of the student, however, might provide symbolic justification for becoming an attractive target. Singer (1981) reasoned that members of a violent subculture might value retaliation. Thus, an individual might alternate offender and victim roles continually, as a criminal act invites retaliation and counter-retaliation. In fact, individual delinquency is an important and consistent correlate of victimization (Lauritsen et al., 1991; Schreck et al., 2002).

31.3.1.3 Guardianship Factors

Schools can affect guardianship in numerous ways and thereby act to reduce victimization risks on their premises. Physical guardianship could be influenced by the presence of security guards, by changing building configurations, and by installing metal detectors and other security devices. However, such target-hardening measures tend to be expensive and have produced mixed results in terms of physical and social protection (Miethe and Meier, 1994; Rosenbaum, 1987).

31.3.2 Social Bonds and Vulnerability

The routine activities perspective looks exclusively at situational sources of risk. Individuals may also possess characteristics that might make them more vulnerable to victimization. In this chapter, we consider social bonds to be an additional determinant of victimization risk. Social bonds refer to emotional and rational ties to society, and individuals perceive them as beneficial and worth protecting. Most criminologists perceive bonds as barriers against crime (e.g., Hirschi, 1969; Sampson and Laub, 1993). That is, the presence of bonds indicates that the individual has something to lose when engaging in crime. Bonds also may deter victimization. Behaving confrontationally and provoking a violent attack, for instance, is a risk to a person's livelihood (injuries can cost a job or money) and may cause distress to their loved ones. People may thus anticipate that negligent or reckless behavior would have detrimental consequences beyond their own pain or discomfort and may thus choose a course of action entailing lower risk of victimization. On the other hand, someone who lacks bonds risks less by facilitating, provoking, or precipitating crime. Those with weaker bonds should therefore, on average, experience a greater degree of victimization.

Social bonds may also determine daily activity patterns (Felson, 1998; Horney et al., 1996). Children who enjoy school and have a high grade point average (GPA), for instance, tend to spend more time at school in the presence of guardians such as teachers and administrators. Conversely, one might expect that children who dislike school would spend more time away from it, by skipping or not participating in school-related activities. Because skipping such activities usually takes place away from the presence of responsible adult guardians, they would be more vulnerable to motivated offenders. In sum, strong bonds of attachment or commitment to school might reduce victimization by: (1) creating a feeling of obligation to take precautions against harm and (2) altering routines and placing students in environments in which risk of victimization is reduced.

The goal of this study is exploratory. We wish to identify correlates of school victimization, as suggested by the routine activity and social bonding theories. The identification of these correlates should help develop victimization theory in the school context and potentially alert policymakers to additional indicators for students with a higher risk of becoming victims of crime.

31.4 The Present Study

We examine the effect of hypothesized school-related predictors of victimization risk using the 1999 Monitoring the Future (MTF) study. The MTF survey is an ongoing (since 1975) annual cross-sectional study of the lifestyles and values of American high school students with a particular focus on drug use, victimization experiences, and delinquency. The MTF uses a 3-stage probability sample of students from approximately 130 schools. In addition to high-school seniors, the MTF samples tenth-graders. A random sample of all tenth-grade participants answered the questionnaire regarding the measure of victimization experienced at school.

Because the MTF study does not sample those who were not at school (either absent or had dropped out), our findings can only be generalized to adolescents in the tenth grade who were attending school. Nevertheless, this limitation concerning generalizability primarily would affect estimates of victimization rates and frequency; we have no reason to expect that the general pattern of relationships between lifestyle and social-bonding variables will differ based on individual characteristics. The MTF data set is therefore among the best methods for investigating victimization during late adolescence.

31.4.1 *Dependent and Independent Variables*

31.4.1.1 *Victimization*

Victimization is a composite index containing seven items. Three items reflect property victimization. Two items measure theft — one less than $50 (36% of the sample reported at least one instance of this type of victimization) and the other greater than $50 (reported by 18% of the sample). The MTF survey also asks about damage to personal property at school (reported by 13% of the sample). The remaining items measure violent victimization. These items include injury with a weapon (6%), threatening with a weapon without causing injury (15%), injury by an unarmed person (15%), and threats from an unarmed person (27%).

31.4.1.2 Demographic Controls

The analyses incorporate controls for three demographic variables often associated with victimization risk: age, gender, and race (see, for instance, U.S. Department of Justice Statistics, 1999). All the afore-mentioned variables have dichotomous coding. Age measures whether the respondent is older or younger than 16 (1 = older than 16). The variable for gender measures whether the respondent is a male (females are the reference category). Finally, the race variable differentiates between black (1) and nonblack (0) respondents. About 45 percent of the sample are males, 56 percent are older than 16, and the majority are white (88 percent) youth.

31.4.1.3 School Environment Characteristics

The MTF data focus primarily on individuals and not on the charac-teristics of the schools attended by students. Nevertheless, there are items that might substitute for disorder at school. In particular, there are three items relating to feelings of safety at, or going to and from, the school campus. Higher scores on each item indicate more frequent feelings that school is unsafe, which suggests exposure to offenders. Another item measures the presence of antidrug education programs at school (1 = drug program present; 0 = no drug program).

31.4.1.4 Delinquency

Delinquency consists of four items: (1) bringing a weapon to school, (2) drug use, (3) substance use at school, and (4) being suspended. Higher scores on these items indicate more frequent delinquent activity.

31.4.1.5 Social Bonds

"Attachment to school" consists of six items. High scores indicate strong attachment to three items (enjoying school, working hard, and finding school interesting) and weaker attachment for the remaining three items (hating school, finding work too challenging, and not getting it done). Items tapping "commitment to school" include: GPA, ambitions of graduating, going to college or to vocational school, as well as two items that include being held back a year and needing summer school. "School involvement" consists of participation in school-related publi-cations, athletics, performing arts, and other activities. Higher scores indicate greater participation.

31.4.1.6 Peer Associations

"Peer context" consists of seven items, including measures of friends who take drugs, pressure to do drugs, friends who have dropped out, and several items that indicate alienation and mischief at school (such as friends doing things to provoke a teacher, dislike of work, and so forth).

31.4.1.7 Absences from School

Finally, four items relate to "absences from school" such as being ill, skipping school altogether, cutting class periodically, or other reasons for being absent.

31.5 Findings

Consistent with our exploratory purposes, we present zero-order Pearson correlation coefficients and partial coefficients, which control for demographic characteristics. As is apparent in Table 31.1, these controls have little influence on the strength of the correlations. Most of the variables stand out as significant predictors of victimization at school. The strongest predictors of victimization appear to be the individual deviance and peer context variables. Actual substance abuse at school (e.g., alcohol consumption or taking other drugs) is the most salient of these, as are friendships with those who have pressured students to use drugs. Nevertheless, any degree of deviance or competition among students or their friends seems to relate to more victimization. In contrast, peer contexts that are more conventional in orientation, such as a social scene where there is opposition to cheating, tend to correspond with a lower risk of victimization.

The remaining predictors tend to have collectively lesser influence on victimization but are still statistically significant. Students who like school, who work hard, and who feel that what they do is interesting tend to report less victimization. Conversely, those who hate school, feel that it is too difficult, and fail to complete their work tend to experience more victimization. Commitment to school appears to matter also. Those with high GPAs and who have ambitions of graduating and going to college tend to be safer. In contrast, schoolchildren who experience educational setbacks by being held back a year, need to attend summer school, and intend to go to a vocational school have enhanced risks. Students who are absent from school, whether for illness, fear, or delinquent reasons, tend to experience higher levels

Table 31.1 Zero-Order and Partial Correlation Coefficients between Predictor Variables and Victimization (N = 2,999)

Item	Zero-Order Correlation	Partial Correlation
Demographics		
Older than 16	.02	—
Male	.14**	—
Black	.01	—
Commitment to school		
Grade point average	−.13**	−.12**
Plans to graduate H.S.	−.09**	−.08**
Attends vocational school	.05**	.04*
Ever held back	.07**	.06**
Ever needed summer school	.08**	.07**
Attachment to school		
Enjoys school	−.11**	−.10**
Hates school	−.10**	.10**
Does not do best work at school	−.16**	−.15**
Feels school is too hard	.06**	.07**
Feels school work is not interesting	−.06**	−.06**
Does not do homework	.17**	.16**
School involvement		
Participates in school publications	.01	.03
Participates in athletics	.01	.00
Participates in performing arts	−.02	.00
Participates in other activities	−.01	.02
Peer context		
Friends do drugs	.17**	.18**
Friends pressure student to do drugs	.22**	.21**

Table 31.1 Zero-Order and Partial Correlation Coefficients between Predictor Variables and Victimization (N = 2,999) (continued)

Item	Zero-Order Correlation	Partial Correlation
Much competition among fellow students to get good grades	.04*	.05**
Fellow students dislike cheating	−.09**	−.08**
Friends like to provoke teacher	−.14**	−.13**
Friends encourage bad behavior against teacher	.26**	.23**
Friends dropped out of school	.19**	.20**
Absences from school		
Illness	.09**	.11**
Cutting classes	.15**	.15**
Other reasons	.11**	.12**
School-related variables		
Attends drug education program	.01	.02
Feels unsafe at school	.18**	.20**
Feels unsafe going to/from school	.14**	.17**
Avoids school because it is unsafe	.18**	.11**
Delinquency		
Uses substances at school	.23**	.22**
Uses drugs away from school	.17**	.16**
Has brought gun to school	.14**	.13**
Was suspended from school	.20**	.18**
Acts up in school	.19**	.17**

* $p < .05$; ** $p < .01$. Partial correlations control for age, gender, and race.

of victimization. Perceptions that school is unsafe also consistently relate to more victimization. One exception is involvement in school-related activities, in which participation is not associated with changes in victimization risk. Similarly, schools with drug education programs do not make individual students safer from victimization.

31.6 Conclusion and Policy Implications

We began with the desire to conduct an exploratory analysis of the correlates of victimization in the school environment. Although victimization at school is not a common experience for students, it is widespread enough to make further research focusing on the school context worthwhile. The routine activities framework that researchers frequently rely on to make sense of victimization provides an empirically grounded explanation that should have relevance in the school context. We also turned to the concept of social bonds between the student and the school as another plausible source of influence. We acknowledge that there may be other interpretations for our results, but we also believe that some theoretically guided interpretation of our analyses is necessary so that readers may better understand the potential substantive importance of these findings.

Results clearly show that students do not, on average, share the same level of victimization risk. Many variables determine the likelihood of whether individual students will become victims of crime at school. The strongest predictors tend to be the delinquent tendencies of individual students, as well as the delinquency of their friends. This supports our explanation that having delinquent friends elevates exposure to motivated offenders and that individual deviance, as well as participation in crime with one's peer group, makes the student a more attractive target. Our proxy for exposure to motivated offenders at school (outside of one's peer group, at least), feelings that one is unsafe, likewise seemed to be associated with higher levels of victimization. Controlling for demographic variables did not substantially influence either of these or any of the predictors' correlation strengths.

Although attachment and commitment to school and school absences did not relate as strongly with victimization as did delinquency, peer context, and feelings of safety, they still had significant relationships with victimization. The results show that students who like school and put effort into their work tend to be safer than those who dislike school and find schoolwork too hard. Readers should be aware that since our analyses cannot resolve causal order, weak attachment to school might be a consequence of victimization as well as a source. Nevertheless these correlations support our claim that strong bonds could promote a sense of obligation to take precautions against victimization, as well as enhance guardianship and inhibit victimization-relevant daily activity. Students struggling in school (as measured by low grade point average, being held back a grade, and the need for summer school) tend to experience more victimization, as do those who have no ambitions of graduating or going to college. Finally, students who are in the habit of missing school, apparently for any reason, tend to have a higher risk of becoming a victim.

One interesting pattern is that involvement in school-related activities does not appear to relate to victimization risk, either for better or worse. One explanation for this finding could be that the participation measures are fairly broad, and not all school-related participation is necessarily supervised by an adult or would take the same amount of time. More specific and detailed measures of such activity could help elucidate which types of activities promote greater safety. Also, individual and school-related risk factors might transcend participation in school activity. Introducing appropriate controls for such risk factors may show that students who take part in school-sponsored activity might be safer.

Whereas these results appear to support a routine activities/social bonding approach to understanding student victimization, readers should be aware that our analysis is exploratory. We rely on a simple analysis, using zero-order and partial correlations, to identify salient variables that predict victimization. These correlations may yet be spurious when other controls are introduced. Moreover, many of the risk factors identified in this study might occur in the same people. Our analyses also rely on cross-sectional data, which means that we cannot determine the causal sequence between independent and dependent variables. We, therefore, rely on theory to guide our interpretation of the variables; other interpretations may also exist.

31.6.1 Policy Implications

Although our study is exploratory, it might be useful to speculate on the policy implications of this study. First, school administrators should benefit from the knowledge that many perpetrators of crime at school and victims are frequently found in the same pool of students.

Nevertheless, we can easily see school officials, and justice officials for that matter, in a quandary relating to which role will be likely occur next for a particular student — will the student assume the role as perpetrator of a crime or the role of a victim? School officials, faced with many competing responsibilities, could easily ignore delinquents as unworthy of guardianship and thus fail to protect those with unusually high chances of becoming a victim. Sparks (1982), in fact, reasoned that police authorities tend to discount crimes committed against delinquents, thus undermining their guardianship and making their victimization more likely.

For school policy makers, there may be an inordinate focus on discipline policies emphasizing strict sanctions for misconduct and visible target hardening. Apart from potentially weakening the bond between students and school, these programs are solely geared toward stopping offenders and do not address the risk factors for victimization. Instead, we concur with Felson (1998), who stated that schools could decrease on-campus crime by, among other things, designing the campus in order to improve surveillance, thus increasing the guardianship of potential victims. Additionally, schools might improve guardianship by striving to decrease hostility between educators and students; closer ties might promote a willingness among students to seek adult protection. In short, crime control efforts at school should also have a victim focus; addressing the offender deals with only part of the problem.

References

Crime rate in the Netherlands 1950–1993. *British Journal of Criminology, 39*, 401–415.

Casella, R. (2001). *At Zero Tolerance: Punishment, Prevention, and School Violence*. New York: Peter Lang Publishing.

Cohen, L.E. and Felson, M. (1979). Social change and crime rate trends: A routine activities approach. *American Sociological Review, 44*(4), 588–608.

Copes, H.A. (1999). Routine activities and motor vehicle theft. *Journal of Crime and Justice, 22*, 125–146.

Davoe, J.F., Peter, K., Kaufman, P., Ruddy, S.A., Miller, A.K., Planty, M., Snyder, D.T., and Rand, M.R. (2002). Indicators of School Crime and Safety, 2002. Washington, D.C.: U.S. Department of Education and Justice.

Felson, M. (1992). Routine activities and crime prevention: armchair concepts and practical action. *Studies on Crime and Crime Prevention, 1*(1), 30–34.

Felson, M. (1998). *Crime and Everyday Life.* Thousand Oaks, CA: Pine Forge.

Fisher, B.S., Sloan, J.J., Cullen, F.T., and Lu, C. (1998). Crime in the ivory tower: the level and sources of student victimization. *Criminology, 36,* 671–710.

Garofalo, J. (1987). Reassessing the lifestyle model of criminal victimization. In Gottfredson, M.R. and Hirschi, T. (Eds.), *Positive Criminology.* Thousand Oaks, CA: Sage. pp. 23–42.

Gottfredson, G.D. and Gottfredson, D.C. (1985). *Victimization in Schools.* New York: Plenum.

Hindelang, M.J., Gottfredson, M.R., and Garofalo, J. (1978). *Victims of Personal Crime: An Empirical Foundation for a Theory of Personal Victimization.* Cambridge, MA: Ballinger Press.

Horney, J., Osgood, D.W., and Marshall, I.H. (1995). Criminal careers in the short-term: intra-individual variability in crime and its relation to local life circumstances. *American Sociological Review, 60,* 655–673.

Jensen, G.F. and Brownfield, D.M. (1986). Gender, lifestyles, and victimization: beyond routine activity theory. *Violence and Victims, 1,* 85–99.

Juvonen, J. (2001). School violence: Prevalence, fears, and prevention. Issue Paper No. 219. Santa Monica, CA: Rand.

Lauritsen, J.L., Sampson, R.J., and Laub, J.H. (1991). Addressing the link between offending and victimization among adolescents. *Criminology, 29,* 265–291.

Lynch, J.P. (1987). Routine activity and victimization at work. *Journal of Quantitative Criminology, 3,* 283–300.

Madiz, E. (1996). Perception of risk in the workplace: A test of routine activity theory. *Journal of Criminal Justice, 24,* 407–418.

McElrath, K., Chitwood, D.D., Comerford, M. (1997). Crime victimization among injection drug users. *Journal of Drug Issues, 27,* 771–783.

Miethe, T.D. and Meier, R.F. (1994). Crime and its social context: toward an integrated theory of offenders, victims, and situations. Albany, New York: State University of New York Press.

Miethe, T.D., Stafford M.C., and Long J.S. (1987). Social differentiation in criminal victimization: a test of routine activities/lifestyles theories. *American Sociological Review, 52,* 184–194.

Mustaine, E. and Tewksbury, R. (1998). Predicting risks of larceny theft victimization: a routine activity analysis using refined lifestyle measures. *Criminology, 36*(4), 829–857.

Rosenbaum, D.P. (1987). Community crime prevention: a review and synthesis of the literature. *Justice Quarterly, 5,* 323–395.

Sampson, R.J. and Laub, J.H. (1993). *Crime in the Making.* Cambridge, MA: Harvard University Press.

Sampson, R.J. and Lauritsen, J.L. (1990). Deviant lifestyles, proximity to crime, and the offender-victim link in personal violence. *Journal of Research in Crime and Delinquency, 27*(2), 110–139.

Sampson, R.J. and Wooldredge, J.D. (1987). Linking the micro- and macro-dimensions of lifestyle-routine activity and opportunity models of predatory victimization. *Journal of Quantitative Criminology, 4,* 371–393.

Schreck, C.J., Wright R.A., and Miller J.M. (2002). A study of the individual and situational antecedents of violent victimization. *Justice Quarterly, 19,* 159–180.

Schreck, C.J., Miller, J.M., and Gibson, C. (2003). Trouble in the schoolyard: A study of the risk factors for victimization at school. *Crime and Delinquency, 49,* 460–484.

Singer, S.I. (1981). Homogeneous victim-offenders populations: a review and some research implications. *Journal of Criminal Law and Criminology, 72,* 779–788.

Snyder, H.N., and Sickmund, M. (1999). Juvenile Offenders and Victims: 1999 National Report. Washington, D.C.: U.S. Office of Juvenile Justice and Delinquency Prevention.

Sparks, R.F. (1982). Research on Victims of Crime. Washington, D.C.

Tewksbury, R. and Mustaine, E.E.(2000). Routine activities and vandalism: a theoretical and empirical study.

Thompson, C.Y. and Fisher, B.S. (1996). Predicting household victimization utilizing a multi-level routine activity approach. *Journal of Crime and Justice, 19,* 49–66.

Tremblay, M. and Tremblay, P. (1998). Social structure, interaction opportunities, and the direction of violent offenses. *Journal of Research in Crime and Delinquency, 35,* 245–267.

Tucker, N. (April 2001). Report says youth violence overplayed. *The Washington Post,* April 11, page B2.

Wallace, L.H. (2001). Reports from rural Mississippi: a look at school violence. *Journal of Security Administration, 24,* 15–32.

Welsh, W.N. (2001). Effects of student and school factors on five measures of school disorder. *Justice Quarterly, 18,* 911–947.

Welsh, W.N., Greene J.R., and Jenkins P.H. (1999). School disorder: the influence of individual, institutional, and community factors. *Criminology, 37,* 73–115.

Welsh, W.N., Stokes R., and Greene J.R. (2000). A macro-level model of school disorder. *Journal of Research in Crime and Delinquency, 37,* 243–283.

Chapter 32

Juvenile Justice: Answering the Question of Black Disproportionality

Everette B. Penn

32.1 Introduction

In 1988 the issue of the overrepresentation of minorities in the juvenile justice system became a federal issue. In that year Congress required states seeking Juvenile Justice and Delinquency Prevention (JJDP) formula grants to show programs and efforts initiated to reduce the numbers of their minority youths detained and confined in lockups, jails, detention, and other correctional facilities. Through a competitive process in 1991, five states were selected to pilot the disproportionate minority confinement (DMC) initiative. With pilot testing in Arizona, Florida, Iowa, North Carolina, and Oregon, the initiative assessed disproportionate confinement, and worked to design and implement corrective actions that could be used on a larger scale (Devine et al., 1998).

The Office of Juvenile Justice and Delinquency (OJJDP) defines disproportionate minority confinement as a situation in which "the proportion of juveniles detained, or confined in secure detention facilities, secure correctional facilities, jails and lockups who are members of minority groups ... exceeds the proportion such groups represented in the general population" (Devine et al., 1998).

Over the years, two major conclusions have come from DMC research. The first is that there is a selection bias in the juvenile justice system that is not racially or culturally neutral. The second is that overrepresentation of minorities is apparent throughout the juvenile justice system. This overrepresentation intensifies as minority juveniles continue through the system at various points such as arrest, detainment, petitioning, and the adjudicated outcome of cases (Devine et al., 1998; Hawkins et al., 2000; Joseph, 2000; Mann, 1994; Pope and Feyerherm, 1990).

There is no racial group that is more severely affected by overrepresentation in the juvenile justice system than African American youth. In every phase of the juvenile justice system African American youth are disproportionately involved (U.S. Department of Justice, 2001). This chapter answers the question of disproportionality from the perspective of black criminology. In examining the traditional criminological responses to African American overrepresentation, it becomes clear that the historical context of African Americans in the United States is missing. Such traditional responses discount the tumultuous past of African Americans in the U.S. Black criminology acknowledges this history and takes the terms African American, black, Negro, and colored as social constructs that affect the entry and processing of these youth into the juvenile justice system.

32.2 African Americans and the Juvenile Justice System

The categorization of people into racial groups gained significance in the 19th and 20th centuries with the publication of Charles Darwin's *On the Origin of Species* (1859). This pivotal text marked the beginning of a departure from a belief in witchcraft and the emergence of the classical theory of crime. From his study of plant and animal typology and classification emerged Social Darwinism, a theory in which races were ranked from inferior to superior (Reasons et al., 2002). Positivist works (Ferri, 1881; Garofalo, 1885; Lombroso, 1876) claimed that heredity, feeblemindedness, customs, and atavistic traits followed family lineages and racial groups. The term "natural crime" came to mean acts that all civilized societies would readily recognize as offensive (Williams and McShane, 1999). This notion of civilized and uncivilized was projected globally as Europeans "discovered" new lands in Africa, Asia, and North America, and throughout the world "civilized" whites dominated and conquered the uncivilized persons of red, yellow, brown, and black skin. Through domination, colonized West African nations became a pool of free labor for the Americas through a slave trade that instilled the dichotomy of black and white races into the law of the United States.

The acting out of white superiority continued in the 20th century with mass extermination of peoples, lynching, and segregation laws. In the United States, the stigma of being black was such that any person with even one drop of black blood in his or her family history was categorized as black regardless of the rest of their lineage or outward skin pigmentation (Bell, 2000).

32.3 Defining Black and White in the United States

In the United States today, blacks are defined as persons descended from any of the black racial groups of Africa (U.S. Office of Management and Budget, 1997). Comparably, whites are defined as persons descended from any of the original peoples of Europe, North Africa, or the Middle East (U.S. Office of Management and Budget, 1997). This socially constructed definition allows persons from the African countries of Algeria, Morocco, and Egypt to be categorized as white, no matter how dark their outward appearance may be. According to the 2000 U.S. census, 76 percent of the U.S. population is white and 12 percent is black, with 9 percent Hispanic, 3 percent Asian, and less than 1 percent Native Americans or from other groups.

According to the DMC definition, any proportion of blacks greater than 12 percent in a juvenile justice category would be problematic and disproportionate because it exceeds the general population proportion. A statistical trip through the juvenile justice system presents an abundantly clear picture of disproportionality.[1]

32.3.1 Arrests

For persons under 18, a total of 1,584,718 arrests were made in the United States in 1999 (U.S. Department of Justice, 2000). A total of

71.9 percent of the arrested youth were white and 25.1 percent were black. Blacks comprised 49 percent of those persons arrested for murder and nonnegligent manslaughter, compared to 47 percent for whites. Black youth also represented the modal category in robbery, with 54 percent of arrests compared to 43 percent for white youth. A comparison of property crime and violent crime statistics shows that whites comprised 69 percent of the arrests for property crimes and 57 percent of arrests for violent crimes, whereas blacks comprised 27 percent of property arrests and 41 percent of violent crime arrests.

32.3.2 Detained Prior to Court Disposition

Prior to having their case heard in court, 16.8 percent of white youth were detained in a facility. This compares with 22.8 percent of black youth detained (U.S. Department of Justice, 2001). A breakdown by type of crime shows that 20.5 percent of whites in violent cases were detained vs. 24 percent of blacks in such cases. White detainees represented 12.8 percent of the property cases as compared to a figure of 19.5 percent for blacks. Finally, 17.8 percent of the white youth in drug cases were detained, as compared to 34.6 percent of the black youth (U.S. Department of Justice, 2001).

32.3.3 Petitioned Cases

In following the *parens patriae* tradition of the juvenile courts, only 56.9 percent of all juvenile cases are petitioned (U.S. Department of Justice, 2001). Petitioning is a formal handling of a case, resulting in an official appearance in court and either a disposition being rendered in a juvenile court or a transfer to an adult court for processing. Of those cases petitioned, 63.4 percent found the youth delinquent and 0.8 percent were transferred to adult courts (U.S. Department of Justice, 2001). Overall, 53.8 percent of white cases were adjudicated delinquent as compared to 64.9 percent of black cases (U.S. Department of Justice, 2001). A comparison of the most serious proceedings possible for a delinquent youth shows that 0.7 percent of white petitioned cases were transferred to an adult court, whereas 1.0 percent of black petitioned cases were transferred (U.S. Department of Justice, 2001).

Table 32.1 Selected Juvenile Justice Points Compared by Race (1999)

Race (U.S. Population Percentage)	Violent Arrest (%)	Property Arrest (%)	Detained prior to Court (%)	Transferred to Adult Court (%)	Adjudicated Placement outside the Home (%)
Black (12)	41	27	22.8	1.0	29.5
White (76)	57	69	16.8	0.07	24.1

Source: From U.S. Department of Justice (2001). *Sourcebook of Criminal Justice Statistics 2000.* Washington, D.C.

32.3.4 *Adjudicated Cases*

The judging of a child delinquent creates an adjudicated case. There are four outcomes of an adjudicated case: (1) placement out of the home, (2) probation, (3) a fine or other court action, or (4) dismissal. Placement out of the home occurred in 25.8 percent of the adjudicated cases; probation occurred in 57.7 percent of cases; some type of fine, restitution, community service, or other service with little or no further court involvement occurred in 11.2 percent; and dismissal occurred in 5.2 percent of cases (U.S. Department of Justice, 2001).

A comparison of whites to blacks shows that dismissal occurred in 5 percent of the white cases as compared to 5.8 percent of the black cases (see Table 32.1). A fine, community service, restitution, etc., occurred in 12.9 percent of white cases and in only 7.5 percent of black cases. Placement on probation occurred in 58 percent of white cases and in 57.2 percent of black cases. Finally, placement outside the home occurred in 24.1 percent of white cases and in 29.5 percent of black adjudicated cases (U.S. Department of Justice, 2001).

A picture of disproportionality emerges from the juvenile justice data (see Table 32.1). Such disproportionality carries through into the adult system, with 58 percent of the persons under 18 to state prison in 1997 being black (U.S. Department of Justice, 2001). Furthermore, 47.5 percent of the prisoners under the jurisdiction of adult state and federal correctional authorities in 1997 were black and 40.7 percent were white (U.S. Department of Justice, 2001).

32.4 Origin of the American Juvenile Justice System

The juvenile justice system in the United States stems from an English *parens patriae* philosophy: "The king is the father of the country." The king, having ultimate power, became the guardian of the children and youth in his kingdom. Thus, the king was allowed to intervene in the lives of children and youth when necessary (Jackson and Knepper, 2003). This concept was imported to the United States and flourished, largely through the work of affluent women responding to the need for treatment of wayward youth in a developing, industrialized urban environment (Platt, 1977). The work of the child-savers peaked with the creation of the first juvenile court in Illinois in 1899 (Platt, 1977). The first court started with 6 paid probation officers and 16 Chicago police officers. In addition, there were 36 private citizens who at times supervised children on probation. Finally, there was one colored woman who worked without pay. Her task was to take charge of all the colored children (Platt, 1977). Thus, even in the founding of the juvenile court, separation between the races occurred.

32.5 Traditional Answers to Disproportionality in Juvenile Justice

When explaining black juvenile disproportionality, the traditional criminological response focuses on issues of economics, social disorganization, and bonding to middle-class values (Hawkins, 1993, 1995; Hirschi, 1969; Sampson, 1987; Shaw and McKay, 1931; Sutherland, 1947; Tonry, 1995). Stemming from the Chicago School, Shaw and McKay moved, in their analysis, from biological factors to social relationships and the concept of social disorganization (Williams and McShane, 1999). Delinquency occurs when there are elements of social disorganization: low economic status, different ethnic groups, mobile residents moving in and out of the neighborhood, and disrupted and broken families (Sampson and Groves, 1989).

Living in a socially disorganized neighborhood does not fully explain juvenile delinquency, because not all youth who live in these areas participate in delinquent behaviors. Thus, an explanation that includes individual choices is necessary. Traditionally, differential association theory and social bond theory are presented as the response. Differential association explains how behavior is learned in a social environment (Sutherland, 1947). Behavior is learned through an interaction occurring within an intimate personal group. Thus, the learning process is directed by motives and drives to create definitions favorable to law violation as opposed to law-abiding behavior (Sutherland, 1947). Because these differential associations vary in frequency, duration, priority, and intensity, the behavior-learning process is as individually variable as any other type of learning (Sutherland, 1947).

Social bonds present the final element of a traditional response to African American juvenile justice disproportionality. Bonding to society means a commitment to and belief in middle-class values (Hirschi, 1969). Persons with limited perceived and actual opportunities become frustrated when success does not follow their attempts to adhere to these social norms. This strain creates a new standard and adaptation for those black youth unable to attain middle-class values and goals (Durkeim, 1893; Merton,1957; Cohen, 1955). This adaptation involves delinquent behavior and a movement away from the traditional attachment, involvement, commitment, and belief (Hirschi, 1969).

With the proportionately larger numbers of black children living in socially disorganized environments, greater opportunities exist for adapting counter-middle-class values and social norms. This creates delinquency, and entry into and processing through the juvenile justice and criminal justice system, in numbers disproportionate to whites. Social disorganization is seen as the seed that lies behind explanations of lack of adequate legal representation, detainment before adjudication, petitioning, placement outside the home, and transfer to adult courts (Bishop and Frazier, 1996; Feld, 1989; Podkopacz and Feld; 1996; Sampson and Laub, 1993; Synder and Sickmound, 1995)

This traditional answer appears to be sound but has three major flaws. The first is that it fails to address the causal factors of social disorganization in black neighborhoods. Second, it fails to adequately address the degree of disproportionality of black juveniles throughout the system. Finally, there is no allowance for the social construct of "being black" in a nation with an abundant history of racial strife and segregation of minority groups, especially black Americans. Black criminology provides a useful philosophical foundation for answering the question of black juveniles' disproportionality in the juvenile justice system.

32.6 Black Criminology

Black criminology goes beyond the race variable to produce a black paradigm. It looks to study "black" as a socially constructed variable in order to explain or refute disproportionality. Black criminology builds upon traditional criminology in order to become solidified into a recognized subfield (George-Abeyie, 1989, 1990; Russell, 1992; Young and Sulton, 1994).

Black criminology presents the common history that many black people in America share. It is a history filled with slavery, segregation, lynching, Jim Crow laws, stereotyping, prejudice, discrimination, and racial profiling. History has firmly cemented the label of an inferior race. Such a history easily creates an American social reality of black people being atavistic and part of a criminal element. In turn, frustration and alienation may lead some blacks to adopt a counterculture that includes delinquency and crime.

Unlike traditional theories, the social construct of being black is the initiating variable that spawns into issues of social disorganization, labor, resources, wealth, and different treatment in the criminal justice system. The major tenet of black criminology is that there is a social reality of being black in the United States, which has an effect on the labeled persons inside and outside the justice system.

32.7 Social Disorganization in the Black Community

Social disorganization is a dominant factor in the lives of many black children and youth. The official poverty level for 2001 was $11,569 for a two-person household, $14,128 for a three-person household, and $18,104 for a four-person household (U.S. Census, 2002). Just over 12 percent of white children live in a family below the poverty level (U.S. Census, 2002). Thirty percent of black children are raised in poverty (U.S. Census, 2002). Thus, in proportional terms, almost three times as many black than white children live in poverty and experience the social disorganization that accompanies it.

Traditional family and middle-class values are an additional area of disparity between whites and blacks. In 2000, 68.5 percent of African American children were born out of wedlock, compared to 27.1 percent of white children (U.S. Census, 2002). This translates into 49 percent of black children and 17 percent of white children living only with their mother (U.S. Census, 2002). The birth circumstances and living situation of children becomes an important factor because of the direct correlation to poverty. A black female in the United States earns $16,282 annually compared to $16,652 for a white female (U.S. Census, 2002). This is less than the $21,466 annually earned by black males and the $30,240 earned by white males (U.S. Census, 2002). It is significantly less than the possible income of both a mother and father in the household. A black family with both parents working would produce $37,748 annually as compared to $46,892 for a white family (U.S. Census, 2002). On the average, a black mother rearing a child alone has an income of just over $16,000 per year. This is a mere $416 per month above the poverty level for a family of two (U.S. Census, 2002). According to Hawkins et al. (2000), such living arrangements lead to female-headed households exhibiting significantly higher levels of violence among youth in the home. The correlation between the high number of black female-headed households and delinquency has been attributed to the belief that such families are dysfunctional and unable to provide proper supervision (Gottfredson and Hirschi, 1990; Hirschi, 1969).

African American youth have the highest number of arrests for murder and nonnegligent manslaughter (U.S. Department of Justice, 2001). These violent crimes carry severe penalties and possible petitioning to adult courts. Even after taking into account controls for type of arrest and comparison of similar circumstances in and out of the juvenile justice system, there still remains an unexplained factor of disproportionality, which lends support to the notion that the unexplained factor is race (Blumstein, 1993; Leiber and Stairs, 1999; Leonard et al., 1995; Pope and Feyerherm, 1990; Sampson and Laub, 1993; Tonry, 1995). Black criminology makes use of existing research to look back at the aspects that have gone into the creation of the social construct of being black in the United States.

32.8 The Development of Black Social Disorganization and Delinquency

Blacks have not always been disproportionately represented in the juvenile justice and criminal justice systems. Before the Civil War, blacks were underrepresented in crime statistics (Young, 1994). W.E.B. Du Bois wrote in 1901 that slavery presented a system in which "there was no crime of any consequence among Negroes" (Gabbidon, Greene, and Young, 2002, p. 83). Because Negroes were considered "property," without the protections and privileges of citizens, their control and handling were at the whim of their white masters, thus eliminating the use of the criminal justice system (Gabbidon, Greene, and Young, 2002). After the emancipation of all blacks from slavery, there was a great migration away from a Jim Crow South to northern urban areas, where blacks hoped to find decent wages (Frazier, 1939). This migration resulted in large numbers of northern blacks living in socially disorganized areas (Wilson, 1987).

For the blacks who stayed in the South, a convict lease system developed (Du Bois, 1901). This system allowed private citizens to hire prison labor. Writing in 1901, Du Bois stated that over 70 percent of Southern prisoners were black. He further stated that these blacks were more easily convicted and received longer sentences (Du Bois, 1901). The convict lease system resembled slavery as the forced labor of a large black population provided low-cost labor to a white southern agriculture economy.

32.9 Child Saving or Child Slaving?

Believing that the child-saving movement was not intended for black children, Ward (2001, p. 47) states that "the rehabilitation of black delinquents was a contradiction in terms." Just as the black man was "invisible," so too was the black child (Ellison, 1952). Traditionally, black children as a group were seen as undeveloped adults who could perform the menial tasks of adults but were incapable of thinking or acting as developed adults in society. A black child in the antebellum South was to become a "good nigger," which had very specific economic, political, and cultural connotations (Ward, 2001). Child saving of black youth in antebellum Mississippi was viewed as a waste of money because there was no use trying to reform a Negro (Oshinsky, 1996). The issue of differential treatment was not confined to the South. During the reform movement, northern reformatories were originally open only to whites, until there developed a need for someone to perform household duties (Ward, 2001). White boys were taught useful occupations, whereas black boys were put to work on meaningless tasks in support of the institutions (Mennel, 1973). Black youth consequently stayed in houses of refuge longer than whites, who gained skills that could be applied to apprenticeships in the community (Ward, 2001). Such practices created a condition of child saving for whites, and "child slaving" for blacks. This slaving comes about through structural oppression and a societal belief in the black race being inferior to the white (Tatum, 2000).

By socially controlling an undesirable element of society in the juvenile justice system, their mainstream evolution can be stunted. The stigmatizing of blacks as a perceived serious threat to public safety is a phenomenon called *Blackophobia* (Gabbidon, 1994). Fears of being robbed, assaulted, or otherwise victimized are typically centered around a picture of a black man or woman as the assailant. Wilson (1990) explains that the ultimate outrage for a white man is for his white woman to be sexually victimized by a black man. This fear is a frequent theme that perpetrates the criminalizing of the race.

In controlling this undesired, and often feared, population, the postemancipation history of the United States is filled with hundreds of examples of night and day raids that ended in lynching of blacks who were deemed out of control by angry mobs (Gabbidon et al., 2002). Shortly after emancipation, the then-governor of South Carolina, Ben Tillman, speaking under a tree from which eight blacks had been lynched in 1 year alone, stated that he would lead a mob to lynch a Negro who had raped a white woman (Gabbidon et al., 2002). Blackophobia, and the media's acceptance of it, allowed the nation to be sympathetic to Susan Smith from South Carolina who in 1994 claimed a black man carjacked her and drove off with her two sons. Nine days after the questioning of several black men in the area, it was found that Smith had drowned her children in a nearby lake (Russell, 1998).

Blackophobia is entrenched in the media, and in the political arena. As recently as 1948, Strom Thurmond was able to run for president of the United States on a platform that called for the "segregation of races." He received 39 electoral votes including those of the state of Mississippi (Goodgame and Tumulty, 2002). A hope that such archaic beliefs had disappeared from the political arena of the United States vanished when Thurmond was praised in 2002 by U.S. Senate Majority Leader Trent Lott as a man to be proud of. "And if the rest of the country followed our [Mississippi] lead, we wouldn't have had all these problems over these years" (Goodgame and Tumulty, 2002, p. 21).

32.10 Continuing a Social Disorganizational Cycle

Racial alienation has produced, and continues to produce, black urban areas filled with decay and social disorganization. A large, mostly black, urban underclass ghetto has appeared (Wilson, 1987). Other racial and ethnic groups developed ghettos, but tended to develop businesses and move on to more affluent neighborhoods (Wilson, 1987). Blacks continued to come to urban areas, despite the change of the American city from a goods-producing environment that was once filled with manufacturing jobs for unskilled workers, to a service-producing economy (Wilson, 1987). Those that could move out of the cities did so in vast numbers. This mass exodus of middle- and working-class families left a void and removed the "social buffer" that guards against elements of social disorganization in urban neighborhoods (Wilson, 1987). Thus, many black children no longer see or emulate practices of the mainstream culture, and the counterculture or "code of the streets" becomes the social norm (Anderson, 1994).

The "streets" produce a culture that values physical toughness so highly that it exists as an external entity which must always be guarded and can be easily lost (Anderson, 1994). Physical ability, fighting, and gun violence are ways to win and keep respect. In these neighborhoods the black youth's ability to fight and win are valuable status symbols that give the youth "juice" (Anderson, 1990, 1994; Canada, 1995; Prothrow-Stith, 1991). Such violence may result in serious injury or even death, as witnessed by the high number of black arrests for assault, murder, and nonnegligent homicide (U.S. Department of Justice, 2001), thus producing a high number of black-on-black homicides in the black community (Loya et al., 1986).

The ease with which violence occurs (and ultimately ends in homicide) can be attributed to the devaluing of a black life (Hawkins, 1983), as seen throughout American history. Slave masters could whip, maim, and even kill disobedient slaves without fear of reprisal from the criminal justice system (Hawkins, 1983). The exact opposite was the case for a black killing of a white person. Through an examination of homicide cases and proceedings, Hawkins (1983) developed a 13-point scale ranking types of homicides involving blacks and whites. The least serious offense was a white killing a black known to the white person intimately. The most serious offense was a black killing a white in authority. This leniency can be attributed to the devaluing of a black life by the assailant, and a more lenient punishment in the juvenile justice or criminal justice system because an inferior being was removed (Hawkins, 1983).

Black children are made aware of their "inferior" status at a very young age. In numerous studies with black children (some under the age of five), skin-color sensitivity led most to choose a white doll instead of a black doll (Clark, K. and Clark, M., 1947; Goodman, 1952; Morland, 1969). Many black children learn early, through media and through a self-assessment of their own living conditions, that beauty, status, and success come with white skin (Kvaraceus, 1965). A review of literary definitions shows how deeply entrenched black/white value contrasts are in the English language. Black is defined as soiled, wicked, or evil, the opposite of white. The white definition yields words such as pure, clean, spotless, clear, and of favorable appearance (Webster, 1989).

A black history in the United States flooded with blatant examples of perceived inferiority, poor economic conditions, and social disorganization creates an environment in which the "street culture" fills the void in a young person's life. For the girl, being a part of the "streets" may mean early motherhood (Anderson, 1990). This serves as a consolation prize for the valued rewards that may be obtained in the traditional culture. Academic success, sports, clubs, organization involvement, college entrance, and other socially normal activities of a teenager disappear as possibilities as the newly created life infuses a state of value in the mind of a girl living in the "street culture" (Anderson, 1990). The all-important peer group becomes a social support group in which the competition centers around comparing the baby's cuteness, features, skin color, grooming, and expensive dresses (Anderson, 1990).

For the male in these "street cultures," sexual exploits increase one's "juice." The woman's body is to be conquered in a sexual game. The "rap" of the male includes his ability to talk to girls, his dress, grooming, looks, and his dancing ability. Responding to media images of the higher society, the "street culture" girl looks for a male who will love her and provide her a middle-class lifestyle. The male, knowing this, raps a story of love and promises. The two engage in sexual intercourse, and the male's rap has been successful. If a baby is created, the male denies responsibility and may be supported by his family and friends in his denial (Anderson, 1994). Because of a father's lack of financial foundation, and a poorly educated and unskilled mother, another black child is raised in social disorganization.

32.11 Conclusion

Alienation, disbelief in middle-class values, counterculture adaptation, and internalization of the most vile characteristics of social disorganization create a "street culture" that is disproportionately present in the black community, thus creating the disproportionality of black youth entering the juvenile justice system. The creation of a social reality that black youth are inferior and undesirable creates disproportionality in the juvenile justice system. Future research should focus on the process of changing the social reality of being black in the United States. As presented earlier, the social construct of being black and its negative meaning are found literally in the English language, the history of the United States, the political arena, and the juvenile and criminal justice systems. A greater understanding of how this social construct remains vibrant throughout all facets presents a starting point to reducing black disproportionality in the juvenile justice system.

References

Anderson, E. (1990). *Street Wise: Race, Class, and Change in an Urban Community*. Chicago, IL: University of Chicago Press.

Anderson, E. (May 1994). The Code of the Streets. *The Atlantic Monthly*, 80–94.

Bell, D. (2000). *Race, Racism and American Law*. New York: Aspen Law and Business.

Bishop, D. and Frazer, C. (1996). Race effects in juvenile justice decision-making: findings of a statewide analysis. *Journal of Criminal Law and Criminology, 86*(2), 392–413.

Blumstein, A. (1993). Making rationality relevant. *Criminology, 31,* 1–16.

Canada, G. (1995). Fist, Stick, Knife, Guns. Boston, MA: Beacon Press.

Cohen, A. (1955). *Delinquent Boys*. New York: Free Press.

Clark, K. and Clark, M. (1947). Racial identification and preference in Negro children. In Newcomb, T. and Hartley, E. (Eds.), *Readings in Social Psychology*. New York: Holt.

Darwin, C. (1859). *The Origin of Species*. Cambridge, MA: Harvard University Press (reprinted 1964).

Devine, P., Coolbaugh, K., and Jenkins, S. (1998). Disproportionate Minority Confinement: Lessons Learned from Five States. Washington, D.C.: U.S. Department of Justice, Office of Justice Programs, Office of Juvenile Justice and Delinquency Prevention.

Du Bois, W.E.B. (1901). *The Black North in 1901: A Social Study*. New York: Arno Press.

Durkheim, E. (1893). *The Division of Labor in Society*. New York: Free Press (reprinted and translated 1933).

Ellison, R. (1952). *Invisible Man*. New York: Random House.

Feld, B. (1989). The right to counsel in juvenile court: an empirical study of when lawyers appear and the difference they make. *Journal of Criminal Law and Criminology, 79*(4), 1185–1346.

Ferri, E. (1881). *Criminal Sociology*. Trans. Joseph Killey and John Lisle. Boston, MA: Little Brown (reprinted 1917).

Frazier, E. (1939). *The Negro Family in the United States*. Chicago, IL: University of Chicago Press.

Gabbidon, S. (1994). Blackaphobia: what is it and who are its victims. In Kedia, P. (Ed.), *Black on Black Crime: Facing Facts-Challenging Fictions*. Bristol, IN: Wyndham Hall Press.

Gabbidon, S., Greene, H., and Young, V. (2002). *African American Classics in Criminology and Criminal Justice.* Thousand Oaks, CA: Sage.

Garofalo, R. (1885). *Criminology.* Trans. Robert W. Millar. Boston, MA: Little Brown (reprinted 1914).

George-Abeyie, D. (1990). The myth of a racist criminal justice system? In MacLean, B. and Milovanovic, D. (Eds.), *Racism, Empiricism, and Criminal Justice* (pp. 11–14). Vancouver: Collective Press.

George-Abeyie, D. (1989). Race, ethnicity, and the spatial dynamic: toward a realistic study of black crime, crime victimization, and criminal justice processing of blacks. *Social Justice 16*(4), 35–54.

Goodgame, D. and Tumulty, K., (December 23, 2002). Tripped Up by History. *Time,* 22–29.

Goodman, M. (1952). *Race Awareness in Young Children.* Cambridge, MA: Addison-Wesley.

Gottfredson, M. and Hirschi, T. (1990). *A General Theory of Crime.* Stanford, CA: Stanford University Press.

Hawkins, D. (1983). Black and white homicide differentials: alternatives to an adequate theory. *Crime and Delinquency, 31,* 83–103.

Hawkins, D. (1993). Crime and ethnicity. In Forst, B. (Ed.), *The Socio-Economics of Crime and Justice* (pp. 89–120). Armonk, New York: M.E. Sharpe.

Hawkins, D. (1995). Ethnicity, race and crime: a review of selected studies. In Hawkins, D. (Ed.), *Ethnicity, Race and Crime: Perspectives across Time and Place* (pp. 11–45). Albany, New York: State University of New York Press.

Hawkins, D., Laub, J., Lauritsen, J., and Cothern, L. (2000). *Race, Ethnicity and Serious and Violent Juvenile Offending.* Washington, D.C.: U.S. Department of Justice, Office of Justice Programs, Office of Juvenile Justice and Delinquency Prevention.

Hirschi, T. (1969). *Causes of Delinquency.* Berkeley, CA: University of California Press.

Jackson, M. and Knepper, P. (2003). *Delinquency and Justice.* Boston, MA: Ally and Bacon.

Joseph, J. (2000). Overrepresentation of minority youth in the juvenile justice system: discrimination or disproportionality of delinquent acts? In Markowitz, M. and Jones-Brown, D. (Eds.), *The System in Black and White: Exploring the Connections Between Race, Crime and Justice* (pp. 227–240). Westport, CT: Praeger.

Kvaraceus, W. (1965). *The Negro Self-Concept: Implications for School and Citizenship.* New York: McGraw-Hill.

Leonard, K., Pope, C., and Feyerherm, W. (Eds.) (1995). *Minorities in Juvenile Justice.* Thousand Oaks, CA: Sage.

Leiber, M.J. and Stairs, J. (1999). Race, contexts, and the use of intake diversion. *Journal of Research in Crime and Delinquency,* 36, 56–86.

Lombroso, C. (1876). *The Criminal Man.* Milan: Hoepli.

Loya, F., Garcia, P., Sullivan, J., Vargas, L., Allen, N., and Mercy, J. (1986). Conditional risks of type of homicide among Anglo, Hispanic, black, and Asian victims in Los Angeles, 1970–1979. In *Report of the Secretary's Task Force on Black and Minority Health: Vol. V* (pp. 117–133). Washington, D.C.

Mann, C. (1994). A minority view of juvenile justice. *Washington and Lee Law Review, 51,* 468–472.

Mennel, R. (1973). *Thorns and Thistles: Juvenile Delinquents in the United States, 1825–1940.* Hanover: University Press of New England.

Merton, R. (1957). *Social Theory and Social Structure* (rev. ed.). New York: Free Press.

Morland, J. (1969). Race Awareness among American and Hong Kong Chinese Children. *American Journal of Sociology, 75,* 360–374.

Oshinsky, D. (1996). *Worse than Slavery: Parchman Farm and the Ordeal of Jim Crow Justice.* New York: Free Press.

Platt, A. (1977). *The Child Savers: Invention of Delinquency* (2nd ed.). Chicago, IL: University of Chicago.

Podkopacz, M., and Feld, B. (1996). The end of the line: an empirical study of judicial waiver. *Journal of Criminal Law and Criminology, 86*(2), 449-492.

Pope, C. and Feyerherm, W. (1990). Minority status and juvenile justice processing: an assessment of the research literature (Parts I and II). *Criminal Justice Abstracts,* June. 327–385; September. 527–542.

Prothrow-Stith, D. (1991). *Deadly Consequences.* New York: Harper Collins.

Reasons, C., Conley, D., and Debro, J. (2002). *Race, Class, Gender, and Justice in the United States.* Boston, MA: Allyn and Bacon.

Russell, K. (1998). *The Color of Crime.* New York: New York University Press.

Russell, K. (1992). The development of black criminology and the role of the black criminologists. *Justice Quarterly 9*(4), 667–683.

Sampson, R. (1987). Urban black violence: the effect of male joblessness and family disruption. *American Journal of Sociology, 93*(2), 348–382.

Sampson, R. and Laub, J. (1993). Structural variations in juvenile court processing: inequality, the underclass, and social control. *Law and Sociology Review, 27,* 285–311.

Sampson, R. and Groves, W. (1989). Community structure and crime: testing social disorganization theory. *American Journal of Sociology, 94,* 774–802.

Shaw, C. and McKay, H. (1931). Report on the Causes of Crime. Vol. 2: Social Factors in Juvenile Delinquency National Commission on Law Observance and Enforcement, Report No. 13. Washington, D.C.

Snyder, H. and Sickmund, M. (1995). Juvenile Offenders and Victims: A National Report. Washington, D.C.: Office of Juvenile Justice and Delinquency Prevention.

Sutherland, E. (1947). *Principles of Criminology* (4th ed.). Philadelphia, PA: Lippincott.

Tatum, B. (2000). *Crime, Violence and Minority Youths*. Brookfield, VT: Ashgate.

Tonry, M. (1995). *Malign Neglect: Race, Crime and Punishment in America*. New York: Oxford University Press.

U.S. Census Bureau (2002). *Population and Household Economic Topics*. Retrieved June 6, 2004: http://www.census.gov/population.html.

U.S. Department of Justice (2001). *Sourcebook of Criminal Justice Statistics 2000*. Washington, D.C.

U.S. Office of Management and Budget (October 30, 1997). Revisions to the standards for classification of federal data on race and ethnicity. *Federal Register 62*, 368–374.

Ward, G. (2001). Color Lines of Social Control: Juvenile Justice Administration in a Racialized Social System, 1825–2000. Doctoral dissertation, University of Michigan (UMI 3029453).

Webster (1989). *New World Thesaurus*. New York: Warner Books.

Williams, F. and McShane, M. (1999). *Criminological Theory* (3rd ed.). Upper Saddle River, NJ: Prentice Hall.

Wilson, A. (1990). *Black-on-Black Violence: The Psychodynamics of Black self-Annihilation in Service of White Domination*. New York: Afrikan World Infosystems.

Wilson, W. (1987). *The Truly Disadvantaged: The Inner City, the Underclass and Public Policy*. Chicago: University of Chicago Press.

Young, V. (1994). The politics of disproportionality. In Sulton, A. (Ed.), *African-American Perspectives On: Crime Causation, Criminal Justice Administration and Crime Prevention*. Englewood, CO: Sulton Books.

Young, V. and Sulton, A. (1994). Excluded: the current status of african-american scholars in the field of criminology and criminal justice. In Sulton, A. (Ed.), *African-American Perspectives on Crime Causation, Criminal Justice Administration, and Crime Prevention*. Englewood, CO: Sulton Books.

Notes

1. It is important to keep in mind that Hispanics are categorized as white in most statistics (U.S. Department of Justice, 2001).

Chapter 33

Kids, Cops, and School-Based Drug Prevention: The Legacy of Drug Abuse Resistance Education (DARE)

David Mueller

33.1 Introduction

In 2002 Project DARE (drug abuse resistance education) marked its 20-year anniversary as a school-based drug education program. Established in 1983 in the wake of the much-maligned "just say no" program, DARE continues to enjoy widespread support from a variety of influential stakeholders including parents, teachers, elected officials, and the law enforcement community. Despite its popularity, however, recent scholarly evaluations of the program indicate that DARE is not particularly effective in preventing adolescent drug use. In light of these negative evaluations, this chapter seeks to identify the reasons behind DARE's continued popularity and to show how administrators have shielded the program from critics both inside and outside academe. This chapter begins by reviewing some recent data on the "war on drugs" and its impact on juvenile drug use. The chapter goes on to show that although many Americans support aggressive supply-side drug enforcement policies, they also believe that proactive demand reduction efforts such as DARE are an attractive alternative to arrest. The chapter concludes with a discussion about DARE's apparent immunity to scholarly criticism and points up a few of the more thorny challenges facing researchers in the field of program evaluation.

33.2 One Step Forward, Two Steps Back

In spite of the government's ongoing battle against illegal drug use in the United States, both official and self-reported crime data indicate that the "war on drugs" has made little substantive progress in the past decade. In 2001, police made an estimated 13.7 million arrests nationwide (Federal Bureau of Investigation, 2002, p. 232). Of these, more than 3 million arrests were for drug- and alcohol-related offenses, including drug abuse violations and driving under the influence (Federal Bureau of Investigation, 2002, p. 233).[1] More troubling is the fact that some 50 to 80 percent of adult males arrested test positive for some form of illegal drug use (U.S. Department of Justice, 2001). Although drug- and alcohol-related offenses are fairly common in the United States, these problems are particularly intractable among juveniles and young adults.

Between 1992 and 2001 arrests for driving under the influence (DUI) decreased by nearly 16 percent among persons over the age of 18 but increased by more than 34 percent among persons under the age of 18. Across this same time period, arrests for drug abuse violations increased by 33 percent among persons over the age of 18 and by more than 121 percent among juveniles under the age of 18 (Federal Bureau of Investigation 2002, p. 238).

To the casual observer, an increase in the number of drug-related arrests is usually seen as an indication of "progress." For example, a Gallup poll taken in April 2001 shows that nearly half (47 percent) of Americans felt that some degree of progress had been made in the nation's efforts to cope with illegal use of drugs in the past year (Maguire and Pastore, 2001, p. 131). Yet, scholars have long recognized that official arrest data such as these are only the proverbial tip of the iceberg. That is, they represent only those violations that came to the attention of law enforcement. Many offenses, particularly illegal drug use, go undetected. Thus, to better understand this so-called dark figure of crime, it is critical that researchers draw on self-reported data in their efforts to gauge the extent of illegal drug use nationwide.

According to a recent self-report study by the National Household Survey on Drug Abuse (NHSDA), 41 percent of Americans admitted to using an illegal substance at some point in their lifetime (U.S. Department of Health and Human Services, 2001). Estimates on lifetime drug use, however, are misleading insofar as they tell us only that an individual has tried an illegal drug once. Measures of more prevalent drug use are estimated by asking respondents if they have used an illegal drug in the past year or in the past 30 days. Here, NHSDA data show that more than 12 percent of all Americans (or some 34 million people) used an illegal substance in the past year and more than 7 percent (or some 20 million people) used an illegal drug in the past 30 days.

Data on the extent of teenage drug use are gleaned primarily from self-report studies conducted in schools. The Monitoring the Future (MTF) study, for example, provides a wealth of self-reported data on the drug-related behaviors of eighth-, tenth-, and twelfth-grade students each year. Longitudinally speaking, MTF data show a general reduction in drug consumption by high school seniors between the late 1970s and the early 1990s. In the early 1990s, however, student drug consumption began to rise again (Johnston et al., 2002). Three out of four high school seniors in the graduating class of 2001 claimed that they hung around with people who "get high" (Johnston et al., 2002). Another study by the National Center on Addiction and Substance Abuse at Columbia University (2001, p. 11) found that more than half (60 percent) of high school seniors claim that drugs are used, kept, or sold at their schools. Not surprisingly, many teens today see drugs as the most important problem facing people their age (National Center on Addiction and Substance Abuse at Columbia University, 2002, p. 29).

So what effect has the drug war had on teenagers' use of proscribed drugs? Are they using substantially more or fewer drugs today? To offer some insight into these questions, Table 33.1 compares 1991 and 2001 MTF data on a select number of illegal drugs. Unfortunately, these data are not very promising, as they appear to indicate that drug use, at least among high school seniors, has risen substantially.

Table 33.1 shows clearly that alcohol, cigarettes, and marijuana are among the three most commonly used substances among high school seniors. What is also clear from this truncated comparison is that, with

Table 33.1 Percentage of High School Seniors Claiming to Have Used Illegal Drugs

| | Period of Use | | | | | |
| | Lifetime | | Past Year | | Past 30 d | |
Drug	1991	2001	1991	2001	1991	2001
Any illicit drug	44.1	53.9	29.4	41.4	16.4	25.7
Alcohol	88.0	79.7	77.7	73.3	54.0	49.8
Has Been Drunk	65.4	63.9	52.7	53.2	31.6	32.7
Cigarettes	63.1	61.0	NA	NA	28.3	29.5
Marijuana/Hashish	36.7	49.0	23.9	37.0	13.8	22.4
LSD	8.8	10.9	5.2	6.6	1.9	2.3
Amphetamines	15.4	16.2	8.2	10.9	3.2	5.6
Methamphetamines	NA	6.9	NA	3.9	NA	1.5
Cocaine	7.8	8.2	3.5	4.8	1.4	2.1
Crack	3.1	3.7	1.5	2.1	0.7	1.1
Heroin	0.9	1.8	0.4	0.9	0.2	0.4

Note: NA = not available.

Source: From Johnston, L., O'Malley, P., and Bachman, J. (2002). *Monitoring the Future: National Survey Results on Drug Use*, 1975–2001. Ann Arbor, MI: Institute for Social Research.

only two isolated exceptions (lifetime alcohol use and being drunk), drug use by high school seniors has increased over the past decade. More than 73 percent of all high school seniors surveyed claimed that they had used alcohol in the past year, and nearly one in three admitted to being drunk in the past 30 days. Additionally, about half of all seniors surveyed claimed that they had smoked marijuana at least once in their lifetime, and nearly one in four said they had smoked marijuana in the past 30 days. These data, crude as they are, indicate that the drug war has actually lost ground over the past 11 years. This finding is all the more disconcerting in light of the fact that federal expenditures for domestic drug enforcement activities have doubled in the past decade.

33.3 Where Drug War Dollars Are (and Are Not) Going

In 1991, federal budgetary allocations for domestic drug enforcement activities (not including international eradication and domestic interdiction efforts) were in excess $4.6 billion (Maguire and Pastore, 2001, p. 15). By 2001, this figure had more than doubled to $9.8 billion. These data, of course, do not include state and local drug enforcement expenditures, nor do they include tax dollars needed to process and house convicted drug offenders. Whereas the federal budget for domestic drug enforcement has more than doubled in the past 10 years, federal expenditures for demand reduction programs (which includes both prevention and treatment programs) have increased by a paltry $2 billion (up from $3.7 billion in 1991 to approximately $5.7 billion in 2001).

Public opinion polls show that many Americans support drug enforcement activities. A poll conducted in March 2001 by the Pew Research Center shows that 82 percent of Americans believed that arresting drug sellers would be either very effective or at least somewhat effective in controlling the drug problem (Maguire and Pastore, 2001, p. 131). Substantially fewer Americans (64 percent) felt that arresting drug users would be an effective deterrent. However, despite the apparent public support for "arresting" the drug problem, 79 and 76 percent of Americans, respectively, felt that drug treatment and drug education programs could be an effective solution to the nation's drug problem.

Theoretically speaking, demand reduction programs such as DARE have a simple and intuitive appeal. Children who are taught to avoid drugs at an early age are expected to mature into drug-free adults. With fewer people using illegal drugs, fewer resources would be needed for drug enforcement, and police agencies would be freer to engage in more proactive crime prevention efforts. If these prevention efforts were successful, fewer people would go to prison and correctional officials could, in turn, use a larger portion of their budgets for more aggressive rehabilitation programs for the remaining offenders. All of these positive outcomes, however, are predicated on the assumption that demand reduction efforts are (or could be) effective. DARE is among the most widely recognized demand reduction programs in existence today. So how does it work? More important, does it work?

33.4 Drug Abuse Resistance Education (DARE)

Many states today require drug education as part of the basic academic curriculum in schools. One of the best-known and most widely adopted drug education programs today is DARE. Though DARE is often discussed as a single unified program, it is actually a compilation of several different programs. The most widely recognized DARE program operating today is the elementary school curriculum, which consists of 17 weeks of drug education for fifth- and/or sixth-grade students. This curriculum is delivered by uniformed police officers and incorporates a wide range of teaching techniques including question-and-answer sessions, role-playing, group discussions, and workbook exercises. The goal of the elementary school curriculum is to prevent adolescent drug use by making students aware of the potential health risks associated with drug use and to heighten their awareness about drug refusal skills.

DARE programs have also been developed for older students. The middle school curriculum, for example, provides students with information on how to resist negative peer pressure and how to resolve conflicts without resorting to violence, drugs, or alcohol. There is also a high school component that is designed to help teens make prudent decisions when faced with high-risk situations.

DARE has also developed two other peripheral programs including the Parent Program and DARE + PLUS (Play and Learn Under Supervision). The Parent Program is designed to help parents identify warning signs indicative of adolescent drug use and to help parents enhance their children's sense of self-esteem. DARE + PLUS is a less structured program that provides after-school supervision and recreational activities for latchkey kids. Despite the addition of these recent DARE "spin-offs," the most widely recognized and most studied of all the DARE programs remains the basic elementary school program.

Since its inception in 1983, DARE has been exported to approximately 80 percent of school districts nationwide, and is estimated to reach some 36 million students each year (Miller, 2001). Although many consider DARE to be a cornerstone in the nation's adolescent drug prevention strategy, recent scholarly evaluations of the program have raised serious questions about its effectiveness (Gottfredson, 1997; Rosenbaum and Hanson, 1998; Rosenbaum et al., 1994).

One of the earliest and least sophisticated evaluations of the program (DeJong, 1987) found that students who were exposed to DARE showed no significant differences in drug knowledge or attitudes toward drugs, or in self-concept ratings, when compared with control groups. However, this study did find that students who were exposed to DARE showed significantly less substance use after the intervention and were better able to resist peer pressure to experiment with certain drugs.

Some years later, Ennett et al. (1994) conducted a meta-analysis of eight methodologically rigorous evaluations of DARE programs across the United States and Canada. The results of this study suggested that DARE had only minimal effect on students' attitudes toward drug use and that the program produced few substantive change in students' social skills, self-esteem, knowledge about drugs, or attitudes toward the police. Additionally, the researchers found that DARE's effectiveness was substantially less than that of similar drug prevention programs that used comparable interactive teaching techniques. Longitudinal evaluations of the program have uncovered similar shortcomings (see Clayton, Cattarello et al., 1996; Kochis, 1995; Lynam et al., 1999; Rosenbaum and Hanson, 1998; Wysong et al., 1994).

One of the more sophisticated longitudinal studies (Rosenbaum et al., 1994) found that DARE instruction had no statistically significant impact on students' use of alcohol or cigarettes only 1 year after "graduation." Although the program did appear to heighten students' awareness of media influences regarding alcohol consumption, and may even have encouraged some girls to quit using alcohol, Rosenbaum and his colleagues noted that boys' consumption of alcohol actually increased following the intervention. A subsequent study by Rosenbaum and Hanson (1998) found that 3 years or more after DARE instruction, even students' positive attitudes toward the police had returned to preintervention levels.

In light of these poor reviews, it is important to emphasize that DARE is the most widely recognized and popular school-based drug education program ever created (Bureau of Justice Assistance, 1995). In terms of name recognition, DARE stands head and shoulders above all other drug education programs currently on the market. This is due in large part to the program's shameless self-promotion through T-shirts, buttons, bumper stickers, pencils, and other forms of "daraphernalia." Additionally, the program has enjoyed a long list of celebrity endorsements from prominent actors, politicians, and sports figures. But why would these people support DARE in the face so many negative evaluations? More important, why is DARE supported by parents, educators, and the law enforcement community? How is this possible?

Parents' support for DARE can be explained in two ways. First, parents are concerned about drugs and violence in school (Rose and Gallup, 2002), and most are apt to feel a sense of security knowing that police officers are in the classroom helping to discourage anti-social behaviors. Second, parents, similar to many Americans, are willing to pin a great deal of hope on the power of "education" to treat and/or ameliorate a variety of complex social ills (Rose and Gallup, 2000). How else would one interpret the proliferation of tertiary educational programs dealing with issues such as sex, health, drug use, and character formation, as well as programs targeted at drivers and gangs?

Teachers and school administrators may support DARE for many of the same reasons. That is, they may feel that the presence of a DARE officer on school grounds will help enhance school safety. Moreover, educators are apt to support virtually any program that keeps parents positive toward schooling and education. Teachers' approval ratings of DARE, in particular, may reflect their desire for additional help in the classroom (Lawrence, 1998). Given DARE officers' specialized training in drug education, this may be a powerful incentive for teachers to positively evaluate the program irrespective of the quality of instruction offered.

Police officers, on the other hand, support DARE because the program is seen as an important community relations tool (Cox and Fitzgerald, 1996). That is, DARE has provided police officers access to community institutions that were once assumed to be off limits to law enforcement personnel (Lawrence, 1998). Additionally, police administrators may see community-based programs such as DARE as an effective way to defuse public mistrust of the police. That is, rather than appearing in schools as law enforcers, DARE officers are cast in the role of mentors who are genuinely concerned about keeping kids drug free.

Given DARE's symbolic mission, its "packaging," and the various sources of support outlined earlier, it would seem to make little difference if the program is effective or not. In fact, some writers have suggested that drug education programs of all types may be virtually immune to negative evaluations and scholarly criticism (Aniskiewicz and Wysong, 1990; Bangert-Drowns, 1988; Clayton, Leukefeld et al., 1996; Elliott, 1995; Klockars, 1988). For example, Aniskiewicz and Wysong (1990, p. 733) write, "When drug education programs are viewed as symbolic actions that have political utility for various sponsoring groups, the continuation of such programs is likely to be only loosely coupled to their actual efficacy." Bangert-Drowns (1988, p. 260) adds, "It is unlikely that drug education will ever be withdrawn from the schools, even if it is shown to be ineffective. It appears to serve other functions … such as the reassurance of parents that the schools are at least trying to control substance abuse among students." These arguments suggest that criticizing DARE for trying (but apparently failing) to keep kids off drugs would be akin to criticizing firefighters for trying to prevent fires, or doctors for trying to prevent disease. In short, it would be like "criticizing the tune selection of the singing dog … It is not that the dog

is singing well that is so remarkable, but that he is in fact singing"
(Klockars, 1988, pp. 257–258).

33.5 Sticks and Stones, Slander and Suits

Though many readers will see DARE's popularity as a classic case of
public faith flying in the face of scholarly "facts," it is important to
note that DARE administrators have actively defended their program
against critics both inside and outside academe. For example, DARE
officials are said to have lobbied both the National Institute of Justice
(NIJ) and the American Journal of Public Health in an effort to quash
the poor programmatic outcomes uncovered by Ennett and her
colleagues (Elliott, 1995). Citing methodological problems with the
study, the NIJ, in fact, refused to publish Ennett's work. However, the
American Journal of Public Health appears to have had no problems
with the study and published her research that same year. Although
this one study was effectively "buried," an onslaught of negative
program evaluations made their way into mainstream criminal justice
journals in the coming years (Clayton, Cattarello et al., 1996; Kochis,
1995; Rosenbaum, et al., 1994; Wysong, et al., 1994).

In an effort to counter this negative publicity, program administrators announced a new and improved version of the DARE curriculum
in the fall of 1994. Given the onslaught of scholarly criticism that
surrounded the program in the mid-1990s, the timing of this curriculum
revision is certainly suspect. A stronger interpretation of these events
suggests that DARE officials were looking for a way to quickly and
effectively invalidate these negative studies. According to Elliott (1995,
p. 15), this "disingenuous attempt to deflect criticism" was nothing
more than a "shell game."

Throughout the 1990s, criticism of the DARE program continued in
various popular magazine articles as well. In an article published in
The New Republic, Stephen Glass (1997, p. 19) wrote that, in an effort
to quell the critics, angry DARE supporters were engaging in "tactics
ranging from bullying journalists to manipulating the facts … to intimidate government officials and stop news organizations, researchers, and
parents from criticizing the program." As evidence of this intimidation
campaign, Glass claimed that "DARE supporters have been accused of
slashing tires, jamming television transmissions, and spray-painting
reporters homes to quiet critics." According to Glass (1997, p. 19), these
critics were said to have been "dared."

In June 1998, DARE America went on the offensive, suing Stephen Glass in U.S. District Court for $10 million for writing what DARE America called false and libelous statements regarding the alleged "strong-arm tactics" of pro-DARE supporters (*DARE America v. Stephen Glass*). Two years later, DARE America sued *Rolling Stone Magazine* for $50 million for printing a similar defamatory article written by Glass (*DARE America v. Rolling Stone Magazine*). Although both defendants were eventually absolved of libel, lawyers for DARE America were able to show that Glass "made up some of his facts." Apparently, this was not an isolated incident; other confirmed cases of journalistic fabrication by Glass came to light, and he was eventually fired from his position as associate editor of *The New Republic* (Pogrebin, 1998).

33.6 Science vs. Symbolic Politics

Fritsch et al. (1999, p. 127) have noted that a common criticism of many contemporary crime prevention programs is that they "sound good, feel good, look good, but do not work good." "What is surprising [however] is that, despite an uninterrupted pattern of failure, alcohol, and drug education [programs] are as popular as ever" (Weisheit, 1983, p. 72). Given the millions of dollars that are currently funneled into school-based drug education programs, it is interesting to note that only a handful of rigorous evaluations have ever attempted to assess DARE's long-term effectiveness.

More than 30 years ago, Alice Rivlin (1970) argued that the lack of comprehensive evaluation data in the public sector stemmed, in large part, from three major factors. First, she argued, program administrators rarely set aside adequate resources for either evaluation or impact analysis. Second, program managers are often hesitant to subject their programs to in-depth scrutiny. That is, program administrators and other interested stakeholders may feel that the value of a particular program simply cannot be adequately measured. Third, systematic evaluations can become highly controversial. This is especially true when a sponsoring agency believes that an evaluator is not inclined to portray a program in a particularly pleasing light (Weiss, 1987).

Because evaluations of popular programs such as DARE are often politicized and become controversial, some scholars have cautioned researchers against attempting to construct scientific assessments of these programs. For example, Weisheit (1983) warns that rigorous evaluations may occasionally draw fire from a variety of interested stakeholders, including the sponsoring agency itself. In a telling example of how badly these kinds of studies can go, Weisheit (1983, p. 76) writes:

> A meticulous "scientific" evaluation may become counter-productive, generating a loss of credibility and even hostility toward the evaluator. The participants "know" that the program works and are convinced that the evaluator, an ivory-tower type who is naive about the "real world," has simply failed to measure this fact in the evaluation.

Evidence of this sentiment was seen in a 1997 *Dateline* television news story in which then "drug czar" General Barry McCaffrey was asked to respond to the various allegations about DARE's ineffectiveness. Unfortunately, McCaffrey shrugged off the question, intimating instead that all people have to do is to look into the eyes of DARE graduates to know the program is working (Schooley, 1997).

33.7 Conclusion

If academics expect to continue meaningful research on popular school-based drug education programs, it is important for them to recognize what Dennis Palumbo (1987) has called the "politics of program evaluation." In his book, Palumbo notes that field studies, particularly those involving program evaluation, are often construed by program administrators (and their partners) as a potential threat. Because program administrators are often expected to be program advocates, they must exercise a great deal of caution when allowing researchers access to politically sensitive data. Moreover, the political milieu in which administrators operate abhors even the slightest risk of failure (Weiss, 1987). Consequently, it should come as no surprise to learn that school district officials are often skeptical of letting neutral, third-party researchers access data as it might adversely affect the continued existence of "their" program (Mueller, 2001). There is simply too much at stake, and too much to lose. Thus, "avoiding political embarrassment rather than accomplishing program goals [may become a school district's] first priority" (Faux, 1971, p. 278).

Although program evaluations are sometimes undertaken with the express desire of building a positive image of a program (Rossi and Freeman, 1993), even the slightest hint of failure can be used as political ammunition to undermine a program's image. As Palumbo (1987, p. 22) rightly points out, "The facts, when made public, may set back [a] program and the policy under which it operates, particularly if there are some negative findings in the evaluation." Although positive findings can be politically useful to program administrators, a finding of "no effect" (e.g., neither positive nor negative) is only useful to the opposition. Although "the finding of little impact (or null results) is pervasive over a wide band of program fields and program strategies" (Weiss, 1987, p. 61), administrators often feel the need to suppress such findings for fear that they will be used against them. Obviously, the political sensitivities of program managers can weaken their receptivity to any kind of study, irrespective of its methodological rigor. As Weiss (1987, p. 58) notes, unanalyzed programs are safe and undisturbed. However, when they are subjected to the scrutiny of a scientific evaluation, a program's continued existence may be jeopardized.

In the end, perhaps it is the competing imperatives under which researchers and program administrators operate that is the primary force behind the politics of program evaluation. Perhaps these competing imperatives can even be said to put academics and practitioners at odds with one another. Crain and Carsud (1985, p. 229) describe the conflict in the area of education this way: "Not only do academics look down their noses at school practitioners, but some practitioners consider academics to be time wasters at best and dangerous at worst." Nevertheless, as contentious as the academic–practitioner relationship may be, we should not lose sight of the fact that this relationship is also symbiotic. That is, academics need access to data that they cannot obtain without the help of practitioners. Practitioners also need the credentials and legitimization that academics can provide. With understanding and compromise from both sides, further rigorous research on drug education programs such as DARE can contribute to our knowledge base, which is necessary for improved school safety, an issue on which we all agree.

References

Aniskiewicz, R. and Wysong, E. (1990). Evaluating D.A.R.E.: drug education and the multiple meanings of success. *Policy Studies Review*, 9(4), 727–747.

Bangert-Drowns, R. (1988). The effect of school-based substance abuse education: a meta-analysis. *Journal of Drug Education*, 18(3), 243–264.

Bureau of Justice Assistance Fact Sheet. (September, 1995). Drug Abuse Resistance Education (DARE). Washington, D.C.: U.S. Department of Justice.

Clayton, R., Cattarello, A., and Johnstone, B. (1996). The effectiveness of drug abuse resistance education: five-year follow-up results. *Preventive Medicine*, 25: 509–527.

Clayton, R., Leukefeld, C., Harrington, N., and Cattarello, A. (1996). DARE (drug abuse resistance education): very popular but not very effective. In McCoy, C., Metsch, L., and Inciardi, J. (Eds.), *Intervening with Drug-involved Youth*. Thousand Oaks, CA: Sage. pp. 101–109.

Cox, S. and Fitzgerald, J. (1996). *Police in Community Relations*. Madison, WI: Brown and Benchmark.

Crain, R. and Carsrud, K. (1985). The role of the social sciences in school desegregation policy. In Shotland, R. and Mark, M. (Eds.), *Social Science and Social Policy*. Newbury Park, CA: Sage. pp. 219–236.

DARE America v. Rolling Stone Magazine. April 27, 2000. Case No. CV 99-1132. United States District Court, Central District of California.

DARE America v. Stephen Glass. June 29, 1998. Case No. CV 98-5230. United States District Court, Central District of California.

DeJong, W. (1987). A short-term evaluation of DARE (Drug Abuse Resistance Education): Preliminary indications of effectiveness. *Journal of Drug Education* 17(4), 279–294.

Elliott, J. (March, 1995). Drug prevention placebo: how DARE wastes time, money, and police. *Reason*, 26(10), 14–21.

Ennett, S., Tobler, N., Ringwalt, C., and Flewelling, R. (1994). How effective is drug abuse resistance education? A meta-analysis of project DARE outcome evaluations. *American Journal of Public Health* 84, 1394–1401.

Faux, G. (1971). Politics and the bureaucracy in community controlled economic development. *Law and Contemporary Problems*. Durham, NC: Duke University School of Law, Spring, 277–296.

Federal Bureau of Investigation. (2002). Crime in the United States 2001: Uniform Crime Reports. Washington, D.C.

Fritsch, E., Caeti, T., and Taylor, R. (1999). Gang suppression through saturation patrol, aggressive curfew, and truancy enforcement: a quasi-experimental test of the Dallas anti-gang initiative. *Crime and Delinquency*, 45(1), 122–139.

Glass, S. (March 3, 1997). Don't you DARE. *The New Republic*, 18–28.

Gottfredson, D. (1997). School-based crime prevention. In Sherman, L., Gottfredson, D., MacKenzie, D., Eck, J., Reuter, P., and Bushway, S. (Eds.), *Preventing Crime: What Works, What Doesn't, What's Promising?* Washington, D.C.: National Institute of Justice. pp. 5-1–5-74.

Johnston, L., O'Malley, P., and Bachman, J. (2002). Monitoring the Future: National Survey Results on Drug Use, 1975–2001. Ann Arbor, MI: Institute for Social Research.

Klockars, C. (1988). The rhetoric of community policing. In Greene, J. and Mastrofski, S. (Eds.), *Community Policing: Rhetoric or Reality?* New York: Praeger. pp. 239–258.

Kochis, D. (1995). Project DARE (drug abuse resistance education): does it work? *Juvenile Justice Update*, 1(4), 5.

Lawrence, R. (1998). *School Crime and Juvenile Justice*. New York: Oxford University Press.

Lyman, D., Milich, R., Zimmerman, R., Novak, S., Logan, T.K., Martin, C., Leukefeld, C., and Clayton, R. (1999). Project DARE: no effects at 10-year follow-up. *Journal of Consulting and Clinical Psychology*, 67, 590–593.

Maguire, K. and Pastore, A. (2001). *Sourcebook of Criminal Justice Statistics, 2000*. Washington, D.C.: Department of Justice.

Miller, D. (October 19, 2001). DARE reinvents itself — with help from its social-science critics. *The Chronicle of Higher Education*, A 12–14.

Mueller, D. (2001). Kids, Cops, and the Politics of School-Based Crime Prevention. Ph.D. dissertation, Washington State University, Pullman, WA.

National Center on Addiction and Substance Abuse at Columbia University. (September 2001). Malignant Neglect: Substance Abuse and America's Schools. New York: National Center on Addiction and Substance Abuse at Columbia University.

National Center on Addiction and Substance Abuse at Columbia University. (August 2002). National Survey of American Attitudes on Substance Abuse VII: Teens, Parents, and Siblings. New York: National Center on Addiction and Substance Abuse at Columbia University.

Palumbo, D. (Ed.) (1987). *The Politics of Program Evaluation*. Newbury Park, CA: Sage.

Pogrebin, R. Rechecking a Writer's Facts: A Magazine Uncovers Fiction. *New York Times*, June 12, 1998, p. A1.

Rivlin, A. (1970). *Systematic Thinking for Social Action*. Washington, D.C.: The Brookings Institute.

Rose, L. and Gallup, A. (September, 2000). The 32nd annual phi delta kappa/gallup poll of the public's attitudes toward the public schools. *Phi Delta Kappan*, 82(1), 41–58.

Rose, L. and Gallup, A. (September, 2002). The 34th annual phi delta kappa/gallup poll of the public's attitudes toward the public schools. *Phi Delta Kappan*, 84(1), 41–56.

Rosenbaum, D., Flewelling, R., Bailey, S., Ringwalt, C., and Wilkinson D. (1994). Cops in the classroom: a longitudinal evaluation of drug abuse resistance education (DARE). *Journal of Research in Crime and Delinquency*, 31(1), 3–31.

Rosenbaum, D. and Hanson, G. (1998). Assessing the effects of school-based drug education: a six-year multilevel analysis of project D.A.R.E. Journal of Research in *Crime and Delinquency*, 35(4), 381–412.

Rossi, P. and Freeman, H. (1993). *Evaluation*. (5th ed.). Thousand Oaks, CA: Sage.

Schooley, D. (Producer). (February 21, 1997). Dateline NBC. "Truth or DARE?" [Television broadcast]. New York: National Broadcasting Company.

U.S. Department of Health and Human Services, Substance Abuse and Mental Health Services Administration (2001). Summary of Findings from the 2000 National Household Survey on Drug Abuse. Rockville, MD: U.S. Department of Health and Human Services.

U.S. Department of Justice (2001). ADAM (Arrestee Drug Abuse Monitoring Program) Preliminary 2000 Findings on Drug Use and Drug Markets: Adult Male Arrestees. Washington, D.C.: National Institute of Justice.

Weisheit, R. (1983). The social context of alcohol and drug education: Implications for program evaluations. *Journal of Alcohol and Drug Education*, 29(1), 72–81.

Weiss, C. (1987). Where politics and evaluation research meet. In Palumbo, D. (Ed.), *The Politics of Program Evaluation*. Newbury Park, CA: Sage. pp. 47–70.

Wysong, E., Aniskiewicz, R., and Wright D. (1994). Truth and DARE: tracking drug education to graduation and as symbolic politics. *Social Problems*, 41(3), 448–473.

Notes

1. These figures reflect only those arrests in which drug possession or sales or driving under the influence was the most serious charge. Undoubtedly, many other arrests resulted in the discovery of illegal drug activity. Additionally, an even higher proportion of arrested individuals were likely to have been under the influence of drugs or alcohol at the time of their arrest.

Chapter 34

Is It Time to Abolish the Juvenile Justice System?

Tory J. Caeti and Eric J. Fritsch

34.1 Introduction

Criticism of the utility of a separate juvenile justice system virtually coincided with its inception in the early 1900s in the United States. The operations and practices of the juvenile court have been tinkered with by politicians throughout its 100-year history. However, the recent shift toward more punitive juvenile sentencing, increased waivers to adult court, and harsher correctional systems (Feld, 1999; Fritsch et al., 1996; Gardner, 1987; Hemmens et al., 1997, 1999; Torbet et al., 1996) has led to a substantial increase in academic attention concerning the fundamental assumptions and philosophies of the juvenile justice system. A reexamination of system operations leads some commentators to conclude that it is time to reinvent the system (Hufstedler, 1984; Krisberg and Austin, 1986), whereas others conclude that it is time to abolish it (Wizner and Keller, 1977; Feld, 1999). The impetus behind such arguments lies in criticisms of the fundamental mission of the juvenile court system and in its current operational status across the United States. This chapter reviews arguments on both sides of the abolition debate, beginning with a discussion of the changes in the juvenile justice system that spawned the most recent arguments about abolition. Following this, an examination of the various arguments on both sides of the debate will be reviewed and discussed.

34.2 Arguments for Abolishing the Juvenile Justice System

34.2.1 The Changing Landscape of Juvenile Justice

Changes in the juvenile justice system since the due process revolution of the 1960s have led some philosophers to conclude that the current state of the system has outlived its usefulness. Those in favor of abolishing the juvenile court as a separate system argue that original foundations of the juvenile system, specifically the focus on rehabilitation and treatment, have given way to ideologies of punishment and accountability that no longer justify a separate system (Ainsworth, 1991, 1995; Federle, 1990; Feld, 1999; Fox, 1977; McCarthy, 1977). A combination of events in the past 40 years led to substantive changes in state legislation on juvenile justice; indeed, many states have rewritten the fundamental purpose of their juvenile justice systems (Hemmens et al., 1997, 1999). Violent crime rates rose sharply beginning in the 1980s, especially among juvenile offenders. Recent changes in state juvenile justice legislation focus on community safety and protection, resulting in the juvenile court increasingly considering the punishment of juveniles in both sentencing and waiver decisions (Federle, 1990; Hemmens et al., 1997, 1999; Taylor et al., 2002; Torbet et al., 1996). In Texas, for example, juveniles accused of serious felonies can be sentenced to up to 40 years of incarceration by the juvenile court (Fritsch, Caeti et al., 1996; Fritsch, Hemmens et al., 1996).

Revised juvenile justice codes emphasize responsibility, accountability, and deterrence of juvenile offenders (Federle, 1990; Feld, 1999; Gardner, 1987; Hemmens et al., 1997, 1999; Taylor et al., 2002) while still refusing to extend to them the full range of due process rights that adults have in criminal proceedings (Ainsworth, 1991, 1995; Feld, 1999; Fox, 1977; McCarthy, 1977). This shift also reflects a change in how the juvenile is reviewed by society as well as the courts, which no longer practice the ideals of *parens patriae* (the State as parent). Abolitionists feel that juveniles are unduly penalized by the two-tiered system and feel they would benefit from a single, unified system giving every offender equal due process rights as entitled by law. The Supreme Court decisions in *Kent v. United States, In re Gault,* and

In re Winship afforded juveniles the basic due process rights adult offenders enjoy in the criminal system. Nonetheless, there are important due process rights still not specifically guaranteed to juveniles, specifically the right to a jury trial (Ainsworth, 1991; Federle, 1990; Feld, 1999; Fox, 1977; McCarthy, 1977). In addition, although one of the primary philosophical foundations of the juvenile court is that juveniles are less culpable than adults because of their age, many states still do not automatically require that an attorney be present when a juvenile waives his or her rights (Caeti et al., 1996; Feld, 1989; Berkheiser, 2002). Indeed, recent research has found that juveniles are far less capable of understanding their rights or what a waiver of rights means in subsequent proceedings against them (Grisso, 1980; Cowden and McKee, 1995). Recent "get-tough-on-crime" laws allow juvenile court judges to hand out harsher sentences, thus narrowing the gap in sentencing between the juvenile and adult systems of justice (Fritsch, Hemmens et al., 1996; Fritsch, Caeti et al., 1996; Torbet et al., 1996).

34.2.1.1 The "New" Juvenile Criminal and the Wave of Violent Juvenile Crime

The driving force behind many of the calls for the abolition of the juvenile system can be found in changing assumptions about the culpability of juvenile offenders and changing assumptions about how to best deal with juvenile crime. Table 34.1 depicts a concise summary of the assumptions that have changed concerning juvenile justice and popular thought concerning how to best deal with juvenile crime. A fundamental paradigm shift (Fritsch, Hemmens et al., 1996) has occurred, resulting in a new conception of the juvenile delinquent and what to do about juvenile crime. This new assumptional framework leads to a fundamentally different perspective from what was envisioned by the founders of the juvenile justice system. The new juvenile justice system might correctly be termed a junior criminal court with all of the punishment of its adult counterpart, but with substantially fewer due process rights and protections.

34.2.2 The Juvenile Justice System Does Not Reflect the Goals of the Founders

The modern calls for abolition can be traced to a commentary on the recommendations by the Joint Commission on Juvenile Justice Standards in the 1970s. The recommendations included abolishing jurisdiction over

Table 34.1   Traditional vs. the New Model of the Juvenile Court

	Traditional Model of the Juvenile Court System	New Model of the Juvenile Court System
Juvenile's level of criminal responsibility	Diminished; juveniles are not capable of forming the same level of criminal intent as adults.	Certain juveniles, especially violent or multiple offenders, are just as culpable as adults.
View of juvenile's development	Disposition of a juvenile's case reflects that juveniles are not as intellectually, socially, or morally developed as adults.	Not as important in decision making about disposition as the offense committed.
Causes of delinquency	The broader social environment — the neighborhood, poverty, urban decay, the family, and child-rearing practices.	In general, delinquency is a matter of a juvenile choosing to commit a crime for which he or she must be held accountable.
Role of the juvenile court	The juvenile court acts *in loco parentis (in place of the parents)* to determine the best interests of the child, tailoring the process to each child's individual needs.	The juvenile court acts *in loco parentis* for the best interests of society. Dispositions are guided by statute in many cases, and the crime committed dictates dispositions.
Level of discretion in the juvenile court	Broad and widespread; necessary to take into account the various causes and cures for delinquency. The juvenile court acts in a medical fashion, diagnosing and treating delinquency as an illness.	The level of discretion is inversely related to the seriousness of the crime committed. Discretion in dealing with serious or violent juveniles is strictly limited, if not eliminated. The court enforces statutory guidelines and attempts to protect society and hold juveniles accountable for their actions.

Table 34.1   Traditional vs. the New Model of the Juvenile Court (continued)

	Traditional Model of the Juvenile Court System	*New Model of the Juvenile Court System*
Juvenile court records	Once the juvenile is rehabilitated, he or she deserves a second chance. Records held to strict confidentiality standards.	The lack of record keeping hinders coordination of the system, which results in juveniles "slipping through the cracks." Records are essential to hold the youth accountable and protect society. Juvenile records are used in future proceedings — in some cases (counting as a strike under three strikes laws).
Goals of the juvenile court system	Prevention of future delinquency through individual treatment and rehabilitation designed to address the unique needs of each juvenile.	Prevention of future delinquency through punishment, incapacitation, deterrence, and holding juveniles accountable. Rehabilitation is not viewed as being in conflict with these other goals.

and deinstitutionalizing status offenders, adopting a determinate sentencing framework over an indeterminate one based on the severity of the offense committed, and the extension of procedural safeguards to juveniles accused of a crime (Wizner and Keller, 1977). Wizner and Keller (1977) noted at the time that although the standards were an admirable attempt to reform a system badly in need of reform, they were the first step in a process that would inevitably lead to the abolition of the system. The argument rests on the notion that duplicating a criminal court, with all of the associated procedures and due process safeguards, for juveniles is unnecessary and woefully inadequate when compared with the adult criminal justice system. In other words, the juvenile court was never designed to deal with crime in such a way owing to its historical roots in a civil system of justice. Hence, once criminal charges, criminal proceedings, and criminal sanctions become available, why not simply use the adult system that is already in place? Reminiscent of the classic observation by Justice Fortas in the *Kent* opinion, Feld (1999) notes that revisions to the juvenile justice system have transformed the juvenile court into a scaled-down, second-class criminal court in which juveniles receive neither therapy nor justice. To Feld (1999), the goals of rehabilitation and punishment are in direct conflict, and he concludes that the juvenile court cannot be both a mechanism of social control and social welfare.

Abolitionists argue that the current juvenile justice system no longer reflects the views of the original founders (Ainsworth, 1991, 1995; Federle, 1990; Feld, 1999; Fox, 1977; McCarthy, 1977; Wizner and Keller, 1977). Ainsworth (1991, 1995) argues that in recent years there has been a reconstructing of the definition of childhood as a developmental continuum in which it has become accepted that the development of different capacities may proceed at different rates. Society is now comfortable in concluding that a particular 15-year-old may have sufficient cognitive and moral maturity to justify holding him or her fully responsible for his or her criminal conduct (Ainsworth, 1991, 1995). The current two-tiered structure demands there be an all-or-nothing choice made in each case categorizing a juvenile as a child or an adult, with no middle ground available (Ainsworth, 1991, 1995). Either the juvenile is retained in juvenile court or certified to adult court. The shift away from bright-line distinctions based on a fixed age such as 17 or 18 to one in which 14-year-olds can be waived to adult court could mean that there is no longer a justification for maintaining a separate system for dealing with these types of offenders (Ainsworth, 1991, 1995). Indeed, many commentators and several states have concluded that certain offenses should be automatically waived to adult court without any discretion (Torbet et al., 1996).

34.2.3 Juveniles Are Denied Basic Due Process Rights

A common observation is that the juvenile system uses juveniles' perceived incapacity as a justification to deny them their legal rights (Federle, 1990). Juveniles' ability to comprehend the proceedings and understand the nature of waiving their rights has been questioned by several authors (Grisso, 1980; Caeti et al., 1996; Feld, 1989; Berkheiser, 2002). Additionally, society no longer views some juvenile offenders as children, and in some proceedings the juvenile may be entitled to additional rights. Many argue that young offenders should receive all of the rights as adult offenders if they are going to be expected to take responsibility for their actions and receive punishment (Ainsworth, 1991, 1995; Federle, 1990; Fox, 1977; Feld, 1999; McCarthy, 1977). In granting them full due process rights, many conclude that a separate system is lacking and redundant.

Because juvenile proceedings have become increasingly punitive, abolitionists contend that juveniles are put in greater jeopardy than their adult counterparts. In addition to facing long terms of incarceration, they are expected to be able to make a knowing and voluntary waiver of their rights. Further, in many cases juveniles waive their rights without the benefit of counsel or in the absence of their parents or legal guardian (Grisso, 1980; Feld, 1989; Caeti et al., 1996). In the past, when a juvenile spoke with police or a juvenile court judge, it was assumed that discussions were of a benevolent nature. Today, these discussions are more fact-finding and investigatory in nature. The willingness of the court to extend due process rights to juveniles including the right to an attorney, the right to notice of charges, the right to confront witnesses, and a protection against self-incrimination reflects the changing view of society as to the role of juveniles and the responsibility they are now expected to take for their actions (Ainsworth, 1991, 1995; Federle, 1990). Abolitionists argue that the rights they are still lacking make it unreasonable for them to be punished for their actions without the full protection of the law. The abolition of the juvenile court would allow them to have access to all of these rights in the adult criminal system.

It has also been argued that the individualized justice in the juvenile courts allows juvenile court judges to substantively and procedurally operate lawlessly (Feld, 1999). Feld (1989, 1999) argues that although statutes and procedural rules exist, these courts operate unconstrained by the rule of law, especially to the extent that disposition decisions are made by judges based on individual assessments. There is no formal restriction on judicial discretion in the juvenile courts that allows for similarly situated offenders to be handled differently based on personal characteristics over which they have no control (Feld, 1999). Abolition would result in the equal protection of juveniles under all laws as well as a more fair system of adjudication.

34.2.3.1 Right to a Jury Trial

The lack of a right to a jury trial is another reason abolitionists feel juveniles would be better off being tried in the adult criminal system (Ainsworth, 1991, 1995; Federle, 1990; Feld, 1999; Fox, 1977; McCarthy,

1977). The jury trial was created to shelter defendants from biased systems as well as to expose the defendant to the symbolic conscience of the community in determining guilt and sentences (Ainsworth, 1991, 1995). The jury system can also remove the political pressures and affiliations associated with judges and prosecutors (Ainsworth, 1991). Because of the closed nature of juvenile proceedings, there is typically no record of the decision-making processes of judges in deciding a juvenile's guilt or innocence, thus making it impossible for an appellate court to review these decisions. Because juries are given instructions as to how to interpret and follow the law, there is a record of what the jury is told, leaving something for an appellate court to examine. For this reason, abolitionists argue that the juvenile's denial of the right to jury is detrimental to the fairness of the adjudication of these offenders (Ainsworth, 1991).

34.2.3.2 Role of Counsel in Juvenile Courts: A Good Thing?

Although *Gault* legally gave juveniles the right to assistance of counsel, the competency of their representation has come into question. Abolitionists argue that acknowledging the punitive reality of the contemporary juvenile court carries with it a concomitant obligation to provide appropriate procedural safeguards, most notably the effective assistance of counsel (Feld, 1989). Studies have found that in some states fewer than 20 percent of 12- and 13-year-olds are represented by counsel in juvenile proceedings (Feld, 1989). In addition, abolitionists argue that there is confusion among attorneys in juvenile court as to their role. Because actors in the juvenile court have traditionally taken a rehabilitative and parental role, attorneys are unsure of their place in the process and unaware of the workings of the system (Feld, 1999). Another common argument is that attorneys assigned to juvenile cases are typically overworked and underpaid and are forced to manage large caseloads. As such, the due process rights of juvenile defendants suffer. The mere fact that these defendants are given an attorney is no guarantee that their rights are being safeguarded, and abolitionists feel that juveniles would receive better representation in the adult system (Ainsworth, 1991, 1995). It has been argued that attorneys are uncertain of their role in juvenile proceedings, because of traditional views that actors in the juvenile system are to play the role of a parent.

Abolitionists also argue that juveniles who are represented by attorneys typically face harsher penalties than those who are not, merely because they have representation, and it is expected that their counsel would ensure their clients receive their legal rights (Ainsworth, 1991).

In fact, some studies have shown that having an attorney present can have negative consequences on dispositions in juvenile court (Feld, 1989). It makes no sense for defendants represented by counsel to face harsher penalties, and it has been argued that this would not be the case if juveniles were defendants in the adult criminal court.

34.2.4 The Punitive Juvenile Justice System: Harsher than the Adult System?

Abolitionists contend that recent demands from the public to get tough on crime have resulted in legislative actions in the adult system to hand out harsher sentences. As a result, sentencing changes have spread into the juvenile system, with many courts focusing on punishment and retribution when determining sentences for juvenile offenders. This has resulted in harsher penalties in many jurisdictions as well as the use of sentencing guidelines (Ainsworth, 1991, 1995; Federle, 1990; Feld, 1999; Fox, 1977). Recent trends in the juvenile court to make use of judicial and statutory waiver procedures have also deprived many young offenders of the supposed lenient sentences of the juvenile court, and as a result more juveniles are being given longer and harsher sentences (Ainsworth, 1991). Fox (1977) argues that the use of determinate sentencing guidelines based on the degree of the offense and the discretion of the judge to impose a particular level of sanction are other examples of the juvenile system's movement away from rehabilitation toward punishment. The sentences young offenders receive in the juvenile court are increasingly resembling those given to their adult counterparts, and as long as the gap between differences in sentencing continues to narrow, the case for a separate system continues to weaken. One study found that juveniles who were retained in the juvenile court in a state with determinate sentencing received longer sentences than those who were waived to adult court for similar crimes (Fritsch, Hemmens et al., 1996).

34.2.5 A Unified System

Abolitionists note that changes to the adult system would have to be made before processing juveniles would be possible. These changes would have to meet the special needs of juveniles facing criminal convictions. Most philosophers arguing for a unified system agree that many juveniles have not developed the full mental capacity of adults, not yet fully comprehending the extent of the possible consequences of their

actions (Ainsworth, 1991, 1995; Feld, 1999). For this reason, many abolitionists argue that there should be some way to adjust sentencing
according to the age of the offender. For example, Feld (1999) suggests
a "youth-discount" sentencing scheme that would be devised to adjust
the level of sentence passed on a particular juvenile offender based on
his or her age. Upon entering the adult criminal court system, juveniles
would be allotted the same due process rights that adults now possess.
Ainsworth (1995) contends that the merger of the juvenile and adult
system would not mean that the court would have to overlook an
offender's age as a mitigating factor in sentencing. Additionally, because
the court would not have to classify young offenders as children, they
would be able to address the individual needs of offenders more effectively. Young offenders would be treated differently, and the system
would adapt to having them in the system by administering shorter and
more appropriate sentences according to the circumstances.

Other commentators oppose any policy that would let young offenders
be treated differently because of their age. Hirschi and Gottfredson (1996)
argue that the public does not see any difference in the seriousness of
a crime based on the offender's age. Rather, those who possess low self-
control are more likely to commit crime at any age after childhood. They
argue that the juvenile court's rehabilitative nature is not a justification
for its existence, because the crimes of young offenders are no less
serious than those of adult offenders. In addition, young offenders should
still be held accountable for their actions, and the juvenile courts' focus
on rehabilitation results in leniency for these offenders without punishing
them for their actions (Hirschi and Gottfredson, 1996).

In sum, abolitionists contend that a unified system of justice would
effectively grant juveniles the rights they are entitled to when facing
criminal sanctions. The net result of this unification would be greater
equity in both the processing and disposition of offenders. Finally, the
shift away from rehabilitation to a punitive and accountability-based
juvenile system has eliminated the need for separation and a second,
less rights-oriented system of justice. Although the move would encounter some problems and issues initially, it is the only way to achieve a
balanced system of justice for juveniles according to the abolitionists.

34.3 Arguments against Abolishing the Separate Juvenile Justice System

Other juvenile justice thinkers would prefer not to throw out the proverbial
baby with the bathwater, arguing instead that the original purpose of the

juvenile justice system is not flawed (Krisberg and Austin, 1986). Rather, current system operation and recent attempts to increase the punitiveness of the system run counter to the original intentions of the founders. The arguments of those opposed to the abolition of the juvenile court are centered around the original tenets of the system, including the juvenile courts' view of juvenile offenders as being inherently different from adult offenders and unable to develop the same levels of intent. Further, the rehabilitation potential of juveniles is seen as being greater than for their adult counterparts. Among those opposing abolition, juveniles are still considered to be different from adults and deserve to be treated differently from adults (Arthur, 1998; Dawson, 1990; Rosenberg, 1993; Springer, 1991; Yellen, 1996). The juvenile system was designed to rehabilitate young offenders by attempting to solve the problems that led to juvenile delinquency through methods beyond punishment. Antiabolitionists argue that even if changes were made to the adult system, juveniles would not be treated fairly, because of plea bargaining and the mitigating factor of age. Hence, eventually juveniles would be treated as adult offenders because the public would continue to complain about lenient sentencing (Rosenberg, 1993). As with the get-tough movement, any violent incident in the news would result in demands for tougher sentencing, leading to the point where juveniles and adults would truly be treated the same. Juveniles have a greater potential for rehabilitation because they have not fully developed emotionally, and their moral and ethical values can still be altered; hence, the need for a separate and different system (Arthur, 1998; Dawson, 1990; Rosenberg, 1993; Yellen, 1996).

Although most would agree that changes need to be made to the juvenile system, anti-abolitionists feel that juveniles would be worse off if faced with the realities of the adult criminal system. Merging the two systems would be an acknowledgment that there is no difference between juvenile and adult offenders and that no special consideration should be given to their individual situations or needs. Other arguments opposing the abolition of a separate juvenile system include the inability of the adult criminal system to reduce recidivism, the current state of the adult criminal court system, the difficulty of providing for individual needs, the fact that the move would entail eliminating the legal protections currently available, and the fact that the juvenile system is largely successful (Arthur, 1998; Dawson, 1990; Rosenberg, 1993; Springer, 1991; Yellen, 1996).

34.3.1 Lessened Responsibility

Because young offenders have not lived long enough to have the life experience of adults, are not fully developed or able to fully understand the long-term consequences of their actions, and do not have the reasoning capacity of adults, many argue they should be treated differently (Arthur, 1998; Dawson, 1990; Rosenberg, 1993; Springer, 1991; Yellen, 1996). Devoting individualized attention to each child's needs and circumstances is in order to determine his or her level of understanding of their actions and the resulting culpability, leading to tailored consequences to meet the needs of the child. Opponents of abolition argue that a merger with the adult system would result in a lack of consideration of these characteristics, resulting in juveniles being treated more for the offense committed and less for their needs.

34.3.2 Greater Rehabilitation Potential

34.3.2.1 Lower Recidivism

Many in favor of maintaining separate systems argue that the juvenile system more effectively reduces recidivism among young offenders (Arthur, 1998). In fact, research reveals that most juveniles who are processed by the police do not return to the system (Taylor et al., 2002). The rehabilitative approach of the juvenile system responds to the special needs of offenders and focuses on making positive changes in these individuals' lives, whereas the adult criminal system does nothing to reduce recidivism, because its primary purpose is punishment (Arthur, 1998; Rosenberg, 1993; Yellen, 1996). The current juvenile system looks at each offender and the crime committed to determine the sentence that would most effectively reduce their chances of re-offending, by giving trained and dedicated judges control over sentencing (Arthur, 1998). The elimination of the juvenile system would result in a loss of attention to these individualized needs as well as impairing the abilities of those judges who serve only juveniles. Because recidivism is not an underlying goal of the adult system, there is no reason to believe the system would change dramatically to provide juveniles the range of services that the current juvenile system provides.

The juvenile courts look to the future when considering treatment options by focusing on the offender who committed the crime, what influenced the child, and what can be done to address these influences in the future (Arthur, 1998). Rehabilitative programs and individualized attention give juveniles the opportunity to become productive members of society by teaching them to make better decisions and to learn skills they may not already possess.

34.3.2.2 State of Adult System: Warehousing Inmates

One observation regarding the abolitionist perspective is that abolitionists argue in support of an idealized version of the adult criminal system without considering the way the adult system actually operates (Springer, 1991). Prisons are overcrowded, dockets are full, and defendants are pushed through as are items on an assembly line, with the primary goal of moving people through to make room for more. Bargaining for justice is the norm in the adult system, which is hard pressed to handle the caseload it already has. How can such a system increase its current load when it has difficulty with the current caseload? The current system would be difficult to alter so that it could adequately address the individual needs of children who come before it (Springer, 1991). The fact is that juveniles would be just another number if the two systems were merged, and they would receive little if any individualized attention.

In response to those who argue that young offenders are unduly penalized because of their denial of the right to a jury trial, defenders of the juvenile system would argue that the reality is that jury trials are seldom used in adult courts, with over 90 percent of convictions being attributed to guilty pleas rather than jury trials (Yellen, 1996). There is no reason to believe that merger of the two courts would result in a more frequent use of the right than currently exists among adults, and certainly there is no reason why a lack of this right should result in abolition of a separate system. Further, as the Supreme Court noted in the *McKeiver* case, the introduction of the jury system would bring with it all of the delay and gamesmanship of the adult system into the juvenile system of justice. Commenting on the competency of juvenile representation, antiabolitionists note that the adult public defender system is not a more attractive option and the competency of their representation would likely be worse than it is now (Rosenberg, 1993). Therefore, the competency of juvenile attorneys should not warrant the abolition of the system.

34.3.3 Protections of the Juvenile Justice System

34.3.3.1 Bail

Dawson (1990) argues that abolishing the juvenile system would deny juveniles protection against unfair legal practices that the current system has fought hard to protect them against, mainly bail practices. He argues that the many problems of the use of bail bondsmen and the workings of the bail system have not been present in the juvenile court. If juveniles were granted the right to bail, many juveniles dependent on their parents, or without reliable guardians, and without a source of income would be at the mercy of a corrupt system. The decision to grant them bail and the amount of bail might then be based on their parents' income, a factor over which the juvenile has no control. Additionally, bail bondsmen would be unlikely to approve most bonds on juveniles because of the risks associated with their being young (Dawson 1990).

34.3.3.2 Harsher Penalties

If the two systems were to merge, those in favor of maintaining a separate system argue that juveniles would no longer be sheltered from the severe sentences of the adult system (Arthur, 1998; Dawson, 1990; Rosenberg, 1993; Springer, 1991; Yellen, 1996). The current juvenile system uses waivers to transfer violent offenders to the adult system if a judge believes the crime warrants a more severe penalty than the juvenile court can levy. An original tenet of the juvenile system was that a judge who was trained and dedicated to serving the best interests of juveniles would make decisions regarding their disposition. The elimination of the juvenile system would mean that every juvenile defendant would be subject to harsh sentencing laws, without the special attention to his or her situation they currently receive in the juvenile court. Juvenile court actors and judges are trained to examine every situation, whereas the adult court only looks at the crime committed in punishing the offense rather than the offender (Arthur, 1998). Many juveniles who have the potential to be rehabilitated would not have that option if the juvenile system were eliminated, and these juveniles would then become throwaways, sentenced to a life of incarceration. Finally, merger with the adult system may also increase the possibility of juveniles receiving the death penalty for murder.

Antiabolitionists argue that merging the two systems would eventually result in juvenile offenders being incarcerated alongside adult offenders (Rosenberg, 1993). This would unnecessarily put the safety of juveniles at risk, with the possibility of nonviolent juveniles being exposed to violent adults. All juveniles would be put at unnecessary risk in that they have not developed fully and are not as physically strong as many adult offenders.

Finally, how would the adult courts handle status offenses? Undoubtedly, the overwhelming burden already placed on the adult courts would preclude the system from addressing such minor laws as curfew and truancy. Nonetheless, it is precisely the punishment of these offenses that has the potential to reduce juvenile crime and juvenile victimization in communities (Taylor et al., 2002).

34.3.3.3 Criminal Records

A primary goal of the juvenile justice system that developed over the course of its existence was to be able to remove the stigma associated with a criminal conviction. In short, the juvenile justice system allows a young person to make a mistake without having to pay for it the rest of his or her life. In recent years, the confidentiality and sealing of juvenile records has been severely curtailed by several states (Torbet et al., 1996; Taylor et al., 2002). For the overwhelming majority of juveniles, however, who are adjudicated in juvenile court, their records are still sealed or destroyed upon reaching adulthood. Although it might be reasonable to hold a juvenile's record for a violent crime for later use in adult proceedings, most juveniles age out of crime, and society is generally forgiving of misdeeds committed by young people. Because we know that the overwhelming majority of youths who commit crimes do not do so into adulthood, do we really want to stigmatize them for the rest of their lives with a conviction for a crime they committed at age 14? Without a separate system that is designed to protect the juvenile and look out for his or her best interests, this would not be the case.

34.3.4 Maintaining a Separate System

Child advocates who have spoken out against the abolition of the juvenile court as a separate system believe it is still the best way of meeting the special needs of children. They argue that although the juvenile system may be in need of some changes, traditional goals of rehabilitation and providing each offender individualized attention will continue to prove effective in reducing rates of recidivism among juvenile offenders. They believe the adult system has too many problems in its current operation to effectively make changes that will allow the court to serve the special needs of juveniles as well (Arthur, 1998; Dawson, 1990; Rosenberg, 1993; Springer, 1991; Yellen, 1996).

It is important to remember that what is commonly referred to as the "juvenile justice system" is really anything but a system. What exists is a mélange of criminal-justice, social-service, and social-welfare agencies at the local level (typically county) that work in combination and separately for the welfare of wayward children. The centerpiece of this "system" is the juvenile court. The wealth of placements and referrals at the disposal of the juvenile court is unavailable in the adult system of justice. Proponents of maintaining a separate system claim that to eliminate the juvenile court from this system would essentially remove the glue holding together a patchwork of agencies designed to serve the needs of juveniles at the local level. In many counties across the United States, the juvenile court is the only juvenile justice service available.

34.3.4.1 The Juvenile Justice Process Is Still More Benign than the Criminal Justice Process

Although abolitionists maintain that the juvenile court has become nothing more than a junior criminal court, this is typically not the case in the court itself. Again, abolitionists focus their arguments on the increased punitiveness and harshness of penalties available in the juvenile court today. These penalties typically only apply to a very small minority of cases. Although records in this area are not reliable estimates of the total number of cases in the juvenile court because of severe underreporting, it is important to note that only 23 percent (387,100 nationally) of all formal referrals for delinquency to the juvenile court were for person or violent offenses (Stahl et al., 2002). The percentage does not include status offenses and does not include cases that were not formally processed. One estimate puts the number of informally handled cases at nearly 700,000 in the year 2000 (Stahl et al., 2002).

When a critical eye is cast on how the juvenile court operates and the statistics beyond the 2 percent of the offenders who commit violent crimes are examined, it becomes clear that the juvenile court is more benign than the adult system. Proponents of maintaining the separate system of justice would thus argue, why should we abolish an entire system of juvenile justice to accommodate the most violent 2 percent of all offenders when the system does a good job of handling the other 98 percent? In short, they would argue that abolitionists are focusing on only the most prominent, violent cases to base their points — arguments that do not reflect the true nature of dispositions within the system. In fact, many would point out that certification to adult court of the 2 percent is the exact remedy already available that would provide the additional due process rights that many abolitionists contend are absent. Finally, and perhaps the most telling argument in favor of maintaining a separate system, of all the person offense (violent) cases formally referred to the juvenile justice system, 40 percent are dismissed at intake and an additional 15 percent are dismissed at adjudication (OJJDP 2003). Only 0.7 percent are waived to adult court, and 10 percent are placed in secure confinement (OJJDP 2003). When compared with nonviolent and status offenses processed by the juvenile justice system, the violent cases that are waived or that result in a juvenile going to secure confinement represent less than one half of one percentage point of the juveniles processed in the system.

34.3.5 *Success of the Juvenile Justice System*

Proponents of maintaining a separate system of juvenile justice are quick to point out that the juvenile justice system is perhaps the more successful system of the two criminal justice systems in the United States. There are several reasons for this statement. First, the cost of the juvenile justice system is far less than that of the adult system of justice. Cases are processed quickly in the juvenile court, for most cases attorneys are not needed, and the time spent on each case is also reduced. Second, as noted previously, there are a multitude of options for juveniles who come into contact with the juvenile justice system compared with the adult system of justice. Third, despite what abolitionists would argue, most people working in the juvenile justice system have the best interests of the child in mind. To repeat, the small proportion of offenders who commit violent offenses might be better served by being waived to adult court, but it simply does not make sense to abolish an entire system to accommodate the less than 1 percent of offenders who are processed through it. Finally, the recidivism rates of juveniles who are referred to some component of the juvenile justice system are extraordinarily lower than those of the adult system of justice. Again, reliable statistics are difficult to ascertain because of the numerous placements used in juvenile court, but the simple fact is that 80 to 90 percent of the juveniles who are sanctioned by the police, schools, and the juvenile court do not come back into the system. In short, the system works.

34.4 Conclusions

Arguments on both sides of this debate have merit. Clearly, the juvenile justice system has issues that must be addressed. It is important to recognize that this debate is ongoing, and there is probably no resolution in sight anytime in the near future. (Table 34.2 summarizes the arguments presented in this chapter.)

Table 34.2   Arguments for and against Abolishing the Juvenile Justice System

Arguments for Abolition	Arguments against Abolition
The current state of the juvenile justice system does not reflect the original intentions of the founders. The system has become increasingly punitive and harsh.	Juveniles are still less culpable than adults and deserve to be treated differently.
Children in juvenile court are denied basic due process rights. The move to a more punitive system has not been accompanied by an increase in the due process rights of children in the juvenile court.	The adult system of criminal justice is not equipped to deal with juveniles. The adult correctional system simply warehouses inmates. There is little, if any, rehabilitation potential.
The current juvenile justice system duplicates the adult system. Juveniles get all of the punishment and none of the protection of the adult system of justice.	Juveniles have a greater rehabilitation potential than adults. They have lower rates of recidivism.
Increasing use of determinate sentencing has led some juvenile courts to become more punitive than their adult counterparts.	The worst aspects of the adult system are not present in the juvenile system, specifically bail and the gamelike adversarial system.
Juveniles are routinely not represented by counsel in proceedings in which their liberty is at stake. The presence of counsel in the juvenile court does not have a positive effect in many cases.	The violent criminals that serve as the basis for arguments about abolishing the juvenile system make up less than 1 percent of the offenders processed by the system. Throwing away an entire system for this tiny minority is not logical.
The distinction between the juvenile and adult systems of justice has become blurred, thus eliminating the need for a separate system of justice.	The juvenile justice system is still more benign than the adult criminal justice system, and this allows the juvenile system to individualize justice for most of the offenders it deals with.

Table 34.2   Arguments for and against Abolishing the Juvenile Justice System (continued)

Arguments for Abolition	Arguments against Abolition
A unified, streamlined system of justice could take age into account as a mitigating factor and provide juveniles with increased due process rights.	The range of placement options and other mechanisms available in the juvenile court far that available in the adult system.
	The juvenile justice system is the most successful system in American criminal justice. Most juveniles who are processed do not come back, and the system enjoys high rates of success in reforming juveniles.

References

Ainsworth, J.E. (1991). Re-imaging childhood and reconstructing the legal order: the case for abolishing the juvenile court. *North Carolina Law Review*, 69, 1083–1133.

Ainsworth, J.E. (1995). Youth justice in a unified court: response to critics of juvenile court abolition. *Boston College Law Review*, 36, 927–951.

Arthur, L.G. (1998). Abolish the juvenile court? *Juvenile and Family Court Journal*, 49, 51–58.

Berkheiser, M. (2002). The fiction of juvenile right to counsel: waiver in the juvenile courts. *Florida Law Review*, 54, 577–686.

Caeti, T.J., Hemmens, C., and Burton, V. (1996). Juvenile right to counsel: a national comparison of state legal codes. *American Journal of Criminal Law*, 23(3), 611–632.

Cowden, V.L. and McKee, G.R. (1995). Competency to stand trial in juvenile delinquency proceedings — cognitive maturity and the attorney-client relationship. *University of Louisville Journal of Family Law*, 33, 629–660.

Dawson, R.O. (1990). The future of juvenile justice: is it time to abolish the system? *Journal of Criminal Law and Criminology*, 81, 136–155.

Federle, K.H. (1990). The abolition of the juvenile court: a proposal for the preservation of children's legal rights. *Journal of Contemporary Law*, 16, 23–51.

Feld, B.C. (1989). The right to counsel in juvenile court: an empirical study of when lawyers appear and the difference they make. *Journal of Criminal Law and Criminology* 79, 1185–1346.

Feld, B.C. (1999). Abolish the juvenile court: sentencing policy when the child is a criminal and the criminal is a child. *Bad Kids,* New York: Oxford University Press. pp. 287–330.

Fox, S.J. (1977). Abolishing the Juvenile Court. *Harvard Law School Bulletin,* 28, 22–27.

Fritsch, E.J., Hemmens, C., and Caeti, T.J. (1996). Violent youth in juvenile and adult court: an assessment of sentencing strategies. *Law and Policy,* 18(1–2), 115–136.

Fritsch, E.J., Caeti, T.J., and Hemmens C. (1996). Spare the needle but not the punishment: the incarceration of waived juveniles in texas prisons. *Crime and Delinquency,* 42(4), 574–592.

Gardner, M.R. (1987). Punitive juvenile justice: some observations on a recent trend. *International Journal of Law and Psychiatry,* 10, 129–151.

Grisso, T. (1980). Juveniles' capacities to waive Miranda rights: an empirical analysis. *California Law Review,* 68, 1134–1142.

Hemmens, C., Fritsch, E.J., and Caeti, T.J. (1999). The rhetoric of juvenile justice reform. *Quinnipiac Law Review,* 18(3), 661–685.

Hemmens, C., Caeti, T.J., Fritsch, E.J. (1997). Juvenile justice purpose clauses: the power of words. *Criminal Justice Policy Review,* 8(2–3), 221–246.

Hirschi, T. and Gottfredson, M.R. (1996). Rethinking the juvenile justice system. In Rojek, D.G. and Jensen, G.F. (Eds.), *Exploring Delinquency: Causes and Control.* Los Angeles, CA: Roxbury. pp. 459-464..

Hufstedler, Shirley M. (1984). Should we give up reform? *Crime and Delinquency,* 30, 5–38.

Krisberg, B. and Austin, J. (1986). *Reinventing Juvenile Justice.* Newbury Park, CA: Sage.

McCarthy, F.B. (1977). Should juvenile delinquency be abolished? *Crime and Delinquency,* 23, 196–203.

Office of Juvenile Justice and Delinquency Prevention (OJJDP) (2003). *Statistical Briefing Book.* Online: http://ojjdp.ncjrs.org/ojstatbb/index.html.

Rosenberg, I.M. (1993). Leaving bad enough alone: a response to the juvenile court abolitionists. *Wisconsin Law Review,* 1, 163–185.

Springer, C.E. (1991). Rehabilitating the juvenile court. *Notre Dame Journal of Law, Ethics, and Public Policy,* 5, 397–420.

Stahl, A., Finnegan, T., and Kang, W. (2002). Easy Access to Juvenile Court Statistics: 1985–2000. Online: http://ojjdp.ncjrs.org/ojstatbb/ezajcs/.

Taylor, R.W., Fritsch, E.J., and Caeti, T.J. (2002). *Juvenile Justice: Policies, Programs, and Practices.* New York: McGraw-Hill.

Torbet, P., Gamble, R., Hurst, H., IV, Montgomery, I., Szymanski, L., and Thomas, D. (1996). State Responses to Serious and Violent Juvenile Crime: Research Report. Washington, D.C.: Office of Juvenile Justice and Delinquency Prevention.

Wizner, S. and Keller, M.F. (1977). The penal model of juvenile justice: is delinquency court jurisdiction obsolete? *New York University Law Review*, 52, 1120–1135.

Yellen, D. (1996). What juvenile court abolitionists can learn from the failures of sentencing reform. *Wisconsin Law Review*, No. 3, 577–602.

Cases Cited

In re Gault 387 U.S. 1 (1967).

In re Winship 397 U.S. 358 (1970).

Kent v. United States 383 U.S. 541 (1966).

McKeiver v. Pennsylvania 403 U.S. 528 (1971).

Part VII Conclusion

DISCUSSION QUESTIONS FOR PART VII

1. Wallace (Chapter 30) discusses three societal changes that may have contributed to school violence. What are they? What are the programs aimed at reducing school violence and why do they not work, according to Wallace?
2. According to the study conducted by Schreck et al. (see Chapter 31), what are some of the strongest predictors of victimization among schoolchildren? What theoretical underpinnings support their findings?
3. According to Penn (see Chapter 32), what role does social disorganization play in the production of delinquency among African American or black young people in the U.S.? What does he mean by the term *child slaving*? Explain.
4. According to Mueller (Chapter 33), what is the appeal of DARE programs? What does he mean by *science vs. symbolic politics*?
5. In Chapter 34, Caeti and Fritsch give the pros and cons for abolishing the juvenile justice system in America. What conclusions do they reach about this important topic? Do you agree or disagree with their conclusions? Why?

Index

A

ABA, 396
abandonment, 129
Abolish Chronic Truancy (ACT), 337
abstinence violation effect (AVE), 393
abuse definition, 128–130
abuse history of sex offenders, 364, 369
academic performance and school crime, 146, 573
accountability, 315
    Balanced and Restorative Justice (BARJ) programs, 23
    goal of probation, 18
    and Preppie Gangs, 215
accountability based sanctions, 513–515
ACT (Abolish Chronic Truancy) program, 337, 338
ADA (Americans with Disabilities Act of 1990), 357
    See also disabled juvenile offenders
Addams, Jane, 43
ADD (attention-deficit disorder), 355
ADHD (attention-deficit hyperactivity disorder), 351
adjustment disorders, 453
adolescent egocentrism, 203
adult criminal procedure vs. juvenile, 45–46
    rights associated with juveniles waivers, 53 (see also Kent v. United States, 383 U.S. 541 (1966))

trends in juvenile transfer, 25, 49
adulticism, 306–307
adult mental retardation, 529–531
adults, stalking
    prevalence, 237–239
    typologies, 239–240
adult sex offenders, 363
adult supervision, 153
    and delinquency, 163
    and gang participation, 162
    See also family conditions
adult vs. juvenile drug usage patterns, 459–460
African Americans and juvenile justice
    about, 619–620
    adjudicated case statistics, 623
    arrest statistics, 622
    black criminology, 625–626
    Blackophobia, 628–629
    definitions of black and white, 621
    detainment, 622
    historical perspectives on justice system, 624, 627–628
    petitioned case statistics, 622
    Social Darwinism, 620–621
    social disorganization in black communities, 626–627, 629–631
    status symbols of street culture, 630
    theoretical responses to disproportionality, 624–625
aftercare programs, 504–505

age
    adulticism, 306–307
    and behavior assessment, 240–241
    childhood *vs.* adolescence, 129
    historical consideration, 8–9, 16–17,
        24–26, 49
    infanticistic, 307
    legal liability, 296
    puberty and delinquent behavior, 223
    status offenses and, 332
    typical female offenders, 97
    See also reasoning power
Agnew, Robert, 88
Aid for Family with Dependent Children,
    438
AIDS treatment, 499
Alaska Supreme Court. *See Davis v. Alaska,*
    415 U.S. 308 (1974)
alcohol abuse, 414, 422, 459
    See also substance abuse
Alcoholics Anonymous (AA), 459
All Handicapped Children Act of 1975,
    348–349
American Association of Mental
        Retardation and the American
        Psychiatric Association, 531
American Bar Association Standards
        Relating to the Administration
        of Criminal Justice, 301–302
American Indian juvenile justice
    about, 409–410, 409–411
    federal arrest data compared with tribal
        data, 421–425
    future policy development, 427–428
    high rates of victimization, 421
    jurisdiction and legal structure, 412–419
    research implications, 425–427
    tribal differences, 419–421
American Indians and Crime (Greenfeld,
    Smith), 421
American Journal of Public Health, 645
American juvenile justice system, 44–46,
    180–181
    African Americans and juvenile justice,
        627–628
    blended sentencing, 180–181
    challenges, 313–315
    court discretion, 476 (*see also*
        prosecutorial discretion)

    doctrine of *void for vagueness,* 42
    historical perspectives, 11–12, 312–313,
        624 (*see also* juvenile court:
        historical perspectives)
    industrialization period, 12–13
    informality in, 333
    jurisdiction, 180–181 (*See also* American
        Indian juvenile justice)
    recent loss of rights, 561
    subjectivity of, 339–341
    See also African Americans and juvenile
        justice; juvenile court;
        prosecutorial discretion;
        reforms in juvenile justice
        (modern); waivers, juvenile
American Psychological Association (APA),
    501
Americans with Disabilities Act (ADA), 347
anger, 568, 575
anomie, 81, 82
anomie theory, 81, 82, 225–226
anonymity, 64–65, 181
antisocial behaviors, 501
antistalking legislation, 236
apprenticeships, 34
Arizona Juvenile Code, 56
    See also In re Gault, 387 U.S. 1 (1967)
atavism, 79
Atkins, Daryl Renard, 531
Atkins v. Virginia, 122 S.Ct. 2242 (2002),
    530–532
attachment theory, 244–245
attention-deficit disorder (ADD), 355
Augustus, John, 18, 39
automatic waiver, 325
autonomy, quest for, 568
aversive conditioning, 393

B

"bad kid" and "good kid," 305–306
bail practices, 39, 50
    See also Kent v. United States, 383 U.S.
        541 (1966)
Balanced and Restorative Justice (BARJ)
    programs, 23, 512–513
battered child syndrome, 127
Beccaria, Cesare, 221

behavioral analysis of sex offenders. *See* sex offenders, behavior analysis
behavioral models of stalking, 244
Behavior Assessment System for Children (BASC), 364
behavior disorder, 350
behavior modification, 495–496
behavior scientific endeavors and causal agents, 17, 44
Bellotti v. Baird, 1979, 283
Berne, Eric, 495
best interests of the juvenile. *See* juvenile's best interests
BIA (Bureau of Indian Affairs), 412–413
BIA Liquor Suppression Office, 414
Big Brothers/ Big Sisters Program, 339
Bill of Rights
  doctrine of *void for vagueness,* 42
  protection under, 20
biological theory, 78–80
biopsychosocial approach, 222–223
black criminology, 625–626
Blackophobia, 628–629
blended sentencing, 25, 180–181, 525
Bloody Code, 532
Blueprints for Violence Prevention, 503
Bonger, William, 227
"boot camps," 22, 459, 503
Boston Municipal Court, 18
Bowen, Louise, 43
Boys Clubs/Girls Clubs Program, 339, 460–461
brain development and adolescents, 531, 532
Braithwaite, John, 89
Breed v. Jones, 421 U.S. 517 (1975)., 20, 61–63
bullying, 242–243, 572, 573, 579–580
Bureau of Indian Affairs (BIA), 412–413
Burger, (Chief Justice), 58
Butler, Brenton, 186–187
Bykofsky v. Borough of Middletown (1976), 279, 282

C

California Supreme Court, 61–62, 63
California Youth Authority program, 516, 517

capital punishment
  about, 521–522, 532–533
  adults, 526
  ban, 531–532
  early American, 14
  historical statistics, 522–523, 524
  juvenile reasoning, 529–531 (*see also* reasoning power)
  prison as alternative solution, 35
  recent trends, 526–529
  standards of decency, 523, 525–526
Capitol Offender Program, 516
case construction, 302–303
case law, 33
caseloads, 18–19, 23
Catholic Church
  first juvenile correctional institution, 11
  Roman-German law system, 8, 10
Causes of Delinquency (Hirschi), 85
Center for Independent Living for Truants (SOAR), 339
Center for Juvenile Alternatives (CJA), 337–338
Center for Restorative Justice and Mediation, 512–513
charging decisions, 301–309
chemical imbalances, 79–80
The Chicago School, 227–228
The Chicago School, 83
child abuse
  and delinquent behavior, 570
  rising rates, 186, 560
  See also maltreatment during childhood
child abuse identification
  about, 130
  data sources, 131
  reporters, 130–131
child labor, 13, 15, 36, 38, 40, 88
child neglect, 128–130, 572
  See also child abuse
children, historically changing attitudes
  Age of Enlightenment, 10–16
  biblical times, 5–7
  cultural customs, 4
  evolution of in America, 16–24
  Industrial Revolution, 10–16
  middle ages and Renaissance periods, 8–10
"children in need of supervision" (CHINS), 333

children's aid societies, 15–16, 38–39
Children's Protective Services, 135, 136,
    139–140
child-saving movement, 15, 38–39, 46, 628
child status, 34
child welfare agencies compared with
        police agencies, 259–260
Child Welfare Agency, 136–137
Child Welfare League of America, 131
CHINS ("children in need of supervision"),
    333
Christ's Hospital (England), 9
Civil War era, 14, 30, 40, 412
Clark County Juvenile Court Services, 339
class barriers
    child saving movement, 15–16
    and critical theory, 87
    intelligence and delinquency, 80
    and law, 33–34
    living up to standards, 82
    parens patrie, 33
classical approach, 221–222
clinical behavior analysis, 403–405
codified law. *See* statutory law
cognitive distortions, 370
    See also intelligence and delinquency
Cohen, Stanley, 24
Columbine High School, 209, 530, 562, 568
common law
    American, 33, 312–313
    English, 31–35
    provision for mental illness, 530–531
    Romano-Germanic, 12
communications theory applied to
        obsessive relational intrusions,
        245–246
community attachment, 576
community environment and
        delinquency, 575–576
community justice. *See* prosecutorial
        discretion
community social control
    and delinquency, 161–162
    and gang participation, 160–161
Computer Fraud and Abuse Act, 230
"Comrade" (cyberdeliquent), 220
concept migration of gang-type activity,
        212–214, 572
conditioned emotional responses (CERs),
        399–400

conduct disorder, 351, 362
conflict resolution, 578, 580
conflict theory, 87, 227
consensus theories, 87
constitution rights and juveniles, 68–70
control theory, 147, 227
convict lease program, 628
Cook County, Illinois, 44, 313
    juvenile court creation, 16–19, 44–46
    juvenile court jurisdiction, 50
    See also juvenile court: historical
        perspectives
correctional facilities, 493
    deinstitutionalization, 333–334
    "juvenile institution," 11
    "minor penitentiaries," 14
    prison as alternative to death penalty,
        35
    See also placement facilities
correctional facility personnel
    about, 537–539
    caseloads, 18–19, 23
    discussion, 546–551
    education, 538
    job satisfaction and organizational
        commitment in adult facilities,
        538–539
    job satisfaction and organizational
        commitment in juvenile
        facilities, 538
    job satisfaction predictors, 538
    study data, 539–542
    study methods, 539
    study results, 542–546
correctional institutions
    adults with disabilities, 357
    establishment of, 11
    population percentage with disabilities,
        347–348
court order violations, 334
"courtship disorder," 239
"crime does not pay," 78
criminal intent *(mens rea),* 34, 332, 355
criminal law, 303
critical theory, 87
Crouse, Mary Ann, 37
Culture of Fear (Glassner), 174
curfews
    about, 275–276, 289–291, 332

efficacy, 336
enforcement, 283–287
example programs, 279, 280–281
legal issues, 279, 281–283
police role, 287–289
purpose and extent, 276–278
routine activity factors, 605
status offense policy, 334–337
custody, number of juveniles in, 491
custody entitlement, 50
cybercrime
    about, 219–221, 231
    anomie theory, 225–226
    biopsychosocial approach, 222–223
    classical approach, 221–222
    control theory, 227
    detection and management, 230–231
    developmental theories, 228–229
    social disorganization, 227–228
    social learning approach, 222–223
    strain theory, 225–226

D

Daily Mail Publishing Company, 64–65
DARE America v. Rolling Stone Magazine,
    646
DARE America v. Stephen Glass, 646
DARE (Drug Abuse Resistance Education),
    461, 637–638, 641–646
Davis v. Alaska, 415 U.S. 308 (1974), 60–61
The Dawes Act, 412, 415
death sentences. *See* capital punishment
death sentences by year (table), 524
decency standards, 525, 528
    See also capital punishment
Defense Threat Reduction Agency (DTRA),
    220
deferred prosecution, 354–355
deinstitutionalization, 333–334
deliberate crime, 528–529
delinquency
    definition, 77
    educational level of offenders, 355–356
    most common offenses, 179, 220
    multifaceted problem, 300
    population growth trends, 176

problems of immediate gratification
    (PIG), 393
statistical reduction in, 176–178
and substance abuse, 457–458
theories of cause, 77–90
    See also female delinquents
Delinquency and Opportunity (Cloward,
    Ohlin), 83
delinquency theory
    biological theory, 78–80
    deterrence theory, 78
    psychological theory, 80–81
    sociological theory, 81–90
Delinquent Boys: The Culture of the Gang
    (Cohen), 82
delinquent girls. *See* female delinquents
demographics, 608–609
detention, 65–66
detention facilities. *See* correctional
    facilities; foster homes;
    institutions; reform schools
deterrence and capital punishment, 528
deterrence theory, 78, 221, 276–277
developmental findings on brain
    development, 531, 532
developmental theory, 228–229
    See also substance addicted juveniles
Deviant Behavior (Akers), 85
differential association and African
    American juveniles, 624–625
differential association and social learning
    theory, 84–85
differential association-reinforcement
    theory, 84–85
differential association theory, 88
differential opportunity theory, 82–83
differential oppression theory, 571
difficult temperaments, 567–568
DiIulio, John, 174, 188
Disabilities Education Act (IDEA), 348–349
disability programs, 348, 352–356
disabled juvenile offenders, 498–500
    about, 347–348, 357
    prevalence, 350–352
    programs, 352–356
    types of, 348–350
disorders, 348
"disruptive students," 577
diversion program research, 481–483

diversion programs, 478–481, 486–487

diversion theories, 476–478

double jeopardy

    and self-incrimination, 61–62 (*see also Breed v. Jones,* 421 U.S. 517 (1975).)

    in tribal and federal courts, 418

Dowling v. United States, 230

Drug Abuse Resistance Education (D.A.R.E), 461, 637–638, 641–646

drug courts, 23

drug education programs, 613

    See also DARE (Drug Abuse Resistance Education); substance abuse

drug violations, 353

due process, 14

    addressed in Fourteenth Amendment, 51–52

    clearly defined for adults, 20

    cross-examination, 59 (*see also Davis v. Alaska,* 415 U.S. 308 (1974); *In re Gault,* 387 U.S. 1 (1967))

    custody entitlement, 50

    double jeopardy (*see Breed v. Jones,* 421 U.S. 517 (1975).; *Miranda v. Arizona,* 384 U.S. 436 (1966))

    in educational environments, 66–70

    Ex parte Crouse, 37

    historical lack of, 16

    importance of *Breed v. Jones,* 62

    and internet privacy, 231

    jury trial, 58–59 (*see also McKeiver v. Pennsylvania,* 403 U.S. 528 (1971))

    notice of charges (*see In re Gault,* 387 U.S. 1 (1967))

    reasonable doubt (*see In re Winship,* 397 U.S. 358 (1970))

    self-incrimination (*See Fare v. Michael C.* 44 U.S. 707 (1979))

    waiver to criminal court, 53–55 (*see also Kent v. United States,* 383 U.S. 541 (1966))

DUIs (1992-2001), 638

Durkheim, Emile, 81

dysfunctional families, 100, 365

    See also family conditions

E

economic disadvantage, 432

    in communities, 576

    immigrants, 35

    strain theory, 225–226

    See also Mexican American female gang affiliations

economic status

    and child abuse rates, 134

    immigrants and impoverishment, 35

    and Preppie Gangs, 194

economic status of victims, 606

economic wealth

    amassing, 225–226

    and law enforcement of Preppie Gang activities, 205–207

Eddings, Monty Lee, 527

Eddings v. Oklahoma, 445 U.S. 104 (1982), 527, 529

Eddy, Thomas, 35

educational institutions

    abuse occurrence, 130–131

    DARE programs, 637–648

    delinquency, 150

    delinquency and social controls, 160

    gang activity and social controls, 159–160

    LEA [local educational agency], 353

    media coverage of violence, 178

    and participation, 151

    school shootings, 178

    "stay-put" rule, 353

    See also school violence; social control study; teachers

educational institutions and constitutional rights

    First Amendment Rights, 66–67

    school suspensions, 68

    search and seizure, 68–70

educational level of institutionalized populations, 355–356, 365

educational neglect, 129

educational programs, 496–498

educational success and delinquency, 573–575

education programs for special needs, 351, 352

egocentrism, 80–81, 203

egoism, 227

Eighth Amendment Rights, 20, 528, 529, 531, 532
emotional disturbance (ED), 349
emotional instability, 81
English juvenile justice, 9, 31–35, 624
  See also juvenile court: historical perspectives; *parens patriae*
environmental influences, 79, 432
  and impoverished conditions, 35
  and substance abuse, 455–457
  vs. innate sin, 11
erotomania, 243
escape behaviors, 399
ethnic identity and gang affiliation, 441
ethnic minorities
  alienation, 631
  black students in school settings, 604–605
  female offenders, 97–98 (*see also* Mexican American female gang affiliations)
  and general strain theory, 434–435
  Hispanic categorization, 635
  incidence of maltreatment, 133–134, 410
  intervention for female offenders, 119–120
  overrepresentation in public institutions, 494
  racial alienation, 629–630
  racial stereotyping, 176
  rates of detention, 182
  routine activities, 605
  and single-parent families, 560
  "street" status symbols, 631
  "zero tolerance" in the school setting, 582
  See also African Americans and juvenile justice; American Indian juvenile justice
ethnic nationalism, 198–199
ex-offenders, 501
Ex parte Crouse, 4 Whart. 9 (Pa. 1838), 14, 37

F

family conditions
  communication quality, 570
  dysfunctional, 100, 365
  moral installation, 569–570
  parental characteristics, 571
  and substance abuse, 455–457
family courts, 22
Family Educational Rights and Privacy Act (FERPA), 259, 354
'family matter' focus
  change over time, 4
  historical roots, 8–9
FAP (functional analytic psychotherapy), 403
Fare v. Michael C. 44 U.S. 707 (1979), 61
fatalities, child, 132–133
FECT (functional analytic psychotherapy-enhanced cognitive therapy), 405
Federal Aviation Association, 220
Federal Bureau of Investigation (FBI), 132, 133
federal funding for drug issues, 462
Federal Handgun Safety Act, 333
Federal Juvenile Delinquency Act (1974), 333
female delinquents
  about, 93–94
  age, 97
  childhood maltreatment, 100
  in the educational environment, 100–104
  ethnicity, 97–98
  internalized victimization, 100
  profiles, 95–97
  rate statistics, 94–95
  risk factors (table), 102
  system bias, 98–99
  truancy rates, 339
  underrated upward trend, 98
  See also Mexican American female gang affiliations
female delinquents and gender-specific intervention. *See* gender-specific intervention (female)
female victims of sexual abuse, 366–367
FERPA (Family Educational Rights and Privacy Act), 354
Ferrell, Rod, 210
Fifth Amendment Rights
  Miranda v. Arizona, 53, 55

protection against self-incrimination, 61
  (*see also Fare v. Michael C.
  44 U.S. 707* (1979); *Gallegos v.
  Colorado,* 370 U.S. 49 (1962);
  Haley v. Ohio, 332 U.S. 596
  (1948))
protection from double jeopardy and
  self-incrimination (*See Breed v.
  Jones,* 421 U.S. 517 (1975).)
First Amendment Rights
  curfew laws, 335 (*see also Qutb et al.
  v. Strauss,* (1994))
  educational institutions, 66–67
  juvenile anonymity, 64–66
first-time offenders
  age, 484
  ethnicity, 483–484
  gender, 484
flag salute, 66–67
Florida Atlantic University (FAU), 512–513
Florida Child Protective System, 128
Ford v. Wainwright, 447 U.S 399 (1986),
  530
foster homes, 46
  child disappearance of, 128
  forerunners of, 35
Fourteenth Amendment Rights, 51–52,
  528, 529, 531
  educational institution settings, 67
  juvenile detention, 65–66
Fourth Amendment Rights, 68–70
free will, 78
Freudian theory, 80–81
functional analysis of stalking, 245
functional analytic psychotherapy-
  enhanced cognitive therapy
  (FECT), 405
functional analytic psychotherapy (FAP),
  403
functionalism, 87
funding
  cuts with rising incarcerations, 183
  drug enforcement, 641
  substance abuse treatment, 462–463

G

Gallegos, Robert, 53
Gallegos v. Colorado, 370 U.S. 49 (1962),
  20, 55

gang members
  affiliate female, 432, 433
  initiations, 433
  victimization of members, 572
gang migration and proliferation
  Preppie Gangs, 210–212
  studies suggestive of, 572
Gang Resistance Education and Training
  program, 166
gangs, 571–573
  activities, 150, 314 (*see also* social
    control study in educational
    and community settings)
  concept migration, 212–214
  curfew laws, 285–286
  definition, 197
  deviant behavior of, 444
  effects of participation in youth group
    activities, 156
  formation, 13
  levels of delinquency, 572
  participation in activities, 504
  See also Mexican American female gang
    affiliations; Preppie Gangs
gateway hypothesis of drug use, 454–455
Gault, Gerald Francis, 55–57
gender comparisons
  delinquency, 94–95
  gang membership (*see* Mexican
    American female gang
    affiliations)
  substance abuse, 452–453
gender-specific intervention (female)
  about, 109–110, 121–122
  abuse and neglect, 113–114
  academics, 117
  economic independence, 117–118
  family relationships, 114
  health and mental health, 115–116
  historically, 110–113
  needs based *vs.* offense-based
    programs, 119–121
  self-esteem, 118–119
  situations involving motherhood and
    childcare, 116–117
  socialization, 118–119
  substance abuse, 115
General Crimes Act, 412
general strain theory, 88, 432, 434–435, 441

general theory of crime, 86

geriatric offenders, 177

"get-tough" ideology, 23–25, 314–315, 328–329, 334, 340–341, 525, 533, 561–562, 564

See also waivers, juvenile

GGI (Guided Group Interaction), 496

Glass, Steven, 645, 646

Glassner, Barry, 174

Glassner, William, 495

Glover, Michael, 187

Good Behavior Game, 503

"good kid" and "bad kid," 305–306

Goss v. Lopez, 419 U.S. 565 (1975)

Goth groups, 199–200, 204, 208

Graham, Gary, 529

Graham v. Collins, 506 U.S. 461 (1993), 527, 529

Graunger, Thomas, 527

Green, Richard, 60–61

Green v. United States 355 U.S. 184, 187–188 (1957), 62

group therapy, 496

Growves, Byron, 88

GST (general strain theory). *See* general strain theory

Guided Group Interaction (GGI), 496

Gun Free Schools Act of 1990, 564

Gun Free Schools Act of 1994, 564

H

habeas corpus, 37

Habitual Truant Act (Nevada), 338

Haley, John, 51–52

Haley v. Ohio, 332 U.S. 596 (1948), 51–52, 55

"halfway houses," 492

handicap, 348

Hannah, Ocunish, 527

Harris, Eric, 209

Hayt (Commissioner of Indian Affairs), 413

hearing-impairment, 357

Hirschi, Travis, 85, 86, 224

Hispanic Stress Inventory (HSI), 432, 435–436

HIV juveniles, 499

Hodgkins et al. v. Peterson et al. (2004), 282

home detention, 503

homicide
by Black Americans, 630
counties reporting homicides, 178
likely times of, 335
rates, 178–179, 561

houses of refuge, 14, 32, 35, 312
associated problems, 38–39
duties and custodianship, 36–37

HSI (Hispanic Stress Inventory), 432, 435–436

Hutchins v. District of Columbia (1999), 282

I

IAP (Intensive Aftercare Programs), 505

Idaho Youth Ranch, 503

IDEA (Disabilities Education Act), 348–349, 353, 357

identity disturbances and stalking behavior, 245

identity work, 203

IEP (individualized educational program), 353

Illinois General Assembly, 188

Illinois Juvenile Court Act 1899 Ill. Laws 132 *et seq.,* 50

immigrants
curfew laws, 335
impoverishment, 35

immigration, 15, 16

immunity, 17
absolute of children, 17, 29, 34
limited of youth, 29

Impact of Crime on Victims, 516

impairment, 348

inclusion/normalization, 396

incorrigible juveniles, 334

indentured service, 9–10, 11
See also child labor

Indian Child Welfare Act (ICWA), 417

Indian Civil Rights Act, 412

Indian Civil Rights Act (ICRA), 416

Indian Reorganization Act of 1934, 412, 415–416

Indian Self-Determination and Education Assistance Act of 1975, 412, 417, 424

Indicators of School Crime and Safety, 2002 (U.S.Dept. of Education and Justice), 563
individualized educational program (IEP), 353
Individuals with Disabilities Education Act Amendments, 565
Industrial Revolution, 40, 312
industrial training schools, 15–16, 42, 312
 See also reform schools
infanticistic behavior, 307
innovators, 82
In re Gault, 387 U.S. 1 (1967), 20, 42, 44, 55–57, 314
In re Holmes, 348 U.S. 973, 75 S.Ct. 535 (1955), 20
In re Winship, 397 U.S. 358 (1970), 20, 57–59
insane asylums, 40
institutionalization
 deinstitutionalization, 22
 education in, 494
 effects of, 334, 494
 efficacy of treatment strategy, 19
 funding cuts with rising incarcerations, 183
 results of incarceration, 334
institutions
 living conditions, 16, 18–19, 332, 494
 number of juveniles in, 491–492
 types of during 19th century, 40
intake officer role, 18
intelligence and delinquency, 80, 223, 567
Intensive Aftercare Programs (IAP), 505
International Covenant on Civil and Human Rights (1989), 521–522, 522
Internet Rapid Response Team (IRRT), 230
interrogations, 51–52
 see also Gallegos v. Colorado, 370 U.S. 49 (1962); *Haley v. Ohio,* 332 U.S. 596 (1948)
Interstate Transportation of Stolen Property, 230
intervention
 point and form of, 4
 programs, 501–504
 See also rehabilitation and treatment

intervention study identifying critical components
 about, 255–256, 270–271
 analysis, 265–270
 data and methods, 263–264
 early onset, 256–257
 program innovation, 257–261
 site descriptions, 262–263
invincibility myth, 203–204
IQ and delinquency, 80, 223, 567
isolation, 20
ISP (intensive supervision probation), 22, 23

J

Jackson, Robert, Attorney General, 295–297
Jehovah's Witnesses, 66–67
JJDP Act, 1974 (Juvenile Justice and Delinquency Prevention Act), 24, 333–334, 418, 512, 619
Job Corps, 504
Job Descriptive Index (JDI), 541
Johnson, Dorsie, 529
Johnson et al. v. City of Opelousas (1981), 282
Johnson v. Texas, 509 U.S. (1993), 527, 529
judges, juvenile, 46
judicial waivers, 180–181, 182, 317, 318–324
"just-say-no-type programs, 461
juvenile court: historical perspectives, 22, 332, 473–475
 constitutional protections, 55
 creation and early days, 16–19, 44–46, 179–180
 informal proceedings and due process, 17, 20–21, 313
 parens patriae power relocation to, 45, 312–313 (*see also parens patriae*)
 probation and effectiveness, 20–21
 program innovation, 22–24
 punishment of serious crimes, 24–26
Juvenile Court Act of the District of Columbia, 55
Juvenile Detention Alternative Initiative (JDAI), 99
"juvenile institution," 11

juvenile justice and American Indian populations. *See* American Indian juvenile justice

Juvenile Justice and Delinquency Prevention Act. *See* JJDP Act, 1974 (Juvenile Justice and Delinquency Prevention Act)

Juvenile Justice Bulletin (OJJDP; 2000), 188

juvenile justice reforms. *See* reforms in juvenile justice (modern)

juvenile offenders as subsequent adult offenders, 19

juvenile's best interests, 301, 311, 525

juvenile status, 16, 26, 34, 50, 176, 187, 240–241, 521, 522, 528

juveniles tried as adults, 175–176, 180, 304–305, 527
    consequences of, 181–182, 185–186
    deterrence benefit, 183–184
    See also waivers, juvenile

juvenile waivers. *See* waivers, juvenile

K

Kennedy, Justice, 532

Kent, Morris, Jr., 53–55

Kentucky Department of Juvenile Justice (DJJ), 538–539

Kent v. United States, 383 U.S. 541 (1966), 20, 42, 46, 53–55, 314

Klebold, Dylan, 209

L

labeled individuals, 626

labeling theory, 86–87, 89, 227

law
    adult criminal procedure *vs.* juvenile, 45–46
    types, 41

law enforcement, 176, 187
    cybercrime, 230–231
    police brutality, 227
    and Preppie Gangs, 205–207
    prevention control points, 287–289
    See also intervention study identifying critical components; police

LEA [local educational agency], 353

LEARN, St. Louis Project, 352–353, 357

learning disabilities (LD), 349, 351, 567

LEARN program, 356

legal counsel rights, 50, 51–52, 57
    See also In re Gault, 387 U.S. 1 (1967)

legislative waivers, 317, 324–328

leniency, 19, 314–315
    historically, 19
    and individuals lacking accountability, 206
    prosecutorial discretion, 296

life sentences
    juvenile quoted on, 173

Life Skills Training, 502

Lockett v. Ohio, 438 U.S. 586 (1978), 527, 529

Lohnes v. Cloud (1973), 416

Lombroso, Cesare, 79, 222–223

looking-glass self, 86–87

Lopez, Dwight, 67

Los Angeles Police Department, 239

Lott, Trent, 629

Louisiana Department of Public Safety and Corrections, 515–516

Lutheran Social Services, 339

M

Major Crimes Act, 412, 414–415

male delinquency compared with females, 93–94
    See also gender comparisons

maltreatment during childhood
    about, 127–128
    explanation models, 137–138
    future needs, 139–140
    identifying, 130–131
    legal definition, 128–130
    links to delinquency, 138–139
    profiles, 132–134
    responses, 134–137

maltreatment profile, 132–134
    correlating circumstances, 133–134
    fatalities, 132–133
    type of maltreatment, 132
    victim-offender relationship, 133

maltreatment response
  intervention programs, 139–140
  investigation and intervention, 134–137
  jurisdiction, 130
Manson, Marilyn, 209
marijuana to cocaine users, 455
Marshall, Chief Justice, 411
Maruschak, Laura, 523
Marx, Carl, 87
McCaffrey, Barry, 647
McKeiver v. Pennsylvania, 403 U.S. 528
    (1971), 58–60, 64
Mead, George Herbert, 86–87
media coverage
  drug education programming, 646
  sensationalism and school violence, 577
  sensationalism and the superpredator
      myth (1990s), 173–176 (*see also*
      superpredator myth (1990s))
  sensationalism of school violence,
      565–566, 577
media violence, 561
medical neglect, 129
MEIM (Multigroup Ethnic Identity Measure),
    432
Meloy, J. Reid, 238
mental health disorders, 356, 362
mental illness, 351, 499–500
mental retardation, 351, 529–531
mentoring, 579
Merton, Robert, 225
Mexican American female gang affiliations
  categories of gangs, 433–435
  ethnic categorization of Hispanics, 635
  factors relating to, 435–436
  study conclusions, 443–444
  study data analysis, 438–439
  study findings, 439–443
  study methods, 436–438
Michigan Juvenile Intervention Initiative
    (MJII), 255–270
"minor penitentiaries," 14
"minors in need of supervision" (MINS),
    333
"minors requiring authoritative
    intervention" (MRAI), 333
MINS ("minors in need of supervision"),
    333
Miranda rights, 53, 55

Miranda v. Arizona, 384 U.S. 436 (1966),
    53, 55
Missouri v. Wilkins, 492 U.S. 361 (1989),
    527, 528
Monitoring the Future (MTF, 1999), 608,
    639
moral culpability, 529–531, 530, 532
moral development, 560
moral entrepreneurs, 86
morality, 81
moral panic, 24, 210, 521, 577
mother-child bonding, 370
Motor City Police Athletic League (PAL),
    263
Mountlake Terrace Neutral Zone, 290–291
MRAI ("minors requiring authoritative
    intervention"), 333
MST (multisystemic therapy), 383, 496
Multigroup Ethnic Identity Measure
    (MEIM), 432
multisystemic therapy (MST), 383, 496
Murder on a Sunday Morning (HBO
    Undercover), 187

N

National Aeronautics and Space
    Administration (NASA), 220
National Center for Juvenile Justice
    (NCSS), 96
National Council on Crime and
    Delinquency (NCCD),
    277–278, 332
National Crime Victimization Survey, 177,
    186
National District Attorneys Association
    (NDAA), 299–300
National Household Survey on Drug
    Abuse (NHSDA), 639
National Incidence Study of Child Abuse
    and Neglect, 186
National Incidence Study of Child Abuse
    and Neglect (NIS-3). *See* NIS-3
    (National Incidence Study of
    Child Abuse and Neglect)
National Incident-Based Reporting System
    (NIBRS), 133
National Institute of Drug Abuse, 437
National Institute of Justice, 645

National Opinion Survey of Crime and
    Justice, 315
National School Safety Center, 166, 178–179
National Victim Assistance Academy, 131,
    132
National Victim Center, 241
Native American Pass-Through Program,
    418
Nazi occultism, 209
neglect, 128–130, 570
    See also child neglect; maltreatment
        response
net widening, 514
New Jersey v. T.L.O., 469 U.S. 325 (1985),
    68–70
New Social Defense Movement, 525
New York City Children's Aid Society, 30
New York House of Refuge, 312
NIS-3 (National Incidence Study of Child
    Abuse and Neglect), 131, 132
Nixon, Richard, 416
notice of charges, 57, 59
    See also In re Gault, 387 U.S. 1 (1967)
Nunez by Nunez v. City of San Diego
    (1997), 282

O

objectivist school of thought in
    prosecution, 303
obsessional follower, 237
obsessive relational intrusion, 237
O'Connell, Daniel, 41–42
offender's individual circumstances,
    304–305
offense exclusion, 325
Office of Juvenile Justice and Delinquency
    Prevention (OJJDP). *See* OJJDP
    (Office of Juvenile Justice and
    Delinquency Prevention)
Ohio Department of Rehabilitation and
    Corrections, 515–516
OJJDP (Office of Juvenile Justice and
    Delinquency Prevention),
    175–176, 188, 279, 333, 419,
    427, 501
Oliphant v. Suquamash, 431 U.S. 964
    (1977), 412, 417

Operation Nightlight (Boston), 277
organizational commitment, 541–542,
    549–551
orphanages, 40, 41
"orphan trains," 30
Ortiz v. Barraza, 512 F.2d 1176 (1975),
    416–417
Outward Bound programs, 22

P

PAIR (Project for Adolescent Intervention
    and Rehabilitation), 356
Palumbo, Dennis, 647
parens patriae, 8, 13–14, 20, 26, 37, 50,
    624
    balancing with juvenile rights, 68–70
    English class applications, 33
    importance of *In re Gault,* 387 U.S. 1
        (1967), 57 (*see also In re Gault,*
        387 U.S. 1 (1967))
    infanticistic behavior, 307
    with regard to capital punishment,
        525–526
    relocated to juvenile court, 45
parental characteristics, 571
parental control
    incorrigible juveniles, 334
    See also family conditions
    See also parens patriae
parental opinions on school violence, 577
parental responsibilities and curfew
        programs, 279, 283, 335
parental responsibilities and truancy, 337
parents and guardians
    historically, 10
    of Preppie Gang members, 204–205
Parker (Commissioner of Indian Affairs),
    413
Parsons, Talcott, 87
"patriot groups," 198
peer association, 150–151, 163–165, 224,
    229
    and delinquent activity, 571–573
    and drug use, 457, 639
    in the school setting, 610, 613
    victimization risk, 606
peer culture, positive, 496

Pennsylvania Department of Corrections et al., petitioners v. Ronald R. Yeskey. No. 97-June 15, 1998, 347
Pennsylvania Supreme court, 59
Penry, Johnny Paul, 530
Penry v. Lynaugh, 492 U.S. 302 (1989), 530
People ex. rel. O'Connell v. Turner, 55 Ill. 280 (1870), 41–42
People v. Turner, 55 Ill. 280 (1879), 14
person-centered planning, 396
personnel in correctional facilities. *See* correctional facility personnel
"persons in need of supervision" (PINS), 333
physical abuse and delinquency, 570
physical fitness education, 580
PINS (Persons in Need of Supervision), 333, 356, 357
placement and programming. *See* correctional facilities; placement facilities; rehabilitation and treatment
placement facilities
    about, 491–492
    aftercare, 504–506
    private, 492–493
    public, 493–495
play groups, 197
Pledge of Allegiance, 66–67
police
    child welfare agencies compared, 259–260
    curfews, 287–289
    Indian police forces, 412, 413–414
    juvenile slain by, 527
    and Preppie Gang members, 205–206
    See also law enforcement
poorhouses, 34, 35
poor laws, 33–34
positive peer culture, 496
positivist theory, 223
post-traumatic stress disorder, 399–400
praise and recognition, 578
predelinquent individuals, 35–36, 41, 43, 45
premeditated crime *vs.* impulsive, 222
Preppie Gangs
    about, 193–194, 216–217

causes of involvement, 201–204
characteristics, 194–195
criminal activity, 197, 207–208
criminal activity examples, 208–210
dangers of membership, 207
enforcing responsibility and accountability, 215–216
gang migration and proliferation, 210–212
ideological, 198–199
law enforcement and, 205–206
member migration *vs.* concept migration, 212–214
occult-based, 199–200
psychosocial perspective on behavior, 200–201
sociological attitude towards, 204–205
wannabes and gonnabes, 195–196
President's Commission on Law Enforcement and Administration of Justice, 313
prevention based programs, 578–579, 613
    See also rehabilitation and treatment
Preventive Intervention (PI), 504
probable cause, 301–302
probation
    early use, 312–313
    efficacy of, 21
    P. Torbet quoted on, 18
    program founding, 18, 39
probation officer role, 63
problems of immediate gratification (PIG), 393
programs
    aftercare, 504–506
    curricular, 580
    Dare, 637–648
    educational and vocational programs, 496–498
    potential programs, 503–504
    special needs programs, 498–500
    successful programs, 501–503
    treatment, 495–496
    unsuccessful programs, 503
Progressive era, 42–44, 312–313
Project Northland, 504
proof beyond reasonable doubt, 57
    In re Winship, 57–59
property crime, 485

property crimes, 157–158, 179
prosecution deferment, 354–355
prosecutorial discretion, 303–305, 476
   about, 295–297, 298, 309
   ideals in juvenile prosecution, 299–301
   offender's behavior, 305–306
   offender's circumstances, 303–305 (*see also* disabled juvenile offenders; family conditions)
   offender's maturity, 306–307
   prosecutorial construction, 301–303
   rehabilitative potential, 307–309
prosecutorial waivers, 317, 318
   See also waivers, juvenile
prosecutor role, 295–299
protection of delinquent, 180–181
psychodynamic model of stalking behavior, 244–245
psychological explanations for delinquency, 80–81
psychological theory, 80–81
The Psychology of Stalking (Meloy), 238
PTSD (post-traumatic stress disorder), 399–400
puberty, 223
public opinions
   juvenile capital punishment, 523, 526
   juvenile crime rates, 561–562
   juvenile laziness and spoiledness, 562
   juvenile waivers, 315–316
   progress against illegal drugs, 638–639
   punishment of mentally retarded, 531
   school violence, 604
punishment
   accountability based sanctions, 513–515
   fairness and adequacy of victim offender mediation, 514–515
   goals, 532
   1975-2003 period, 21–24
      see also reforms in juvenile justice (modern)
Purvis, Johnny, Dr., 194

Q

Quakers, 12, 35, 43
Quinney, Richard, 227
Qutb et al. v. Strauss, (1994), 282
Qutb v. City of Dallas (1993), 282

R

racist gangs, 198
Rahway State Prison (NJ), 21–22
Ramos v. Town of Vernon et al. (2003), 282
rational choice model of substance abuse, 461
rational choice theory, 78
reality therapy, 495
reasoning power
   adolescent egocentrism, 203
   contradictory judgments, 187
   determined age, 12, 26, 33, 86
   and drug use choices, 461
   juvenile *vs.* adult, 222
   legal liability, 296
   and status offenses, 332
   of wannabes under the influence, 196
recidivism, 316–317, 484–487
   drugs, 485
   property crime, 485
   running away from home, 485
   tobacco or alcohol, 485
   traffic offenses, 485
   value of diversion programs, 486–487
   violent crime, 485
   of violent crime offenders, 500
reform movement (early), 35–42, 628
reform schools, 14, 17, 18, 312, 628
   about, 39–42
   establishment of, 11
reforms in juvenile justice (modern)
   about, 653–654, 669–671
   arguments against abolishment of juvenile system, 662–663
   arguments for unified system, 661–662
   currently not reflecting goals of founders, 655–658
   current punitive focus, 654–655
   denial of due process, 658–660
   jury trials, 659–660
   maintaining current system, 667–669
   new assumptional framework, 655
   now more successful than adult justice system, 669
   protections of juvenile system, 665–667
   punitive juvenile system *vs.* adult system, 661
   reasoning and responsibility of juveniles, 663–664

rehabilitation potential, 664–665
right of counsel, 660–661
superpredator myth (1990s), 183–185
rehabilitation and treatment, 260
aftercare programs, 504–505
co-occurring substance abuse, 351
efficacy of, 313, 314
emphasis on education, 353
focus of early juvenile court, 17–18
funding for substance abuse, 462–463
goals, 49
group therapy, 496
historical ideology, 15–16, 49
loss of philosophy, 461
probation goal, 18
punishment rather than treatment,
180–181
purpose of juvenile court, 505–506
substance addicted juveniles, 458–463
See also disabled juvenile offenders;
Kent v. United States, 383 U.S.
541 (1966); placement facilities
rehabilitation potential, 307–309
reintegration into society, 494
reintegration shaming theory, 89
relational frame theory (RFT), 400–401
relative deprivation, 87
religious beliefs and freedom of expression
in medical situations, 129
in school situations, 66–67
religious groups, 199
religious influence on juvenile law, 5–10,
11, 188
See also Jehovah's Witnesses;
medical neglect; Quakers
reoffendors, 316–317
responsibility for actions, 215, 522
restorative justice
about, 517–518
accountability-based sanctions,
513–515
advantages over traditional, 511
balanced approach, 510
definition, 509–510
history, 510
traditional, 511
restorative justice programs
Impact of Crime on Victims, 517

Restorative Justice Project (LA),
515–517
Restorative Justice Project (LA), 515–517
"Revenge of the Goths" incident, 209
reverse waiver, 317
right to remain silent, 55
right-wrong differentiation ability, 86, 296,
332
See also reasoning power
Rilya, disappearance of, 128
risk factors
children in school settings, 578, 603–604
female delinquency, 102
Rivlin, Alice, 646
Romano–Germanic law, 8, 10
Roper v. Simmons, 543 U.S. 633 (2005), 532
routine activities theory, 78, 605, 614
routine activity theory of victimization,
605–606
conclusions, 613–614
dependent and independent variables,
608–610
findings, 610–613
policy implications, 614–615
study description, 608–609
RTF (relational frame theory), 400–401
rule-governed behavior, 404
running away, 485, 492

S

Safe School Report, 562
Safe Schools Act of 1994, 603–604
Safe Streets Coalition, 173
Sampson, Robert, 88
SAP (Student Assistance Program),
Westchester, NY, 460
SARA model (scanning, analysis,
response, and assessment), 256
Scalia, Justice, 532
scanning, analysis, response, and
assessment (SARA) model, 256
Scapegoat Generation (Males), 562
Scared Straight program, 21–22
Scared Straight Programs, 503
Schall v. Martin, 467 U.S. 253 (1984).,
65–66
*Schleifer ex rel. Schleifer v. City of
Charlottesville*, (1999), 282

school age, 337
school commitment, 613
school involvement, 609
school shootings, 178, 209, 530
school suspensions, 67
school truancy. *See* truancy
school violence, 209
    associated behaviors, 563
    explaining school violence, 566–569
    failed programs addressing violence,
        581–583
    peer influence, 571–573
    protection and fear factors, 146
    recommended programs addressing
        violence, 583–584
    responses to school violence, 577–579
    risk factors, 566–567
    school climate, 573–575, 609
    school settings, 562–565
    sensationalism of school violence,
        565–566
    statistical decrease, 563
    successful programs addressing
        violence, 579–581
    and teacher authority, 574
    See also social control study;
        socialization of children
school violence, victims of. *See* victims of
        school violence
search and seizure in school
        environments, 68–70
Second amendment, 20
secure-building" policies, 582
self-control, 86, 461, 501
self-control theory, 85–86
self-determination, 12, 21, 26, 44
"self-determination" era of Indian policy,
        416, 417
self-esteem, 403–405, 572–573
self-fulfilling prophecy, 86–87
self-incrimination, 53, 57, 61–62
    See also Fifth Amendment Rights
self-medication hypothesis, 453
sentencing forms, 316–317
"sentinels," 131
separatist groups, 199
seventh amendment, 20
severely emotionally disturbed (SED), 350
sex offender profile

about, 359–360
    abuse history, 364
    age, 361
    family dysfunction, 365
    gender, 360–361
    profiling the offender, 360
    psychiatric diagnosis, 362–363
    school difficulties, 365
    socialization, 363–364
    socioeconomic status, 361–362
    substance abuse, 365–366
sex offenders, behavior analysis
    about, 391–392, 405–406
    assumptions and characteristics of PBS,
        396–398
    aversive conditioning and satiation
        behavioral treatment approach,
        394
    clinical behavior analysis, 403–405
    functional assessment and analysis, 402
    PBS approach, 395–396, 398
    PBS goals, 396–397
    PBS origin, 396
    relapse-prevention approach, 393–394
    relational frame theory, 400–401
    sexual abuse cycle approach, 392–393
    victim to victimizer, 399–400
sex offenders, treatment
    about, 375–377, 384
    assessing offenders, 381
    characteristics, 377–380
    treatment programs, 381–384
    typologies, 380–381
sex offense causative factors
    about, 368–369, 371–372
    developmental factors, 370–371
    offenses, 367–368
    psychiatric diagnosis, 369–370
    sexual victimization, 369
    socialization, 371
    substance abuse, 370
sex offense victims, 399–400
    age, 366–367
    gender, 366
sexual abuse
    involving family members, 133
    involving strangers, 128
    and sexual offenses, 364
sexual harassment, 241–242

sexually aggressive behavior in children, 242
sexually reactive children, 369, 399–400
shaming process, 89
Simmons, Christopher, 531
Simmons v. Missouri, Missouri SC 84454 (2002), 531
single-parent households, 432, 560
Sixth amendment, 20, 58–60
    See also Davis v. Alaska, 415 U.S. 308 (1974); McKeiver v. Pennsylvania, 403 U.S. 528 (1971)
slavery, 12–13
Smart Moves, 460–461
Smith, John L., 413
Smith, Susan, 629
Smith v. Daily Mail Publishing Company, 443 U.S. 97 (1979), 64–65
smoking and cigarettes, 187
    gateway hypothesis, 454–455
    6 month expulsion from school for, 181
    status offense, 332
Snell, Tracey, 523
social accountability
    and delinquency, 163–164
    and gang participation, 163
social bonding theory, 85, 614, 624–625
social bonds, 150–151, 163–165, 229
social communitarianism, 89
social control study in educational and community settings
    conclusion, 166
    data analysis, 153–154
    dependent variables, 150–151
    discussion, 164–166
    hypotheses, 147–148
    independent variables, 151–153
    measures, 149–150
    methodology, 148–149
    results, 154–164
social control theory, 85–86, 146–147
Social Darwinism, 620–621
social disorganization, 227–228, 576
    in black communities, 625–627
    disorganized neighborhoods, 624
social disorganization theory, 83
social illness, 44

socialization of children
    about, 559
    changing roles, 560–562
    explaining school violence, 566–569
    failed programs addressing violence, 581–583
    family expectations, 569–571
    family structure, 560
    peer influence, 571–573
    recommended programs addressing violence, 583–584
    responses to school violence, 577–579
    school environments, 573–575
    school settings, 562–565
    sensationalism of school violence, 565–566
    successful programs addressing violence, 579–581
social learning approach, 222–223
social norms, 86, 87, 215
societal morality, 224, 226, 560–562, 584
societal protection, 298–299
society interests
    goal of probation, 18
    and juvenile anonymity, 181
    punishment and, 20–21
    vs. best interest of juvenile, 25–26, 50
        (*See also Kent v. United States, 383 U.S. 541 (1966)*)
sociological theories of delinquency (macro perspectives)
    about, 81–82
    differential opportunity, 82–83
    social disorganization, 83
sociological theories of delinquency (micro perspectives)
    about, 84
    differential association and social learning, 84–85
    self-control, 85–86
    social control, 85–86
socio-structural theory, 434
special education programs, 348
specific learning disabilities (SLD), 349
St. Louis Project LEARN, 352–353
stalkers
    about, 235, 246
    behavioral definition, 236–237
    legal definition, 236

technical definition, 235–236
stalking by adults
  prevalence, 237–239
  typologies, 239–240
stalking by juveniles
  obsessional behavior, 241–243
  prevalence, 240–241
  theoretical models, 244–246
  typologies, 243–244
Stanford v. Kentucky, 492 U.S. 361 (1989),
    527, 528
Starkweather, Charles Raymond, 523
state jurisdiction in abuse and neglect of
    children, 130
  See also Children's Protective Services
state-run institutions. *see* institutions
status offenses, 5, 22, 276
  about, 331, 339–341
  curfew violations, 334–337
  definition, 332
  impacts of confinement, 332–334
  juvenile status, 331–332
  ratio of female to male, 492
  truancy, 337–339
Statute of Artificers (1563), 9–10
statutory exclusion. *See* legislative waivers
statutory law, 33
statutory reverse onus in waiver process, 25
"stay-put" rule, 353
Stephens, Mary Ann, 186–187
Stewart, (Justice), 58
stigmata, 79
strain theory, 82, 88, 225–226
strain theory, general. *See* general strain
    theory
Strategic Approaches to Community
    Safety Initiative (SACSI), 270
street gangs, 314
  general characteristics, 212, 214
  vs. preppy gangs, 194
  See also gangs
substance abuse, 525
  and adolescent development, 138–139
  adult *vs.* juvenile punishments, 451
  and American Indian youth, 422, 423
  clinical *vs.* legal definition sets, 450
  and delinquent behavior, 498–499, 567
  and development stages, 452
  drug enforcement funding, 641

gender comparisons, 115, 452–453
indications, 156–157
"just-say-no-type programs, 461
most commonly abused, 639–640
and non-Indian youth, 423
parental, 129, 571
rational choice model, 461
recidivism, 485
rehabilitation and treatment, 115, 351,
    458–463, 462–463
at school, 609, 610
and sex offenders, 365–366, 370,
    383–384
statistical arrest information, 638
user *vs.* nonuser activities, 156–157
substance addicted juveniles
  about, 449–450
  environmental factors, 455–457
  gateway hypothesis, 454–455
  genetics and personality, 452–453
  personality and self-medication, 453
  prevention and treatment, 458–463
  relationship to delinquency, 457–458
  risk and protective factors, 451–452
  treatment context, 450–451
superpredator myth (1990s)
  about, 173–176, 187–189
  disproving the myth, 176–179, 210
  juveniles in custody, 182–183
  restructuring of juvenile justice system
    based upon, 179–182
  resulting punishment of victims,
    185–187
  results of restructuring the juvenile
    justice system, 183–185
  "superpredators," 173, 175
supremacist groups, 198
Svendberg v. Stamness (1994), 243
symbolic interaction, 86–87
systemic/social disorganization theory,
    88–89
Szasz, Thomas, 306

T

teachers
  authority and school violence, 574
  and student relationships, 579
  student victimization by, 575

"teaching of lower-class skills and middle-class values," 13–14

teen courts, 23, 24

television, 561

Terry, Edward, 59

Texas Youth Commission's Giddings State Home and School, 516

"The New Republic" (Glass), 645, 646

theoretical integration, 88

Thompson, William Wayne, 527–528

Thompson v. Oklahoma, 487 U.S. 815 (1988), 523, 526, 527

Thurmond, Strom, 629

Tillman, Ben, 629

Tinker v. Des Moines School District, 393 U.S. 503 (1969), 67

Title 18, Section 1030 of the U.S. Code, 220, 224

Torbet, Patricia, 18

traffic offenses, 485

training schools, 15, 17, 313, 493
   population by percent offenses, 494

transactional analysis therapy, 495

transitional assistance programs, 504–505

treatment, 44
   See also rehabilitation; sex offenders, behavior analysis

treatment of sex offenders. *See* sex offenders, treatment

treatment programs, 495–496

"Trench Coat Mafia" incident, 209

The Tribal Youth Program, 419–420

truancy, 610
   status offense policy, 337–339

Tuilaepa v. California, 512 U.S. (1994)

U

unemployment, 432

Uniform Crime Report, 177

United Nations Convention on the Rights of the Child and the International Covenant on Civil and Political Rights, 532

United States v. Kagama, 1886, 415

University of Michigan's Institute for Social Research, 177

University of Minnesota, 513

Unraveling Juvenile Delinquency (Gluecks), 80–81

U.S. Supreme Court positions, 313–314
   1870, 41–42
   1955-1975, 20
   1975-2003, 21–24
   decisions on anonymity of juveniles, 64 (*see also Smith v. Daily Mail Publishing Company,* 443 U.S. 97 (1979))
   decisions on capital punishment (*see* capital punishment)
   decisions on curfew laws, 282–283
   decisions on double jeopardy, 62
   decisions on school suspensions, 68
   decisions on search and seizure in educational institutions, 68–70
   decisions on self-incrimination, 63
   disabled offenders, 347
   on Indian affairs, 415
   jury trial, 59–60
   mid-20th century, 51
   R. Jackson on prosecutors, 295
   rights in cross-examination (*See Davis v. Alaska, 415 U.S. 308 (1974)*)
   and U.S. Indian policy, 411

U.S. v. Lopez (1995), 564

V

Vagabonds Act (1597), 9

"Vampire Murders," 209

victimization, 568, 608–609

victimization in school settings, 582
   as commonly viewed by authorities, 615
   peer association, 606
   risk control and guards, 606–607
   routine activities, 605–606
   security guards, 606–607
   social bonds, 607–608
   statistical incidence, 604
   target attractiveness, 606
   See also routine activity theory of victimization

Victim Offender Mediation, 512, 513, 514

victims
   disproportion of American Indian youth, 410

offender relationship in abusive
situations, 133
sex offense, 366–367, 399–400
victims of school violence
about, 603–604
routine activities, 605–606
trends, 604–605
victim's rights, 512
See also restorative justice
Victim's Rights and Restitution Act of 1990,
512
Violent and Repeat Juvenile Offender Act,
181
violent crimes
capital punishment, 522–523
and most likely times, 335–336
and perpetrator activities, 158–159
and public opinion, 315–316
rates and gender comparisons, 96
rates between 1994-1999, 24
and recidivists, 500
recidivism, 485, 500
See also capital punishment
vocational programs, 496–498
void for vagueness
doctrine of, 42
VOM (Victim Offender Mediation), 512

W

waivers, juvenile
about, 311–312
effects, 316–317
forms of, 317–329
other terms used for, 315

public support, 315–316
Wall Street Journal, 188
war on drugs, 638
weapons
confiscation, 525
Federal Handgun Safety Act, 333
Individuals with Disabilities Education
Act Amendments, 565
of Preppie Gangs, 197
in school, 146, 178–179, 353, 564
"street" culture, 630
U.S. v. Lopez (1995) (in school), 564
Wendorf, Heather, 210
Westchester Student Assistance Program
(SAP), 460
*West Virginia State Board of Education v.
Barnette,* 319 U.S. 624 (1943),
66–67
West Virginia Supreme Court of Appeals,
64–65
wilderness challenge programs, 22
Wilkins, Health, 528
Winship, Samuel, 57–59
women and influence on juvenile law, 15,
43
Wootton, James, 173–174
work camps, 494
Wraparound Milwaukee program, 356
wrongful conviction, 186–187

Z

zero-tolerance policies, 564, 565, 579–580,
603
Zimring, Franklin, 175